ELECTRIC CIRCUIT THEORY

Dr. M. Arumugam & Dr. N. Premakumaran
Deptt. of Electrical & Electronics Engineering
Regional Engineering College,
Trichy-T.N.

KHANNA PUBLISHERS
Operational Office :
B-35/9, G.T. Karnal Road Industrial Area,
(Near Telephone Exchange), Delhi-110033
Phones : 011-27224179, 011-45033819 • *Mob*. 09811541460
email : contactus@khannapublishers.in

Published by :

Romesh Chander Khanna & Vineet Khanna
for **KHANNA PUBLISHERS**
2-B, Nath Market, Nai Sarak
Delhi- 110 006 (India)

Website : www.khannapublishers.in

Hologram & Description

To all readers of our books, to prevent yourself from being defrauded by piraters, please make sure that there is an Hologram on the cover of our books with the below specifications. If you find any book without Hologram and Description, please mail us at **contactus@khannapublishers.in**

Thanking you

ISBN No. 978-81-7409-077-5

First Edition : 1979
Fifth Edition : 2000
Fourteenth Reprint : 2021

***Price :* ₹ 279.00**

ACKNOWLEDGEMENT

The authors wish to express their sincere thanks to Prof. P.S. Mani Sundaram, Principal, Regional Engineering College, Tiruchirapalli, for his encouragement.

Our thanks are due to the friends who have helped us in this endeavour.

AUTHORS

CONTENTS

ONE

INTRODUCTION

In the study of electric circuits we are interested in the flow of electricity from one device to another. The simplest of electric devices will have a pair of terminals. 'Electricity' enters at one terminal and leaves from the other. The parameters of the device such as resistance etc., are assumed to be lumped or concentrated at one point. This is not quite true as is evident in the case of transmission lines. The resistance and other parameters of a transmission line are distributed throughout its length.

The energy associated with an electric system is measured by quantities like electric charge, potential and current. Historically electric charges were first observed by rubbing certain dry substances together. Atomic physicists now picture the electric charge as one of the building blocks of the universe. The negatively charged electron is one of the constituents of the atom. Its mass is 9.107×10^{-28} gm. As the electron is a very small unit, the practical unit of charge is the coulomb.

$$1 \text{ coulomb} = 6.24 \times 10^{18} \times Q_e$$

where Q_e is the electronic charge. The flow of electric charge (electrons) constitutes a current. The rate of flow of charge is defined as current (i) and its unit is the ampere. If one coulomb of charge is transferred in one second, the current is said to be one ampere.

$$i = \frac{dQ}{dt}$$

Current has direction depending on the flow of charge.

Potential Difference (e). This is defined with respect to any two points and is measured in volts. Numerically, this is equal to the work done (in joules per coulomb) in moving a coulomb of charge between the two points.

$$1 \text{ volt} = 1 \text{ joule/coulomb.}$$

$$V = \frac{dW}{dQ}$$

Power can be obtained as a product of current and potential difference as

$$p = e \cdot i. \qquad ...(1)$$

The extent to which conduction of current (electrons) takes place is determined by the number of electrons which are free to move. In metals, a comparatively large current will be transmitted under a given applied electric pressure, as they have a larger number of free electrons. Silver, Copper and Aluminium are excellent conductors. In contrast rubber and porcelain are extremely poor conductors.

Electric Current

When one coulomb of electric charge continuously passes a given point every second, the electric current is said to be one ampere.

$$I = \frac{Q}{t} \qquad ...(2)$$

where I = current in amperes

Q = charge in coulombs

t = time in seconds.

Electromotive force (*EMF*)

This term represents the electric pressure or potential difference between two ends of a conductor that tends to create an electron flow. EMF may be developed in a battery or in a generator.

Electrical Resistance and Resistivity

Resistance in a circuit is the parameter which dissipates energy. Typical examples are the heating elements in stoves, filament bulbs etc. The amount of current passing through a conductor depends not only on the impressed voltage but on the properties of the conductor also. Electrical conductivity varies with different material. All substances may therefore be assumed to have a property which tends to oppose the flow of a current. This is called electrical resistance of a material and is very much like any other property of a material.

The unit of resistance is the ohm. The international ohm is defined to be the resistance at zero degrees centigrade of a column of mercury of uniform cross section, having a length of 106.3 cm and a mass of 14.4521 grams. The resistance of a conductor depends upon :

1. The material of the conductor.
2. Its length.
3. Cross-sectional area, and
4. The temperature.

The resistance of electrical materials are usually given per unit cross-sectional area and per unit length. This is called specific resistance or resistivity of the material represented by the letter ρ. Thus the resistivities of silver, copper and aluminium are 0.0147, 0.0173 and 0.0283 μ Ω-m. If ρ of a material is specified, then the resistance of conductor of that material with length l and area of cross-section a is

$$R = \frac{\rho l}{a} \quad \text{...(3)}$$

In the MKS system of units, l is in metres a in square metres, and hence the unit of specific resistance is ohm-metre.

Example 1.1. *Find the resistance of a copper wire 1 km long and 0.5 cm dia given the specific resistance of copper as 1.7 × 10⁻⁸ Ω-m*

Solution.
$$R = \frac{\rho l}{a}$$

$$l = \text{length in metres} = 1000$$

$$R = \frac{1.7 \times 10^{-8} \times 1000}{\frac{\pi}{4} \times \left(\frac{0.5}{100}\right)^2}$$

$$= \mathbf{0.866\ ohm}$$

Example 1.2. *A copper wire whose diameter is 0.162 cm has a resistance of 0.4 ohm. If the wire is drawn through a series of dies until its diameter is reduced to 0.032 cm, what is the resistance of the lengthened conductor ? Assume ρ remains constant.*

Solution. Let l_1 and a_1 be the original length and area of cross section of the conductor and let l_2 and a_2 be the corresponding values after passing through the dies.

$$0.4 = \frac{\rho l_1}{a_1}$$

where $$a_1 = \frac{\pi}{4}\left(\frac{0.162}{100}\right)^2$$

New Resistance $$R = \frac{\rho l_2}{a_2}$$

where $$a_2 = \frac{\pi}{4}\left(\frac{0.032}{100}\right)^2$$

As the volume of copper remains unchanged in the process,

$$a_1 l_1 = a_2 l_2$$

or
$$l_2 = \frac{a_1}{a_2} l_1$$

$$\therefore \quad \frac{R}{0.4} = \frac{l_2}{l_1}\frac{a_1}{a_2} = \left(\frac{a_1}{a_2}\right)^2 = \left(\frac{0.162}{0.032}\right)^4$$

i.e.
$$R = 0.4\left(\frac{0.162}{0.032}\right)^4 = \mathbf{262.7\ ohms.}$$

Example 1.3. *A bread toaster has a Nichrome unit ($\rho = 112 \times 10^{-8}$ Ω-m) of resistance 32 ohms. What is the resistance of a copper conductor of equal area of cross section but 10 times as long as the Nichrome wire ?*

Solution.
$$\rho_{Cu} = 1.7 \times 10^{-8} \text{ ohm–m}$$

$$\rho_{Ni} = 112 \times 10^{-8} \text{ ohm–m}$$

$$R_{Ni} = 32 = 112 \times 10^{-8} \times \frac{l_{Ni}}{a_{Ni}}$$

$$R_{Cu} = \rho_{Cu}\frac{l_{Cu}}{a_{Cu}}$$

$$\frac{R_{Cu}}{32} = \frac{\rho_{Cu}}{\rho_{Ni}} \cdot \frac{l_{Cu}}{l_{Ni}} \cdot \frac{a_{Ni}}{a_{Cu}}$$

$$= \frac{1.7 \times 10^{-8}}{112 \times 10^{-8}} \times 10 = \frac{17}{112}$$

$$\therefore \quad R_{Cu} = \frac{32 \times 17}{112} = \mathbf{4.857\ ohms.}$$

Example 1.4. *An overhead busbar of copper is a tube with 3 cm internal diameter and 0.5 cm thickness. Find the resistance between the two ends of the busbar, if its length is 10 metres.*

Solution.
$$R = \frac{\rho l}{a}$$

$$\rho = 1.7 \times 10^{-8} \text{ ohm–m for copper}$$

$$l = 10 \text{ m}$$

$$a = \frac{\pi}{4}\left(\frac{4^2 - 3^2}{100 \times 100}\right) \text{sq. m}$$

$$\therefore \quad R = \frac{1.7 \times 10^{-8} \times 10 \times 4 \times 10000}{\pi \times 7}$$

$$= \mathbf{3.09 \times 10^{-4}\ ohm.}$$

Example 1.5. *A 240 V generator supplies a motor through a pair of aluminium wires each 400 metres long. The terminal* *voltage at the motor is 230 V and the current supplied is 20 A. Find the area of cross-section of the wires required (specific resistance of aluminium 2.83×10^{-8} ohm-m).*

Solution. Voltage drop in the wires

$$= 240 - 230 = 10 \text{ V}$$

Drop in each conductor $= 5$ V

Current flowing $= 20$ A

$$\therefore \text{ Resistance of each wire} = \frac{5}{20} = 0.25\ \Omega$$

$$= \frac{\rho l}{a}$$

$$\therefore \quad a = \frac{2.83 \times 10^{-8} \times 400}{0.25} \text{ sq. m}$$

$$= \mathbf{0.4528\ sq.\ cm.}$$

Conductance and Conductivity

The reciprocal of resistance is called conductance, it is represented by the letter G and its unit is the mho (Ω) siemens.

$$G = \frac{1}{R}$$

The reciprocal of resistivity is called conductivity and is represented by the symbol ν

$$\nu = \frac{1}{\rho} \text{ mho/metre.}$$

Temperature-Resistance Effect

It has been experimentally found that the resistance of most of the metals increases as the temperature is raised. This change is approximately proportional to the temperature change, except for very low and very high temperatures. Therefore within the usual operating range, the resistance may be said to vary linearly with temperature changes.

The change in resistance per ohm per degree temperature variation is called temperature co-efficient of resistance and is represented by the symbol α.

α itself varies with temperature. Thus α for copper is 0.00402 per °C at 20°C.

If R_1 is the resistance of a conductor at t_1 °C and

R_2 is its resistance at t_2 °C, then

$$R_2 = R_1\,[1 + \alpha_1(t_2 - t_1)] \qquad \ldots(4)$$

The value of α_1 is the temperature co-efficient of resistance at the temperature t_1 °C.

Example 1.6. *The resistance of a coil of wire increases from 50 ohms at 25°C to 62 ohms at 75°C. Calculate the temperature coefficient of the material of the wire at 0°C.*

Solution. The resistance at 25°C, $R_{25} = 50 = R_0\,[1 + \alpha_0\,(25 - 0)]$ and at 75°C, $R_{75} = 62 = R_0\,[1 + \alpha_0\,(75 - 0)]$

Dividing one by the other,

$$\frac{62}{50} = \frac{1 + 75\,\alpha_0}{1 + 25\,\alpha_0}$$

$$1.24\,(1 + 25\,\alpha_0) = 1 + 75\,\alpha_0$$

$$0.24 = \alpha_0\,(75 - 31) = 44\,\alpha_0$$

or $$\alpha_0 = 0.24/44 = 0.00545.$$

Example 1.7. *An incandescent lamp takes 2.5 Amps at 240 V at the instant of switching it on. At the normal operating temperature the current drops to 0.2 Amp. Find the temperature of the heated filament. Take room temperature as 20°C and the corresponding temperature co-efficient of the filament as 0.005 per °C.*

Solution. Let t be the normal operating temperature.

$$R_{20} = \frac{240}{2.5} = 96 \text{ ohms.}$$

$$R_t = \frac{250}{0.2} = 1200 \text{ ohms}$$

$$R_t = R_{20}\,[1 + \alpha_{20}\,(t - 20)]$$

$$1200 = 96\,[1 + 0.005\,(t - 20)]$$

or $$t = \frac{1113.6}{0.48} = \mathbf{2320°C.}$$

Example 1.8. *Two conductors, one of copper and the other of iron, are connected in parallel. At 20°C, they carry equal currents. If the temperature is now raised to 150°C, what proportion of the total current will each conductor carry ?*

$\alpha_{Cu} = 0.0043;$ $\quad \alpha_{Fe} = 0.0063$ *per°C at 20°C.*

Solution. At 20°C, the currents carried by the 2 conductors are equal. Hence their resistances are equal at 20°C say R.

Let R_{Cu} be the resistance of the copper conductor at 150°C, and R_{Fe} the corresponding resistance of the iron conductor at 150°C.

$$R_{Cu} = R\,[1 + 0.0043\,(150 - 20)] = 1.559\,R$$

$$R_{Ee} = R\,[1 + 0.0063\,(150 - 20)] = 1.819\,R$$

The currents will be in the inverse proportion of the resistances.

Hence current in the copper conductor : Current in the iron conductor

i.e. 1.819 : 1.559

∴ Current in the copper conductor

$$= \frac{1.819}{1.819 + 1.559} = \frac{1.819}{3.378}$$

$$= \textbf{0.539 of the total current.}$$

Example 1.9. *The resistance temperature co-efficient for a certain copper wire is 0.004 and for carbon filament it is 0.0003. How many ohms of carbon filament in series with a 75 ohm copper wire will make the total combined resistance invariant with temperature.*

Solution. Let the required carbon filament resistance be R ohms. The resistance of the copper wire increases with temperature and is given by

$$R_{Cu} = 75\,(1 + 0.004\,t)$$

where t is the difference of temperature.

The increase in copper wire resistance is

$$75\,(1 + 0.004\,t) - 75 = 0.3\,t.$$

The resistance of the carbon filament decreases with temperature

$$R_c = R\,(1 - 0.0003\,t)$$

The decrease $= R - R\,(1 - 0.0003\,t) = 0.0003\,Rt.$

If the total resistance of copper wire and the carbon filament is to remain constant, the increase of resistance of the copper wire with temperature must be compensated by the decrease of resistance of the carbon filament.

i.e., $0.3\,t = 0.0003\,Rt$

$$\therefore \quad R = \frac{0.3}{0.0003} = \textbf{1000 ohms.}$$

Example 1.10. *Show that α_1, the resistance temperature co-efficient at t_1 °C is given by*

$$\frac{1}{\alpha_1} = \frac{1}{\alpha_0} + t,$$

where α_0 is the resistance temperature co-efficient at 0°C.

Solution. Let R_0, R_1 and R_2 be the resistances at temperatures 0°, t_1° and t_2°C respectively.

Then $R_1 = R_0(1 + \alpha_0 t_1)$

$R_2 = R_0(1 + \alpha_0 t_2)$

Also $R_2 = R_1[1 + \alpha_1(t_2 - t_1)]$

Substituting for R_1 and R_2.

$$R_0(1 + \alpha_0 t_2) = R_0(1 + \alpha_0 t_1)[1 + \alpha_1(t_2 - t_1)]$$

$$1 + \alpha_0 t_2 = (1 + \alpha_0 t_1)[1 + \alpha_1(t_2 - t_1)]$$

or
$$0 = \alpha_1(t_2 - t_1) - \alpha_0(t_2 - t_1) + \alpha_0\alpha_1(t_2 - t_1)t_1$$

i.e.,
$$\alpha_0\alpha_1 t_1 + \alpha_1 = \alpha_0$$

or
$$\frac{1}{\alpha_1} = \frac{1}{\alpha_0} + t_1.$$

Similarly it can be shown that α_2, the temperature co-efficient at t_2°C is given by

$$\frac{1}{\alpha_2} = \frac{1}{\alpha_1} + (t_2 - t_1)$$

Insulation Resistance

Current carrying cable conductors are provided with one or more layers of insulating material over them. Although the normal current is along the length of the conductor, small cross wire currents called leakage currents, exist and flow radially outward through the insulation. This is not a desirable condition and is as a result of the insulating material not being perfect. The resistance offered to the flow of the leakage current is called insulation resistance.

To compute the insulation resistance of a cable of length '*l*' metres, conductor radius r_1 metres, outer cable radius r_2m, consider an annular strip at a distance of *r* metres from the centre and of thickness *dr* metres, as shown in Fig. 1.1.

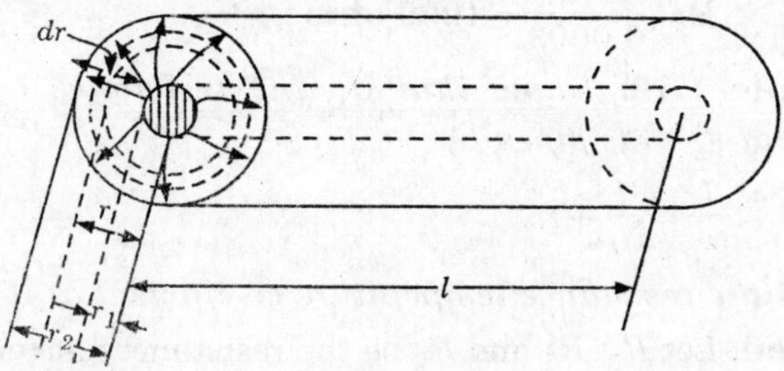

Fig. 1.1

The length of leakage current flow in the strip = dr metres (radially out)

area of cross-section = $2\pi rl$

Resistance of the annular strip

$$= \frac{\rho dr}{2\pi rl} \text{ ohms.}$$

where ρ is the specific resistance of the insulating material used. The total resistance offered by the insulating material is

$$R_{in} = \int_{r_1}^{r_2} \frac{\rho dr}{2\pi rl} = \frac{\rho}{2\pi l} \ln\left(\frac{r_2}{r_1}\right) \text{ohms} \qquad ...(5)$$

The insulation resistance decreases with increase of length of cable.

Example 1.11. *An insulated cable has an insulation resistance of 600 Mega ohms-per km. The internal and external diameters of the insulation are 1.5 and 3 cms. Calculate the specific resistance of the insulation material used.*

If the insulation resistance is to be increased by 50% by using another layer of insulating material of resistivity 6×10^{12} Ω-m, find the additional thickness of insulation required.

Solution. $l = 1000$ metres

$r_2 = 1.5$ cm $\quad r_1 = 0.75$ cm

$$R = 600 \times 10^6 = \frac{\rho}{2\pi\, 1000} \log_e \frac{1.5}{0.75}$$

$$\rho = \frac{2\pi \times 1000 \times 600 \times 10^6}{\log_e 2}$$

$$= 5.44 \times 10^{12} \text{ ohm–m.}$$

Extra insulation resistance

$$= 300 \times 10^6$$

$$= \frac{\rho}{2\pi \times 1000} \log_e \frac{D/2}{3/2}$$

$$300 \times 10^6 = \frac{6 \times 10^{12}}{2\pi \times 1000} \log_e \frac{D}{3}$$

$$\log_e \frac{D}{3} = \frac{\pi}{10} = 0.314$$

Solving $\quad D = 4.12$ cm.

thickness of insulation required

$$= \frac{4.12 - 3}{2} = \mathbf{0.56\ cm.}$$

EXERCISES

1.1. A coil of copper wire ($\rho = 1.7 \times 10^{-8}$ ohm-m) has a length of 600 metres. What is the length of an aluminium conductor ($\rho = 2.83 \times 10^{-8}$ ohm-m) if its area of cross-section and the resistance are the same as those of the copper wire. [**Ans.** 360.4 m]

1.2. A copper wire of a certain length and diameter having a resistance of 4 ohms is drawn successively through dies till its diameter is halved. What is the resistance of the lengthened conductor. Assume that the resistivity remains unchanged. [**Ans.** 64 ohms]

1.3. A copper wire of unknown length has a diameter of 0.25 cm and a resistance of 0.28 ohm. By passing through several successive dies the diameter is reduced to 0.05 cm. Assume ρ to remain unchanged. Find the resistance of the reduced size wire. [**Ans.** 175 ohms]

1.4. The copper field winding of an electric machine has a resistance of 46 ohms at 22°C. What will be its resistance at 75 °C ($\alpha = 0.0043$ per °C)

[**Ans.** 56.5 Ω]

1.5. An incandescent lamp has a tungsten filament whose resistance is 1000 ohms at the operating temperature of 2800°C. Calculate the resistance of the filament just before switching on the lamp at room temperature of 20°C. $\alpha_{20} = 0.005$ per °C. [**Ans.** 67.1 Ω]

1.6. The resistance of a given electric device is 40 ohms at 25°C. If the temperature co-efficient of resistance of the material is 0.00454 at 20°C, determine the temperature at which the resistance of the device is 80 ohms.

[**Ans.** 250.3°C]

1.7. A platinum resistance thermometer has a resistance of 20 ohms at 20°C. When placed in a furnace, the resistance increases to 134 ohms. Find the temperature of the furnace assuming temperature co-efficient of resistance of platinum at 20°C as 0.0032 per °C. [**Ans.** 1801.25°C]

1.8. Repeat Problem 1.7 if α is given as 0.00342 per°C. [**Ans.** 1800.67°C]

1.9. The conductor and insulation resistances of a cable 100 meter long are 0.001 Ω and 2000 Mega Ω respectively. What will these resistances be for a similar cable 100 km long. [**Ans.** 1 Ω, 2 M Ω]

1.10. Find the conductor and insulation resistances of a cable 15 km long given the following : conductor diameter = 1.5 cm thickness of insulation 0.5 cm, resistivity of conductor material = 1.7×10^{-8} Ω-m ; resistivity of insulation material = 6×10^{12} Ω-m. If the cable is cut into two equal bits what are the values of the conductor and insulation resistances of each bit ?

[**Ans.** 1.443 Ω, 32.5 MΩ, 0.7215Ω, 65 MΩ]

1.11. If three lengths of cable having insulation resistances of 330, 660 and 990 Mega ohms respectively are joined together to form a single cable, what is its insulation resistance. [**Ans.** 180 MΩ]

TWO

DIRECT CURRENT CIRCUITS–I

Ohm's Law—Power—Energy

As already pointed out, an electric current is a flow of electrons. Electrons are negatively charged and we know they move from the negative electrode in a battery to the positive electrode as shown below.

However, the conventional current direction is assumed to be from the positive terminal of the battery as shown in the Fig. 2.1. This is the direct opposite of the actual direction of electron motion. To suit this generally adopted direction (opposite to that of the electron motion), we shall throughout this book adopt the conventional practice of current flowing from the positive to the negative electrode through external wires.

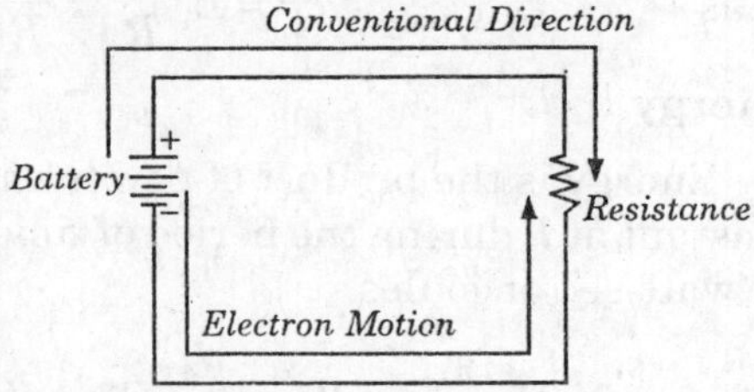

Fig. 2.1

Ohm's Law

The current flowing in an electric circuit depends on two quantities, the applied emf and the resistance in the circuit. The law connecting the three factors was established first by G.S. Ohm in 1826 and is popularly known as the Ohm's law.

Statement of Ohm's Law

Temperature remaining constant, the potential difference (E) across the ends of a conductor is proportional to the current (I) flowing through it.

Mathematically $\qquad E \propto I$

In equation form, this becomes

$$E = RI$$

where the constant of proportionality, R, by a proper choice of units, is the resistance of the conductor in ohms.

The law is subject to temperature remaining constant as otherwise R tends to vary with temperature.

Electrical Power

Power is the rate of doing work and its unit is *watt* in honour of the inventor James Watt. The unit of electric power is defined in terms of the joule per second. 1 joule per second is the work done when one coulomb of electricity is moved through a potential difference of one volt in one second. As one coulomb per second is 1 ampere, 1 joule per second = 1 watt, and this is the product of E (volt) and I (current). In general therefore, the power in an electric circuit is

$$P = EI \text{ watts}$$

As $$E = IR,$$

P may also be written as

$$P = (IR)\, I = I^2R \text{ watts}$$

or as $$P = E\left(\frac{E}{R}\right) = \frac{E^2}{R} \text{ watts}$$

Energy

Energy is the product of power and time. If the power remains constant at P during the period of time t seconds, the energy equals Pt watt-sec or joules.

$$\text{Energy} = W = Pt = EIt = I^2Rt = \frac{E^2}{R}\, t \text{ joules.}$$

Since the watt-secs is too small for practical use, the kilowatt hour (kWh) is generally used. This unit is very often called simply one Electrical unit. (Board of Trade or B.O.T. unit)

$$1 \text{ unit} = \text{kWh}$$

$$\therefore \quad \text{Energy} = \frac{\text{Power in watts} \times \text{Time in sec}}{1000 \times 60 \times 60} \text{ kWh}$$

Example 2.1. *Find the current flowing through the circuit shown in Fig. 2.2.*

Solution. From the Fig. 2.2 it is evident that the emf's of the two batteries oppose each other. Therefore the net voltage acting in the clockwise direction is $(12 - 6) = 6$ V.

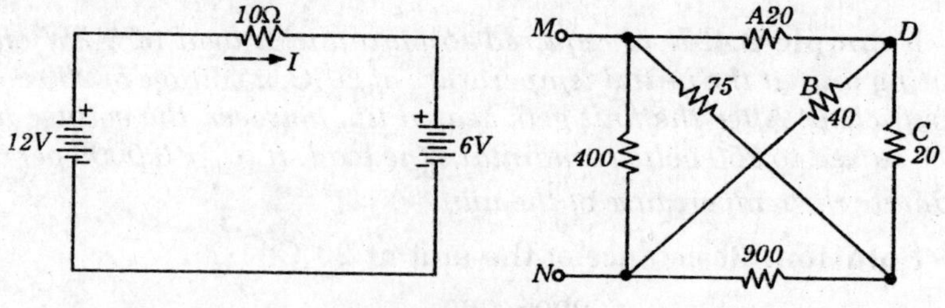

Fig. 2.2

Using Ohm's law $I = \frac{E}{R} = \frac{6}{10} = \mathbf{0.6\ A.}$

Example 2.2. *An electric iron is rated 1000 W, 240 V. Find the current drawn and the resistance of the heating element.*

Solution.
$$P = \frac{E^2}{R}$$
$$1000 = \frac{(240)^2}{R}$$
$$\therefore \quad R = \frac{240 \times 240}{1000} = 57.6 \text{ ohms.}$$
$$I = \frac{E}{R} = \frac{240}{57.6} = \mathbf{4.17\ Amps.}$$

Example 2.3. *Find the current flowing at the instant of switching on a 40 watt filament lamp on to a 240 volt circuit if the filament temperature at normal operating conditions is 2800°C. Resistance temperature co-efficient of the filament at room temperature of 20°C is 0.005 per °C.*

Solution. Under normal operating conditions (*i.e.*, at the temperature of 2800°C), the resistance of the lamp is
$$R = \frac{E^2}{P} = \frac{240 \times 240}{40} = 1440 \text{ ohms.}$$

Let the resistance at normal room temperature (at the instant of switching on) be R_{20}. Then
$$R = R_{20}\,[1 + \alpha_{20}\,(2800 - 20)]$$
$$1440 = R_{20}\,[1 + 0.005\,(2780)]$$
$$\therefore \quad R_{20} = \frac{1440}{14.90} = 96.64 \text{ ohms.}$$

Current flowing at the instant of switching on
$$= \frac{240}{R_{20}} = \frac{240}{96.64} = \mathbf{2.48\ Amps.}$$

Example 2.4. *It is required to maintain a load of 5 kW on a heating unit at the initial temperature of 20°C, a voltage of 200 volts is sufficient. After the unit gets heated up, however, the voltage has to be raised to 250 volts to maintain the load. If $\alpha_{20} = 0.0005$ per °C, estimate the temperature of the unit.*

Solution. Resistance of the unit at 20°C

$$= \frac{200 \times 200}{5000} = 8\ \Omega$$

Resistance of the heated up unit

$$= \frac{250 \times 250}{5000} = 12.5\ \Omega$$

If t is the temperature of the unit,

$$R_t = 12.5 = R_{20}\,[1 + 0.0005\,(t - 20)]$$
$$= 8\,[1 + 0.0005\,(t - 20)]$$
$$12.5 = 8 + 0.004t - 0.08$$
$$\therefore \quad t = \frac{4.58}{0.004} = \mathbf{1145°\ C.}$$

Example 2.5. *A building has the following loads : twenty 100 watt lamps operated 4 hours daily, thirty 60 watt lamps operated 3 hours daily, twenty 40 watt lamps operated 4 hours daily and ten 40 watt fans operated 8 hours daily, all connected to a 230 volt source. Calculate (a) the total power (b) the total current (c) the monthly consumption of electrical energy and (d) the monthly electrical energy charges at 35 paise per unit.*

Solution.

(*a*) Total Power $= 20 \times 100 + 30 \times 60 + 20 \times 40 + 10 \times 40$
$= 5{,}000$ watts $= 5$ kW

(*b*) Total current $= \dfrac{5{,}000}{230} = 21.74$ Amps.

(*c*) Energy consumption daily

$$= 20 \times 100 \times 4 + 30 \times 60 \times 3 + 20 \times 40 \times 4 + 10 \times 40 \times 8$$
$$= 19{,}800 \text{ watt-hours.}$$

Monthly consumption

$$= \frac{19{,}800 \times 30}{1000} \text{ kilo watt hour} = 594 \text{ kWh.}$$

(*d*) Monthly charges $= 594 \times 0.35 =$ **Rs. 207.90** .

Resistors in Series and Parallel

Resistances may be connected in two fundamental ways. When they are connected together end to end so that the *same* current passes from one to the other, they are said to be connected in series, as shown in Fig. 2.3.

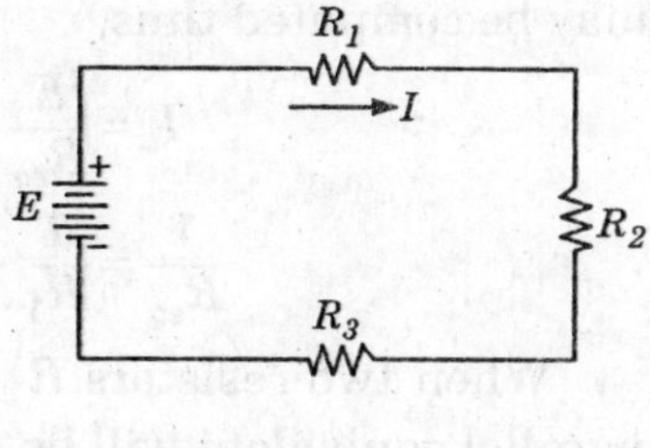

Fig. 2.3

In such a circuit, $I = \dfrac{E}{R_1 + R_2 + R_3}$

so that $R_1 + R_2 + R_3$ will be total effective resistance of the three resistances in series.

The power expended in $R_1 = I^2 R_1$

Power expended in $R_2 = I^2 R_2$

Power expended in $R_3 = I^2 R_3$

Total Power $= I^2 (R_1 + R_2 + R_3)$

$$= \frac{E^2}{(R_1 + R_2 + R_3)}$$

However for computing the power in each resistance we cannot use the total voltage E. The voltage drop across R_1 is only IR_1 and for calculating the power spent in it, we may use this voltage drop.

Power in $R_1 = \dfrac{(IR_1)^2}{R_1} = I^2 R_1$ as before.

When resistances are connected across one another, so that the same voltage is applied to each resistance, then they are said to be in parallel. (Fig. 2.4). The total current I_t in the circuit divides to pass through the individual resistances.

$$I_1 = \frac{E}{R_1}$$

$$I_2 = \frac{E}{R_2}$$

$$I_3 = \frac{E}{R_3}$$

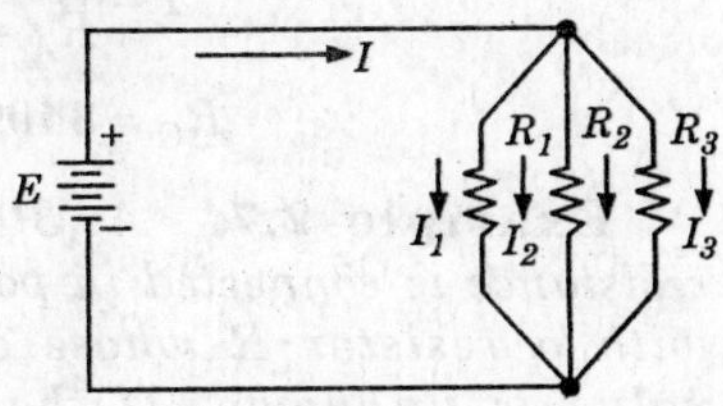

Fig. 2.4

The total current $I_t = I_1 + I_2 + I_3 = \dfrac{E}{R_1} + \dfrac{E}{R_2} + \dfrac{E}{R_3}$

The equivalent resistance of the three resistances in parallel may be computed thus,

$$I_t = \frac{E}{R_{eq}} = \frac{E}{R_1} + \frac{E}{R_2} + \frac{E}{R_3}$$

$$\therefore \quad \frac{1}{R_{eq}} = \frac{1}{R_1} + \frac{1}{R_2} + \frac{1}{R_3}$$

When two resistors R_1 and R_2 are connected in parallel, their parallel equivalent will be given by

$$\frac{1}{R_{eq}} = \frac{1}{R_1} + \frac{1}{R_2}$$

$$R_{eq} = \frac{R_1 R_2}{R_1 + R_2}$$

If $\quad R_1 = R_2 = R,$

then $\quad R_{eq} = \frac{R}{2}$

The equivalent resistance of a number of resistors in parallel, is always less than the magnitude of the smallest one.

Example 2.6. *Three resistors A, B and C are connected in series to a 240 volts source, as shown in Fig. 2.5. If R_A = 60 ohms and E_B = 40 volts when the current is 0.5 amp, calculate the resistances R_B and R_C.*

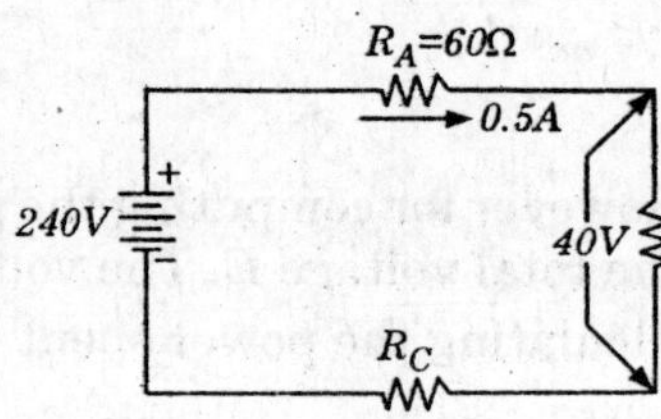

Fig. 2.5

Solution. $\quad E_B = 40 \text{ V} = IR_B$

$$\therefore \quad R_B = \frac{40}{0.5} = 80\Omega$$

$$I = \frac{E}{R_A + R_B + R_C} = \frac{240}{60 + 80 + R_C} = 0.5\,A$$

$$\therefore \quad R_C = 340\Omega$$

Example 2.7. *A 30-ohm resistance is connected in parallel with a resistor R whose ohmic value is unknown. If the total current taken is 10.5 amps when the circuit voltage is 210 V, calculate R, shown in Fig. 2.6.*

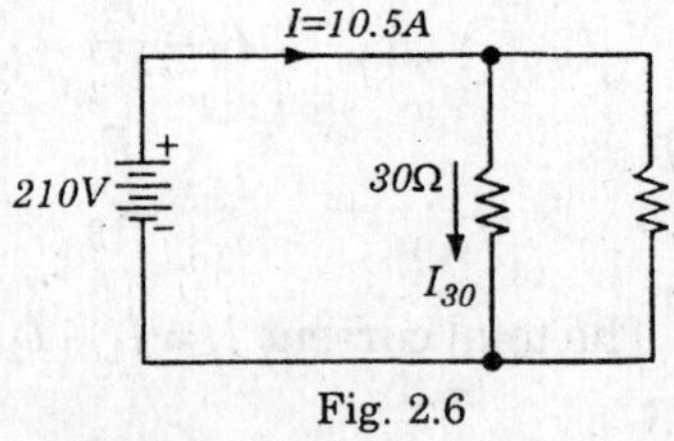

Fig. 2.6

Solution. $I_{30} = \frac{210}{30} = 7$ A.

$$I_R = 10.5 - 7 = 3.5 \text{ A.}$$

$$\therefore \quad R = \frac{210}{3.5} = \mathbf{60\ \Omega}.$$

Example 2.8. *Three loads A, B and C are connected in parallel to a 240 volt source. Load A takes 9.6 kW, load B takes 60 amp and load C is a resistance of 4.8 Ω. Calculate (a) R_A and R_B (b) the total current (c) the total power and (d) the total equivalent resistance of the three loads.*

Solution. (*a*) $R_A = \frac{E^2}{P_A} = \frac{240 \times 240}{9.6 \times 1000} = \frac{240 \times 240}{9600} = 6$ ohms.

$$R_B = \frac{240}{60} = 4 \text{ ohms.}$$

(*d*)
$$\frac{1}{R_{eq}} = \frac{1}{R_A} + \frac{1}{R_B} + \frac{1}{R_C}$$

$$= \frac{1}{6} + \frac{1}{4} + \frac{1}{4.8}$$

$$\therefore \quad R_{eq} = 1.06 \text{ ohms.}$$

(*b*)
$$I_t = \frac{240}{R_{eq}} = 150 \text{ amps.}$$

(*c*) Total Power
$$= 9600 + 240 \times 60 + \frac{240 \times 240}{4.8}$$

$$= 36{,}000 \text{ Watts or } 36 \text{ kW.}$$

Example 2.9. *Three resistors A, B and C are connected in parallel and take a total current of 7.9 amp. R_A = 48 Ω and takes 2.5 amps, $I_B = 2I_C$. Calculate (a) I_B and I_C (b) the line voltage and (c) R_B and R_C.*

Solution.

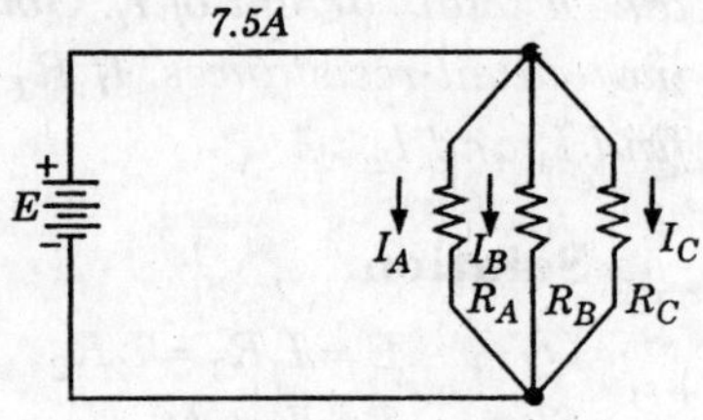

Fig. 2.7

$$E = 48 \times 2.5 = 120 \text{ volts.}$$

$$I_B = \frac{120}{R_B}$$

$$I_C = \frac{120}{R_C}$$

$$I_B = 2I_C$$

$$\therefore \quad R_B = \frac{R_C}{2}$$

$$I_A + I_B + I_C = 7.9 \text{ A}$$

$$I_B + I_C = 7.9 - 2.5 = 5.4 \text{ amps.}$$

$$\therefore \quad I_B = 3.6 \text{ A}$$

$$I_C = 1.8 \text{ A}$$

$$R_B = \frac{120}{3.6} = 33.33 \text{ ohms}$$

$$R_C = \frac{120}{1.8} = 66.67 \text{ ohms.}$$

Example 2.10. *Two 50-ohms resistors are connected in series. When a resistor R is connected across one of them, the total circuit resistance is 60 ohms. Calculate the value of R, shown in Fig. 2.8.*

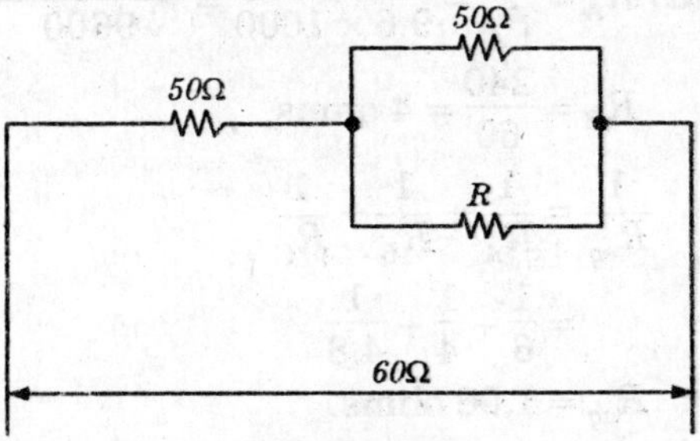

Fig. 2.8

Solution. Total resistance = 60 Ω

The effective value of the parallel combination

$$= \frac{50\,R}{50 + R} = 10\ \Omega$$

$$\therefore \quad R = 12.5 \text{ ohms.}$$

Example 2.11. *Two resistances R_1 and R_2 connected in parallel take a total current of I_t. Obtain expressions for the currents in the individual resistances. If $R_1 = 1.95\ \Omega$; $R_2 = 0.05$ ohm and $I_t = 50$ A, find I_1 and I_2.*

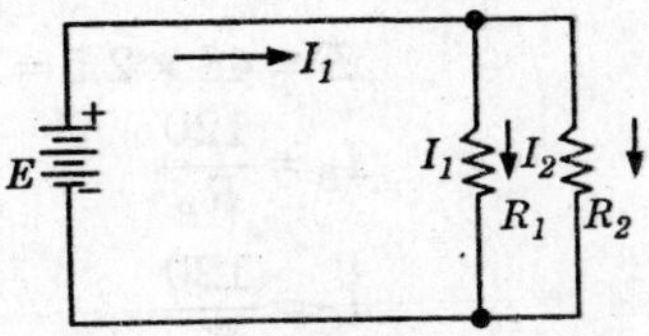

Fig. 2.9

Solution.

$$E = I_1 R_1 = I_2 R_2 \qquad \text{...(1)}$$

Also $\quad I_t = I_1 + I_2 \qquad \text{...(2)}$

Substituting for I_2 from (1)

$$I_2 = I_1 \frac{R_1}{R_2}$$

$$I_t = I_1 + I_1 \frac{R_1}{R_2} = I_1 \left(1 + \frac{R_1}{R_2}\right)$$

$$\therefore \quad I_1 = I_t \frac{R_2}{R_1 + R_2} \text{ and similarly } I_2 = \frac{I_t R_1}{R_1 + R_2}$$

In the problem $R_1 = 1.95\ \Omega$

$$R_2 = 0.05\ \Omega$$

$$I_t = 50\ \text{A}$$

$$I_1 = \frac{50 \times 0.05}{2} = 1.25\ \text{A}$$

$$I_2 = \frac{50 \times 1195}{2} = \mathbf{48.75\ A.}$$

Example 2.12. *Two resistors R_A = 20 ohms and R_B variable are connected in parallel. The combination is connected through a 5-ohm line resistor to a 240 volts source. For what value of R_B is (a) the power supplied to the load a maximum (b) the power in R_B a maximum.*

Solution. (*a*) The total resistance in the circuit

$$R_t = 5 + \frac{20\,R_B}{20 + R_B}$$

$$= \frac{100 + 25R_B}{20 + R_B}$$

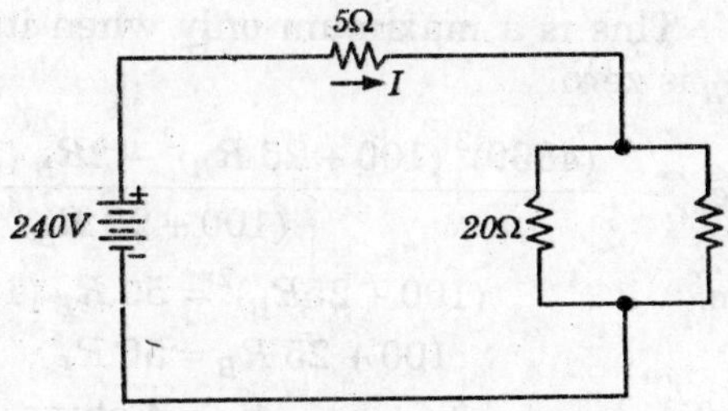

Fig. 2.10

Current $\quad I = \dfrac{E}{R}$

$$= \frac{240\,(20 + R_B)}{(100 + 25\,R_B)}$$

Power supplied by the load

$$P_L = I^2 \frac{20\,R_B}{20 + R_B} = \left[\frac{240\,(20 + R_B)}{100 + 25R_B}\right]^2 \cdot \frac{20\,R_B}{(20 + R_B)}$$

$$= (240)^2 \times \frac{(20 + R_B)\,20\,R_B}{(200 + 25\,R_B)^2}$$

for this power to be maximum.

$$\frac{dP_L}{dR_B} = 0 = 20 \times (240)^2\ [(100 + 25\,R_B)^2\,(20 + 2R_B)$$

$$- \frac{(20\,R_B + R_B^2)\,2\,(100 + 25R_B) \times 25]}{(100 + 25\,R_B)^4}$$

i.e. $\quad (100 + 25\,R_B)^2\,(20 + 2R_B) = (20R_B + R_B^2)\,50\,(100 + 25R_B)$

$$(100 + 25R_B)(20 + 2R_B) = 50\, R_B\, (20 + R_B)$$

$$2000 + 500\, R_B + 200\, R_B + 50\, R_B = 1000\, R_B + 50\, R_B$$

$$R_B = \frac{2000}{300} = 6.67 \text{ ohms.}$$

(*b*) As before, $I = \dfrac{240\,(20 + R_B)}{100 + 25\, R_B}$

This current divides into I_1 and I_2

$$I_2 \text{ flowing through } R_B = \frac{240\,(20 + R_B)}{(100 + 25\, R_B)} \times \frac{20}{(20 + R_B)}$$

$$= \frac{4800}{100 + 25\, R_B}$$

$$\text{Power in } R_B = I_2^{\,2} R_B = \frac{4800^2\, R_B}{(100 + 25\, R_B)^2}$$

This is a maximum only when its differential with respect to R_B is zero.

i.e. $$\frac{(4800)^2\,(100 + 25\, R_B)^2 - 2R_B\,(100 + 25\, R_B)\, 25}{(100 + 25\, R_B)^4} = 0$$

i.e. $$(100 + 25R_B)^2 = 50\, R_B\,(100 + 25\, R_B)$$

$$100 + 25\, R_B = 50\, R_B$$

or $$R_B = 4 \text{ ohms.}$$

Example 2.13. *A filament lamp is rated for 110 volts, 60 watts. Find the series resistance necessary to operate this lamp on a 230 volt mains. What is the power lost in this resistance?*

Solution. Let R be the resistance necessary. Current in the lamp is

$$I = \frac{60}{110} \text{ Amps.}$$

The voltage to be dropped in R is

$$230 - 110 = 120 \text{ V.}$$

$$\therefore \quad R = \frac{120}{I} = \frac{120}{60/110}$$

$$= \frac{120 \times 110}{60} = 220\ \Omega$$

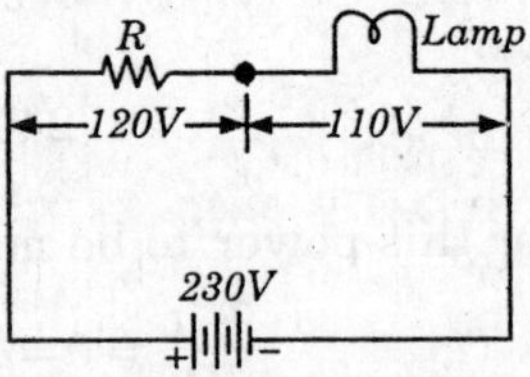

Fig. 2.11

Power dissipated in R is

$$\frac{60}{110} \times 220 = \frac{720}{11} = 65.45 \text{ Watts.}$$

Example 2.14. *An ammeter gives full scale deflection for a current of 10 mA. Its resistance is 50 ohms. Find the value of (a) the shunt resistance required to measure upto 25 A. (b) the series resistance required to use it as a voltmeter to read upto 250 volts range.*

Solution. (*a*) The maximum current that can be taken by the meter = 0.01 A.

If it is to read upto 25 A, then the shunt must take

$$= 25 - 0.01 = 24.99 \text{ A}$$

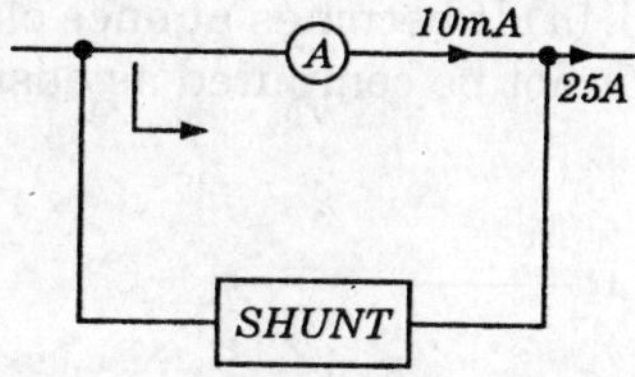

Fig. 2.12

The instrument resistance = 5 ohms

∴ Shunt resistance

$$= \frac{0.01 \times 5}{24.99} = 0.002\ \Omega$$

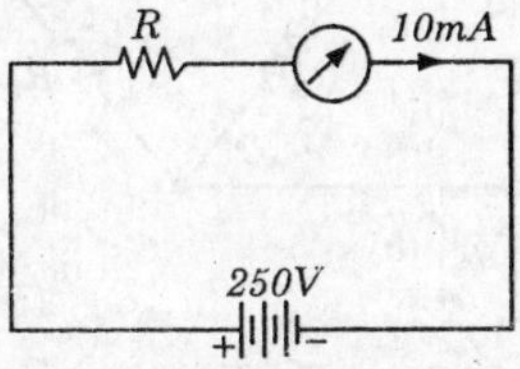

Fig. 2.13

(*b*) The voltage drop in the instrument

$$= 0.01 \times 5 = 0.05 \text{ V}.$$

∴ the voltage drop in $R = 250 - 0.05 = 249.95$ V.

As current in the meter is 0.01 A

$$R = \frac{249.95}{0.01} = 24995\ \Omega$$

Δ-Y transformation

Take the circuit of Fig. 2.14. Let it be required to find the total resistance between *A* and *B*.

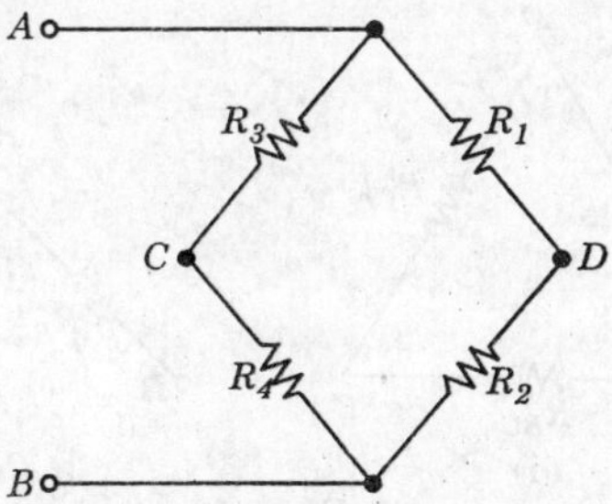

Fig. 2.14

It is clear that R_1 and R_2 are in series and the combination is in parallel with combination of R_3 and R_4 in series. Hence

$$R_{AB} = \frac{(R_1 + R_2)(R_3 + R_4)}{(R_1 + R_2) + (R_3 + R_4)}$$

Now add a resistance R_5 connected between C and D as in Fig. 2.15. (a) It becomes at once clear that the resistance between A and B cannot be computed as easily as before.

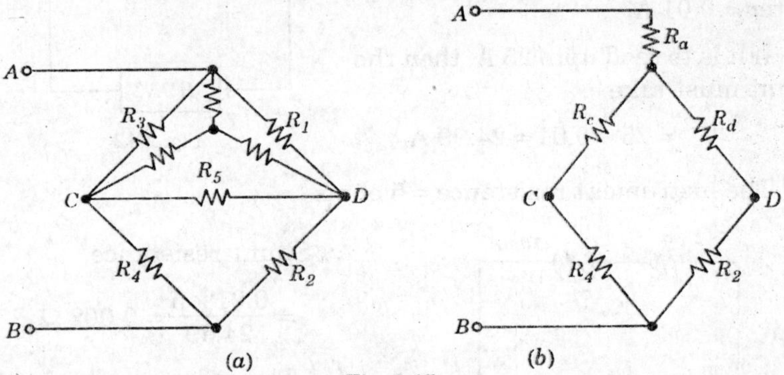

Fig. 2.15

If however, the three resistances R_1, R_3 and R_5 forming a closed loop (called a Δ) can be converted into a star (Y) as in Fig. 2.15 (b), so that they can be effectively replaced by R_a, R_c and R_d, then the computation is easier. In some cases, three resistances meeting at a point forming a star may have to be converted to a Δ. How is this conversion achieved ?

Consider three resistors R_{AB}, R_{BC} and R_{CA} forming a Δ. Let R_A, R_B and R_C be their Y equivalent which when connected to A, B and C replace the three original resistances [Fig. 2.16 (a) and (b)].

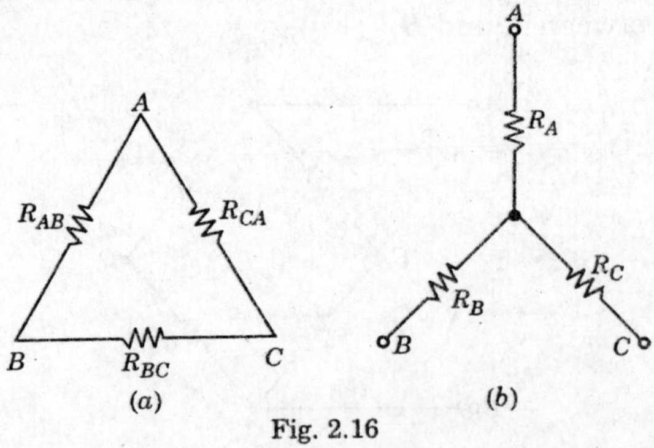

Fig. 2.16

The equivalent resistance between A and B in the Δ

$$= \frac{R_{AB}\,(R_{BC}+R_{CA})}{R_{AB}+(R_{BC}+R_{CA})}$$

effective resistance between A and B in the $Y = R_A + R_B$

As the two circuits are to be identical

$$R_A + R_B = \frac{R_{AB}\,(R_{BC}+R_{CA})}{R_{AB}+R_{BC}+R_{CA}} \qquad ...(1)$$

Similarly, considering the effective resistance between B and C and C and A in the two cases, we get two more equations.

$$R_B + R_C = \frac{R_{BC}\,(R_{CA}+R_{AB})}{R_{AB}+R_{BC}+R_{CA}} \qquad ...(2)$$

and
$$R_C + R_A = \frac{R_{CA}\,(R_{AB}+R_{BC})}{R_{AB}+R_{BC}+R_{CA}} \qquad ...(3)$$

Now (3) – (2) $\Rightarrow (R_C + R_A) - (R_B + R_C)$

$$= \frac{R_{CA}\,(R_{AB}+R_{BC}) - R_{BC}\,(R_{CA}+R_{AB})}{R_{AB}+R_{BC}+R_{CA}}$$

$$\therefore \qquad R_A - R_B = \frac{R_{AB}\,(R_{CA}-R_{BC})}{R_{AB}+R_{BC}+R_{CA}} \qquad ...(4)$$

(1) + (4) gives
$$2R_A = \frac{2R_{AB}\cdot R_{CA}}{R_{AB}+R_{BC}+R_{CA}}$$

or
$$R_A = \frac{R_{AB}\cdot R_{CA}}{R_{AB}+R_{BC}+R_{CA}}$$

R_B and R_C are obtained as

$$R_B = \frac{R_{BC}\cdot R_{AB}}{R_{AB}+R_{BC}+R_{CA}}$$

and
$$R_C = \frac{R_{CA}\cdot R_{BC}}{(R_{AB}+R_{BC}+R_{CA})}$$

If it is desired to convert the Y into Δ, then the equations (1), (2) and (3) have to be re-arranged to solve for R_{AB}, R_{BC} and R_{CA} from known R_A, R_B and R_C. It can be shown that

$$R_{AB} = \frac{R_A R_B + R_B R_C + R_C R_A}{R_C}$$

$$R_{BC} = \frac{R_A R_B + R_B R_C + R_C R_A}{R_A}$$

and
$$R_{CA} = \frac{R_A R_B + R_B R_C + R_C R_A}{R_B}$$

Example 2.15. *Transform a set of Y connected identical resistances into a Δ connection, as shown in Fig. 2.17*

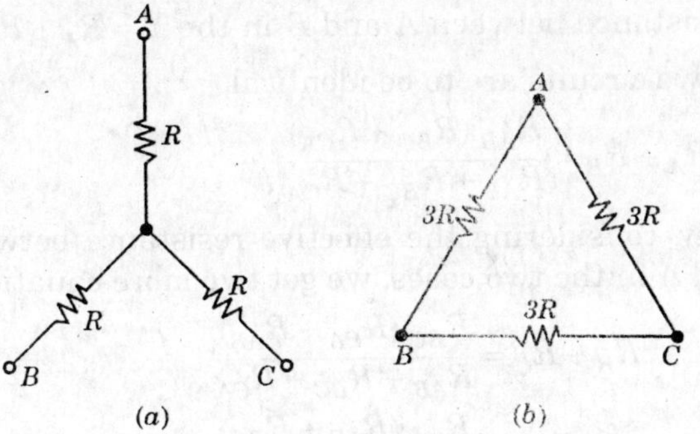

Fig. 2.17

$$R_{AB} = R_{BC} = R_{CA} = \frac{R \times R + R \times R + R \times R}{R} = \frac{3R^2}{R} = \mathbf{3R}.$$

Example 2.16. *In the circuit of Fig. 2.18, find (a) the equivalent resistance of the circuit (b) the total current and (c) the current in the resistor between points B and C. The applied voltage is 200 V.*

Solution. We shall transform the resistors connected between *AB, BC and CA into a set of Y connected resistors, R_A, R_B and R_C.*

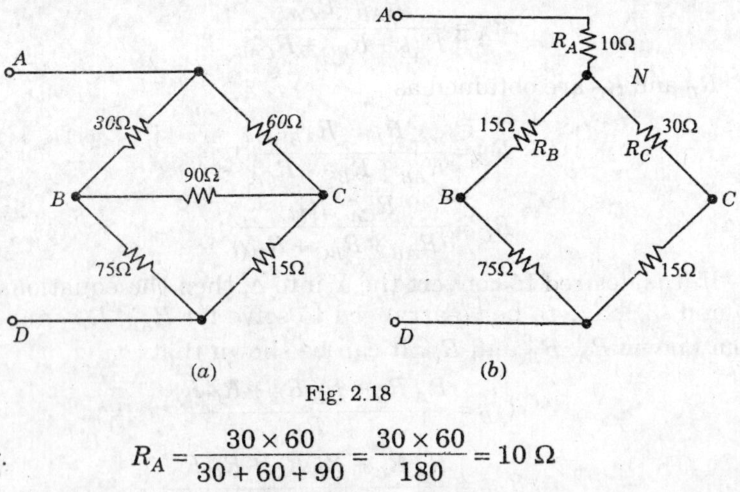

Fig. 2.18

$$\therefore \quad R_A = \frac{30 \times 60}{30 + 60 + 90} = \frac{30 \times 60}{180} = 10\ \Omega$$

$$R_B = \frac{30 \times 90}{180} = 15\ \Omega$$

$$R_C = \frac{60 \times 90}{180} = 30\ \Omega$$

(a) $$R_{eq} = 10 + \frac{(75+15)\times(30+15)}{90+45} = 40 \text{ ohms.}$$

(b) The total current is

$$I = \frac{200}{40} = 5 \text{ A.}$$

(c) To find the current through the 90 ohm resistor, we shall find the potential difference between B and C. For this we shall compute the currents through the two parallel branches of Fig. 2.18 (b).

$$I_{90} \text{ (left branch)} = \frac{5\times 45}{90+45} = \frac{5}{3} \text{ A.}$$

$$I_{45} \text{ (right branch)} = \frac{5\times 90}{135} = \frac{10}{3} \text{ A.}$$

Voltage drop across NB

$$= \frac{5}{3}\times 15 = 25 \text{ volts.}$$

Voltage drop across NC

$$= \frac{10}{3}\times 30 = 100 \text{ volts.}$$

Therefore, the voltage drop between B and C

$$= 100 - 25 = 75 \text{ volts.}$$

$$\therefore \quad I_{90} = \frac{75}{90} = \frac{5}{6} \text{ Amps.}$$

Example 2.17. *In the circuit of Fig. 2.19 find the equivalent resistance between (a) A and B (b) A and N.*

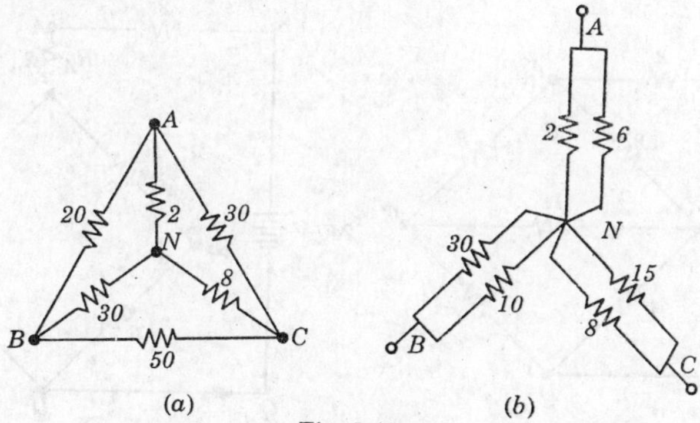

Fig. 2.19

Solution. Fig. 2.19 (b) shows the circuit equivalent to Fig. 2.19 (a) after converting the Δ resistors into equivalent Y.

$$R_A = \frac{20\times 30}{20+30+50} = 6\ \Omega$$

$$R_B = \frac{50 \times 20}{100} = 10\ \Omega$$

$$R_C = \frac{50 \times 30}{100} = 15\ \Omega$$

(*a*) Equivalent resistance between *A* and *B*

$$= \frac{2 \times 6}{2+6} + \frac{30 \times 10}{30+10} = \frac{3}{2} + \frac{30}{4} = 9\ \Omega$$

(*b*) Equivalent resistance between *A* and *N*

$$= \frac{2 \times 6}{2+6} = \frac{3}{2}\ \Omega.$$

Example 2.18. *In the Wheatstone bridge circuit of Fig. 2.20 find (a) the equivalent resistance between P and Q (b) the total current and (c) the current through the 18 ohm resistor.*

Solution. The equivalent *Y* connection has

$$R_A = \frac{12 \times 6}{12+18+6} = \frac{12 \times 6}{36} = 2\ \Omega$$

$$R_B = \frac{12 \times 18}{36} = 6\ \Omega$$

$$R_C = \frac{6 \times 18}{36} = 3\ \Omega$$

(*a*)
$$R_t = 2 + 2 + \frac{(6+6)(21+3)}{6+6+21+3}$$

$$= 4 + \frac{12 \times 24}{36} = 12\ \Omega.$$

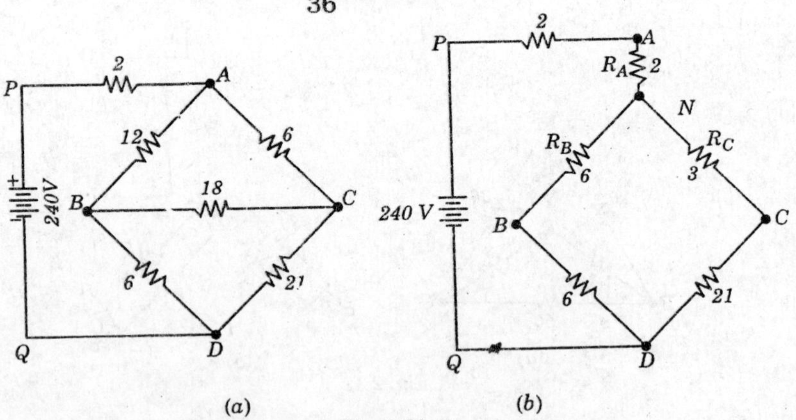

Fig. 2.20

(*b*)
$$I = \frac{240}{12} = 20\ \text{A}$$

(c) To find I_{18}, we shall first find the potential difference between B and C.

$$I_{24} \text{ (right branch)} = \frac{20 \times 12}{12 + 24} = \frac{20}{3} \text{ A}$$

$$I_{12} \text{ (left branch)} = \frac{20 \times 24}{36} = \frac{40}{3} \text{ A}$$

$$\text{Voltage drop } NB = \frac{40}{3} \times 6 = 80 \text{ volts}$$

$$\text{Voltage drop } NC = \frac{20}{3} \times 3 = 20 \text{ volts}$$

Voltage drop between B and C

$$= 80 - 20 = 60 \text{ volts} \qquad (C \text{ positive})$$

$$\therefore \qquad I_{CB} = \frac{60}{18} = \frac{10}{3} \text{ amps.}$$

Example 2.19. *Fig. 2.21 shows 6 resistors connected to form a circuit. Find the equivalent resistance between points M and N.*

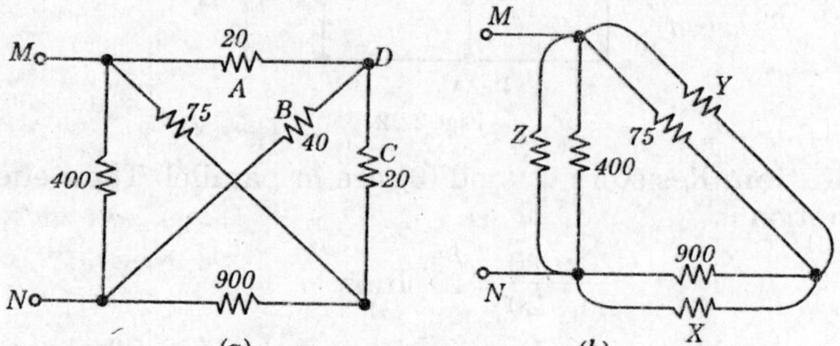

Fig. 2.21

Solution.

Converting the resistance A, B and C into a Δ,

$$X = \frac{40 \times 20 + 20 \times 20 + 20 \times 40}{20}$$

$$= \frac{2000}{20} = 100\ \Omega$$

$$Y = \frac{2000}{40} = 50\ \Omega$$

and $$Z = \frac{2000}{20} = 100\ \Omega$$

R_{MN} can now be determined from Fig. 2.21 (b)

$$\frac{50 \times 75}{50 + 75} = 30\ \Omega$$

$$\frac{100 \times 90}{100 \times 900} = 90\ \Omega$$

$$\frac{100 \times 400}{100 \times 400} = 80\ \Omega$$

$$\therefore \qquad R_{MN} = \frac{80 \times (90 + 30)}{80 + 90 + 30} = 48 \text{ ohms.}$$

Example 2.20. *In the electric circuit of Fig. 2.22, find the currents in each resistor. All resistors are in ohms.*

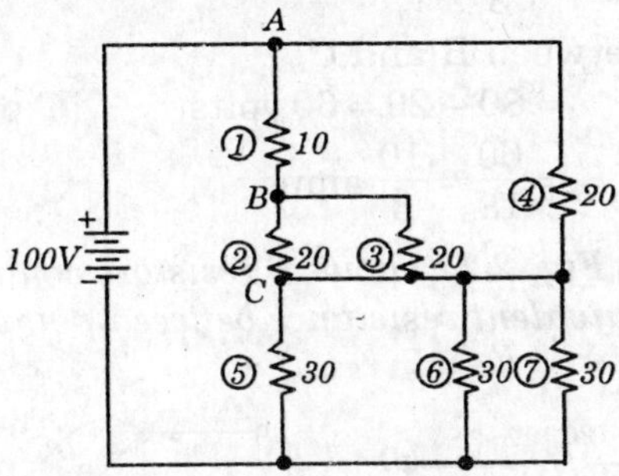

Fig. 2.22

Solution. Resistors (2) and (3) are in parallel. Their effective combination is

$$\frac{20 \times 20}{20 + 20} = 10 \text{ ohms.}$$

This is added with (1) being in series giving 20 ohms. This combination is in parallel with element (4). The effective resistance = **10 ohms.**

Similarly the combination of resistors (5), (6) and (7) gives 10 ohms.

Total effective resistance= 10 + 10 = 20 ohms.

$\therefore$ Current from source $I = \dfrac{100}{20} = 5$ amps.

This current splits into I_1 and I_4 at junction A equally as the resistances in the two paths are identical.

Hence $\qquad I_1 = I_4 = 2.5$ A

I_1 splits into 2 equal components at B

$$I_2 = I_3 = \frac{2.5}{2} = 1.25 \text{ A.}$$

At C, $\qquad I_5 = I_6 = I_7 = \dfrac{5}{3}$ amps.

Example 2.21. *In the circuit of Fig. 2.23, the power consumed in the 3Ω resistor is 12 watts. Find the value of R.*

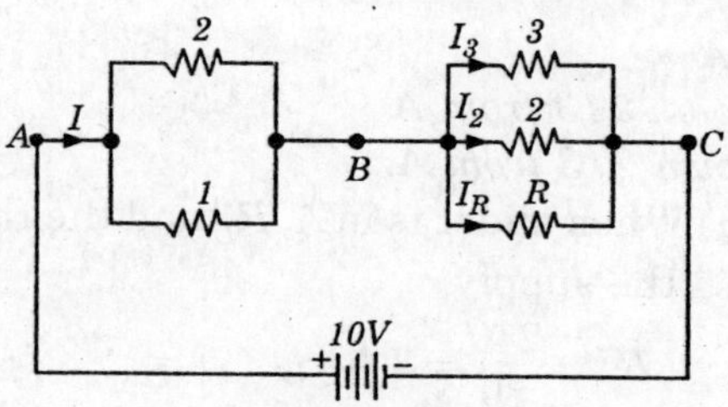

Fig. 2.23

Solution. Power in the 3 Ω resistor

$$= I_3^2 \times 3 = 12 \text{ Watts}$$

$$\therefore \quad I_3 = 2 \text{ Amps.}$$

Voltage drop between BC

$$= I_3 \times 3 = 2 \times 3 = 6 \text{ Volts.}$$

$$\therefore \quad I_2 = \frac{V_{BC}}{2} = \frac{6}{2} = 3 \text{ A.}$$

The voltage drop $V_{AB} = 10 - V_{BC} = 4$ V.

The total effective resistance between A and B

$$= \frac{2 \times 1}{2 + 1} = \frac{2}{3} \Omega$$

$$\therefore \quad I = \frac{V_{AB}}{R_{AB}} = \frac{4}{\frac{2}{3}} = 6 \text{ A.}$$

and $$I_R = I - (I_3 + I_2) = 1 \text{ A}$$

Hence $$R = \frac{V_{BC}}{I_R} = \mathbf{6 \text{ ohms.}}$$

Example 2.22. *Fig. 2.24 represents a load resistance $R_L = 80$ ohms being loaded through a slide wire rheostat. The slide wire*

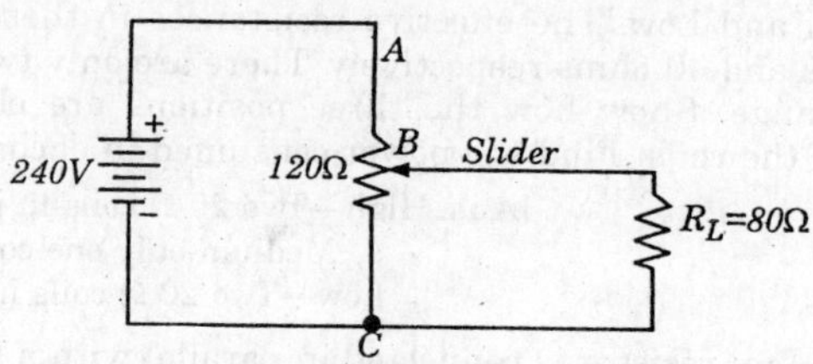

Fig. 2.24

rheostat has a total resistance of 120 ohms uniformly wound. Calculate the power delivered to R_L when the slider is in

(*a*) *position A*
(*b*) *moved down 1/3 from A*
(*c*) *moved down 2/3 from A.*

Solution. (*a*) When slider is in *A*, R_L and the rheostat are both in parallel across the supply.

$$\text{Current in} \quad R_L = \frac{240}{80} = 3\text{ A}$$

$$P_L = 3^2 \times 80 = 720 \text{ Watts.}$$

(*b*) Slider moved down 1/3 from A.

$$\text{Total resistance} = 40 + \frac{80 \times 80}{80 + 80} = 80\ \Omega$$

$$\text{Current drawn} = \frac{240}{80} = 3\text{ A.}$$

This current divides into 2 paths at the slider.

$$I_L = 1.5\text{ A}$$

$$P_L = (1.5)^2 \times 80 = 180 \text{ Watts.}$$

(*c*) Slider moved down 2/3 from A.

$$\text{Total resistance} = 80 + \frac{80 \times 40}{80 + 40} = 106.667\ \Omega$$

$$\text{Current drawn} = \frac{240}{106.667} = 2.25\text{ A}$$

$$I_L = 2.25 \times \frac{40}{120} = 0.75\text{ A}$$

$$P_L = (0.75)^2 \times 80 = 45 \text{ Watts.}$$

EXERCISES

2.1. Calculate the resistance of (*a*) a 100 watt 230 V lamp (*b*) a 1 kW 250 V iron. **[Ans.** 529 Ω, 62.5 Ω]

2.2. A 250 V electric cooking range has three positions of the switch – High, Medium and Low. The effective resistances in these positions are 10 ohms, 20 ohms and 40 ohms respectively. There are only two identical heater coils in the range. Show how the three positions are obtained by proper connections of the coils. Find the power consumed in each position.

[**Ans.** High—Two 20 Ω coils in parallel — 6.25 kW.
Medium-only one coil is used-3.125 kW.
Low—Two 20 Ω coils in series-1.5625 kW.]

2.3. A 18-ohm resistor is connected in parallel with a series combination of resistors of 10 and 26 ohms. If the drop across the 10 ohms is 50 Volts, find the total applied voltage and the total current. [**Ans.** 180 V, 15 A]

2.4. Two resistors R_A and R_B are connected in series across a 240 volt source. When a 30,000-ohm. Voltmeter is connected across R_A and then across R_B, the voltmeter reads, 96 V in each case. Find the ohmic values of the resistors. [**Ans.** 15,000 Ω]

2.5. Three resistors R_A, R_B and R_C are connected to a 240 volt source. If $R_A = 2R_C$; $R_B = 3R_C$, and the total power taken by the circuit is 800 watts, calculate (*a*) R_A, R_B, R_C, (*b*) the power in each resistor.

[**Ans.** 24, 36 and 12 Ω, 266.67, 400 and 133.33 W]

2.6. Two 30-ohm resistors are connected in parallel. What should be the resistance to be connected in series with this parallel combination such that the power in each 30 ohm resistor is one-fourth of the total power.

[**Ans.** 15 Ω]

2.7. It is required to operate a 1 kW, 220 volt electric heater from 250 volt mains. What is the value of the resistance to be used in series ? What is the percentage of power wasted in the series resistance ? [**Ans.** 6.6 Ω, 13.64]

2.8. Four resistances of values 2, 3, 4 and 5 ohms are all in parallel with a common supply. If the total power absorbed in all of them is 4620 watts, find the applied voltage and the power absorbed in each resistor.

[**Ans.** 60 V; 1.8, 1.2, 0.9 and 0.72 kW]

2.9. When two resistors are connected in series the total equivalent is 90 ohms; when in parallel, the equivalent is 20 ohms. What is the value of each resistor. [**Ans.** 30, 60 Ω]

2.10. Referring to the circuit in Fig. 2.25; calculate (*a*) the total equivalent resistance at *AB*, (*b*) the supply current I_S, (*c*) load current I_L and (*d*) the load power. [**Ans.** 20 A, 12 A, 3 A, 108 W]

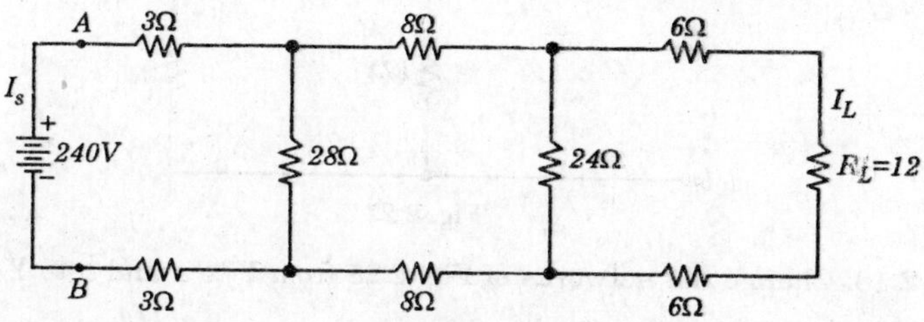

Fig. 2.25

2.11. Two voltmeters having resistances of 10,000 Ω and 15,000 Ω respectively are joined in series across as 240 V supply. What is the reading of each voltmeter ? [**Ans.** 96, 144V]

2.12. Two coils connected in parallel have a common applied voltage of 240 V. The total current taken is 30 A and the power taken by one coil is 2.4 kW. What is the resistance of each coil ? [**Ans.** 24 ; 12 Ω]

2.13. A resistor *R* is connected in series with a parallel combination of two resistors of 24 and 8 ohms. The total power dissipated in the circuit is 64 W when the applied voltage is 24 Volts. Calculate *R*. [**Ans.** 3 Ω]

2.14. If AB and CD represent two resistances R_1 and R_2 show that EF represents, to the same scale, the value of their parallel combination.

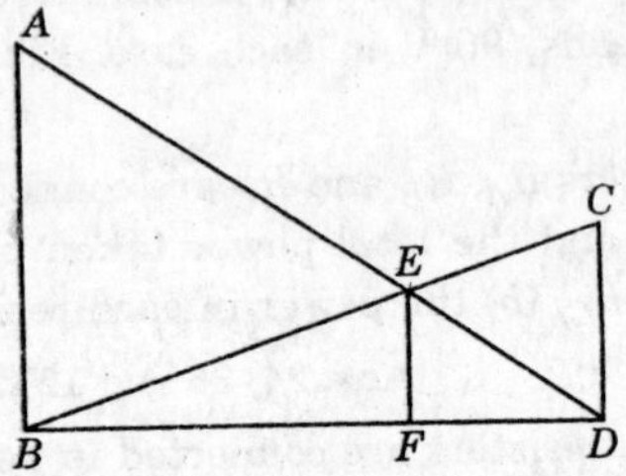

Fig. 2.26

2.15. Two resistors $R_1 = 2{,}000\ \Omega$ and $R_2 = 4{,}000\ \Omega$ are joined in series and connected to a 100 volt supply. The voltage drops across R_1 and R_2 are measured successively by a voltmeter of resistance 50,000 Ω. Find the sum of the two readings. **[Ans. 97.4 Volts]**

2.16. A wheatstone bridge circuit is made up of the following arms. $AB = 260\ \Omega$, $BC = 325\ \Omega$, $AC = 260\ \Omega$, $BD = 110\ \Omega$, $CD = 20\ \Omega$. A voltage of 240 volts is applied between A and D. Find (a) the total equivalent resistance between A and D. (b) the total current supplied by the source and (c) the current through the element BC. $\left[\textbf{Ans. } 160\ \Omega,\ 1.5\ \text{A},\ \frac{2}{13}\ \text{A}\right]$

2.17. In the circuit of Fig. 2.27, find R_{ab}. **[Ans. 1.3 Ω]**

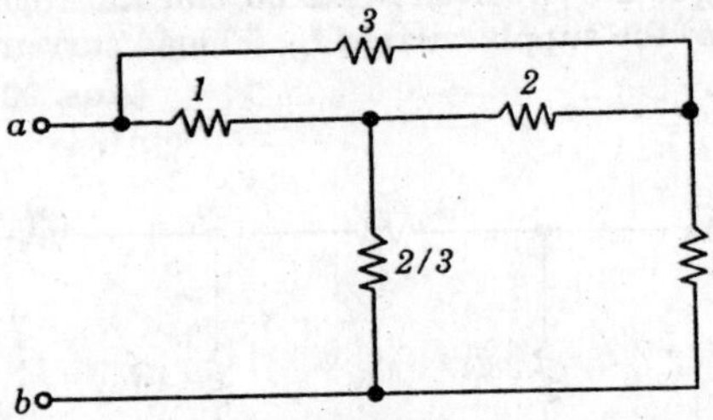

Fig. 2.27

2.18. Change the networks of Fig. 2.28 from Y to Δ and Δ to Y

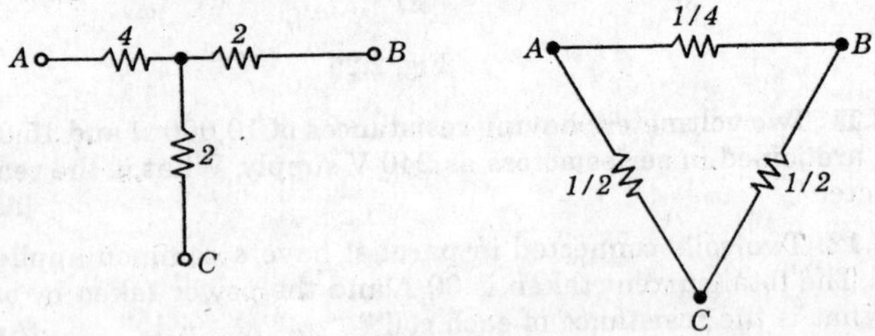

Fig. 2.28

[Ans. 5, 10, 10 ohms 0.2, 0.1, 0.1 Ω**]**

2.19. Reduce the network of Fig. 2.29 into a single resistance.

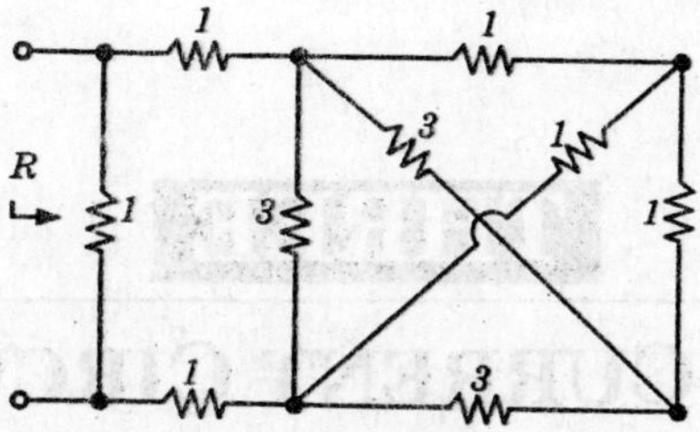

Fig. 2.29

[Ans. 3/4 ohms)

2.20. A battery of 10 volts *DC* is applied between points *A* and *B* in the circuit in Fig. 2.30. Find by star delta transformation, the current supplied by the battery. **[Ans. 1.56 A]**

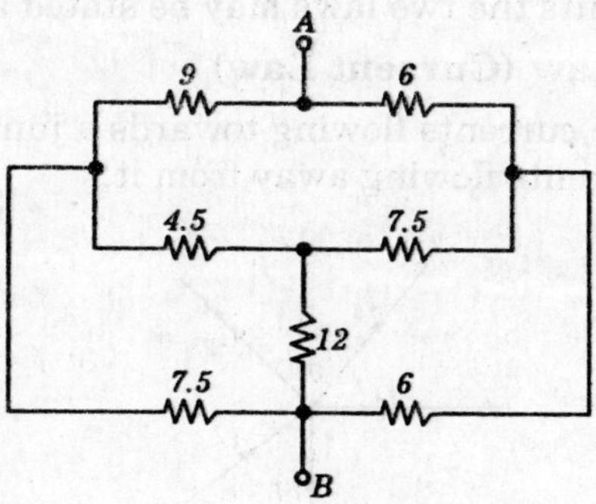

Fig. 2.30

2.21. Twelve 1 Ω resistors are connected to form the sides of a cube. Find the equivalent resistance between two opposite corners of opposite faces.

THREE

DIRECT CURRENT CIRCUITS–II

Kirchhoff's Laws

Kirchhoff stated two simple laws, one for currents meeting at any electrical junction and the other for voltages around closed loops. For d.c. circuits the two laws may be stated as follows :

Kirchhoff's 1st Law (Current Law)

The sum of the currents flowing towards a junction is equal to the sum of the currents flowing away from it.

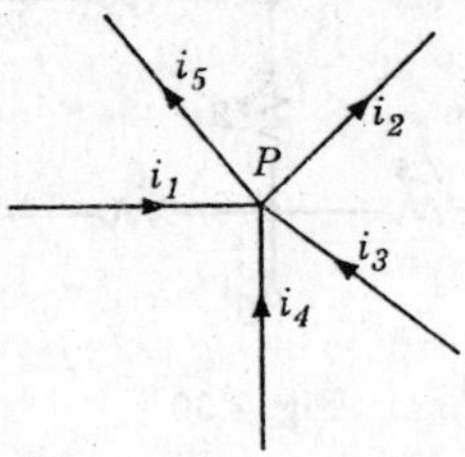

Fig. 3.1

In Fig. 3.1, the currents i_1, i_2 and i_4 flow towards the junction P; i_2 and i_5 flow away from the junction. According to Kirchhoff's 1st law,

$$i_1 + i_2 + i_4 = i_2 + i_5.$$

Kirchhoff's 2nd Law (Voltage Law)

In a closed circuit the sum of the potential drops is equal to the sum of the potential rises.

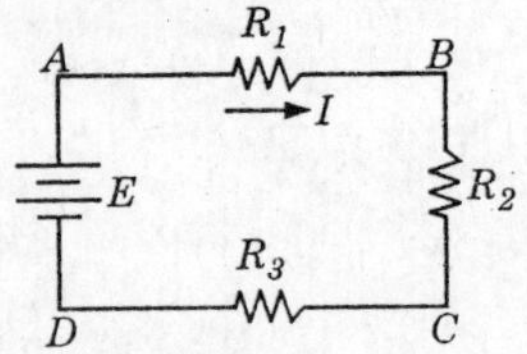

Fig. 3.2

In the closed loop *ABCDA*,

Branch	*Pot. Drop*	*Pot. Rise*
AB	IR_1	—
BC	IR_2	—
CD	IR_3	—
DA	—	*E*

Hence $$IR_1 + IR_2 + IR_3 = E$$

Note. Current flowing from *A* to *B* implies a potential drop from *A* to *B*. When we go from *D* to *A* (from the negative terminal to the positive terminal of the battery) there is a potential rise of *E* volts.

Several electric circuits can now be solved with the help of these two laws.

Example 3.1. *Fig. 3.3 shows two batteries P and Q supplying a common load through their internal resistances. Calculate (a) the load current and the currents supplied by the batteries (b) the voltage at the load and (c) the power delivered to the load.*

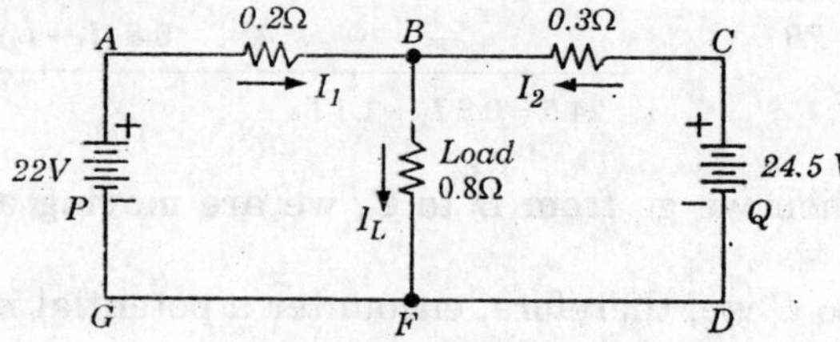

Fig. 3.3

Solution. In all such problems, the method of attack will be as follows :

Step 1. Name the circuit. Here *ABCDFG*.

Step 2. Mark arbitrarily the currents in the circuit.

(Use Kirchhoff's 1st law at all junctions.)

Here at node *B*, $I_L = I_1 + I_2$.

Step 3. Check the number of unknown currents

Here 2 ; I_1 and I_2.

Step 4. Write using Kirchhoff's 2nd law equations for as many closed loops as there are number of unknowns. Care must be taken as will be seen later, in choosing the closed loops.

Step 5. Solve the equations for the unknown quantities.

This method of solution is called the branch-current method. For the problem at hand, we must write two equations choosing 2 closed loops.

For the loop *ABFGA*,

Branch	*Pot. drops*	*Pot. rises*
AB	$I_1 \times 0.2$	—
BF	$(I_1 + I_2)\ 0.8$	—
FG	—	—
GA	—	22

$$\therefore \quad 0.2\, I_1 + 0.8\, (I_1 + I_2) = 22$$

For the loop *BCDFB*

Branch	*Pot. drop*	*Pot. rise*
BC	—	$0.3\, I_2$
CD	24.5	—
DF	—	—
FB	—	$0.8\, (I_1 + I_2)$

$$\therefore \quad 24.5 = 0.8\, I_1 + 1.1\, I_2$$

Note. When we go from *B* to *C*, we are moving against the current.

From *B* to *C* we, therefore, encounter a potential rise.

Solving the two equations,

$$I_1 = 10 \text{ amps.}$$
$$I_2 = 15 \text{ amps.}$$

(*b*) The voltage at the load

$$= I_L \times 0.8$$
$$= (10 + 15)\ 0.8 = 20 \text{ V.}$$

(*c*) Power delivered to the load

$$= \text{Current} \times \text{Voltage at load}$$
$$= 25 \times 20 = 500 \text{ W} = 25^2 \times 0.8 \text{ (also).}$$

Example 3.2. *Fig. 3.4 shows a 125 V D.C. generator connected to charge two storage batteries to* E_A = *114 V and* E_B = *110 V; Calculate (a)* I_A, I_B *and I (b) the power loss in the resistors (c) the power delivered by the generator and (d) the efficiency of the charging system.*

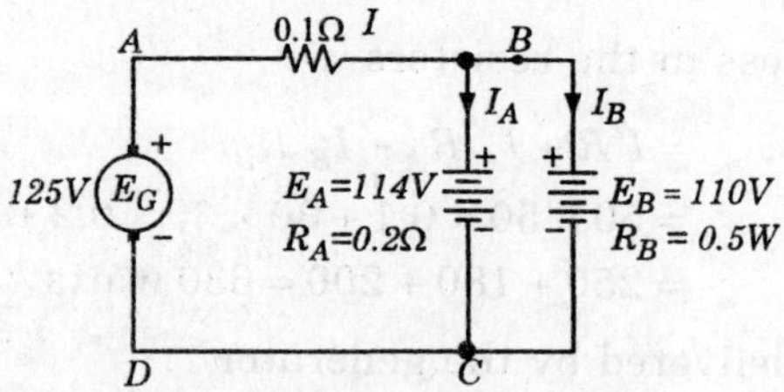

Fig. 3.4

Solution.

1. Name the circuit *ABCD*
2. Mark the currents—using Kirchhoff's I law at *B*.
3. The number of unknowns is 2 (I_A and I_B)
4. Closed loop equations for loop (*a*) *ABCDA* through E_A and (*b*) *ABCDA* through E_B.

ABCDA through battery A.

Branch	Pot. drop	Pot. rise
AB	$(I_A + I_B)\ 0.1$	—
BC	$114 + 0.2\ I_A$	—
CD	—	—
DA	—	125

$$\therefore \quad 0.1\ (I_A + I_B) + 0.2\ I_A + 114 = 125$$

or $$0.3\ I_A + 0.1\ I_B = 11 \qquad ...(1)$$

ABCDA through battery B

Branch	Pot. drop	Pot. rise
AB	$(I_A + I_B)\ 0.1$	—
BC	$110 + 0.5\ I_B$	—
CD	—	—
DA	—	—

$$\therefore \quad 0.1\ I_A + 0.6\ I_B = 15..(2)$$

Solving, $I_A = 30$ A

$I_B = 20$ A

$I = I_A + I_B = 50$ A

(*b*) Power loss in the resistors

$$= I^2R + I_A{}^2R_A + I_B{}^2R_B$$
$$= 50 \times 50 \times 0.1 + 30 \times 30 \times 0.2 + 20 \times 20 \times 0.5$$
$$= 250 + 180 + 200 = 630 \text{ watts.}$$

(*c*) Power delivered by the generator

$$= 125 \times 50 = 6250 \text{ watts.}$$

(*d*) Efficiency $= \dfrac{\text{Output}}{\text{Input}} = \dfrac{\text{Input–Losses}}{\text{Input}}$

$$= \left(1 - \frac{\text{Losses}}{\text{Input}}\right) = 1 - \frac{630}{6250}$$
$$= 0.8992 \quad \text{or} \quad 89.92 \text{ per cent.}$$

Example 3.3. *For the circuit of Fig. 3.5, calculate* E_A *and* E_B.

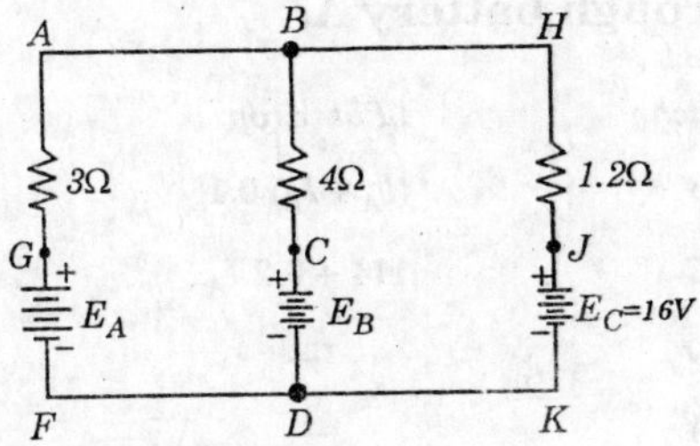

Fig. 3.5

Solution. There are two unknowns E_A and E_B. Hence we write two closed-loop equations.

For the loop *ABCDFGA*

Branch	*Pot. drop*	*Pot. rise*
AB	—	—
BC	—	6×4
CD	E_B	—
DF	—	—
FG	—	E_A
GA	5×3	—
∴	$E_B + 15$ =	$E_A + 24$

or $\quad E_B - E_A = 9$

For the loop *BHJKDCB*

Branch	Pot. drop	Pot. rise
BH	—	—
HJ	11×1.2	—
JK	16	—
KD	—	—
DC	—	E_B
CB	6×4	—

$\therefore \quad 13.2 + 16 + 24 = E_B$

Hence $\quad E_B = 53.2$ V.

and $\quad E_A = 44.2$ V.

Example 3.4. *Two batteries A and B are properly connected to supply a current of 160 amps to a load resistance R_L. $E_A = 120$ V $R_A = 0.15$, $R_B = 0.10\ \Omega$ and $I_B = 60$ A. Calculate (a) E_B and (b) the load power, shown in Fig. 3.6.*

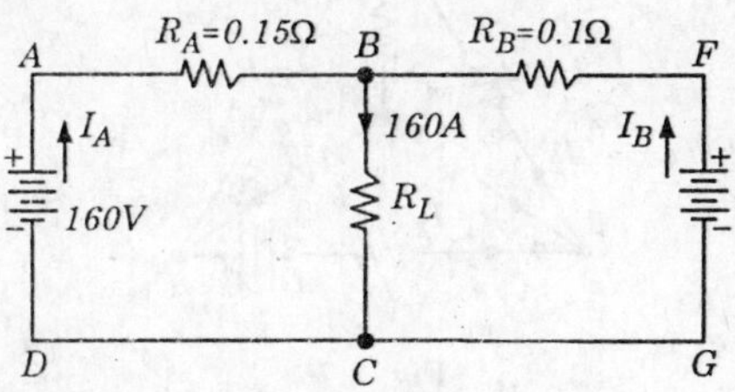

Fig. 3.6

Solution. As $I_B = 60$ A, $\quad I_A = 100\,A$.

Writing the closed loop equation for *ABCDA*.

Branch	*Pot. drop*	*Pot. rise*
AB	100×0.15	—
BC	$160\,R_L$	—
CD	—	—
DA	—	120

$\therefore \quad 15 + 160\,R_L = 120$

or $\quad 160\,R_L = 105$

For the loop *FBCGF*

Branch	*Pot. drop*	*Pot. rise*
FB	60×0.1	—
BC	$160 \times R_L$	—
CG	—	—
CF	—	E_B

$\therefore \quad 6 + 160\, R_L = E_B$

Substituting for R_L

(*a*) $\quad 6 + 105 = E_B = 111$ **volts.**

(*b*) load power $\quad$ = Voltage at load × load current

$= 160\, R_B \times 160$ watts

$= 105 \times 160 = 16{,}800$ watts.

Example 3.5. *Find the value of R in the circuit of Fig. 3.7 if the current through branch AO is zero. Find also the current in R.*

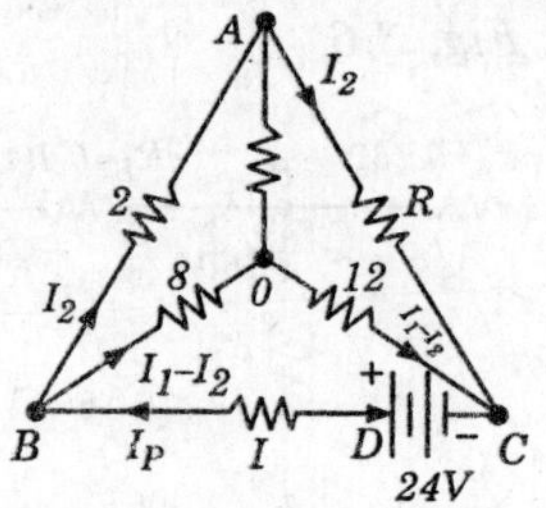

Fig. 3.7

Solution. The currents are marked as in figure keeping in view that the current in *AO* is zero.

Voltage drop $V_{BA} = V_{BO}$, as *A* and *O* must be at the same potential.

$$V_{BA} = 2\, I_2 = 8\, (I_1 - I_2) \qquad ...(1)$$

Similarly $\quad V_{AC} = V_{OC}$

i.e., $\quad I_2 R = 12\, (I_1 - I_2) \qquad ...(2)$

Divide (1) by (2), we get

$$\frac{2}{R} = \frac{8}{12}$$

$\therefore \quad R = 3.$

From (1), $\quad 10 I_2 = 8 I_1$

$$I_1 = \frac{10}{8} I_2$$

Consider the closed loop *BACDB*.

Branch	*Pot. Drop*	*Pot. Rise*
BA	$2I_2$	—
AC	$3I_2$	—
CD	—	24
DB	$1 \times I_1$	—
$\therefore$	$5I_2 + I_1 = 24$	

Substituting for I_1 in terms of I_2

$$5I_2 + \frac{10}{8} I_2 = 24$$

$$\frac{50}{8} I_2 = 24$$

$$I_2 = \frac{24 \times 8}{50} = 3.84 \text{ Amps.}$$

Maxwell's Mesh Method (Loop Method)

This method first proposed by Maxwell simplifies the solution for several networks. In this method, we consider loop or mesh currents instead of the currents in the various elements in the previous section. In the circuit of Fig. 3.7, two batteries are connected in a five resistor network. We shall name the three loop currents I_1, I_2 and I_3. The directions of the loop currents are arbitrarily chosen. Note that the actual current flowing through R_A is neither I_1 nor I_2 but $(I_1 - I_2)$ in a downward direction. (Because I_1 and I_2 are flowing in opposite direction through R_A).

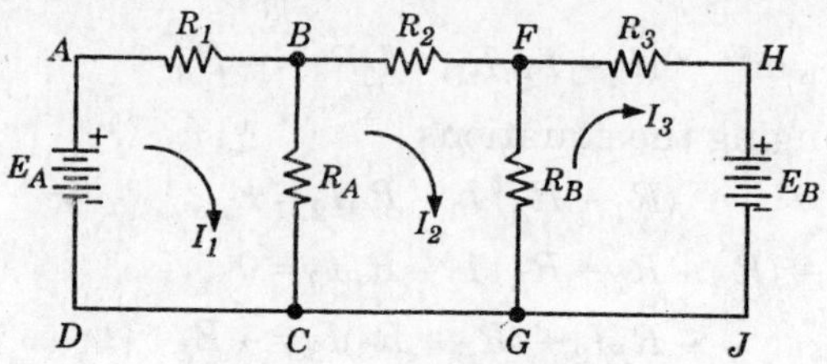

Fig. 3.7

For the first loop, we may write (*ABCDA*)

$$I_1R_1 + (I_1 - I_2)\, R_A = E_A$$

For the second loop (*BFGCB*) :

Branch	*Pot. drop*	*Pot. rise*
BF	I_2R_2	—
FG	$(I_2 - I_3) R_B$	—
GC	—	—
CB	—	$(I_1 - I_2) R_A$

$$\therefore \quad I_2R_2 + (I_2 - I_3) R_B = (I_1 - I_2) R_A$$

or $$I_2R_2 + (I_2 - I_3)R_B + (I_2 - I_1) R_A = 0.$$

Note that when we consider the nett current in R_A to be $(I_1 - I_2)$ directed downwards, then if we move from C to B, we encounter current flowing against us. Hence this is a potential-rise of $(I_1 - I_2) R_A$. However, instead of $(I_1 - I_2)$ downwards, we could have considered $(I_2 - I_1)$ upwards, in which case moving from C to B we meet a current flowing along with us which means a potential drop of $(I_2 - I_1) R_A$. Both give us the same results. A potential rise of $(I_1 - I_2) R$ is identical with a potential drop of $(I_2 - I_1) R$.

For the third loop (*FHJGF*)

Branch	Pot. drop	Pot. rise
FH	I_3R_3	—
HJ	E_B	—
JG	—	—
GF	—	$(I_2 - I_3) R_B$

$$\therefore \quad I_3R_3 + E_B = (I_2 - I_3) R_B$$

or $$(I_3 - I_2) R_B + I_3R_3 = - E_B$$

Re-arranging the equations

$$(R_1 + R_A) I_1 - R_AI_2 = E_A$$

$$- R_AI_1 + (R_A + R_2 + R_B) I_2 - R_BI_3 = 0$$

$$- R_BI_2 + (R_B + R_3)I_3 = - E_B$$

These equations may be put in matrix form

$$\begin{bmatrix} (R_1 + R_A) & - R_A & 0 \\ - R_A & (R_A + R_2 + R_B) & - R_B \\ 0 & - R_B & (R_B + R_3) \end{bmatrix} \begin{bmatrix} I_1 \\ I_2 \\ I_3 \end{bmatrix} \begin{bmatrix} E_A \\ 0 \\ - E_B \end{bmatrix}$$

If values of the resistances and voltages are known the currents can be solved by the Kramer's rule.

Matrix Solution.

Consider the 3 equations

$$A_1x + A_2y + A_3z = P$$
$$B_1x + B_2y + B_3z = Q$$
$$C_1x + C_2y + C_3z = R$$

where x, y and z are unknowns, the A_i's, B_i's and C_i's are known co-efficients and P, Q and R are also known. These three equations may be put in matrix form, thus

$$\begin{bmatrix} A_1 & A_2 & A_3 \\ B_1 & B_2 & B_3 \\ C_1 & C_2 & C_3 \end{bmatrix} \begin{bmatrix} x \\ y \\ z \end{bmatrix} = \begin{bmatrix} P \\ Q \\ R \end{bmatrix}$$

By Kramer's rule, x is the ratio of 2 determinants. For the numerator determinant we have the same numbers as in the co-efficient matrix, with the first column replaced by P, Q and R.

$$x = \frac{\begin{vmatrix} P & A_2 & A_3 \\ Q & B_2 & B_3 \\ R & C_2 & C_3 \end{vmatrix}}{\begin{vmatrix} A_1 & A_2 & A_3 \\ B_1 & B_2 & B_3 \\ C_1 & C_2 & C_3 \end{vmatrix}}$$

$$y = \frac{\begin{vmatrix} A_1 & P & A_3 \\ B_1 & Q & B_3 \\ C_1 & R & C_3 \end{vmatrix}}{\begin{vmatrix} A_1 & A_2 & A_3 \\ B_1 & B_2 & B_3 \\ C_1 & C_2 & C_3 \end{vmatrix}}$$

$$z = \frac{\begin{vmatrix} A_1 & A_2 & P \\ B_1 & B_2 & Q \\ C_1 & C_2 & R \end{vmatrix}}{\begin{vmatrix} A_1 & A_2 & A_3 \\ B_1 & B_2 & B_3 \\ C_1 & C_2 & C_3 \end{vmatrix}}$$

In all the cases the denominator determinant is the same.

To find determinants of orders 2 and 3.

$$\textit{Order 2}: \text{Det} = \begin{vmatrix} A & B \\ C & D \end{vmatrix} = AD - BC$$

$$\textit{Order 3}: \text{Det} = \begin{vmatrix} A_1 & A_2 & A_3 \\ B_1 & B_2 & B_3 \\ C_1 & C_2 & C_3 \end{vmatrix}$$

For a third order determinant first find the following :

$$D_1 = A_1 (B_2C_3 - B_3C_2)$$
$$D_2 = A_2 (B_1C_3 - B_3C_1)$$
$$D_3 = A_3 (B_1C_2 - B_2C_1)$$

Then determinant $= D_1 - D_2 + D_3$

Example 3.6. *Solve the following set of simultaneous equations :*

$$2x + 3y = 13$$
$$x + y - z = 0$$
$$x - y + z = 4.$$

Solution. In matrix from

$$\begin{bmatrix} 2 & 3 & 0 \\ 1 & 1 & -1 \\ 1 & -1 & 1 \end{bmatrix} \begin{bmatrix} x \\ y \\ z \end{bmatrix} = \begin{bmatrix} 13 \\ 0 \\ 4 \end{bmatrix}$$

$$x = \frac{\begin{vmatrix} 13 & 3 & 0 \\ 0 & 1 & -1 \\ 4 & -1 & 1 \end{vmatrix}}{\begin{vmatrix} 2 & 3 & 0 \\ 1 & 1 & -1 \\ 1 & -1 & 1 \end{vmatrix}}$$

Numerator Determinant

$$D_1 = 13 (1 - 1) = 0$$
$$D_2 = 3 (0 + 4) = 12$$
$$D_3 = 0$$

$\therefore$ Determinant $= 0 - 12 + 0 = -12$

Denominator Determinant

$$D_1 = 2 (1 - 1) = 0$$
$$D_2 = 3 (1 + 1) = 6$$
$$D_3 = 0$$

$\therefore$ Determinant $= 0 - 6 + 0 = -6$

$$x = \frac{-12}{-6} = 2$$

$$y = \frac{\begin{vmatrix} 2 & 13 & 0 \\ 1 & 0 & -1 \\ 1 & 4 & 1 \end{vmatrix}}{\begin{vmatrix} 2 & 3 & 0 \\ 1 & 1 & -1 \\ 1 & -1 & 1 \end{vmatrix}}$$

Numerator Determinant

$$D_1 = 2\,(0 \times 1 \times 4) = 8$$

$$D_3 = 13\,(1 + 1) = 26$$

$$D_3 = 0$$

Determinant $= 8 - 26 = -18$

Denominator Determinant

$= -6$ **(as before)**

$$y = \frac{-18}{-6} = 3.$$

$$z = \frac{\begin{vmatrix} 2 & 3 & 13 \\ 1 & 1 & 0 \\ 1 & -1 & 4 \end{vmatrix}}{-6 \text{ (as before)}}$$

Numerator $D_1 = 2\,(4 - 0) = 8$

$$D_2 = 3\,(1 \times 4 - 0) = 12$$

$$D_3 = 13\,(-1 - 1) = -26$$

Determinant $= 8 - 12 - 26 = -30$

$$z = \frac{-30}{-6} = 5$$

$$x = 2 \;\; y = 3 \;\; z = 5.$$

Example 3.7. *Solve simultaneously*

$$3x + 2y = 0$$

$$2x + 3y = -10.$$

Solution. In matrix form

$$\begin{bmatrix} 3 & 2 \\ 2 & 3 \end{bmatrix} \begin{bmatrix} x \\ y \end{bmatrix} = \begin{bmatrix} 0 \\ -10 \end{bmatrix}$$

$$x = \frac{\begin{vmatrix} 0 & 2 \\ -10 & 3 \end{vmatrix}}{\begin{vmatrix} 3 & 2 \\ 2 & 3 \end{vmatrix}} = \frac{0 \times 3 - (-10 \times 2)}{3 \times 3 - 2 \times 2} = \frac{20}{5} = 4$$

$$y = \frac{\begin{vmatrix} 3 & 0 \\ 2 & -10 \end{vmatrix}}{\begin{vmatrix} 3 & 2 \\ 2 & 3 \end{vmatrix}} = \frac{3 \times (-10) - 0}{5} = \frac{-30}{5} = -6.$$

Maxwell's Equations in Matrix Form by Inspection

Let us look at the circuit of Fig. 3.7 and the corresponding matrix equations. It is possible to form these set of equations without having to go through the procedure.

First we recognise that the matrix equations are written in the form

$$[R]\ [I] = [V]$$

where R is a resistance matrix, shown in Fig. 3.8.

I is a current matrix

and V is a voltage matrix

If the circuit has three loops, and three loop currents, then $[I]$ will have 3 elements being the 3 loop-currents. $[R]$ will be a 3×3 matrix. $[V]$ has 3 elements being the voltages of the 3 loops. Let us look at $[R]$ carefully. $[R]$ is a 3×3 matrix for a 3 loop network.

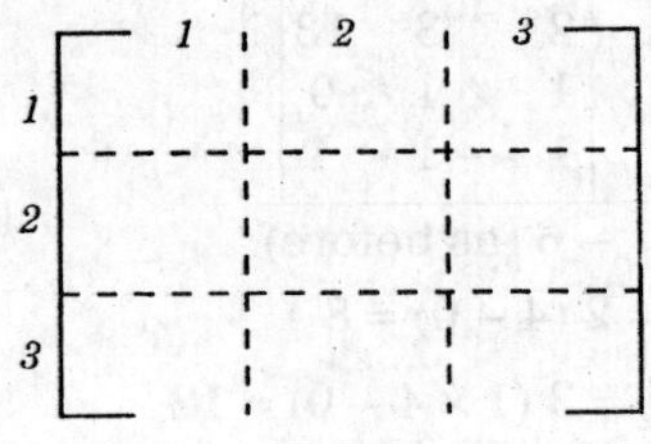

Fig. 3.8

On inspection, it is found that the first element is the sum of all the elements (resistances) in the first loop, in this case $(R_1 + R_A)$. The next element in this row (the 1-2 element) is the element or elements common to the 1st and 2nd loops. The sign of this entry is fixed this way : if the currents in the 2 loops flowing in the common element, are in the same direction the entry is positive otherwise it is negative. In this case the common element is R_A and it is negative as I_1 and I_2 flow in opposite direction. The next entry in the same row (1-3 entry) is the element common to the first and the third loops, the sign being fixed as before. In case there is no common element, the entry is zero.

Similarly, we fix the entries in the 2nd and 3rd rows. The first entry in the 2nd row (2 – 1), is the element common to the 2nd and 1st loops, the sign being fixed as before. The entry will be identical to the 1-2 entry. The 2-2 entry will be the sum of the resistances forming the 2nd loop just as the 3-3 entry is the sum of the resistances in the 3rd loop.

Note the following points :

1. All diagonal entries (sums of resistances in the respective loops) will be positive.

2. All off-diagonal entries (resistances common between loops) will have symmetry about the diagonal.

3. The signs of off diagonal elements will depend on the directions of the currents in the 2 loops.

The Voltage Matrix [V]. There are three entries being the voltages in the 3 loops. (If there is no voltage as in loop 2 put a zero).

In the first loop, we have E_A and in the third E_B.

The sign is again fixed by convention. If in the direction of the flow of the current in a loop, there is a potential rise at the voltage source then we put a positive sign (in loop 1 the current, I_1 is assumed arbitrarily to flow in the clockwise direction). In the voltage source, in the direction of flow of I_1 there is a voltage rise E_A. Hence we use $+E_A$. In loop 3, the current I_3, assumed clockwise, gives a voltage drop at the voltage source. Hence $-E_B$.

Example 3.8. *Form the Maxwell's mesh matrix for the network shown in Fig. 3.9.*

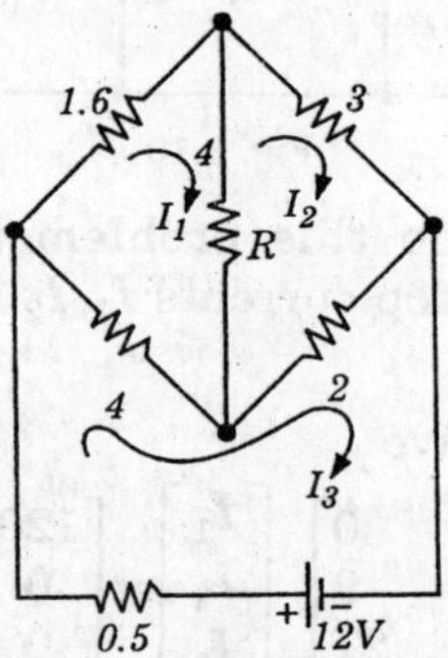

Fig. 3.9

Solution. By inspection

$$\begin{bmatrix} 9.6 & -4 & -4 \\ -4 & 9 & -2 \\ -4 & -2 & 6.5 \end{bmatrix} \begin{bmatrix} I_1 \\ I_2 \\ I_3 \end{bmatrix} = \begin{bmatrix} 0 \\ 0 \\ +12 \end{bmatrix}$$

Now we may solve for any of the currents by using Kramer's rule.

To solve for the currents

$$I_1 = \frac{\begin{vmatrix} 0 & -4 & -4 \\ 0 & 9 & -2 \\ 12 & -2 & 6.5 \end{vmatrix}}{\begin{vmatrix} 9.6 & -4 & -4 \\ -4 & 9 & -2 \\ -4 & -2 & 6.5 \end{vmatrix}} = \frac{528}{211.2} = 2.5 \text{ A}$$

$$I_2 = \frac{\begin{vmatrix} 9.6 & 0 & -4 \\ -4 & 0 & -2 \\ -4 & 12 & 6.5 \end{vmatrix}}{\begin{vmatrix} 9.6 & -4 & -4 \\ -4 & 9 & -2 \\ -4 & -2 & 6.5 \end{vmatrix}} = \frac{422.4}{211.2} = 2 \text{ A.}$$

The net current through the resistance 4Ω is 2.5 – 2 = 0.5 ampere flowing down.

Example 3.9. ***In the circuit of Fig. 3.10, obtain the load current and the power delivered to the load.***

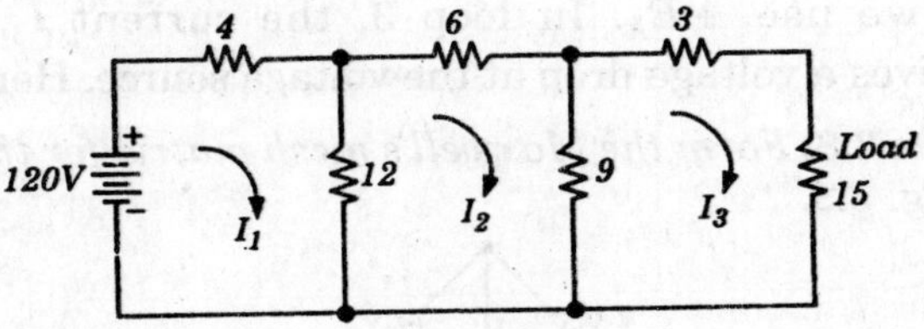

Fig. 3.10

Solution. Let us do this problem by the Mesh method. Considering the three loop currents I_1, I_2 and I_3 as shown in Fig. 3.10.

By inspection, we have

$$\begin{bmatrix} 16 & -12 & 0 \\ -12 & 27 & -9 \\ 0 & -9 & 27 \end{bmatrix} \begin{bmatrix} I_1 \\ I_2 \\ I_3 \end{bmatrix} = \begin{bmatrix} 120 \\ 0 \\ 0 \end{bmatrix}$$

$$I_3 = \frac{\begin{vmatrix} 16 & -12 & 120 \\ -12 & 27 & 0 \\ 0 & -9 & 0 \end{vmatrix}}{\begin{vmatrix} 16 & -12 & 0 \\ -12 & 27 & -9 \\ 0 & -9 & 27 \end{vmatrix}} = \frac{12{,}960}{6480} = 2 \text{ A.}$$

Power in the load $= I_3^2 \times R_L = 2 \times 2 \times 15 = 60$ Watts.

Example 3.10. *In the network of Fig. 3.11 find the direction and magnitude of current in the ammeter of resistance 10Ω.*

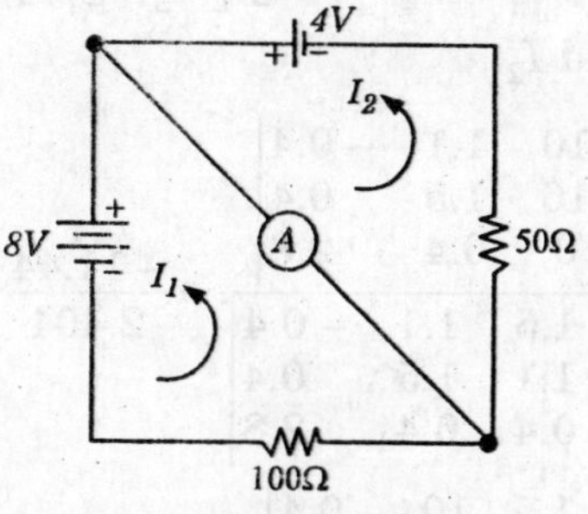

Fig. 3.11

Solution. Putting Kirchhoff's voltage. Law equations in matrix form, we have

$$\begin{bmatrix} 110 & -10 \\ -10 & 60 \end{bmatrix} \begin{bmatrix} I_1 \\ I_2 \end{bmatrix} = \begin{bmatrix} -8 \\ 4 \end{bmatrix}$$

$$I_1 = \frac{\begin{vmatrix} -8 & -10 \\ 4 & 60 \end{vmatrix}}{\begin{vmatrix} 110 & -10 \\ -10 & 60 \end{vmatrix}} = \frac{-480+40}{6600-100} = \frac{-440}{6500} \text{ A.}$$

$$I_2 = \frac{\begin{vmatrix} 110 & -8 \\ -10 & 4 \end{vmatrix}}{6500} = \frac{440-80}{6500} = \frac{360}{6500} \text{ A}$$

The current through the Ammeter $= I_1 - I_2 = -\dfrac{800}{6500}$ A.

Example 3.11. *Find the power delivered by the batteries of Fig. 3.12.*

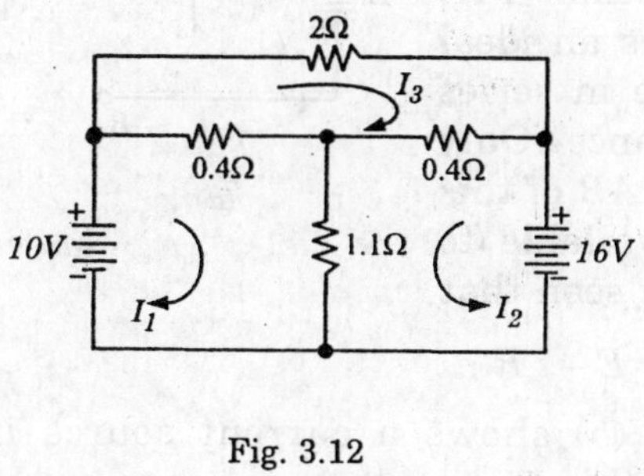

Fig. 3.12

Solution. The three loop currents, I_1, I_2 and I_3 are arbitrarily chosen to be as in figure.

Then $\begin{bmatrix} 1.5 & 1.1 & -0.4 \\ 1.1 & 1.5 & 0.4 \\ -0.4 & 0.4 & 2.8 \end{bmatrix} \begin{bmatrix} I_1 \\ I_2 \\ I_3 \end{bmatrix} = \begin{bmatrix} 10 \\ 16 \\ 0 \end{bmatrix}$

Solve for I_1 and I_2

$$I_1 = \frac{\begin{vmatrix} 10 & 1.1 & -0.4 \\ 16 & 1.5 & 0.4 \\ 0 & 0.4 & 2.8 \end{vmatrix}}{\begin{vmatrix} 1.5 & 1.1 & -0.4 \\ 1.1 & 1.5 & 0.4 \\ -0.4 & 0.4 & 2.8 \end{vmatrix}} = \frac{-11.44}{2.404} = -4.76 \text{ A}$$

$$I_2 = \frac{\begin{vmatrix} 1.5 & 10 & -0.4 \\ 1.1 & 16 & 0.4 \\ -0.4 & 0 & 2.8 \end{vmatrix}}{2.404} = \frac{32.24}{2.404} = 13.41 \text{ A.}$$

Power in batteries.

Battery 1 : – 4.76 × 10 = – 47.6 watts.

(The negative sign indicates it is consuming power instead of delivering)

Battery 2 : 13.41 × 16 = 241.56 watts.

Equivalence of Sources

It can be seen that for the mesh method of analysis, it is easier if the circuit has voltage sources and in the nodal method, it is easier if we have only current sources. In several cases, we may have to transform one source to another. Fig. 3.13 (*a*), shows an ideal voltage source in series with a resistance. Only the terminals *AB* of this device are available to us. It is easily seen that

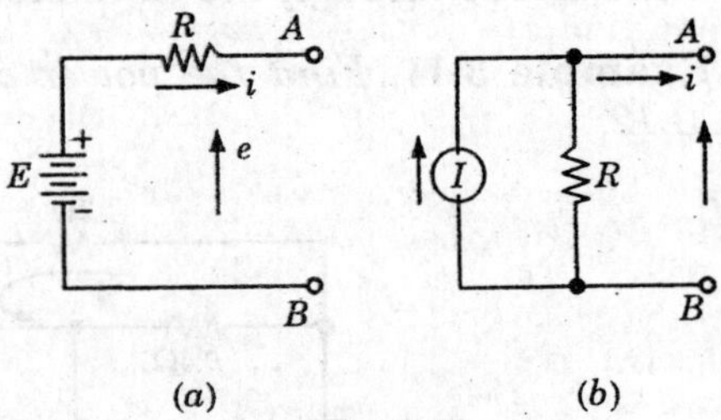

Fig. 3.13

$$e = E - i\,R \;....$$

Fig. 3.13 (*b*) shows a current source in parallel with a resistance. In this case,

$$e = (I - i)\,R = IR - i\,R.$$

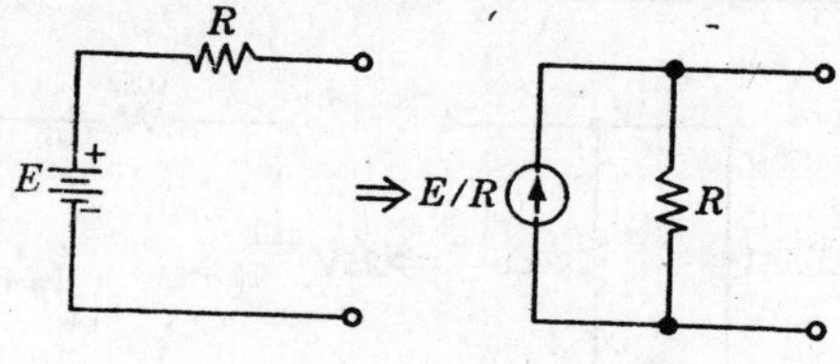

Fig. 3.14 (*a*)

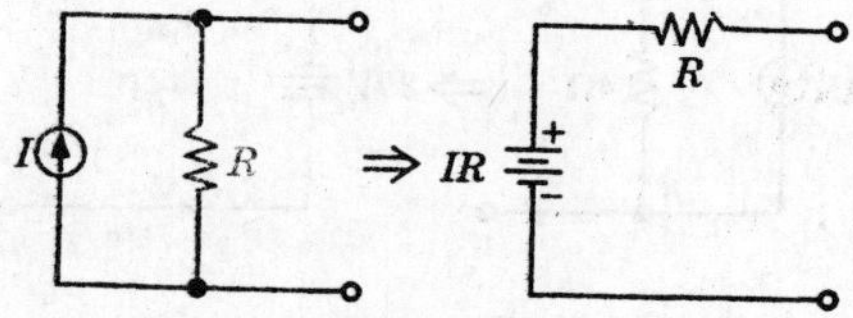

Fig. 3.14 (*b*)

The above equations are identical if $E = IR$. Thus a current source in parallel with a resistor is equivalent to a voltage source in series with the same resistor, provided that the value of the voltage source is equal to the value of the current source multiplied by the resistance. The transformation is valid in either direction and is shown in Fig. 3.14 (*a*) and (*b*). The polarities are clear from the examples worked below.

Example 3.12. *Convert the following voltage sources into current sources.*

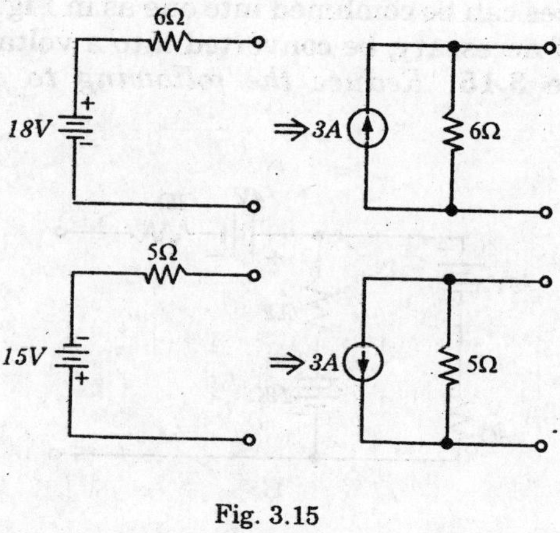

Fig. 3.15

Example 3.13. *Convert the following current sources into voltage sources.*

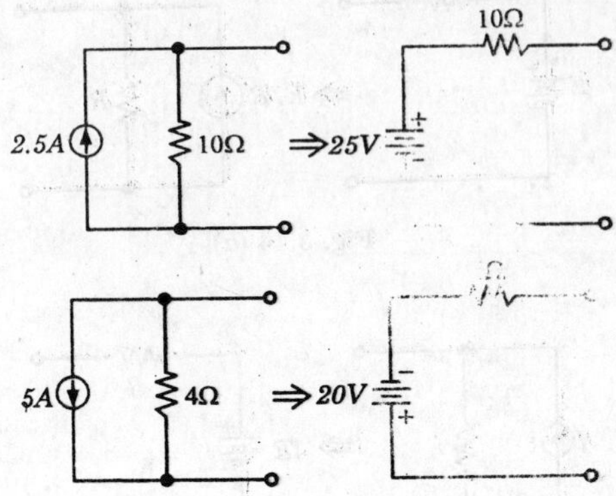

Fig. 3.16

Example 3.14. *Reduce the following to a single source.*

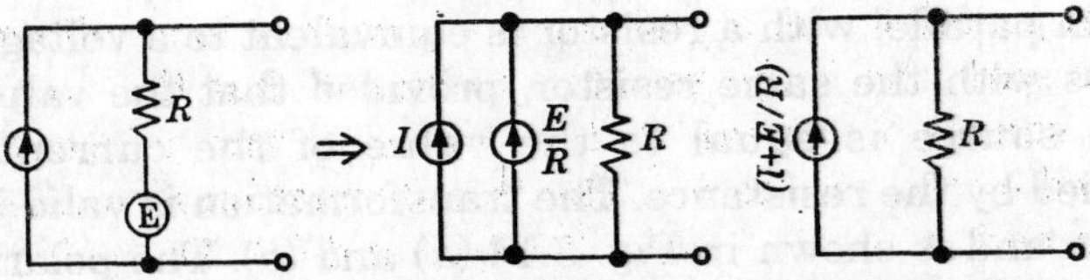

Fig. 3.17

The reduction procedure is shown in Fig. (*b*) and (*c*). The voltage source is first converted into a current source. The two current sources can be combined into one as in Fig. (*c*). The current source can, if necessary, be converted into a voltage source.

Example 3.15. *Reduce the following to a single source equivalent.*

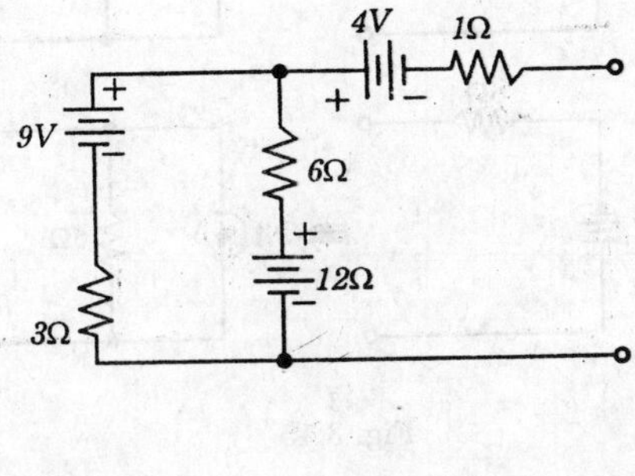

(*a*)

Solution. The reduction procedure is shown as a series of steps in Fig. 3.18 (*b*) to (*e*).

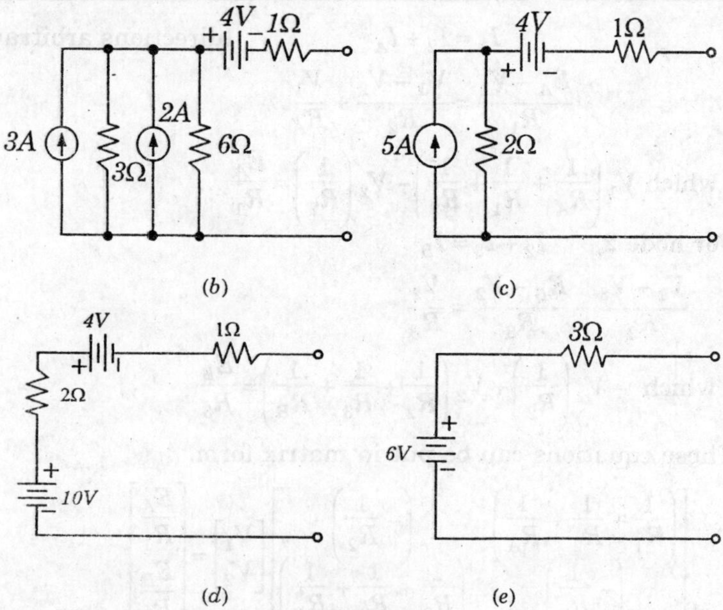

Fig. 3.18

The Nodal Method

For the nodal method, we consider the nodes of networks. A junction representing a connection of three or more branches is regarded as a node. One of the nodes is taken as the reference node. The voltages of the other nodes are assumed V_1, V_2 ... etc., with respect to the reference node. If n is the total number of nodes including the reference node, current equations for these $(n-1)$ nodes are then written and solved. Consider again the net work of Fig. 3.19. There are three nodes.

Node 3 may be chosen as the reference node. Let V_1 and V_2 be the voltages of nodes 1 and 2 with respect to node 3.

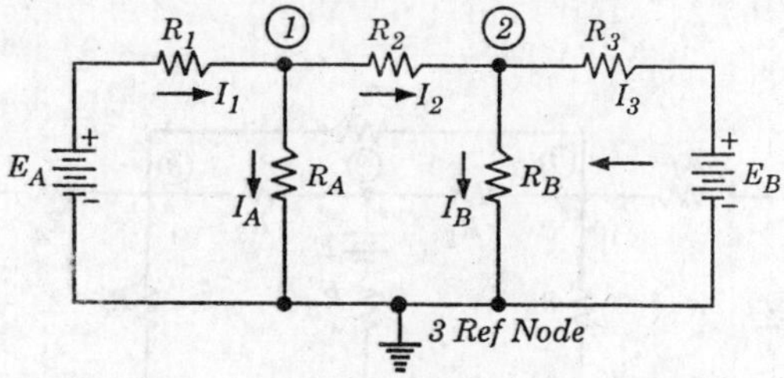

Fig. 3.19

Node 1 is the junction of R_1, R_2 and R_A and we may write the current equation for it as

$$I_1 = I_2 + I_A \qquad \text{(directions arbitrary)}$$

i.e. $$\frac{E_A - V_1}{R_1} = \frac{V_1 - V_2}{R_2} + \frac{V_1}{R_A}$$

from which $$V_1\left(\frac{1}{R_A} + \frac{1}{R_1} + \frac{1}{R_2}\right) - V_2\left(\frac{1}{R_2}\right) = \frac{E_A}{R_1} \ldots$$

For node 2, $I_2 + I_3 = I_B$

i.e. $$\frac{V_1 - V_3}{R_2} + \frac{E_B - V_2}{R_3} = \frac{V_2}{R_B}$$

from which $$-V_1\left(\frac{1}{R_2}\right) + V_2\left(\frac{1}{R_2} + \frac{1}{R_3} + \frac{1}{R_B}\right) = \frac{E_B}{R_3}$$

These equations can be put in matrix form.

$$\begin{bmatrix} \left(\frac{1}{R_1} + \frac{1}{R_2} + \frac{1}{R_A}\right) & \left(-\frac{1}{R_2}\right) \\ \left(-\frac{1}{R_2}\right) & \left(\frac{1}{R_2} + \frac{1}{R_3} + \frac{1}{R_B}\right) \end{bmatrix} \begin{bmatrix} V_1 \\ V_2 \end{bmatrix} = \begin{bmatrix} \frac{E_A}{R_1} \\ \frac{E_B}{R_3} \end{bmatrix}$$

and are of the form [*G*] [*V*] = [*I*]

The matrix can be formed by inspection if we remember that each element in the diagonal is the sum of the reciprocals of the resistances connected to each node. The off-diagonal element is the reciprocal of the resistance connecting two nodes. These off-diagonal terms (mutual terms) are *all* negative. The right hand matrix is the equivalent current entering the node. (This may be computed by replacing the voltage sources E_A and E_B by their corresponding current sources). Let us now try another network by the nodal method. We shall write out the nodal matrix by inspection for the circuit shown in Fig. 3.20.

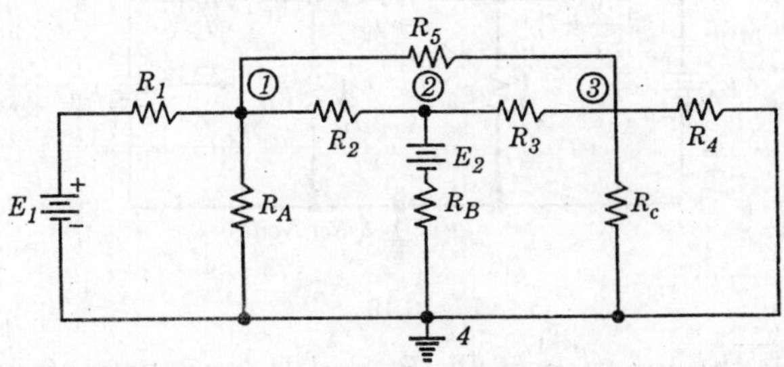

Fig. 3.20

$$\begin{bmatrix} \left(\frac{1}{R_1}+\frac{1}{R_2}+\frac{1}{R_5}+\frac{1}{R_A}\right) & \left(-\frac{1}{R_2}\right) & \left(-\frac{1}{R_5}\right) \\ \left(-\frac{1}{R_2}\right) & \left(\frac{1}{R_2}+\frac{1}{R_3}+\frac{1}{R_B}\right) & \left(-\frac{1}{R_3}\right) \\ \left(-\frac{1}{R_5}\right) & \left(-\frac{1}{R_3}\right) & \left(\frac{1}{R_3}+\frac{1}{R_4}+\frac{1}{R_5}+\frac{1}{R_C}\right) \end{bmatrix}$$

$$\begin{bmatrix} V_1 \\ V_2 \\ V_3 \end{bmatrix} = \begin{bmatrix} E_1/R_1 \\ E_2/R_B \\ 0 \end{bmatrix}$$

It is seen that all diagonal elements are positive and the all off-diagonal elements (mutual) are negative. There is no source attached to node 3 and hence the last element in the right hand matrix is zero.

Example 3.16. *Find by the nodal method, the currents I_A and I_B for the circuit shown in Fig. 3.21.*

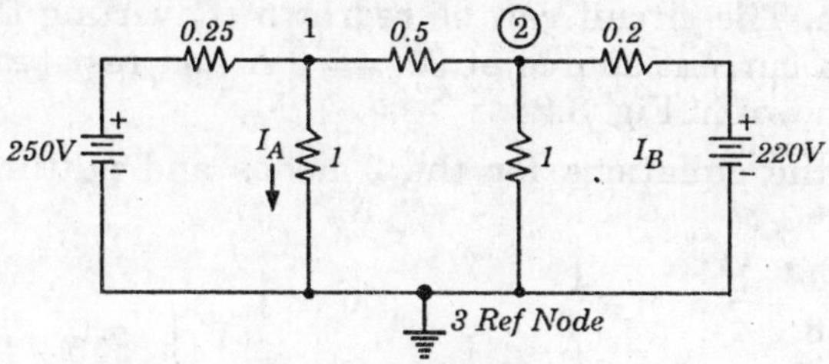

Fig. 3.21

Solution. There are 3 nodes. Select node 3 as reference node and then, writing the nodal equations for nodes 1 and 2 in matrix form, we have

$$\begin{bmatrix} \frac{1}{0.25}+\frac{1}{0.5}+\frac{1}{1} & -\frac{1}{0.5} \\ -\frac{1}{0.5} & \frac{1}{0.2}+\frac{1}{0.5}+\frac{1}{1} \end{bmatrix} \begin{bmatrix} V_1 \\ V_2 \end{bmatrix} = \begin{bmatrix} \frac{250}{0.25} \\ \frac{220}{0.2} \end{bmatrix}$$

i.e.

$$\begin{bmatrix} 7 & -2 \\ -2 & 8 \end{bmatrix} \begin{bmatrix} V_1 \\ V_2 \end{bmatrix} = \begin{bmatrix} 1000 \\ 1100 \end{bmatrix}$$

$$V_1 = \frac{\begin{vmatrix} 1000 & -2 \\ 1100 & 8 \end{vmatrix}}{\begin{vmatrix} 7 & -2 \\ -2 & 8 \end{vmatrix}} = \frac{8000+2200}{52} = \frac{10200}{52} = 196.154 \text{ V}$$

$$V_2 = \frac{\begin{vmatrix} 7 & 1000 \\ -2 & 1100 \end{vmatrix}}{52} = \frac{7700 + 2000}{52} = \frac{9700}{52} = 186.54 \text{ V}.$$

$$I_A = \frac{V_1}{1} = 196.154 \text{ Amps.}$$

$$I_B = \frac{V_2}{1} = 186.54 \text{ Amps.}$$

Example 3.17. *Find the power dissipated in the 10 ohms resistor shown in Fig. 3.22.*

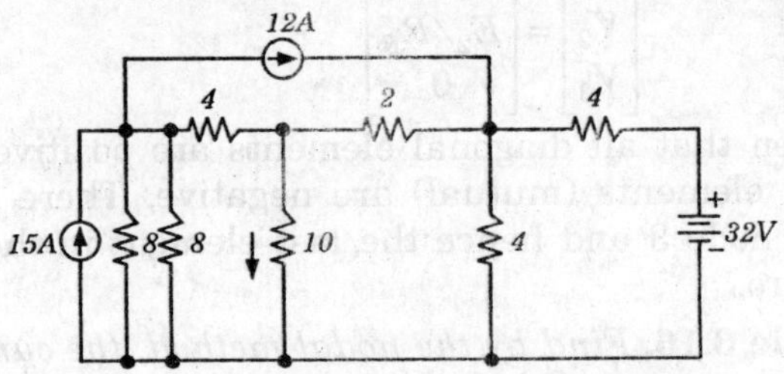

Fig. 3.22

Solution. The circuit can be redrawn converting the voltage source into a current source of 32/4 = 8 A and resistance 4 Ω in parallel as shown in Fig. 3.23.

Writing the equations for the 3 nodes and putting them in matrix form.

$$\begin{bmatrix} \frac{1}{8}+\frac{1}{8}+\frac{1}{4} & -\frac{1}{4} & 0 \\ -\frac{1}{4} & \frac{1}{4}+\frac{1}{2}+\frac{1}{10} & -\frac{1}{2} \\ 0 & -\frac{1}{2} & \frac{1}{2}+\frac{1}{4}+\frac{1}{4} \end{bmatrix} \begin{bmatrix} V_1 \\ V_2 \\ V_3 \end{bmatrix} = \begin{bmatrix} 15-12 \\ 0 \\ 12+8 \end{bmatrix}$$

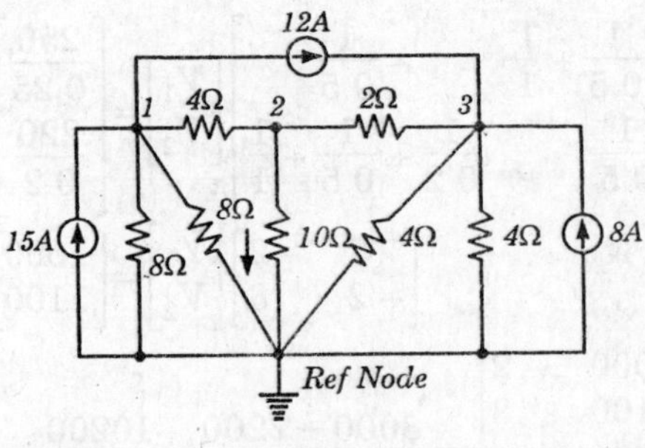

Fig. 3.23

The current entering node 1 is 15 A and the current leaving it is 12 A. Similarly the total current entering node 3 is 12 + 8 = 20 A. There is no source connected to node 2.

Thus $$\begin{bmatrix} 0.5 & -0.25 & 0 \\ -0.25 & 0.85 & -0.5 \\ 0 & -0.5 & 1 \end{bmatrix} \begin{bmatrix} V_1 \\ V_2 \\ V_3 \end{bmatrix} = \begin{bmatrix} 3 \\ 0 \\ 20 \end{bmatrix}$$

To find the power in the 10 ohms resistor, we must find V_2 and then find the current through it.

$$V_2 = \frac{\begin{vmatrix} 0.5 & 3 & 0 \\ -0.25 & 0 & -0.5 \\ 0 & 20 & 1 \end{vmatrix}}{\begin{vmatrix} 0.5 & -0.25 & 0 \\ -0.25 & 0.85 & -0.5 \\ 0 & -0.5 & 1 \end{vmatrix}} = 24.21 \text{ V}$$

Current in the 10 Ω = 2.421 A.

Power in the 10 ohms resistance = $(2.421)^2 \times 10 = 58.6$ Watts.

Example 3.18. *Solve the network of Fig. 3.24.*

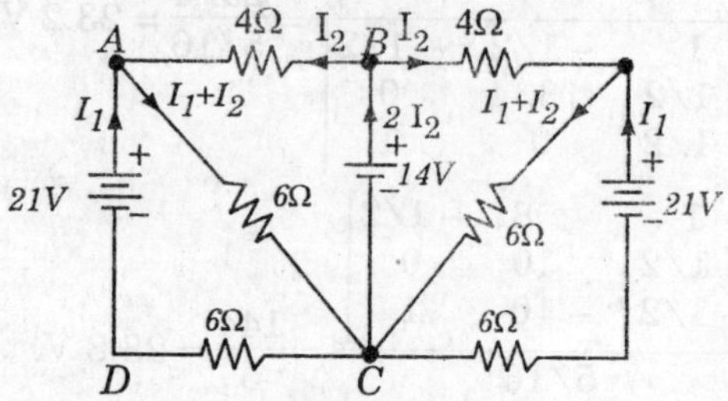

Fig. 3.24

Solution. We shall use the symmetry of the circuit to solve it. The currents are marked as shown. We have 2 unknown currents I_1 and I_2 for which we may write 2 loop equations.

$$6\,(I_1 + I_2) + 6I_1 = 21 \text{ for loop } ACDA$$

$$12I_1 + 6I_2 = 21$$

$$4I_2 + 6\,(I_1 + I_2) = 14 \text{ for loop } BACB$$

$$6I_1 + 10I_2 = 14$$

Solving these equations

$$I_1 = 1.5 \text{ A} \quad I_2 = 0.5 \text{ A}.$$

The currents in all the elements may be marked using these values.

Example 3.19. *Solve the network of Fig. 3.25 by nodal analysis and find the powers supplied by the sources.*

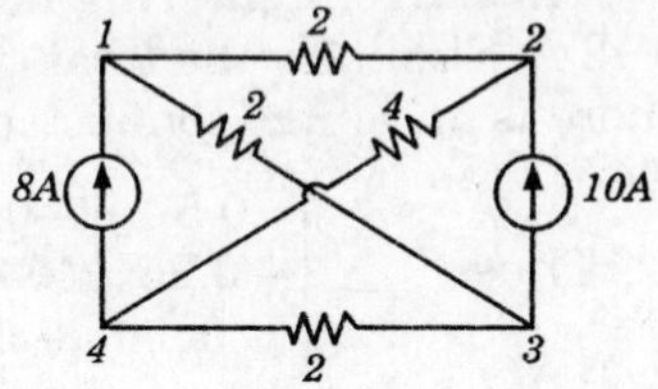

Fig. 3.25

Solution. Choosing node 4 as reference and the voltages of the other nodes as V_1, V_2 and V_3 w.r.t. 4, and writing the equations in matrix form.

$$\begin{bmatrix} 1/2+1/2 & -1/2 & -1/2 \\ -1/2 & 1/2+1/4 & 0 \\ -1/2 & 0 & 1 \end{bmatrix} \begin{bmatrix} V_1 \\ V_2 \\ V_3 \end{bmatrix} = \begin{bmatrix} 8 \\ 10 \\ -10 \end{bmatrix}$$

or

$$\begin{bmatrix} 1 & -1/2 & -1/2 \\ -1/2 & 3/4 & 0 \\ -1/2 & 0 & 1 \end{bmatrix} \begin{bmatrix} V_1 \\ V_2 \\ V_3 \end{bmatrix} = \begin{bmatrix} 8 \\ 10 \\ -10 \end{bmatrix}$$

$$V_1 = \frac{\begin{vmatrix} 8 & -1/2 & -1/2 \\ 10 & 3/4 & 0 \\ -10 & 0 & 1 \end{vmatrix}}{\begin{vmatrix} 1 & -1/2 & -1/2 \\ -1/2 & 3/4 & 0 \\ -1/2 & 0 & 1 \end{vmatrix}} = \frac{29/4}{5/16} = 23.2 \text{ V.}$$

$$V_2 = \frac{\begin{vmatrix} 1 & 8 & -1/2 \\ -1/2 & 10 & 0 \\ -1/2 & -10 & 1 \end{vmatrix}}{5/16} = \frac{144}{5} = 28.8 \text{ V.}$$

$$V_3 = \frac{\begin{vmatrix} 1 & -1/2 & 8 \\ -1/2 & 3/4 & 10 \\ -1/2 & 0 & -10 \end{vmatrix}}{5/16}$$

$$= \frac{1/2}{5/16} = 1.6 \text{ Volts.}$$

Power supplied by 8 A source,

$$V_1 \times 8 = 23.2 \times 8 = 185.6 \text{ W}$$

Power supplied by 10 A source,

$$(V_2 - V_3) \times 10 = (28.8 - 1.6)\, 10 = 272 \text{ W.}$$

Example 3.20. *Set up the nodal equations for the network of Fig. 3.26. Hence find the potential difference between nodes 2 and 4.*

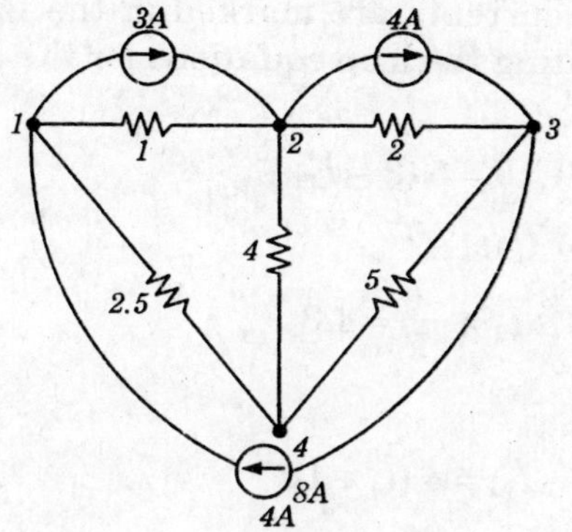

Fig. 3.26

Solution. Let node 4 be the reference node and let the voltages of nodes 1, 2 and 3 be V_1, V_2 and V_3 with respect to node 4. Writing the nodal equations directly in matrix form.

$$\begin{bmatrix} \frac{1}{1}+\frac{1}{2.5} & -\frac{1}{1} & 0 \\ -1 & \frac{1}{1}+\frac{1}{2}+\frac{1}{4} & -\frac{1}{2} \\ 0 & -\frac{1}{2} & \frac{1}{2}+\frac{1}{5} \end{bmatrix} \begin{bmatrix} V_1 \\ V_2 \\ V_3 \end{bmatrix} = \begin{bmatrix} 4-3=1 \\ 3-4=-1 \\ 4-4=0 \end{bmatrix}$$

or

$$\begin{bmatrix} 1.4 & -1 & 0 \\ -1 & 1.75 & -0.5 \\ 0 & -0.5 & 0.7 \end{bmatrix} \begin{bmatrix} V_1 \\ V_2 \\ V_3 \end{bmatrix} = \begin{bmatrix} 1 \\ -1 \\ 0 \end{bmatrix}$$

$$V_2 = \frac{\begin{vmatrix} 1.4 & 1 & 0 \\ -1 & -1 & -0.5 \\ 0 & 0 & 0.7 \end{vmatrix}}{\begin{vmatrix} 1.4 & -1 & 0 \\ -1 & 1.75 & -0.5 \\ 0 & -0.5 & 0.7 \end{vmatrix}} = \frac{-0.7 \times 0.4}{0.665} = -0.42 \text{ V.}$$

Example 3.21. *Find the power consumed in the 4 ohm resistor in Fig. 3.27. Find also the power supplied by the current source.*

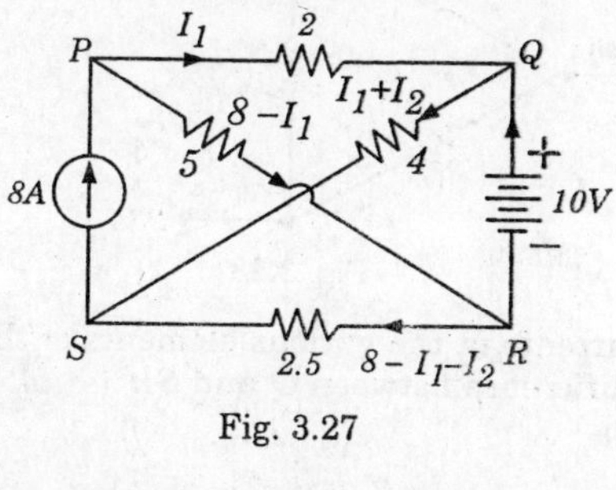

Fig. 3.27

Solution. The currents are marked in the figure. There are two unknowns. Writing the loop equations for the loops *PQRP* and *QRSQ*, we get

PQRP $\quad 2I_1 + 10 = 5\,(8 - I_1)$

i.e. $\quad 7I_1 = 30$

or $\quad I_1 = \dfrac{30}{7} = 4.3$

QRSQ

$$10 + 2.5\,(8 - I_1 - I_2) = 4\,(I_1 + I_2)$$

$$6.5\,I_1 + 6.5I_2 = 30$$

$$I_1 + I_2 = \frac{30}{6.5} = 4.6.$$

Substituting for I_2, we have

$$I_2 = 0.3 \text{ A}$$

Current in the 4 ohm resistor

$$= I_1 + I_2 = 4.3 + 0.3 = 4.6 \text{ amps.}$$

∴ Power consumed = 84.64 watts.

Voltage drop across the current source

$$= V_{PS}$$

$$= V_{PR} + V_{RS}$$

$$= 3.7 \times 5 + 3.4 \times 2.5 = 27 \text{ volts.}$$

Power supplied by current source

$$= 27 \times 8 = 216 \text{ watts.}$$

EXERCISES

3.1. Find the power dissipated in each resistor of the circuit shown in Fig. 3.28.

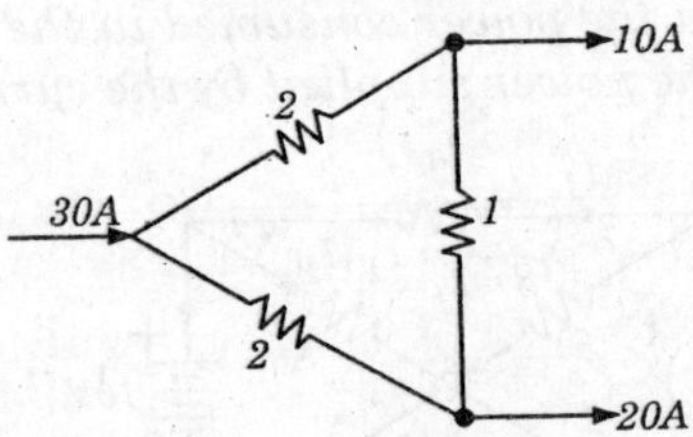

[**Ans.** *AB* : 392 W
BC : 16 W
AC : 512 W]

Fig. 3.28

3.2. Find the currents in the various elements of the circuit of Fig. 3.29. Find the potential difference between *Q* and *S*.

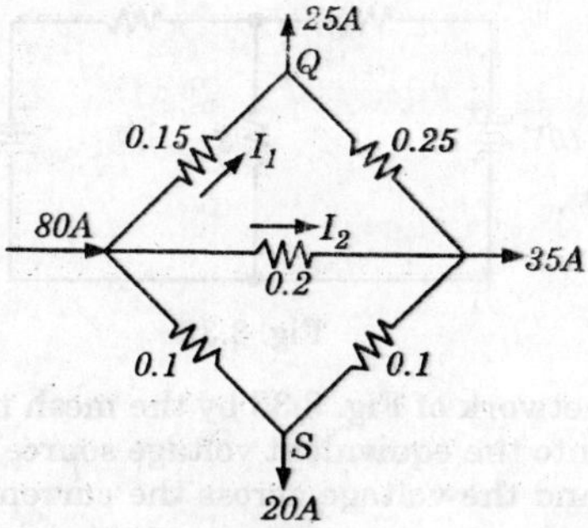

Fig. 3.29

[Ans. $I_1 = 26.5$, $I_2 = 21.75$, $V_{QS} = 0.8$ V, S +ve]

3.3. A Wheatstone bridge circuit is made up of the following resistance elements AB = 3 ohms, BC = 6 ohms, CD = 5 ohms and DA = 4 ohms. A 4 V battery is connected between A and C. Find the current through a 10 ohms. Galvanometer connected between B and D. [Ans. 31.25 mA]

3.4. In the circuit of Fig. 3.30, find the potential difference between B and D. The numerical values are the resistances of the conductors in ohms.

[Ans. 0.96 volts, B + ve]

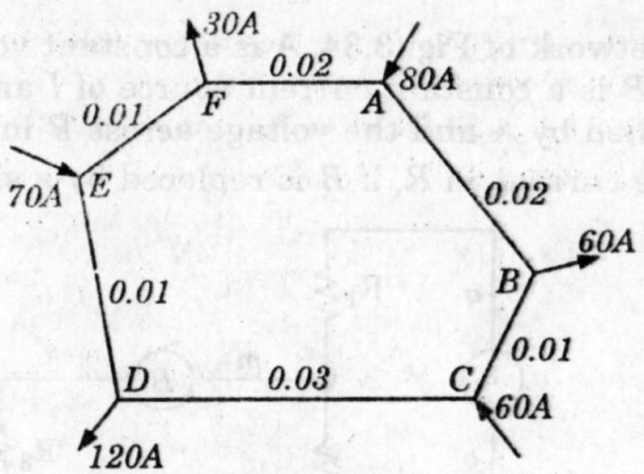

Fig. 3.30

3.5. In the circuit of Fig. 3.31, find the current I by the mesh method.

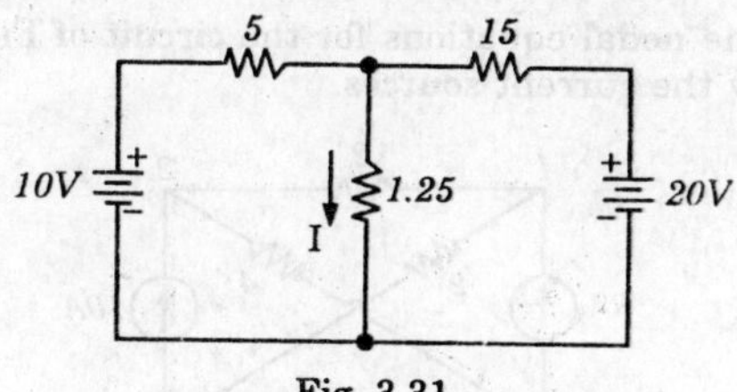

Fig. 3.31

[Ans. 2.5 A]

3.6. Write the mesh equations for the circuit of Fig. 3.32 in the matrix form. Find the current in the 3 ohm resistor. Also find the power supplied by the batteries. [Ans. 0 amp, 100 W, 200 W]

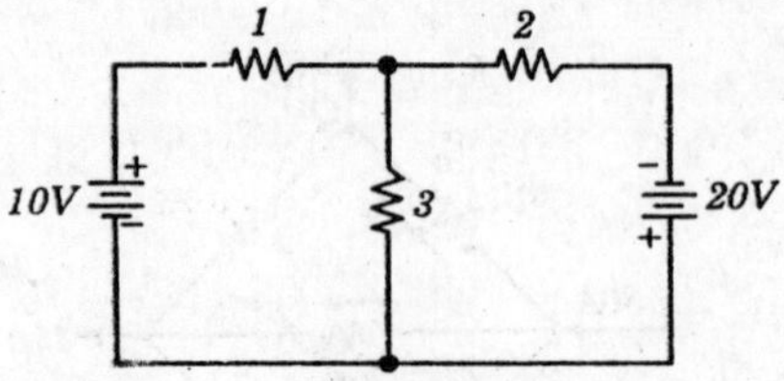

Fig. 3.32

3.7. Solve the network of Fig. 3.33 by the mesh method and find (convert the current source into the equivalent voltage source) the current supplied by the voltage source and the voltage across the current source.

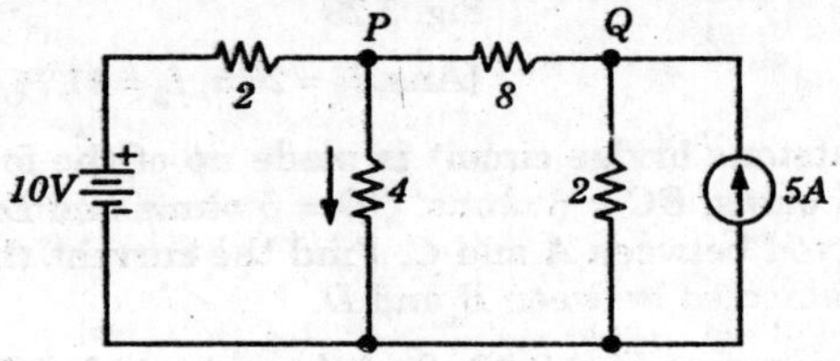

Fig. 3.33

[Ans. 1.47 A, 9.42 V]

3.8. In the network of Fig. 3.34, *A* is a constant voltage source of *E* volts (*q*, positive) and *B* is a constant current source of *I* amps. from *m* to *n*. Find the current supplied by *A* and the voltage across *B* in terms of *I*, R_1, R_2 and *R*. Hence find the current in *R*, if *B* is replaced by a short circuit.

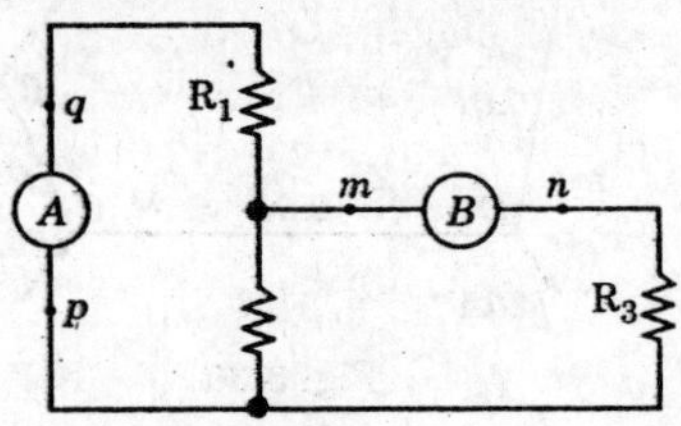

Fig. 3.34

3.9. Set up the nodal equations for the circuit of Fig. 3.35, and find the power supplied by the current sources.

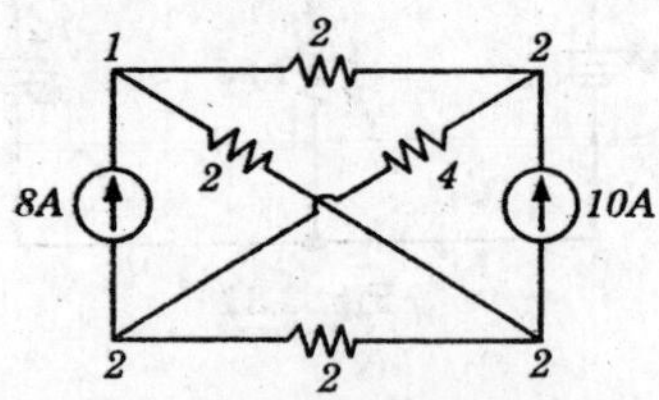

Fig. 3.35

[Ans. $V_1 = 21.6$ $V_2 = 27.2$ $V_3 = 1.6$ $P_8 = 185.6$ W $P_{10} = 272$ W]

3.10. Solve problem 3.7 by the nodal method and find the currents in the various elements.

3.11. Write and solve the node-voltage equations for the circuit of Fig. 3.36.

[Ans. $V_1 = \frac{1}{2}$ V, $V_2 = -1$ V**]**

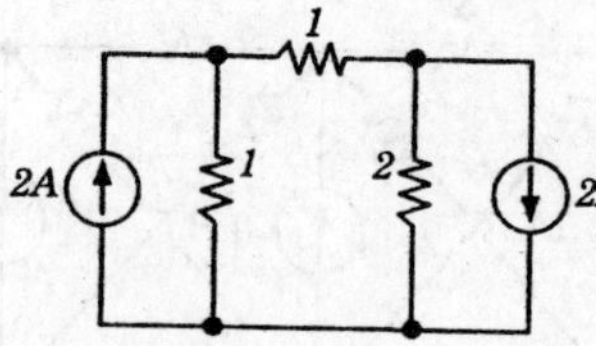

Fig. 3.36

3.12. Write and solve the node voltage equations for the circuit of Fig. 3.37 (make necessary source transformations). **[Ans.** $V_1 = 3.6$ V, $V_2 = -1.2$ V**]**

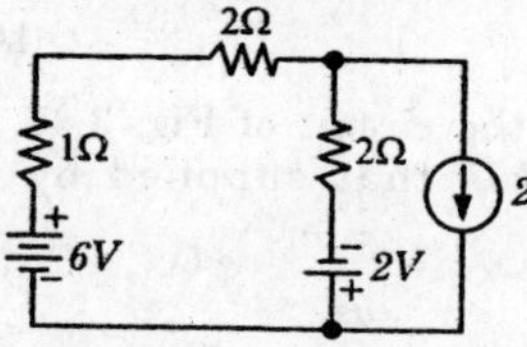

Fig. 3.37

3.13. Solve for V_1, V_2 and V_3 in the circuit of Fig. 3.38 using the nodal method. **[Ans.** –6, 1, 3**]**

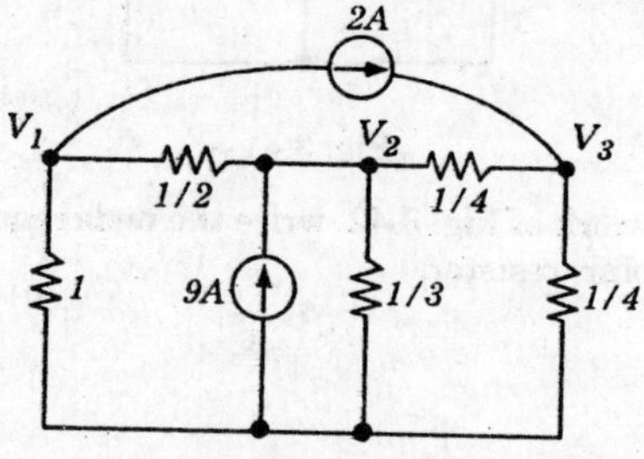

Fig. 3.38

3.14. Obtain the currents in all the branches of the network of Fig. 3.39 by (*a*) the mesh method (*b*) the nodal method.

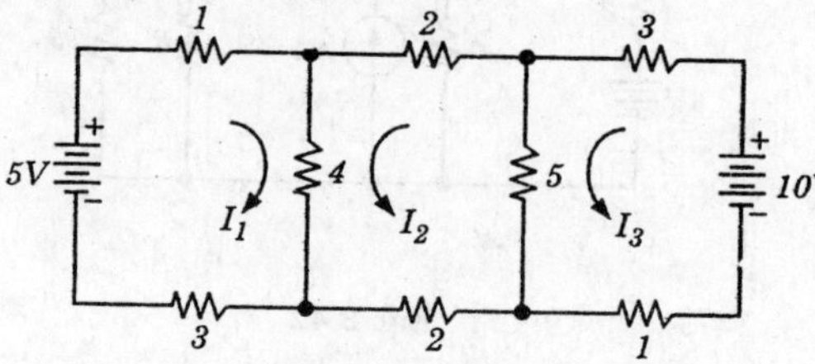

Fig. 3.39

[Ans. $I_1 = 0.44$ V $I_2 = 0.37$ A $I_3 = 1.32$ A**]**

3.15. Using the symmetry of the circuit, of Fig. 3.40 solve for the currents completely. Find the power supplied by the current sources.

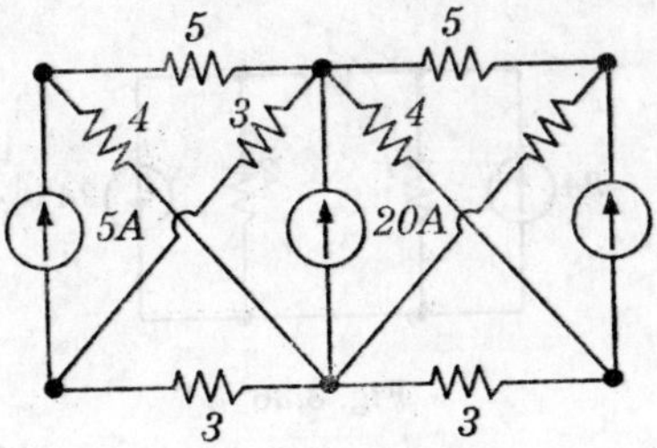

Fig. 3.40

[Ans. $P_5 = 80$ W $P_{20} = 726.7$ W]

3.16. Show that in the circuit of Fig. 3.41, the power supplied by the current source is double that supplied by the voltage source when $R = \dfrac{10}{3}$ ohms.

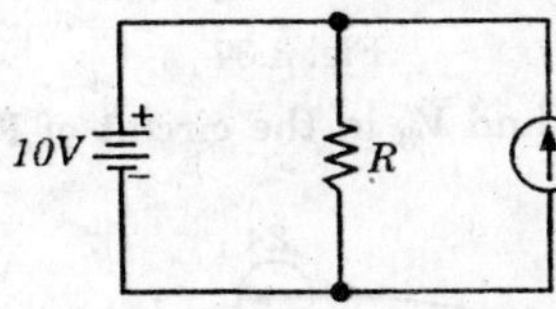

Fig. 3.41

3.17. For the network of Fig. 3.42, write the nodal equations and determine the current in the 3 ohm resistor. [Ans. 3.27 A]

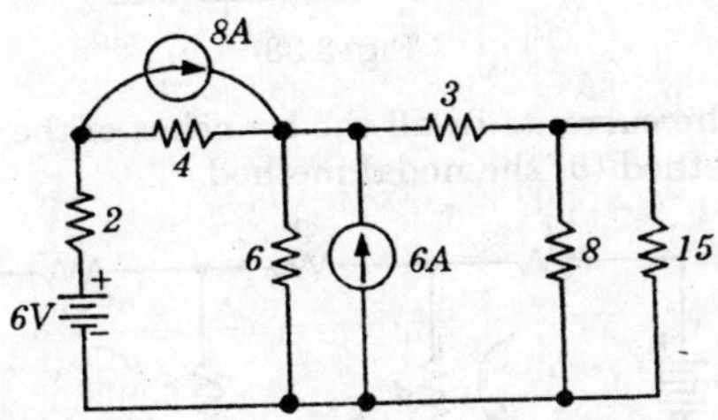

Fig. 3.42

3.18. Using nodal method, find the current in the 2 ohm resistor of the circuit of Fig. 3.43. [Ans. 0.325 A (*A* to *B*)]

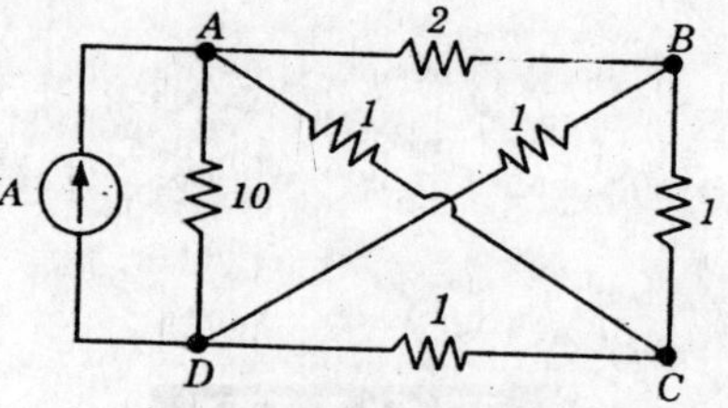

Fig. 3.43

3.19. Find V_2 by the nodal method of Fig. 3.44

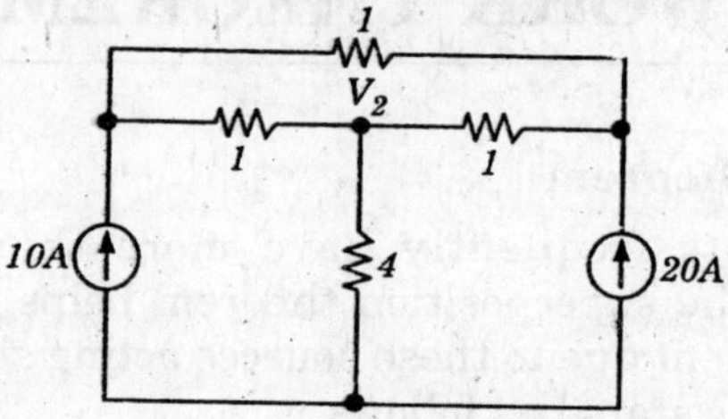

Fig. 3.44

[Ans. 120 V]

FOUR

NETWORK THEOREMS

Super Position Theorem

Electric circuits frequently have more than one source energising them. The superposition theorem helps us to find the current in any element due to these sources acting simultaneously. The theorem may be stated as follows :

"In a linear, lumped element, bilateral electric circuit that is energized by two or more sources the current in any resistor is equal to the algebraic sum of the separate currents in the resistor when each source acts separately. While one source is applied, the other sources are replaced by their respective internal resistances."

To replace the other sources by their respective internal resistances, the voltage sources are short-circuited and the current sources are open-circuited.

Example 4.1. *Find (a) the current, I_L (b) the load voltage V_L and (c) the load power P_L in the circuit of Fig. 4.1 (a) by the principle of superposition.*

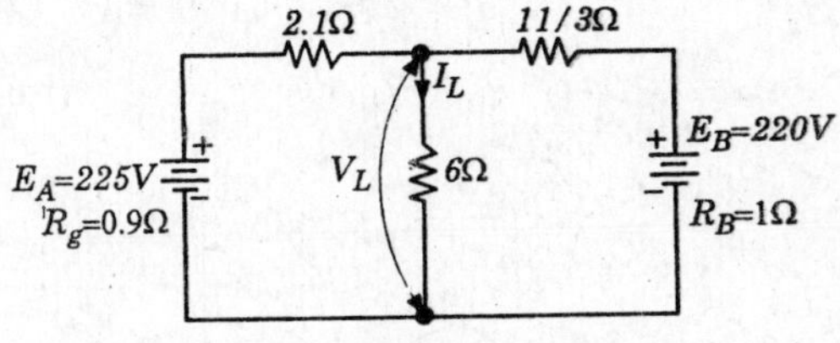

Fig. 4.1 (*a*)

Solution. Superposition Theorem is applied to this problem. At first, battery *A* alone is present, the battery *B* being short circuited (replaced by its internal resistance). The current I_1 in the load resistance is calculated. Next this is repeated with battery B alone in circuit (I_2).

The total current $I_1 + I_2 = I_L$. The steps are illustrated in Fig. 4.1 (b) and (c).

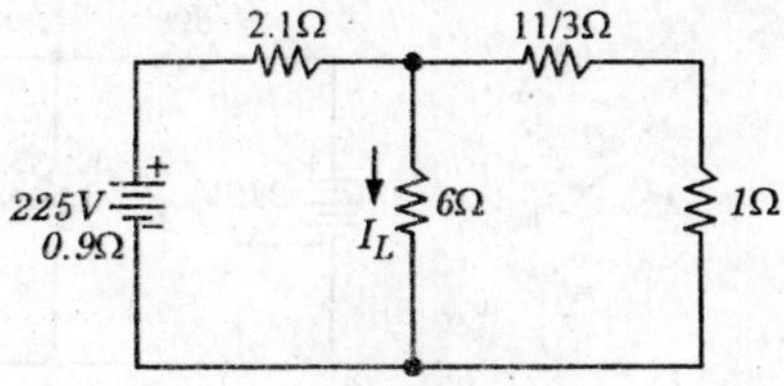

Fig. 4.1 (b)

In Fig. 4.1 (b) the total resistance of the circuit is

$$R_t = (2.1 + 0.9) + \frac{6 \times (11/3 + 1)}{(6 + 14/3)} = 5.625 \text{ ohms.}$$

and the total current,

$$I_t = \frac{225}{5.625} = 40 \text{ A.}$$

$$\therefore \quad I_1 = \frac{40 \times 14/3}{(6 + 14/3)}$$

$$= \frac{40 \times 14/3}{32/3}$$

$$= \frac{40 \times 14}{32}$$

$$= 17.5 \text{ Amps.}$$

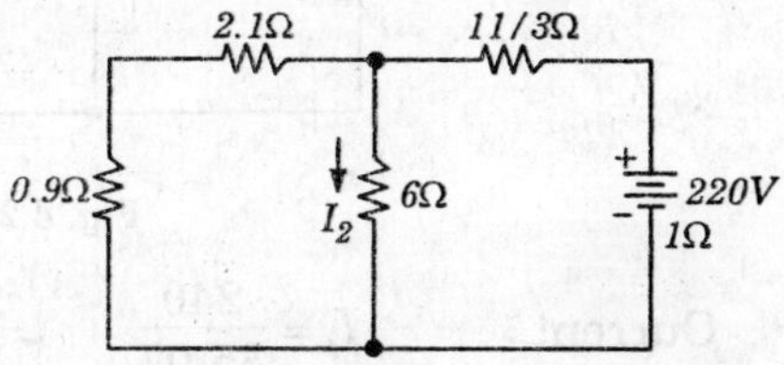

Fig. 4.1 (c)

In Fig. 4.1 (c), the total resistance of the circuit

$$R_t = \frac{11}{3} + 1 + 6 \times \frac{(2.1 + 0.9)}{6 + 3} = 6\frac{2}{3}$$

$$I_t = \frac{220}{6\frac{2}{3}} = 33 \text{ amps.}$$

$$I_2 = 33 \times \frac{3}{9} = 11 \text{ amps.}$$

$\therefore$ Algebraically combining the currents, I_1 and I_2, we get I_L

(a) $\quad I_L = 17.5 + 11 = 28.5$ amps.

(b) $\quad V_L = 28.5 \times 6 = 171.0$ volts.

(c) Power, $\quad P_L = (28.5)^2 \times 6 = 4873.5$ watts.

Example 4.2. *Find the current in the 150 ohms load resistor and the power consumed in it by the principle of superposition.*

Solution. The circuit can be re-drawn with only one source acting at a time as in Fig. 4.2 (b) and (c).

In Fig. 4.2 (b), the total resistance,

$$R_t = 10 + \frac{30 \times 152.5}{30 + 152.5} = 10 + 25.07 = 35.07 \text{ ohms.}$$

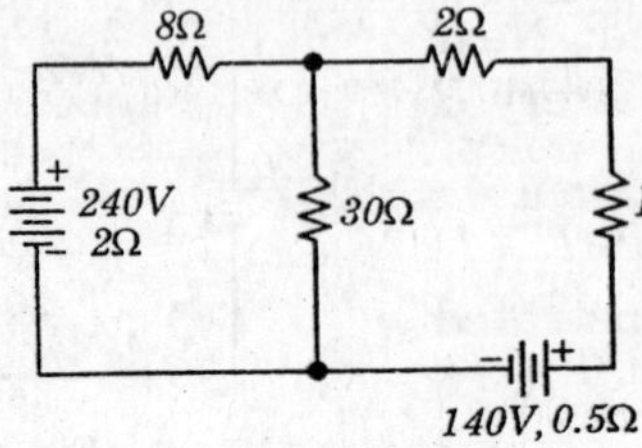

Fig. 4.2 (*a*)

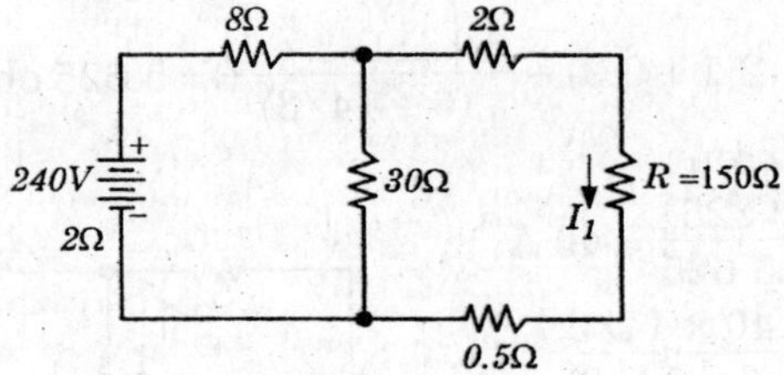

Fig. 4.2 (*b*)

Current $$I_t = \frac{240}{35.07}$$

$$I_1 = \frac{240}{35.07} \times \frac{30}{182.5} = 1.125 \text{ A}$$

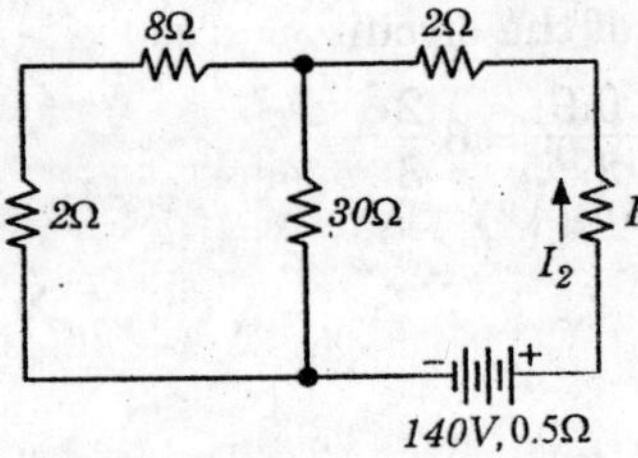

Fig. 4.2 (*c*)

In Fig. 4.2 (*c*)

The total resistance,

$$R_t = \frac{30 \times 10}{30 + 10} + 152.5 = 160$$

$$I_2 = \frac{140}{160} = 0.875.$$

$$I_L = I_1 - I_2$$

(as the two currents are in the opposite directions)

$$I_L = 1.125 - 0.0875 = 0.25 \text{ A}.$$

Thevenin's Theorem

A complex network consisting of linear, bilateral active or passive elements with two accessible terminals can be reduced to a simple circuit as shown in Fig 4.3. V_0 is the open circuit voltage at terminals *AB* and

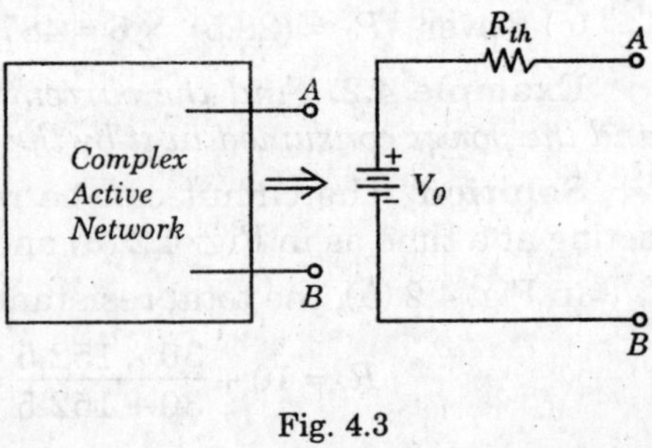

Fig. 4.3

R_{th} is the looking back resistance or Thevenin's resistance. R_{th} is the resistance of the network between terminals A and B replacing all sources by their respective internal resistances.

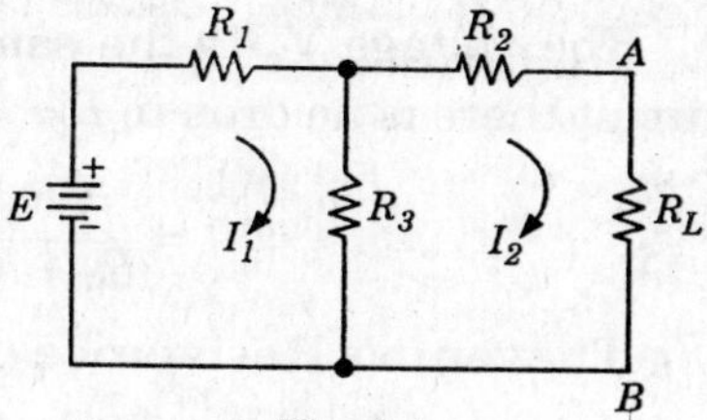

Fig. 4.4

The theorem will now be illustrated by the circuit of Fig. 4.4. Let us say, we are interested in finding the current in R_L.

By mesh analysis $\begin{bmatrix} (R_1+R_3) & -R_3 \\ -R_3 & (R_2+R_L+R_3) \end{bmatrix} \begin{bmatrix} I_1 \\ I_2 \end{bmatrix} = \begin{bmatrix} E \\ 0 \end{bmatrix}$

$$I_2 = \frac{\begin{vmatrix} R_1+R_3 & E \\ -R_3 & 0 \end{vmatrix}}{\begin{vmatrix} (R_1+R_3) & -R_3 \\ -R_3 & (R_2+R_L+R_3) \end{vmatrix}}$$

$$= \frac{ER_3}{(R_1+R_3)(R_2+R_L+R_3)-R_3^2}$$

$$I_2 = \frac{ER_3}{R_1(R_2+R_L+R_3)+R_3(R_2+R_L)}$$

$$= \frac{ER_3}{R_1R_3+(R_1+R_3)(R_2+R_L)}$$

By Thevenin's theorem, the circuit can be reduced at AB to the circuit of Fig. 4.5.

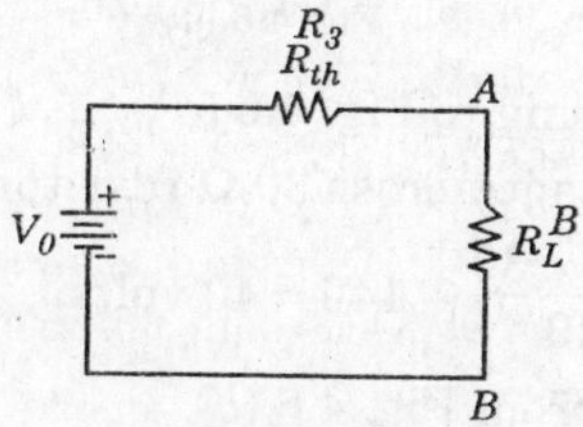

Fig. 4.5 (*a*)

Open Circuit Voltage (V_0)

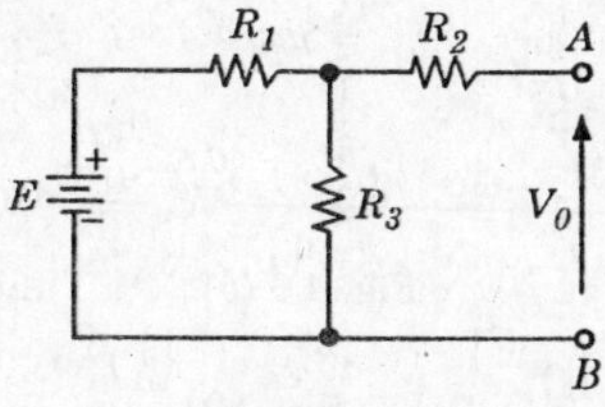

Fig. 4.5 (*b*)

The voltage V_0 is the same as voltage across R_3 as on open circuit there is no drop in R_2.

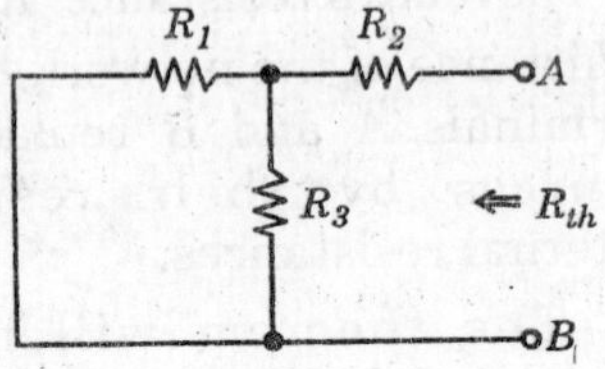

Fig. 4.5 (c)

$$V_0 = \frac{ER_3}{R_1 + R_3}$$

Thevenin's Resistance (R_{th})

$$R_{th} = R_2 + \frac{R_1 R_3}{R_1 + R_3}$$

$$I_L = \frac{V_0}{R_{th} + R_L} = \frac{\dfrac{ER_3}{(R_1 + R_3)}}{R_L + R_2 + \dfrac{R_1 R_3}{R_1 + R_3}}$$

$$= \frac{ER_3}{(R_1 + R_3)(R_L + R_2) + R_1 R_3}$$

This is the same as I_2, determined by the mesh method.

Example 4.3. *Solve Example 4.2 by the Thevenin's theorem.*

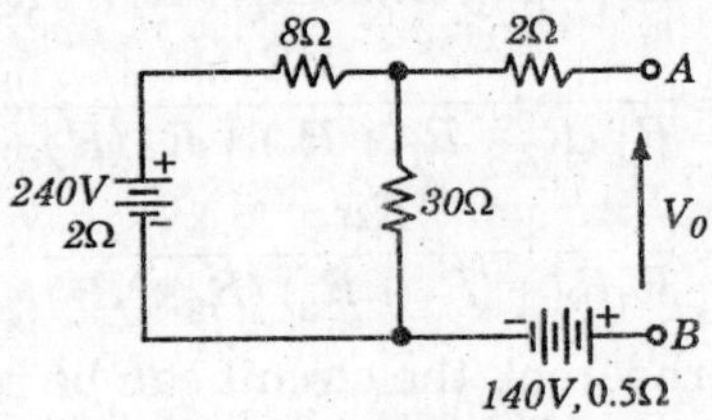

Fig. 4.6 (a)

Solution. Referring to Fig. 4.6 (*a*)

$$V_0 = \text{Voltage across 30 } \Omega \text{ resistor} - 140 \text{ volts}$$

$$= \frac{240 \times 30}{40} - 140 = 40 \text{ volts.}$$

R_{th} is computed from Fig. 4.6 (*b*).

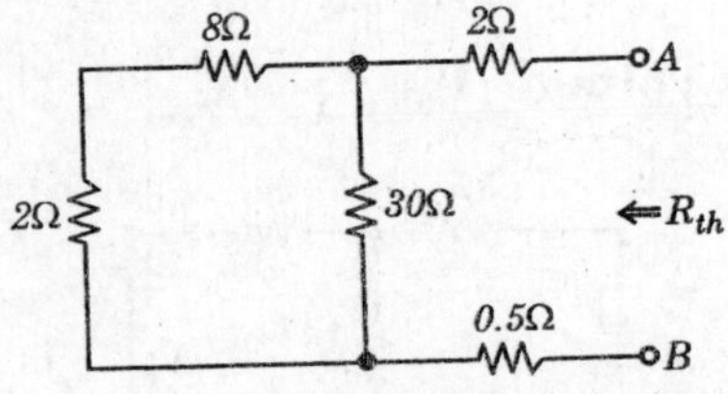

Fig. 4.6 (b)

$$R_{th} = \frac{30 \times 10}{30 + 10} + 2 + 0.5 = 10$$

The circuit is redrawn as shown in Fig. 4.6 (*c*).

$$I_L = \frac{V_0}{R_L + R_{th}}$$

$$= \frac{40}{150 + 10} = 0.25 \text{ Amp.}$$

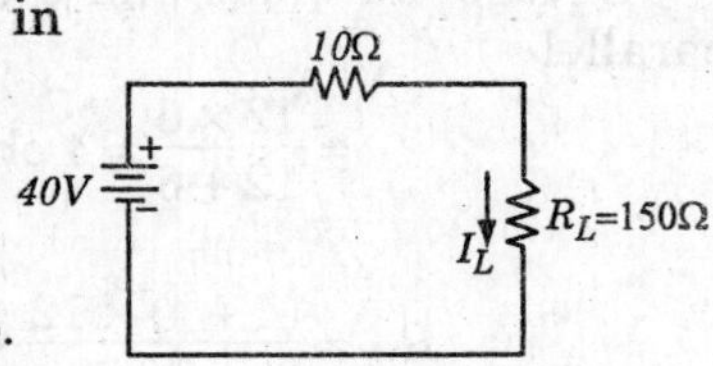

Fig. 4.6 (*c*)

Example 4.4. *For the circuit shown in Fig. 4.7 (a) determine*

(*a*) *the open circuit emf at the load terminals PQ.*

(*b*) *the Thevenin's resistance at PQ*

(*c*) *the load current and*

(*d*) *load power.*

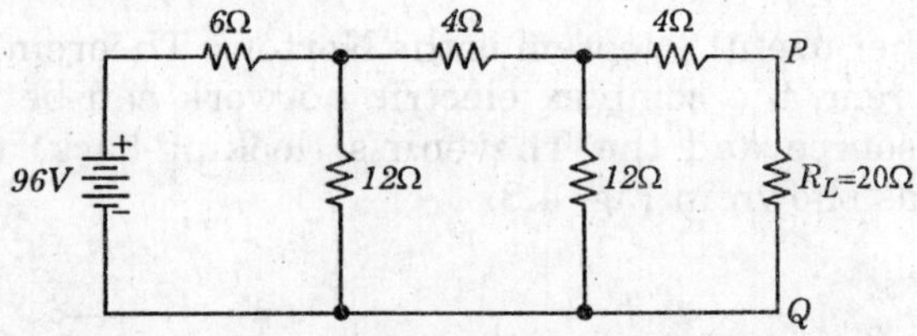

Fig. 4.7 (*a*)

Solution. Under open circuit conditions, the circuit may be re-drawn as in Fig. 4.7 (*b*).

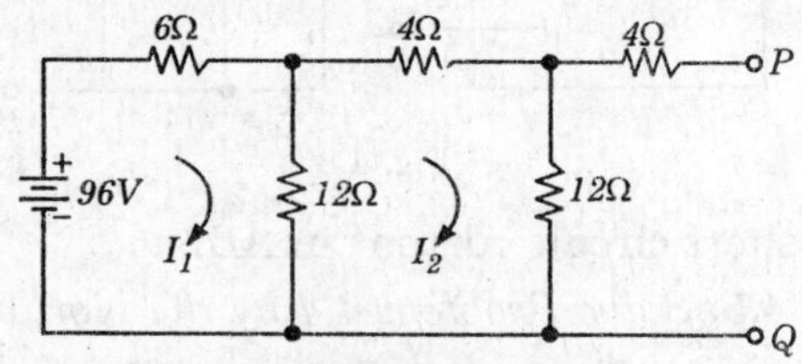

Fig. 4.7 (*b*)

V_0 = the voltage across the 12 ohm resistor $= I_2 \times 12$

By mesh method, we have

$$\begin{bmatrix} 18 & -12 \\ -12 & 28 \end{bmatrix} \begin{bmatrix} I_1 \\ I_2 \end{bmatrix} = \begin{bmatrix} 96 \\ 0 \end{bmatrix}$$

$$I_2 = \frac{\begin{vmatrix} 18 & 96 \\ -12 & 0 \end{vmatrix}}{\begin{vmatrix} 18 & -12 \\ -12 & 28 \end{vmatrix}} = \frac{96 \times 12}{18 \times 28 - 12 \times 12} = 3.2 \text{ A.}$$

$$V_0 = 3.2 \times 12 = 38.4 \text{ Volts.}$$

R_{th} is obtained from the circuit of 4.7 (*b*) after short circuiting the source.

Eqvt. of 12 ohms and 6 ohms in parallel

$$= \frac{12 \times 6}{12 + 6} = 4 \text{ ohms.}$$

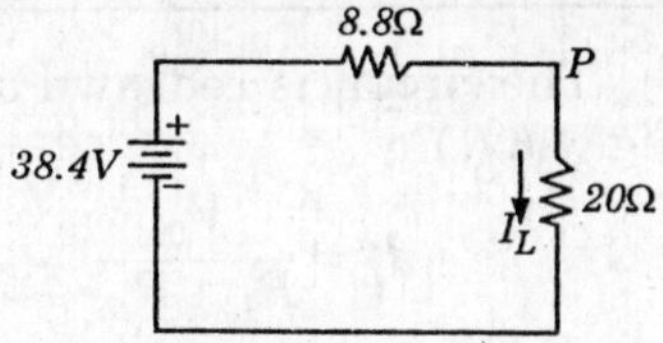

Fig. 4.7 (c)

$$R_{th} = \frac{(4 + 4) \times 12}{20} + 4$$

$$= \frac{9}{20} + 4 = 8.8$$

$$I_L = \frac{38.4}{8.8 + 20} = 1.333 \text{ A.}$$

Load Power $= I_L^2 \times 20 = 35.6$ Watts.

Norton's Theorem

Another useful Theorem is the Norton's Theorem. By applying this theorem, the complex electric network can be reduced to a current source and the Thevenin's (looking-back) resistance in parallel as shown in Fig. 4.8.

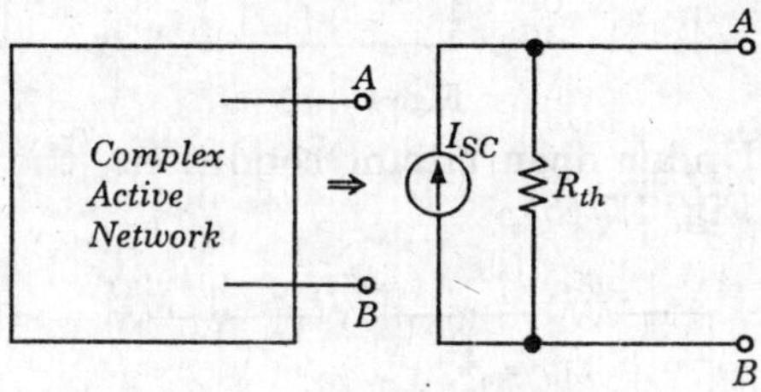

Fig. 4.8

I_{SC} is the short circuit current in *AB*.

Example 4.5. *Solve Problem 4.4 by the Norton's Theorem.*

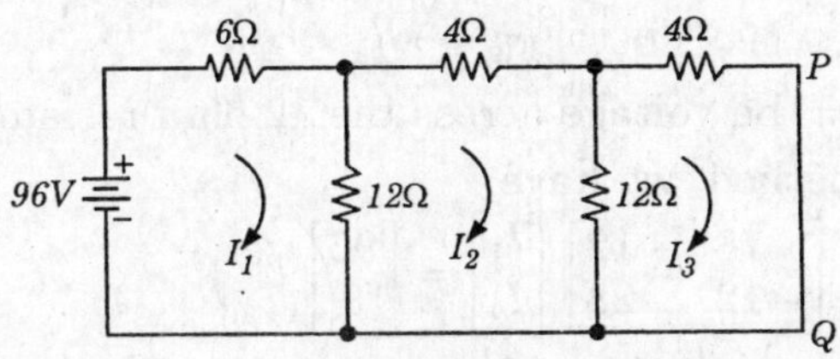

Fig. 4.9

Solution. In Fig. 4.9 *PQ* is shorted and the current I_3 is solved by mesh method.

$$\begin{bmatrix} 18 & -12 & 0 \\ -12 & 28 & -12 \\ 0 & -12 & 16 \end{bmatrix} \begin{bmatrix} I_1 \\ I_2 \\ I_3 \end{bmatrix} = \begin{bmatrix} 96 \\ 0 \\ 0 \end{bmatrix}$$

$$I_3 = \frac{\begin{vmatrix} 18 & -12 & 96 \\ -12 & 28 & 0 \\ 0 & -12 & 0 \end{vmatrix}}{\begin{vmatrix} 18 & -12 & 0 \\ -12 & 28 & -12 \\ 0 & -12 & 16 \end{vmatrix}}$$

$$= \frac{96 \times 144}{18 \times 304 - 18 \times 128} = \frac{96 \times 144}{18 \times 176}$$

$$= \frac{144}{33} = \frac{48}{11}$$

$R_{th} = 8.8$ as before.

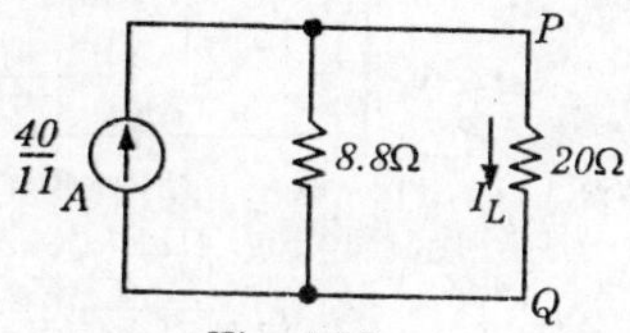

Fig. 4.10

From Fig. 4.10, $I_L = \dfrac{(48/11) \times 8.8}{28.8}$

$= 1.333$ amp.

Example 4.6. *Find by Norton's Theorem, the current in the arm BD of Fig. 4.11.*

Solution. $I_{SC} = I_1 + I_2$ of Fig. 4.11 (*b*)

By mesh method, $\begin{bmatrix} 5.6 & 0 & -4 \\ 0 & 5 & 2 \\ -4 & 2 & 6.5 \end{bmatrix} \begin{bmatrix} I_1 \\ I_2 \\ I_3 \end{bmatrix} = \begin{bmatrix} 0 \\ 0 \\ 12 \end{bmatrix}$

$$\therefore \quad I_1 = \frac{\begin{vmatrix} 0 & 0 & -4 \\ 0 & 5 & 2 \\ 12 & 2 & 6.5 \end{vmatrix}}{\begin{vmatrix} 5.6 & 0 & -4 \\ 0 & 5 & 2 \\ -4 & 2 & 6.5 \end{vmatrix}} = \frac{12 \times 20}{5.6\,(5 \times 6.5 - 4) - 4 \times 20}$$

$$= \frac{12 \times 20}{5.6 \times 28.5 - 80} = 3.015 \text{ A}$$

$$I_2 = \frac{\begin{vmatrix} 5.6 & 0 & -4 \\ 0 & 0 & 2 \\ -4 & 12 & 6.5 \end{vmatrix}}{5.6 \times 28.5 - 80} = \frac{-12 \times 11.2}{5.6 \times 28.5 - 80} = -1.688 \text{ A}$$

$$\therefore \quad I_{SC} = I_1 + I_2 = 1.326 \text{ A}$$

R_{TH} is the resistance between BD and is found from the circuit of Fig. 4.11 (*c*).

The circuit is re-drawn to facilitate easy computation, as shown in Fig. 4.11 (*d*).

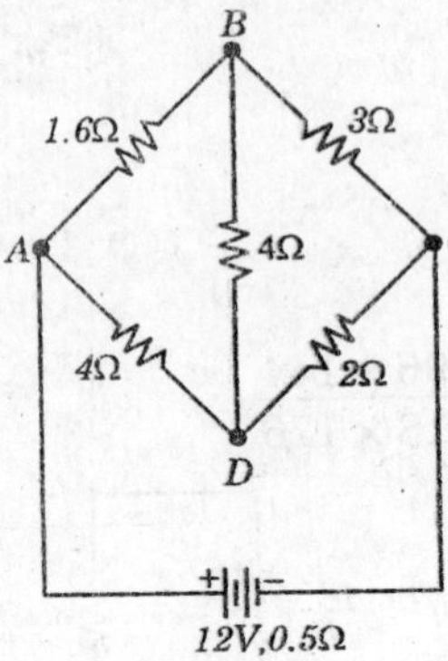

Fig. 4.11 (*a*)

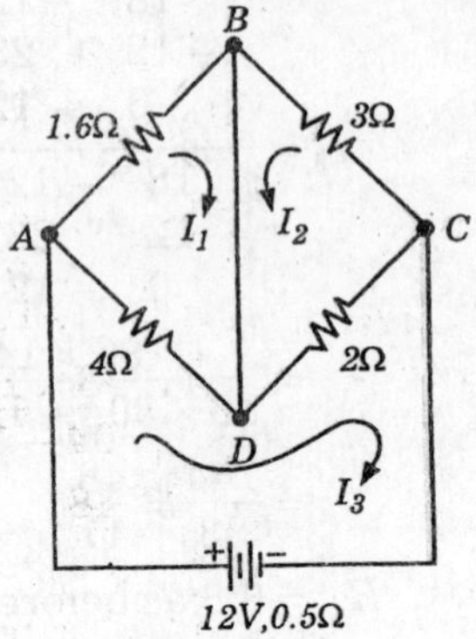

Fig. 4. 11 (*b*)

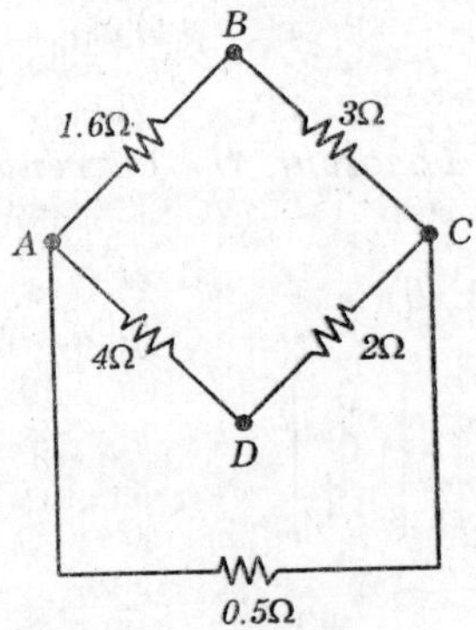

Fig. 4.11 (*c*)

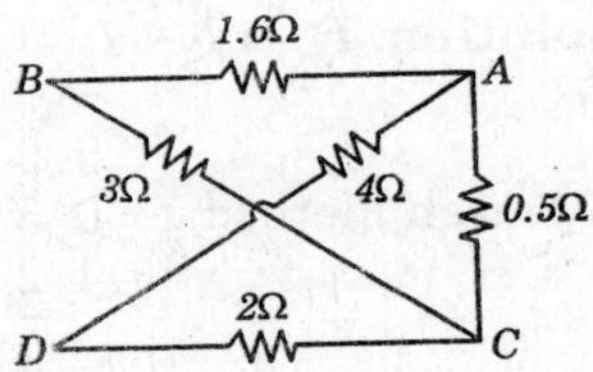

Fig. 4.11 (*d*)

The resistance between *BD* can be obtained only after a star-delta conversion at *A* or *C* as shown in Fig. 4.11 (*c*).

The resistance 1.6, 4 and 0.5 ohm in star at *A* can be converted into a delta as follows.

$$R_x = \frac{1.6 \times 4 + 4 \times 0.5 + 1.6 \times 0.5}{1.6} = 5.75$$

$$\therefore \qquad R_{TH} = \frac{1.84 \times (1.302 + 1.484)}{1.84 + 1.302 + 1.484} = 2.42$$

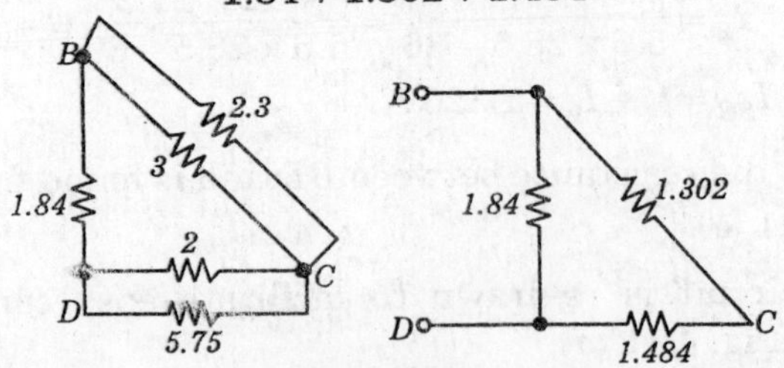

Fig. 4.11 (*e*)

The Norton's equivalent circuit is shown in Fig. 4.11 (*f*).

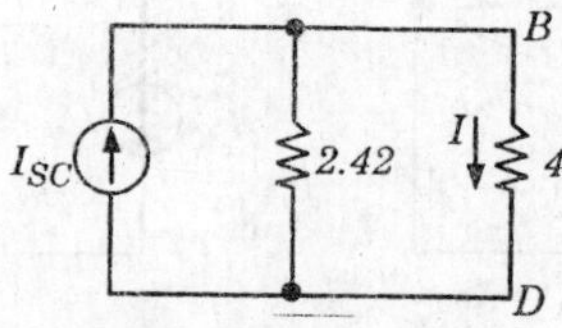

Fig. 4.11 (*f*)

$$I = \frac{264}{199} \times \frac{2.42}{6.42} = 0.5 \text{ amp.}$$

Example 4.7. *Draw the Norton's equivalent at terminals PQ for the circuit of Fig. 4.12 (a). Hence find the power consumed in a 1 ohm resistor connected between P and Q.*

Solution. I_{SC} is found in the short circuit at PQ from the circuit of Fig. 4.12 (*b*).

By mesh method $\begin{bmatrix} 14 & 0 & -8 \\ 0 & 6 & 2 \\ -8 & 2 & 10 \end{bmatrix} \begin{bmatrix} I_1 \\ I_2 \\ I_3 \end{bmatrix} = \begin{bmatrix} 0 \\ 0 \\ 20 \end{bmatrix}$

$$\therefore \quad I_1 = \frac{\begin{vmatrix} 0 & 0 & -8 \\ 0 & 6 & 2 \\ 20 & 2 & 10 \end{vmatrix}}{\begin{vmatrix} 14 & 0 & -8 \\ 0 & 6 & 2 \\ -8 & 2 & 10 \end{vmatrix}} = \frac{20 \times 48}{14\,(60-4) - 8\,(48)}$$

$$= \frac{20 \times 48}{14 \times 56 - 8 \times 48} = 2.4 \text{ A}$$

$$I_2 = \frac{\begin{vmatrix} 14 & 0 & -8 \\ 0 & 0 & 2 \\ -8 & 20 & 10 \end{vmatrix}}{14 \times 56 - 8 \times 48} = \frac{-20 \times 28}{14 \times 56 - 8 \times 48} = -1.4 \text{ A.}$$

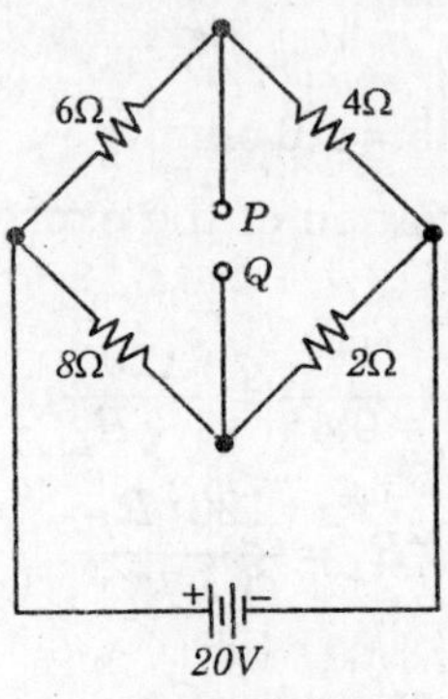

Fig. 4.12 (*a*)

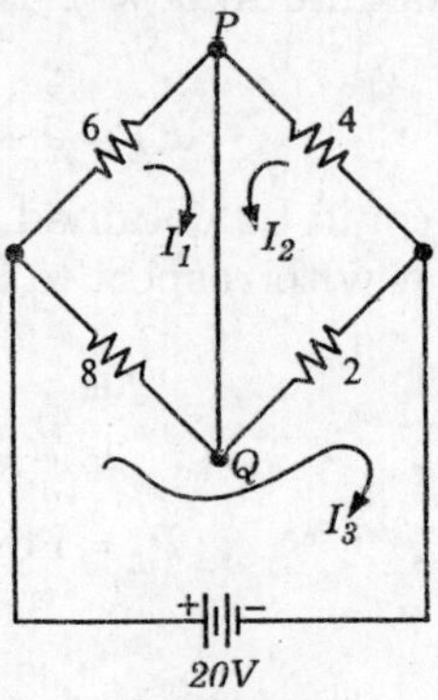

Fig. 4.12 (*b*)

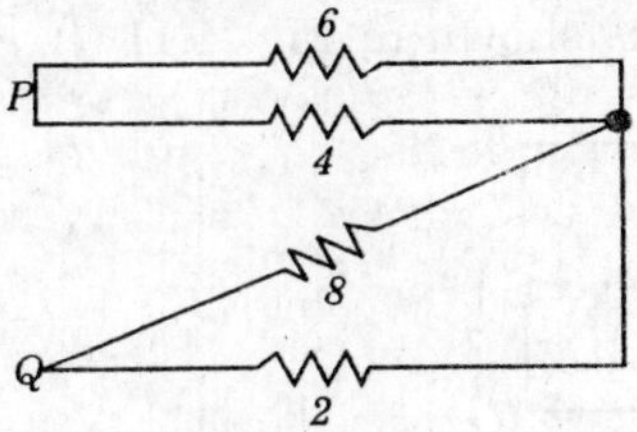

Fig. 4.12 (*c*)

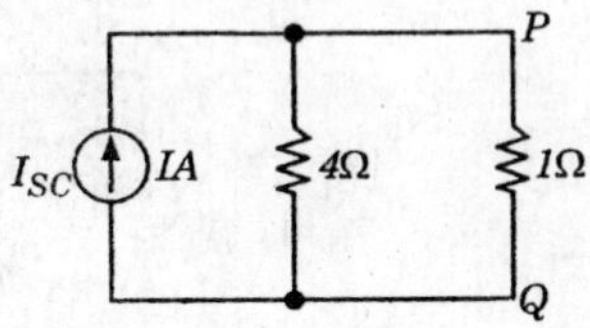

Fig. 4.12 (*d*)

$$I_{SC} = I_1 + I_2 = 2.4 - 1.4 = 1.0 \text{ A}.$$

R_{TH} is obtained between PQ after shorting the source [Fig. 4.12 (*c*)].

$$R_{TH} = \frac{6 \times 4}{6 + 4} + \frac{8 \times 2}{8 + 2} = 4\ \Omega$$

Fig. 4.12 (*d*) gives the Norton's equivalent. The current through 1 ohm resistor connected between P and Q.

$$= 1 \times \frac{4}{5} = 0.8 \text{ A}$$

Maximum Power Transfer Theorem

The maximum power transferred to a load resistor occurs when it has a value equal to the resistance of the network looking back at it from the load terminals (all sources being replaced by their respective internal resistances).

Example 4.8. *A battery of 120 volts and internal resistance 0.1 ohm supplies a load resistor R_L through two wires of resistance 0.45 ohm each. Find the value of R_L which consumes maximum power, as shown in Fig. 4.13.*

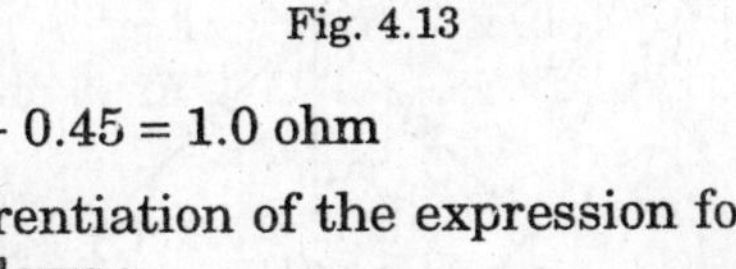

Fig. 4.13

Solution. From an application of the maximum power transfer theorem

$$R_L = 0.45 + 0.1 + 0.45 = 1.0 \text{ ohm}$$

This could be obtained by differentiation of the expression for load power with respect to R_L as follows :

$$I = \frac{120}{0.1 + 0.45 + R_L + 0.45} = \frac{120}{1 + R_L}$$

$$P_L = \text{Power in } R_L = I^2 R_L = \frac{120^2 R_L}{(1 + R_L)^2}$$

$$\frac{dP_L}{dR_L} = (120)^2 \times \frac{R_L \times 2 \times (1+R_L) - (1+R_L)^2}{(1+R_L)^4}$$

$$= 0 \text{ for maximum } P_L.$$

$\therefore \quad 2R_L (1+R_L) = (1+R_L)^2$

i.e. $\quad 2R_L = 1 + R_L$

$$R_L = 1 \text{ ohm.}$$

Example 4.9. *Find the ohmic value of R_L in the circuit of Fig. 4.14 when its power is a maximum. Find also*

(*i*) *the maximum load power*

(*ii*) *the total power delivered by both the batteries and*

(*iii*) *the overall efficiency.*

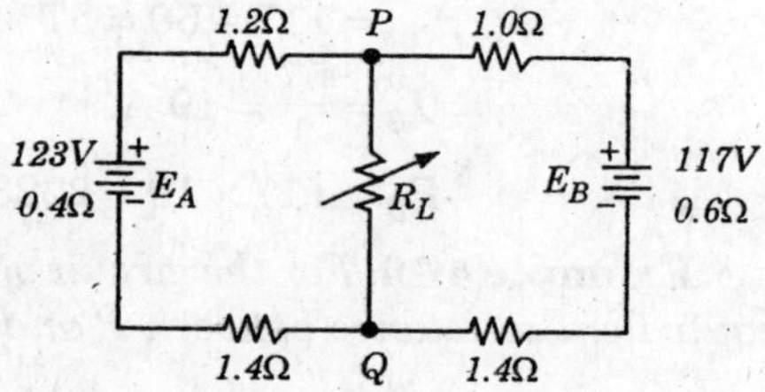

Fig. 4.14 (*a*)

Solution. The circuit can be represented by a Thevenin's equivalent at PQ as in Fig. 4.14 (*b*). To find V_0, R_L is disconnected from Fig. 4.14 (*a*).

$$I = \frac{123 - 117}{(0.4 + 1.2 + 1.0 + 0.6 + 1.4 + 1.4)} = \frac{6}{6} = 1 \text{ A.}$$

$$V_0 = 123 - I \times (1.2 + 0.4 + 1.4)$$
$$= 123 - 3 = 120 \text{ volts.}$$

Looking back from PQ with the two batteries short circuited, the two 3-ohm resistances on either side are in parallel

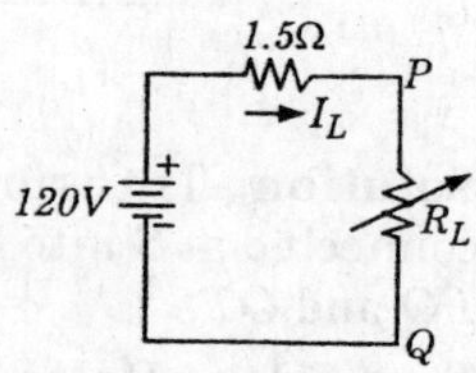

Fig. 4.14 (*b*)

$$\therefore \quad R_{Th} = \frac{3 \times 3}{3+3} = \frac{3}{2} = 1.5 \text{ ohms.}$$

For maximum power in R_L, $R_L = 1.5$

Under this condition,

$$I_L = \frac{120}{1.5 + 1.5} = \frac{120}{3} = 40 \text{ amps.}$$

(*i*) $\quad P_L = (40)^2 \times 1.5 = 2400$ watts.

(*ii*) Power supplied by the source

$$= 120 \times 40 = 4800 \text{ watts}$$

$$\therefore \quad \text{Efficiency} = \frac{2400}{4800} = 50\%.$$

(*iii*) Referring to Fig. 4.14 (*a*)

$$E_L = I_L R_L = 40 \times 1.5 = 60 \text{ V}.$$

$\therefore$ Drop of voltage between battery *A* and the terminals *PQ*,

$$= 123 - 60 = 63 \text{ V}$$

$$\therefore \quad I_A = \frac{63}{3} = 21 \text{ A}.$$

and $$P_A = 123 \times 21 = 2583 \text{ watts}.$$

As the drop of voltage between battery *B* and *PQ*

$$= 117 - 60 = 57$$

$$I_B = \frac{57}{3} = 19 \text{ A}.$$

$$P_B = 117 \times 19 = 2223 \text{ watts}.$$

Example 4.10. *For the circuit of Fig. 4.15, calculate (a) the total equivalent resistance between P and Q (b) the battery current.*

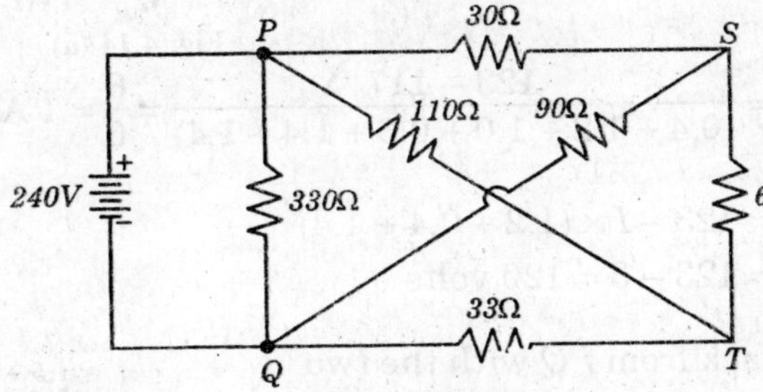

Fig. 4.15 (*a*)

Solution. Transform the 3 resistances *PS*, *QS* and *TS* starconnected at *S* into an equivalent delta to be connected between *PT*, *PQ* and *QT*.

Equivalent Delta

The three equivalent values are

$$R_{QT} = \frac{30 \times 60 + 60 \times 90 + 90 \times 30}{30}$$

$$= \frac{9900}{30} = 330\ \Omega$$

$$R_{PT} = \frac{9900}{90} = 110\ \Omega$$

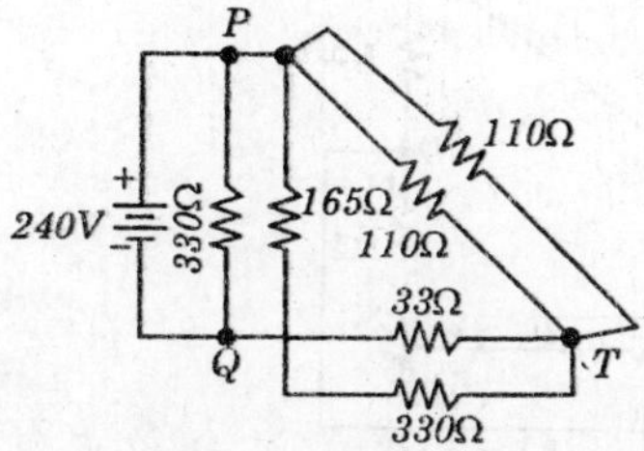

Fig. 4.15 (b)

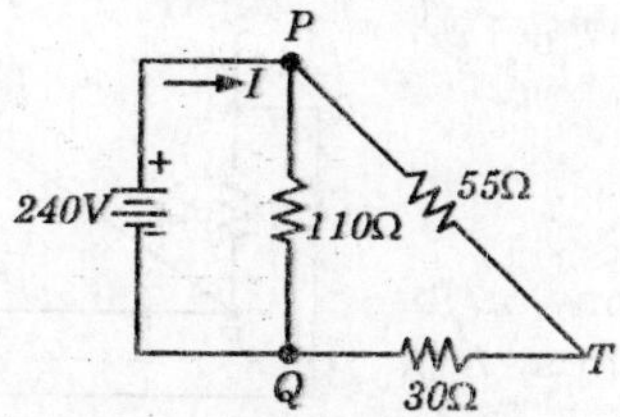

Fig. 4.15 (c)

$$R_{PQ} = \frac{9900}{60} = 165\ \Omega$$

From Fig. 4.15 (c), $R_{PQ} = \dfrac{110 \times (55 + 30)}{110 + 55 + 30}$ 48 ohms

$$I = \frac{240}{48} = 5\text{ A.}$$

Example 4.11. *A resistor R is connected in parallel with another of value 20 Ω. This combination is then connected to a 120 volt source through a 4-ohm line resistor. For what value of R will its power be a maximum. Find this maximum power.*

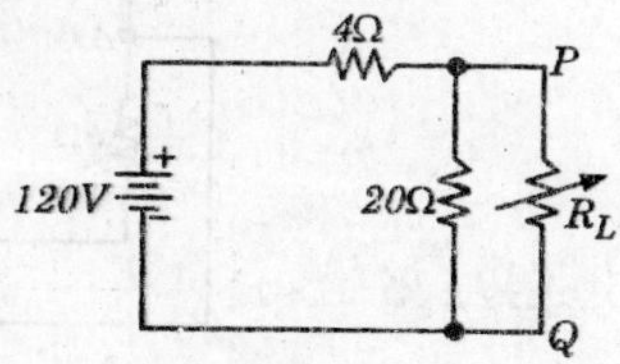

Fig. 4.16 (a)

Solution. Consider Fig. 4.16 (a) an open circuit PQ and replac the circuit by a Thevenin's equivalent as shown in Fig. 4.16 (b).

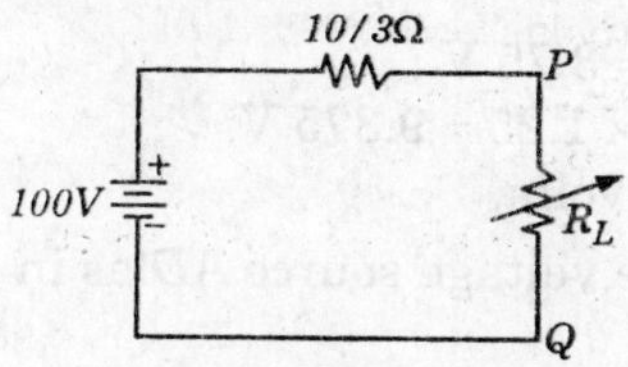

Fig. 4.16 (b)

$$V_0 = \frac{120}{24} \times 20 = 100\text{ V.}$$

$$R_{th} \text{ at } PQ = \frac{20 \times 4}{20 + 4} = \frac{80}{24} = \frac{10}{3}\ \Omega$$

For maximum power,

$$R = \frac{10}{3}\text{ ohm}$$

Current $= \dfrac{100}{\dfrac{10}{3} + \dfrac{10}{3}} = 15$ amps.

Power $= 15 \times 15 \times \dfrac{10}{3} = 750$ watts.

Example 4.12. *Calculate using Thevenin's Theorem, the current in the branch FC for the circuit of Fig. 4.17 (a).*

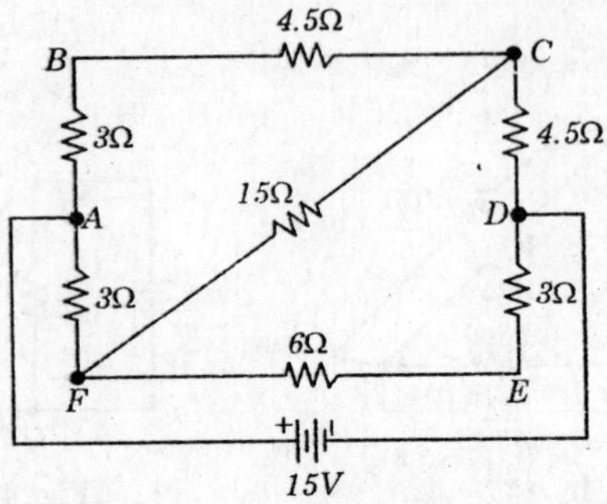

Fig. 4.17 (*a*)

Solution. Considering *FC* as an open circuit. It reduces to a 15 Volt battery supplying two parallel branches each of resistance 12 ohms as in Fig. 4.17 (*b*). The current in each branch is

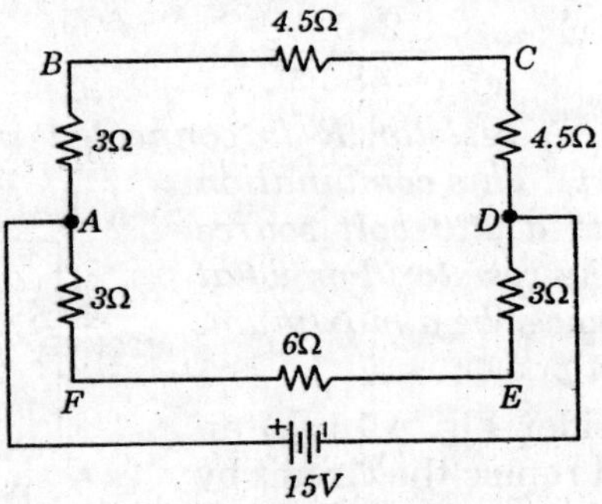

Fig. 4.17 (*b*)

$$= 15/12 = 1.25 \text{ amp.}$$

Voltage drop from A to F is $3 \times 1.25 = 3.75$ V

Voltage drop from A to C is $(3 + 4.5) \times 1.25 = 9.375$ V.

$$\therefore \quad V_0 = 9.375 - 3.75 = 5.625 \text{ volts.}$$

R_{Th} is obtained by short circuiting the voltage source *AD* as in 4.17 (*c*)

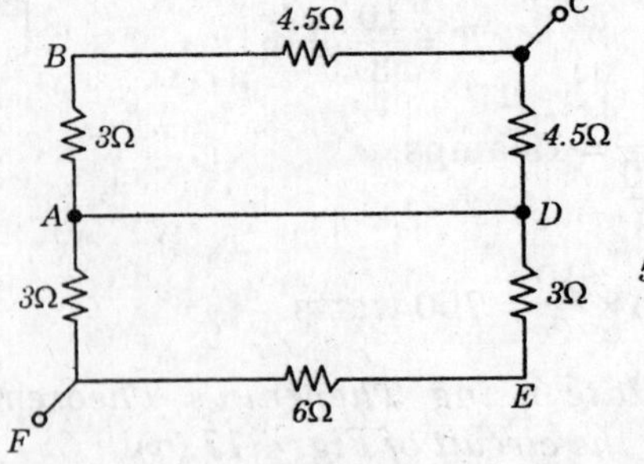

Fig. 4.17 (*c*)

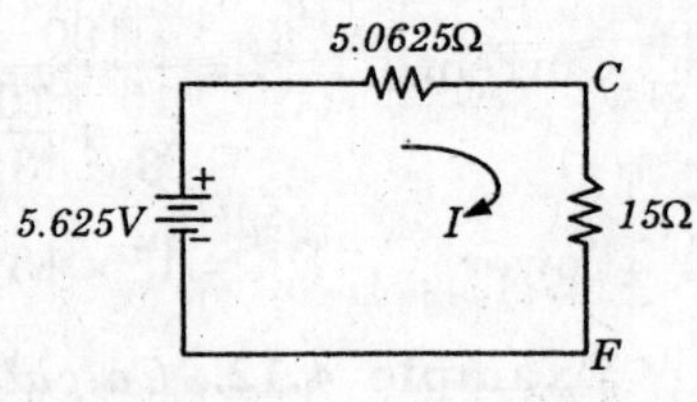

Fig. 4.17 (*d*)

$$R_{Th} = \frac{7.5 \times 4.5}{7.5 + 4.5} + \frac{9 \times 3}{9 + 3} = 5.0625\ \Omega$$

From Fig. 4.17 (*d*) $I = \dfrac{5.625}{20.0625}$

$$= 0.0281\ \text{A}.$$

Example 4.13. *Find the voltage across the 15 Ω resistor using Norton's Theorem in the circuit of Fig. 4.18 (a).*

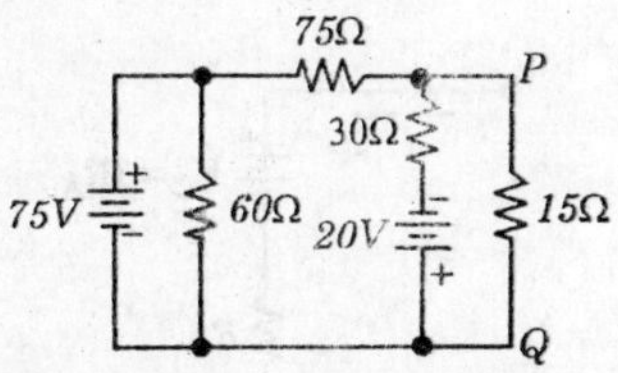

Fig. 4.18 (*a*)

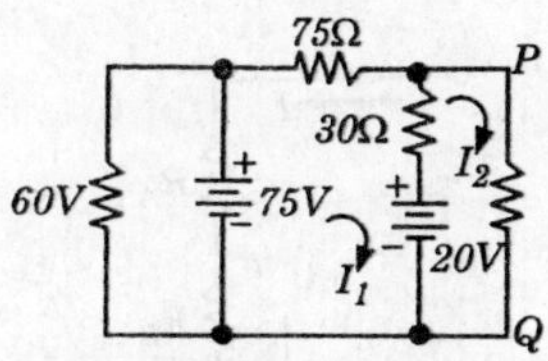

Fig. 4.18 (*b*)

Solution. We shall re-draw the circuit bringing out the 60 ohm resistor as it is just in parallel with the 75 V battery and short circuiting *PQ* to find I_{SC} as in Fig. 4.18 (*b*).

$$\begin{bmatrix} 105 & -30 \\ -30 & 30 \end{bmatrix} \begin{bmatrix} I_1 \\ I_2 \end{bmatrix} = \begin{bmatrix} 75 + 20 \\ -20 \end{bmatrix}$$

$$\therefore \quad I_2 = \frac{\begin{vmatrix} 105 & 95 \\ -30 & -20 \end{vmatrix}}{\begin{vmatrix} 105 & -30 \\ -30 & 30 \end{vmatrix}} = \frac{-20 \times 105 + 95 \times 30}{105 \times 30 - 30 \times 30} = \frac{1}{3}\ \text{A}.$$

R_{TH} is obtained from Fig. 4.18 (*c*)

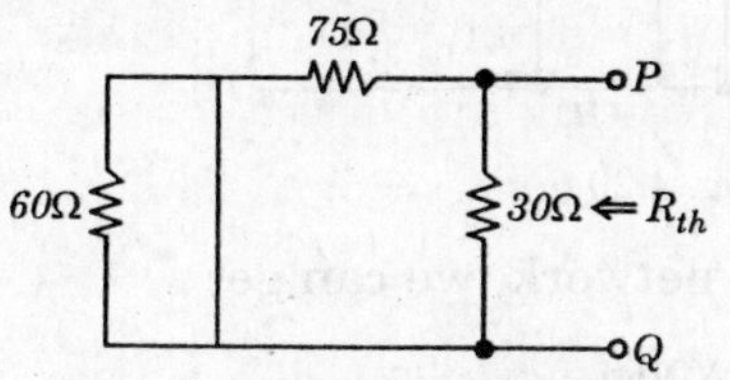

Fig. 4.18 (*c*)

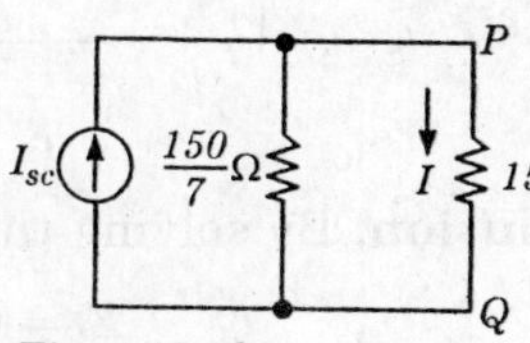

Fig. 4.18 (*d*)

$$R_{TH} = \frac{75 \times 30}{75 + 30} = \frac{150}{7}\ \text{ohms}.$$

Norton's equivalent is drawn in Fig. 4.18 (*d*)

$$I = \frac{\frac{5}{3} \times \frac{150}{7}}{\frac{150}{7} + 15} = \frac{50}{51}\ \text{A}.$$

$$V_{PQ} = \frac{50}{51} \times 15 = \frac{250}{17} \text{ volts.}$$

Substitution Theorem (*Compensation Theorem*)

A known voltage in a circuit can be replaced by an ideal voltage source and a known current can be replaced by an ideal current source. A resistor R carrying a current I has a voltage drop of IR. Then according to this theorem, this resistor can be replaced by a compensation e.m.f. equal to IR. Similarly if the voltage across an element R is V, the element can be replaced by a current source $I = V/R$. No other part of the net work is affected by this substitution.

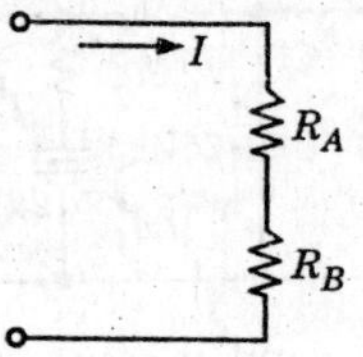

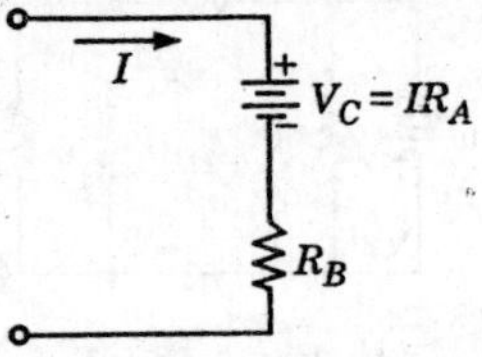

Fig. 4.19

In Fig. 4.19 (a) the resistance R_A can be replaced by compensation voltage source $V_C = IR_A$ as in Fig. 4.19 (b) with the polarity as shown.

Example 4.14. *Let us illustrate the use of this theorem by solving a problem shown in Fig. 4.20.*

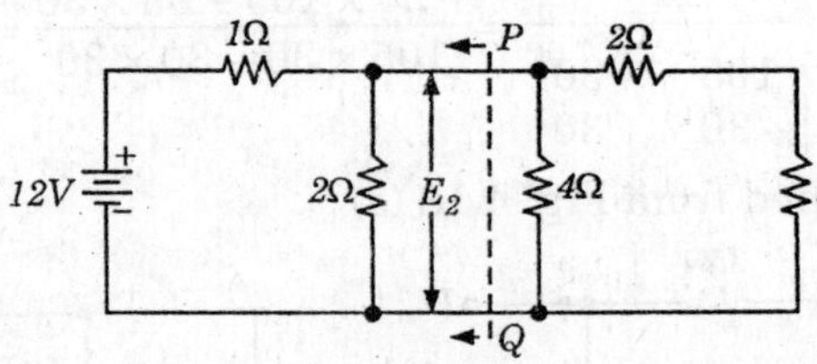

Fig. 4.20 (a)

Solution. By solving the network, we can get

$$E_2 = 6 \text{ volts.}$$

The part of the network to the left of section PQ can now be replaced by an ideal voltage source of 6 volts as in Fig. 4.20 (b).

$$E = 1.5 \times 2 = 3 \text{ volts.}$$

This method leads us to a method of partitioning complicated circuits into smaller sub-sections. These sections can be handled individually and then recombined.

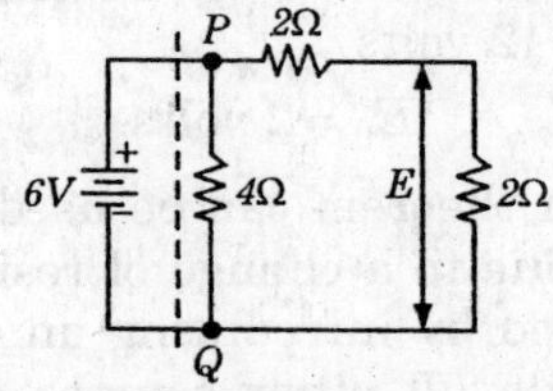

Fig. 4.20 (*b*)

Example 4.15. *Find the voltage E_0 of circuit 4.21 (a) by means of the substitution theorem.*

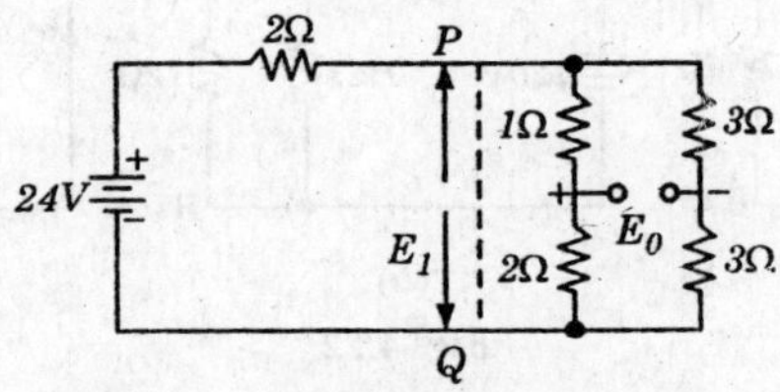

Fig. 4.21 (*a*)

Solution. We shall find E_1 in the section *PQ*.

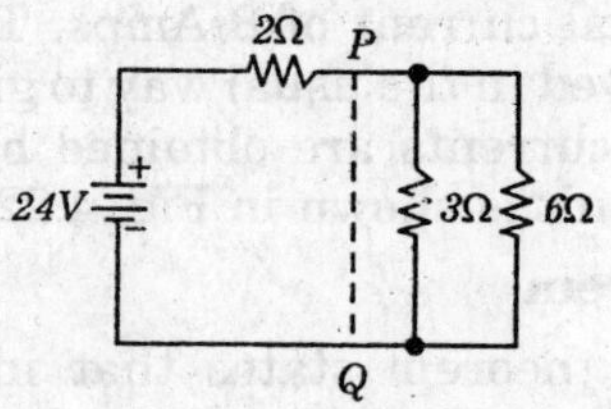

Fig. 4.21 (*b*)

$$E_1 = 12 \text{ V}.$$

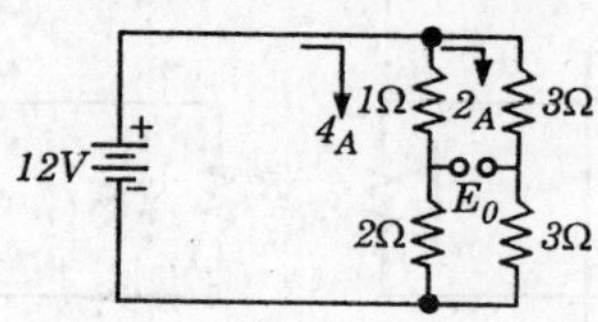

Fig. 4.21 (*c*)

Now the section of the network to the left of PQ can be replaced by a voltage source of 12 volts.

Now $$E_0 = 2 \text{ volts.}$$

The compensation theorem can be used to find the change of current in a branch due to a change of resistance in any branch. This may be calculated by introducing an e.m.f. $(-I\Delta R)$ into the changed branch, while all other sources are replaced by their respective internal resistances.

Example 4.16. *Find the currents in the circuit of Fig. 4.22 if the resistor R_{AB} is changed from 6 to 12 ohms.*

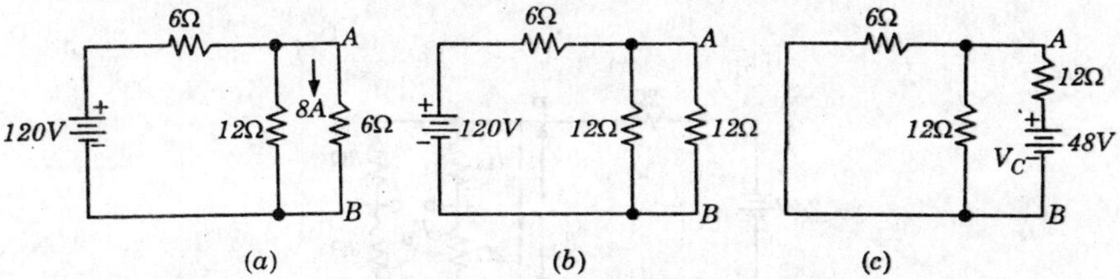

Fig. 4.22

Solution. The currents are first solved for in the usual way and marked as in Fig. 4.22 (*a*). If the resistor *AB* is now changed to 12 ohms, $\Delta R = 12 - 6 = 6$ ohms. The e.m.f. to be introduced is $(-8 \times 6) = -48$ volts. The negative sign indicates that the emf is to oppose the original current of 8 Amps. This is shown in Fig. 4.22 (*c*). which is solved in the usual way to give the compensating currents. The final currents are obtained by adding (*a*) and (*b*) together and the result is shown in Fig. 4.22 (*c*).

Reciprocity Theorem

The reciprocity theorem states that in a linear, bilateral, network a voltage source V volts in a branch gives rise to a current I in another branch, the ratio V/I is constant when the positions of V and I are interchanged.

It is found that on changing the voltage source from branch 1 to branch 2, the current I in the branch 2 appears in branch 1 as shown in Fig. 4.23.

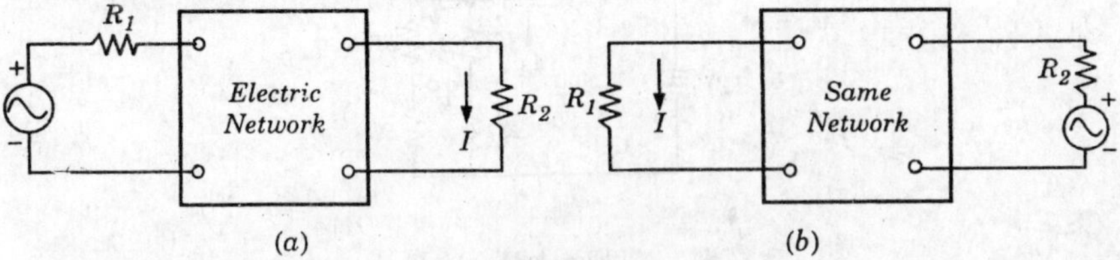

Fig. 4.23

Example 4.17. *In the network shown in Fig. 4.24, find the currents in the 4 ohm resistor. Verify the reciprocity theorem. What change results in the current through the 5 ohm and 10 ohm branches ?*

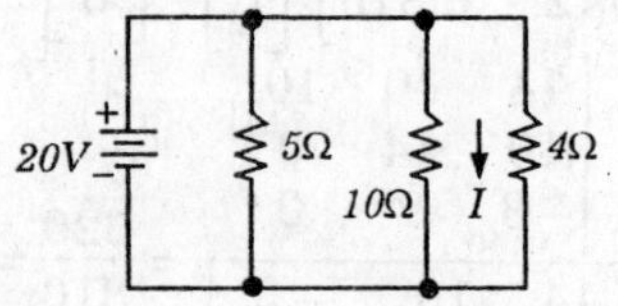

Fig. 4.24 (*a*)

Solution. Current through the 4 Ω resistor $= \frac{20}{4} = 5$ A.

$$I_5 = \frac{20}{5} = 4 \text{ A.}$$

$$I_{10} = \frac{20}{10} = 2 \text{ A.}$$

On changing the voltage source to the 4 Ω branch,

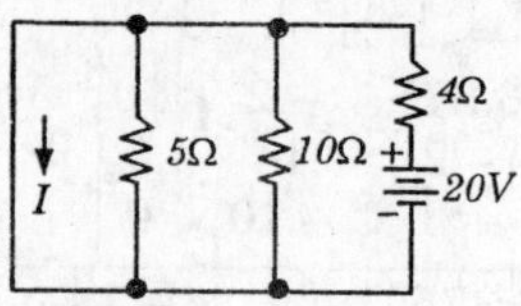

Fig. 4.24 (*b*)

the current through the short = 5 A

Thus Reciprocity Theorem is verified

$$I_5 = I_{10} = 0.$$

Example 4.18. *In the circuit of Fig. 4.25 find I_3 and verify the Reciprocity Theorem.*

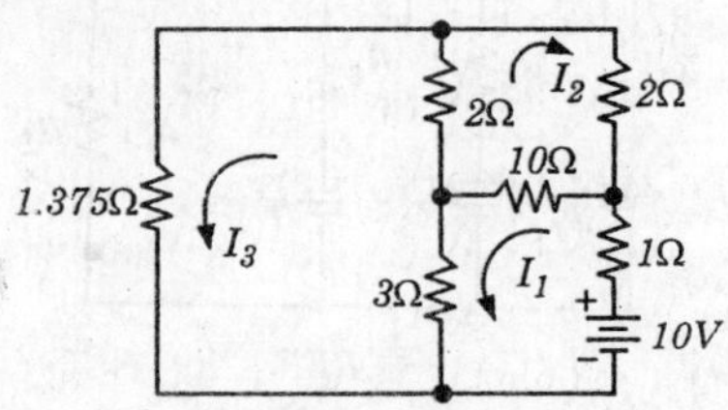

Fig. 4.25 (*a*)

Solution. The current I_3 is found by the Maxwell's loop method as follows :

$$\begin{bmatrix} 14 & 10 & -3 \\ 10 & 14 & 2 \\ -3 & 2 & 6.375 \end{bmatrix} \begin{bmatrix} I_1 \\ I_2 \\ I_3 \end{bmatrix} = \begin{bmatrix} 10 \\ 0 \\ 0 \end{bmatrix}$$

$$\therefore \quad I_3 = \frac{\begin{vmatrix} 14 & 10 & 10 \\ 10 & 14 & 0 \\ -3 & 2 & 0 \end{vmatrix}}{\begin{vmatrix} 14 & 10 & -3 \\ 10 & 14 & 2 \\ -3 & 2 & 6.375 \end{vmatrix}} = \frac{620}{310} = 2 \text{ A}$$

Now transferring the battery to the branch with 1.375 ohm resistor, we get the circuit of Fig. 4.25 (*b*).

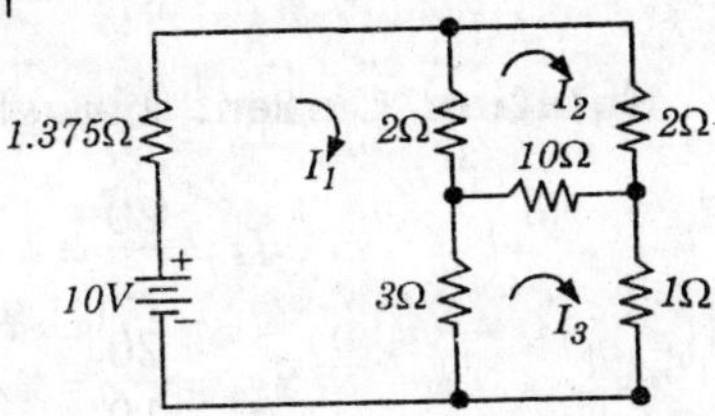

Fig. 4.25 (*b*)

We shall again find I_3 by the loop method

$$\begin{bmatrix} 6.375 & -2 & -3 \\ -2 & 14 & -10 \\ -3 & -10 & 14 \end{bmatrix} \begin{bmatrix} I_1 \\ I_2 \\ I_3 \end{bmatrix} = \begin{bmatrix} 10 \\ 0 \\ 0 \end{bmatrix}$$

$$\therefore \quad I_3 = \frac{\begin{vmatrix} 6.375 & -2 & 10 \\ -2 & 14 & 0 \\ -3 & -10 & 0 \end{vmatrix}}{\begin{vmatrix} 6.375 & -2 & -3 \\ -2 & 14 & -10 \\ -3 & -10 & 14 \end{vmatrix}} = \frac{620}{310} = 2 \text{ A.}$$

which illustrates the Reciprocity Theorem.

Millman's Theorem

Consider the circuit of Fig. 4.26.

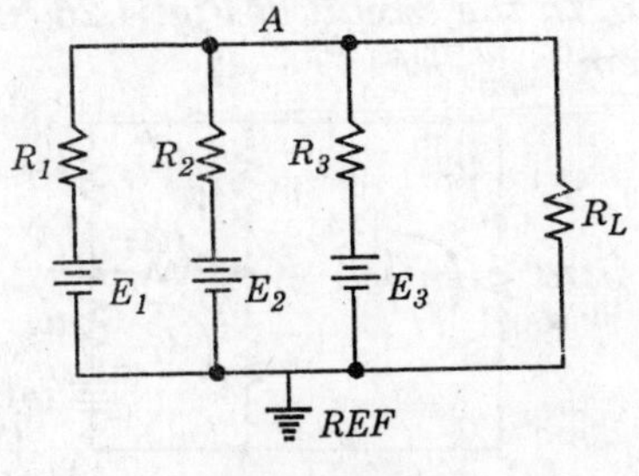

Fig. 4.26

If the voltage of the terminal A is assumed as V then we may write the Kirchhoff's current law to that node as

$$\frac{E_1 - V}{R_1} + \frac{E_2 - V}{R_2} + \frac{E_3 - V}{R_3} = \frac{R}{R_L}$$

or
$$\frac{E_1}{R_1} + \frac{E_2}{R_2} + \frac{E_3}{R_3} = \frac{V}{R_1} + \frac{V}{R_2} + \frac{V}{R_3} + \frac{V}{R_L}$$

Hence
$$V = \frac{\left(\frac{E_1}{R_1} + \frac{E_2}{R_2} + \frac{E_3}{R_3}\right)}{\left(\frac{1}{R_1} + \frac{1}{R_2} + \frac{1}{R_3} + \frac{1}{R_L}\right)}$$

The above equation is referred to as Millman's Theorem. Having found out V, we may find the currents.

Example 4.19. *Solve Example 4.13 using Millman's Theorem.*

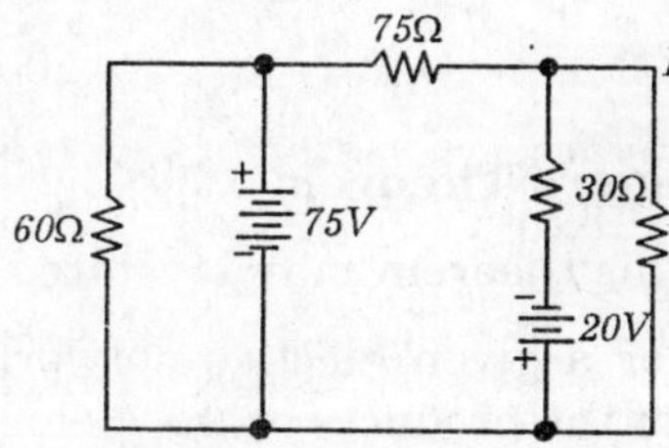

Fig. 4.27

Solution. Using Millman's Theorem for the circuit of Fig. 4.27.

$$V\left(\frac{1}{75} + \frac{1}{30} + \frac{1}{15}\right) = \frac{75}{75} - \frac{20}{30}$$

$$V\left(\frac{2+5+10}{150}\right) = \frac{1}{3}$$

$$\therefore \qquad V = \frac{50}{17} \text{ volts.}$$

Example 4.20. *Using Millman's Theorem, calculate the voltage across AB and the power in each of the four resistors in the circuit of Fig. 4.28.*

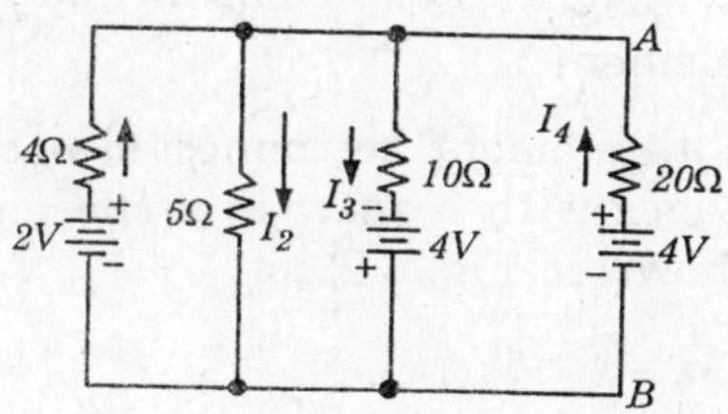

Fig. 4.28

Let the Voltage across $AB = V$.

then
$$V\left(\frac{1}{4} + \frac{1}{5} + \frac{1}{10} + \frac{1}{20}\right) = \frac{2}{4} - \frac{4}{10} + \frac{4}{20}$$

Solving, $V = 0.5$ Volts.

$$I_1 = \frac{2-0.5}{4} = \frac{3}{8}\text{ A}$$

$$I_2 = \frac{0.5}{5} = 0.1\text{ A}$$

$$I_3 = \frac{4.5}{10} = 0.45\text{ A}$$

$$I_4 = \frac{4-0.5}{20} = \frac{7}{40}\text{ A.}$$

$$P_4 = I_1^2 \times 4 = \frac{3}{8} \times \frac{3}{8} \times 4 = \frac{9}{16}\text{ Watts.}$$

$$P_5 = (0.1)^2 \times 5 = 0.05\text{ watts}$$

$$P_{10} = (0.45)^2 \times 10 = 2.025\text{ watts.}$$

$$P_{20} = \left(\frac{7}{20}\right)^2 \times 20 = \frac{49}{80}\text{ watts.}$$

Tellegen's Theorem

This theorem may be stated as follows :

For a given electric network satisfying Kirchoff's Laws, the sum of the products of the element currents and element voltages for all the elements is zero.

If a given network has n elements, with voltages $V_1, V_2, \ldots V_j \ldots V_n$ and currents $i_1, i_2, i_j, \ldots i_n$,

then $$\sum_{j=1}^{n} V_j i_j = 0.$$

V_j is the voltage across the jth element and i_j, is the current through the same element.

Proof. Let the jth element be connected between two nodes x and y whose voltages with respect to a chosen reference node are V_x and V_y, as shown in Fig. 4.29.

Then, $$V_j = V_x - V_y$$

If the current i, is assumed to be the current flowing through the jth element and leaving node x,

then $(-i_j)$ is the current leaving node y.

$$\therefore \quad V_j i_j = (V_x - V_y)\, i_j$$

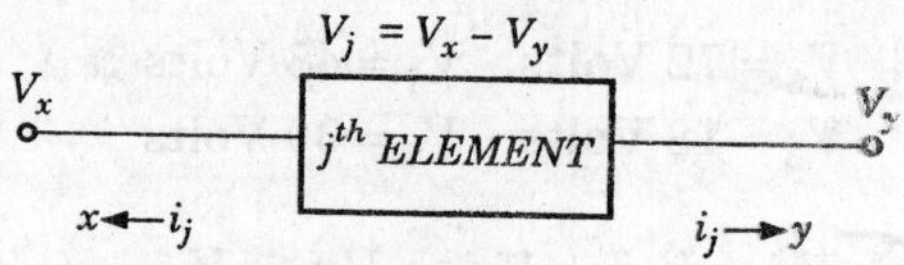

Fig. 4.29

$$= V_x i_j - V_y i_j$$

$$= V_x \text{ [current leaving node } x]$$

$$+ V_y \text{ [current leaving node } y]$$

$$\therefore \quad \sum_{j=1}^{n} V_j i_j$$

V_1. [algebraic sum of all current leaving node 1] + V_2 [algebraic sum of all currents leaving node 2] + ... + V_n [algebraic sum of all currents leaving node n].

But the algebraic sum of all currents at a node is zero by Kirchhoff's current law.

Hence $\sum_{j=1}^{n} V_j i_j = 0$

This theorem is valid for networks so long as Kirchhoff's laws are valid. It is equally valid for non-linear and active networks also. The theorem states in other words the principle of conservation of power. The algebraic sum of the power absorbed by the elements of a network at any time is zero. Or, the total power absorbed by the passive elements must equal the power given out by the active elements.

Example 4.21. *Ilustrate Tellegen's Theorem by the circuit shown in Fig. 4.30.*

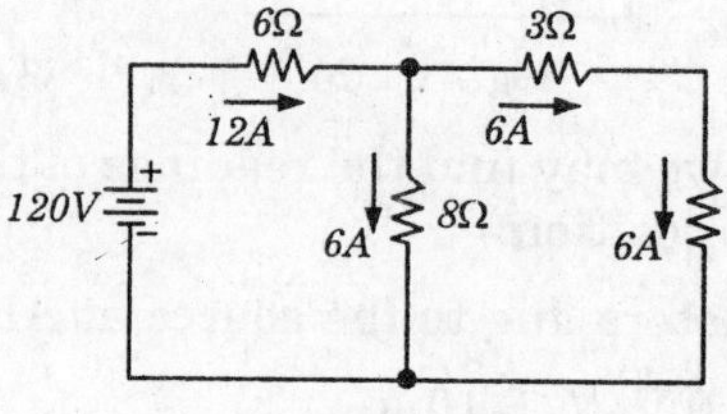

Fig. 4.30

Solution: The currents are solved for in the usual way and are marked in the figure. We may now write the voltage drops across the individual resistors as

$$V_6 = 72 \text{ Volts} \quad V_7 = 48 \text{ Volts}$$

$$V_3 = 18 \text{ Volts} \quad V_5 = 30 \text{ Volts}$$

$$\sum_{j=1}^{4} V_j i_j = V_6 i_6 + V_8 i_8 + V_3 i_3 + V_5 i_5 + (-120 \times 12)$$

Voltage drop in the source = – 120 (negative sign for rise)

$\therefore\ 72 \times 12 + 48 \times 6 + 18 \times 6 + 30 \times 6 - 120 \times 12 = 0.$

Example 4.22. *The network of Fig. 4.31 (a) is built up of linear resistors. When a voltage source is connected at terminals AB and CD short circuited the readings are $V_1 = 10$ V $I_1 = 10$ A, $I_2 = -2$ A and $V_2 = 0$. When the source and the short circuit are interchanged, the readings are $V_1 = 0$, $I_1 = -2$ A, $I_2 = 5$A and $V_2 = 10$ V. Find using the principles of substitution, superposition and linearity, the meter readings when the above source is connected between A and B and a 10 ohm resistor is connected between C and D.*

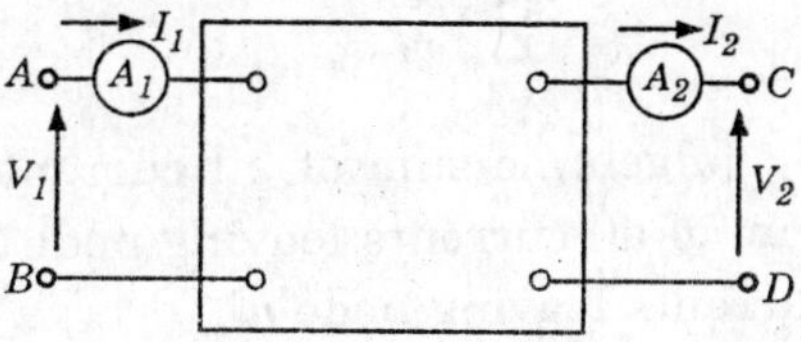

Fig. 4.31 (a)

Solution. The effect of the 10 ohm resistor at CD can be replaced by a voltage source of $10 \times (-2) = -20$ Volts. The negative sign indicates that this e.m.f. is to oppose the original current I_2 to the Voltage source as in Fig. 4.31 (*b*).

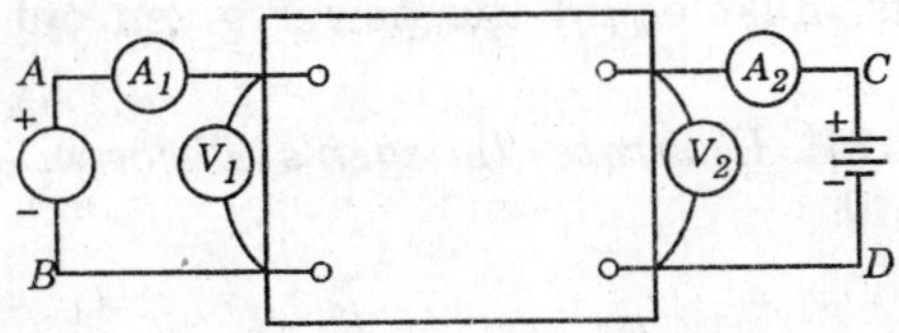

Fig. 4.31 (*b*)

Due to the 2 sources, we may find the readings of the meters using the principle of superposition.

Reading of the meters due to the source at AB

$$V_1 = 10 \text{ V} \quad I_1 = 10 \text{ A}$$

$$V_2 = 0 \text{ V} \quad I_2 = -2 \text{ A}$$

Readings of the meters due to the source at CD

$$V_1 = 0$$

$$I_1 = -2 \times 2 = -4 \text{ A}$$

$$V_2 = 20 \text{ Volts.}$$
$$I_2 = 5 \times 2 = 10 \text{ A.}$$

The readings given in the problem are for 10 volts.

For 20 volts source multiply by 2 ... Linearity.

Hence readings of the instruments are

$$V_1 = 10 \text{ volts ;}$$
$$I_1 = 10 - 4 \text{ A} = 6 \text{ A}$$
$$V_2 = 20 \text{ volts ; } I_2 = -2 + 10 = 8 \text{ A.}$$

EXERCISES

4.1. Solve Prob. 3.5 (Fig. 3.32) by the principle of superposition.

4.2. Solve Prob. 3.6 (Fig. 3.33) by the principle of superposition.

4.3. Find the current in the 2 ohm resistor of Fig. 4.32 by the principle of superposition. **[Ans.** 5 A]

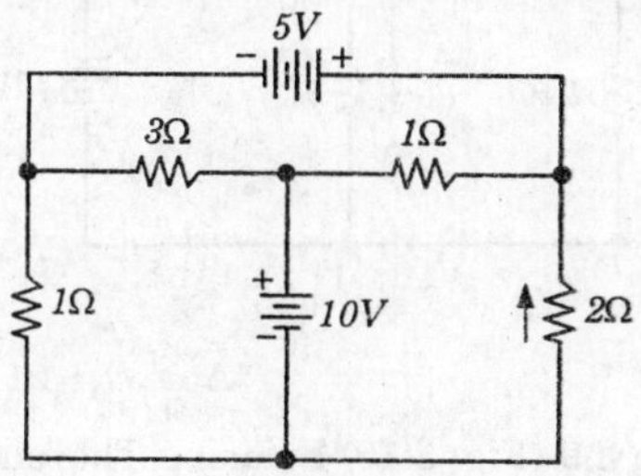

Fig. 4.32

4.4. Find the current in the 5 ohm resistor of Fig. 4.33 using the superposition Theorem. **[Ans.** 30 A]

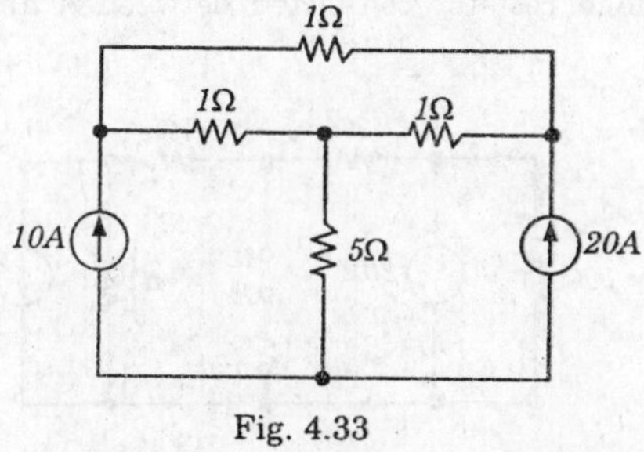

Fig. 4.33

4.5 Use the principle of superposition to find the current in the 8 ohms resistor of Fig. 3.34 (Prob. 3.7). **[Ans.** 0.294 A from Q to P]

4.6. Find in the circuit of Fig. 4.34, the current I using Thevenin's Theorem. **[Ans.** 1 A]

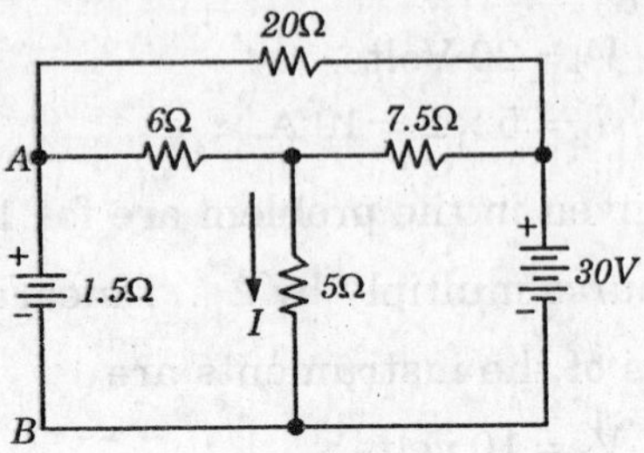

Fig. 4.34

4.7. Solve Prob. 1 (Fig. 3.32) using Thevenin's Theorem.

4.8. In the circuit of Fig. 4.35, (*a*) find the open circuit voltage at *AB*, (*b*) the looking back (Thevenin's) resistance at *AB*, (*c*) the current through the resistance *AB*. Draw the Thevenin's equivalent circuit.

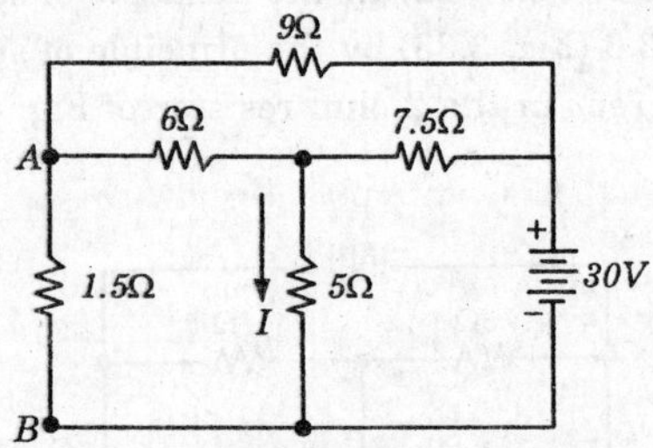

Fig. 4.35

[**Ans.** $E_o = 21$ V $R_{th} = 4.5\ \Omega$ $I = 3.5$ A]

4.9. Solve example 3.9 (Fig. 3.10) by using Thevenin's Theorem.

[**Ans.** 2 A, 60 W]

4.10. From the circuit of Fig. 4.36 compute the open circuit voltage, the short circuit current and the equivalent resistance at the terminals *A* – *B*. Draw the Thevenin's and Norton's equivalent circuits. Hence, find the current through a 2 ohm load resistor connected between *A* and *B* using any one equivalent circuit.

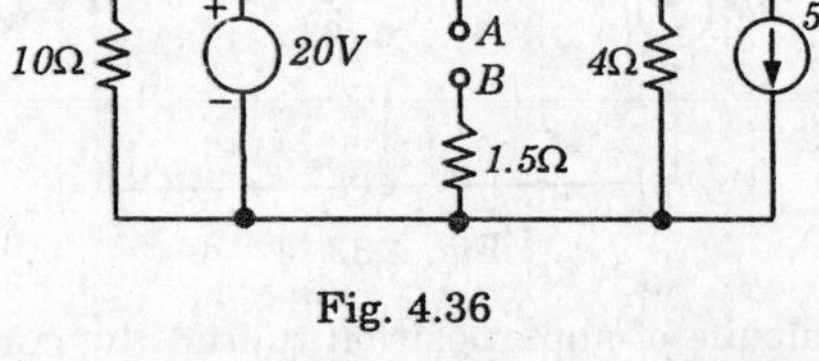

Fig. 4.36

[**Ans.** 10 V, 10/3 A, $I_L = 2$ A]

4.11. Obtain the Thevenin's equivalent circuit at the terminals *PQ* in the network of Fig. 4.37.

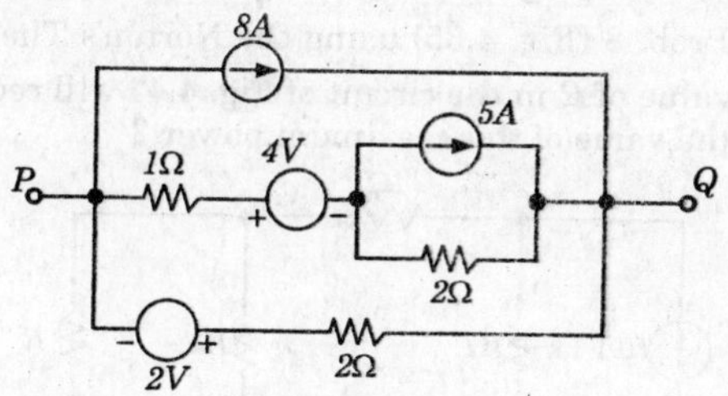

Fig. 4.37

[Ans. $E_{QP} = 6$ V, $R_{TH} = 1.2\ \Omega$**]**

4.12. In the circuit of Fig. 4.38, find using Thevenin's Theorem the current flowing in a 0.5 ohm ammeter placed across $a - b$. **[Ans.** 3 A**]**

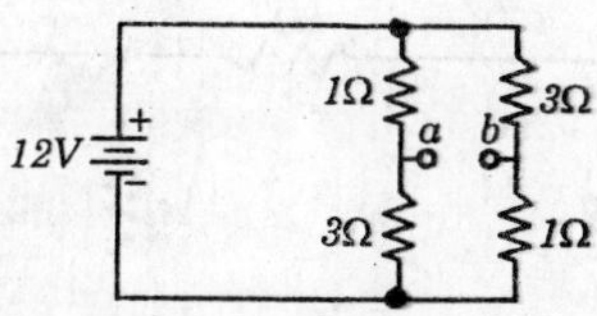

Fig. 4.38

4.13. Find the Thevenin's and Norton's equivalent circuit at terminals $a - b$ for the network of Fig. 4.39. **[Ans.** $E_{ab} = 5$ V, $R_{TH} = 1\ \Omega$, $I_{SC} = 5$ A**]**

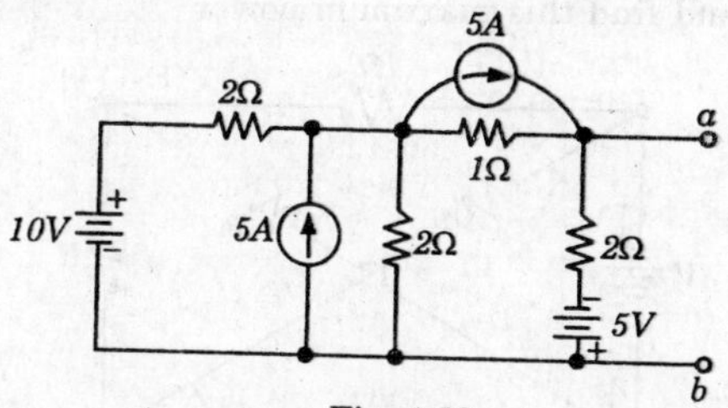

Fig. 4.39

4.14. Obtain the Thevenin's and Norton's equivalent circuit at PQ in the network of Fig. 4.40. **[Ans.** $E_{PQ} = 6$ V, $R_{TH} = 1.6\ \Omega$, $I_{SC} = 3.75$ A**]**

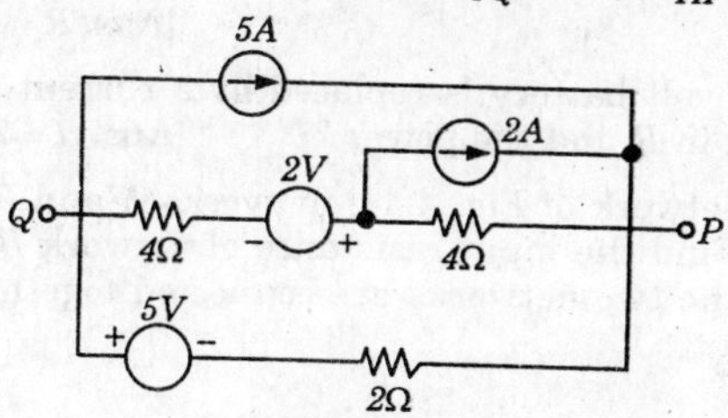

Fig. 4.40

4.15. Solve Prob. 3 (Fig. 4.32) by using the Norton's Theorem.

4.16. Solve Prob. 8 (Fig. 4.35) using the Norton's Theorem.

4.17. What value of R in the circuit of Fig. 4.41 will receive the maximum power ? What is the value of this maximum power ?

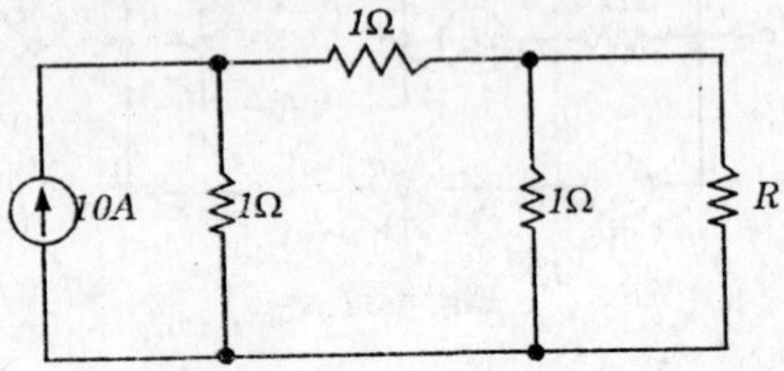

Fig. 4.41

[Ans. $R = 2/3\ \Omega$, **Power** = 25/6 W**]**

4.18. For what value of R in Fig. 4.42 will it receive the maximum power. Find this maximum power.

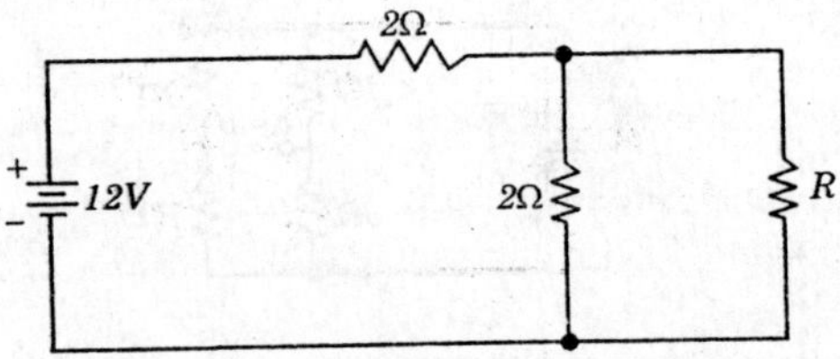

Fig. 4.42

[Ans. $R = 1\ \Omega$ **Power** = 16 W**]**

4.19. Find the value of R for which it receives maximum power in the circuit of Fig. 4.43 and find this maximum power.

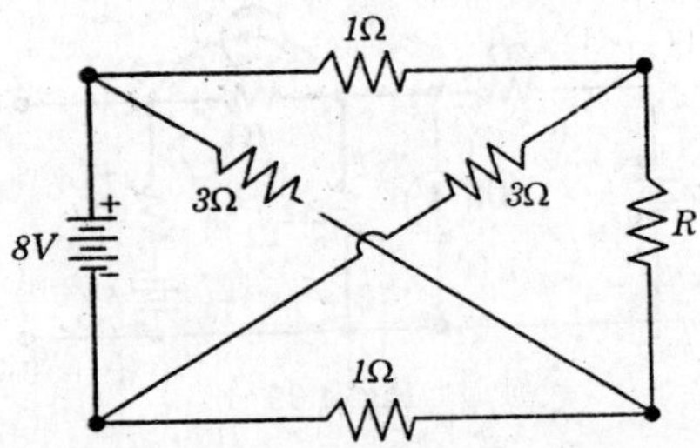

Fig. 4.43

[Ans. $R = 1\ \Omega$, **Power** = 8/3 W**]**

4.20. If the 8 volt battery is replaced by a current source of 8 A, what will be the change in R and the power ? **[Ans.** R = 2 ohms, **Power** = 8 W**]**

4.21. In the network of Fig. 4.44, networks A and B may be considered to be in cascade. Find the input resistance of network B and hence find the voltage E_1 when the two networks are connected together. Use substitution theorem to find E_2. **[Ans.** 2 Ω, 10 V, 2.5 V**]**

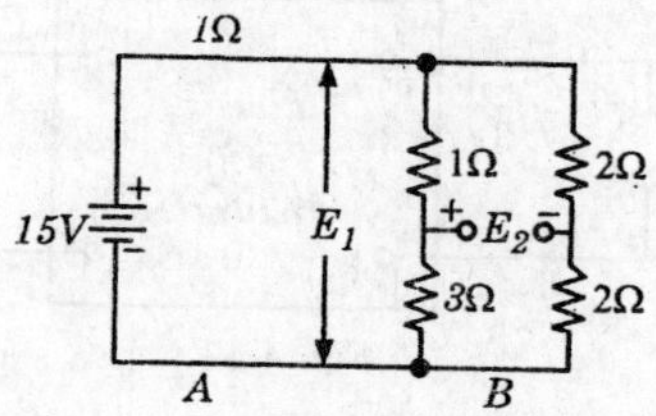

Fig. 4.44

4.22. In the network of Fig. 4.45. Find the input resistance of section B and the voltage E. Find using the substitution theorem, the current I.

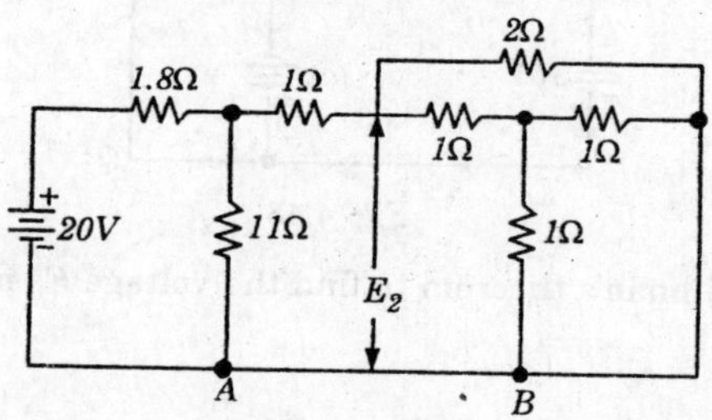

Fig. 4.45

[Ans. 7/4 Ω, 7 V 5/3 A]

4.23. In the circuit of Fig.4.46 compute the current through the zero resistance ammeter. Interchange the ammeter and the voltage source and verify reciprocity theorem. **[Ans.** I = (6/4.1 A)]

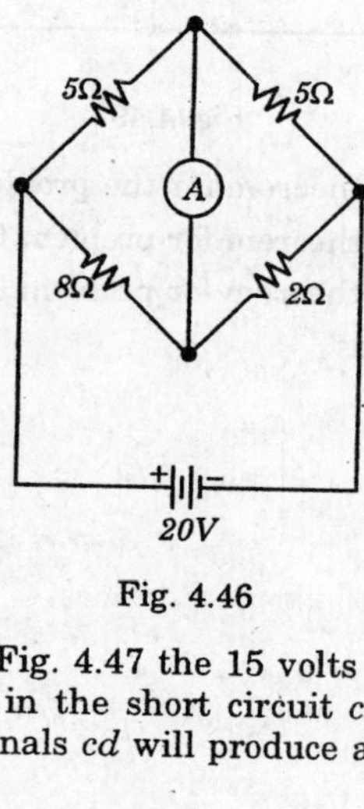

Fig. 4.46

4.24. In the circuit of Fig. 4.47 the 15 volts source E, placed across ab, gives a current of 3 amps in the short circuit cd. Determine what voltage source applied to the terminals cd will produce a short circuit current of 25 amps at ab.

[Ans. 125 volts]

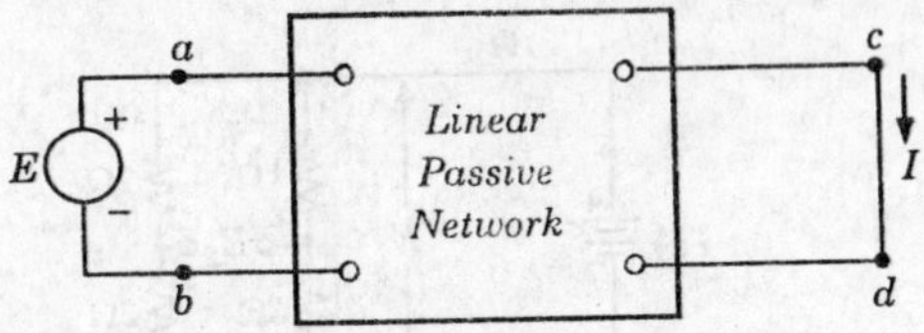

Fig. 4.47

4.25. Find the current in the 5 ohm resistor of the circuit in the Fig. 4.48 using Millman's Theorem. [Ans. 0.8 A from Q to P]

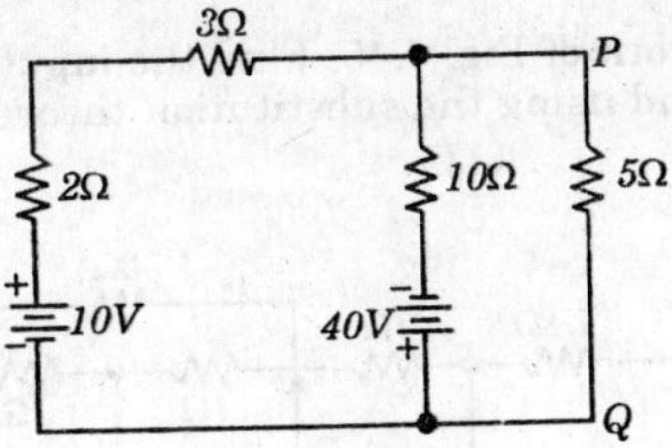

Fig. 4.48

4.26. Use Millman's theorem to find the voltage E_0 in the circuit of Fig. 4.49. [Ans. 20 volts]

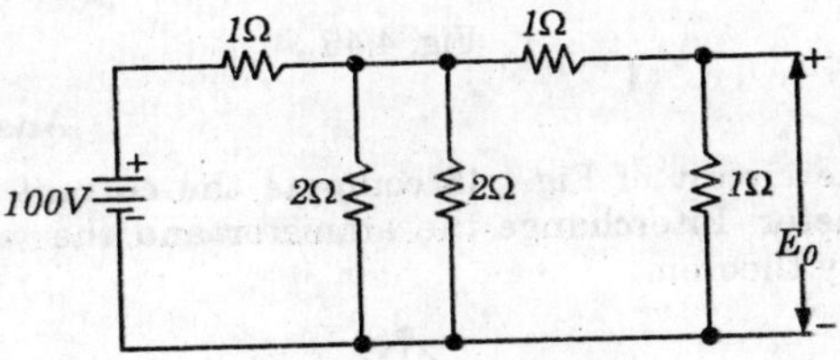

Fig. 4.49

4.27. Verify Tellegen's theorem for the problem 3 (Fig. 4.32)

4.28. Verify Tellegen's theorem for problem 6. (Fig. 4.38)

4.29. Verify Tellegen's theorem for problem 19. (Fig. 4.43) with R = 1.5 ohms.

FIVE

ALTERNATING CURRENT FUNDAMENTALS

We are so far concerned with electric circuits with D.C. sources. By D.C. sources, we mean current and voltage sources which have a fixed polarity and a constant magnitude. In practice, however, alternating current circuits are in wide use. The voltages and currents then become time-varying. They not only vary in magnitude but may also change their polarity from instant to instant. A few waveforms are shown in Fig. 5.1 contrasted with the familiar D.C. voltage waveform of Fig. 5.1 (*a*).

Voltage, current, power etc., represented as in Fig. 5.1 as a function of time t is called waveform. These quantities are generally periodic in nature. *i.e.*, they repeat after a constant interval of time. $f(t) = f(t + T) = f(t + 2T)$ etc. $f(t) = f(t + kT)$, k is an integer. The time taken to complete one cycle is called the period of the wave, represented by T. The number of such cycles occurring in one second is called frequency, f.

Hence $$f = \frac{1}{T}$$

Fig. 5.1 (*a*) shows a constant D.C. voltage. Other waveforms are all time varying with (*b*) and (*c*) indicating also change of

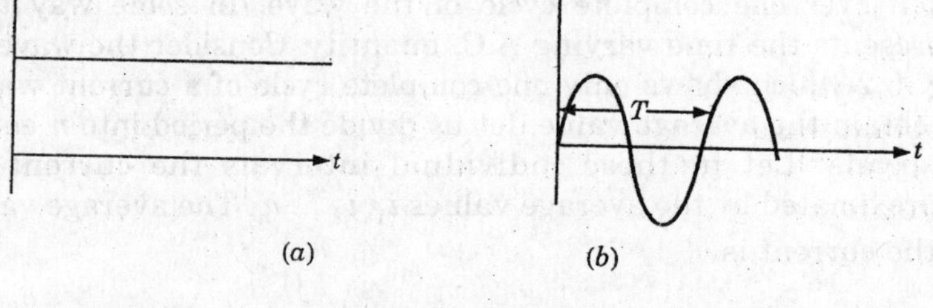

(*a*) (*b*)

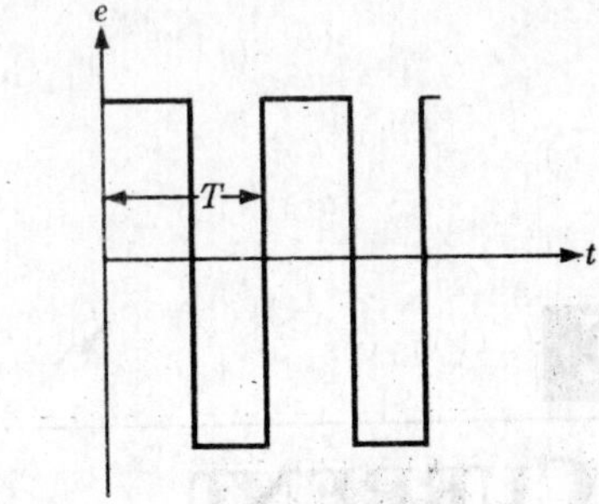

(c)

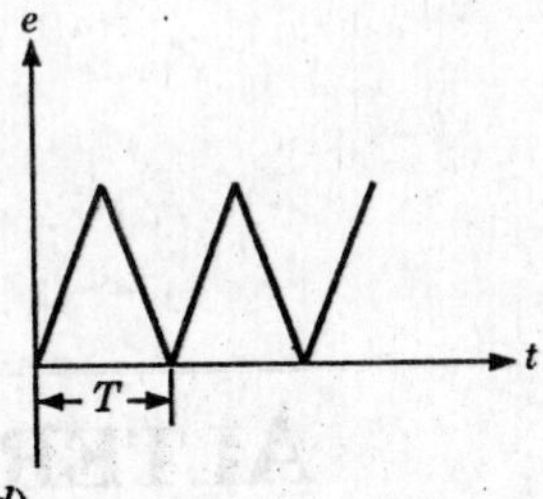

(d)

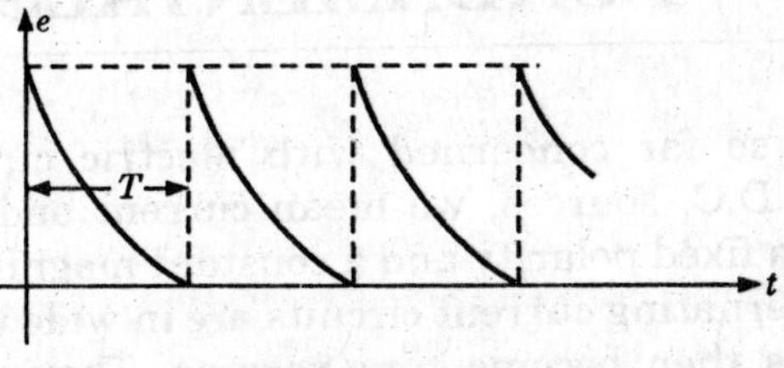

(e)

Fig. 5.1

polarity at regular intervals of time (the voltage becomes negative every half a cycle). (*d*) and (*e*) represent merely time varying (without change of polarity) voltages. An alternating quantity is one which changes sign or polarity.

Average and Effective Values

As the current or voltage in an A.C. circuit is varying from instant to instant it becomes very difficult to specify the quantity. When we say, the current is 5 Amperes or the voltage is 200 Volts, we should also specify the time at which it reaches these values. We shall use small letters i and e to specify instantaneous values. Two normal ways are used to express A.C. quantities : (1) the average value and (2) the effective (RMS) value.

Average Value

This is some kind of the average of the instantaneous values taken over one complete cycle of the wave. In some way this represents the time varying A.C. quantity. Consider the wave in Fig. 5.2 which shows only one complete cycle of a current wave. To obtain the average value, let us divide the period into n equal intervals. Let in these individual intervals the current be approximated by the average values $i_1, i_2 \ldots i_n$. The average value of the current is

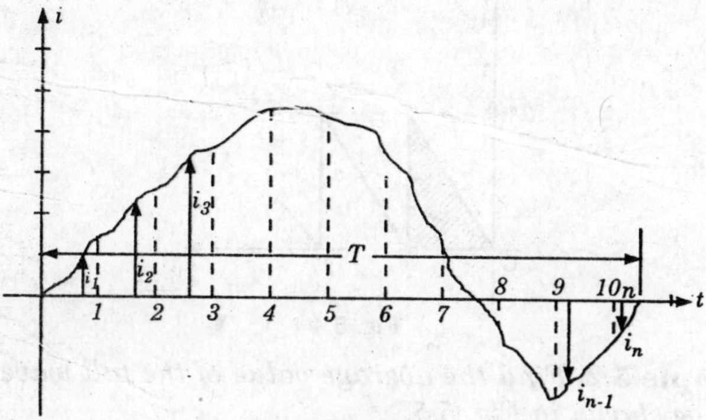

Fig. 5.2

$$I_{av} = \frac{i_1 + i_2 + i_3 + \ldots\ i_n}{n}$$

The average value can also be obtained by finding the area under the curve and dividing it by the base (period).

$$\text{Average value} = \frac{\text{Area under the curve}}{\text{Base (period)}}$$

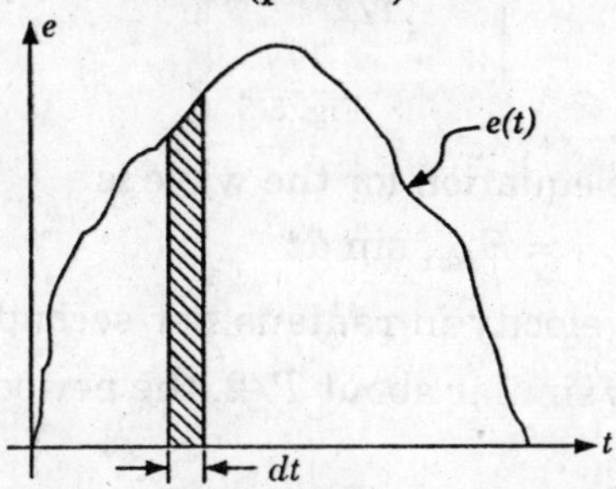

Fig. 5.3

The area can be found by an integration process if the equation of the wave form is known as follows. (Refer to Fig. 5.3)

$$E_{av} = \frac{1}{T}\int_0^T e\ (t)\ dt$$

Example 5.1. *Find the average value of the saw-tooth wave illustrated in Fig. 5.4.*

Solution.

$$\text{Average value} = \frac{\text{Area hatched}}{\text{Base (T)}}$$

$$\text{Area} = \tfrac{1}{2} \times 50 \times T$$

$$\text{Average value} = I_{av} = \frac{50\ T/2}{T} = \mathbf{25\ A}$$

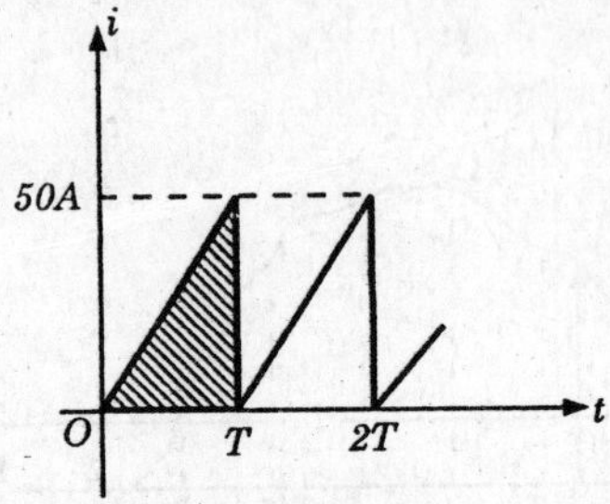

Fig. 5.4

Example 5.2. *Find the average value of the full wave rectified sine voltage shown in Fig. 5.5.*

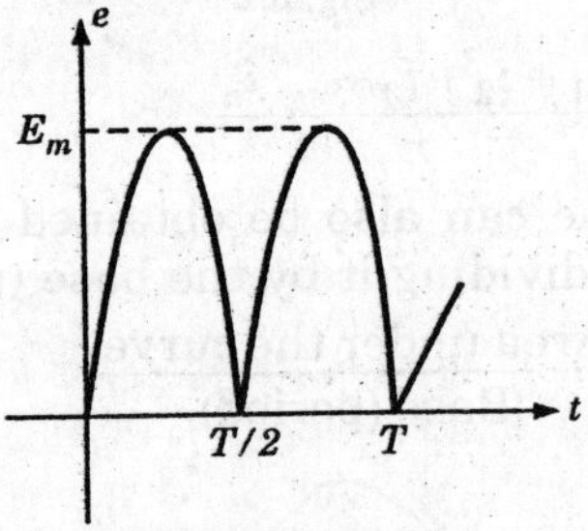

Fig. 5.5

Solution. The equation for the wave is

$$e = E_{max} \sin \omega t$$

ω is the angular velocity in radians per second.

As the wave is similar about $T/2$, the period can be taken to be $T/2$ sec.

$$\text{Area under the curve} = \int_0^{T/2} e\,(t)\,dt$$

$$\text{Average value} = \frac{\text{Area}}{\text{Base}} = \frac{\int_0^{T/2} e\,(t)\,dt}{T/2} = 2.\,E_m/\pi.$$

The Sine Wave

Fig. 5.6 shows a sine wave. The equation for the current is

$$i = I_m \sin \omega t$$

This may also be written as

$$i = I_m \sin \theta$$

where $\theta = \omega t$

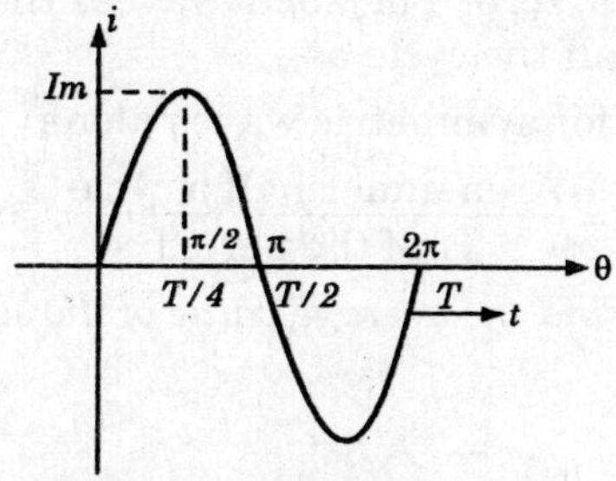

Fig. 5.6

The x-axis can, therefore, be written also in terms of the angle θ in radians. The period T, then is 2π radians.

Example 5.3. *Find the average value of the half-rectified sine wave of Fig. 5.7.*

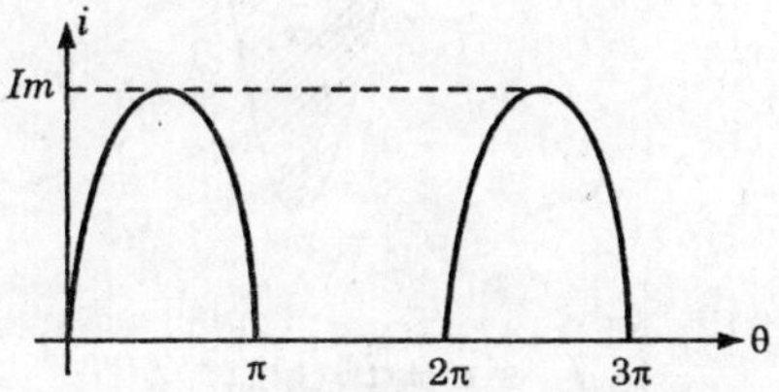

Fig. 5.7

Solution. Here, the area under the curve

$$= \int_0^{\pi} i d\theta = \int_0^{\pi} I_m \sin\theta \, d\theta = 2 I_m$$

Period $= 2\pi$

$\therefore$ Average value $= \dfrac{2 I_m}{2\pi} = \dfrac{I_m}{\pi}$

Example 5.4. *Find the average value of the triangular wave shown in Fig. 5.8.*

Solution. Area under one

Complete cycle $= \frac{1}{2} \times 50 \times T$

Average Value $= \dfrac{1}{2} \times \dfrac{50 \times T}{T}$

$= \mathbf{25\ V}$.

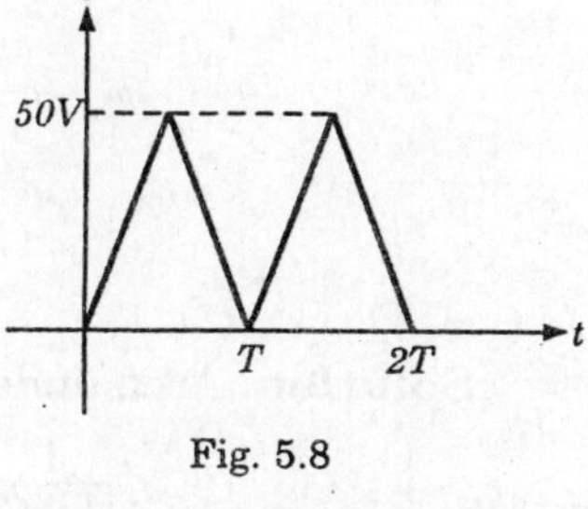

Fig. 5.8

For waves that are symmetrical about the x-axis, the definition originally given would present a problem. the positive area on the top cancels with the negative area below x-axis and the average value then becomes zero. For such waves, the average value is defined over only half the cycle as

Average value (for symmetric waves alone)

$$= \frac{\text{Area under half a cycle}}{\text{Half the period}}.$$

Example 5.5. *Find the average value of the sine wave of Fig. 5.9.*

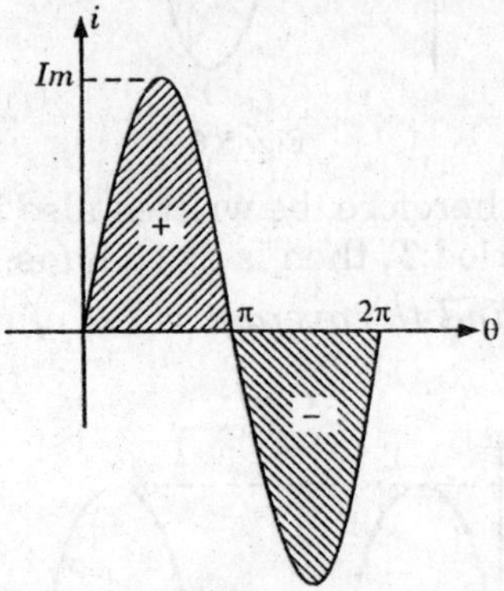

Fig. 5.9

$$\text{Average value } = \frac{\int_0^{\pi} I_m \sin\theta \, d\theta}{\pi} = \frac{2I_m}{\pi}$$

Example 5.6. *Find the average value of the wave shown in Fig. 5.10.*

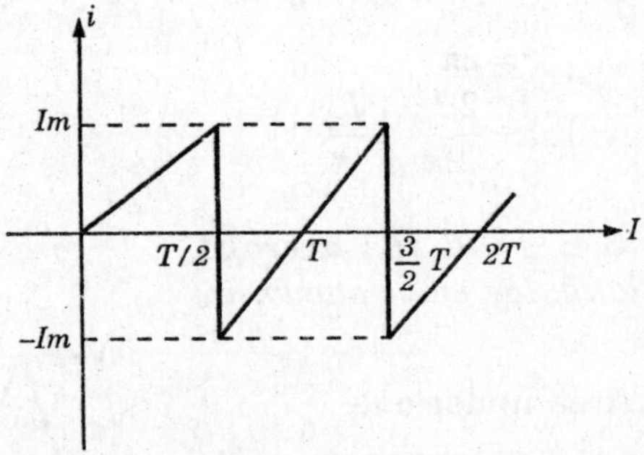

Fig. 5.10

Solution. Area under half the cycle

$$= \frac{1}{2} \times I_m \times \frac{T}{2}$$

$$\text{Average value } = \frac{1}{2} \times \frac{I_m \times T/2}{T/2} = \frac{I_m}{2} \textbf{ Amps.}$$

Effective (RMS) Value

The current passing through a resistor produces heat regardless of its direction. The heat produced by an alternating current of say maximum value 10 amps will not be equal to that produced by a direct current of 10 amps. The heating effect produced may be used to specify alternating (and time varying) currents (or voltages). The effective value of an A.C. is defined as that value of D.C. which on passing through a resistance R ohms for a given time T seconds, produces the same heat as the A.C. passing through R for the same time T.

If $i(t)$ is the A.C., then the heat produced by it for a small interval of time dt seconds, is

$$dH = i^2(t)\,R \cdot dt$$

Over the entire time period,

$$H = \int_0^T dH = \int_0^T i^2(t)\,R\,dt$$

If this heat is equal to that produced by a steady d.c. of I amps, passing through R, for time T seconds, then,

$$I^2RT = R\int_0^T i^2(t)\,dt$$

$$\therefore \qquad I_{eff} = \sqrt{\frac{1}{T}\int_0^T i^2(t)\,dt} \qquad \text{...(5)}$$

The effective value of the current $i(t)$ is also called the root mean square value (RMS) because of its definition in equation 5.

This value for the wave in Fig. 5.2, may be found by equation 5.

$$I_{RMS} = \sqrt{\frac{(i_1^{\,2} + i_2^{\,2} + i_3^{\,2} + \ldots i_n^{\,2})}{n}} \qquad \text{...(6)}$$

An alternate method of evaluating the effective value is to find the area under the squared curve.

$$I_{RMS} = \sqrt{\frac{\text{Area under the squared wave}}{\text{Period}}}$$

Example 5.7. *Find the RMS value of the sine wave of Fig. 5.6.*

Solution. $I_{RMS} = \sqrt{\frac{1}{2\pi}\int_0^{2\pi} (I_m \sin\theta)^2\,d\theta}$

$$= \sqrt{\frac{I_m^{\,2}}{2\pi}\int_0^{2\pi} \sin^2\theta\,d\theta}$$

$$= \sqrt{\frac{I_m^2}{2\pi}\int_0^{2\pi} \tfrac{1}{2}(1-\cos 2\theta)\, d\theta}$$

$$= \sqrt{\frac{I_m^2}{4\pi}\left[\left(\theta - \frac{\sin 2\theta}{2}\right)\right]_0^{2\pi}}$$

$$= \sqrt{\frac{I_m^2}{4\pi}\cdot 2\pi} = \sqrt{2}\, I_m$$

Example 5.8. *Find the R.M.S. value of the saw tooth wave of Fig. 5.11.*

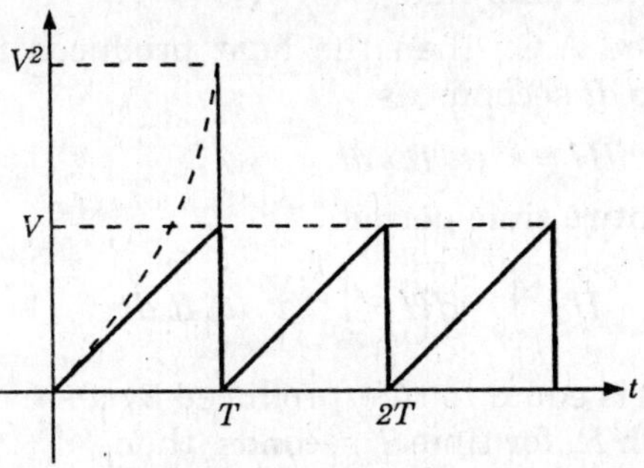

Fig. 5.11

Solution. Area under the squared curve = Area under the parabola

$$= \tfrac{1}{3} V^2 \times T$$

$$\text{RMS value} = \sqrt{\frac{1}{3}\frac{V^2T}{T}} = \frac{V}{\sqrt{3}}$$

Example 5.9. *Find the r.m.s. value of the wave of Fig. 5.12.*

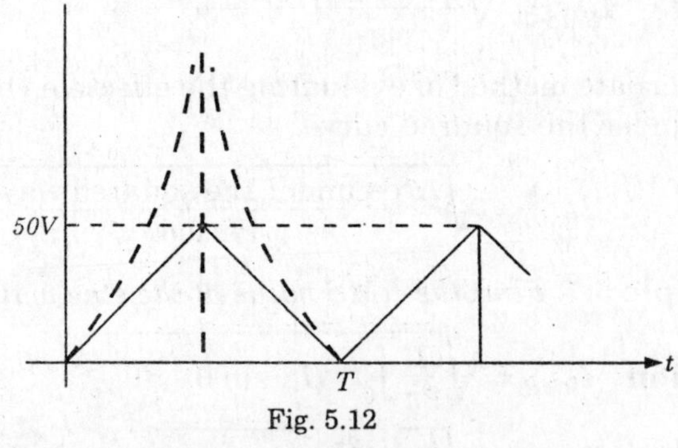

Fig. 5.12

Solution. Area under the squared curve

$$= 2 \times \tfrac{1}{3} \times 50^2 \times T/2$$

$$\text{RMS value} = \sqrt{\frac{50^2 \times T}{3 \times 1}} = \frac{50}{\sqrt{3}} \textbf{ volts.}$$

Example 5.10. *A conductor carries a sinusoidal A.C. of peak value 10 Amps superimposed on a direct current of amplitude 10 Amps. Find the r.m.s. value of the resultant current.*

Solution. The resultant current,

$$i = 10 + 10 \sin \theta$$

where $\theta = \omega t$

$$\therefore \quad I_{RMS} = \sqrt{\frac{1}{2\pi} \int_0^{2\pi} (10 + 10 \sin \theta \, d\theta)^2 \, d\theta}$$

$$= \sqrt{\frac{1}{2\pi} \int_0^{2\pi} 100 + 100 \sin^2 \theta + 200 \sin \theta) \, d\theta}$$

$$= \sqrt{\frac{100}{2\pi} \left(\theta - 2 \cos \theta + \frac{\theta}{2} - \frac{\sin 2\theta}{4} \right)_0^{2\pi}}$$

$$= \sqrt{150} = \mathbf{12.25\ A.}$$

The effective value of the total of two or more currents superimposed on each other can be found by a simpler method. Let n currents (or voltage) each of RMS value $I_1, I_2, I_3, \ldots I_n$ be superimposed and let I be the total effective value. Then

$$I = \sqrt{I_1^2 + I_2^2 + \ldots I_n^2}$$

In this problem $I = \sqrt{10^2 + \left(\frac{10}{\sqrt{2}}\right)^2} = \sqrt{150} = 12.25$ amps.

The following factors are defined.

$$\text{Form factor} \quad = K_f = \frac{\text{RMS value}}{\text{Average value}}$$

$$\text{Peak factor} \quad = K_p = \frac{\text{Maximum value}}{\text{RMS value}}$$

These factors for a sine wave are

$$K_f = \frac{I_m/\sqrt{2}}{2I_m/\pi} = \frac{\pi}{2\sqrt{2}} = 1.11$$

$$K_p = \frac{I_m}{I_m/\sqrt{2}} = 1.414$$

For the triangular wave of Fig. 5.12.

$$K_f = \frac{50/\sqrt{3}}{25} = \frac{2}{\sqrt{3}} = 1.155$$

$$K_p = \frac{50}{50/\sqrt{3}} = \mathbf{1.732.}$$

Example 5.11. *Find the form factor and peak factor of the trapezoidal wave shown in Fig. 5.13.*

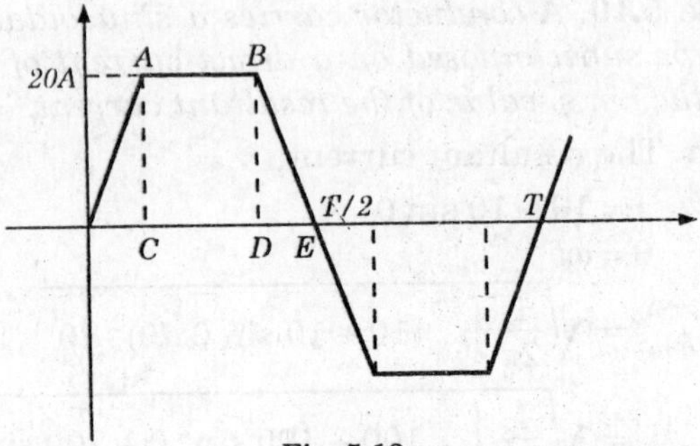

Fig. 5.13

Solution. As the wave is symmetrical, the average value is found over one half cycle,

Area under one half cycle

$$= \text{Area of } \Delta OAC + \Delta\, BDE + \text{rectangle } ABDC$$

$$= \frac{1}{2} \times \frac{T}{8} \times 20 + \frac{1}{2} \times \frac{T}{8} \times 20 + \frac{T}{4} \times 20$$

$$= \frac{T}{8} 60$$

$$\text{Average value} = \frac{60\, T/8}{T/2} = \mathbf{15\ amps.}$$

For the RMS value, we draw the squared curves for one complete cycle. As the two halves are identical on squaring, the rms value may be calculated for one half only.

Area under the squared curve

$$= \frac{1}{3} \times 20^2 \times \frac{T}{8} + \frac{1}{3} \times 20^2 \times \frac{T}{8} + 20^2 \times \frac{T}{4}$$

$$= 400 \times \frac{T}{8} \times \frac{8}{3}$$

$$\text{RMS value} = \sqrt{\frac{400 \times T/3}{T/2}} = \sqrt{\frac{800}{3}} = 16.33 \text{ amps.}$$

$$K_f = \frac{\text{RMS value}}{\text{Average value}} = 1.089$$

$$K_p = \frac{\text{Maximum value}}{\text{RMS value}} = \frac{20}{16.33} = 1.225.$$

Example 5.12. *Find the average and rms values of the wave shown in Fig. 5.14.*

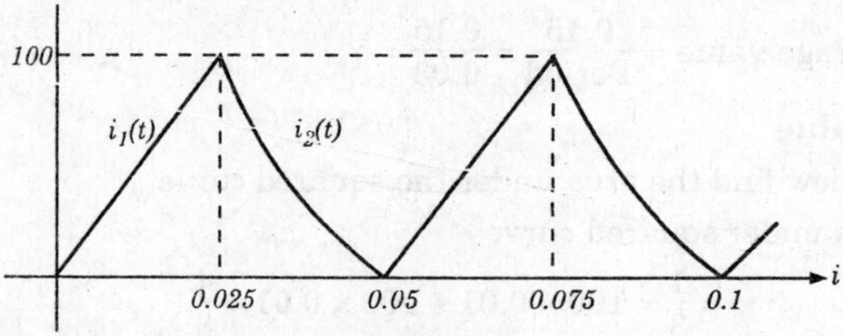

Fig. 5.14

Solution. $i(t)$ is represented by

$$i_1(t) = 4000\,t\ ;\ 0 < t < 0.025$$

$$i_2(t) = 100\,\varepsilon^{-1000\,(t-0.025)}\ ;\ 0.025 < t < 0.05$$

$$I_{average} = \frac{1}{0.05}\int_0^{0.05} i(t)\,dt$$

$$= \frac{1}{0.05}\left[\int_0^{0.025} i_1(t)\,dt + \int_{0.025}^{0.05} i_2(t)\,dt\right]$$

$$= \frac{1}{0.05}\left[\left(4000\,\frac{t^2}{2}\right)_0^{0.025} + \left(\frac{-100}{1000}\,\varepsilon^{-1000\,(t-0.025)}\right)_{0.025}^{0.05}\right]$$

$$= \frac{1}{0.05}\,(1.25 + 0.1) = 27 \text{ amps.}$$

$$I_{RMS} = \sqrt{\frac{1}{0.05}\int_0^{0.05} i(t)^2\,dt} = \mathbf{42\ A.}$$

Example 5.13. *Find the average and effective values of the waveform shown in Fig. 5.15.*

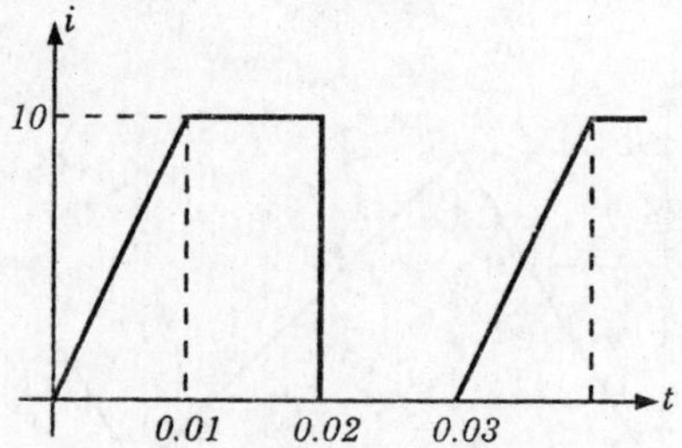

Fig. 5.15

Solution. The period of one complete cycle = 0.03 sec.

Area within one cycle

$$= \text{Area of triangle} + \text{Area of rectangle}$$

$$= \tfrac{1}{2} \times 10 \times 0.01 + 10 \times 0.01 = 0.05 + 0.1 = 0.15$$

$$\text{Average value} = \frac{0.15}{\text{Period}} = \frac{0.15}{0.03} = 5.$$

RMS Value

We now find the area under the squared curve

Area under squared curve

$$= \frac{1}{3} \times 100 \times 0.01 + 100 \times 0.01 = \frac{4}{3}$$

$$\text{RMS value} = \sqrt{\frac{4/3}{0.03}} = \mathbf{6.67}$$

Example 5.14. *A time varying current shown in Fig. 5.16 is passing through a 2 ohm resistor. Find the average and effective values of the voltage across the resistor.*

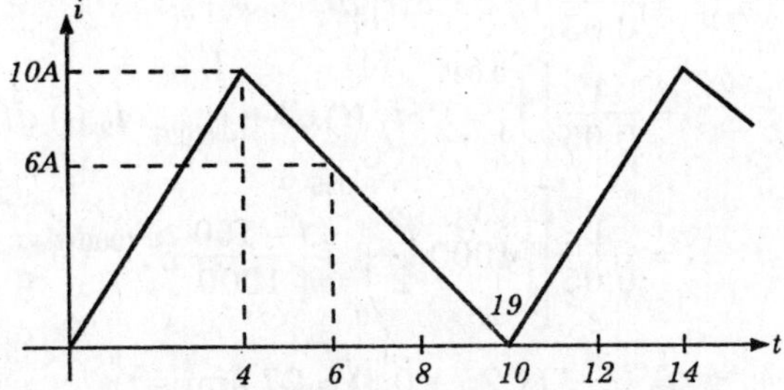

Fig. 5.16

Solution. If the current is i amperes, the voltage

$$e = i\,R \text{ volts} = 2\,i \text{ volts.}$$

The voltage wave form for one complete cycle is shown in Fig. 5.17.

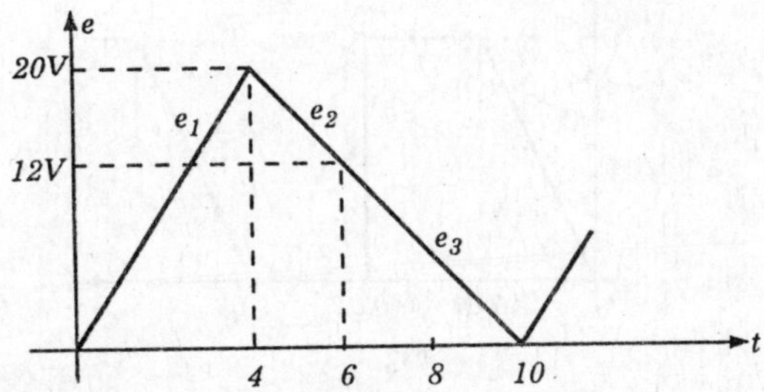

Fig. 5.17

To find the average value, we may integrate and obtain the area under the voltage wave

The area may also be obtained by adding the three areas too.

Area under one cycle

$$= \left(\frac{1}{2} \times 20 \times 4\right) + \left(\frac{20 + 12}{2}\right) 2 + \frac{1}{2} \times 4 \times 12$$

$$= 40 + 32 + 24 = 96$$

$$\text{Average value} = \frac{96}{\text{Period}} = \frac{96}{10} = \mathbf{9.6 \text{ volts.}}$$

RMS Value

Area under the squared curve

$$= \int_0^4 e_1 (t)^2 \, dt + \int_4^6 e_2 (t)^2 \, dt + \int_6^{10} e_3 (t)^2 \, dt$$

$$e_1 = 5t \quad e_2 = 36 - 4t \quad e_3 = 30 - 3t$$

Area under squared curve

$$= \int_0^4 (5t)^2 \, dt + \int_4^{10} (30 - 4t)^2 \, dt + \int_6^{10} (30 - 3t)^2 \, dt$$

$$= \left[25 \frac{t^3}{3}\right]_0^4 + \left[\frac{(36 - 4t)^3}{-12}\right]_4^6 + \left[\frac{(30 - 3t)^3}{-9}\right]_6^{10}$$

$$= \frac{25 \times 64}{3} + 1296 \times 2 - 144 \times 20 + \frac{16 \times 152}{3}$$

$$+ 900 \times 4 - 90 \times 64 + 3 \times 784 = 1248$$

$$\therefore \quad \text{RMS value} = \sqrt{\frac{1248}{10}} = \mathbf{11.17 \text{ volts.}}$$

Example 5.15. *Detemine K (K < 1) in the waveform shown in Fig. 5.18 such that the effective value is (a) 2 (b) 4. What is the highest possible effective value for the waveform as K varies ?*

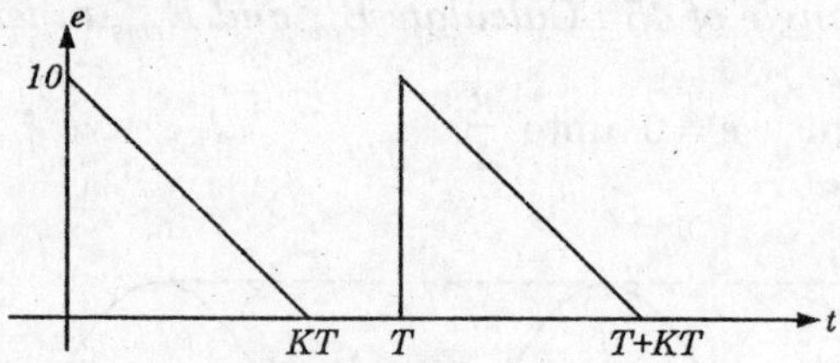

Fig. 5.18

Solution. Equation for the wave form is given by

$$\frac{e}{10} + \frac{t}{KT} = 1$$

or

$$e = 10\left(1 - \frac{t}{KT}\right)$$

$$= 10\,(1 - at) \qquad \text{where } a = \frac{1}{KT}$$

For effective value, we need the integral $\int_0^T e^2(t)\,dt$

$$= \int_0^{1/a} 100\,(1 - at)^2\,dt = 100\left[\frac{(1 - at)^3}{-3a}\right]_0^{1/a}$$

$$= \frac{100}{3} KT.$$

$$\text{RMS value} = \sqrt{\frac{100}{3}\frac{KT}{T}} = \sqrt{\frac{100\,K}{3}}$$

(a) $\sqrt{\dfrac{100\,K}{3}} = 2$

$\therefore$ $\dfrac{100\,K}{3} = 4$

or $K = 0.12$

(b) $\sqrt{\dfrac{100\,K}{3}} = 4$

$\dfrac{100\,K}{3} = 16$

or $K = 0.48$

For $K = 1$, RMS value

$$= \sqrt{\frac{100\,K}{3}} = \sqrt{\frac{100}{3}} = \frac{10}{\sqrt{3}} = 5.774 \text{ V}$$

Example 5.16. *The full rectified sine wave shown in figure 5.19 has a delay angle of 45°. Calculate E_{av} and E_{rms} in terms of E_m.*

Solution. $e = 0$ upto $\dfrac{\pi}{4}$

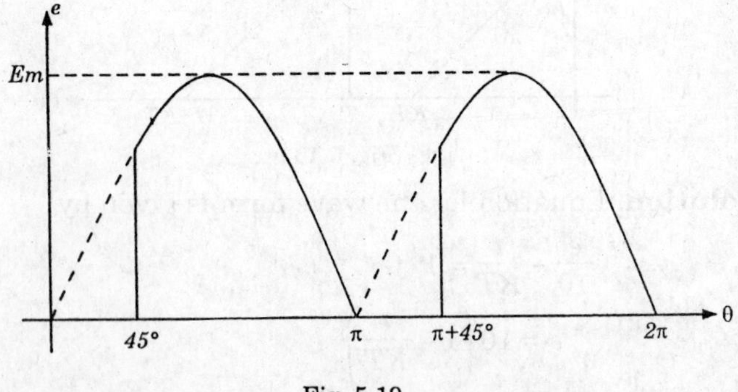

Fig. 5.19

$$e = E_m \sin \theta \text{ from } \frac{\pi}{4} \text{ to } \pi$$

Area under half a cycle

$$= \int_{\pi/4}^{\pi} E_m \sin \theta \, d\theta$$

$$= E_m (\cos \pi/4 - \cos \pi) = E_m \, 1.707$$

$$\text{Average value} = \frac{E_m (1.707)}{\pi} = 0.5434 \, E_m$$

For effective value, we need the integral

$$= \int_{\pi/4}^{\pi} Em^2 \sin^2 \theta \, d\theta = \frac{E_m^{\ 2}}{2} \int_{\pi/4}^{\pi} \left[1 - \cos 2\theta\right] d\theta$$

$$= \frac{E_m^{\ 2}}{2} \left(\theta - \frac{\sin 2\theta}{2}\right)_{\pi/4}^{\pi} = E_m^{\ 2} \left[\frac{3\pi}{4} + \frac{1}{2}\right]$$

$$\text{RMS Value} = \sqrt{\frac{E_m^{\ 2} (3\pi/4 + \frac{1}{2})}{\pi}} = \mathbf{0.674 \, E_m}.$$

Example 5.17. *A full rectified sine wave is clipped as shown in Fig. 5.20. Find the average and effective values of the function.*

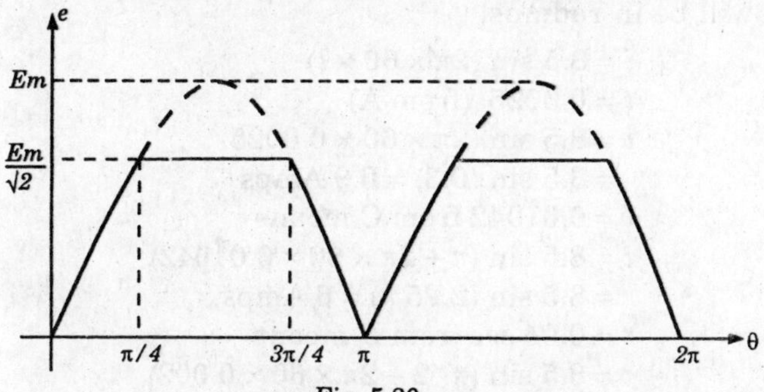

Fig. 5.20

Solution.
$$E_{av} = \frac{2}{\pi} \int_0^{\pi/4} E_m \sin \theta \, d\theta + \frac{E_m}{\sqrt{2}\pi} \left(\frac{3\pi}{4} - \frac{\pi}{4}\right)$$

$$= \frac{E_m}{\pi} \left[2 \times 0.293 + \frac{\pi}{2\sqrt{2}}\right] = 0.54 \, E_m$$

$$E_{RMS}^{\ 2} = \frac{1}{\pi} \left[2 \int_0^{\pi/4} E_m^{\ 2} \sin^2 \theta \, d\theta + \frac{E_m^{\ 2}}{2} \left(\frac{3\pi}{4} - \frac{\pi}{4}\right)\right]$$

$$= \frac{E_m^{\ 2}}{\pi} \left[0.2854 + 0.7854\right] = E_m^{\ 2} (0.34085)$$

$$E_{RMS} = \mathbf{0.584 \, E_m}.$$

Example 5.18. *A sinusoidal wave of frequency 60 Hz, has a maximum value of 8.5 amps. What will be its value (a) 0.0025 sec after it passes through zero in a positive direction (b) 0.01042 sec after the wave passes through zero in a negative direction (c) 0.004 sec after the wave reaches its positive maximum (refer Fig. 5.21).*

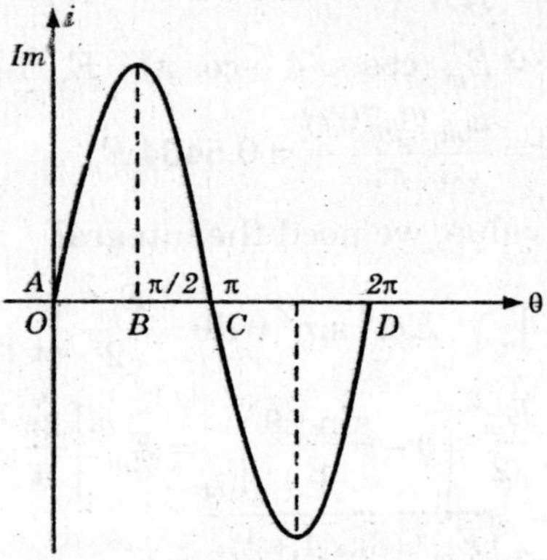

Fig. 5.21

Solution. $i = I_{max} \sin \omega t$

where $\omega = 2\pi f$

and ωt will be in radians.

$$i = 8.5 \sin (2\pi \times 60 \times t)$$

(*a*) $t = 0.0025$ (from A)

$$i = 8.5 \sin (2\pi \times 60 \times 0.0025)$$
$$= 8.5 \sin (0.3) = 6.9 \text{ Amps.}$$

(*b*) $t = 0.01042$ from C means

$$i = 8.5 \sin (\pi + 2\pi \times 60 \times 0.01042)$$
$$= 8.5 \sin (2.25\ \pi) = 6 \text{ Amps.}$$

(*c*) $t = 0.04$ sec from B means

$$i = 8.5 \sin (\pi/2 + 2\pi \times 60 \times 0.002)$$
$$= 8.5 \sin (0.74\ \pi) = \mathbf{6.2\ Amps.}$$

In-phase and out-of-phase quantities : Phase difference

We shall be more interested in sinusoidally varying electrical quantities. When two voltage or current sine-waves of the same frequency reach their maxima and minima at the same instants of time they are said to be in-phase. Otherwise they are out of phase. Two or more such waves may be added to yield a sine wave of the same frequency (Fig. 5.22).

$$i = i_1 + i_2 = (I_{m1} + I_{m_2}) \sin \theta$$

The resultant wave has for its maximum value $(I_{m1} + I_{m2})$.

The RMS value of the resultant wave is as before given by

$$I = \sqrt{I_1^2 + I_2^2 + I_3^2 + \ldots}$$

where $I_1, I_2, I_3 \ldots$ are the RMS values of the individual waves.

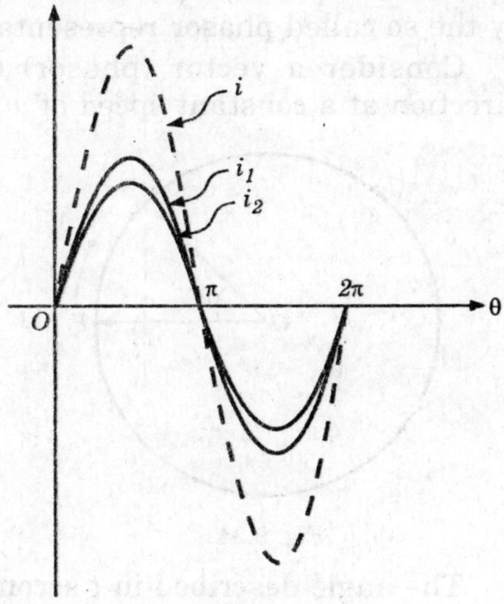

Fig. 5.22

The two voltage waves e_1 and e_2 shows in Fig. 5.23 are out of phase. They are said to have a phase difference of $\pi/3$ radians or 60°. e_2 is said to lag behind e_1 by 60° as it reaches its maximum value 60° after e_1.

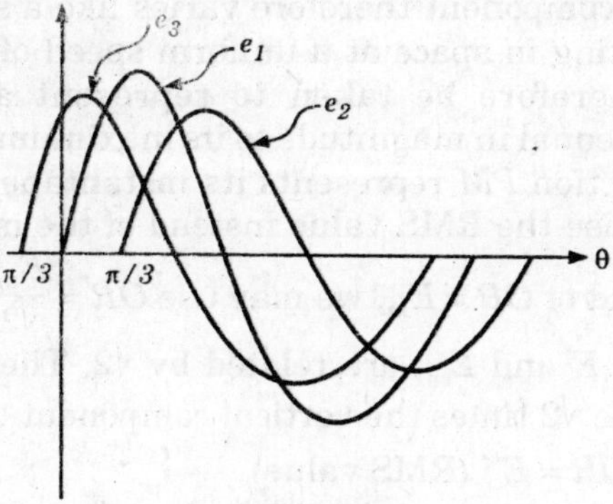

Fig. 5.23

$$e_1 = E_{m1} \sin \theta$$

and $$e_2 = E_{m2} \sin (\theta - \pi/3)$$

The resultant wave

$$= e = e_1 + e_2 = E_{m1} \sin \theta + E_{m2} \sin (\theta - \pi/3)$$

Consider the wave e_3 whose equation is

$$e_3 = E_{m3} \sin (\theta + \pi/3)$$

This wave leads e_1 by 60° as it has already reached its maximum value 60° before e_1.

Phasor Representation of Alternating Quantities

In analysing A.C. circuits, we are often required to add or subtract or multiply in-phase and out-of-phase A.C. quantities. To do this through drawing the wave-forms and writing their equations is quite complicated. The procedure is greatly simplified by the so called phasor representation of such quantities.

Consider a vector (phasor) OP rotating in anti-clockwise direction at a constant speed of w radians per second (Fig. 5.24).

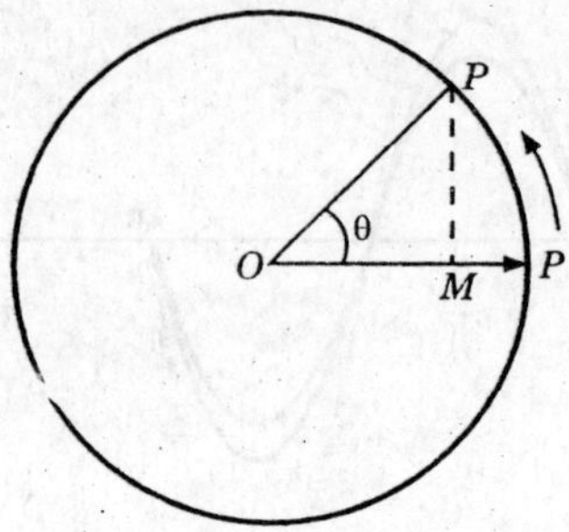

Fig. 5.24

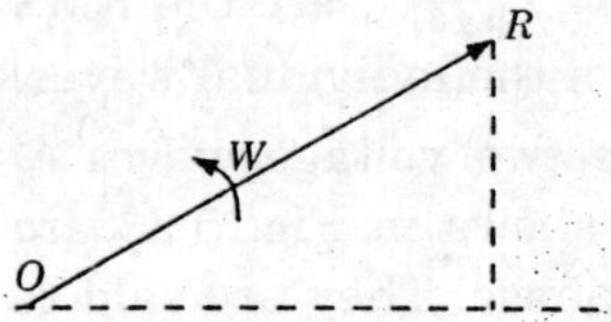

Fig. 5.25

The angle described in t seconds $= \theta = wt$ radians.

The vertical component $PM = OP \sin\theta$

The vertical component therefore varies like a sine curve. The phasor OP (rotating in space at a uniform speed of w radians per second) may therefore be taken to represent an alternating quantity if OP is equal in magnitude to its maximum value (to some scale). The projection PM represents its instantaneous value. It is conventional to use the RMS value instead of the maximum value and hence instead of $OP = E_m$, we may use $OR = \frac{E_m}{\sqrt{2}} = E$. This may be allowed since E and E_m, are related by $\sqrt{2}$. The instantaneous value will then be $\sqrt{2}$ times the vertical component of OR.

$$OR = E \quad \text{(RMS value)}$$

If there are two currents i_1 and i_2 given by

$$i_1 = I_{m1} \sin\theta$$

and

$$i_2 = I_{m2} \sin\theta$$

both in phase with each other, they may be represented by two phasors as shown in Fig. 5.26.

$$OP = \frac{I_{m1}}{\sqrt{2}} = I_1$$

$$OQ = \frac{I_{m2}}{\sqrt{2}} = I_2$$

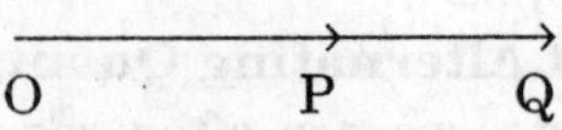

Fig. 5.26

If however, there are two or more quantities which are out-of phase, then they may be represented by two or more phasors which are displaced as in Fig. 5.27.

$$e_1 = E_{m1} \sin \theta \;\Rightarrow OP$$

$$e_2 = E_{m2} \sin (\theta - \pi/3) \;\Rightarrow OQ$$

$$e_3 = E_{m3} \sin (\theta + \pi/3) \;\Rightarrow OR$$

$$OP = \frac{E_{m1}}{\sqrt{2}}, \qquad OQ = \frac{E_{m2}}{\sqrt{2}}, \qquad OR = \frac{E_{m3}}{\sqrt{2}}$$

The angle between OP and OQ is called the phase difference between them.

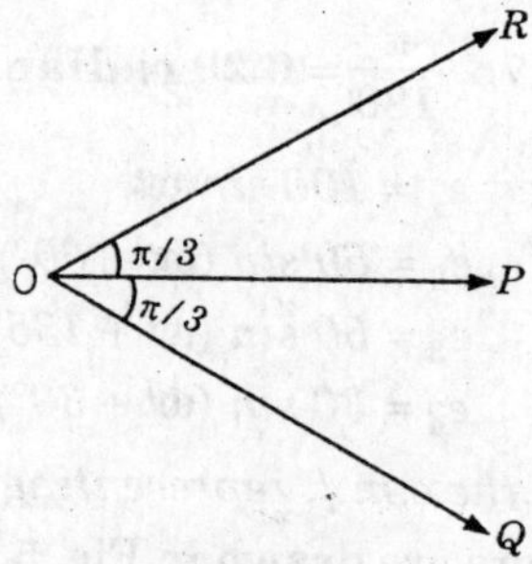

Fig. 5.27

Vector Addition/Subtraction

A number of e.m.f.'s (or a number of currents) acting in a circuit can be added vectorially just as a number of forces acting together at a point. Thus OC is the resultant of e.m.f. phasors OA and OB (Fig. 5.28). Subtraction is also done vectorially.

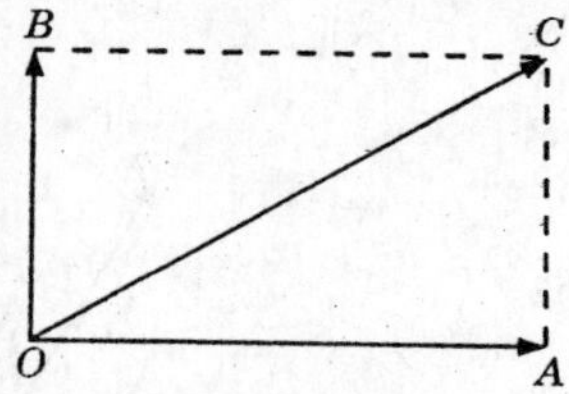

Fig. 5.28

Example 5.19. *Two e.m.f.'s $e_1 = 80 \sin \omega t$ and $e_2 = 100 \sin (\omega t - \pi/6)$ act together in a circuit. Find the resultant voltage.*

Solution. The phasors are shown in Fig. 5.29.

$$OP = \frac{80}{\sqrt{2}} = 56.6 \text{ volts}$$

$$OQ = \frac{100}{\sqrt{2}} = 70.7 \text{ volts}$$

$$OR = 123 \text{ volts.}$$

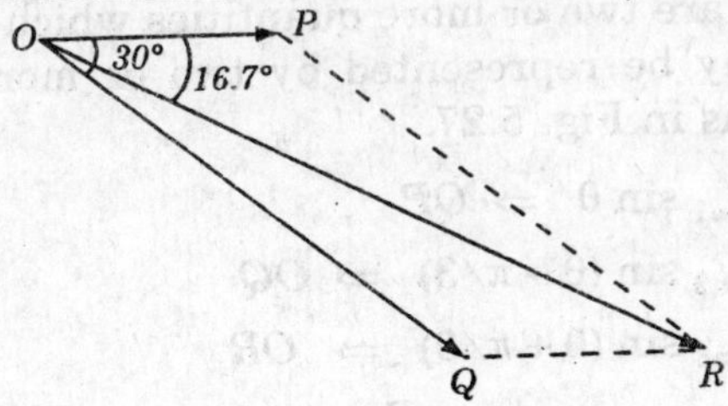

Fig. 5.29

$\therefore$ the resultant voltage

$$= 123\sqrt{2}\sin(\theta - 16.7°)$$
$$= 174\sin(\theta - 0.29)$$
$$\left(16.7° = 16.7 \times \frac{\pi}{180} = \mathbf{0.29\ radian}\right)$$

Example 5.20. *Given* $e_1 = 100 \sin \omega t$

$$e_2 = 60 \sin(\omega t + 60°)$$
$$e_3 = 50 \sin(\omega t + 135°)$$
$$e_4 = 30 \sin(\omega t + 30°)$$

Find the equation of the e.m.f. representing their sum.

Solution. The phasors are drawn in Fig. 5.30. We shall find the total *X*-component and the total *Y*-component.

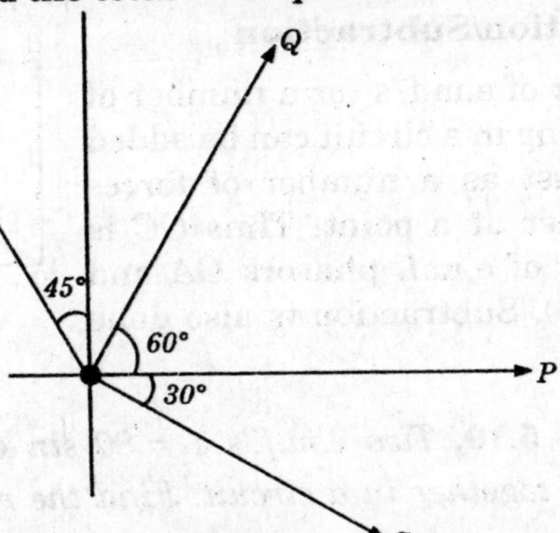

Fig. 5.30

$$OP = \frac{100}{\sqrt{2}} = 70.7 \qquad OQ = \frac{60}{\sqrt{2}} = 42.4$$

$$OR = \frac{50}{\sqrt{2}} = 35.4 \qquad OS = \frac{30}{\sqrt{2}} = 21.2$$

Total *X*-component

$$= |OP| + |OQ| \cos 60° + |OS| \cos 30° - |OR| \cos 45°$$
$$= 70.7 + 21.2 + 18.4 - 25 = 85.3$$

Total Y-component

$$= |OQ| \sin 60° + |OR| \sin 45° - |OS| \sin 30°$$
$$= 36.7 + 25 - 10.6 = 51.1.$$

Resultant voltage

$$= \sqrt{X\text{-comp.})^2 + (Y\text{-comp.})^2}$$
$$= \sqrt{(85.3)^2 + (51.1)^2}$$
$$= 99.4 \text{ (RMS) or } 140.6 \text{ (Max.)}$$
$$\theta = \tan^{-1}\left(\frac{51.1}{85.3}\right) = 31° = 0.54 \text{ radian.}$$

Equation for resultant e.m.f.

$$= \mathbf{140.6 \sin (\omega t - 0.54)}$$

Polar Notation

An alternate method of expressing sinusoidally varying quantities is the polar notation whereby the magnitude and phase angle is expressed as $A \angle\theta$. The magnitude is A and the angle is θ as shown in Fig. 5.31.

$B \angle -\phi$ is the vector OQ.

Angles are measured positive in the anticlockwise direction. The quantities may also be written as $A\varepsilon^{+j\theta}$ or $B\varepsilon^{-j\phi}$ meaning the same as before.

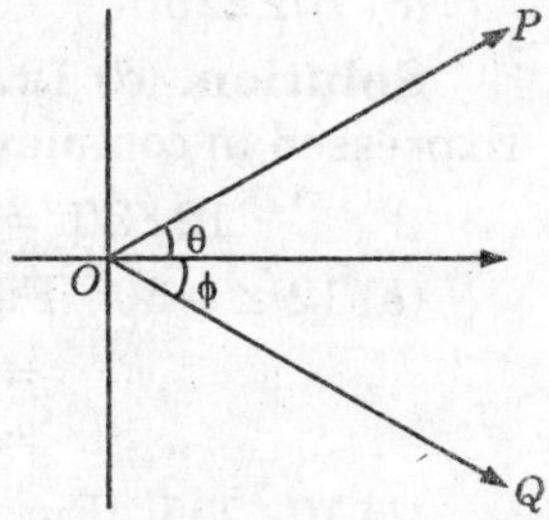

Fig. 5.31

Complex Notation (*j* form)

Consider the phasor $OP = 3\angle 0°$. This is shown as a horizontal line of magnitude 3 units as in Fig. 5.32.

This vector if rotated through 90° (anti-clockwise) becomes $OQ = 3\angle 90°$ and can be represented as $j3$. The symbol j represents an operator whereby the phasor $3\angle 0°$ is rotated through an angle of 90° (anticlockwise). The phasor, OA can, therefore, be considered to have 2 components a and jb and can be written as phasor $OA = a + jb$, where

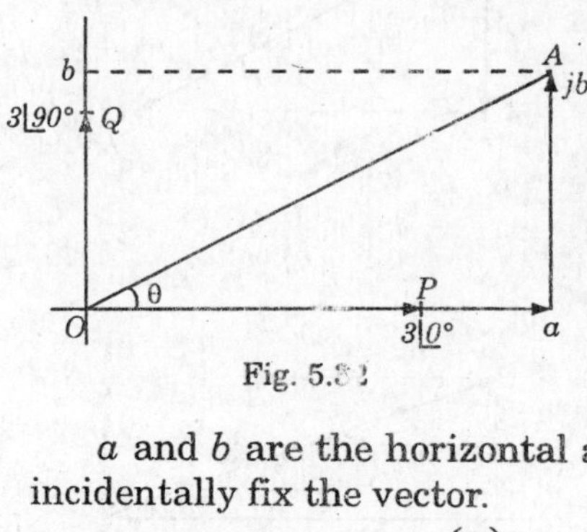

Fig. 5.32

a and b are the horizontal and vertical components of OA and incidentally fix the vector.

$$\theta = \tan^{-1}\left(\frac{b}{a}\right)$$

If as before we rotate the vector OQ once again through 90 (anti-clockwise), we get $j^2\,(OP) = j^2\,(3\angle 0°) = -3$

$$\therefore \qquad j^2 = -1$$

or $\qquad j = \sqrt{-1}$ and is complex.

Two or more electrical quantities can be easily added or subtracted using the j notation. For example, if two currents are $a + jb$ and $c + jd$, then their sum is $(a + c) + j\,(b + d)$ as it involves summing up the horizontal and vertical quantities separately. For multiplication and division of two quantities, however, the polar form is more convenient.

$$A\angle\theta \times B\angle\phi = AB\angle\theta + \phi$$

and $$A\angle\theta / B\angle\phi = A/B\angle\theta - \phi.$$

Example 5.21. *Express the following in j form (complex form)*

(*a*) $12\angle 30°$ (*b*) $12\angle -30°$

(*c*) $10\angle 225°$ (*d*) $8\angle -200°$.

Solution. (*a*) $12\angle 30°$. This quantity is shown in Fig. 5.33 (*a*). Expressed in complex form

$$12\angle 30° = 12\cos 30° + j\,12\sin 30° = 10.4 + j\,6.$$

(*b*) $12\angle -30°$ [Fig. 5.33 (*b*)]

$$= 12\,[\cos(-30°) + j\sin(-30°)]$$
$$= 10.4 - j\,6.$$

(*c*) $10\angle 225°$ [Fig. 5.33 (*c*)]

$$= 10\,(\cos 225° + j\sin 225°)$$
$$= -7.07 - j\,7.07.$$

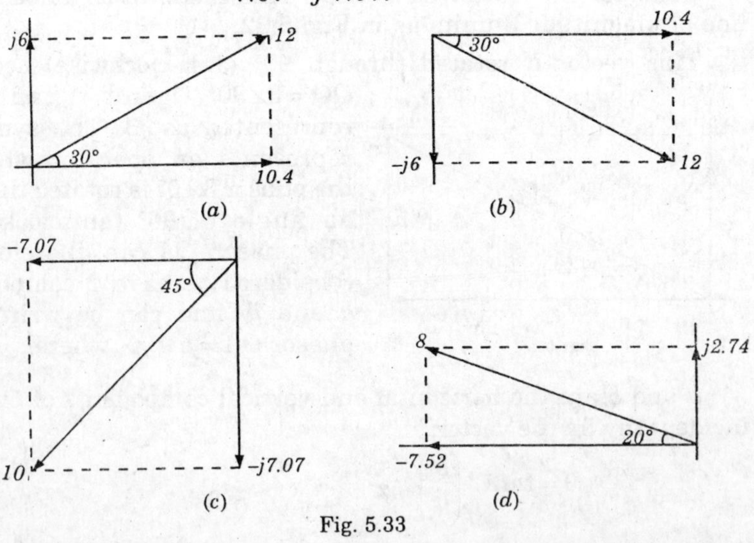

Fig. 5.33

(*d*) $8\angle -200°$ [Fig. 5.33 (*d*)]

$$= 8 [\cos (-200°) + j \sin (-200°)]$$
$$= -7.52 + j\,2.74.$$

Example 5.22. *Express in polar form*

(*a*) $-10 - j\,10$ (*b*) $-10 + j\,7.5$

(*c*) $8 - j6$ (*d*) $25.4 - j\,1.2$.

Solution. The respective vectors are shown in Fig. 5.34.

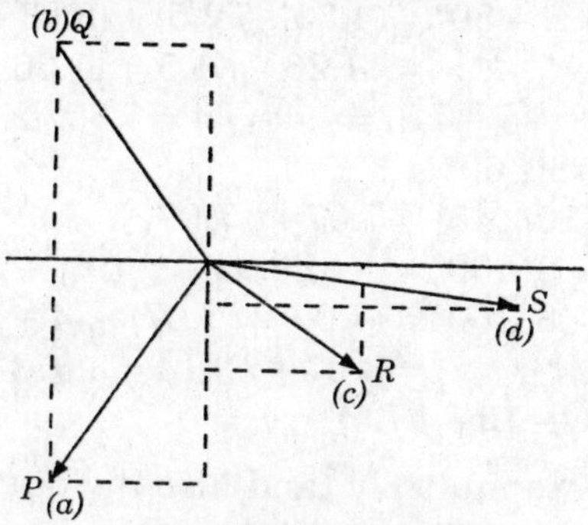

Fig. 5.34

To express (10 – *j*10) in polar form, we need to find the magnitude *OP* and the angle θ

$$OP = \sqrt{10^2 + 10^2} = 14.14$$
$$\theta = 225°$$
$$\therefore \quad 10 - j10 = \mathbf{14.14 \angle 225°.}$$

Note. This may also be written as $14.14\angle -135°$ (angle measured in the clockwise direction).

Similarly, the other vectors evaluated in polar form are

$$|-10 + j\,7.5| = \sqrt{(10)^2 + (7.5)^2} = 12.5$$
$$\text{Angle} = \theta = 143.1°$$
$$\therefore \quad -10 + j7.5 = 12.5 \angle 143.1°$$
$$8 - j6 = \sqrt{8^2 + 6^2} \angle -36.9° = 10 \angle -36.9°$$
$$25.4 - j\,1.2 = \sqrt{(25.4)^2 + (1.2)^2} \angle \tan^{-1}\left(\frac{-1.2}{25.4}\right)$$
$$= \mathbf{25.43 \angle -2.7°.}$$

Example 5.23. *Perform the following operations. The final result may be given in polar form*

(*a*) $5 \angle 30° + 8 \angle -30°$

(*b*) $(3 + j4) + (-7 - j8)$

(*c*) $10\ \angle 45° - 8\ \angle 60°$

(*d*) $(8 + j6) \times (-10 - j7.5)$

(*e*) $10\ \angle 30°/5\ \angle -60°$

(*f*) $(4 - j\,3)/(3 + j4)$.

Solution. (*a*) $5\ \angle 30° + 8\ \angle -30°$. For addition and subtraction, the j form is simpler. Hence

$$5\ \angle 30 = 5\ (\cos 30 + j \sin 30°) = 4.33 + j\,2.5$$
$$8\ \angle -30° = 8\ [\cos(-30) + j \sin(-30)] = 6.93 - j4$$
$$\therefore\ 5\ \angle 30° + 8\ \angle -30° = (4.33 + j\,2.5) + (6.93 - j\,4)$$
$$= 11.26 - j\,1.5 = 11.36\ \angle -7.6°$$

(*b*) $(3 + j\,4) + (-7 - j\,8) = -4 - j\,4 = 5.657\ \angle 225°$.

(*c*) $10\ \angle 45° - 8\ \angle 60°$

$$10\ \angle 45° = 7.07 + j\,7.07$$
$$8\ \angle 60° = 4 + j\,6.93$$
$$10\ \angle 45° - 8\ \angle 60° = (7.07 + j\,7.07) - (4 + j\,6.93)$$
$$= 3.07 + j\,0.14 = 3.073\ \angle 2.6°$$

(*d*) $(8 + j\,6) \times (-10 - j\,7.5)$

It is possible to multiply (and also divide) two quantities in j form, but it is easier to do so in the polar form

$$(8 + j6) = \sqrt{(8^2 + 6^2}\ \angle \tan^{-1}\left(\tfrac{6}{8}\right) = 10\ \angle 36.9°$$
$$(-10 - j\,7.5) = \sqrt{(10)^2 + (7.5)^2}\ \angle 216.9°$$
$$= 12.5\ \angle +216.9°$$
$$(8 + j\,6)\,(-10 - j\,7.5) = 10\ \angle 36.9° \times 12.5\ \angle 216.9°$$
$$= 125\ \angle 36.9° + 216.9° = 125\ \angle 253.8°$$

(*e*)
$$\frac{10\ \angle 30°}{5\ \angle -60°} = 2\ \angle 30° - (-60°) = 2\ \angle 90° = j\,2$$

(*f*)
$$\frac{(4 - j\,3)}{(3 + j\,4)} = \frac{4\ \angle -36.9°}{5\ \angle 53.1°}$$
$$= 1\ \angle -36.9° - 53.1°$$
$$= 1\ \angle -90° = \mathbf{-j\,1}.$$

Example 5.24. *A sinusoidal alternating current of frequency 50 Hz has an RMS value of 20 A. What is the equation for its instantaneous value ? Find this value (a) 0.0025 sec (b) 0.0125 sec after passing through a positive maximum value.*

At what time measured from a positive maximum value will the instantaneous current be 14.14 amps ?

Solution. The wave is shown in Fig. 5.35.

The instantaneous current is given by the equation

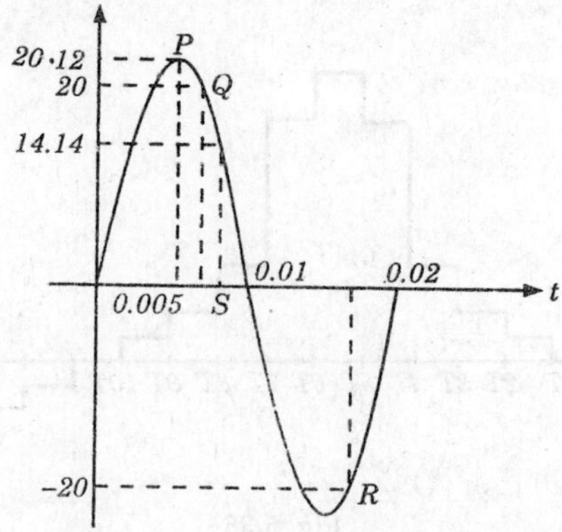

Fig. 5.35

$$i = I\sqrt{2}\sin(\omega t) = 20\sqrt{2}\sin 2\pi\, ft$$
$$= 28.28 \sin 314.16\, t \text{ amperes.}$$

The wave passes through its positive maximum at

$$t = 0.005 \text{ sec } (P)$$

(*a*) At $= 0.0025$ sec,

after passing through the positive maximum

$$t = 0.005 + 0.0025 = 0.0075 \text{ sec (point } Q)$$
$$i = 20\sqrt{2}\sin 2\pi \times 50 \times 0.0075 = 20 \text{ amps.}$$

(*b*) At *R*, 0.0125 sec from *P*,

$$t = 0.005 + 0.0125 = \mathbf{0.0175\ sec.}$$
$$i = 20\sqrt{2}\sin 100\,\pi \times 0.0175 = \mathbf{-20\ amps.}$$

Let the current be 14.14 *A* at *S* (time *t* sec from *P*)

Then $14.15 = 20\sqrt{2}\sin 100\pi\,(0.005 + t)$

i.e. $\sin(0.005 + t)\,100 = 0.5$

or $t = \mathbf{0.0033\ sec.}$

Example 5.25. *Calculate the RMS value, the form and peak factors of a periodic voltage having the following values at equal time intervals. 0, 5, 10, 20, 50, 60, 20, 10, 5, 0, – 5, – 10, – 20, etc. The values change from one to another suddenly. What would be the RMS value of a sine wave having the same peak value ?*

Solution. The wave is shown in Fig. 5.36.

Period of the wave = 20 *T*

$$\text{Average value} = \frac{\text{Area under the wave for half period}}{10\,T}$$

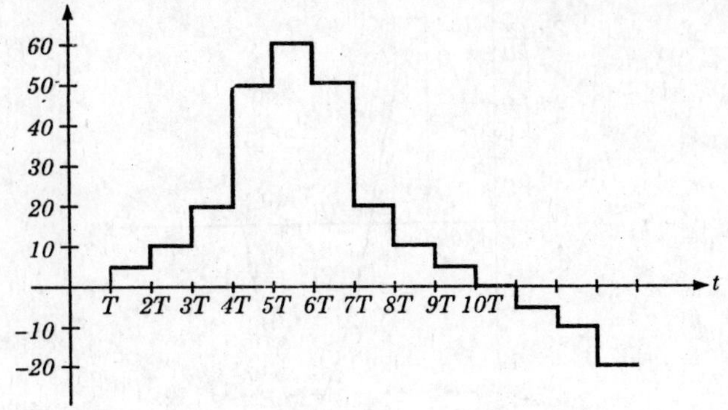

Fig. 5.36

Average value

$$= \frac{0 + 5T + 10T + 20T + 50T + 60T + 50T + 20T + 10T + 5T}{10\ T}$$

$$= \frac{230\ T}{10\ T} = \mathbf{23\ Volts.}$$

For RMS value, we need the area under the squared curve

$$= 2\ [0 + 25T + 100T + 400T + 2500T + 3600T + 2500T + 400T + 100T + 25T]$$

$$= 2 \times 9650\ T$$

$$\text{RMS value} = \frac{2 \times 9650\ T}{20\ T}$$

$$= \mathbf{31.06\ Volts.}$$

$$\text{Form factor} = \frac{\text{RMS value}}{\text{Av. value}} = \frac{31.06}{23} = \mathbf{1.35}$$

$$\text{Peak factor} = \frac{\text{Peak value}}{\text{RMS value}} = \frac{60}{31.06} = \mathbf{1.93.}$$

EXERCISES

5.1. A 50 Hz sinusoidal current has a peak value of 100 A. Write the equation for the current wave and find the current at time (*a*) $t = 0.0025$. (*b*) $t = 0.005$ and (*c*) 0.01 sec. after $i = 0$ and is increasing. Find also the rate of change of current in amperes per second at these instants.

5.2. The current through a 10 ohm resistor is given by $i = 141.4 \sin 377\ t$. Find (*a*) the frequency, (*b*) rms value of the current, (*c*) the equation for the voltage across the resistor. **[Ans.** 60 c/s, 100 A, 1414 sin 377 *t*]

5.3. Find the relative heating effects of two current waves of the same maximum value, one sinusoidal and the other rectangular. **[Ans.** 1 : 2]

5.4. Find the average and effective values of the following wave form (Fig. 5.37). Find also the form factor and peak factor.

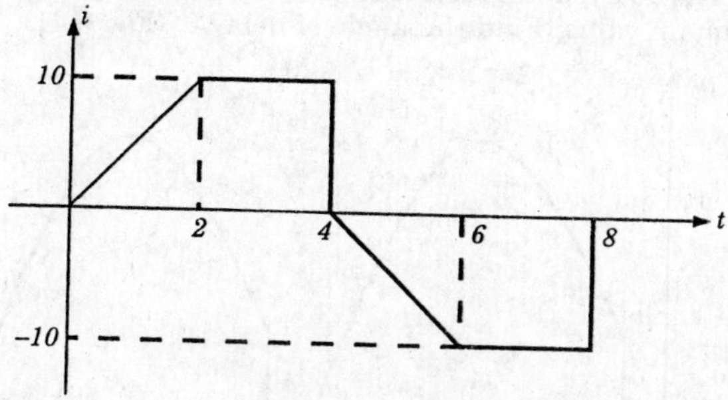

Fig. 5.37

[**Ans.** 7.5 A, 8.165 A, 1.09, 1.225]

5.5. Obtain the average and effective values of the voltage wave of Fig. 5.38.

[**Ans.** 25 V, 28.87 V]

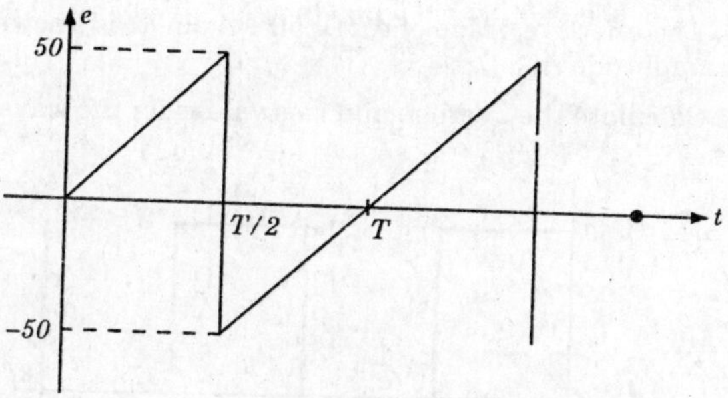

Fig. 5.38

5.6. Determine the average and rms values of the wave form of Fig. 5.39, where in the first interval $e = E_m \varepsilon^{-200t}$

[**Ans.** 0.1 E_m, 0.224 E_m]

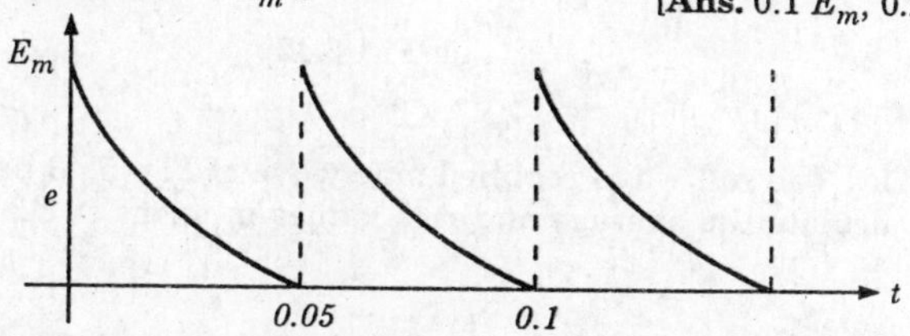

Fig. 5.39

5.7. Find the average and effective values of the wave of Fig. 5.40.

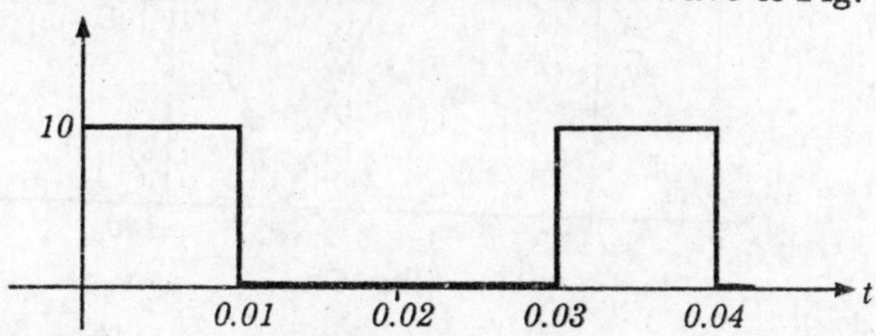

Fig. 5.40

[**Ans.** 3.33, 5.77]

5.8. The delayed full rectified sine wave has an average value of 0.6 times the maximum value. Find the angle of delay θ. (Fig. 5.41) [**Ans.** θ = 27.75°]

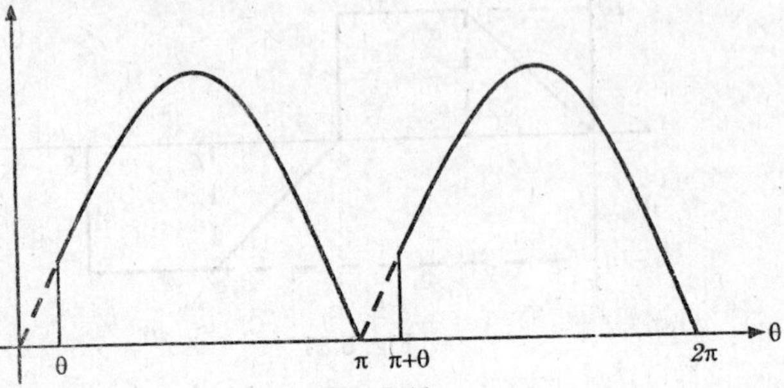

Fig. 5.41

5.9 Determine the effective value of the voltage function given by $e(t) = 100 + 100 \sin 3\omega t + 25 \sin 5\omega t$. [**Ans.** 123.74 Volts]

5.10. The effective value of $e(t) = 50 + A \sin \omega t$ is known to be 65.6 Volts. Find the amplitude A. [**Ans.** 60]

5.11. Calculate the average and rms values for the wave form of Fig. 5.42.

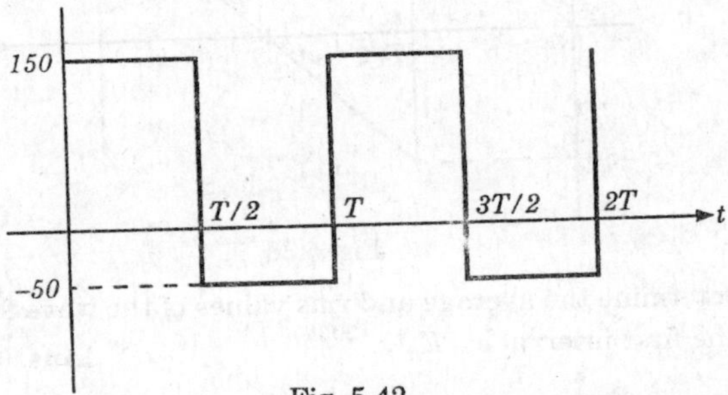

Fig. 5.42

[**Ans.** 50, 111.8]

5.12. The full wave rectified sine wave of Fig. 5.43 has a delay angle of 60°. Calculate the average and rms values in terms of E_m.

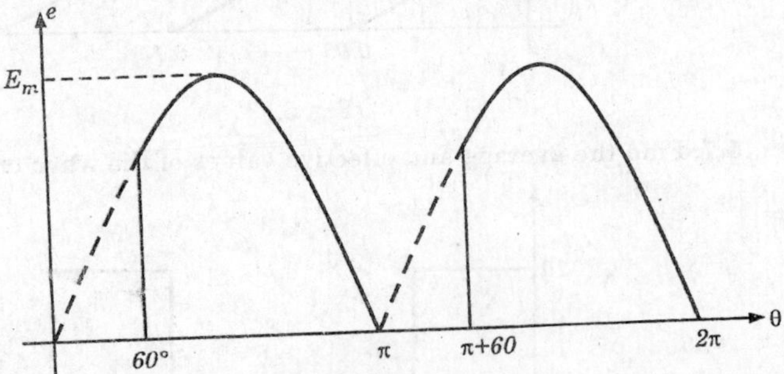

Fig. 5.43

[**Ans.** 0.478 E_m ; 0.633 E_m]

5.13. Two currents, $i_1 = 50 \sin \omega t$ and $i_2 = 100 \sin (\omega t + 45°)$ are super imposed in a conductor. Find the expression for the total current.

[**Ans.** 140 sin $(\omega t + 30.4°)$]

5.14. Two voltages are given by

$\varepsilon_1 = 100 \sin (\omega t + \pi/6)$

and $e_2 = 50 \sin (\omega t - \pi/3)$

Draw the two vectors and find their sum. [**Ans.** 111.8 $\angle 3.4°$]

5.15. Express in polar form

(*a*) $15\varepsilon^{j\pi/4}$ (*b*) $5\varepsilon^{-j2\pi/3}$ (*c*) $-12 + j\,16$

(*d*) $700 + j\,200$ (*e*) $-69.4 - j\,40$ (*f*) $0.048 - j\,0.153°$

[**Ans.** 15 $\angle 45°$, 5 $\angle -120°$, 20 $\angle 126.9°$ 726 $\angle 16°$, 80 $\angle 210°$, 0.1604 $\angle -72.6°$]

5.16. Express in rectangular (Complex or *j*) form :

(*a*) 12 $\angle 30°$ (*b*) 53°160° (*c*) 20 $\angle -45°$

(*d*) 0.02 $\angle 210°$ (*e*) 0.003 $\angle 80°$ (*f*) 8 $\angle 90°$

[**Ans.** $10.4 + j\,6$; $-49.8 + j\,18.13$; $14.14 - j\,14.14$; $-0.0173 - j\,0.01$; $0.00052 + j\,0.00295$; $0 + j\,8$]

5.17. Convert from polar to complex form.

(*a*) 400 $\angle 181°$ (*b*) 100 $\angle -93°$ (*c*) 45 $\angle -179°$

(*d*) 0.05 $\angle -5°$ (*e*) 40 $\angle 10°$ (*f*) 80 $\angle 98°$

[**Ans.** $-399.94 - j\,6.98$; $-5.23 - j\,99.86$; $-44.99 - j\,0.785$; $0.0498 - j\,0.00436$; $39.39 + j\,6.95$; $-11.13 + j\,79.22$]

5.18. Convert from *j* to polar form.

(*a*) $20 + j\,700$ (*b*) $10 + j\,0.55$ (*c*) $-200 - j\,3.5$

(*d*) $0.02 - j\,0.001$ (*e*) $-10 - j\,240$ (*f*) $0.75 - j\,0.075$

[**Ans.** 700.3 $\angle 88.4°$; 10.02 $\angle 3.15°$; 20.003 $\angle 181°$ 0.020025 $\angle -2.86°$; 240.2 $\angle 267.6°$; 0.754 $\angle -5.7°$]

5.19. Perform the following operations.

(*a*) $(3 - j\,2)(1 - j\,4)$ (*b*) $(10 \angle 5.31°) + (4 + j\,2)$

(*c*) $(-4 - j\,6) + (2 + j\,4)$ (*d*) $(5 + j\,5)/(1 - j\,1)$

(*e*) $(8 + j\,12)/j\,2$ (*f*) $(3 \angle 20°)(8 \angle -65°)$.

[**Ans.** (*a*) $-5 - j\,10$ (*b*) $10 + j\,10$ (*c*) $-2 - j\,2$ (*d*) $j\,5$ (*e*) $6 - j\,4$ (*f*) 24 $\angle -45°$]

SIX

A.C. CIRCUITS

Resistance

The potential difference, e across the terminals of a resistor is directly proportional to the current i flowing in it. This is ohm's law. The relation may be written as before

$$e = Ri$$

where e and i now vary with time. When a sinusoidal current $i = I_m \sin \omega t$ is applied to a resistor, the potential across it will be

$$e = I_m R \sin \omega t = E_m \sin \omega t.$$

The r.m.s. value $E = IR$. The wave forms of the current and voltage are shown in Fig. 6.1 (b) and the phasors E and I in Fig. 6.1 (c). The voltage and current waves in resistor are clearly in phase with each other. We shall now obtain the power dissipated in R.

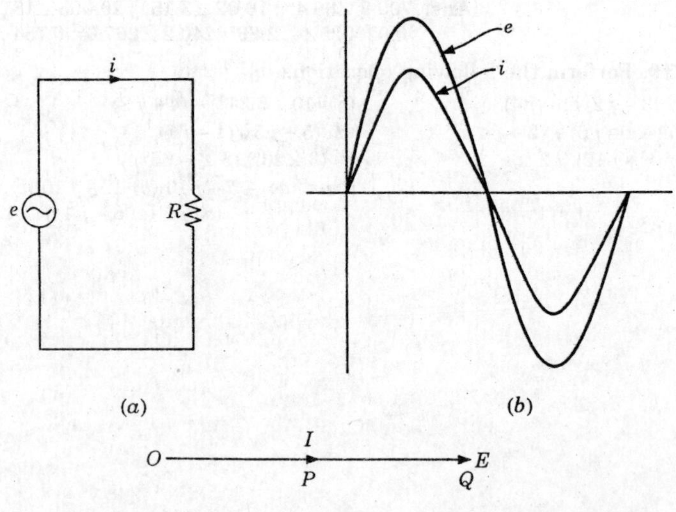

Fig. 6.1

The instantaneous power $p = ei$

$$= E_m \sin \omega t \, I_m \sin \omega t$$

$$= E_m I_m \sin^2 \omega t.$$

A wattmeter measures the average power given by

$$P = \frac{1}{2\pi} \int_0^{2\pi} E_m I_m \sin^2 \theta \, d\theta$$

$$= \frac{E_m I_m}{2\pi} \int_0^{2\pi} \left(\frac{1 - \cos 2\theta}{2} \right) d\theta$$

$$= \frac{E_m \cdot I_m}{4\pi} \left[\theta - \frac{\sin 2\theta}{2} \right]_0^{2\pi}$$

$$= \frac{E_m \cdot I_m}{2} = \mathbf{E \cdot I}.$$

The average power in a resistor is the product of the RMS values of the voltage and current.

Power can also be written as

$$P = EI = I^2R = \mathbf{E^2/R \text{ watts.}}$$

Example 6.1. *A voltage e = 200 sin ωt is applied to a 25 ohm resistor. Find the current i, the instantaneous power p and the average power P.*

Solution. $e = 200 \sin \omega t$

$$i = \frac{e}{R} = \frac{200}{25} \sin \omega t = 8 \sin \omega t$$

$$p = e \cdot i = (200 \sin \omega t)(8 \sin \omega t)$$

$$= 1600 \sin^2 \omega t$$

$$P = \frac{1}{2\pi} \int_0^{2\pi} 1600 \sin^2 \theta \, d\theta$$

$$= \mathbf{E.I}$$

$$= \frac{200}{\sqrt{2}} \cdot \frac{8}{\sqrt{2}} = \mathbf{800 \text{ watts.}}$$

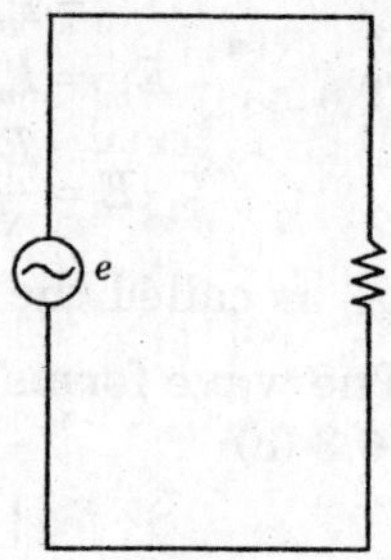

Fig. 6.2

Inductance

If the current flowing in a circuit changes with time, the magnetic flux produced by the current also changes. This change in flux linkages causes an e.m.f. to be induced in the circuit. The induced e.m.f. is equal to the rate of change of flux linkages.

i.e. $$e = -\frac{d\psi}{dt}$$

$d\psi$ is the change in flux linkages in dt time. The flux linkages are produced by the current

$$\therefore \qquad e \propto -\frac{di}{dt}$$

$$\text{or} \qquad e = -L\frac{di}{dt} \text{ and } i = \frac{-1}{L}\int e\,dt$$

where L is the constant of proportionality called self-inductance or simply inductance of the circuit. The applied voltage will be equal and oppocite to indual emf.

Therefore, $L = \frac{d\psi}{di}$ which is the change of flux linkage per ampere change of current.

For a linear magnetic circuit (permeability constant)

$$I = \frac{\psi}{I} \qquad \text{(flux linkages per ampere).}$$

The unit of inductance is Henry. Inductance is 1 Henry if the e.m.f. induced is one volt when the current changes at the rate of 1 Ampere per second. When a sinusoidal current $i = I_m \sin \omega t$ is applied to an inductance, the applied voltage

$$v = L\frac{di}{dt} = L\,\omega\,I_m \cos \omega t$$

$$= I_m\,\omega L \cos \omega t = E_m \sin(\omega t + \pi/2)$$

$$\text{where} \qquad E_m = I_m X_L \text{ and } X_L = \omega L = 2\pi fL$$

$$E = \frac{E_m}{\sqrt{2}} = \frac{I_m}{\sqrt{2}} X_L = IX_L$$

(X_L is called the inductive reactance and its unit is the ohm.)

The wave forms are shown in Fig. 6.3 (b) and the phasors in Fig. 6.3 (c).

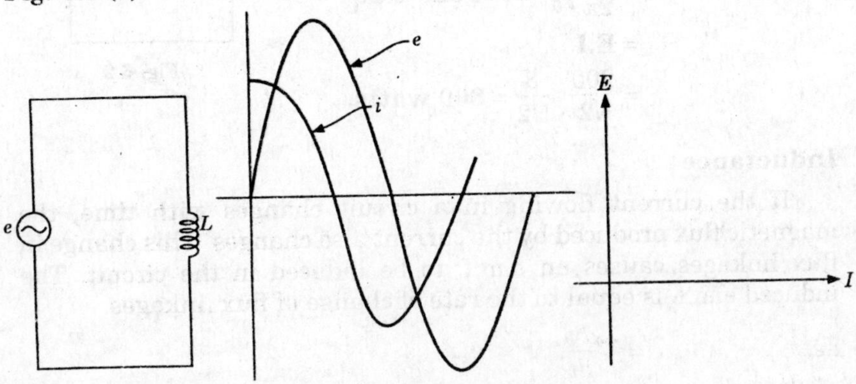

(a) (b) (c)

Fig. 6.3

Clearly, the voltage across an inductor leads the current through it by 90° ($\pi/2$ radians)

Instantaneous power,

$$p = e \cdot i = E_m \sin(\omega t + \pi/2)\, I_m \sin \omega t$$
$$= E_m I_m \sin \omega t \cdot \cos \omega t$$
$$= \frac{E_m I_m}{2} \sin 2\omega t$$

Average power, $P = \dfrac{1}{2\pi}\displaystyle\int_0^{2\pi} E_m I_m \sin\theta \cos\theta \, d\theta$

$$= \frac{1}{2\pi}\int_0^{2\pi} \frac{E_m I_m}{2} \sin 2\theta \, d\theta = 0$$

Example 6.2. *A pure inductance L = 0.1 H has an applied voltage of e = 200 sin 314t. Find the current, the instantaneous and average power. Find also the inductive reactance and the RMS current.*

Solution. $e = L\dfrac{di}{dt}$

or $\quad i = \dfrac{1}{L}\displaystyle\int e dt$

$$= \frac{1}{0.1}\int 200 \sin 314\, t\, dt$$
$$= \frac{-2000}{314} \cos 314t$$
$$= \mathbf{-6.37 \cos 314t}$$

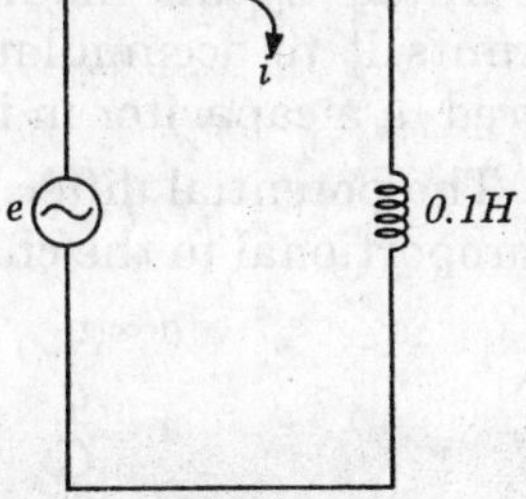

Fig. 6.4

$$p = (200 \sin 314t)(-6.37 \cos 314t)$$
$$= -1274 \sin 314t \times \cos 314t$$
$$= -637 \sin 618t \qquad (\text{as } \sin x \cos x = \tfrac{1}{2}\sin 2x)$$

$$P = 0$$
$$X_L = \omega L = 314 \times 0.1 = 31.4\ \Omega$$

R.M.S. current $I = \dfrac{E}{X_L} = \dfrac{200/\sqrt{2}}{31.4} = \mathbf{4.5\ Amps.}$

Energy Stored in an Inductive Circuit

The power in a pure inductive circuit varies at double the frequency. During the positive half of the double-frequency power wave, energy is delivered by the source to the inductor and stored in the magnetic field ; then during the negative half this stored energy is returned to the source.

$$\text{Energy} = p \cdot dt$$

Energy in half a cycle $= \int_0^{T/4} p\,dt$, where T is the period.

We use $T/4$ because power is a double frequency wave.

Energy, $$W = \int_{\omega t = 0}^{\omega t = T/4} \frac{E_m I_m}{2} \sin 2\omega t \, dt$$

$$W = \frac{E_m I_m}{2} \left[\frac{-\cos 2\omega t}{2\omega} \right]_0^{\pi/2}$$

$$= \frac{I_m X_L \cdot I_m}{2\omega} = \frac{\omega L \cdot I_m^2}{2\omega}$$

$$= \frac{1}{2} L I_m^2 \text{ Joules.}$$

or $$= \mathbf{LI^2}.$$

Capacitive Circuits

A capacitor is formed by two metallic conductors or plates separated by an insulating medium, and the property which permits it to accumulate charge is called capacitance. Energy is stored in a capacitor in its electric field.

The potential difference e between the terminals of a capacitor is proportional to the charge q on it

i.e. $$e \propto q$$

or $$e = \frac{q}{C}$$

The constant C is called the capacitance. q is in coulombs, e in volts and C in coulombs/volt or farad. The capacitance is 1 farad if it requires 1 coulomb of charge per volt of p.d. between the plates.

As $$i = \frac{dq}{dt} = C\frac{de}{dt}$$

$$e = \frac{1}{C}\int i\,dt.$$

Generally capacitance values are expressed in sub-multiples of the farad as

$$1\ \mu f = 1 \text{ micro farad} = 10^{-6} f$$

$$1\ \mu\mu f = 1 \text{ pico farad} = 10^{-12} f$$

consider a voltage $e = E_m \sin \omega t$ applied to capacitor of C farads.

$$i = C\frac{de}{dt} = C\frac{d}{dt}[E_m \sin \omega t]$$

$$= E_m \omega C \cos \omega t = I_m \sin(\omega t + \pi/2)$$

where $\quad I_m = E_m\, \omega C$

or $\quad E_m = \dfrac{I_m}{\omega C} = I_m X_C$

where $\quad X_C$ = capacitive reactance = $\dfrac{1}{\omega C}$ ohms

RMS value, $E = IX_C$

The wave forms and phasors are shown in Fig. 6.5 (*b*) and (*c*).

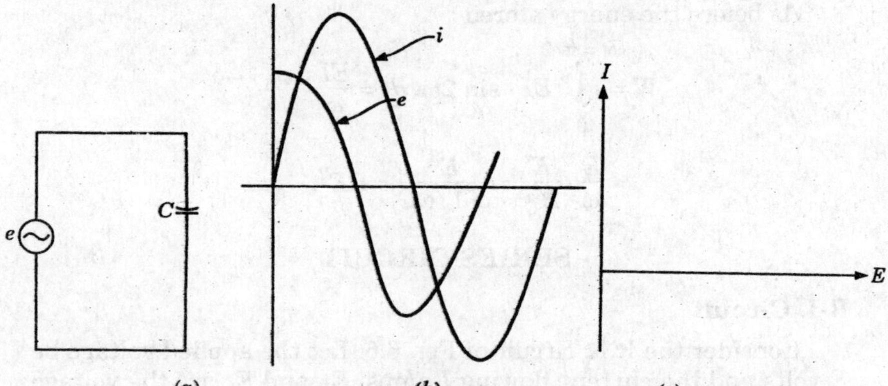

Fig. 6.5

It is obvious that the current in the capacitor leads the voltage by 90° or alternately the voltage lags behind the current.

Power $\quad p = E_m I_m \sin \omega t \cdot \sin (\omega t + \pi/2)$

$$= \frac{E_m I_m}{2} \sin 2\omega t = EI \sin 2\omega t.$$

As in an inductance the average power is zero. The instantaneous power varies at twice the frequency.

Example 6.3. *A 127 μf capacitor has a 125 volts 50 Hz supply. Calculate (a) the capacitive reactance, (b) the equation for the current, (c) the RMS current, (d) the instantaneous power (e) the average power, (f) the maximum power delivered to the capacitor.*

Solution.

(*a*)
$$X_C = \frac{1}{\omega C} = \frac{1}{2\pi f C} = \frac{1}{2\pi \times 50 \times 127 \times 10^{-6}}$$

$$= \frac{10^6}{2\pi \times 50 \times 127} = 25 \text{ ohms.}$$

(*b*) current equation

$$i = 5\sqrt{2} \sin (\omega t + \pi/2)$$
$$= 5\sqrt{2} \sin (314t + \pi/2)$$

(*c*) RMS current $= I = \frac{E}{X_C} = \frac{125}{25} = 5$ A

(*d*) $p = E\,I \sin 2\omega t = 125 \times 5 \sin 628t$

$= 625 \sin 528t$

(*e*) Average power $P = 0$

(*f*) Maximum power = **625 VA.**

Energy Stored in a Capacitive Circuit

As before the energy stored

$$W = \int_0^{\omega t = \pi/2} EI \cdot \sin 2\omega t \, dt = \frac{EI}{\omega}$$

$$= \frac{E}{\omega} \cdot \frac{E}{X_C} = \frac{E^2}{\omega \cdot 1/\omega C} = CE^2.$$

SERIES CIRCUIT

R-L Circuit

Consider the R.L. circuit of Fig. 6.6. Let the applied voltage be E volts and the current flowing I amps. E_R and E_L are the voltage drops across the individual elements.

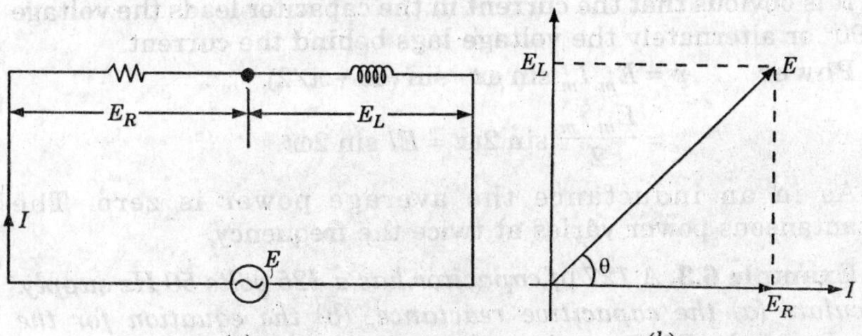

Fig. 6.6

The following are obvious

$$E_R = IR \quad \text{(in phase with } I\text{)}$$

$$E_L = IX_L \quad \text{(leads by } 90°\text{)}$$

We may, therefore, write

$$E = E_R + j\,E_L = IR + j\,IX_L$$

$$= I\,(R + j\,X_L) = IZ.$$

where Z is called the impedance of the RL circuit.

$Z = R + jX_L$ and has a magnitude and phase angle.

$$|Z| = \sqrt{R^2 + X_L^2}$$

$$\angle Z = \theta = \tan^{-1}\left(\frac{X_L}{R}\right)$$

$$Z = |Z| \angle\theta.$$

θ is the angle by which the total voltage E is out of phase from the current I. The phasors are given in Fig. 6.6 (*b*).

The equations for the current and voltage would be

$$i = I_m \sin \omega t \qquad \text{(reference phase or horizontal)}$$

$$e = E_m \sin (\omega t + \theta)$$

$$E_m = I_m |Z|$$

$$p = e \cdot i = E_m I_m \sin \omega t \cdot \sin (\omega t + \theta)$$

$$P = \frac{1}{2\pi}\int_0^{2\pi} E_m I_m \sin \omega t \cdot \sin (\omega t + \theta)\, d(\omega t)$$

$$= \frac{E_m I_m}{2} \cos\theta = EI \cos\theta.$$

$\cos\theta$ is called the power factor of the circuit. It is the factor by which EI, the apparent power must be multiplied to get the real power.

Apparent power = EI

True power = $EI \cos\theta$

$$\text{Power factor} = \frac{\text{True power}}{\text{Apparent power}}$$

$$= \cos\theta = \frac{R}{|Z|}$$

The power factor of the circuit varies between 0 and 1 for different R and L. When $L = 0$, the circuit is purely resistive and the voltage is in phase with the current, $\theta = 0°$ and $\cos\theta = 1$. When $R = 0$, the circuit is purely inductive, and the voltage leads the current by 90° ; $\theta = 90°$ and $\cos\theta = 0$. Then circuit power under this condition is zero.

Example 6.4. *A series RL circuit with R = 25 ohms, and L = 0.02 henry is connected to a 250 volt, 50 Hz source. Calculate (a) the impedance, (b) current, (c) power, (d) power factor.*

Solution. $X_L = 2\pi f L = 2\pi \times 50 \times 0.02 = 6.28\ \Omega$

(*a*) $Z = \sqrt{R^2 + X_L^2} = 25.78$ ohms

(*b*) Current $I = \dfrac{250}{25.78} = 9.7$ Amps.

(*c*) Power factor $= \dfrac{R}{Z} = \dfrac{25}{25.78} = 0.97$

(*d*) Power $= E \cdot I \cdot \cos\theta$

$= (250 \times 9.7)\,(0.97) = \mathbf{2352.0\ watts.}$

Also as power is spent only in the resistor (not in the inductor)

$$\text{Power} = I^2R = (9.7)^2 \times 25 = \mathbf{2352\ watts.}$$

Example 6.5. *A load of 20 kW operates at 0.8 lag power factor lag when connected to a 400 volts 50 Hz cycle source. Find (a) the current in the load, (b) the power factor angle, (c) the impedance, (d) the resistance and (e) the reactance of the load. Write the equations for the voltage and current.*

Solution. $P = 20{,}000 \text{ watts} = EI\cos\theta$

(*a*) $I = \dfrac{P}{E\cos\theta} = \dfrac{20{,}000}{400 \times 0.8} = 62.5$ Amps.

(*b*) Power factor angle $= \theta = \cos^{-1} 0.8 = 36.8°$

(*c*) $Z = \dfrac{E}{I} = \dfrac{400}{62.5} = 6.4$ ohms

(*d*) $R = Z\cos\theta = 6.4 \times 0.8 = 5.12$ ohms

(*e*) $X_L = Z\sin\theta = 6.4 \times 0.6 = 3.84$ ohms

$= \sqrt{Z^2 - R^2} = \sqrt{(6.4)^2 - (5.12)^2} = \mathbf{3.84\ ohms.}$

Equations $e = 400\sqrt{2}\sin(314t)$

$i = 62.5\sqrt{2}\sin(314t - 36.8°)$

R.C. Circuit

Consider the *RC* series circuit of Fig. 6.7 (*a*). The equations are given below and phasor diagram shown in Fig. 6.7 (*b*).

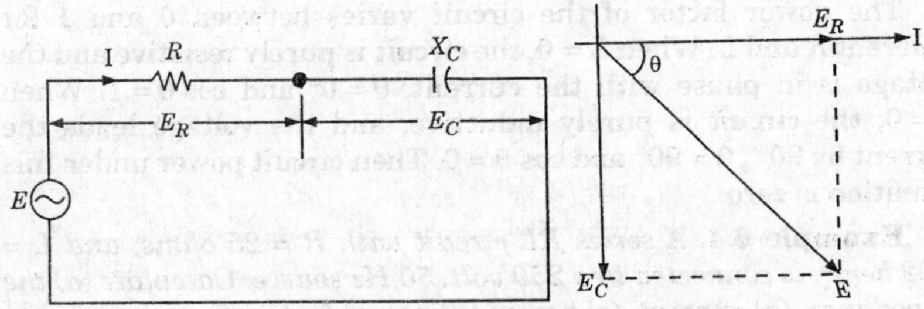

Fig. 6.7

$$E_R = IR, \quad E_C = IX_C$$

where $X_C = \dfrac{1}{\omega_C}$

E_R and E_C are not in the phase as they are drops in the resistance and capacitance.

$$E = IR - j\,IX_C = I\,(R - jX_C) = IZ$$

$$|\,Z\,| = \sqrt{R^2 + X_C{}^2}$$

$$\theta = \tan^{-1}\left(\frac{E_C}{E_R}\right) = \tan^{-1}\left(\frac{X_C}{R}\right).$$

The total voltage E lags behind the current I by θ.

The impedance is written as

$$Z = |\,Z\,| \angle -\theta$$

Again the average power can be proved to be

$P = EI \cos\theta$ and $\cos\theta$ is called the power factor of the circuit

$$\cos\theta = \frac{R}{|\,Z\,|}$$

Example 6.6. *A 200 volt 50 Hz source supplies a series RC circuit, R = 30 ohms and C = 79 μf. Find (a) the impedance, (b) the current, (c) Power factor and (d) Power*

Solution.

(*a*) $X_C = \dfrac{1}{2\pi fC} = \dfrac{10^6}{100\pi \times 79.5} = 40$ ohms

$$Z = \sqrt{R^2 + X_C{}^2} = \sqrt{(30)^2 + (40)^2} = 50 \text{ ohms}.$$

(*b*) $I = \dfrac{E}{Z} = \dfrac{200}{50} = 4$ Amp.

(*c*) Power factor $= \dfrac{R}{Z} = \dfrac{30}{50} = 0.6$ (leading capacitive current)

(*d*) Power $= EI\cos\theta = 200 \times 4 \times 0.6 =$ **480 watts.**

Example 6.7. *A series RC load takes a power of 6400 watts when connected to a 250 volts 25 Hz mains. The voltage drop across the resistor is 160 volts ; calculate (a) the current, (b) the power factor, (c) the impedance, (d) the resistance and (e) the capacitance. Write the equations for the voltage and current.*

Solution.

(*a*) Volt drop across resistor $= E_R = 160 = IR$

$$\text{Power} = I^2R = 6400 \text{ watts}$$

$$\therefore \quad I = \frac{P}{E_R} = \frac{I^2R}{IR} = \frac{6400}{160} = 40 \text{ A}$$

(*b*) Power factor $= \dfrac{P}{EI} = \dfrac{6400}{250 \times 40} = 0.64$

Power factor angle

$$= \cos^{-1}(0.64) = 50°$$

(c) $$Z = \frac{E}{I} = \frac{250}{40} = 6.25 \text{ ohms}$$

(d) $$R = Z\cos\theta = 6.25 \times 0.64 = 4 \text{ ohms}$$

(e) $$X_C = \sqrt{Z^2 - R^2} = 4.8 \text{ ohms} = \frac{1}{2\pi fC}$$

$$C = \frac{1}{2\pi f \times 4.8}$$

$$= \frac{1}{2\pi \times 25 \times 4.8} = 1.326 \times 10^{-3} \text{ farads}$$

$$= \mathbf{1326\ \mu f.}$$

Equations $e = 250\sqrt{2} \sin 2\pi ft = 354 \cdot \sin 157t$

$$i = 40 \cdot \sqrt{2} \sin(157t + 50°) = 56.6 \sin(157t + 50°).$$

R.L.C. Circuit

Consider the *RLC* series circuit of Fig. 6.8 (*a*).

The equations and phasor diagrams are shown,

$$E_R = IR, \quad E_L = IX_L \quad \text{and} \quad E_C = IX_C$$

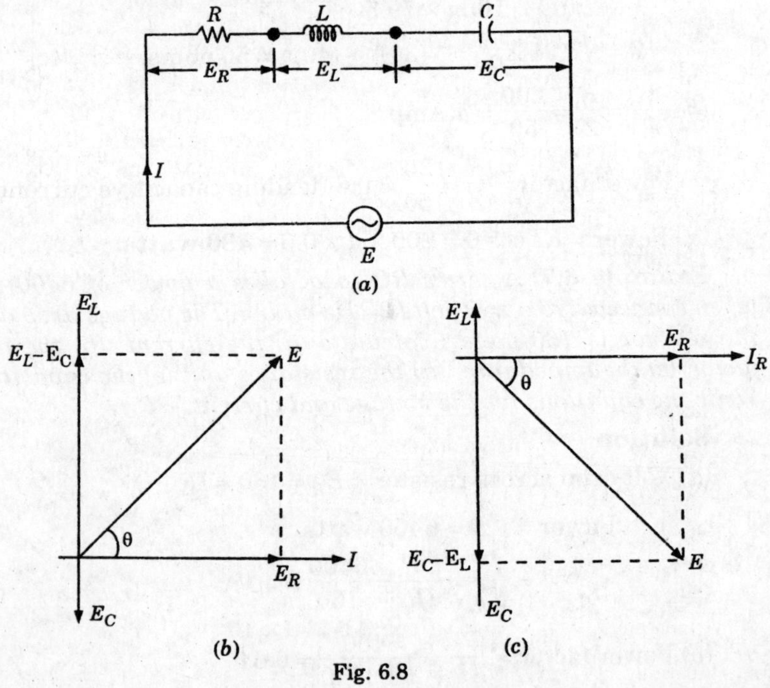

Fig. 6.8

$$E = E_R + jE_L - jE_C = IR + jIX_L - jIX_C$$
$$= I\,[R + j\,(X_L - X_C)] = IZ,$$

where $Z = R + j\,(X_L - X_C)$ ohms

$$|\,Z\,| = \sqrt{R^2 + (X_L - X_C)^2}$$

$$\theta = \tan^{-1}\left[\frac{(X_L - X_C)}{R}\right]$$

If $X_L > X_C$ then the circuit behaves like an *R-L* circuit and the phasor diagram is shown in Fig. 6.8 (*b*). If $X_C > X_L$ the circuit is like an *R-C* circuit and the phasor diagram is shown in Fig. 6.8 (*c*).

Example 6.8. *A series circuit has R = 10 OMEA, L = 50 mh and C = 100 μf and is supplied with 200 V 50 Hz. Find (a) the impedance, (b) the current, (c) the power, (d) the power factor and (e) the voltage drops across each element.*

Solution. The circuit is shown in Fig. 6.9.

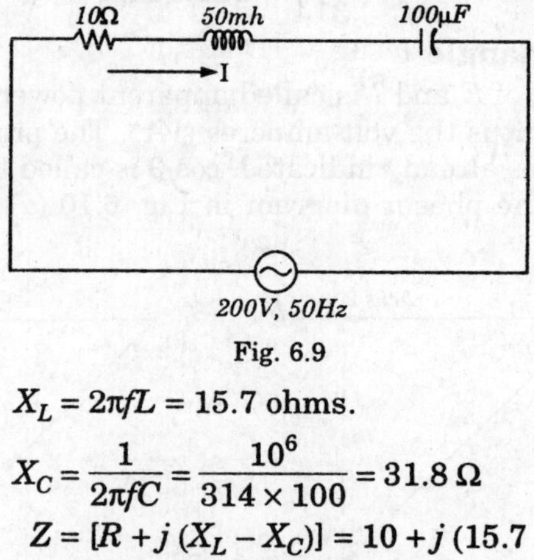

Fig. 6.9

$$X_L = 2\pi fL = 15.7 \text{ ohms.}$$

$$X_C = \frac{1}{2\pi fC} = \frac{10^6}{314 \times 100} = 31.8\ \Omega$$

$$Z = [R + j\,(X_L - X_C)] = 10 + j\,(15.7 - 31.8)$$
$$= 10 - j\,16.1 = 18.95\ \angle -58°.$$

(*a*) Impedance = 18.95 ohms

(*b*) Current, $I = \dfrac{200}{18.95} = 10.55$ Amps.

(*c*) Power $= I^2R = 1113$ watts.

(*d*) Power factor = cos 58° = 0.53 (leading)

Also p.f. $= \dfrac{R}{|\,Z\,|} = \dfrac{10}{18.95} = 0.53$ (lead)

Also Power $= E \cdot I \cos\theta = 200 \times 10.55 \times 0.53 = 1113$ W

(*e*) $E_R = IR = 10.55 \times 10 = 105.5$ Volts.

$$E_L = jIX_L = j\,(10.55 \times 15.7)$$
$$= j\ 165.64 \text{ Volts}$$
$$E_C = -jIX_C = -j\,(10.55 \times 31.8)$$
$$= \mathbf{-j\ 335.5\ Volts.}$$

Example 6.9. *It is desired to have the circuit of Problem 6.8, take the same current and power but operate at a power factor of 0.53 (lagging). For what value of inductance will this be satisfied, all other values remaining unchanged ?*

Solution. Since all values must remain unchanged and p.f. must be 0.53 (lagging).

$$Z = 10 + j\ 16.1 = R + j(X_L - X_C)$$

$\therefore \quad X_L - X_C = 16.1\ \Omega$

i.e. $\quad X_L = 16.1 + X_C = 16.1 + 31.8 = 47.9\ \Omega$

$$L = 2\pi f L$$

$\therefore \quad L = \dfrac{47.9}{2\pi f} = \dfrac{47.9}{314} = \mathbf{152.5\ mh.}$

The Power Triangle

The product of E and I is called apparent power denoted by the symbol S. Its unit is the volt-amperes (*VA*). The product $EI \cos\theta$ is the true power as already indicated. $\cos\theta$ is called the power factor of the circuit. The phasor diagram in Fig. 6.10 (*a*) is for a lagging circuit.

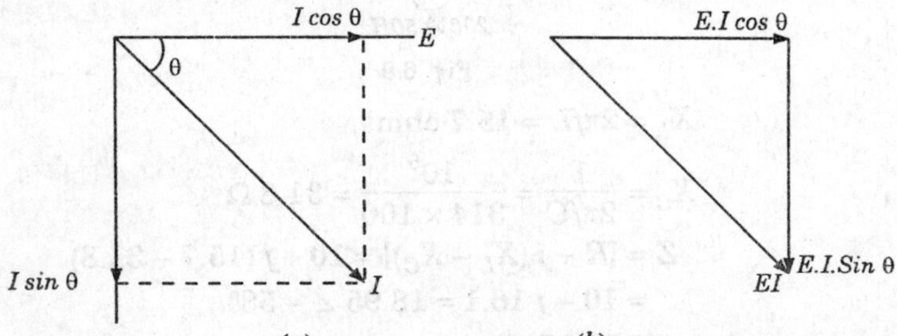

Fig. 6.10

$I\cos\theta$ is the component of current along the voltage phasor and $I\sin\theta$ the component in quadrature (at 90°).

$$EI = \text{Apparent power, } S \text{ (Volt amperes)}$$
$$E{\cdot}I{\cdot}\cos\theta = \text{True power, } P \text{ (average power) watts}$$
$$E{\cdot}I{\cdot}\sin\theta = \text{Reactive Power, } Q \quad \text{(Volt-amperes-reactive)}$$
$$S = P + jQ = EI^*$$

where E and I are complex voltage and current respectively. I^* is the conjugate of I

$$P = \text{Real Part } [EI^*]$$
$$Q = \text{Imaginery Part } [EI^*].$$

Example 6.10. *In an a.c. circuit consisting of two elements in series, the equations for voltage and current are e = 180 sin 314t and i = 28.4 sin (314t – π/3). Calculate (a) the effective voltage and current, (b) the frequency, (c) the power factor, (d) the power and (e) the values of the circuit constants.*

Solution. (*a*) Maximum value of voltage = 170 Volts

$$\text{Effective value} = E = \frac{170}{\sqrt{2}} = 120 \text{ Volts.}$$

Maximum current = 28.4 A

$$\therefore \quad I = \frac{28.4}{\sqrt{2}} = 20 \text{ Amps.}$$

(*b*) Frequency $\omega = 314 = 2\pi f$

$$\therefore \quad f = \frac{314}{2\pi} = 50 \text{ Hz}$$

(*c*) Power factor = cosine of the angle between voltage and current

(Here the current lags the voltage by π/3 rad or 60°)

$$= \cos(\pi/3) = 0.5 \text{ (lag)}$$

(*d*) Power $= E \cdot I \cdot \cos\theta = 120 \times 20 \times 0.5 = 1200$ watts.

(*e*) The circuit constants must be *R* and *L* as the current is lagging behind the voltage.

$$\text{Power} = I^2R = 1200 \text{ Watts}$$

$$\therefore \quad R = \frac{1200}{20^2} = 3 \text{ ohms}$$

$$\text{Impedance} \quad Z = \frac{E}{I} = \frac{120}{20} = 6 \text{ ohms}$$

$$Z = 6 = \sqrt{R^2 + X_L{}^2}$$

$$\therefore \quad X_L = \sqrt{Z^2 - R^2} = \sqrt{6^2 - 3^2}$$

$$= 5.2\ \Omega = 2\pi fL$$

$$\therefore \quad L = \frac{5.2}{2\pi \times 50} = \mathbf{16.6\ mh.}$$

Example 6.11. *Repeat Problem 6.10 above for*

$$e = 50 \sin(2000t - 25)$$
$$i = 8 \sin(2000t + 5)$$

Solution. (*a*) $E = \frac{50}{\sqrt{2}} = 35.36$ Volts.

$$I = \frac{8}{\sqrt{2}} = 5.66 \text{ Amps}$$

(*b*) Frequency $\omega = 2\pi f = 2{,}000$

$$f = \frac{2000}{2\pi} = 318.3 \text{ Hz}$$

(*c*) The angle between voltage and current is 30°

The current leads voltage by 30°

Power factor $= \cos 30° = 0.866$ (lead)

(*d*) Power $= E \cdot I \cdot \cos\theta = 35.36 \times 5.66 \times 0.866$

$= 173.2$ Watts

(*e*) The circuit is series *RC*

$$\text{Power} = I^2 R = 173.2 \text{ Watts}$$

$$R = \frac{173.2}{I^2} = \frac{173.2}{(5.66^2)} = 5.41 \text{ ohms}$$

$$Z = \frac{E}{I} = 6.25 = \sqrt{R^2 + X_C{}^2}$$

$$\therefore \quad X_C = \sqrt{Z^2 - R^2} = \sqrt{(6.25)^2 - (5.41)^2} = 3.13\ \Omega = \frac{1}{\omega C}$$

$$\therefore \quad C = \frac{1}{3.13\ \omega} = \frac{1}{3.13 \times 2000} = \mathbf{160\ \mu f.}$$

Example 6.12. *A series R – L circuit takes 384 watts at a power factor of 0.8 from a 120 volt 60 Hz source. (a) What are the values of R and L ? (b) What additional inductance should be inserted in series to reduce the overall circuit power factor to 0.5 ? (c) What will be the current and power under this condition ?*

Solution. Power $= E \cdot I \cdot \cos\theta$

$$I = \frac{P}{E \cdot \cos\theta} = \frac{384}{120 \times 0.8} = 4 \text{ Amps.}$$

$$\text{Power} = I^2 R$$

$$R = \frac{P}{I^2} = \frac{384}{4^2} = 24 \text{ ohms}$$

$$Z = \frac{E}{I} = \frac{120}{4} = 30\ \Omega$$

$$\therefore \quad X_L = \sqrt{Z^2 - R^2} = \sqrt{(30)^2 - (24)^2} = 18 \text{ ohms}$$

$$L = \frac{X_L}{2\pi f} = \frac{18}{2\pi \times 60} = 47.74 \text{ mh.}$$

(*b*) Let the additional inductive reactance be *X* ohms so that the power factor

$$= \cos\theta = 0.5$$

i.e. $\theta = 60°$

Power factor angle is given by

$$\tan\theta = \frac{X_L}{R} = \left(\frac{18+X}{24}\right)$$

$$\tan 60° = \frac{18+X}{24}$$

$$\sqrt{3} = \frac{18+X}{24}$$

or $X = 23.57$ ohms.

Additional inductance required

$$= \frac{23.57}{2\pi \times 60} = 62.5 \text{ mh}$$

(*c*) *Z* under this condition

$$= \sqrt{R^2 + X_L{}^2} = \sqrt{(24)^2 + (18+23.57)^2}$$

$$= 48 \text{ ohms}$$

$$I = \frac{120}{48.00} = 2.50 \text{ Amps.}$$

$$\text{Power} = I^2R = (2.5)^2 \times 24 = \mathbf{150\ Watts.}$$

Example 6.13. *A resistor R is in the series with a 177 μf capacitor. The combination is supplied at 60 Hz, and the power consumed by the circuit is 500 watts. The voltage drop across the capacitor is 75 volts. Find (a) the current (b) the value of R (c) the supply voltage and (d) the power factor.*

Solution.

(*a*) $X_C = \frac{1}{2\pi fC} = \frac{10}{2\pi \times 60 \times 177} = 15$ ohms

$E_C = 75$ V

$\therefore \quad I = \frac{E_C}{X_C} = \frac{75}{15} = 5$ Amps.

(*b*) Power $= I^2R = 500$ Watts.

$$R = \frac{500}{I^2} = \frac{500}{5^2} = 20 \text{ ohms.}$$

(*c*) Impedance $= 20 - jX_C = 20 - j15$

$|Z| = 25$ ohms.

Supply voltage $= I\,|Z| = 5 \times 25 = 125$ Volts.

(*d*) Power factor $= \dfrac{R}{|Z|} = \dfrac{20}{25} = \mathbf{0.8.}$

Example 6.14. *A series circuit has R = 8 Ω are C = 30 μf. At what frequency will the current lead the voltage by 30°.*

Solution. The impedance $Z = R - jX_C$

$$= R - j\frac{1}{\omega C}$$

$$\text{P.f. angle} = \tan^{-1}\left(\frac{X_C}{R}\right) = \tan^{-1}\left(\frac{1}{\omega CR}\right) = 30°.$$

i.e.
$$\frac{1}{\omega CR} = \tan 30° = 0.57735$$

$$f = \frac{1}{2\pi \times 0.57735 \times C \times R}$$

$$= \frac{10^6}{2\pi \times 0.57735 \times 30 \times 8} = \mathbf{1149\ Hz.}$$

Example 6.15. *An RL series circuit with R = 10 ohms has an angle of 30° for the impedance at a frequency of f_1 = 100 Hz. At what frequency will the impedance be twice that at f_1 in magnitude.*

Solution. Let us denote the impedance at frequency f_1 as Z_1.

$$Z_1 = R + j\,2\pi fL = 10 + j\,628\,L$$

$$\text{Angle of } Z_1 = \tan^{-1}\left(\frac{X_L}{R}\right)$$

$$= \tan^{-1}\left(\frac{628\,L}{10}\right) = \tan^{-1}(62.8L) = 30°$$

$\therefore$
$$62.8\,L = 0.57735$$

$$L = 9.2 \text{ mh}$$

$\therefore$
$$Z_1 = 10 + j\,628 \times 9.2 \times 10^{-3}$$

$$|Z_1| = \sqrt{10^2 + (5.78)^2} = \mathbf{11.55\ ohms.}$$

Let the frequency required be f_2 and the impedance at this frequency is 2 × 11.55 = 23.1 Ω

$$= \sqrt{R^2 + X_L{}^2}$$

$$X_L = \sqrt{(23.1)^2 - (10)^2} = 20.8 \text{ ohms.}$$

$$20.8 = 2\pi f_2 \times 9.2 \times 10^{-3}$$

$\therefore$
$$f_2 = \frac{20.8}{2\pi \times 9.2 \times 10^{-3}} = \mathbf{360\ Hz.}$$

Example 6.16. *A two element series circuit has the following voltage and current for ω = 200 rad / sec ; E = 150 ∠ – 45° and I = 4.74*

∠– 116.6°. A second voltage source results in an angle of 45° between voltage and current. Determine 'ω' for the second source.

Solution. As the current lags behind the voltage by 71.6° it should be an *RL* circuit.

$$Z = \frac{V}{I} = \frac{150}{4.74} = 31.65 \text{ ohms.}$$

Impedance angle = 71.6°

$$Z = 31.65\angle 31.6°$$
$$= 10 + j\,30 \text{ ohms}$$

$$\therefore \quad X_L = 30 = \omega L$$

$$\therefore \quad L = \frac{30}{\omega} = \frac{30}{2{,}000} = 15 \text{ mh.}$$

For the second source, the impedance angle

$$= \tan^{-1}\left(\frac{\omega L}{R}\right) = \tan^{-1}\left(\frac{15 \times 10^{-3}\,\omega}{10}\right) = 45°$$

$$\therefore \quad \frac{15 \times 10^{-3}\,\omega}{10} = 1$$

Hence $w = \dfrac{10}{15 \times 10^{-3}} =$ **667 rad/sec.**

Example 6.17. *A series circuit consisting of a 25 μf capacitor and 15 mh inductor is connected to a 150 V, 60 Hz source. (a) Calculate the circuit current and indicate whether leading or lagging, (b) What value of L will make an equal current lag behind the same voltage with the same capacitor ?*

Solution. $X_C = \dfrac{10^6}{2\pi \times 60 \times 25} = 106.1\ \Omega$

$$X_L = 2\pi \times 60 \times 15 \times 10^{-3} = 5.7\ \Omega$$

$$\text{Impedance} = j\,(X_L - X_C) = 5.7 - 106.1$$
$$= (-j\,100.4)\ \Omega \ \text{(capacitive)}$$

$$\text{Current} = \frac{150}{-j\,100.4} = j\,1.5 \text{ Amps} = 1.5\angle 90°$$

(Current leads the voltage by 90°)

(*b*) For the same current to lag behind the voltage

$$\text{Impedance} = +j\,100.4 = j\,(X_L - X_C)$$

$$\therefore \quad X_L = 106.1 + 100.4 = 206.5 \text{ ohms}$$

Hence $L = \dfrac{206.5}{2\pi \times 60} =$ **0.55 h.**

Example 6.18. *An L-C series circuit is connected to a sinusoidal voltage of constant magnitude but variable frequency. (a) Plot the* *variation of X_L and X_C with frequency. (b) At what frequency is $X_L = X_C$? (c) If L = 0.4 h and C = 200 μf and the supply is 125 volts, at what frequency will the circuit take a lagging current of 2.5 Amps ?*

Solution. (*a*) $X_L = 2\pi fL$

Varies as a straight line passing through the origin.

$$X_C = \frac{1}{2\pi fC}$$

Varies inversely with frequency (Fig. 6.11)

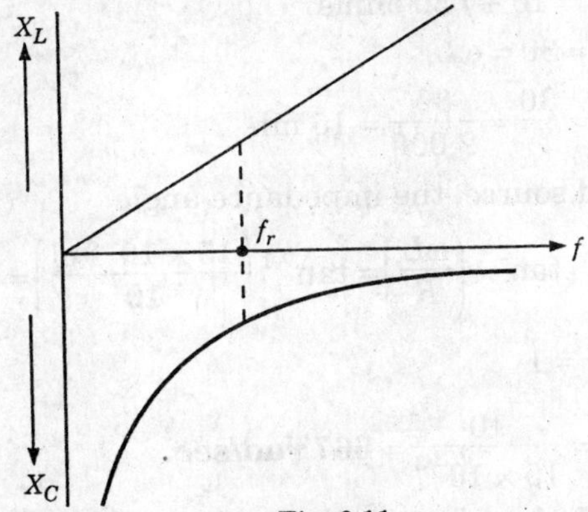

Fig. 6.11

(*b*) Let $X_L = X_C$ at a frequency f_r.

$$2\pi f_r L = \frac{1}{2\pi f_r C}$$

$$\therefore \quad f_r = \frac{1}{2\pi\sqrt{LC}}$$

(*c*) $\quad E = 125 \text{ V} \quad I = 2.5 \text{ A (lag)}$

$$Z = \frac{125}{2.5} = 50 \text{ ohms}$$

$$= X_L - X_C \quad \text{(for lagging } X_L > X_C\text{)}$$

$$\omega L - \frac{1}{\omega C} = 50$$

$$\frac{\omega^2 LC - 1}{\omega C} = 50$$

or $\quad w^2 LC - 50\omega C - 1 = 0$

Solving, we get two values of ω.

The two values are $\omega_{1,2}$

$$= \frac{50\,C + \sqrt{2500\,C^2 + 4LC}}{2LC} = 190 \text{ Hz and} - 65.5 \text{ Hz}$$

∴ The current is lagging at 190 rad/sec and $f = 30.2$ Hz.

Example 6.19. *A series circuit has a 63.7 μf capacitor and a variable resistor. For what two values of the resistance will the power taken by the circuit be 160 watts, if the impressed voltage is 200 volts, 50 Hz.*

Solution. $X_C = \dfrac{1}{2\pi fC} = \dfrac{10^6}{2\pi \times 50 \times 63.7} = 50$ ohms

$$\text{Impedance} = R - jX_C$$

$$|Z| = \sqrt{R^2 + X_C^{\,2}}$$

$$I = \frac{E}{|Z|} = \frac{200}{\sqrt{R^2 + X_C^{\,2}}}$$

$$\text{Power} = I^2 R$$

$$= \left(\frac{200}{R^2 + 50^2}\right)^2 R = \frac{40000\,R}{R^2 + 50^2} = 160 \text{ Watts}$$

i.e. $160\,R^2 - 40000\,R + 160\,(50)^2 = 0$

or $R^2 - 250\,R + 2500 = 0$

Solving, $R = 239.5$ or **$R = 10.5$ ohms.**

Example 6.20. *A series RLC circuit has R = 25 ohms, L = 0.221 h and C = 66.3 μf and is supplied at 150 volts 60 Hz. Find (a) the equivalent impedance, (b) the power factor, (c) the current, (d) the power and (e) the reactive power.*

Solution.

(*a*) $X_L = 2\pi fL = 83.3$ ohms

$$X_C = \frac{1}{2\pi fC} = \frac{10^6}{2\pi \times 60 \times 66.3} = 40 \text{ ohms}$$

$$Z = R + j\,(X_L - X_C) = 25 + j\,(83.3 - 40)$$

$$= 25 + j\,43.3 = 50\angle 60^\circ\ \Omega.$$

(*b*) Power factor

$$= \cos\theta = \cos 60^\circ = 0.5 \text{ (lag) as } X_L > X_C$$

(*c*) $\text{Current} = I = \dfrac{150}{50} = 3$ amps

(*d*) $\text{Power} = E \cdot I \cdot \cos\theta$

$$= 150 \times 3 \times 0.5 = 225 \text{ Watts}$$

(*e*) Reactive Power

$$= EI\sin\theta = 150 \times 3 \times 0.866$$

$$= \textbf{390 reactive V.A.}$$

Example 6.21. *An RLC series circuit has a current which lags behind the applied voltage by 45°. The voltage across the inductance has a maximum value equal to twice the maximum of the voltage across the capacitor. $e_L = 30 \sin 1000t$. If R = 20 ohms, find the values of L and C.*

Solution. The impedance of the *RLC* series circuit

$$= R + j(X_L - X_C) = 20 + j(X_L - X_C).$$

As the current lags behind the applied voltage by 45°

$X_L > X_C$ and $\tan\theta = \tan 45° = 1$

$$= \frac{X_L - X_C}{R}$$

$$\therefore \quad (X_L - X_C) = R = 20 \text{ ohms}.$$

The voltage (maximum) across the inductor is twice the voltage (maximum) across the capacitor. As it is the same current that is passing through both the elements.

$$X_L = 2X_C$$

$$\therefore \quad 2X_C - X_C = X_C = 20 \text{ ohms}$$

$$X_L = 40 \text{ ohms} = \omega L$$

$$\therefore \quad L = \frac{40}{\omega} = 40 \text{ mh as } \omega = 1000$$

$$X_C = 20 \text{ ohms} = \frac{1}{\omega C}$$

$$\therefore \quad C = \frac{1}{1000 \times 20} \text{ farads or } \mathbf{50\ \mu f}$$

SERIES AND PARALLEL CIRCUITS

Series Circuit

Consider a circuit of Fig. 6.12 with three impedance Z_1, Z_2 and Z_3 connected in series to an A.C., source of *E* volts. Let the current

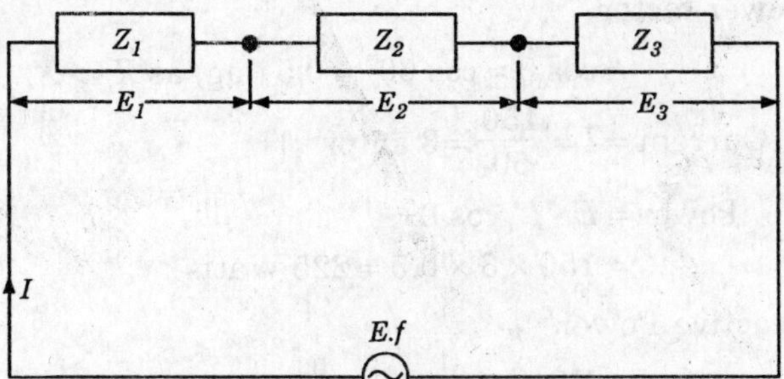

Fig. 6.12

flowing in the circuit be denoted by I. Applying Kirchhoff's voltage law to the circuit,

$$E = E_1 + E_2 + E_3$$

This addition must, however, be performed vectorially and not arithmatically as each one of them is a phasor (complex quantity)

i.e. $$E = IZ_1 + IZ_2 + IZ_3 = I\,(Z_1 + Z_2 + Z_3)$$

$$E = I\,(Z_{eq})$$

or $$I = \frac{E}{Z_{eq}}$$

where $$Z_{eq} = Z_1 + Z_2 + Z_3$$

This may be extended to any number of impedance in series.

Example 6.22. *For the circuit of Fig. 6.12, if $Z_1 = 5\angle 30°$, $Z_2 = 4\angle 60°$, $Z_3 = 10\angle 90°$ and $E = 100$ volts, calculate the current I and the voltage drops across the various impedances. Find the overall power factor.*

Solution. $Z_{eq} = Z_1 + Z_2 + Z_3$

$$= 5\angle 30° + 4\angle 60° + 10\angle 90°$$
$$= (4.33 + j\,2.5) + (2 + j\,3.46) + j\,10$$
$$= 6.33 + j\,15.96 = 17.2\angle 68.4°\ \Omega$$

If we choose the voltage as reference vector

$$E = 100\angle 0°$$

$$I = \frac{E}{Z} = \frac{100\angle 0°}{17.2\angle 68.4°}$$

$$= 5.8\angle -68.4° \text{ amps.}$$

Voltage drops $E_1 = IZ_1$

$$= 5.8\angle -68.4° \times 5\angle 30° = 29\angle -38.4° \text{ V}$$

$$E_2 = IZ_2 = 5.8\angle -68.4° \times 4\angle 60° = 23.2\angle -8.4° \text{ V}$$

$$E_3 = IZ_3 = 5.8\angle -68.4° \times 10\angle 90° = 58\angle 21.6° \text{ V.}$$

It may be noted that

$$E \neq E_1 + E_2 + E_3 \text{ in magnitude}$$

Overall power factor for the circuit

$= \cos(-68.4°) =$ **0.368 (lag)**

Example 6.23. *An impedance coil is connected in series with a fixed resistor and a 240 volt 50 Hz source is then impressed across the combination. If the voltage drops across the coil and resistor are 140 and 160 volts respectively, when the circuit current is 2.5 ampere, calculate the resistance and inductance of the impedance coil.*

Solution. The circuit is shown in Fig. 6.13 (*a*). We shall assume the current I as the reference vector and the phasor diagram is drawn as shown in Fig. 6.13 (*b*).

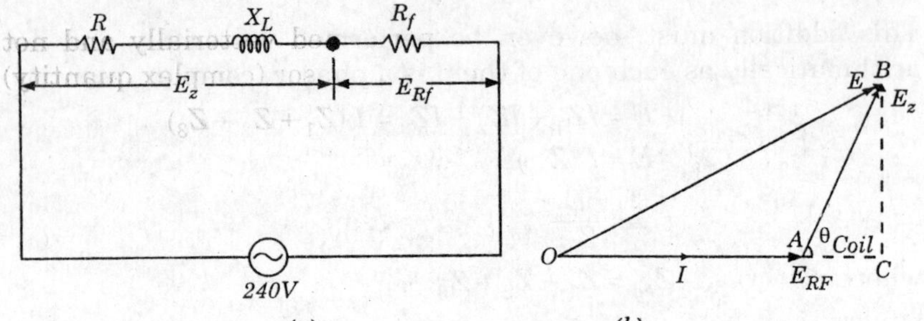

(*a*) (*b*)

Fig. 6.13

$E_{Rf} = IR_f$, in phase with Phasor OA. With A as centre and radius $= E_Z$ draw an arc. With centre O and radius E, draw an arc to intersect the previous arc at B. Join OB and AB.

AB represents E_Z and OA represents E.

$$\text{Power factor angle of the coil} = \tan^{-1}\left(\frac{X_L}{R}\right) = \theta_{\text{coil}}$$

Considering the triangle OBC

$$E^2 = E_{Rf}^{\;2} + E_Z^{\;2} + 2E_{Rf}E_Z \cos\theta_{COIL}$$

i.e. $$(240)^2 = (160)^2 + (140)^2 + 2 \times 140 \times 160 \cdot \cos(\theta_{\text{COIL}})$$

$$\cos(\theta_{\text{COIL}}) = 0.277$$

$$\therefore \quad \theta_{\text{COIL}} = 73.9°$$

$$E_Z = 140 = IZ$$

$$Z = \frac{140}{I} = \frac{140}{2.5} = 56\ \Omega$$

$$R = Z \sin\theta_{\text{COIL}}$$

$$= 56 \cos 73.9° = 15.5 \text{ ohms}$$

$$X_L = Z \sin\theta_{coil} = 56 \sin 73.9° = 53.8 \text{ ohms}$$

$$L = \frac{53.8}{\omega} = \frac{53.8}{2\pi \times 50} = \mathbf{171.3\ mh.}$$

Parallel Circuits

Fig. 6.14 shows a voltage E applied to a parallel connected set of impedance Z_1, Z_2 and Z_3.

Applying Kirchhoff's Current law,

$$I = \vec{I_1} + \vec{I_2} + \vec{I_3}$$ (the arrows on top indicate phasors.)

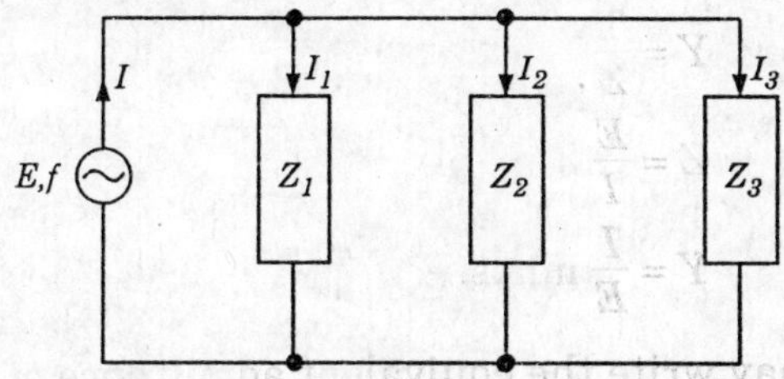

Fig. 6.14

i.e. $$I = \frac{E}{Z_1} + \frac{E}{Z_2} + \frac{E}{Z_3}$$

$$= E\left(\frac{1}{Z_1} + \frac{1}{Z_2} + \frac{1}{Z_3}\right) = \frac{E}{Z_{eq}}$$

where $$\frac{1}{Z_{eq}} = \frac{1}{Z_1} + \frac{1}{Z_2} + \frac{1}{Z_3}.$$

This relationship is identical to what we had for parallel connected resistors.

Two Branch Parallel Circuit

Consider the two branch parallel circuit of Fig. 6.15.

$$\frac{1}{Z_{eq}} = \frac{1}{Z_1} + \frac{1}{Z_2}$$

$$I = I_1 + I_2 = \frac{E}{Z_1} + \frac{E}{Z_2}.$$

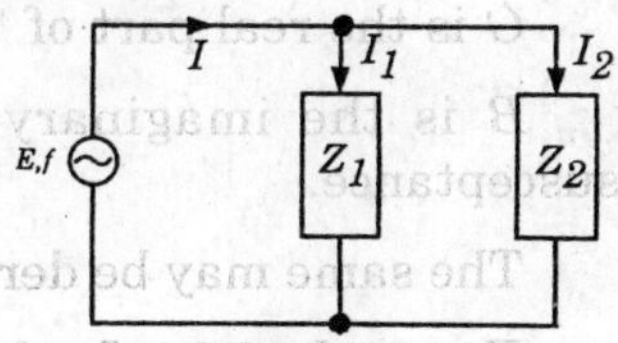

Fig. 6.15

Solving for the branch currents, we get

$$I_1 = I \cdot \frac{Z_2}{Z_1 + Z_2}$$

and $$I_2 = I \cdot \frac{Z_1}{Z_1 + Z_2}.$$

These relations are once again identical to those we had for resistances (in D.C. circuits). The only point to remember is that all arithmetic operations have to be performed with complex quantities.

Admittance

In calculations involving parallel circuits, we come across reciprocal of complex impedances. It is convenient to denote reciprocal of these complex impedances by what are called admittances (Y).

$$Y = \frac{1}{Z}$$

and since $$Z = \frac{E}{I}$$

$$Y = \frac{I}{E} \text{ mhos.}$$

Hence we may write the equivalent admittance of the parallel circuit of Fig. 6.14 as

$$Y_{eq} = Y_1 + Y_2 + Y_3$$

and $$I = Y_{eq}E$$

Further as $Z = R + jX_L$ for an inductive circuit.

$$Y = \frac{1}{Z} = \frac{1}{R + jX_L}$$

$$= \frac{R - jX_L}{(R + jX_L)(R - jX_L)}$$

$$= \frac{R}{R^2 + X_L^2} - \frac{-jX_L}{R^2 + X_L^{\,2}} = G + jB.$$

G is the real part of the admittance and is called conductance

B is the imaginary part of the admittance and is called susceptance.

The same may be derived for capacitive circuits too.

Example 6.24. *In the circuit of Fig. 6.16, R_L = 3.6 ohms, X_L = 4.8 ohms, R_C = 3 ohms and X_C = 4 ohms. Calculate (a) the conductance and susceptance of each branch (b) the total conductance, susceptance and admittance, (c) the total current I and (d) the currents I_L and I_C. The applied voltage E = 150 Volts.*

Solution. (*a*)

$$Z_L = R_L + jX_L = 3.6 + j4.8$$

$$Y_L = \frac{1}{Z_L} = \frac{1}{3.6 + j\,4.8}$$

$$= \frac{3.6 - j\,4.8}{(3.6)^2 + (4.8)^2}$$

$$= 0.1 - j\,0.1333$$

G_L = 0.1 mho; B_L = – 0.133 mho.

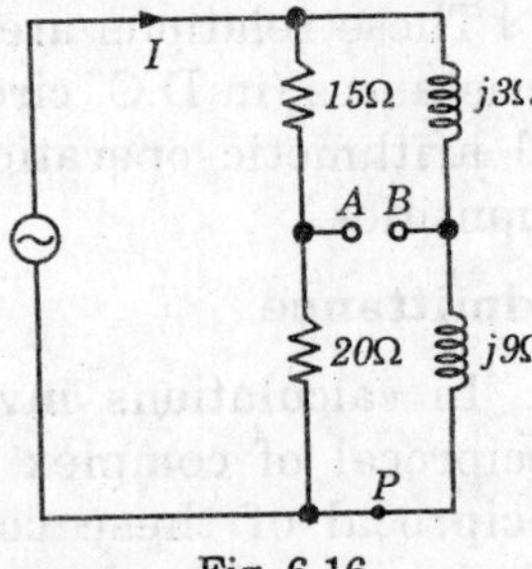

Fig. 6.16

$$Y_C = \frac{1}{Z_C} = \frac{1}{3 - j4} = \frac{3 + j4}{3^2 + 4^2} = 0.12 + j\,0.16$$

$$G_C = 0.12 \text{ mho}; \quad B_C = 0.16 \text{ mho}$$

(*b*) $$Y_{eq} = Y_L + Y_C$$
$$= (0.1 - j\,0.1333) + (0.12 + 0.16)$$
$$= 0.22 + j\,0.0267$$

Total $G = 0.22$; total $B = 0.0267$

(*c*) $$I = E/Z_{eq} = E\,Y_{eq} = 150\,(0.22 + j\,0.0267)$$
$$= (33 + j\,4) \text{ amps.} = 33.24\,\angle 6.9° \text{ A.}$$

(*d*) $$I_L = EY_L = 150\,(0.1 - j\,0.1333)$$
$$= (15 + j\,20) \text{ Amps} = 25\,\angle -53.1° \text{ A}$$
$$I_C = EY_C = 150\,(0.12 + j\,0.16)$$
$$= 18 + j\,24 = 30\,\angle 53.1° \text{ A}$$

Check $I_L + I_C = I$;

i.e. $$(15 - j\,20) + (18 + j\,24) = \mathbf{33 + j\,4\,A}$$

Example 6.25 *A unity power factor load of 3,000 watts is connected in parallel with a load of 2,700 watts operating at a lagging power factor of 0.6. If the supply voltage is 150-V, calculate (a) the current in each load (b) the total current (c) the total power (d) the overall factor and (e) the reactive power.*

Solution. The circuit is shown in Fig. 6.17.

(*a*) $E \cdot I_1 = 3{,}000$ Watts

$$I_1 = \frac{3{,}000}{150} = 20 \text{ A}$$

$$EI_2 \cos\theta = 2{,}700 \text{ Watts}$$

$$I_2 = \frac{2{,}700}{150 \times 0.6} = 30 \text{ Amps.}$$

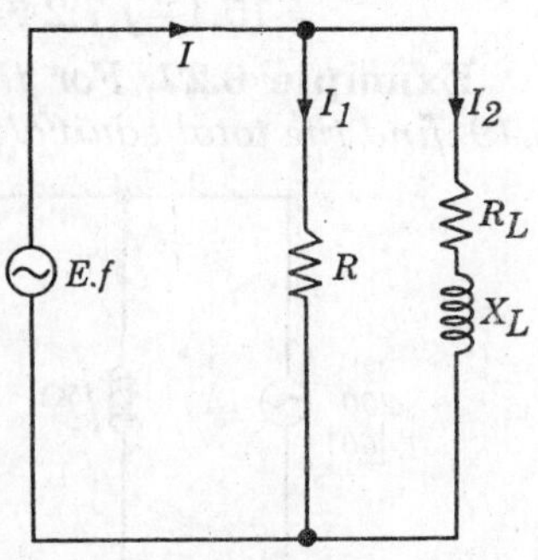

Fig. 6.17

as I_2 is a lagging current (lagging by 0.6)

$$\cos\theta = 0.6$$
$$I_2 = 30\,(0.6 - j\,0.8)$$
$$= 18 - j\,24 \text{ Amps}$$

(*b*) $$I = I_1 + I_2$$
$$= (20) + (18 - j\,24) = 38 - j\,24 \text{ Amps.}$$
$$= 44.94\,\angle -32.3° \text{A}$$

(*c*) Total power
$$= 3{,}000 + 2{,}700 = 5{,}700 \text{ Watts.}$$

(*d*) Overall power factor
$$= \cos 32.3 = 0.845 \text{ (lag)}$$

(*e*) Reactive power $= E \cdot I \cdot \sin\theta$

$= 150 \times 44.94 \times \sin(-32.3°)$

$= -$ **3600 Watts. (3600 VA lag).**

Example 6.26. *In the circuit of Fig. 6.18, the voltage across the 5 ohm register is 60 Volts. Find the total current.*

Solution. If the voltage across the 5 Ω resistor is 60 V, the current through it

$$= I_2 = \frac{60}{5} = 12 \text{ Amps.}$$

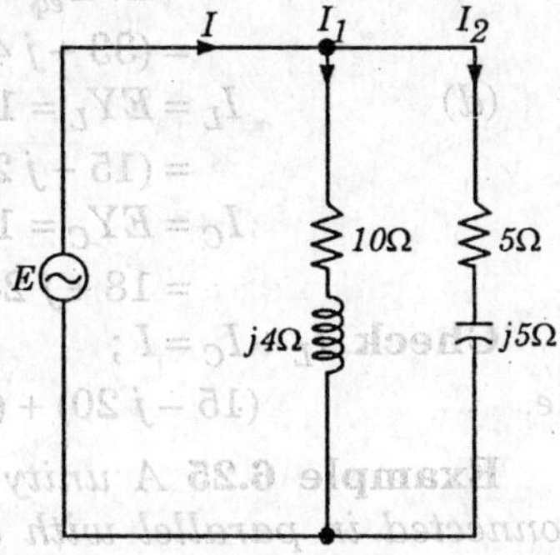

Fig. 6.2

Let this current be assumed as reference, then

$$I_2 = 12 \angle 0° \text{ A}$$

$$E = I_2 (5 - j\,5)$$

$$= 12 \angle 0° (5 - j\,5)$$

$$= 12 \angle 0° \times 5\sqrt{2} \angle -45°$$

$$= 84.9 \angle -45° \text{ V.}$$

$$I_1 = E/(10 + j4) = \frac{84.9 \angle -45°}{10.7 \text{ V} \angle 21.8°}$$

$$= 7.88 \angle -66.8° = (3.1 - j\,7.24) \text{ Amps.}$$

$$I = I_1 + I_2 (3.1 - j\,7.24)(12 + j0)$$

$$= 15.1 - j\,7.24 = \mathbf{16.75 \angle -25.6° \text{ A}}$$

Example 6.27. *For the four branch parallel network of Fig. 6.19, find the total equivalent impedance and the current.*

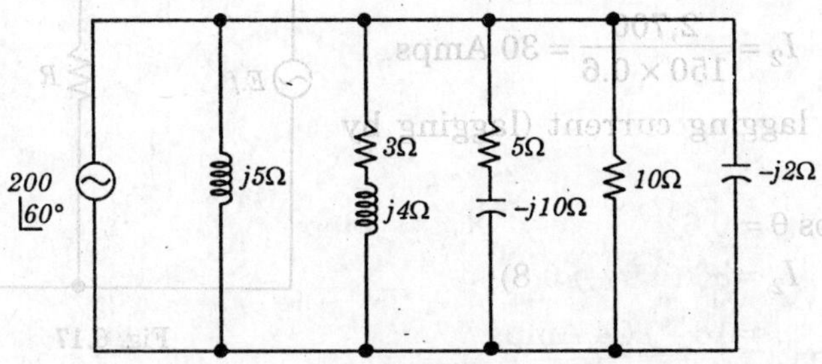

Fig. 6.19

Solution. $Y_1 = \dfrac{1}{j5} = -j\,0.2$ mho

$$Y_2 = \frac{1}{3 + j4} = \frac{3 - j4}{3^2 + 4^2} = (0.12 - j\,0.16) \text{ mho}$$

$$Y_3 = \frac{1}{5 - j\,10} = \frac{5 + j\,10}{5 + 10^2} = (0.04 + j\,0.08) \text{ mho}$$

$$Y_4 = \frac{1}{10} = 0.1 \text{ mho}$$

$$Y_5 = \frac{1}{-j\,2} = j\,0.5 \text{ mho}$$

$$Y_{eq} = Y_1 + Y_2 + Y_3 + Y_4 + Y_5$$

$$= (-j\,0.2) + (0.12 - j\,0.16) + (0.4 + j\,0.08) + (0.1) + (j\,0.5)$$

$$= (0.26 + j\,0.22) = 0.3406\,\angle 40° \text{ mho}$$

$$Z_{eq} = \frac{1}{Y_{eq}} = \frac{1}{0.3406\,\angle 40°} = 2.936\,\angle -40°\ \Omega$$

$$I = \frac{E}{Z_{eq}} = \frac{200\,\angle 60°}{2.936\,\angle -40°} = \mathbf{68.12\,\angle 100°\ A.}$$

Example 6.28. *The total current I in Fig. 6.20 is 20 ∠30°. Find the potential difference between points A and B.*

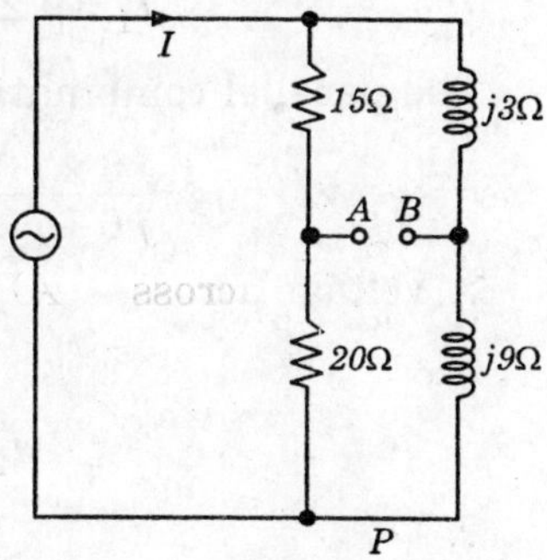

Fig. 6.20

Solution. $I_A = \left(\frac{Z_B}{Z_A + Z_B}\right) \cdot I$

$$= 20\,\angle 30° \left(\frac{j\,12}{35 + j\,12}\right)$$

$$= 6.5\,\angle 101° \text{ A}$$

$$I_B = I\left(\frac{Z_A}{Z_A + Z_B}\right)$$

$$= 20\,\angle 30° \left(\frac{35}{35 + j\,12}\right)$$

$$= 18.9\,\angle 11° \text{ A.}$$

The voltage drop between A and B

$$= E_{AB} = E_{AP} + E_{PB}$$

i.e. $E_{AB} = E_{AP} - E_{BP}$

$$E_{AP} = I_A \times 20 = 6.5\,\angle 101° \times 20 = 130\,\angle 101° \text{ V.}$$

$$E_{BP} = I_B \times (j\,9)$$

$$E_{BP} = 18.9\,\angle 11° \times j\,9 = 170\,\angle 101° \text{ V}$$

$\therefore$ $E_{AB} = E_{AP} - E_{BP}$

$$= 130\,\angle 101° - 170\,\angle 101° = -40\,\angle 101°$$

$$= 40\,\angle 180° + 101° = 40\,\angle 281°$$

$$= \mathbf{40\,\angle -79°\ V.}$$

Example 6.29. *A voltmeter-connected across the 5 ohm resistor in Fig. 6.21 reads 45 volts. Find the current I*

Solution. $I_1 = \frac{45}{5} = 9$ Amps

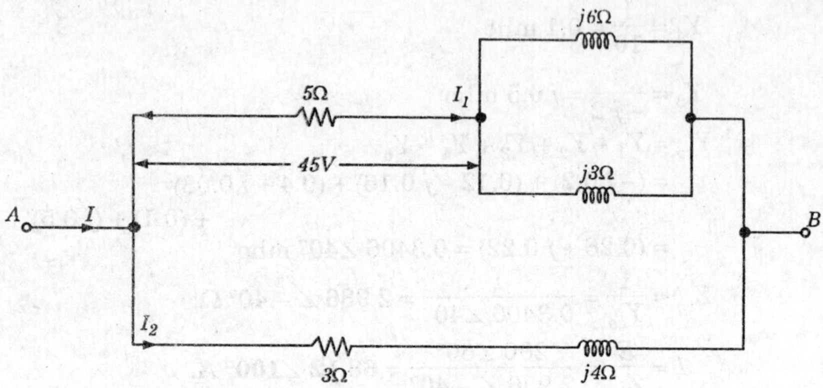

Fig. 6.21

Taking this as reference

$$I_1 = 9\angle 0^\circ \text{ A}$$

The parallel combination of $j\,6$ and $j\,3$ gives,

$$\frac{j\,6 \times j\,3}{j\,6 + j\,3} = j2 \text{ ohms}$$

$\therefore$ Voltage across $\quad AB = I_1\,(5 + j\,2)$

$$= 9\,(5 + j\,2) = (45 + j\,18) \text{ Volts}$$

$$I_2 = \frac{45 + j\,18}{3 + j\,4} = 8.28 - j\,5.04 \text{ A}$$

$\therefore$ $\quad I = 9 + 8.28 - j\,5.04$

$$= \mathbf{17.28 - j\,5.04 \text{ Amp.}}$$

Example 6.30. *In the circuit of Fig. 6.22, the readings of the voltmeters V, V_1 and V_2 are 141.4, 100 and 100 Volts respectively. The ammeter reads 10 A and the wattmeter 600 W. Find the ohmic values of the capacitive reactance X_C and the resistor R in parallel with it.*

Solution. We know $W = V_2 \cdot I \cdot \cos\theta$

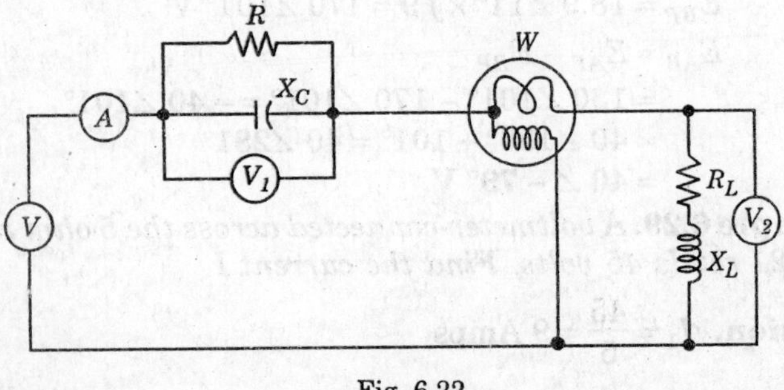

Fig. 6.22

where θ is the phase angle between V_2 and I. This is the power factor angle of the R_L and X_L coil.

$$\cos\theta = \frac{W}{V_2 I} = \frac{600}{100.10} = 0.6 \text{ (lag)}$$

I lags V_2 by 53.1°

By Kirchhoff's Voltage law,

$$V = V_1 + V_2$$

The phasors must form the sides of a right angle triangle (Fig. 6.23).

The current I lags behind V_2 by 53.1°

I can be split into two components I_R and I_C through R and C respectively.

The current I_R is in phase with V_1 and I_C leading V_1 by 90°

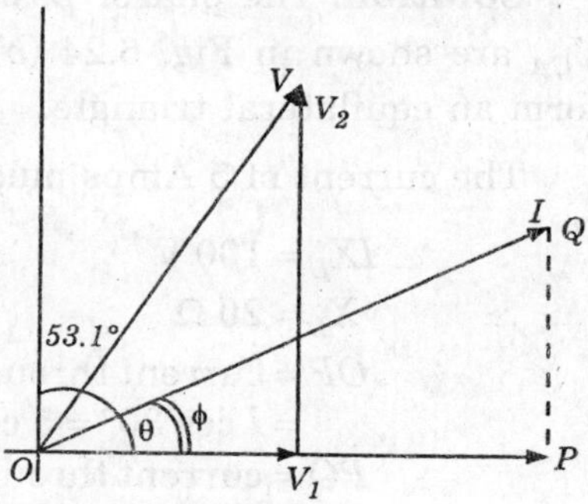

Fig. 6.23

$$OP = I_R = I\cos\phi$$
$$= I\cos 36.9° = 8 \text{ amps.}$$
$$PQ = I_C = I\sin\phi = 10\sin 36.9° = 6 \text{ Amps.}$$

$$\therefore \quad R = \frac{V_1}{I_R} = \frac{100}{8} = 12.5\ \Omega$$

$$X_C = \frac{V_1}{I_C} = \frac{100}{6} = \mathbf{16.7\ \Omega.}$$

Example 6.31. *Given that the voltages V_{AB} and V_{BC} in the circuit of Fig. 6.24 (a) are 100 volts each, find the values of R, L and C in the circuit and the power consumed. The line current is 5 Amps.*

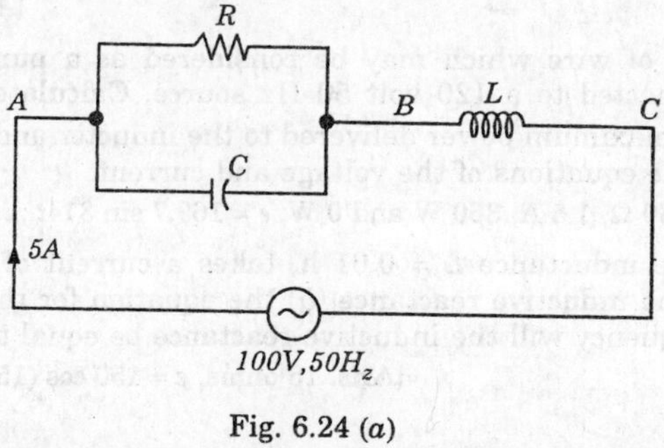

Fig. 6.24 (a)

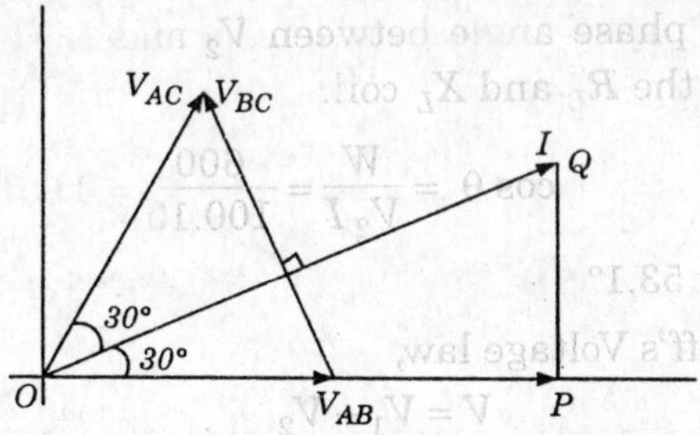

Fig. 6.24 (b)

Solution. The phasor positions of the voltages V_{AB}, V_{BC} and V_{CA} are shown in Fig. 6.24 (b). The three voltage phasors must form an equilateral triangle.

The current of 5 Amps must lag V_{BC} by 90°

$$IX_L = 100 \text{ V}$$

$$\therefore \quad X_L = 20\ \Omega$$

$$OP = \text{current through } R$$

$$= I \cos 30° = 5 \cos 30° = 4.33 \text{ A.}$$

$$PQ = \text{current through } C = I \sin 30° = 2.5 \text{ A.}$$

$$L = \frac{20}{\omega} = \frac{20}{314} = 63.7 \text{ mh}$$

$$R = \frac{100}{4.33} = 23\ \Omega$$

$$X_C = \frac{100}{2.5} = 40\ \Omega$$

$$C = \frac{1}{314 \times 40} = \mathbf{79.6\ \mu f.}$$

EXERCISES

6.1. A voltage $e = 340 \sin 314t$ is applied to a resistor and the current is $i = 42.5 \sin 314t$. Find the ohmic value of the resistor and the power consumed.

[**Ans.** 8 Ω, 7225 W]

6.2. A coil of wire which may be considered as a pure inductance of 0.225 h is connected to a 120 volt 50 Hz source. Calculate (*a*) X_L, (*b*) the current (*c*) the maximum power delivered to the inductor and (*d*) the average power. Write the equations of the voltage and current.

[**Ans.** 80 Ω, 1.5 A, 360 W and 0 W; $e = 169.7 \sin 314t$; $i = -2.12 \cos 314t$]

6.3. A pure inductance L = 0.01 h, takes a current of $i = 10 \cos 1500t$. Calculate (*a*) the inductive reactance (*b*) the equation for the voltage across it. At what frequency will the inductive reactance be equal to 40 ohms ?

[**Ans.** 15 ohms, $e = 150 \cos (1500t + 90°)$; 637 Hz]

6.4. In a series *RL* circuit $R = 15\ \Omega$ and $L = 0.1$ h, the voltage across the inductance is $e_L = 25 \sin 200t$. Find (*a*) the total voltage, (*b*) the current (*c*) the power factor angle (*d*) the power factor (*e*) power and (*f*) the impedance.

[**Ans.** $i = 1.25 \sin (200t - 90)$; $\theta = 53.1°$ (lag) ;
p.f. = 0.6 (lag) ; $e = 31.25 \sin (200t - 39.9°)$;
Power = 11.72 watts ; $Z = 25 \angle 53.1°\ \Omega$]

6.5. A resistor *R* of 8 ohms and an unknown capacitor *C* are in series. If $e_R = 34 \sin (2000t + 45°)$ and the current leads the applied voltage by 60°, find the value of *C*. [**Ans.** 36 μ *f*]

6.6. An *RL* circuit takes a current of 9 amperes lagging behind the 288 volts supply by 25°. Calculate (*a*) the power factor, (*b*) the impedance (*c*) the power, (*d*) resistance and (*e*) inductive reactance of the circuit.

[**Ans.** 0.906, 32 Ω, 2348 W, 29 Ω, 13.5 Ω]

6.7. In the circuit of Fig. 6.25, $E = 100$ V and $I = 25$ amps and the two are in phase. Find X_L. [**Ans.** 40 ohms]

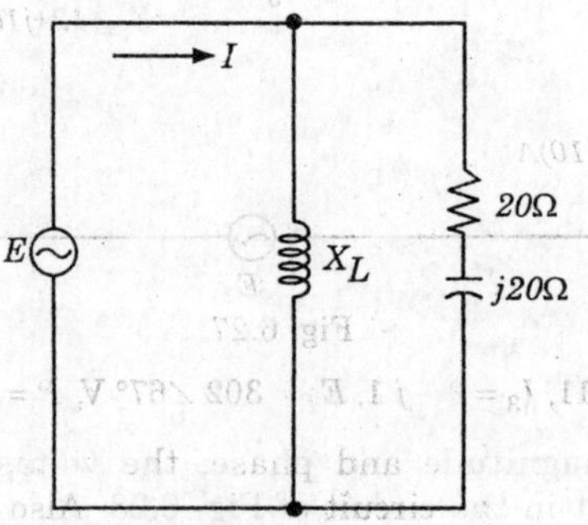

Fig. 6.25

6.8. In the circuit of Fig. 6.26, the effective voltage between points *A* and *B* is 50 volts. Find the values of *E* and *I*. [**Ans.** $E = 10.38$ V, $I = 19.54$ A]

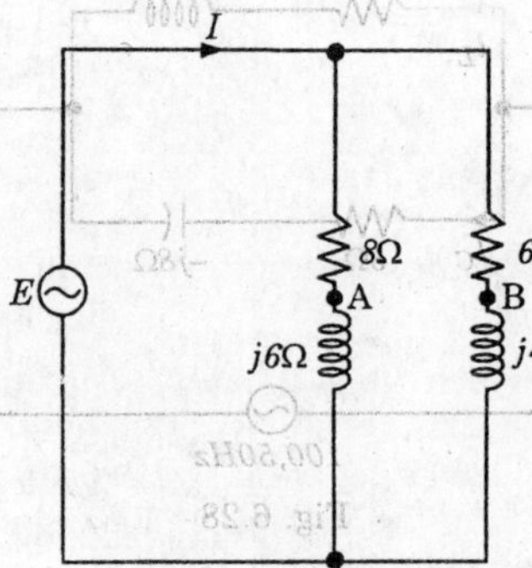

Fig. 6.2

(Assume $E = 100$ V and find E_{AB}. Then for $E_{AB} = 50$ V ; $E = \dfrac{50}{E_{AB}} \times 100$)

6.9. A 50 Hz A.C. voltage expressed in complex form with respect to some reference has the value $(3 + j\,4)$ volts. Find the instantaneous value of this voltage as a function of time. If the above voltage produces a current of $(1 + j1)$ amps in a circuit with respect to the same reference, find the following (*a*) power factor (*b*) impedance of the circuit (*c*) real and reactive powers.

[Ans. $5\sqrt{2}\sin(314t + 53.1°)$ 0.99, 3.54 ohms, ; 7 W, 0.99 VAr.]

6.10. For the circuit of Fig. 6.27, find the total impedance. Determine the currents in the various elements, the total applied voltage, power and power factor.

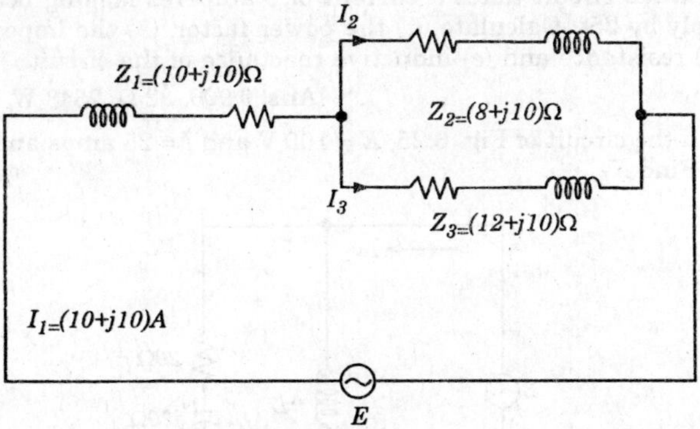

Fig. 6.27

[Ans. $I_2 = 1 + j\,11$, $I_3 = 9 - j\,1$, $E_T = 302\,\angle 67°$ V, $P = 3960$ W, p.f. = 0.927 lag]

6.11. Find in magnitude and phase, the voltage across and current through each element in the circuit of Fig. 6.28. Also find the total current, power and power factor of the circuit. Draw a phasor diagram showing all quantities.

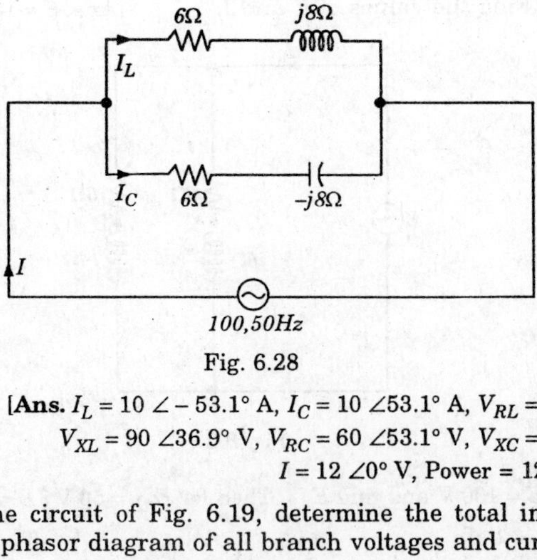

Fig. 6.28

[Ans. $I_L = 10\,\angle -53.1°$ A, $I_C = 10\,\angle 53.1°$ A, $V_{RL} = 60\,\angle -53.1°$ V
$V_{XL} = 90\,\angle 36.9°$ V, $V_{RC} = 60\,\angle 53.1°$ V, $V_{XC} = 80\,\angle -36.9°$ V
$I = 12\,\angle 0°$ V, Power = 1200 W, p.f. = 1]

6.12. For the circuit of Fig. 6.19, determine the total impedance and current. Draw a phasor diagram of all branch voltages and currents.

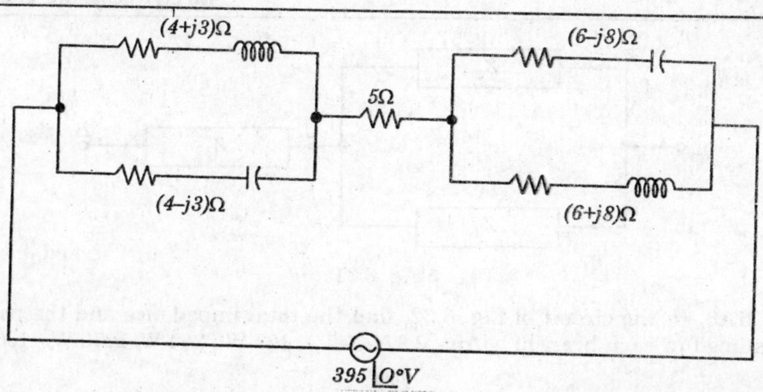

Fig. 6.29 [Ans. 16.4583 Ω, 24 A]

6.13. In a particular circuit, a voltage of 100 V at 25 Hz, produces 1.24 A. The same voltage at 100 Hz, produces 0.983 A. Draw the circuit and obtain the values of constants. [Ans. R = 79.8 Ω, L = 0.1 h]

6.14. A coil of power factor 0.8 is in series with a 100 μf capacitor and then connected to a 50 Hz supply. The potential difference across the coil is found equal to that across the capacitor by measurement. Find the resistance and inductance of the coil. [Ans. 25.5 ohms, 60.8 mh]

6.15. A voltage of 120 V at 50 Hz applied to a choking coil A, gives rise to a current of 8 Amperes and a power of 480 watts. The same source when applied to a coil B, gives I = 10 A, and P = 720 watts. What current and power will be taken when the source is applied to the coils in series.

[Ans. 4.45 A, 291 W]

6.16. Find the values of R and L so that $V_b = 2V_a$ and V_b and V_a are in quadrature, of the circuit shown in Fig. 6.30.

[Ans. R = 32 ohms L = 19 mh]

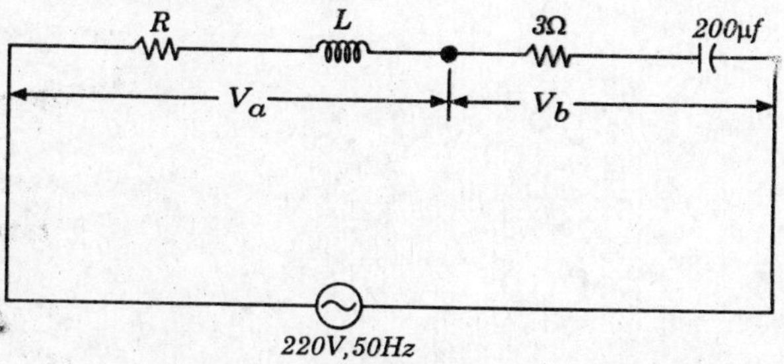

Fig. 6.30

6.17. When 240 volts is applied across AB, in the circuit of Fig. 6.31, the total power input is 4.2 kW and the current is 25 A. With E_{AC} as reference obtain expressions for I_2 and I_3, If $Z_1 = 10 + j\,15$ and $Z_2 = 10 + j\,20$.

[Ans. 9.76 ∠ – 63.4° A ; 34.74 ∠ – 246.5° A]

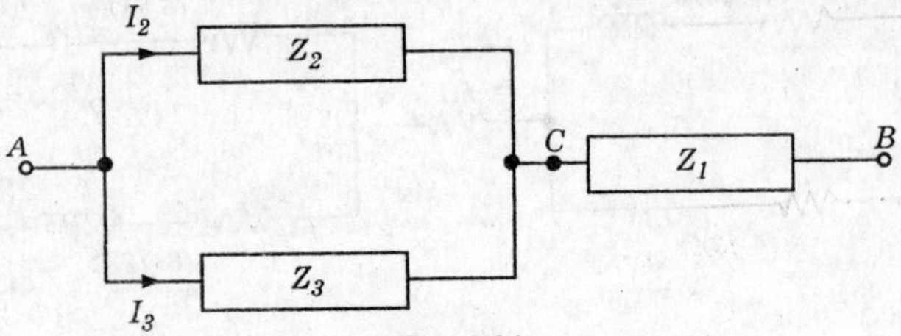

Fig. 6.31

6.18. In the circuit of Fig. 6.32, find the total impedance and the power consumed in each branch. [**Ans.** 2.97 ∠34° Ω, 127 W ; 254 W, 1270 W, 1136 W]

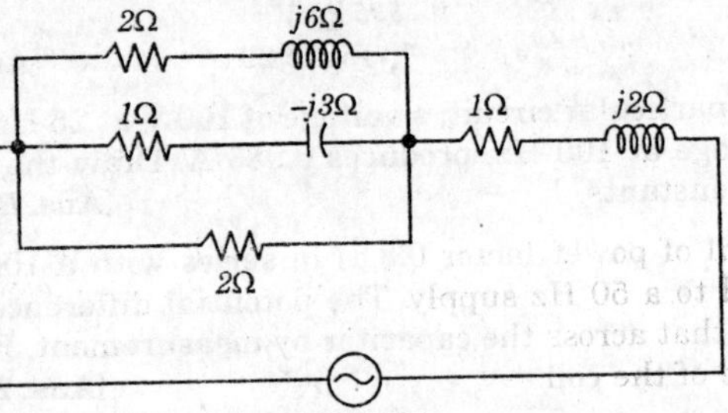

Fig. 6.32

SEVEN

RESONANCE IN A.C. CIRCUITS

An A.C. circuit is said to be in resonance if it behaves in effect like a purely resistive circuit. The total current drawn by the circuit is then in phase with the applied voltage and the power factor will then be unity. Thus at resonance, the equivalent complex impedance of the circuit has no j component.

Series Resonance

Consider the RLC series circuit of Fig. 7.1 (a). Its complex impedance

$$Z = R + j\,(X_L - X_C)$$

where $\quad X_L = \omega L \quad \text{and} \quad X_C = \dfrac{1}{\omega C}$

X_L and X_C have directly opposing actions. Also frequency affects X_L and X_C in different ways as in Fig. 7.1 (b).

$$|\,Z\,| = \sqrt{R^2 + (X_L - X_C)^2}$$

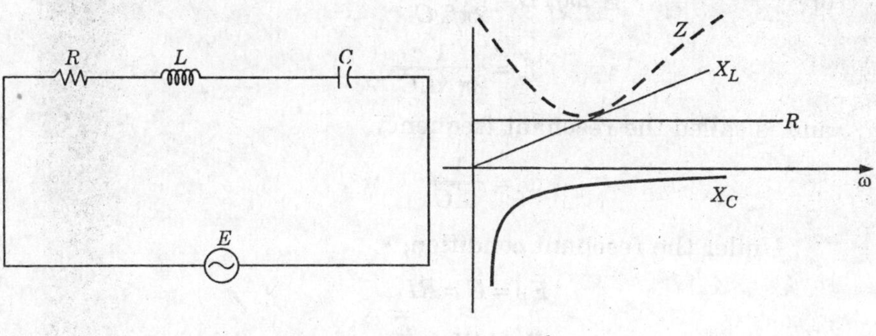

(a) (b)

Fig. 7.1

When $X_L = X_C$ $Z = R$.

The circuit then behaves like a pure resistor.

$$I = \frac{E}{Z} = \frac{E}{R}$$

The voltage drop across L and C are both equal and cancel each other.

$$E_L = IX_L$$
$$E_C = IX_C$$
$$E_R = E = IR$$

The phasor diagram under the resonant condition is shown in Fig. 7.2.

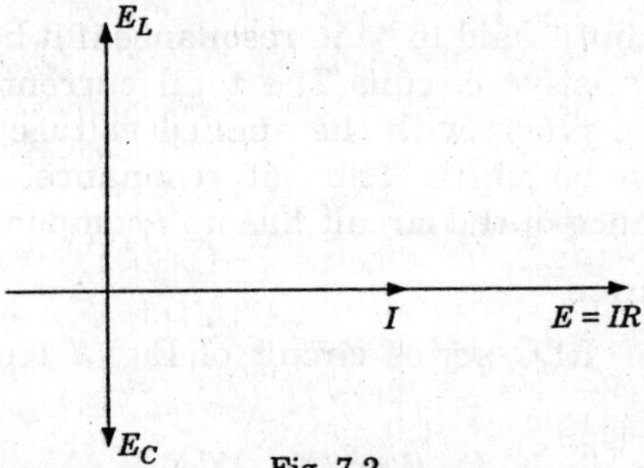

Fig. 7.2

To attain resonance, we may either (1) change the frequency of supply or (2) change the value of inductance L or (3) change the capacitance C.

Frequency Variation in RLC Series Circuit

If the supply frequency in the circuit of Fig. 7.1 (*a*) is varied, resonance occurs when $X_L = X_C$

or $$2\pi f_r L = \frac{1}{2\pi f_r C}$$

$\therefore$ $$f_r = \frac{1}{2\pi \sqrt{LC}}$$

and is called the resonant frequency.

$$\omega_r = \frac{1}{\sqrt{LC}}$$

Under the resonant condition,

$$E_R = E = RI$$

$$E_L = IX_L = \frac{E}{R} w_r L$$

$$= \frac{E}{R} \frac{L}{\sqrt{LC}} = \frac{E}{R}\sqrt{\frac{L}{C}} = E_C.$$

As the frequency of the applied voltage is varied, the current I in the circuit varies as shown in Fig. 7.3.

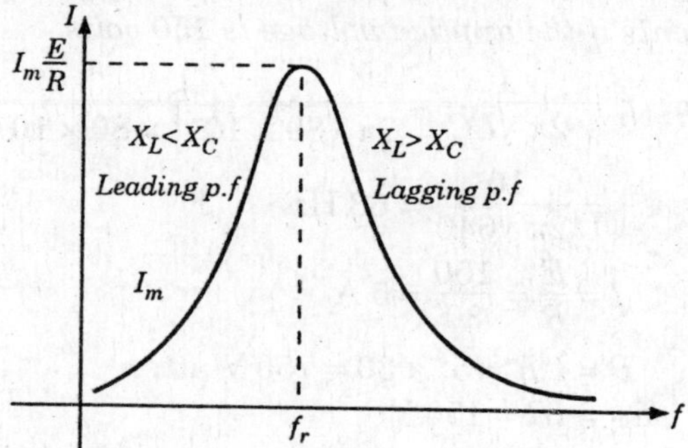

Fig. 7.3

The current is a maximum at the resonant frequency, f_r and is equal to $\frac{E}{R}$ Amps. At f_r, $X_L = X_C$ and the impedance is purely resistive. For frequencies less than f_r, $X_L < X_C$ and, therefore, $(X_L - X_C)$ will in effect be capacitive. The circuit behaves like an RC circuit with leading power factor. For frequencies greater than f_r, $X_L > X_C$, and the circuit behaves in effect like an *RL* circuit taking lagging current. If the value of resistance R in the circuit is increased, the maximum of the current becomes less. The frequency of resonance is not dependent on R. The curves in Fig. 7.4 show how the maximum current varies with the ohmic value of resistance. The current varies most sharply around f_r for low values of resistance. This sharpness is not visible when the resistance is

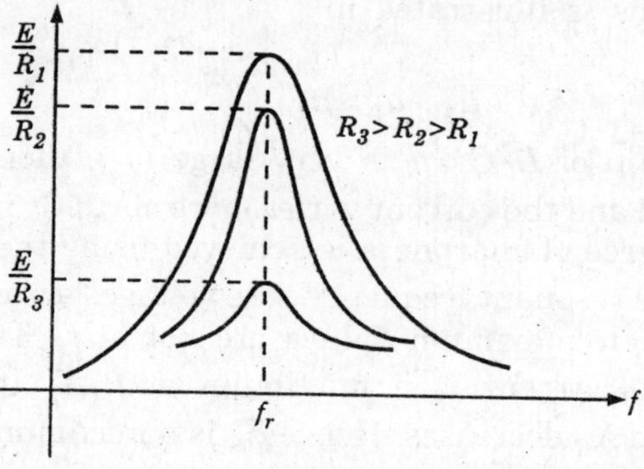

Fig. 7.4

increased. Hence a series resonant circuit is said to be sharply tuned for low R and broadly tuned for high R.

Example 7.1. *An RLC series circuit has $R = 30\ \Omega$, $L = 80\ mH$ and $C = 80\ \mu f$. Find the resonant frequency. Under resonant condition obtain the current, power, the voltage drops across the various elements if the applied voltage is 150 volts.*

Solution. $f_r = \dfrac{1}{2\pi\sqrt{LC}} = \dfrac{1}{2\pi\sqrt{80 \times 10^{-3} \times 80 \times 10^{-6}}}$

$$= \frac{10^4}{2\pi\sqrt{640}} = 63 \text{ Hz.}$$

$$I = \frac{E}{R} = \frac{150}{30} = 5 \text{ A}$$

$$P = I^2R = 5^2 \times 30 = 750 \text{ Watts.}$$

$$E_R = IR = 150 \text{ V}$$

$$E_L = IX_L = 5\ (2\pi \times 63 \times 80 \times 10^{-3}) = 158 \text{ V}$$

$$E_C = IX_C = 5\left(\frac{1}{2\pi \times 63 \times 80 \times 10^{-6}}\right)$$

$$= \frac{5 \times 10^6}{2\pi \times 63 \times 80} = \mathbf{158\ Volts.}$$

The resonant frequency remains the same if L and C are so changed that the product LC is constant. In the above problem the resonant frequency would be the same 63 Hz if $L = 100$ mH and $C = 64\ \mu$F or if $L = 40$ m and $C = 160\ \mu f$. The sharpness of tuning is also affected by the ratio of L to C, with the value of R and the product LC remaining the same. This is illustrated in Fig. 7.5.

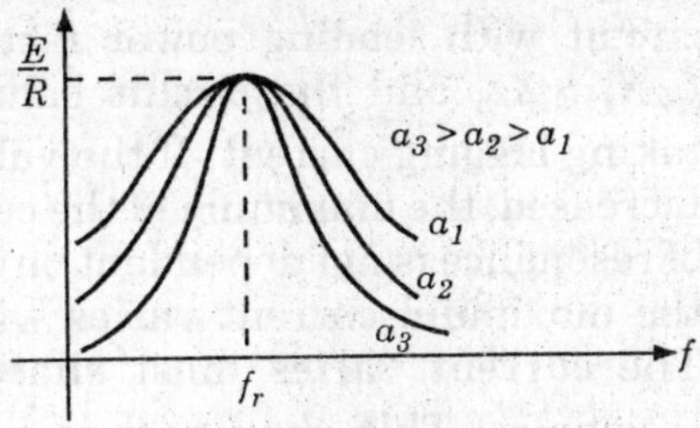

Fig. 7.5

$$a_3 > a_2 > a_1$$

If the ratio of $L/C = a$ is very large (a_3), then the curve is sharply tuned and the current varies more abruptly in the region of f_r. Proper degree of sharpness is achieved using these aspects for design. At the resonant frequency., the voltages across L and C are equal, but their maximum values are not at f_r. This is because although the current is a maximum at f_r, X_L increases with frequency and X_C decreases. Hence E_C is a maximum before f_r and E_L is a maximum after f_r (Fig. 7.6).

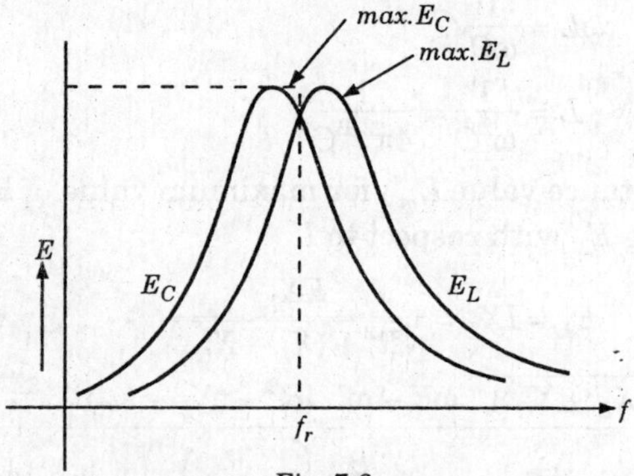

Fig. 7.6

Inductance Variation in Series R-L-C Circuits

When a constant voltage, constant frequency source is impressed across a series *RLC* circuit with the inductance varied, X_C will be constant. The value of X_L increases directly with the value of L. When the inductance is zero, the current is restricted by R and C alone. As X_L increases, the effective reactance $|X_L = X_C|$ reduces and the current increases. At $X_L = X_C$ the current is restricted by the resistance alone and is a maximum equal to $\frac{E}{R}$. This is the resonant condition. As L increases from zero, the impedance increases and the current falls to zero as L approaches infinity. Typical curves showing I, E_C and E_L with respect to L are shown in Fig. 7.7. As X_C is a constant, E_C is a maximum when the current is a maximum ; *i.e.* at resonance.

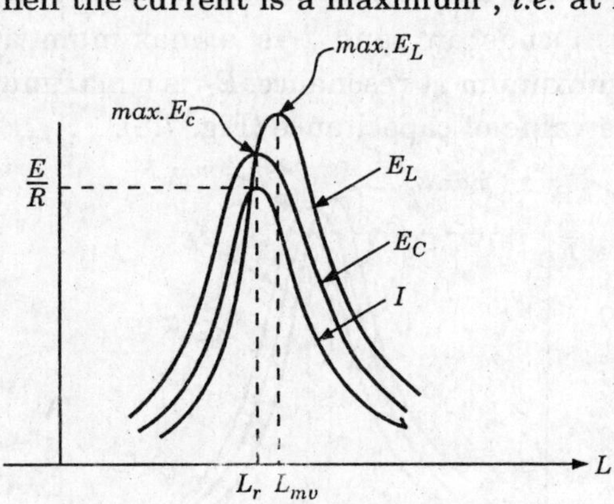

Fig. 7.7

L_r is the value of inductance at resonance and is given by

$$X_L = X_C$$

i.e. $$\omega L = \frac{1}{\omega C}$$

or $$L = \frac{1}{\omega^2 C} = \frac{1}{4\pi^2 f^2 C}$$

The inductance value L_{mV} for maximum value of E_L is given by differentiating E_L with respect to L

$$E_L = IX_L = \frac{EX_L}{\sqrt{R^2 + (X_L - X_C)^2}}$$

$$\frac{dE_L}{dX_L} = \frac{\sqrt{R^2 + (X_L - X_C^2)} \cdot \omega E - \omega L\,[R^2 + (X_L - X_C)^2]^{-3/2} \cdot 2\,(X_L - X_C)\,\omega}{R^2 + \left(\omega L - \dfrac{1}{\omega C}\right)^2}$$

$$= 0$$

or $$R^2 + (X_L - X_C)^2 = X_L\,(X_L - X_C)$$

$$R^2 + X_L{}^2 + X_C - 2X_LX_C = X_L{}^2 - X_LX_C$$

or $$L = C\,(R^2 + X_C{}^2) = L_{mv}$$

Capacitance Variation in RLC Series Circuit

When a series *R-L-C* circuit with constant frequency, constant voltage source has its capacitance alone varied, the following points may be noted (1) X_L is constant. (2) X_C varies inversely as the value of C. (3) When C is very small, X_C is very large and the current is very small. As C is increased, X_C decreases and when $X_C = X_L$, the current $I = E/R$ and is a maximum. As C approaches infinity, $X_C \to 0$ and the current is restricted by R and L.

As X_L is a constant and I is a maximum at resonance, $E_L = IX_L$ is a maximum at resonance. E_C is a maximum just before the resonance value of capacitance (Fig. 7.8).

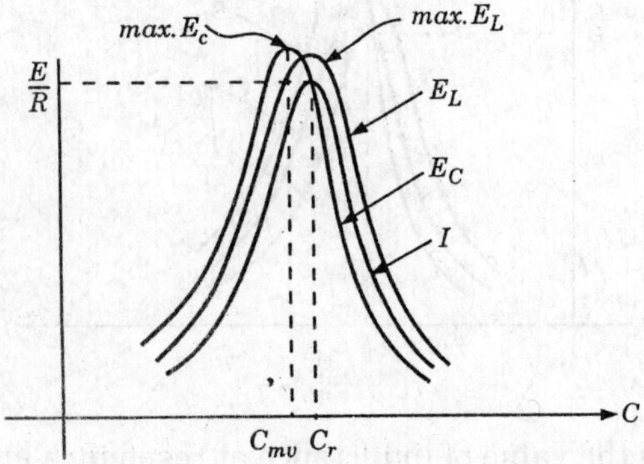

Fig. 7.8

As before $$C_r = \frac{1}{4\pi^2 f^2 L}$$

and C_{mv} (for maximum E_C) may be obtained by differentiating E_C

$$\therefore \quad C_{mv} = \frac{1}{R^2 + X_L^2}$$

Selectivity-Q-Half Power Frequencies-Bandwidth

The current V_S frequency curve of an *RLC* series circuit is symmetrical about the resonance frequency. At resonant frequency $X_L = X_C$ and the equivalent reactance $(X_L - X_C)$ is zero and the current $I = E/R$. There will be two frequencies f_1 and f_2 equally spaced to either side of the resonant frequency f_r at which the equivalent reactance is equal to the resistance itself (Fig. 7.9). Under this condition

$$Z = \sqrt{R^2 + (X_L - X_C)^2} = \sqrt{R^2 + R^2} = \sqrt{2}R$$

$$I = \frac{E}{\sqrt{2}R} \text{ A}$$

Power $$P = I^2 R = \left(\frac{E}{\sqrt{2}R}\right)^2 R = \frac{E^2}{2R}$$

which is half the power at resonance. Obviously f_1 and f_2 are called the lower and upper half-power frequencies respectively.

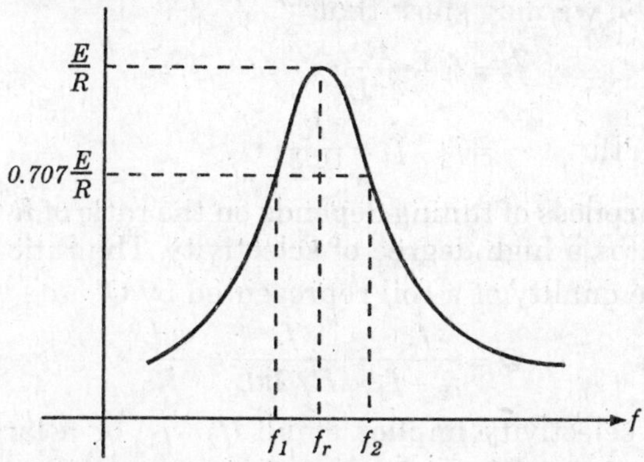

Fig. 7.9

The value $(f_2 - f_1)$ is called bandwidth of the circuit. The bandwidth is an indication of the sharpness of tuning. The half-power frequencies are determined by analysing the following equation.

$$|X_L - X_C| = R \text{ at } f_1 \text{ and } f_2.$$

At the lower half power frequency $X_C > X_L$

$$\therefore \quad \omega_1 L - \frac{1}{\omega_1 C} = -R$$

or $$\omega_1^2 LC - 1 = -\omega_1 RC$$

$$\omega_1^2 LC + \omega_1 RC - 1 = 0$$

$$\omega_1 = \frac{-RC \pm \sqrt{R^2C^2 + 4LC}}{2LC}$$

$$= \frac{-R}{2L} \pm \sqrt{\left(\frac{R}{2L}\right)^2 + \frac{1}{LC}}$$

Only + sign is applicable.

Usually $\frac{R}{2L}$ is small compared to $\frac{1}{LC}$ so that $\left(\frac{R}{2L}\right)^2$ can be neglected in comparison with the latter.

$$\therefore \quad \omega_1 \cong \frac{-R}{2L} + \sqrt{\frac{1}{LC}}$$

or $$f_1 = -\frac{R}{4\pi L} + f_r \qquad \left(\text{Since } \frac{1}{2\pi\sqrt{LC}} = f_r\right)$$

$$\therefore \quad f_1 = f_r - \frac{R}{4\pi L}$$

Similarly, we may show that

$$f_2 = f_r + \frac{R}{4\pi L}$$

Bandwidth $$= f_2 - f_1 = \frac{R}{2\pi L}$$

The sharpness of tuning depends on the ratio of R to L, a small ratio indicates a high degree of selectivity. The ratio f_r to $(f_2 - f_1)$ is called the quality of a coil represented by Q.

$$Q = \frac{f_r}{f_2 - f_1} = \frac{f_r}{R/2\pi L} = \frac{\omega_r L}{R}$$

A good selectivity implies small $(f_2 - f_1)$ or a large Q, which means that the coil has a large inductive reactance compared to its resistance.

Q can also be expressed in terms of R, L and C by substituting for ω

$$Q = \frac{\omega_r L}{R} = \frac{\frac{1}{\sqrt{LC}} L}{R} = \frac{1}{R}\sqrt{\frac{L}{C}}$$

The Q factor of a circuit can also be defined as

$$Q = 2\pi \times \frac{\text{Maximum energy stored}}{\text{Energy dissipated per cycle}}$$

In terms of inductance

$$Q = 2\pi \frac{\frac{1}{2} LIm^2}{\frac{I_m^2}{2} R/f} = \frac{\omega L}{R}$$

In terms of the capacitance,

$$Q = 2\pi \frac{\frac{1}{2} CEm^2}{\frac{I_m^2}{2} R/f} = \frac{1}{\omega CR}$$

Example 7.2. *A series RLC circuit with R = 10 ohms, L = 10 mh, and C = 1 Mf has an applied voltage of 200 V at resonant frequency. Calculate the resonant frequency, the current in the circuit and the voltages across the elements at resonance. Find also the quality factor and bandwidth.*

Solution. $f_r = \frac{1}{2\pi\sqrt{LC}} = \frac{1}{2\pi\sqrt{10 \times 10^{-3} \times 1 \times 10^{-6}}}$

$$= \frac{10^4}{2\pi} = 1592 \text{ Hz.}$$

At resonance $X_L = X_C$

Hence $Z = R + j(X_L - X_C) = R$

$$I = \frac{E}{R} = \frac{200}{10} = 20 \text{ A}$$

$$E_R = IR = E = 200 \text{ V}$$

$$E_L = IX_L = I\omega_r L = 20 \times 10^4 \times 1 \times 10^3 = 2000 \text{ V}$$

$$E_C = IX_C = IX_L = 2000 \text{ Volts}$$

$$Q = \frac{\omega_r L}{R} = \frac{10^4 \times 10 \times 10^{-3}}{10} = 10$$

$$= \frac{f_r}{f_2 - f_1}$$

$\therefore$ Bandwidth $= f_2 - f_1 = \frac{f_r}{Q} = \frac{1592}{10} = 159.2$ Hz.

Example 7.3. *Show that in a series R-L-C circuit, $f_1 f_2 = fr^2$ where f_r is the resonant frequency and f_1, f_2 are the half power frequencies.*

Solution. $\omega_1 = -\frac{R}{2L} + \sqrt{\left(\frac{R}{2L}\right)^2 + \frac{1}{LC}}$

$$\omega_2 = \frac{R}{2L} + \sqrt{\left(\frac{R}{2L}\right)^2 + \frac{1}{LC}}$$

$$\therefore \quad \omega_1\omega_2 = -\left(\frac{R}{2L}\right)^2 + \left(\frac{R}{2L}\right)^2 + \frac{1}{LC}$$

$$= \frac{1}{LC} = \left(\frac{1}{\sqrt{LC}}\right)^2 = \omega_r^2$$

Hence $\quad f_1 f_2 = f_r^2$

Example 7.4. *A series RLC circuit has R = 5 ohms, L = 40 mH and C = 1 μf. Calculate (a) the Q of the circuit (b) the separation between half power frequencies (c) the resonant frequency and (d) the half power frequencies f_1 and f_2.*

Solution. (*a*) $Q = \frac{1}{R}\sqrt{\frac{L}{C}}$

$$= \frac{1}{5}\sqrt{\frac{40 \times 10^{-3}}{1 \times 10^{-6}}} = 40$$

(*b*) $$f_2 - f_1 = \frac{R}{2\pi L} = \frac{5}{2\pi \times 40 \times 10^{-3}} = 20 \text{ Hz}$$

(*c*) $$f_r = Q\,(f_2 - f_1) = 40 \times 20 = 80 \text{ Hz}$$

(*d*) $$f_1 = 900 - \frac{20}{2} = 790 \text{ Hz}$$

$$f_2 = 800 + \frac{20}{2} = 810 \text{ Hz.}$$

Example 7.5. *A series circuit consisting of a 12-ohm resistor, a 84.4 μf capacitor and a variable inductor is connected to a 100 volt 50 Hz source. (a) For the condition of resonance, determine the inductance current and voltage drop across the inductor, (b) Determine the inductance current and the voltage drop across the inductor when this voltage drop is a maximum.*

Solution.

(*a*) For resonance $X_L = X_C$

$$\omega L = \frac{1}{\omega C}$$

$$L = \frac{1}{\omega^2 C} = \frac{1}{(2\pi \times 50)^2 \times 84.4 \times 10^{-6}}$$

$$= \frac{10^6}{2\pi^2 \times 2500 \times 84.4} = 0.12 \text{ h}$$

$$I = \frac{E}{R} = \frac{100}{2} = 8.33 \text{ amps.}$$

$$E_L = IX_L = \frac{100}{12} \times 2 \times 50 \times 0.12 = 314 \text{ volts.}$$

(*b*) E_L is a maximum when

$$L = C\,(R^2 + X_C^{\,2})$$

$$X_C = \frac{10^6}{2 \times 50 \times 84.4 \times \pi} = 37.7 \text{ ohms}$$

$$L = C\,(R^2 + X_C^{\,2}) = 84.4 \times 10^{-6}\,[12^2 + 37.7^2]$$

$$= 0.132 \text{ H}$$

$$I = \frac{E}{\sqrt{R^2 + (X_L - X_C)^2}} = \frac{100}{\sqrt{12^2 + (41.5 - 37.7)^2}}$$

$$= 7.94 \text{ amps}$$

$$E_L = IX_L = 7.94 \times 41.5 = 330 \text{ volts.}$$

Example 7.6. *An impedance coil takes 144 watts at 0.6 lagging power factor. What values of capacitance and resistance should be connected in series with the coil if the power input to the latter is to remain unchanged and the overall circuit power factor is to be unity. The circuit is energized by a 120 volt 60 Hz source.*

Solution. When the coil alone is connected,

$$E \cdot I \cdot \cos\theta = 144$$

$$I = \frac{144}{120 \times 0.6} = 2 \text{ amps.}$$

$$\text{Impedance of coil} = \frac{E}{I} = \frac{120}{2} = 60 \text{ ohms}$$

$$= 60\,(0.6 + j\,0.8) = (36 + j\,48) \text{ ohms.}$$

After connecting, an R-C combination in series, the power factor must be unity. Therefore

$$X_C = 48$$

or $$C = \frac{1}{2\pi f \times 48} = \frac{1}{2\pi \times 60 \times 48} = 55.3\ \mu\text{F}$$

The power to the coil should still be 144 watts

i.e. $$I^2 \times 36 = 144$$

or $$I = 2 \text{ amps}$$

$$Z = \frac{120}{2} = 60 \text{ ohms} \qquad \text{(at unity p.f.)}$$

$\therefore$ The new resistance to be added

$$= 60 - 36 = \mathbf{24 \text{ ohms.}}$$

Example 7.7. *The Q factor of a series resonant circuit resonant at 50 Hz is 1.5. If this circuit is supplied with a voltage of constant magnitude and variable frequency, find the frequency at which the capacitor voltage in the circuit is a maximum.*

Solution. The expression for current

$$I = \frac{E}{\sqrt{R^2 + (X_L - X_C)^2}}$$

$$E_C = IX_C = \frac{EX_C}{\sqrt{R^2 + (X_L - X_C)^2}}$$

$$= \frac{E}{\omega C \sqrt{R^2 + (\omega L - 1/\omega C)^2}}$$

$$E_C{}^2 = \frac{E^2}{R^2C^2\omega^2 + \omega^2C^2\,(\omega L - 1/\omega C)^2}$$

For E_C to be a maximum, $E_C{}^2$ is also a maximum. The frequency condition for this may be obtained by differentiating $E_C{}^2$ with respect to ω, or by differentiating the denominator alone with respect to ω.

$$\therefore\ 2R^2\omega C^2 + 2\omega C^2\left(\omega L - \frac{1}{\omega C}\right)^2 + 2\omega^2 C^2\left(\omega L - \frac{1}{\omega C}\right)\left(1 + \frac{1}{\omega^2 C}\right) = 0$$

or $$4L^2C^2\omega^2 = 2\,(LC - R^2C^2)$$

$$\omega^2 = \frac{1}{2}\left[\frac{1}{LC} - \left(\frac{R}{L}\right)^2\right] = \frac{\omega_r{}^2}{2}\left[1 - \frac{1}{Q^2}\right]$$

$$\therefore\quad \omega = \omega_r \sqrt{\frac{Q^2 - 1}{2Q^2}}$$

$$\omega = 2\pi \times 50 \sqrt{\frac{1.5^2 - 1}{2 \times 1.5^2}}$$

$$= 2\pi \times 50 \sqrt{\frac{1.25}{4.5}}$$

$$\therefore\quad f = 50 \sqrt{\frac{1.25}{4.5}} = 26.4 \text{ Hz.}$$

Parallel Resonance

The parallel circuit of Fig. 7.10, consisting of branches with single pure elements is an ideal circuit.

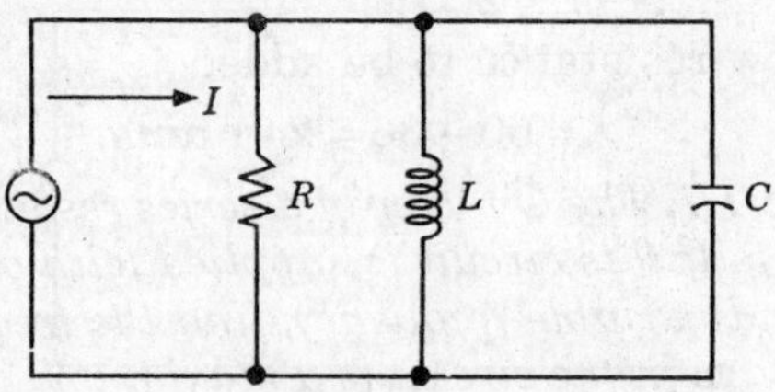

Fig. 7.10

When the overall power factor of the circuit (cosine of the phase angle between E and I) is unity, the circuit is resonant. This will be achieved when I_L and I_C are equal and cancel each other. This will be true when

$X_L = X_C$. This condition is similar to *R-L-C* series circuits.

Two Branch Parallel Circuits

Consider the circuit of Fig. 7.11 (*a*). For this circuit to be in resonance, *i.e.* for E and I to be in phase, the components BP and

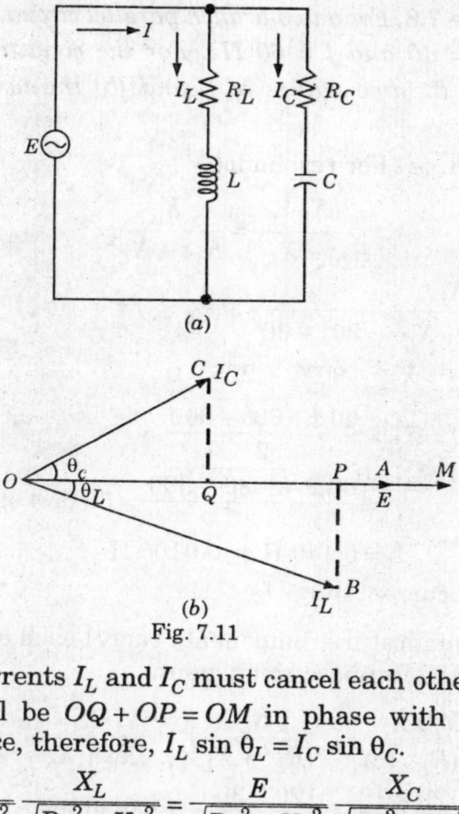

Fig. 7.11

CQ of the two currents I_L and I_C must cancel each other. Then the total current will be $OQ + OP = OM$ in phase with the voltage OA. For resonance, therefore, $I_L \sin \theta_L = I_C \sin \theta_C$.

i.e.
$$\frac{E}{\sqrt{R_L^2 + X_L^2}} \frac{X_L}{\sqrt{R_L^2 + X_L^2}} = \frac{E}{\sqrt{R_C^2 + X_C^2}} \frac{X_C}{\sqrt{R_C^2 + X_C^2}}$$

or
$$\frac{X_L}{R_L^2 + X_L^2} = \frac{X_C}{R_C^2 + X_C^2}$$

Which is the same as

$$\frac{\omega L}{R_L^2 + \omega^2 L^2} = \frac{\omega C}{1 + \omega^2 C^2 R_C^2}$$

or the frequency of resonance

$$\omega_r = \frac{1}{\sqrt{LC}} \sqrt{\frac{R_L{}^2 C - L}{R_C{}^2 C} - L}$$

frequency of resonance

$$f_r = \frac{1}{2\pi\sqrt{LC}} \sqrt{\frac{R_L{}^2 C - L}{R_C{}^2 C - L}}$$

If $R_L = R_C$, then the frequency of resonance is the same as for a series *R-L-C* circuit.

Example 7.8. *For a two-branch parallel circuit $R_L = 15$, $R_C = 30$, $X_C = 30$, $E = 10$ and $f = 60$ Hz. For the condition of resonance, calculate (a) the two values of L and (b) the two values of total current.*

Solution. (*a*) For resonance

$$\frac{X_L}{R_L{}^2 + X_L{}^2} = \frac{X_C}{R_C{}^2 + X_C{}^2}$$

i.e. $$\frac{X_L}{15^2 + X_L{}^2} = \frac{30}{30^2 + 30^2} = \frac{1}{60}$$

$\therefore$ $$X_L{}^2 - 60X_L + 225 = 0$$

$$X_L = \frac{60 \pm \sqrt{60^2 - 900}}{2}$$

$$= \frac{60 \pm \sqrt{3630 - 900}}{2} = 56 \text{ or } 4 \text{ ohms}$$

Hence $L = 0.149$ H *or* 0.0106 H

(*b*) Total current $= I_L + I_C$

As the quadrature components cancel each other, it is enough if we know the in phase components.

$$I = \frac{E}{\sqrt{R_L{}^2 + X_L{}^2}} \cdot \frac{R_L}{\sqrt{R_L{}^2 + X_L{}^2}} + \frac{E}{\sqrt{R_C + X_C{}^2}} \cdot \frac{R_C}{\sqrt{R_C{}^2 + X_C{}^2}}$$

$$= \frac{120 \times 15}{15^2 + 56^2} + \frac{120 \times 30}{30^2 + 30^2} = 2.536 \text{ amps.}$$

or $$I = \frac{120 \times 15}{15^2 + 4^2} + \frac{120 \times 30}{30^2 + 30^2} = 9.47 \text{ amps.}$$

Resistance Variation in Two-branch Parallel Circuits

Unlike the *R-L-C* series circuit, it is often possible to adjust a two-branch parallel circuit to resonance by varying R_L or R_C. This is evident on a close look at the condition for resonance.

$$\frac{X_L}{R_L{}^2 + X_L{}^2} = \frac{X_C}{R_C{}^2 + X_C{}^2}$$

$$(R_L{}^2 + X_L{}^2)\,X_C = X_L\,(R_C{}^2 + X_C{}^2)$$

Therefore $$R_L = \sqrt{\frac{X_L}{X_C} R_C{}^2 + X_L X_C - X_L{}^2}$$

$$R_C = \sqrt{\frac{X_C}{X_L} R_L + X_L X_C - X_C{}^2}$$

Parallel Resonance at All Frequencies

It was shown previously that a two branch parallel circuit with $R_L = R_C$ is resonant at $f = \frac{1}{2\pi\sqrt{LC}}$ just as in a series *R-L-C* circuit.

Further, if $R_L = R_C = \sqrt{\frac{L}{C}}$ the parallel circuit will resonate at all frequencies as shown below. At resonance

$$\frac{\omega L}{R_L{}^2 + \omega^2 L^2} = \frac{\omega C}{1 + \omega^2 C^2 R_C{}^2}$$

This becomes

$$\omega^2 C^2 R_C{}^2 L + L = C R_L{}^2 + \omega^2 L^2 C$$

Dividing both sides by LC,

$$\omega^2 C R_C{}^2 + \frac{1}{C} = \omega^2 L + \frac{R_L{}^2}{L}$$

(capacitive branch) (inductive branch)

The left hand side contains C term and applies to the capacitive branch. Likewise, the right hand side applies to the inductive branch.

If $$R_C{}^2 = R_L{}^2 = \sqrt{\frac{L}{C}}$$

then, $$\omega^2 C \frac{L}{C} + \frac{1}{C} = \omega^2 L + \frac{L}{CL}$$

$$\omega^2 L + \frac{1}{C} = \omega^2 L + \frac{1}{C}$$

(capacitive branch) (inductive branch)

Both sides of the equality sign are identical and each branch is affected identically by a change in the frequency. The resonance condition is therefore satisfied for all frequencies.

Example 7.9. *Find the resonant frequency for the circuit of Fig. 7.12. If R_C is increased, find its maximum value for which there is a resonant frequency.*

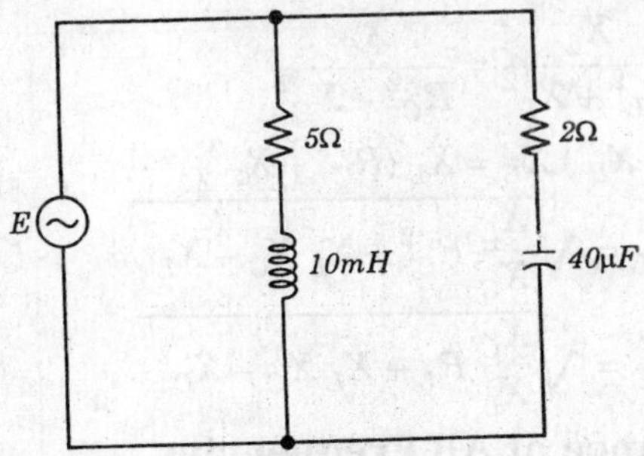

Fig. 7.12

Solution.

$$f_r = \frac{1}{2\pi\sqrt{LC}}\sqrt{\frac{CR_L^2 - L}{CR_C^2 - L}}$$

$$= \frac{1}{2\pi\sqrt{10\times10^{-3}\times40\times10^{-6}}}\times\sqrt{\frac{40\times10^{-6}\times5^2 - 10\times10^{-3}}{40\times10^{-6}\times2^2 - 10\times10^{-3}}}$$

$$= \mathbf{240\ Hz.}$$

If R_L is increased, keeping the other parameters constant, the numerator within the radical sign is

$$CR_L^2 - L = -0.009$$

The radical will have a real root, only if the denominator is also negative. The denominator will be negative if $CR_C^2 < L$

or $$R_C^2 < \frac{L}{C} < \frac{10\times10^{-3}}{40\times10^{-6}} < 250$$

or $$R_C < 15.8 \text{ ohms}$$

The maximum value of R_C is 15.8 ohms.

Tuned Circuits

Series-parallel circuits can be adjusted to act selectively to one or more frequencies and to reject another (or others). That is the circuit offers low impedance (high current) to the selected frequency and high impedance, almost infinite to other frequencies. Such combination of networks are called filters. Fig. 7.13 shows a few combinations used for tuning purposes. The following points are made use of for proper design of filters.

1. When a series circuit is in resonance, its impedance is low, and the current is high.

2. When a parallel circuit is tuned to resonance, its impedance is high and the current is low.

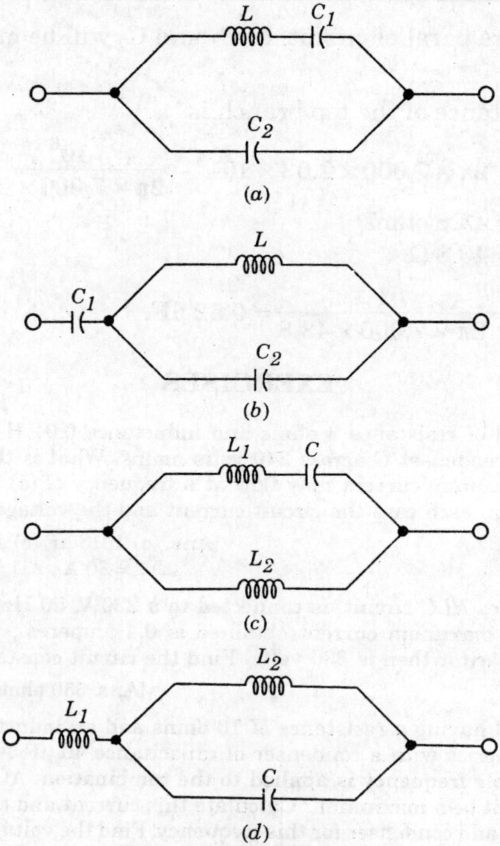

Fig. 7.13

To pass a frequency f_p, the circuit of Fig. 7.13 (*a*) must be tuned to series resonance of L and C_1 at f_p.

To block a frequency f_b, the combination L, C_1 and C_2 must be tuned to parallel resonance at f_b.

Example 7.10. *The circuit of Fig. 7.13 (a) has $C_1 = 0.5\ \mu F$. It has to pass a 5,000 Hz wave and block a 7,000 Hz wave, determine the values of L and C_2*

Solution. The series L and C_1 must be tuned to be resonant at 5,000 Hz.

$$\therefore \qquad 5{,}000 = \frac{1}{2\pi\sqrt{LC_1}} = \frac{1}{2\pi\sqrt{L \times 0.5 \times 10^{-6}}}$$

$$L = 2.03 \text{ mH}$$

The entire parallel circuit, L, C_1 and C_2 will be made resonant to 7,000 Hz.

The reactance of the top branch is

$$= 2\pi \times 7{,}000 \times 2.03 \times 10^{-3} - \frac{10^6}{2\pi \times 7{,}000 \times 0.5}$$

$$= 43.8 \text{ ohms}$$

$$X_{C_2} = 43.8\ \Omega$$

$$\therefore \quad C_2 = \frac{1}{2\pi \times 7{,}000 \times 43.8} = \mathbf{0.52\ \mu F.}$$

EXERCISES

7.1. A coil of resistance 3 ohms and inductance 0.01 H is connected in series with a condenser C across 240 volts mains. What is the value of C in order that maximum current may flow at a frequency of (*a*) 50, (*b*) 60 (*c*) 80 Hz ? (*d*) Find in each case the circuit current and the voltage across C.

[**Ans.** (*a*) 1013 μF (*b*) 704 μ*f* (C) 396 μF (*d*) I = 80 A ; 251 V, 302 V ; 402 V.]

7.2 A series RLC circuit, is connected to a 220 V, 50 Hz supply, when L is varied, the maximum current obtained is 0.4 amperes ; and the voltage across the capacitor then is 330 volts. Find the circuit constants.

[**Ans.** 550 ohms, 2.63 H, 3.9 μF]

7.3. A coil having a resistance of 10 ohms and an inductance of 0.4 H is connected in series with a condenser of capacitance 40 μF. A voltage of 2000 volts at variable frequency is applied to the combination. At what frequency will the current be a maximum ? Calculate this current and the voltage drops across the coil and condenser for this frequency. Find the voltage magnification at resonance. [**Ans.** 39.8 Hz, 20 A, 2010 V, 2000 V, 10]

7.4. A series RLC circuit has R = 5 ohms, L = 0.01 H, and C = 10 μ*f*. Calculate the resonant frequency, Q factor, and the half power frequencies f_1 and f_2. [503, 6.3, 463, 543]

7.5. A series RLC circuit has a Q of 80 and a bandwidth of 160 Hz. Calculate the resonant frequency and the two half power frequencies.

[**Ans.** 12,800; 12,720; 12,880]

7.6. An RLC series circuit is supplied with a constant voltage of variable frequency. Show that the voltage across the inductance is a maximum at a frequency given by

$$\omega = \frac{1}{\sqrt{LC}}\sqrt{\frac{2Q^2}{2Q^2 - 1}}$$

7.7. An RLC series circuit with R = 50 Ω, L = 5 mH and C = 20 μF has an applied voltage of 100 volts at a frequency. The frequency is varied until the voltage across the capacitance is a maximum. Find this frequency and the capacitor voltage.

7.8. Obtain the resonant frequency for the circuit of Fig. 7.14.

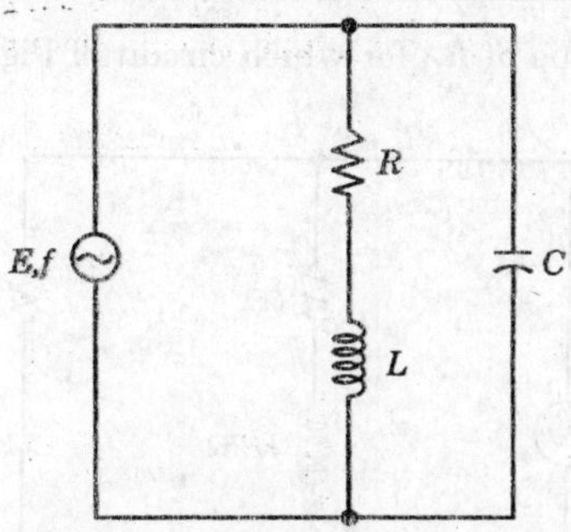

Fig. 7.14

7.9. If in problem 7.8, $L = 2$ mH and $C = 10\ \mu F$, find the value of R which will make the circuit resonant at 200 Hz. **[Ans. 139.17 ohms]**

7.10. What resistance in series with the capacitor of Problem 7.9 will make the circuit resonate at 1600 Hz. **[Ans. 12.1 ohms]**

7.11. Find the value of R_L for which the parallel circuit of Fig. 7.15 will be resonant. **[Ans. 24.5 ohms]**

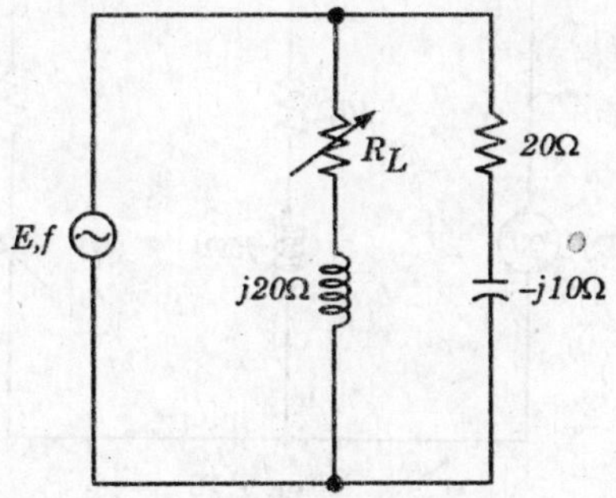

Fig. 7.15

7.12. A variable inductive reactance X_L is connected in parallel with a series combination of resistance R and capacitance reactance X_C. For resonance, derive an expression for X_L in terms of R and X_C. **[Ans. $(R^2 + X_C^2)/X_C$]**

7.13. At what value of X_L will the parallel circuit of Fig. 7.16 be resonant ? **[Ans. 16.6 Ω, 2.2 Ω]**

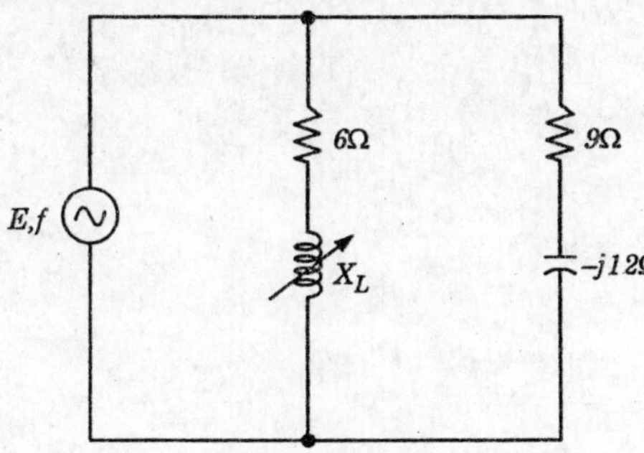

Fig. 7.16

7.14. Find the value of R_C for which circuit of Fig. 7.17 is in resonance.

[Ans. $R_C = 0$**]**

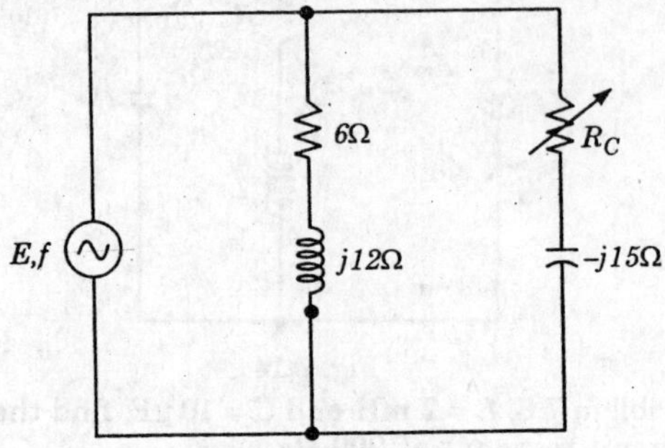

Fig. 7.17

7.15. Determine the value of the capacitance C in order that the circuit of Fig. 7.18 is resonant at 6366 Hz. **[Ans.** $X_C = 12.5\ \Omega$; $C = 2\ \mu F$**]**

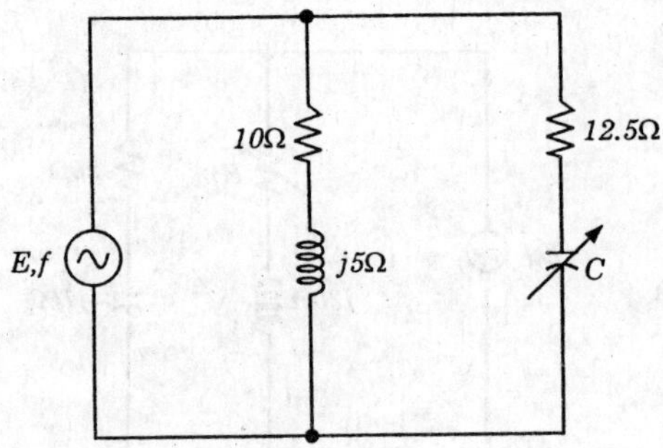

Fig. 7.18

EIGHT

A.C. NETWORK ANALYSIS — LOCUS DIAGRAM

As in D.C. circuits, A.C. circuits too could be analysed through Mesh and Node methods. These methods already discussed in Chapter 3 for D.C. circuits must now be modified to include A.C. sources and complex impedances.

Mesh (Loop) Current Method

As before, we may select loop currents and write the Kirchhoff's law voltage equations and put them in matrix form. For the circuit, of Fig. 8.1,

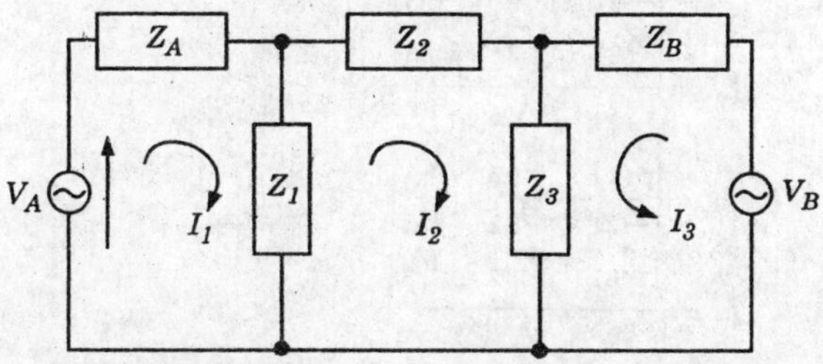

Fig. 8.1

we may write the matrix equation as

$$\begin{bmatrix} (Z_A+Z_1) & -Z_1 & 0 \\ -Z_1 & (Z_1+Z_2+Z_3) & Z_3 \\ 0 & Z_3 & (Z_B+Z_3) \end{bmatrix} = \begin{bmatrix} I_1 \\ I_2 \\ I_3 \end{bmatrix} = \begin{bmatrix} V_A \\ 0 \\ V_B \end{bmatrix}$$

The signs of the off diagonal terms of the impedance matrix is decided as before, *i.e.*, if the two currents in the two loops are in the same direction, it is positive, otherwise negative. The sign of the voltage entry is also decided as before. If there is a rise of voltage in the direction of the assumed current, we use a positive sign.

These equations can be solved for I_1, I_2 and I_3 by using Kramer's rule.

Consider the following general matrix equation

$$[Z]\ [I] = [V]$$

which if expanded gives

$$\begin{bmatrix} Z_{11} & Z_{12} & Z_{13} \\ Z_{21} & Z_{22} & Z_{23} \\ Z_{31} & Z_{32} & Z_{33} \end{bmatrix} \begin{bmatrix} I_1 \\ I_2 \\ I_3 \end{bmatrix} = \begin{bmatrix} V_1 \\ V_2 \\ V_3 \end{bmatrix}$$

for a 3-loop circuit.

Z_{ii} is called the self impedance of the ith loop and is the sum of all impedances in that loop. Z_{ij} is the impedance common to the ith loop and the jth loop, and its sign is determined by the directions of I_i and I_j. The impedance matrix Z is symmetrical as $Z_{ij} = Z_{ji}$. The solutions for the currents may be written as under.

$$I_1 = \frac{\begin{vmatrix} V_1 & Z_{12} & Z_{13} \\ V_2 & Z_{22} & Z_{23} \\ V_3 & Z_{32} & Z_{33} \end{vmatrix}}{\Delta}$$

$$I_2 = \frac{\begin{vmatrix} Z_{11} & V_1 & Z_{13} \\ Z_{21} & V_2 & Z_{23} \\ Z_{31} & V_3 & Z_{33} \end{vmatrix}}{\Delta}$$

and

$$I_3 = \frac{\begin{vmatrix} Z_{11} & Z_{12} & V_1 \\ Z_{21} & Z_{22} & V_2 \\ Z_{31} & Z_{32} & V_3 \end{vmatrix}}{\Delta}$$

where

$$\Delta = \begin{vmatrix} Z_{11} & Z_{12} & Z_{13} \\ Z_{21} & Z_{22} & Z_{23} \\ Z_{31} & Z_{32} & Z_{33} \end{vmatrix}$$

Expanding the Numerator determinants about the columns containing the Voltages,

$$I_1 = V_1 \frac{\Delta_{11}}{\Delta} + V_2 \frac{\Delta_{21}}{\Delta} + V_3 \frac{\Delta_{31}}{\Delta}$$

$$I_2 = V_1 \frac{\Delta_{12}}{\Delta} + V_2 \frac{\Delta_{22}}{\Delta} + V_3 \frac{\Delta_{32}}{\Delta}$$

$$I_3 = V_1 \frac{\Delta_{13}}{\Delta} + V_2 \frac{\Delta_{23}}{\Delta} + V_3 \frac{\Delta_{33}}{\Delta}$$

Driving Point Impedance

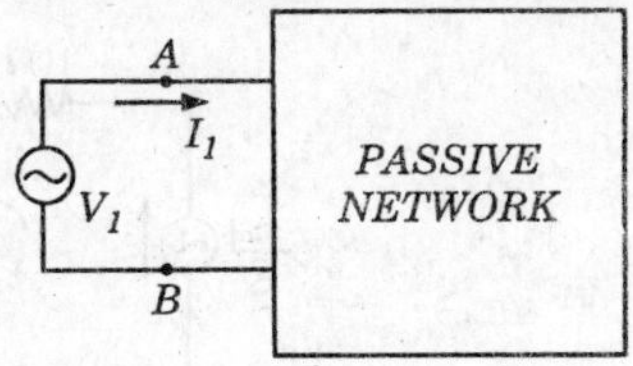

Fig. 8.2

Consider a passive or source-free network with two terminals A and B as in Fig. 8.2. Apply a voltage source V_1 and let the resulting loop current be I_1. As there is no other source in the network.

$$I_1 = V_1 \frac{\Delta_{11}}{\Delta} + 0\frac{\Delta_{21}}{\Delta} + \ldots = V_1 \frac{\Delta_{11}}{\Delta}$$

The ratio $\frac{V_1}{I_1} = Z$ -input or driving point impedance at AB.

$$\frac{V_1}{I_1} = \frac{\Delta}{\Delta_{11}} = \text{Driving point impedance}$$

For active networks, the other voltage sources are short circuited (replaced by their internal impedances) when one terminal pair is considered.

Transfer Impedance

A voltage source in one loop of a network causes currents to flow in all other loops. The ratio of the driving voltage in one loop to the resulting current in another loop is called the transfer impedance between the two loops (all other sources must be set to zero)

$$I_j = (0)\frac{\Delta_{1j}}{\Delta} + 0\frac{V_{2j}}{\Delta} + \ldots + V_i \frac{\Delta_{ij}}{\Delta} + 0 \ldots$$

$$= V_i \frac{\Delta_{ij}}{\Delta}$$

or $$Z_{transfer,\, i,j} = \frac{V_i}{I_j} = \frac{\Delta}{\Delta_{ij}}$$

The subscript ij denotes that the voltage source is in mesh i and the current in mesh j, as shown in Fig. 8.3.

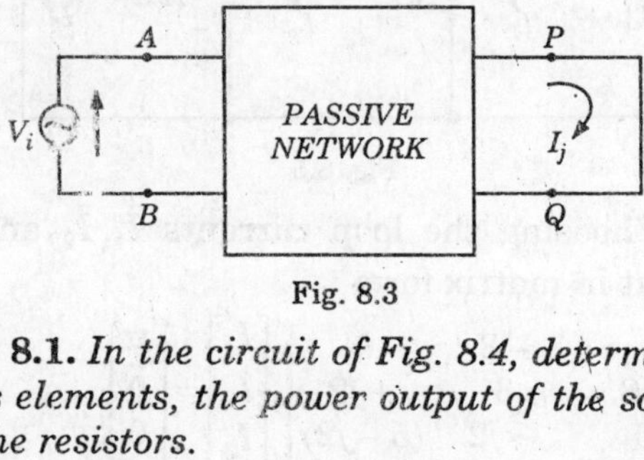

Fig. 8.3

Example 8.1. *In the circuit of Fig. 8.4, determine the currents in the various elements, the power output of the source and power expended in the resistors.*

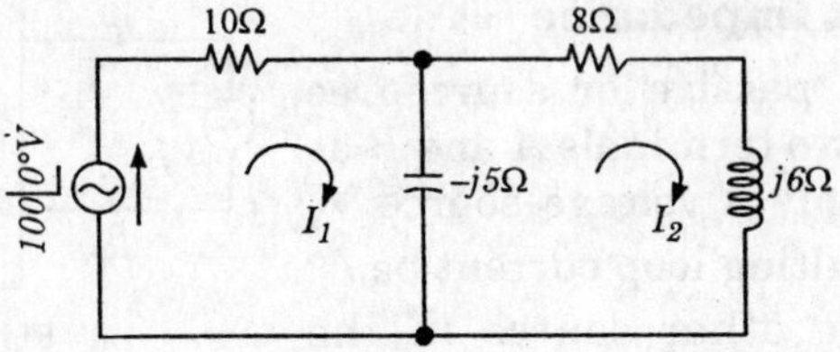

Fig. 8.4

Solution. Select the mesh currents as shown (This choice and the direction is quite arbitrary). The matrix equation may be written as

$$\begin{bmatrix} 10-j5 & j5 \\ j5 & 8+j1 \end{bmatrix}\begin{bmatrix} I_1 \\ I_2 \end{bmatrix} = \begin{bmatrix} 100\angle 0^\circ \\ 0 \end{bmatrix}$$

$$I_1 = \frac{\begin{vmatrix} 100\angle 0^\circ & j5 \\ 0 & 8+j1 \end{vmatrix}}{\begin{vmatrix} 10-j5 & j5 \\ j5 & 8+j1 \end{vmatrix}} = \frac{800+j100}{110-j30} = 7.07\angle 22.38^\circ$$

$$I_2 = \frac{\begin{vmatrix} 10-j5 & 100\angle 0^\circ \\ j5 & 0 \end{vmatrix}}{110-j30} = \frac{-j500}{110-j30} = 4.39\angle -74.74^\circ$$

Source Power

$$= VI\cos\theta = 100 \times 7.07 \cos(22.28) = 653.75 \text{ W}$$

$$P_{10} = I_1^{\ 2} \times 10 = 499.85 \text{ watts}$$

$$P_8 = I_2^{\ 2} \times 8 = 154 \text{ watts.}$$

Example 8.2. *Find the magnitude of the voltage source V of Fig. 8.5 below which results in an effective voltage of 20 volts across the 5 ohm resistor.*

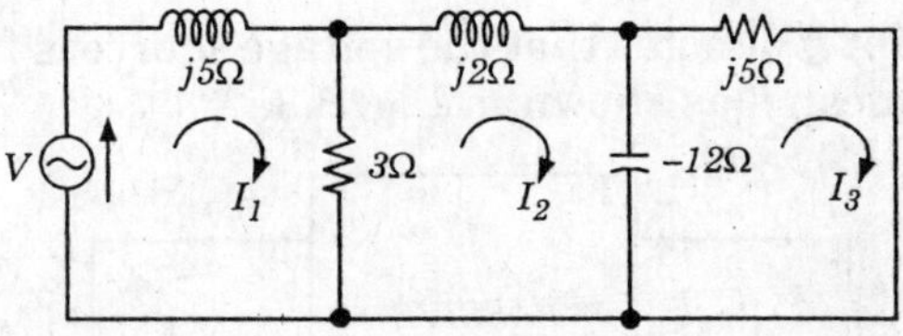

Fig. 8.5

Solution. Choosing the loop currents I_1, I_2 and I_3 the loop equations are put in matrix form :

$$\begin{bmatrix} (3+j5) & -3 & 0 \\ -3 & 3 & +j2 \\ 0 & +j2 & (5-j2) \end{bmatrix}\begin{bmatrix} I_1 \\ I_2 \\ I_3 \end{bmatrix} = \begin{bmatrix} V \\ 0 \\ 0 \end{bmatrix}$$

Solving for I_3

$$I_3 = \frac{\begin{vmatrix} 3+j5 & -3 & V \\ -3 & 3 & 0 \\ 0 & +j2 & 0 \end{vmatrix}}{\Delta} = \frac{-j6V}{42+j95}$$

$$|\, I_3 \,| = \frac{6V}{\sqrt{42^2+95^2}}$$

Voltage across the 5 ohm resistor $= |\, I_3 \,| \times 5$

$$= \frac{6V}{\sqrt{42^2+95^2}} \times 5 = 20 \text{ V}$$

$$\therefore \quad V = \frac{20\sqrt{42^2+95^2}}{30} = \mathbf{69.25 \text{ volts.}}$$

Example 8.3. *Find the current in the arm BD of the bridge network of Fig. 8.6.*

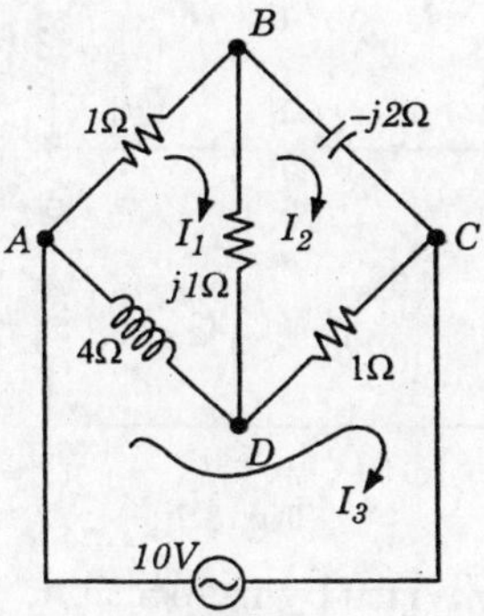

Fig. 8.6

Solution. Choosing the loop currents I_1, I_2 and I_3 as shown, we may write the loop equations by inspection as follows :

$$\begin{bmatrix} (2+j1) & -1 & -j1 \\ -1 & (2-j2) & -1 \\ -j1 & -1 & (1+j1) \end{bmatrix} \begin{bmatrix} I_1 \\ I_2 \\ I_3 \end{bmatrix} = \begin{bmatrix} 0 \\ 0 \\ 10\angle 0^\circ \end{bmatrix}$$

Current in arm $BD = I_1 - I_2$

We have to solve for I_1 and I_2

$$I_1 = \frac{\begin{vmatrix} 0 & -1 & -j1 \\ 0 & (2-j2) & -1 \\ 10 & -1 & (1+j1) \end{vmatrix}}{\Delta} = \frac{10\,(3+j2)}{(7-j2)}$$

$$= \frac{10\,(3+j2)\,(7+j2)}{(7-j2)\,(7+j2)} = \frac{170+j200}{53}$$

$$I_2 = \frac{\begin{vmatrix} (2+j1) & 0 & -j1 \\ -1 & 0 & -1 \\ -j1 & 10 & (1+j1) \end{vmatrix}}{\Delta} = \frac{20\,(1+j1)}{(7-j2)}$$

$$= \frac{100+j180}{53}$$

Current in $BD = I_1 - I_2$

$$= \frac{(170+j200)-(100+j180)}{53} = \frac{70+j20}{53}$$

$= \mathbf{1.374}$ **amps.**

Example 8.4. *In the network of Fig. 8.7, find the currents I_A, I_B and I_C.*

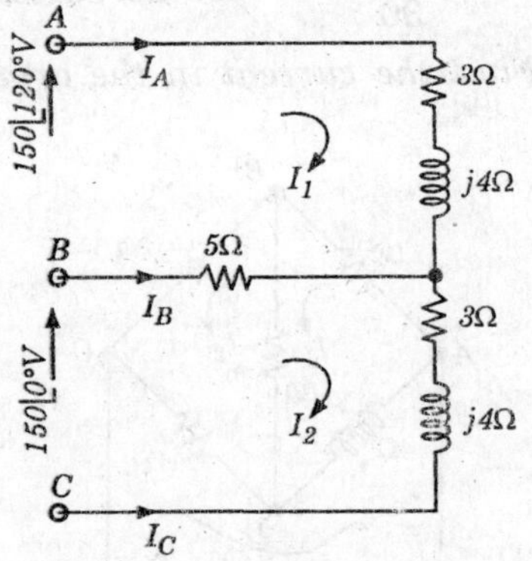

Fig. 8.7

Solution. We may write by inspection,

$$\begin{bmatrix} (8+j4) & -5 \\ -5 & (8+j4) \end{bmatrix} \begin{bmatrix} I_1 \\ I_2 \end{bmatrix} = \begin{bmatrix} 150\angle 120^\circ \\ 150\angle 0^\circ \end{bmatrix}$$

$$I_1 = \frac{\begin{vmatrix} 150\angle 120^\circ & -5 \\ 150\angle 0^\circ & (8+j4) \end{vmatrix}}{\Delta} = \frac{-369.6+j739.2}{23+j64}$$

$$= 12.15\angle 46.3^\circ$$

$$I_2 = \frac{\begin{vmatrix} (8+j4) & 150\angle 120^\circ \\ -5 & 150\angle 0^\circ \end{vmatrix}}{23+j64} = 22.0\angle -13.7^\circ$$

$$I_A = I_1 = 12.15\angle 46.3^\circ$$

$$I_B = I_2 - I_1 = 22\angle -13.7^\circ - 12.15\angle 46.3^\circ$$

$$= 29.09\angle -47.1^\circ$$

$$I_C = -I_2 = 22\angle 163.7^\circ.$$

Example 8.5. *In the Fig. 8.8 below, find the value of 'V' such that the power in the 8 ohm resistor is 200 Watts.*

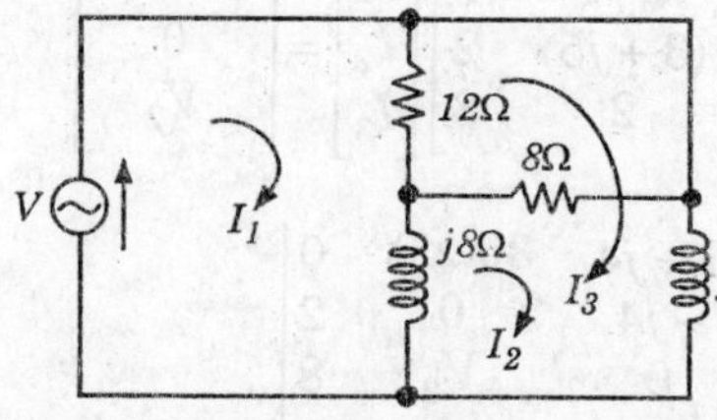

Fig. 8.8

Solution. Let the choice of loop currents be made as shown. The loop equations are

$$\begin{bmatrix} (12+j8) & -V & -(12+j8) \\ -j8 & (8+j14) & j14 \\ -(12+j8) & j14 & (12+j14) \end{bmatrix} \begin{bmatrix} I_1 \\ I_2 \\ I_3 \end{bmatrix} = \begin{bmatrix} V \\ 0 \\ 0 \end{bmatrix}$$

We must solve for I_2 alone

$$I_2 = \frac{\begin{vmatrix} (12+j8) & -j8 & -(12+j8) \\ -j8 & 0 & j14 \\ -(12+j8) & 0 & (12+j14) \end{vmatrix}}{\Delta}$$

$$= \frac{-j\,72\,V}{-5664 - j2560}$$

$$P_8 = 200 = I_2^{\,2} \times 8$$

$$\therefore \quad I_2 = 5A$$

$$5 = \frac{72\,V}{\sqrt{(5664)^2 + (2560)^2}}$$

$$\therefore \quad V = \frac{5\sqrt{(5664)^2 + (2560)^2}}{72} = \mathbf{431.6\ volts.}$$

Example 8.6. *In the network of Fig. 8.9, the voltage $V_1 = 30\angle 0°$. Find V_2 such that the current in the $(1+j1)$ branch is zero.*

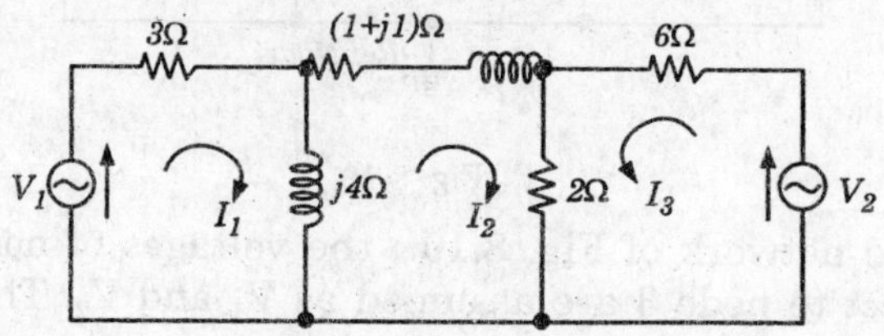

Fig. 8.9

Solution. The mesh equations are

$$\begin{bmatrix} (3+j4) & -j4 & 0 \\ -j4 & (3+j5) & 2 \\ 0 & 2 & 8 \end{bmatrix} \begin{bmatrix} I_1 \\ I_2 \\ I_3 \end{bmatrix} = \begin{bmatrix} 30\angle 0^\circ \\ 0 \\ V_2 \end{bmatrix}$$

from which

$$I_2 = \frac{\begin{vmatrix} 3+j4 & 30\angle 0^\circ & 0 \\ -j4 & 0 & 2 \\ 0 & V_2 & 8 \end{vmatrix}}{\Delta}$$

$$= \frac{(3+j4)(-2V_2) + j4\,(240)}{\Delta} = 0$$

$\therefore$

$$(3+j4)(-2V_2) + j\,960 = 0$$

or

$$V_2 = \frac{j\,960}{2\,(3+j4)}$$

$$= 96\angle 36.87^\circ$$

Nodal Method

The nodal method explained in Chapter 3 for D.C. circuits can be extended to A.C. circuits as well. As before one of the nodes is chosen as the reference node and the voltages of the other nodes with respect to the reference node are the unknowns. The nodal equations expressed in matrix form are of the form.

$$[Y]\,[V] = [I]$$

where $[Y]$ is the admittance matrix.

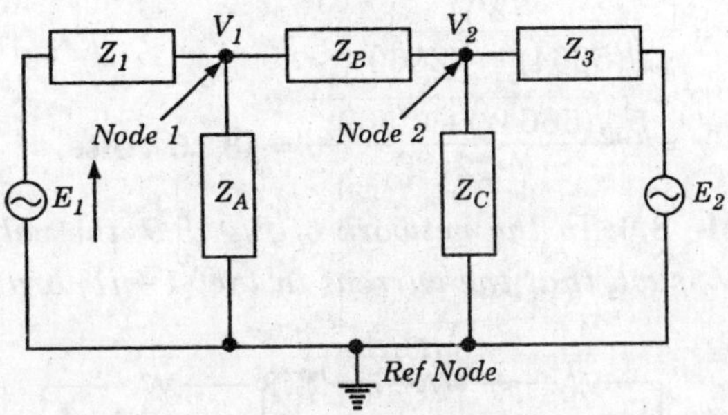

Fig. 8.10

For the network of Fig. 8.10 ; the voltages of nodes 1 and 2 with respect to node 3 are assumed as V_1 and V_2. The equations are (in matrix form)

$$\begin{bmatrix} \left(\frac{1}{Z_1}+\frac{1}{Z_A}+\frac{1}{Z_B}\right) & -\frac{1}{Z_B} \\ -\frac{1}{Z_B} & \left(\frac{1}{Z_B}+\frac{1}{Z_C}+\frac{1}{Z_2}\right) \end{bmatrix} \begin{bmatrix} V_1 \\ V_2 \end{bmatrix} = \begin{bmatrix} \frac{E_1}{Z_1} \\ \frac{E_2}{Z_2} \end{bmatrix}$$

In general, the no nodal equations are of the form

$$\begin{bmatrix} Y_{11} & Y_{12} & Y_{13} \\ Y_{21} & Y_{22} & Y_{23} \\ Y_{31} & Y_{33} & Y_{33} \end{bmatrix} \begin{bmatrix} V_1 \\ V_2 \\ V_3 \end{bmatrix} = \begin{bmatrix} I_1 \\ I_2 \\ I_3 \end{bmatrix}$$

for a network with 3 nodes plus a reference node, Y_{ii}'s are the self admittance of the ith node and this is the sum of all the admittances connected to that node. Y_{ij} $(i \neq j)$ is the mutual admittance between the nodes 'i' and 'j' and is taken as negative.

The node voltages V_1, V_2 and V_3 are solved by using Kramer's rule

As before we may write :

$$V_1 = I_1 \frac{\Delta_{11}}{\Delta} + I_2 \frac{\Delta_{21}}{\Delta} + I_3 \frac{\Delta_{31}}{\Delta}$$

$$V_2 = I_1 \frac{\Delta_{12}}{\Delta} + I_2 \frac{\Delta_{22}}{\Delta} + I_2 \frac{\Delta_{32}}{\Delta}$$

$$V_3 = I_1 \frac{\Delta_{13}}{\Delta} + I_2 \frac{\Delta_{23}}{\Delta} + I_3 \frac{\Delta_{33}}{\Delta}$$

Driving Point Admittance

For a passive multi node network with 2 external terminals A and B as in Fig. 8.11, let the current into node 1 be I_1 and let its voltage be V_1.

Then $\quad V_1 = I_1 \frac{\Delta_{11}}{\Delta}$

all other sources being open circuited.

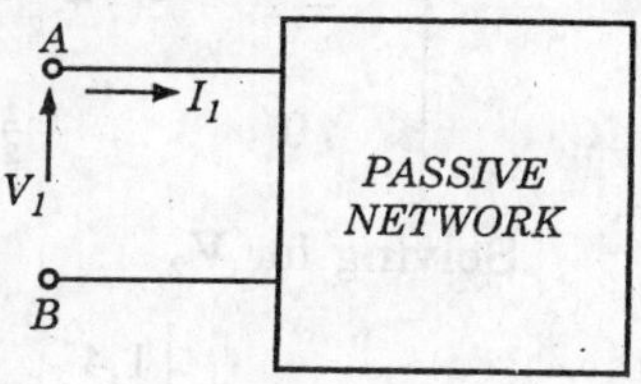

Fig. 8.11

The ratio, $\frac{I_1}{V_1} = \frac{\Delta}{\Delta_{11}} = Y_{\text{input 1}}$

= Driving point admittance.

Transfer Admittance

A current flowing into one node gives rise to voltages at all other nodes. The transfer admittance is defined as the ratio of current flowing into one node to the resulting voltage at another node (all other sources set to zero)

$$V_j = I_i \frac{\Delta_{ij}}{\Delta}$$

$$\frac{I_i}{V_j} = \frac{\Delta}{\Delta_{ij}} = Y_{\text{transfer i, j}}.$$

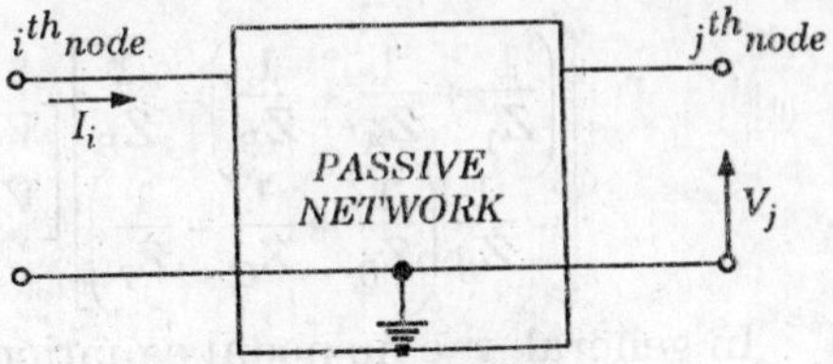

Fig. 8.12

Example 8.7. *Frame the nodal equations of the network in Fig. 8.13. Hence find the difference of potential, between nodes 2 and 4.*

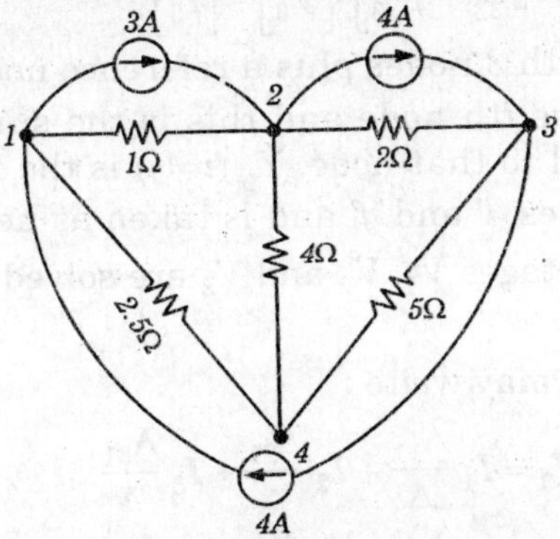

Fig. 8.13

Solution. Choosing node 4 as reference node and the voltages of nodes. 1, 2 and 3 as V_1, V_2 and V_3 with reference to node 4, we may write the nodal equations in matrix form as

$$\begin{bmatrix} \left(\frac{1}{1}+\frac{1}{2.5}\right) & -1 & 0 \\ -1 & \left(\frac{1}{1}+\frac{1}{2}+\frac{1}{4}\right) & -\frac{1}{2} \\ 0 & -\frac{1}{2} & \left(\frac{1}{2}+\frac{1}{5}\right) \end{bmatrix} \begin{bmatrix} V_1 \\ V_2 \\ V_3 \end{bmatrix} = \begin{bmatrix} 4-3 \\ 3-4 \\ 4-4 \end{bmatrix} = \begin{bmatrix} 1 \\ -1 \\ 0 \end{bmatrix}$$

Solving for V_2

$$V_2 = \frac{\begin{vmatrix} 1.4 & 1 & 0 \\ -1 & -1 & -\frac{1}{2} \\ 0 & 0 & 0.7 \end{vmatrix}}{\begin{vmatrix} 1.4 & -1 & 0 \\ -1 & 1.75 & 0.5 \\ 0 & -0.5 & 0.7 \end{vmatrix}} = \frac{-0.28}{0.665} = -0.421 \text{ volts.}$$

Example 8.8. *For the network of Fig. 8.14, find the line currents I_A, I_B and I_C.*

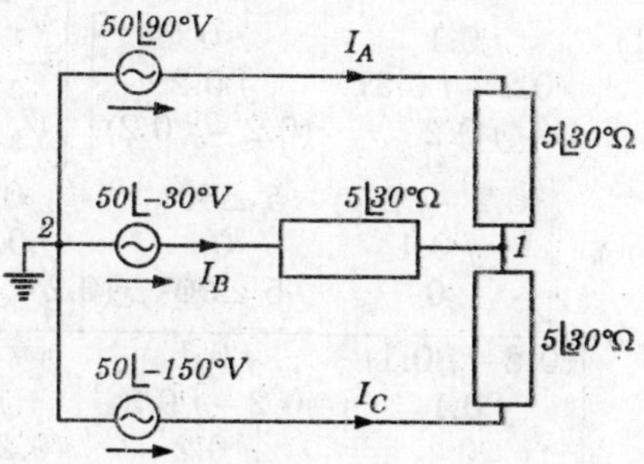

Fig. 8.14

Solution. For node 1, we may write,

$$\frac{V_1 - 50\angle 90^\circ}{5\angle 30^\circ} + \frac{V_1 - 50\angle -30^\circ}{5\angle 30^\circ} + \frac{V_1 - 50\angle -150^\circ}{5\angle 30^\circ} = 0$$

Hence $V_1 = \dfrac{50\angle 90^\circ + 50\angle -30^\circ + 50\angle -150^\circ}{3} = 0$

$$\therefore \quad I_A = \frac{50\angle 90^\circ}{5\angle 30^\circ} = 10\angle 60^\circ \text{ A}$$

$$I_B = \frac{50\angle -30^\circ}{53\angle 0^\circ} = 10\angle -60^\circ \text{ A}$$

$$I_C = \frac{50\angle -150^\circ}{5\angle 30^\circ} = 10\angle 180^\circ \text{ A.}$$

Example 8.9. *In the network of Fig. 8.15, obtain the voltage V_2.*

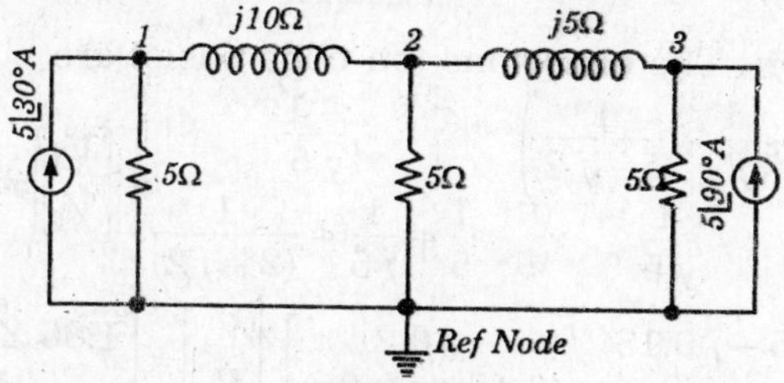

Fig. 8.15

Solution. The nodal equations are :

$$\begin{bmatrix} \left(\frac{1}{5} + \frac{1}{j\,10}\right) & \frac{-1}{j\,10} & 0 \\ \frac{-1}{j\,10} & \left(\frac{1}{5} + \frac{1}{j\,10} + \frac{1}{j\,5}\right) & \frac{-1}{j\,5} \\ 0 & \frac{-1}{j\,5} & \left(\frac{1}{5} + \frac{1}{j\,5}\right) \end{bmatrix} \begin{bmatrix} V_1 \\ V_2 \\ V_3 \end{bmatrix} = \begin{bmatrix} 5\angle 30^\circ \\ 0 \\ 5\angle 90^\circ \end{bmatrix}$$

$$\begin{bmatrix} (0.2-j\,0.1) & j\,0.1 & 0 \\ j\,0.1 & (0.2-j\,0.3) & j\,0.2 \\ 0 & j\,0.2 & (0.2-j\,0.2) \end{bmatrix} \begin{bmatrix} V_1 \\ V_2 \\ V_3 \end{bmatrix} = \begin{bmatrix} 5\,\angle 30° \\ 0 \\ 5\,\angle 90° \end{bmatrix}$$

$$\therefore \quad V_2 = \frac{\begin{vmatrix} (0.2-j\,0.1) & 5\,\angle 30° & 0 \\ j\,0.1 & 0 & j\,0.2 \\ 0 & 5\,\angle 90° & (0.2-j\,0.2) \end{vmatrix}}{\begin{vmatrix} (0.2-j\,0.1) & j\,0.1 & 0 \\ j\,0.1 & (0.2-j\,0.3) & j\,0.2 \\ 0 & j\,0.2 & (0.2-j0.2) \end{vmatrix}}$$

$$= \frac{0.1634 - j\,0.2366}{-\,0.004 - j\,0.024}$$

$$= \frac{0.29\,\angle 55.4°}{0.024\,\angle 260.6°} = 11.8\,\angle 44°\text{ V.}$$

Example 8.10. *In the network of Fig. 8.16, find the node voltages V_1 and V_2 and the current supplied by the voltage source.*

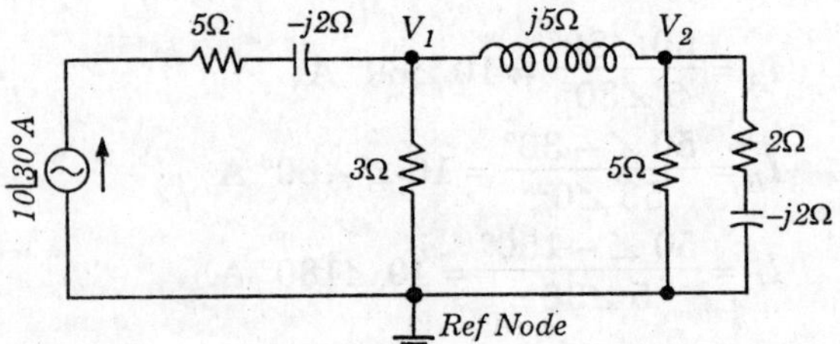

Fig. 8.16

Solution. The equations (on node basis) are

$$\begin{bmatrix} \left(\dfrac{1}{3}+\dfrac{1}{j5}+\dfrac{1}{5-j\,2}\right) & \dfrac{-1}{j\,5} \\ -\dfrac{1}{j\,5} & \dfrac{1}{5}+\dfrac{1}{j\,5}+\dfrac{1}{(2-j\,2)} \end{bmatrix} \begin{bmatrix} V_1 \\ V_2 \end{bmatrix} = \begin{bmatrix} \dfrac{10\,\angle 30°}{(5-j\,2)} \\ 0 \end{bmatrix}$$

i.e.

$$\begin{bmatrix} (0.5-j\,0.13) & +j\,0.2 \\ +j\,0.2 & (0.45-j\,0.05) \end{bmatrix} \begin{bmatrix} V_1 \\ V_2 \end{bmatrix} = \begin{bmatrix} 1.86\,\angle 52° \\ 0 \end{bmatrix}$$

$$V_1 = \frac{\begin{vmatrix} 1.86\,\angle 52° & j\,0.2 \\ 0 & (0.45-j\,0.05) \end{vmatrix}}{\begin{vmatrix} (0.5-j\,0.13) & (j\,0.2) \\ (j\,0.2) & (0.45-j\,0.05) \end{vmatrix}}$$

$$= \frac{0.842\,\angle 46°}{0.272\,\angle -18°} = 3.1\,\angle 63.6°\text{ volts}$$

$$V_2 = \frac{\begin{vmatrix} (0.5-j\,0.13) & 1.86\,\angle 52° \\ j\,0.2 & 0 \end{vmatrix}}{0.272\,\angle -18°}$$

$$= \frac{-0.372 \angle 142°}{0.272 \angle -18°}$$

$$= 1.37 \angle 160° = 1.37 \angle -20°.$$

Locus Diagram

Very often, we have to analyse circuits with one or more parameters varying. We shall in this section consider basic circuits with combinations of resistance, inductance, and capacitance, in which one of the elements varies. The resulting currents when plotted are called phasor loci.

Series Circuits

1. R-L Circuits : (A) 'R' Variable. Consider the series R-L circuit of Fig. 8.17 (*a*) to which is applied a constant voltage at constant frequency. Let R be variable over a wide range between zero and an extremely large value.

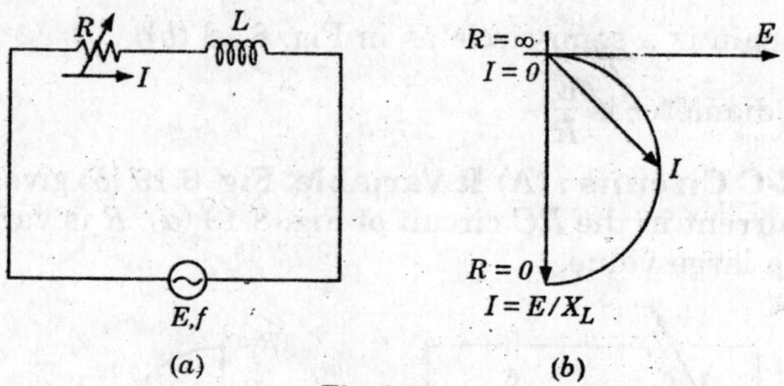

Fig. 8.17

When $R = 0$, the current will be E/X_L lagging behind the voltage by 90°. As the resistance is increased to infinity, the current drops to zero, and the angle by which the current lags behind the voltage reduces. The tip of the phasors when joined is the locus diagram of the current as R varies and is a semi-circle with E/X_L as diameter.

The general expression for the current is

$$I = \frac{E}{Z} = \frac{E}{\sqrt{R^2 + X_L{}^2}} = \frac{E}{X_L}\frac{X_L}{Z}$$

$$= \frac{E}{X_L} \sin \theta$$

This is the polar equation of a circle with E/X_L as diameter and is shown in Fig. 8.17 (*b*).

(B) 'L' Variable. Fig. 8.18 (*a*) illustrates a constant resistance variable L circuit fed from a constant voltage and frequency supply.

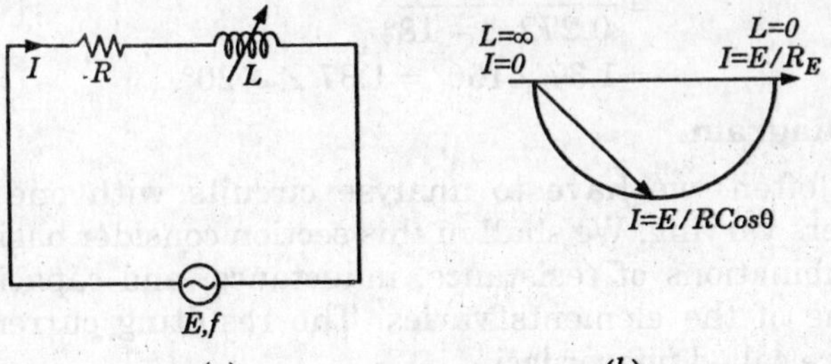

(a) (b)

Fig. 8.18

The current will obviously be E/R when $L = 0$ ($X_L = 0$, in phase with voltage) and reduces to zero as L (X_L) is increased to infinity,

$$I = \frac{E}{Z} = \frac{E}{R}\,\frac{R}{Z} = \frac{E}{R}\cos\theta$$

which again is a semi-circle as in Fig. 8.18 (*b*).

The diameter is $\frac{E}{R}$.

2. R-C Circuits : (A) R Variable. Fig. 8.19 (*b*) gives the locus of the current in the *RC* circuit of Fig. 8.19 (*a*). *R* is variable from zero to a large value.

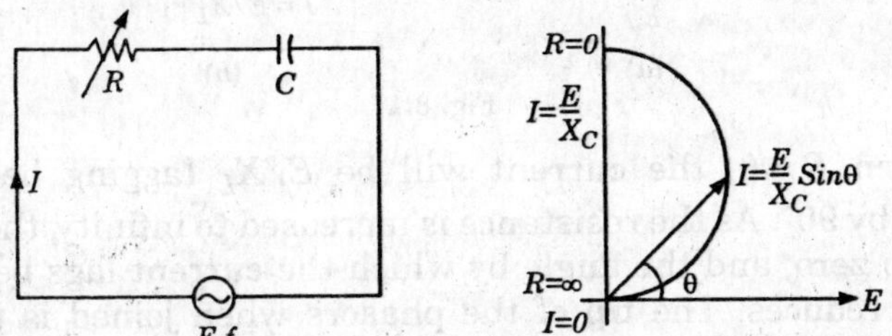

(a) (b)

Fig. 8.19

(B) C variable. The locus is shown in Fig. 8.20 (*b*).

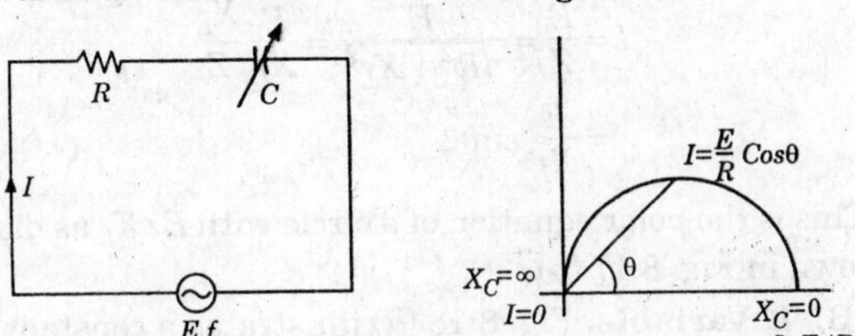

(a) (b)

Fig. 8.20

3. R-L-C. Circuits. When such a circuit is studied with variable resistance, it may be considered as RL or RC series circuit depending on which is larger. X_L or X_C. However, when L is variable R and C being constants, we get the following current locus shown in Fig. 8.21.

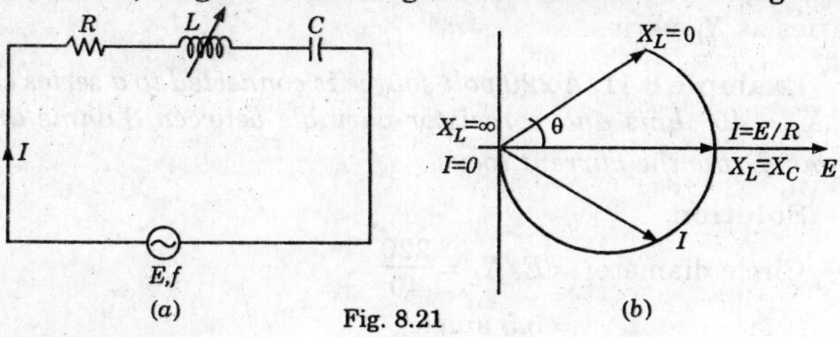

Fig. 8.21

Parallel Circuits

Consider the parallel circuit of Fig. 8.22 (a). Let X_L be constant and R variable. The total current (I_t) locus is the sum of a constant current phasor (I_L) and a variable current locus (I_R). When R is infinite I_R is zero and the total current $I_t = I_L$ (lagging behind E by 90°).

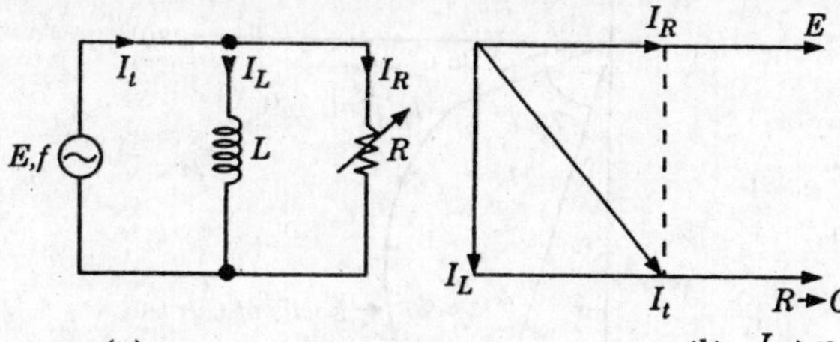

Fig. 8.22

As R decreases, I_R increases (in phase with E) and the total current I_t lies along a straight line. The power factor approaches

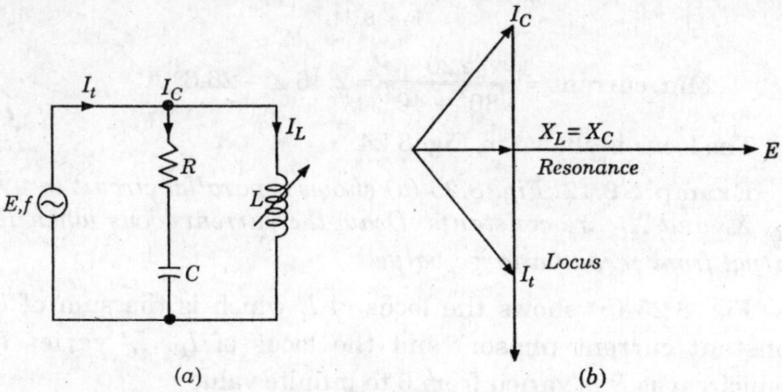

Fig. 8.23

unity as R is decreased to low values. Such a circuit cannot be tuned to resonance as u.p.f. is never practically achieved.

In the circuit of Fig. 8.23 (a), however, the condition of resonance is achieved. The current I_C is a fixed phasor while I_L varies as X_L varies.

Example 8.11. *A 220 volt source is connected to a series circuit of $X_L = 40$ ohms and a resistor variable between 8 ohms and 80 ohms. Draw the current locus.*

Solution.

$$\text{Circle diameter} = E/X_L = \frac{220}{40}$$

$$= 5.5 \text{ amps.}$$

$$\text{Max. current} = \frac{220}{\sqrt{8^2 + 40^2}} = 5.39 \text{ A}$$

$$\text{Angle} = \tan^{-1}\frac{40}{8} = 78.7° \text{ (lag)}$$

$$I_{max} = 5.39 \angle -78.7° \text{ A}$$

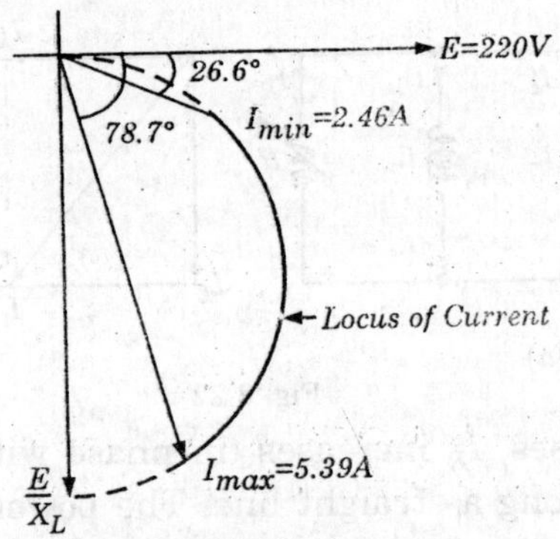

Fig. 8.24

$$\text{Min. current} = \frac{220}{\sqrt{80^2 + 40^2}} = 2.46 \angle -26.6° \text{ A}$$

The locus is shown in Fig. 8.24.

Example 8.12. *Fig. 8.25 (a) shows a parallel circuit in which R_L, X_L and X_C are constants. Draw the current locus when R_C is varied from zero to a large value.*

Fig. 8.25 (b) shows the locus of I_t which is the sum of I_L (a constant current phasor) and the locus of I_C. I_C varies as a semicircle as R is varied from 0 to infinite value.

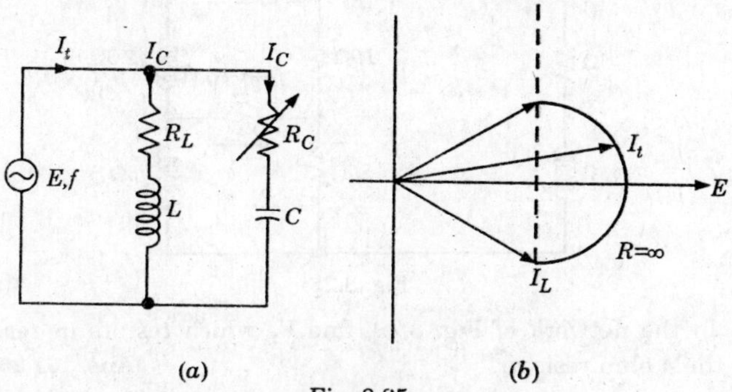

Fig. 8.25

EXERCISES

8.1. The circuit shown in Fig. 8.26 has voltages given between each pair of the three lines A, B and C. The impedances are $20 \angle 45°$ ohms each. With the mesh currents indicated, determine I_A, I_B and I_C.

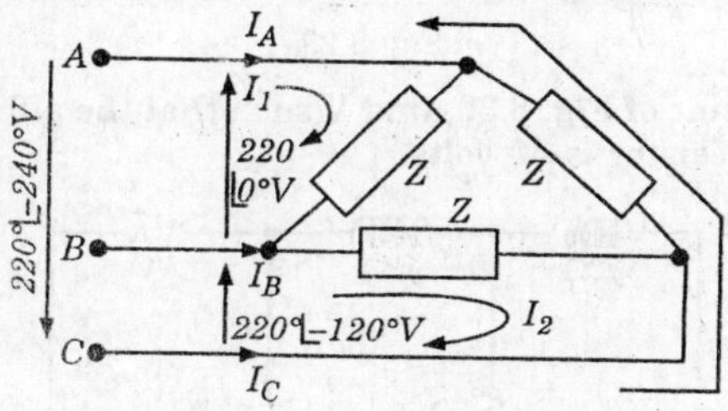

Fig. 8.26

[**Ans.** $I_A = 19.05 \angle -75°$, $I_B = 19.05 \angle 165°$, $I_C = 19.05 \angle 45°$]

8.2. In the network of Fig. 8.27, find the voltage V_{AB} and V_{BC}.

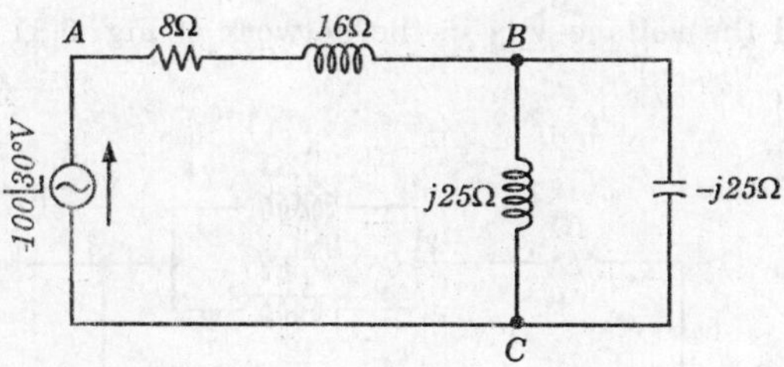

Fig. 8.27

[**Ans.** $V_{AB} = 0$, $V_{BC} = 100 \angle 30°$]

8.3. In the circuit of Fig. 8.28 find the current through the $(5 + j5)$ impedance. [**Ans.** 0]

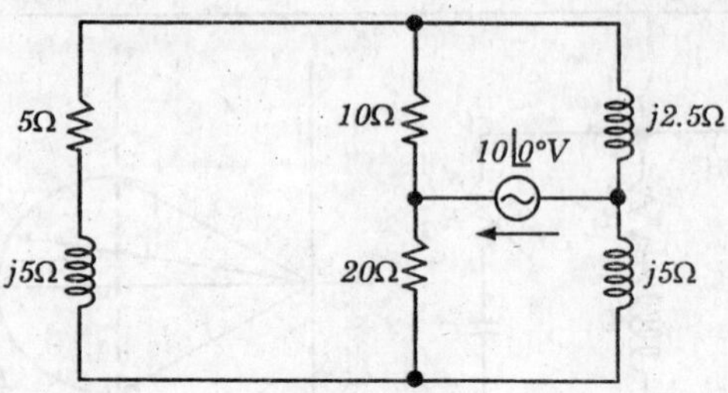

Fig. 8.28

8.4. In the network of Fig. 8.29, find V_2 which results in zero current through the 4 ohm resistor. **[Ans.** 161.25 ∠ – 82.9]

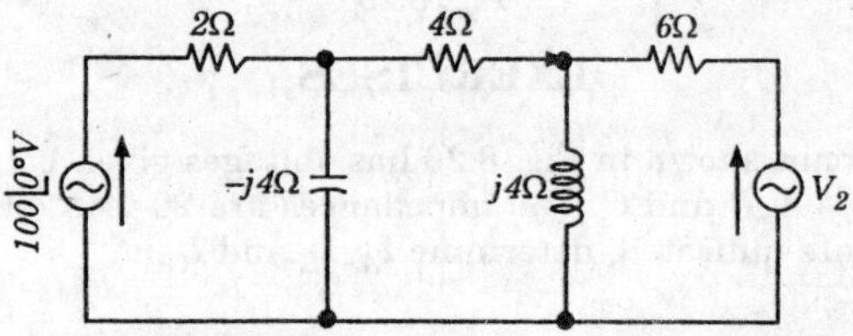

Fig. 8.29

8.5. In the circuit of Fig. 8.30, find V such that the effective voltage drop across the 4 ohm resistor is 30 volts. **[Ans.** 100 V]

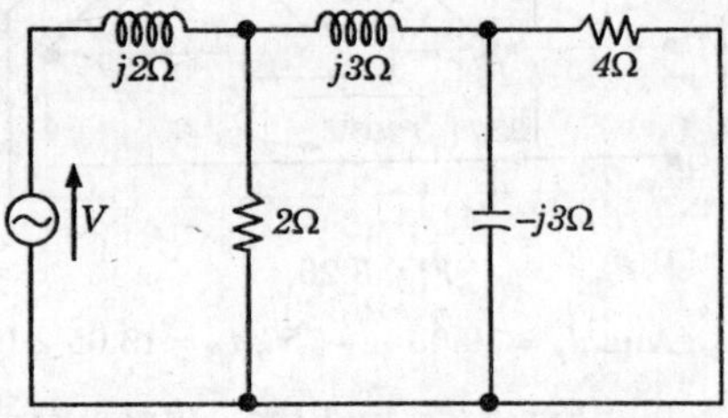

Fig. 8.30

8.6. Find the voltage V_{PQ} in the network of Fig. 8.31 using the nodal method. **[Ans.** 15.19 ∠102.5°]

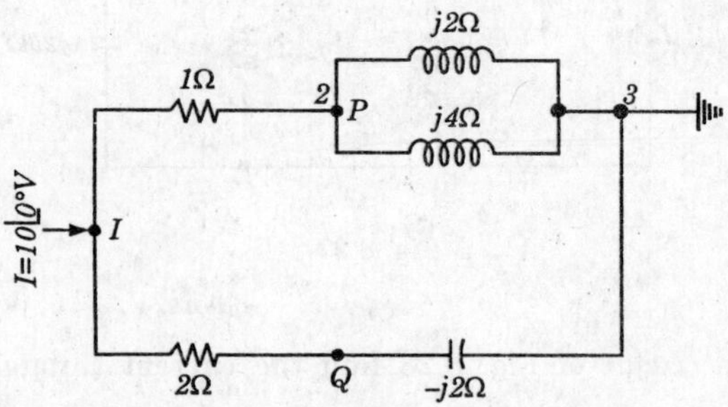

Fig. 8.31

8.7. For the circuit of Fig. 8.32 find the voltage V_{AB} using the nodal method.

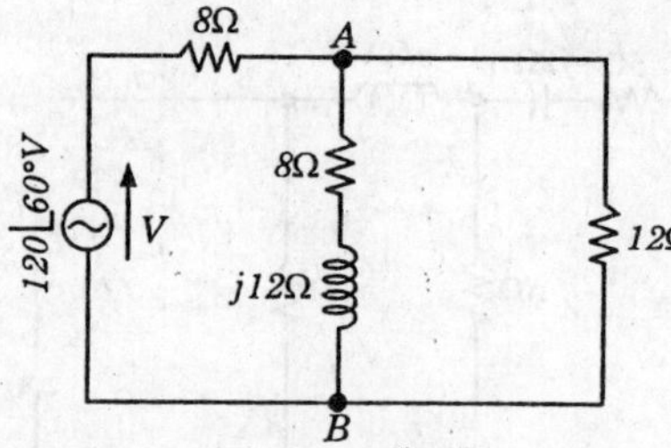

Fig. 8.32

8.8. In the circuit of Fig. 8.33, find V_2 such that the current supplied by it is zero.

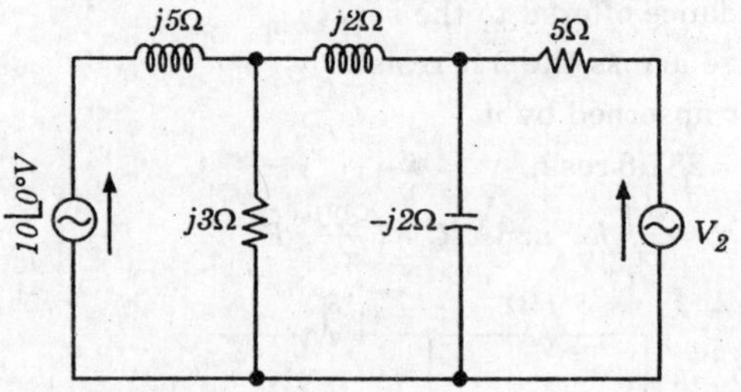

Fig. 8.33

8.9. In Fig. 8.34, find the current I_3.

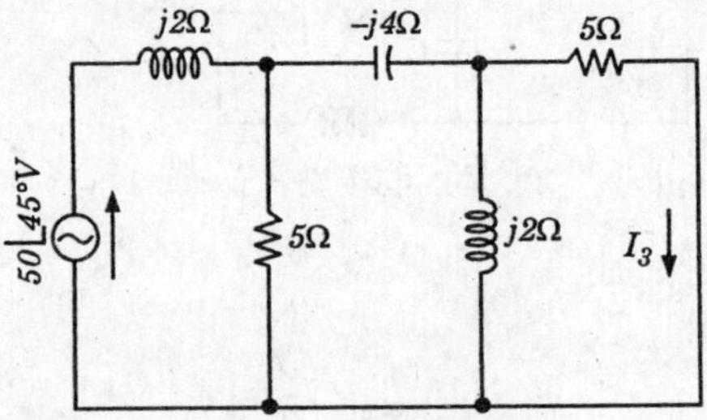

Fig. 8.34

8.10. Apply the mesh current method and determine the currents through the three resistors of the network of Fig. 8.35.

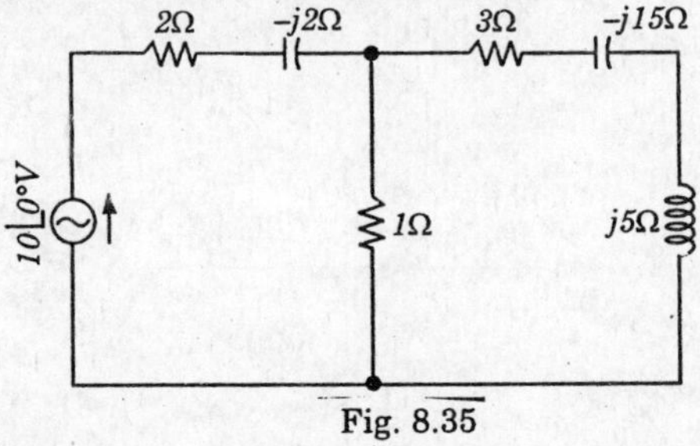

Fig. 8.35

8.11. In the network of Fig. 8.36, find the node-voltages V_1 and V_2. Find also the current supplied by the source.

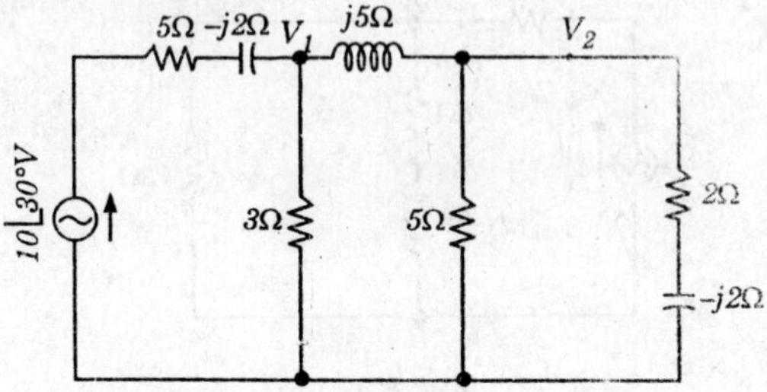

Fig. 8.36

8.12. In the circuit of Fig. 8.37, calculate

(*a*) The impedance offered to the source.

(*b*) The voltage across the 2 Ω resistor.

(*c*) The power absorbed by it.

Given that $e = 281.8 \cos t$,

$$L = \frac{0.1}{\pi} h \quad \text{and} \quad C = \frac{2000}{\pi} \mu F$$

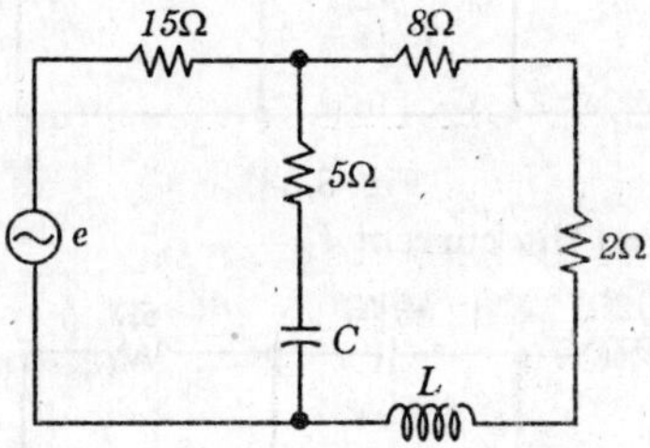

Fig. 8.37

NINE

NETWORK THEOREMS

The analysis of a.c. circuits with large number of branches often with many sources becomes exceedingly difficult by the methods discussed in the previous chapters. With loop and node methods all circuit problems can nearly be solved. Several helpful laws, theorems and principles have been developed to simplify the analysis of large networks. These helpful tools have been discussed with respect to D.C. circuits in an earlier chapter and are equally applicable for A.C. circuits.

Kirchhoff's laws have already been discussed for the solution of network, using the mesh and node methods. The other theorems are dealt with in the following sections.

Thevenin's Theorem and Norton's Theorem

A network with fixed impedances can be solved by either the node or the mesh method. An A.C. network consisting of bilateral linear impedances and a number of sources may present two load terminals. We may be interested in computing the current through an impedance connected to these load terminals. If this load impedance is of variable value, the current has to be calculated afresh for every value. Much of the tedious work involved in this repeated calculations can be avoided if we can replace the whole network by a simple equivalent network at the load terminals. This is done using the Thevenin's and Norton's Theorems.

Thevenin's Theorem

Any linear bilateral network with output terminals *AB* as shown in Fig. 9.1 (*a*) can be replaced by a simple equivalent circuit

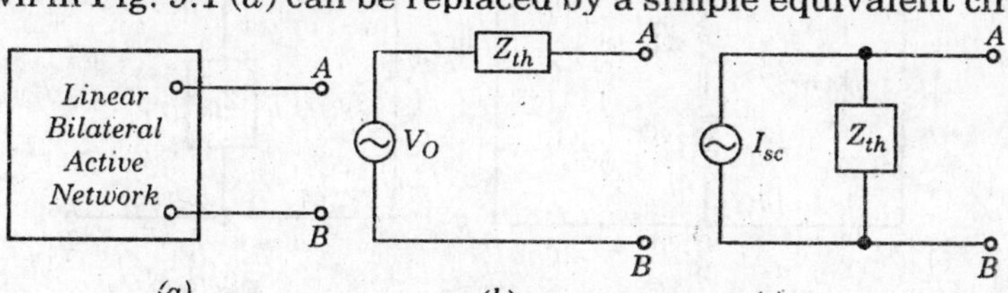

Fig. 9.1

with single voltage source V_0 in series with a single impedance (Z_{th}) about the terminals AB, as in Fig. 9.1 (*b*).

As before V_0 is the open circuit voltage at terminals AB and Z_{th} is the driving point impedance of the network at terminals AB, when all sources are replaced by their internal impedance.

Norton's Theorem

The bilaterial linear active network of Fig. 9.1 (*a*) may also be replaced by the equivalent circuit of Fig. 9.1 (*c*). The current source I_{SC} is given by the short circuit current at terminals AB and Z_{th} is the same as before.

Example 9.1. *Obtain the Thevenin's equivalent circuit for the network of Fig. 9.2.*

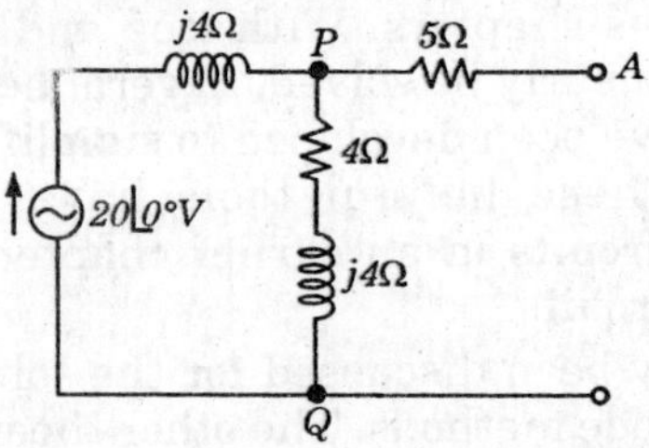

Fig. 9.2

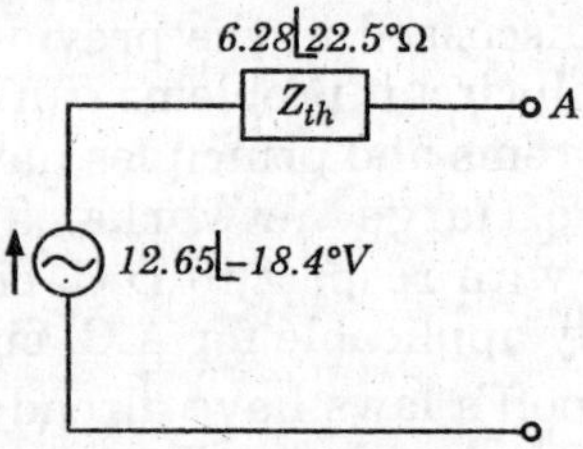

Fig. 9.3

Solution. V_0 is the open circuit voltage at $AB = V_{PQ}$

$$V_0 = V_{PQ} = \frac{20\ \angle 0°\ (4 + j4)}{(j4 + 4 + j4)}$$

$$= 12.65 \angle -18.4°\ \text{V}$$

$$Z_{th} = 5 + \frac{(4 + j4)\, j4}{(4 + j8)} = 6.28\ \angle 22.5°\ \Omega.$$

The equivalent circuit is given in Fig. 9.3.

Example 9.2. *Obtain the Norton's equivalent circuit for the network given by Fig. 9.2, at terminals AB.*

Solution. Apply a short circuit to the terminal AB as in Fig. 9.4.

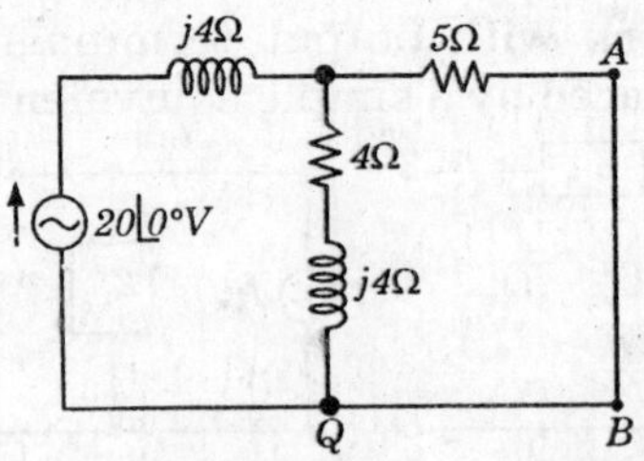

Fig. 9.4

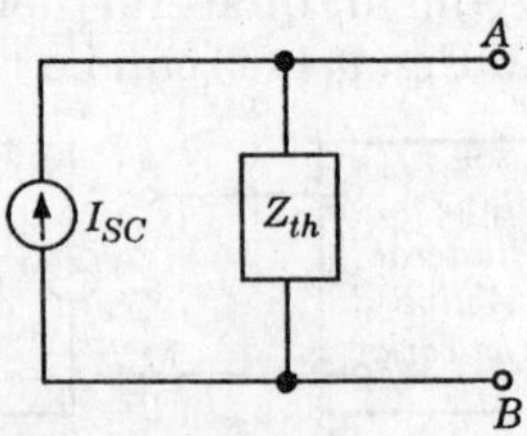

Fig. 9.5

The total impedance presented to the source

$$= Z_T = j4 + \frac{(4+j4)\,5}{4+j4+5} = \frac{4+j56}{9+j4}$$

$$I_T = \frac{20\angle 0°}{Z_T} = \frac{20\,(9+j4)}{(4+j56)}$$

$$I_{SC} = I_T\frac{(4+j4)}{(9+j4)} = 20\,\frac{(4+j4)}{4+j56}$$

$$= 2.015 \angle -40.9° \text{ amps.}$$

The equivalent circuit is given in Fig. 9.5.

Example 9.3. *Using Thevenin's theorem for the bridge network of Fig. 9.6 (a) find the current through a galvanometer of resistance 1 ohm connected between B and D.*

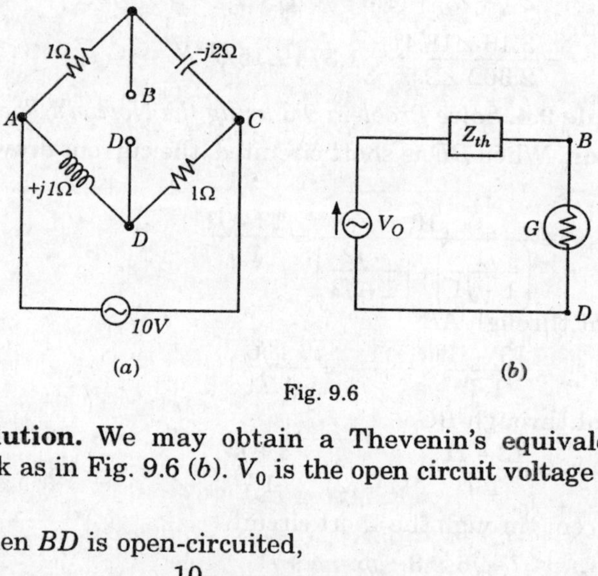

Fig. 9.6

Solution. We may obtain a Thevenin's equivalent of the network as in Fig. 9.6 (*b*). V_0 is the open circuit voltage between *B* and *D*.

When *BD* is open-circuited,

$$I_1 = \frac{10}{1-j2} = 2\,(1+j2)\text{ A}$$

$$I_2 = \frac{10}{1+j1} = 5\,(1-j1)\text{ A}$$

$$V_{BD} = V_{AD} - V_{AB} = 5\,(1-j1)\,j1 - 2\,(1+j2)\times 1$$

$$= (3+j1) = 3.16\angle 18.4° \text{ volts}$$

Z_{th} is the driving point impedance with *AC* shorted.

$$Z_{th} = \frac{-j2}{1-j2} + \frac{j1}{1+j1} = \frac{13+j1}{10}$$

$$= (1.3+j0.1)\text{ ohm.}$$

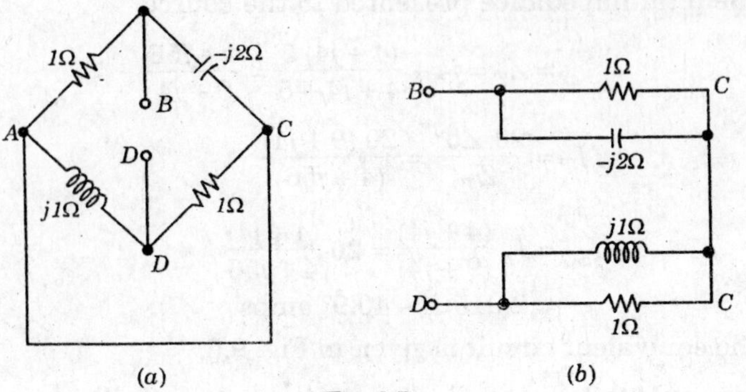

Fig. 9.7

$$I_g = \frac{V_0}{Z_{th} + Z_L} = \frac{3.16 \angle 18.4^\circ}{(1.3 + j0.1) + 1} = \frac{3.16 \angle 18.4^\circ}{2.3 + j0.1}$$

$$= \frac{3.16 \angle 18.4^\circ}{2.302 \angle 2.5^\circ} = 1.374 \angle 15.9^\circ \text{ A.}$$

Example 9.4. *Solve Problem 9.3 using the Norton's Theorem.*

Solution. When *BD* is short circuited, the current drawn from supply

$$= \frac{10}{\left(\frac{j1}{1+j1}\right) + \left(\frac{-j2}{1-j2}\right)} = \frac{13 - j1}{1.7}$$

Current through *AB*

$$= \frac{13 - j1}{1.7} \times \frac{j1}{1 + j1} = \frac{7 + j6}{1.7}$$

Current through *BC*

$$= \frac{13 - j1}{1.7} \times \frac{1}{(1 - j2)} = \frac{3 + j5}{1.7}$$

∴ Current through the short circuit,

$$I_{SC} = \frac{7 + j6}{1.7} - \frac{3 + j5}{1.7} = \frac{4 + j1}{1.7}$$

The equivalent circuit is shown in Fig. 9.8.

$$I_g = \frac{I_{SC} \times Z_{th}}{Z_{th} + 1}$$

$$= \frac{(4 + j1)}{1.7} \times \frac{(1.3 + j0.1)}{2.3 + j0.1}$$

$$= \frac{4.123 \angle 14^\circ \times 1.303 \angle 4.4^\circ}{1.7 \times 2.302 \angle 2.5^\circ}$$

$$= \mathbf{1.374 \angle 15.9^\circ \text{ A.}}$$

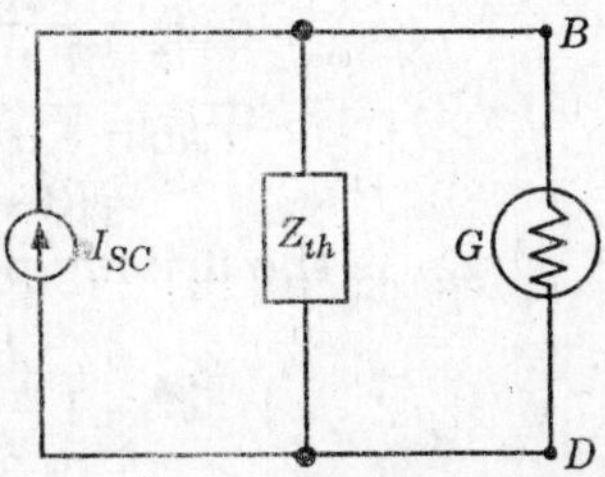

Fig. 9.8

Reciprocity Theorem

In a linear bilateral active network with a single source, the ratio of excitation to response is constant when the positions of these two are interchanged. The excitation may be a voltage or current source. The response may be the current through or voltage across any branch.

Using matrix approach, the loop current in any loop is given by

$$I_r = V_1 \frac{\Delta_{1r}}{\Delta} + V_2 \frac{\Delta_{2r}}{\Delta} + \ldots + V_r \frac{\Delta_{rr}}{\Delta} + \ldots$$

If only V_j is present, then

$$I_r = V_j \frac{\Delta_{jr}}{\Delta}$$

Then $$\frac{V_j}{I_r} = \frac{\Delta}{\Delta_{jr}}$$

When the excitation and response are interchanged, the source is V_r and response is I_j

$$I_j = V_r \frac{\Delta_{rj}}{\Delta}$$

$$\therefore \quad \frac{V_r}{I_j} = \frac{\Delta}{\Delta_{rj}}$$

The ratios are the transfer impedances between *jr* and *rj* loops respectively. But the network impedance matrix *Z*, is symmetrical for linear bilateral network. Therefore

$$\Delta_{rj} = \Delta_{jr}$$

Example 9.5. *Verify the reciprocity theorem for the network of Fig. 9.9. Find the current in the (3 – j4) ohm impedance.*

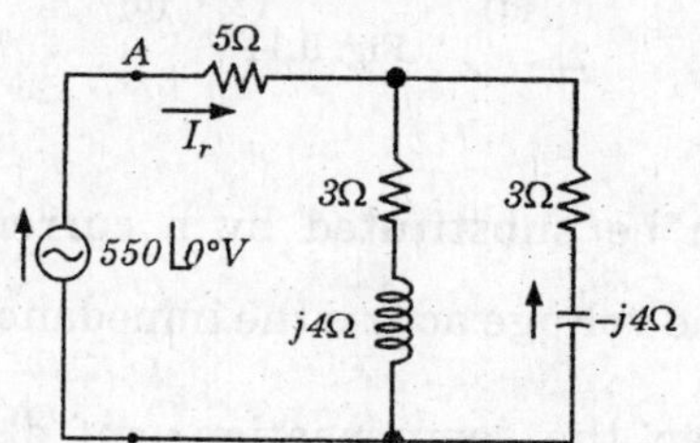

Fig. 9.9

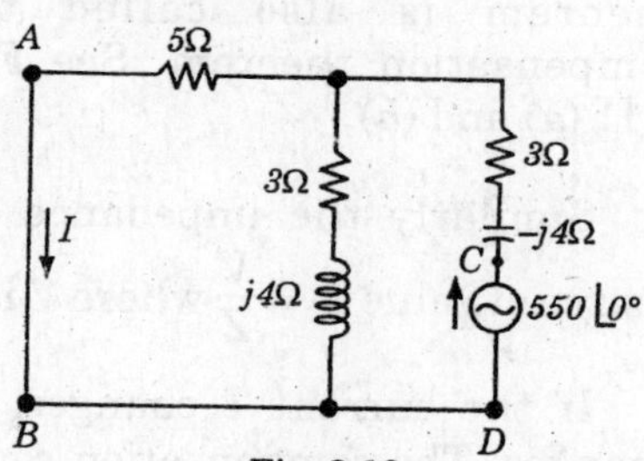

Fig. 9.10

Solution. The equivalent impedance of the network between *A* and *B*

$$Z_{eq} = 5 + \frac{(3+j4)\,(3-j4)}{6} = \frac{55}{6}$$

$$I_T = \frac{550\,\angle 0^\circ}{55/6} = 60 \text{ amps}$$

$$I = I_T\,\frac{(3+j4)}{6}$$

$$= \frac{60}{6}\,(3+j4) = (30+j40) \text{ amps.}$$

If the voltage source is shifted as shown in Fig. 9.10 the current I would shift to the branch AB. The impedance between CD

$$= (3-j4) + \frac{5\,(3+j4)}{8+j4}$$

$$= \frac{11}{4}\,(2-j1) \text{ ohms}$$

$$I = \frac{550}{\frac{11}{4}\,(2-j1)} \times \frac{(3+j4)}{(8+j4)}$$

$$= \frac{50\,(3+j4)}{(2-j1)\,(2+j1)} = \mathbf{(30+j40)\ amps.}$$

Thus the reciprocity theorem is verified.

Substitution Theorem

Any network containing an impedance Z carrying a current I has a voltage drop $I{\cdot}Z$ across it. Hence this impedance may be replaced by a voltage source of emf $V_C = IZ$ called the compensation voltage of proper polarity. This theorem is also called the compensation theorem. See Fig. 9.11 (*a*) and (*b*).

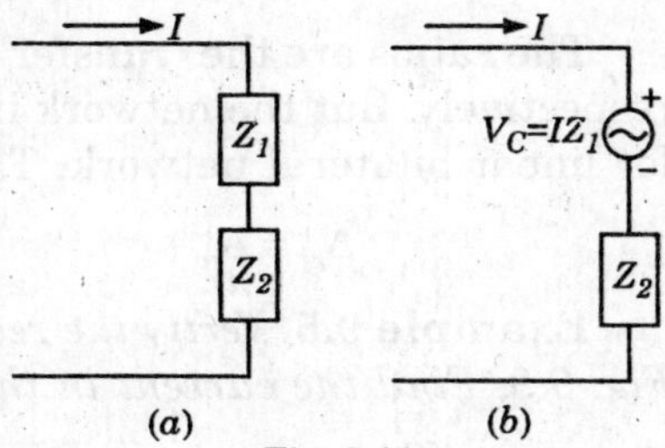

Fig. 9.11

Similarly the impedance can be substituted by a current source of value $I_C = \dfrac{V}{Z}$ where V is the voltage across the impedance.

If the current I changes, then the compensation emf also changes. The compensation source is a dependent source.

This theorem is useful in determining the changes in currents or voltages when the network elements are changed, as in the case of potentiometer or bridge circuits.

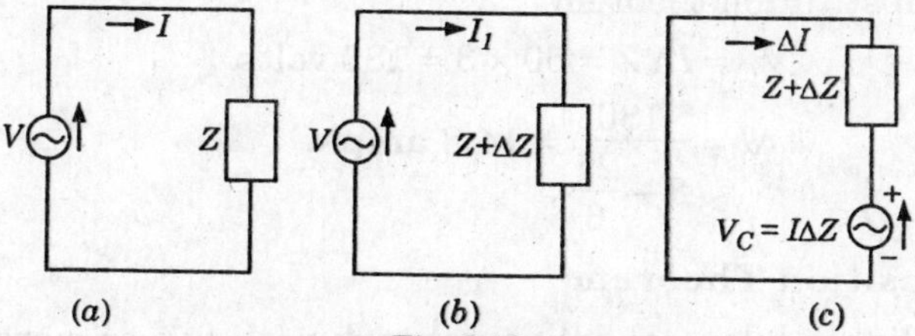

Fig. 9.12

Consider the network shown in Fig. 9.12.

$$I = V/Z$$

$$I_1 = V/(Z + \Delta Z)$$

where ΔZ is the change in the impedance Z.

Then, the change in the current, $\Delta I = I_1 - I$

$$\Delta I = \frac{V}{Z + \Delta Z} - \frac{V}{Z} = -\frac{V\Delta Z}{Z\,(Z + \Delta Z)}$$

$$= -I\frac{\Delta Z}{Z + \Delta Z}$$

The change in current ΔI, can be obtained as the current in the network of Fig. 9.12 (*c*), by replacing the e.m.f. by a compensation emf $V_C = I\,\Delta Z$.

Example 9.6. *Determine the change in the current I of Fig. 9.13 when the 5 ohms resistor is changed to 8 ohms. Verify by the substitution theorem.*

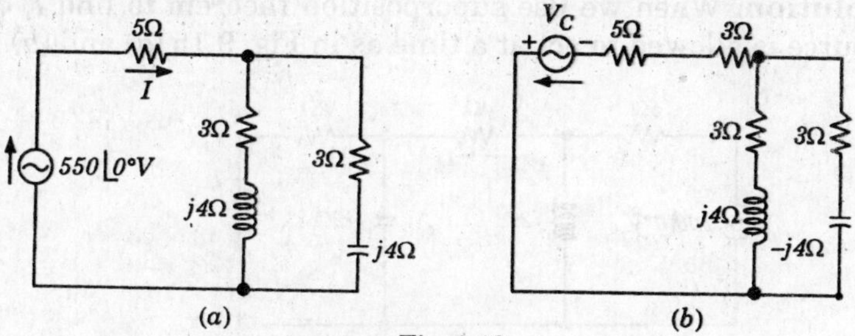

Fig. 9.13

$$I = \frac{550}{5 + \dfrac{(3 + j4)\,(3 - j4)}{(3 + j4) + (3 - j4)}} = \frac{550}{4 + \dfrac{25}{6}} = 60 \text{ amps}$$

$$I_1 = \frac{550}{8 + \dfrac{25}{6}} = 45.2 \text{ amps}$$

$$\Delta I = 60 - 45.2 = 14.8 \text{ amps.}$$

By substitution theorem,

$$V_C = I\Delta Z = 60 \times 3 = 180 \text{ volts.}$$

$$\Delta I = \frac{180}{8 + \frac{25}{6}} = \mathbf{14.8\ amps.}$$

Superposition Theorem

In a linear bilateral active network with two or more sources, the current through (or voltage across) any element is equal to the vector sum of the currents through (or voltages across) the element when each source is applied separately. The other sources are in turn replaced by their respective internal impedances. The application of this theorem has already been dealt with for D.C. circuits. The theorem can be applied only for linear relations and as such cannot be applied for power calculations.

Example 9.7. *Using the principle of superposition, calculate the current I in the network of Fig. 9.14.*

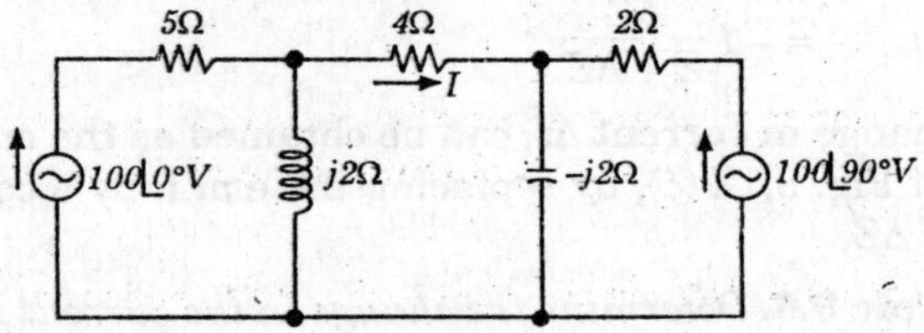

Fig. 9.14

Solution. When we use superposition theorem to find I, only one source is allowed to act at a time as in Fig. 9.15 (a) and (b).

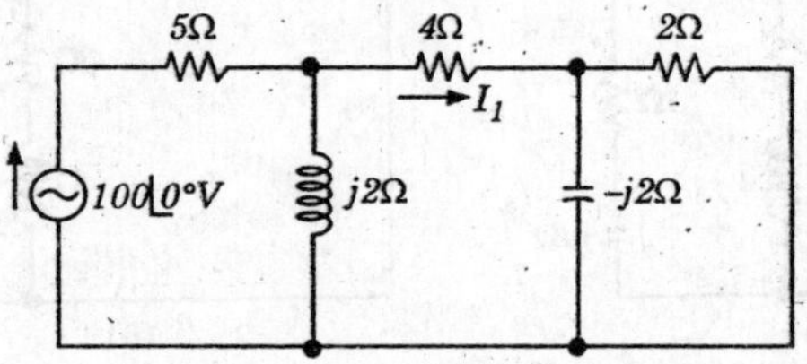

(a)

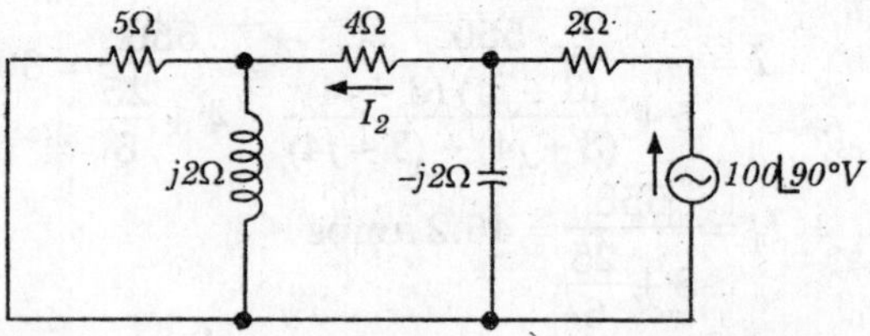

(b)

Fig. 9.15

As the two currents are marked in the opposite directions

$$I = I_1 - I_2$$

From Fig. 9.15 (*a*). Total impedance presented to the source.

$$= 5 + \frac{j2\left[4 + \dfrac{2 \times (-j2)}{2 - j2}\right]}{j2 + 4 + \dfrac{2 \times (-j2)}{2 - j2}}$$

$$= 5 + \frac{j2\,(5 - j1)}{j2 + 4 + (1 - j1)} = \frac{75 + j24}{13}\ \Omega$$

$$I_1 = \frac{100\ \angle 0^\circ \times 13}{75 + j24} \times \frac{j2}{5 + j1} = 6.475\ \angle 61^\circ$$

$$= \mathbf{(3.14 + j\ 5.66)\ amps.}$$

From Fig. 9.15 (*b*) equivalent impedance presented to the source.

$$= 2 + \frac{(-j2)\left[4 + \dfrac{5 \times j2}{5 + j2}\right]}{-j2 + 4 + \dfrac{5 \times j2}{5 + j2}}$$

$$= 2 + \frac{100 - j272}{136 - j8} = 2.85 - j1.95\ \Omega$$

$$I_2 = \frac{100\ \angle 90^\circ}{2.85 - j1.95} \times \frac{-j2 \times 19}{136 - j8}$$

$$= \frac{200 \times 29}{(2.85 - j1.95)\,(136 - j8)} = 12.3285\ \angle 37.75^\circ\ \text{A}$$

$$= 9.75 + j7.55\ \text{A}$$

$$\therefore \quad I = I_1 - I_2 = (3.14 + j5.66) - (9.75 + j7.55)$$

$$= (-6.61 - j1.89)\ \text{amps.}$$

$$= \mathbf{6.875\ \angle 196^\circ\ A.}$$

Maximum Power Transfer Theorem

Large electrical systems are designed for maximum efficiency conditions and not for maximum power transfer conditions. But small battery circuits and communication circuits are designed for maximum power transfer conditions because the maximum utilization of the equipments is more important. Unlike the case of D.C. circuits, here the load may be a variable pure resistance or a complex impedance. We shall consider the two cases separately.

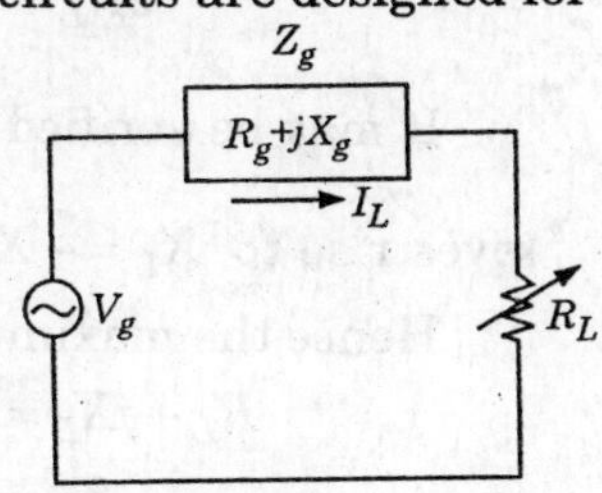

Fig. 9.16

Case (*i*) Variable pure resistance loads, as shown in Fig. 9.16.

Load current, $I_L = \dfrac{V_g}{\sqrt{(R_g + R_L)^2 + X_g^2}}$

Power dissipated in the load

$$P_L = I_L^2 R_L = \frac{V_g^2 R_L}{(R_g + R_L)^2 + X_g^2}$$

P_L is maximum when $\dfrac{dP_L}{dR_L} = 0$

i.e. $$\frac{V_g^2 \left[(R_g + R_L)^2 + X_g^2\right] - R_L 2X (R_g + R_L)}{\left[(R_g + R_L)^2 + X_g^2\right]^2} = 0$$

$$R_g^2 + R_L^2 + 2R_g R_L \times X_g^2 - 2R_L R_g - 2R_L^2 = 0$$

or $$R_g^2 + X_g^2 = R_L^2$$

or $$R_L = \sqrt{R_g^2 + X_g^2} = |\, Z_g \,|$$

For maximum power transfer to the load, its resistance must be equal to the magnitude of the source impedance. If $X_g = 0$, then $R_L = R_g$ as in the D.C. case.

Case (*ii*) Load is a complex impedance as shown in Fig. 9.17.

$$I_L = \frac{V_g}{\sqrt{(R_g + R_L)^2 + (X_g + X_L)^2}}$$

$$P_L = \frac{V_g^2 R_L}{(R_g + R_L)^2 + (X_g + X_L)^2}$$

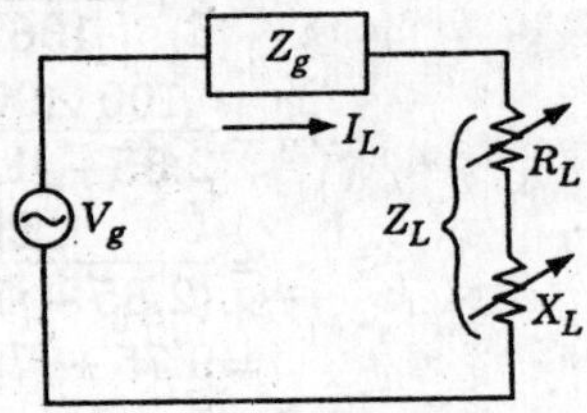

Fig. 9.17

P_L is a maximum (when R_L and X_L are both varied) when the partial derivatives satisfy the following conditions :

$$\frac{\partial P_L}{\partial R_L} = 0 \quad \text{and} \quad \frac{\partial P_L}{\partial X_L} = 0$$

As before $\dfrac{\partial P_L}{\partial R_L} = 0$ gives rise to $R_L = R_g$

It may be verified that $\dfrac{\partial P_L}{\partial X_L} = 0$

gives rise to $X_L = -X_g$

Hence the maximum Power Transfer condition is

$$R_L + jX_L = R_g - jX_g$$

or $$Z_L = Z_g^*$$

The load impedance must equal the conjugate of the internal impedance.

Case (*iii*) Load impedance with fixed reactance, but variable resistance

$$P_L = \frac{V_g^2 R_L}{(R_L + R_g)^2 + (X_L + X_g)^2}$$

and is a maximum when $\dfrac{dP_L}{dR_L} = 0$

This gives rise to

$$R_L^2 = R_g^2 + (X_L + X_g)^2$$

or $$R_L = \sqrt{R_g^2 + (X_L + X_g)^2}.$$

Example 9.8. *Show that the power supplied by the current source in Fig. 9.18 would be double that supplied by the voltage source when R = 10/3 ohms.*

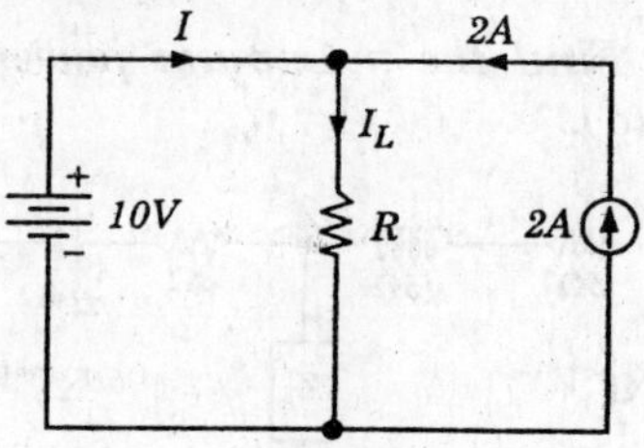

Fig. 9.18

Solution. $I = I_L - 2 = \dfrac{10}{R} - 2$

Power supplied by the current source = 10 × 2 = 20 W

Power supplied by the voltage source

$$= 10\left(\frac{10}{R} - 2\right)$$

Given that $$20 = 2\left[10\left(\frac{10}{R} - 2\right)\right]$$

∴ $$R = \frac{10}{3} \text{ ohms.}$$

Example 9.9. *In the circuit of Fig. 9.19, find the value of Z_L for maximum power transfer to it if (a) Z_L is a pure resistor (b) if Z_L is a complex impedance with both variable real and imaginary parts. Determine in each case the maximum power.*

Solution. (*a*) Maximum power transfer occurs when

$$Z_L = R_L = |\, Z_g \,|$$
$$R_L = |\, 5 + j10 \,|$$
$$= \mathbf{11.18\ ohms.}$$

Under this condition

$$I = \frac{100\ \angle 90°}{5 + j10 + 11.18}$$
$$= 5.258\ \angle 58.28°\ \text{A}.$$

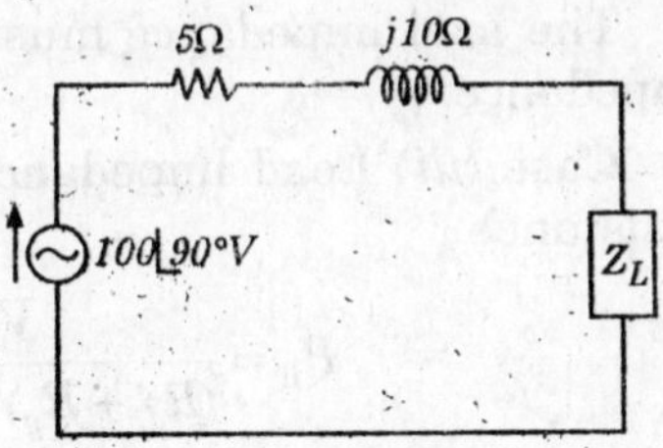

Fig. 9.19

$$\text{Load Power} = I^2 R_L$$
$$= (5.258)^2\ 11.18 = \mathbf{309\ watts}$$

(b) If Z_L is complex, maximum power transfer occurs

when $\quad Z_L = Z_g^* = 5 - j10$

$$I = \frac{100\ \angle 90°}{(5 + j10) + (5 - j10)} = 10\ \angle 90°\ \text{A}$$

$$\text{Load Power} = I^2\ R_L = (10)^2 \times 5 = \mathbf{500\ watts.}$$

Example 9.10. *Find the maximum power transferred to the load Z_L of Fig. 9.20 (a).*

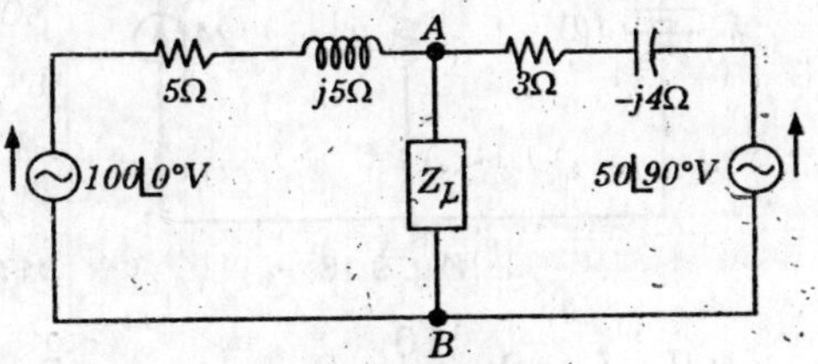

Fig. 9. 20 (a)

Solution. We shall first obtain a Thevenin's equivalent of the above circuit about *AB* as in Fig. 9.20 (*b*).

When *AB* is open circuited, current in the circuit is

$$= \frac{100 - j50}{5 + j5 + 3 - j4} = \frac{100 - j50}{8 + j1}$$

$$V_{AB} = V_0 = 100 - \frac{100 - j50}{8 + j1} \times (5 + j5)$$

$$= \frac{50 - j250}{13}\ \text{V}.$$

$$Z_{th} = \frac{(5 + j5)(3 - j4)}{8 + j1} = \frac{55 - j15}{13}$$

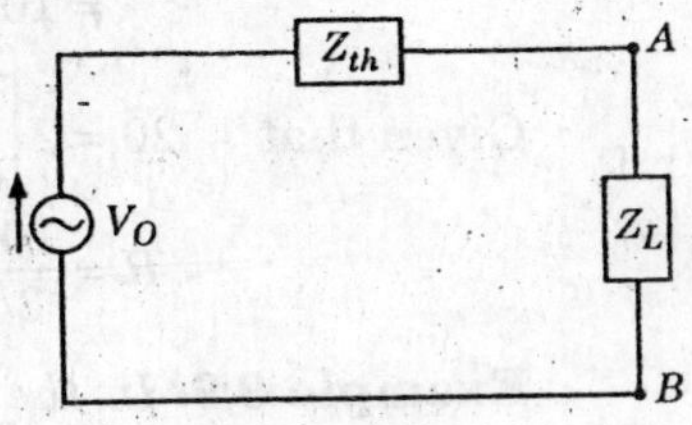

Fig. 9.20 (b)

Power transferred to the load is a maximum when

$$Z_L = Z_{th}^* = \frac{55 + j15}{13}$$

For this condition,

$$I = \frac{V_0}{Z_{th} + Z_L} = \frac{(50 - j250)}{13\left(\frac{55 - j15}{13} + \frac{55 + j15}{13}\right)}$$

$$= \frac{50 - j250}{110} = 2.32 \angle -78.7° \text{ A}$$

$$\text{Load Power} = I^2 R_L$$

$$= (2.32)^2 \times \frac{55}{13}$$

$$= \mathbf{22.73 \text{ watts.}}$$

Example 9.11. *In the network of Fig. 9.21, the load across AB consists of a variable resistance R_L and a capacitive reactance, variable between 1.5 and 6 ohms. Determine the value of R_L and X_C for which the power transfer is a maximum and calculate the maximum power transferred to the load.*

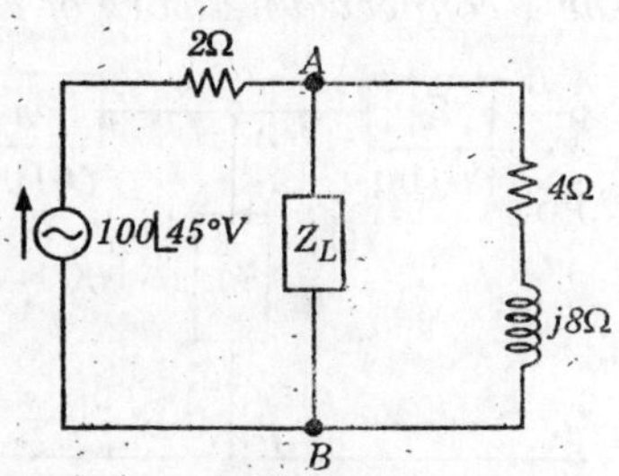

Fig. 9.21

Solution. We shall again obtain a Thevenin's equivalent of the above circuit about terminals *AB*.

$$V_0 = \frac{100 \angle 45°}{2 + 4 + j8}(4 + j8)$$

$$= 100 \angle 45° \left(\frac{4 + j8}{6 + j8}\right)$$

$$= 89.4 \angle 55.3° \text{ V}$$

$$Z_{th} = \frac{2\,(4 + j8)}{2 + 4 + j8} = 1.76 + j0.32 \,\Omega$$

For maximum power transfer

$$Z_L = Z_{th}^* = 1.76 - j0.32 \,\Omega$$

But the minimum value of $X_C = 1.5$ ohms and therefore the closest value possible for X_C is 1.5 ohms and

$$R_L = |\, Z_{th} - jX_C \,|$$

$$= |\, 1.76 - j0.32 - j1.5 \,|$$

$$= |\, 1.76 - j1.18 \,| = 2.12 \text{ ohms}$$

$$I_L = \frac{V_0}{Z_{th} + Z_L} = \frac{89.4 \angle 55.3°}{(1.76 + j0.32) + (2.12 - j1.5)}$$

$$= 22.055 \angle 38.4° \text{ A}$$

$$P_L = I_L^2 R_L = \mathbf{1031 \text{ watts.}}$$

Star-Delta Transformation

The same formulae derived in Chapter 2 for D.C. circuits are valid here too, with the difference that we must consider complex impedances in A.C. as compared to pure resistance in D.C.

Example 9.12. *Determine the Δ-connected equivalent circuit for the Y connected network of Fig. 9.22.*

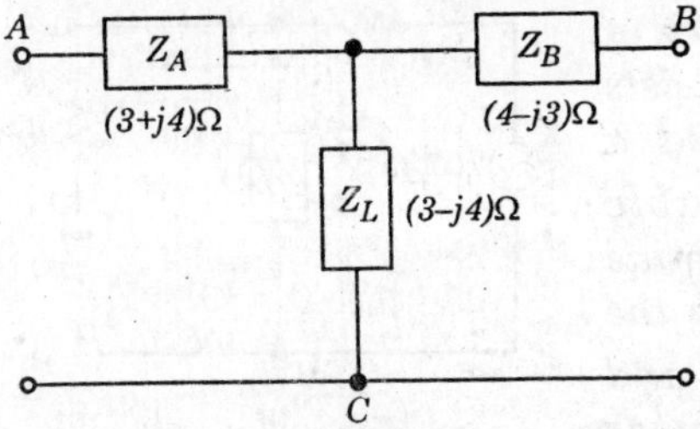

Fig. 9.22.

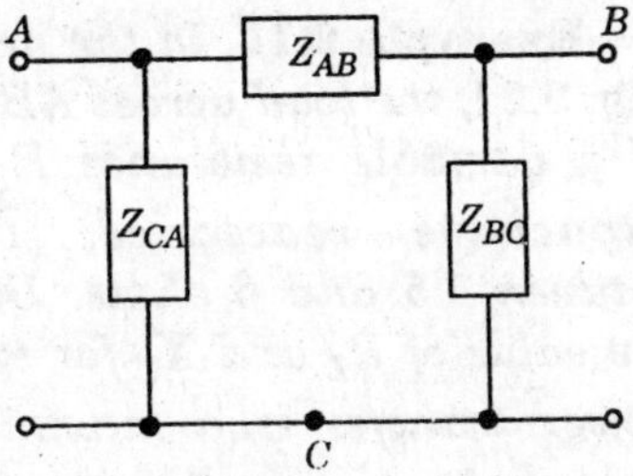

Fig. 9.23

Solution.

$$Z_{AB} = \frac{Z_A Z_B + Z_B Z_C + Z_C Z_A}{Z_C}$$

$$= Z_A + Z_B + \frac{Z_A Z_B}{Z_C}$$

$$= (3 + j4) + (4 - j3) + \frac{(3 + j4)(4 - j3)}{3 - j4}$$

$$= (8.8 + j5.7)\ \Omega$$

$$Z_{BC} = Z_B + Z_C + \frac{Z_B Z_C}{Z_A}$$

$$= (4 - j3) + (3 - j4) + \frac{(4 - j3)(3 - j4)}{3 + j4}$$

$$= (3 - j10)\ \Omega$$

$$Z_{CA} = Z_C + Z_A + \frac{Z_C Z_A}{Z_B}$$

$$= (3 - j4) + (3 + j4) + \frac{(3 - j4)(3 + j4)}{4 - j3}$$

$$= (10 + j3)\ \Omega.$$

Example 9.13. *Obtain the Y connected equivalent of the Δ connected circuit shown in Fig. 9.24.*

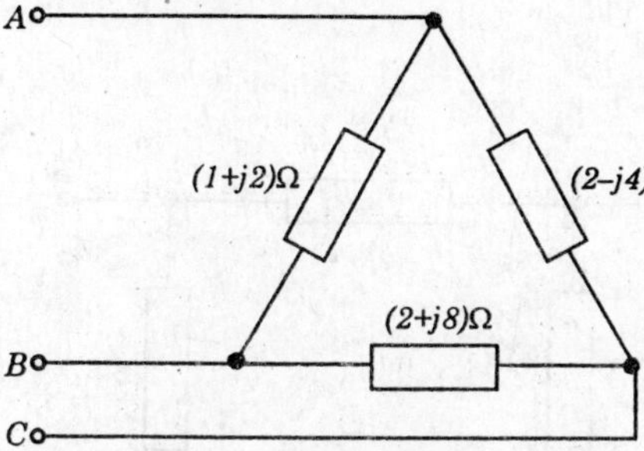

Fig. 9.24

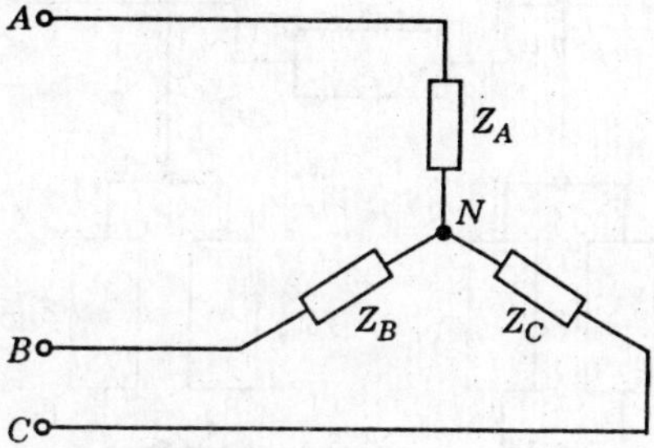

Fog. 9.25

$$Z_A = \frac{Z_{AB}\, Z_{CA}}{Z_{AB} + Z_{BC} + Z_{CA}} = \frac{(1 + j2)\,(2 - j4)}{(1 + j2) + (2 + j8) + (2 - j4)}$$

$$= (0.82 - j0.98)\ \Omega$$

$$Z_B = \frac{(2 + j2)\,(2 + j8)}{5 + j6} = (0.033 + j2.36)\ \Omega$$

$$Z_C = \frac{(2 + j8)\,(2 - j4)}{5 + j6} = (3.74 - j2.39)\ \Omega$$

Example 9.14. *The network of Fig. 9.26 consists of two Y connected circuits in parallel. Obtain the single delta connected equivalent circit.*

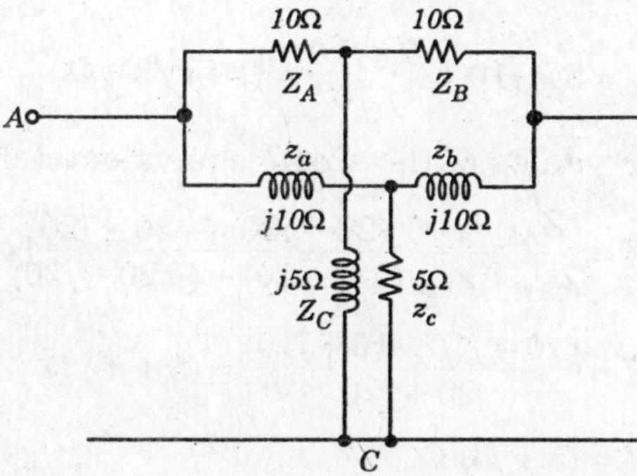

Fig. 9.26

Solution. We shall convert the two sets of Y circuits into two sets of parallel-circuits first and then obtain the single equivalent delta. See Fig. 9.27 (*a*) and (*b*).

$$Z_{AB} = Z_A + Z_B + \frac{Z_A Z_B}{Z_C}$$

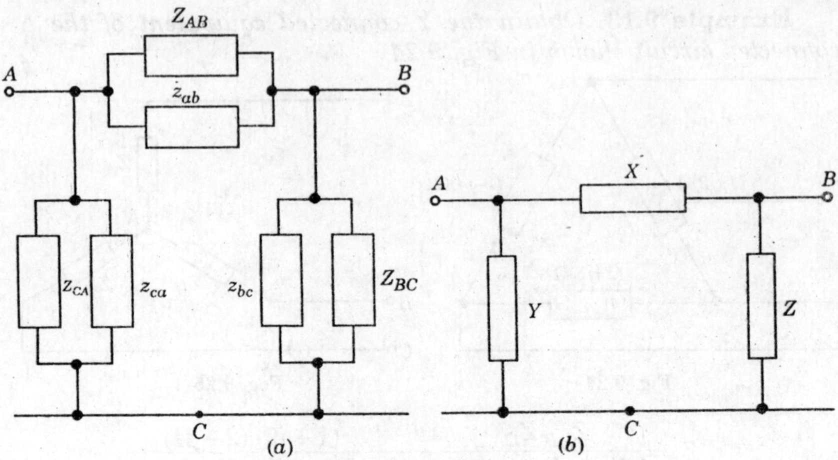

Fig. 9.27

$$= 10 + 10 + \frac{10 \times 10}{j5} = (20 - j20)\ \Omega$$

Similarly, $$Z_{BC} = 10 + j5 + \frac{10 \times j5}{10} = (10 + j10)\ \Omega$$

$$Z_{CA} = j5 + 10 + \frac{j5 + 10}{10} = (10 + j20)\ \Omega$$

$$z_{AB} = j10 + j10 + \frac{j10 \times 10}{4} = (-20 + j20)\ \Omega$$

$$z_{BC} = j10 + 5 + \frac{j10 \times 5}{j\,10} = (10 + j10)\ \Omega$$

$$z_{CA} = 5 + j10 + \frac{5 \times j10}{j\,10} = (10 + j10)\ \Omega$$

The impedance values of the single equivalent delta are :

$$X = \frac{Z_{AB}\, z_{AB}}{Z_{AB} + z_{AB}} \frac{(20 - j20)\,(-20 + j20)}{(20 - j20) + (-20 + j20)} = \infty$$

$$Y = \frac{(10 + j10)\,(10 + j10)}{20 + j20} = (5 + j5)\ \Omega$$

$$Z = (5 + j5)\ \Omega.$$

Example 9.15. *Show that a multi-mesh passive three terminal network may be replaced with a Δ connection of three impedances.*

Solution. Apply a voltage V_1 to the left terminals and let the current be I_1 as shown in Fig. 9.28. Let the corresponding values at the right terminals be V_2 and I_2 respectively. As the network is passive all other driving voltages are zero.

(a)

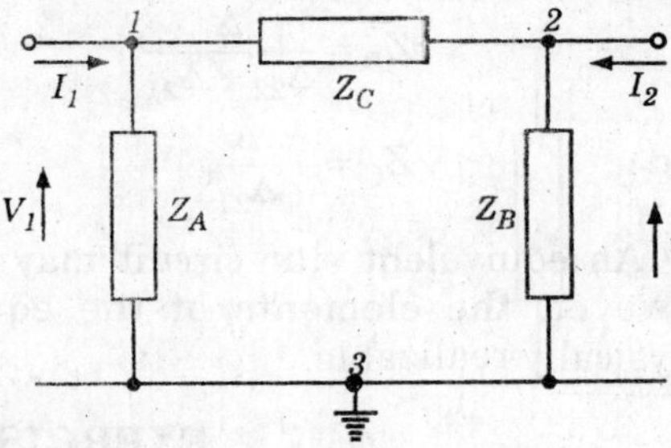

(b)

Fig. 9.28

$$\therefore \quad \begin{bmatrix} Z_{11} & Z_{12} & Z_{13} \ldots Z_{1n} \\ Z_{21} & Z_{22} & Z_{23} \quad Z_{2n} \\ & \ldots\ldots\ldots\ldots & \\ Z_{n1} & Z_{n2} & Z_{n3} \quad Z_{nn} \end{bmatrix} \begin{bmatrix} I_1 \\ I_2 \\ \ldots \\ I_n \end{bmatrix} = \begin{bmatrix} V_1 \\ V_2 \\ \ldots \\ 0 \end{bmatrix}$$

By determinants, $I_1 = V_1 \dfrac{\Delta_{11}}{\Delta} + V_2 \dfrac{\Delta_{21}}{\Delta}$

and $$I_2 = V_1 \frac{\Delta_{12}}{\Delta} + V_2 \frac{\Delta_{22}}{\Delta}$$

which may be put in matrix form as

$$\begin{bmatrix} \dfrac{\Delta_{11}}{\Delta} & \dfrac{\Delta_{21}}{\Delta} \\ \dfrac{\Delta_{12}}{\Delta} & \dfrac{\Delta_{22}}{\Delta} \end{bmatrix} \begin{bmatrix} V_1 \\ V_2 \end{bmatrix} = \begin{bmatrix} I_1 \\ I_2 \end{bmatrix}$$

This set of equation is similar to the node voltage equations of the network of Fig. 9.28 (*b*).

$$\begin{bmatrix} \left(\dfrac{1}{Z_A} + \dfrac{1}{Z_C}\right) & \left(-\dfrac{1}{Z_c}\right) \\ \left(-\dfrac{1}{Z_C}\right) & \left(\dfrac{1}{Z_B} + \dfrac{1}{Z_c}\right) \end{bmatrix} \begin{bmatrix} V_1 \\ V_2 \end{bmatrix} = \begin{bmatrix} I_1 \\ I_2 \end{bmatrix}$$

Comparing the two equations, we have

$$\frac{1}{Z_A} + \frac{1}{Z_C} = \frac{\Delta_{11}}{\Delta}; \qquad -\frac{1}{Z_C} = \frac{\Delta_{21}}{\Delta}$$

and $$\frac{1}{Z_B} + \frac{1}{Z_C} = \frac{\Delta_{22}}{\Delta}$$

These may be used to solve for Z_A, Z_B and Z_C given by

$$Z_A = \frac{\Delta}{\Delta_{11} + \Delta_{21}}$$

$$Z_B = \frac{\Delta}{\Delta_{22} + \Delta_{21}}$$

and $$Z_C = -\frac{\Delta}{\Delta_{21}}$$

An equivalent star circuit may also be obtained. Sometimes, however, the elements of the equivalent circuit may not be physically realizable.

EXERCISES

9.1. Obtain the Thevenin's equivalent for the circuit of Fig. 9.29 at the terminals AB. [**Ans.** $V_0 = 38.4 \angle 16.4°$ V, $Z_{th} = 4.435 \angle -58.9°$ Ω]

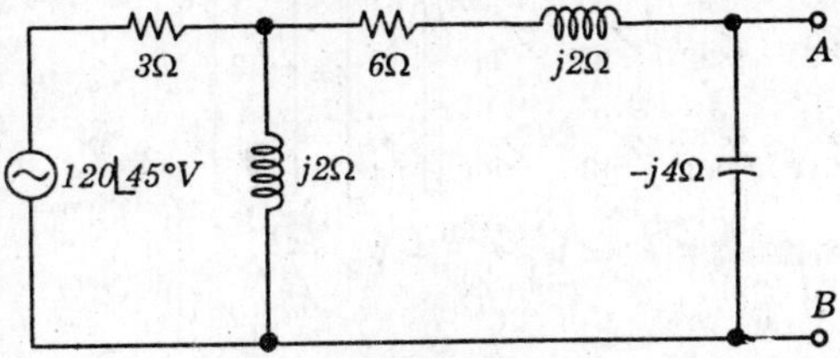

Fig. 9.29

9.2. The active network shown in Fig. 9.30 is supplied by a current source $I = 5 \angle 30°$. Find the Thevenin's equivalent at terminals AB.

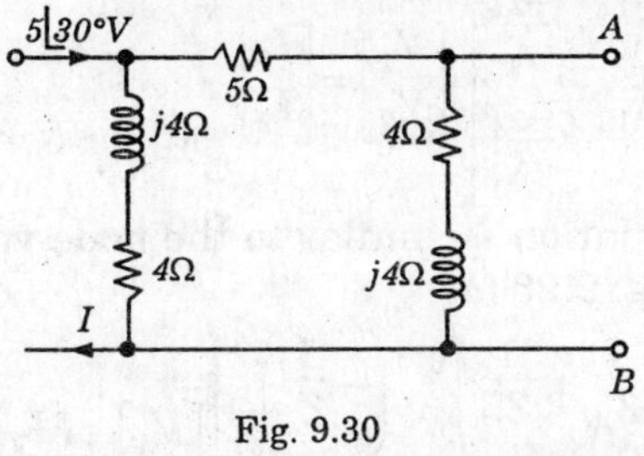

Fig. 9.30

[**Ans.** $V_0 = 10.5 \angle 88.4°$ V, $Z_{th} = 3.65 \angle 37.4°$ Ω]

9.3. In the circuit in Fig. 9.31, a load impedance of $5 \angle 60°$ is connected to terminal PQ. Find the power consumed in it using Thevenin's theorem.

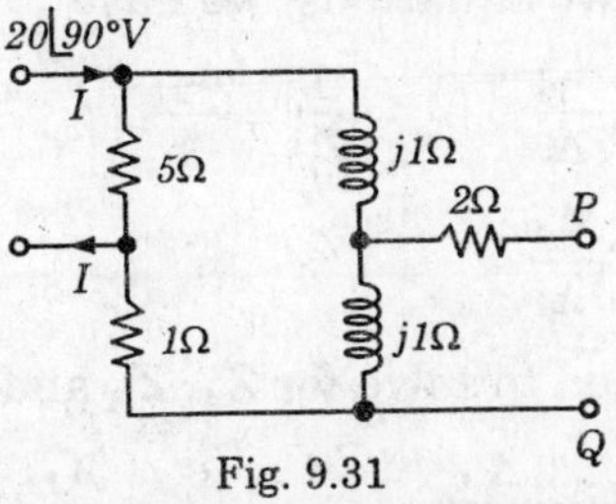

Fig. 9.31

[**Ans.** $V_0 = 1518 \angle 161.6°$ V, $Z_{th} = 2.15 + j0.95$ Ω Power = 12.6 Watts]

9.4. Find the Norton's equivalent for the circuit of Fig. 9.29.

[**Ans.** $I_{SC} = 8.66 \angle 75.3°$ A]

9.5. Find the Norton's equivalent for the circuit of Fig. 9.30.

[**Ans.** 2.88 $\angle 51°$ A]

9.6. Repeat Problem 9.3 using Norton's Theorem. [**Ans.** $I_{SC} = 6.722 \angle 137.8°$ A]

9.7. In the circuit shown in Fig. 9.32, find the current I. Apply the reciprocity theorem and compare the results. [**Ans.** $I = 3.52 \angle -92.4°$ A]

9.8. In the network of Fig. 9.33, determine the voltage V_C. Then apply reciprocity theorem and compare the two voltages.

[**Ans.** $V_C = 67.3 \angle -104.6°$ V]

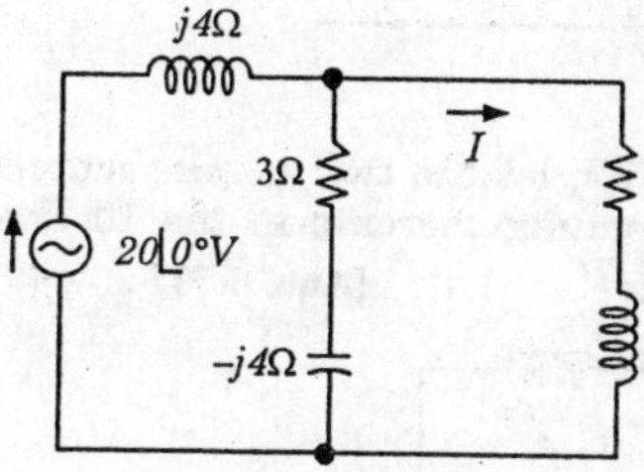

Fig. 9.32

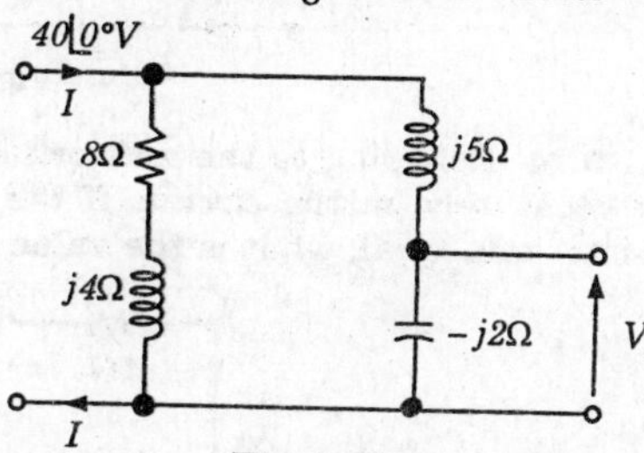

Fig. 9.33

9.9. In the network of Fig. 9.34, determine the node voltage V_2. Apply the reciprocity theorem and compare the results. [**Ans.** $V_2 = 4.2 \angle 104°$ V]

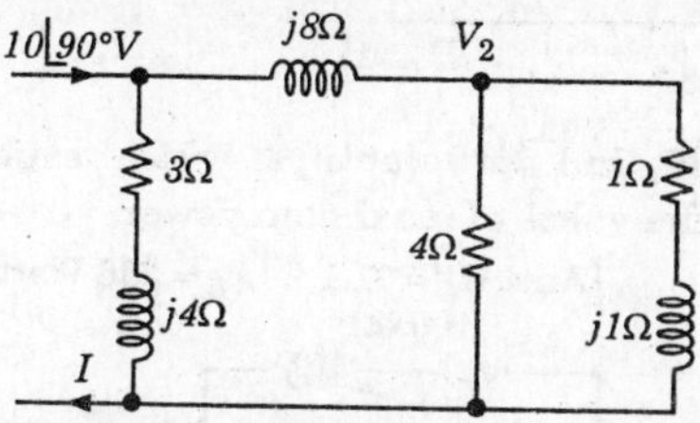

Fig. 9.34

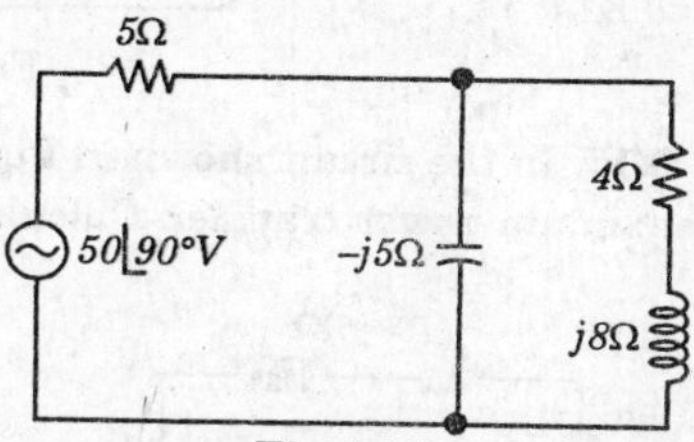

Fig. 9.35

9.10. In Fig. 9.35, replace the $j8$ ohm reactor by a compensation e.m.f.

[**Ans.** $V_C = 33.22 \angle 94.7°$ V]

9.11. In Fig. 9.36, the 10 ohm resistor is changed to 5 ohms. Using compensation theorem find V_C and the change in the current through it.

[**Ans.** $V_C = 7.8 \angle -128.66°$ V, $\Delta I = 0.872 \angle 173.35°$ A]

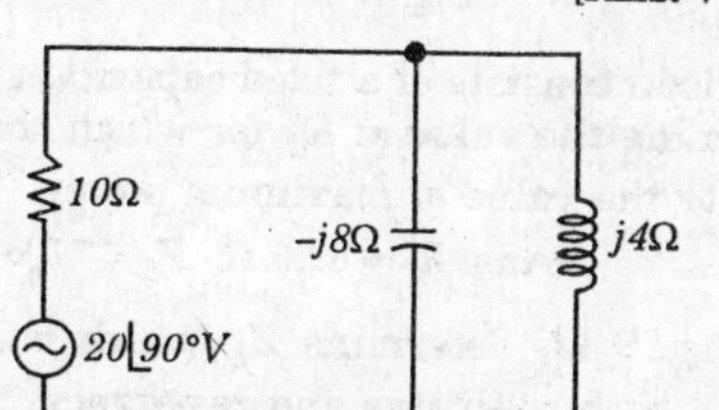

Fig. 9.36

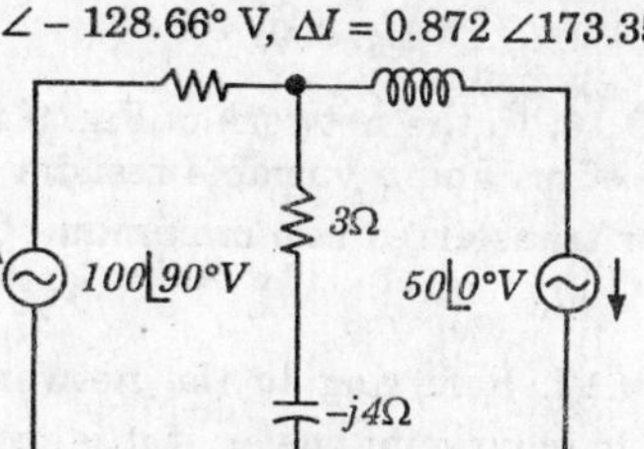

Fig. 9.37

9.12. Apply the principle of superposition to obtain the current I through the $(3 - j4)$ ohm impedance of Fig. 9.37. [Ans. $I = 17 \angle 144.7°$ A]

9.13. In the network of Fig. 9.38, determine V_B by means of the principle of superposition. [Ans. $V_B = 62.1 \angle 66.8°$ Volts]

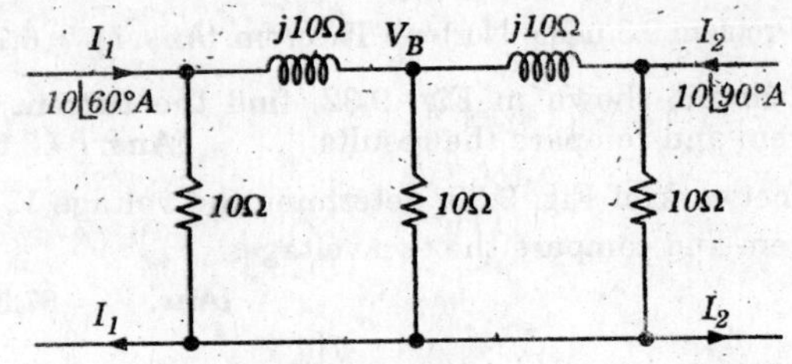

Fig. 9.38

9.14 Referring to the network of Fig. 9.39, let the two voltage sources act separately on the circuit. If the corresponding currents in the 10 ohm resistor are equal, what is the value of V_1/V_2 ? [Ans. $0.707 \angle -45°$]

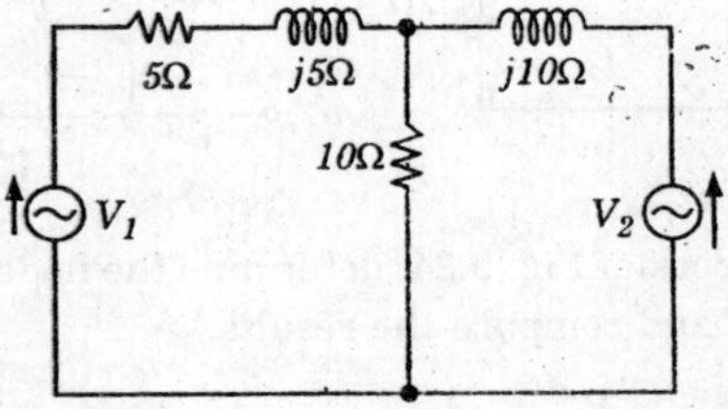

Fig. 9.39

9.15. In the circuit shown in Fig. 9.40, find the value of R_L which results in maximum power transfer. Calculate the value of maximum power. [Ans. $R_L = 11.1$ Ω, $P_L = 236$ Watts]

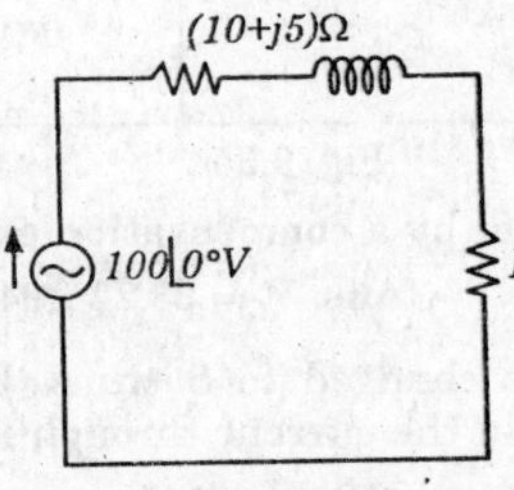

Fig. 9.40

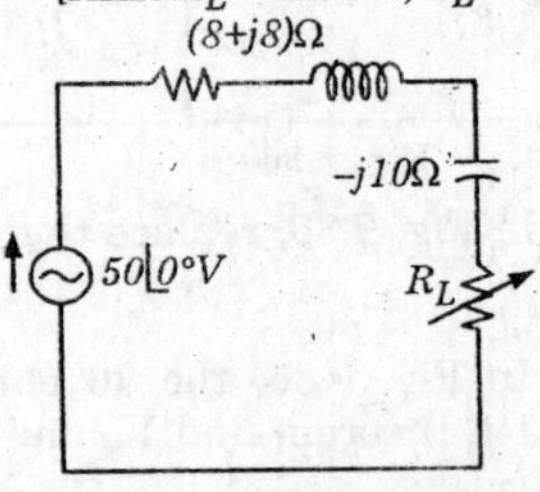

Fig. 9.41

9.16. In the network of Fig. 9.41, the load consists of a fixed capacitance of 10 ohms and a variable resistor. Determine the value of R_L for which the power transferred is a maximum. Calculate the value of maximum power. [Ans. $R_L = 8.25$ Ω, $P_L = 77$ W]

9.17. Referring to the network of Fig. 9.42, determine Z_L which will receive maximum power, if it is variable in both reactance and resistance. [Ans. $(4.64 - j2.06$ Ω$)$]

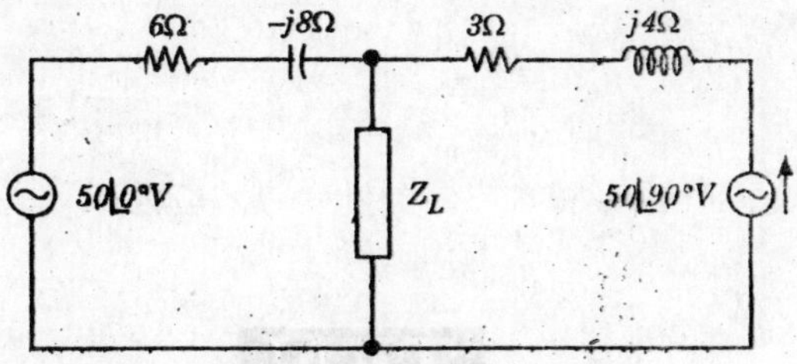

Fig. 9.42

9.18. Three impedances each of value 10 ∠30° Ω are connected in delta. Find the equivalent star value. $\left[\textbf{Ans. } \frac{10}{3} \angle 30°\ \Omega\right]$

91.19. Obtain the Δ-connected equivalent circuit for the network of Fig. 9.43. [**Ans.** 21 + *j*12 Ω, 5.4 + *j*0.3 Ω, – 12 + *j*21 Ω]

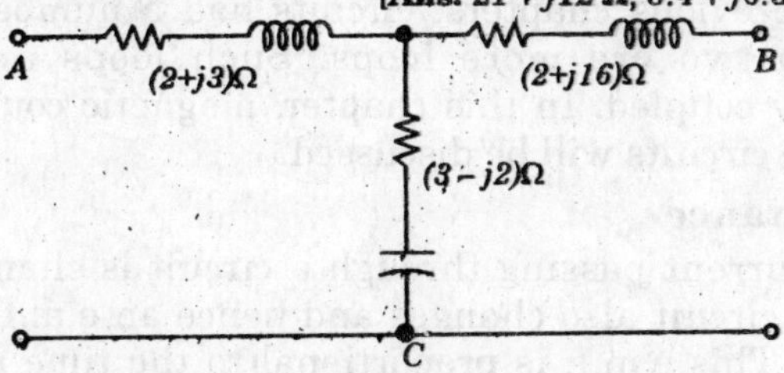

Fig. 9.43

TEN

COUPLED CIRCUITS

In the previous chapters, circuits had a number of branches common to two ore more loops. Such loops are said to be conductively coupled. In this chapter, magnetic coupling between two or more circuits will be discussed.

Self Inductance

If the current passing through a circuit is changing, the flux linking the circuit also changes and hence an e.m.f. is induced in the circuit. This e.m.f. is proportional to the time rate of change of current.

i.e. $$\nu \propto \frac{di}{dt}$$

or $$\nu = L\frac{di}{dt}$$

where the constant of proportionality, L is the self inductance of the circuit and ν is called the self induced e.m.f. If the coil has N turns the e.m.f. induced is also given by

$$\nu = N\frac{d\phi}{dt}$$

where ϕ is the flux linking the circuit. Hence

$$L = N\frac{d\phi}{di}$$

If the permeability is constant, then

$$L = \frac{N\phi}{i}$$

Mutual Inductance

Consider the circuit shown in Fig. 10.1. The changing current i_1 produces a flux ϕ_1. If a second coil is placed near the first coil, some of the flux links coil 2 also say ϕ_{12}. An e.m.f. will be induced in coil 2, given by

$$v_2 = N_2 \frac{d\phi_{12}}{dt}$$

Since ϕ_{12} is produced by i_1, v_2 will be proportional to the time rate of change of current i_1.

Therefore $$v_2 = M \frac{di_1}{dt}$$

where the constant of proportionality M, is called the mutual inductance between the two coils and has the unit of Henry. v_2 is a mutually induced e.m.f.

Hence $$M = N_2 \frac{d\phi_{12}}{di_1}$$

As before, if the permeability is constant

$$M = \frac{N_2\,\phi_{12}}{i_1}$$

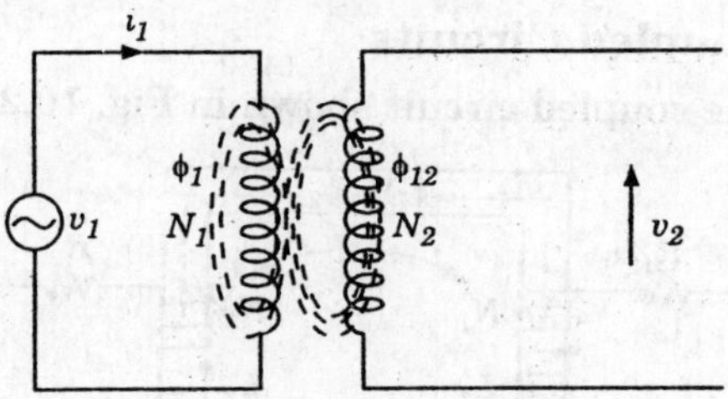

Fig. 10.1

The mutual coupling is bilateral and analogous results are obtained if a current i_2 flows in coil 2, an e.m.f. v_1 will be induced in coil 1.

$$v_1 = M \frac{di_2}{dt}$$

Hence $$M = N_1\,\phi_{21}/i_2.$$

The lines of flux which do not link both the coils are called leakage lines.

Coefficient of Coupling

The fraction of the total flux produced by one coil linking a second coil is called the coefficient of coupling, K. Thus

$$K = \frac{\phi_{12}}{\phi_1} = \frac{\phi_{21}}{\phi_2}$$

Since $\phi_{12} < \phi_1$ or $\phi_{21} < \phi_2$, the value of K is always less than or equal to 1.

$$M = \frac{N_2 \phi_{12}}{i_1}$$

Also $$M = \frac{N_1 \phi_{21}}{i_2}$$

Therefore multiplying together

$$M^2 = \left(\frac{N_2 \phi_{12}}{i_1}\right)\left(\frac{N_1 \phi_{21}}{i_2}\right)$$

$$= \left(\frac{N_2 K \cdot \phi_1}{i_1}\right)\left(\frac{N_1 K \cdot \phi_2}{i_2}\right)$$

$$= K^2 \left(\frac{N_1 \phi_1}{i_1}\right)\left(\frac{N_2 \phi_2}{i_2}\right) = K^2 \cdot L_1 L_2$$

or $$M = K \sqrt{L_1 L_2}$$

Analysis of Coupled Circuits

Consider the coupled circuit shown in Fig. 10.2.

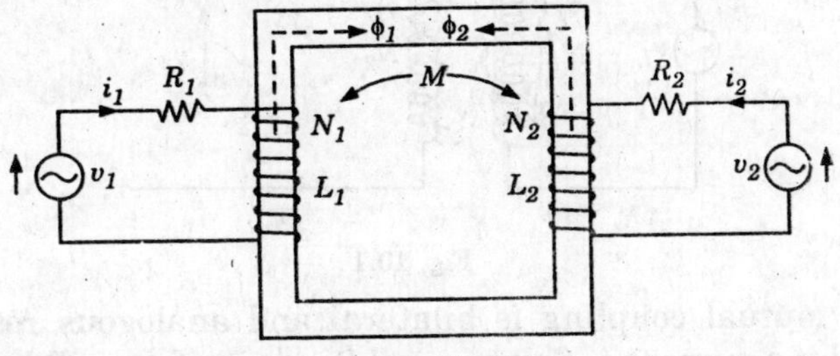

Fig. 10.2

The mutually induced e.m.f. may be of either polarity. If the fluxes ϕ_1 and ϕ_2 produced by currents i_1 and i_2 for the assumed current directions and winding sense, aid one another then the signs of the voltages of mutual inductances are the same as the signs of the voltages of self inductances. If they oppose each other, their signs are opposite of the voltages of self inductances.

The direction of flow of flux can be determined by right hand rule. Wrap around the conductor by right hand with thumb pointing in the direction of current flow. Then the fingers will point in the direction of lines of flux. For the Fig. 10.2, the loop equations are

$$R_1 i_1 + L_1 \frac{di_1}{dt} - M \frac{di_2}{dt} = v_1$$

$$-M\frac{di_1}{dt}+R_2i_2+L\frac{di_2}{2dt}=v_2$$

For sinusoidal steady state analysis, the above equations reduces to

$$(R_1+jwL_1)I_1-j\omega MI_2=V_1$$
$$-jwM I_1+(R_2+j\omega L_2)I_2=V_2$$

Fig. 10.2 shows that there is no electrical coupling between the two coils, but the equations show that there is coupling between the two loops. Thus, the coupling is said to be mutual or magnetic coupling.

Natural Current

Consider the coupled circuit shown in Fig. 10.3. The alternating current I_1 flowing in circuit 1 induces an e.m.f. in the second circuit due to magnetic coupling. If the second circuit is closed, current I_2 will flow in the circuit 2.

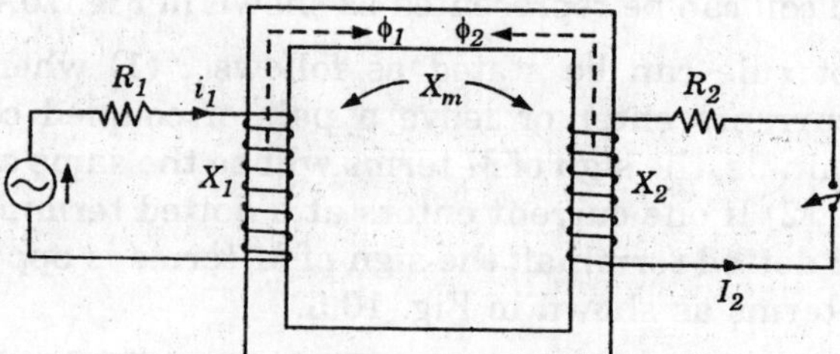

Fig. 10.3

I_2 will flow in such a direction as to oppose the cause producing it. *i.e.* the changing flux ϕ_1. Therefore, the flux ϕ_2 produced by I_2, will oppose ϕ_1, as shown in Fig. 10.3. From this, the direction of the current flow can be determined by applying right hand rule. This current is called the natural current. The loop equations are written as

$$V_1=(R_1+jX_1)I_1-jX_M I_2$$
$$O=-jX_M I_1+(R_2+jX_2)I_2$$

Dot Rule for Coupled Coils

The polarity of voltage of mutual induction is determined from the sketches of the core with winding senses and the directions of current flow. To simplify the representation of coupled circuits, coils are marked with dots to identify the polarity of mutual e.m.fs. Selecting a current direction in one coil, a dot is placed at the

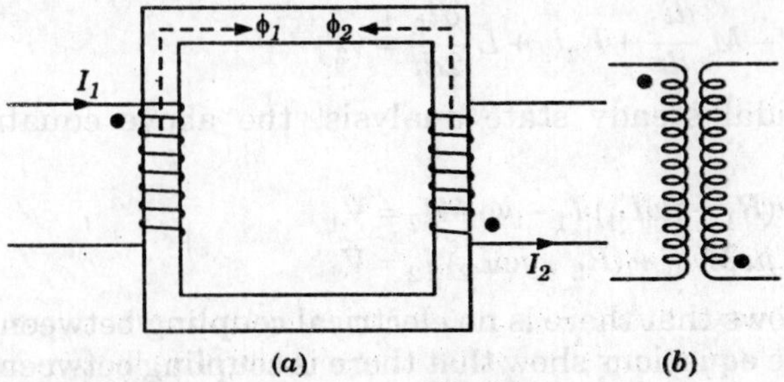

Fig. 10.4

terminal where this current enters the winding. Applying the hand rule, the direction of flux is obtained. According to Lenz's Law, the flux in the second coil will oppose the original flux. The direction of the natural current can be determined by hand rule. The voltage of mutual induction is positive at the terminal where the current leaves the winding. Hence, a dot is placed at the terminal where the natural current leaves the winding as shown in Fig. 10.4 (*a*). Then the coupled coil can be represented as shown in Fig. 10.4 (*b*).

The dot rule can be stated as follows : (1) when both the assumed currents enter or leave a pair of coupled coils at the dotted terminals, the sign of *M* terms will be the same as the signs of *L* terms. (2) If one current enters at a dotted terminal and one leaves by a dotted terminal, the sign of *M* terms is opposite to the signs of *L* terms as shown in Fig. 10.5.

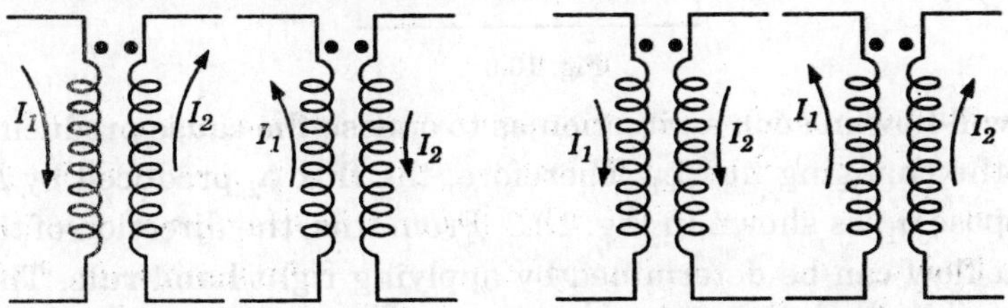

Fig. 10.5

Equivalent circuit of coupled coil

A conductively coupled equivalent circuit can be obtained for a coupled circuit. The loop equation in matrix form for Fig. 10.6 (*a*) is given by

$$\begin{bmatrix} (R_1 + jwL_1) & -jwM \\ -jwM & (R_2 + jwL_2) \end{bmatrix} \begin{bmatrix} I_1 \\ I_2 \end{bmatrix} = \begin{bmatrix} V_1 \\ V_2 \end{bmatrix}$$

The mesh equation for Fig. 10.6 (*b*) is

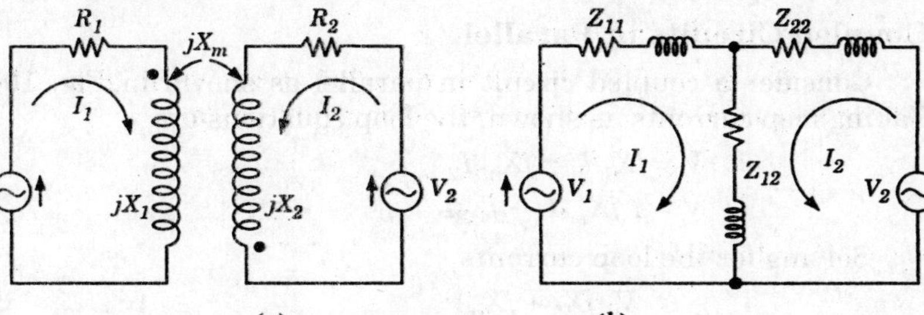

Fig. 10.6

$$\begin{bmatrix} Z_{11}+Z_{12} & -Z_{12} \\ -Z_{12} & Z_{22}+Z_{12} \end{bmatrix}\begin{bmatrix} I_1 \\ I_2 \end{bmatrix}=\begin{bmatrix} V_1 \\ V_2 \end{bmatrix}$$

If the circuit shown in Fig. 10.6 (*b*) is to represent an equivalent conductively coupled circuit of the given coupled coil, the following relation must hold good.

$$Z_{12} = jwM$$

$$Z_{11} = (R_1 + jwL_1 - jwM)$$

$$Z_{22} = (R_2 + jwL_2 - jwM)$$

Hence, an equivalent circuit can be obtained using the above relation. A physically realizable equivalent circuit for any coupled circuit is not always possible. This is true when $M > L_1$ or $M > L_2$ which requires a negative value of inductance.

Coupled Circuits in Series

Consider two coupled coils connected in series as shown in Fig. 10.7. The loop equation is written as

$$V = IX_1 + IX_2 \pm 2IX_m = I\,(X_1 + X_2 \pm 2X_m)$$

Hence, the equivalent reactance of the coupled coils in series is

$$X_{eq} = \frac{V}{I} = X_1 + X_2 \pm 2X_m$$

or the equivalent inductance

$$L_{eq} = L_1 + L_2 \pm 2M$$

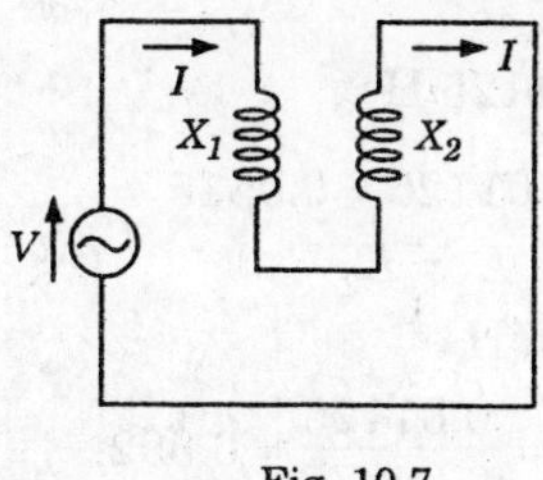

Fig. 10.7

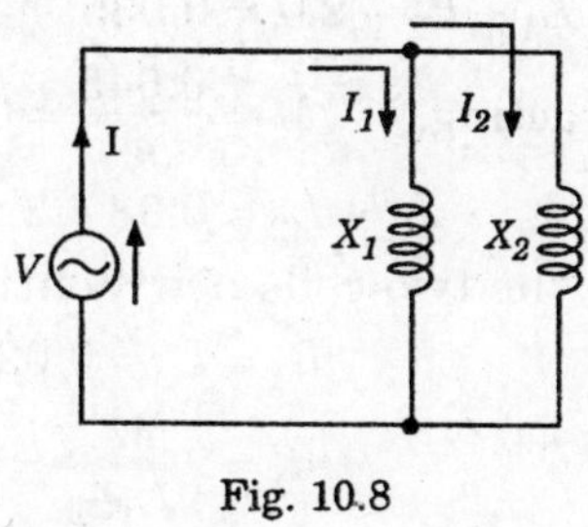

Fig. 10.8

Coupled Circuits in Parallel

Consider a coupled circuit in parallel as shown in Fig. 10.8. Taking loop currents as shown, the loop equations are

$$V = jX_1 I_1 \pm jX_m I_2$$
$$V = \pm jX_m I_1 + jX_2 I_2$$

Solving for the loop currents

$$I_1 = \frac{V(jX_2 \mp jX_m)}{(jX_1 jX_2 + X_m{}^2)}$$

$$I_2 = \frac{V(jX_1 \mp jX_m)}{(-X_1 X_2 + X_m{}^2)}$$

Therefore $\quad I = I_1 + I_2 = \dfrac{V(jX_1 + jX_2 \mp j2X_m)}{-X_1 X_2 + X_m{}^2}$

The equivalent reactance

$$X_{eq} = \frac{V}{I} = \frac{-X_1 X_2 + X_m{}^2}{jX_1 + jX_2 \mp j\,2X_m}$$

$$X_{eq} = \frac{j(X_1 X_2 - X_m{}^2)}{(X_1 + X_2 \mp 2X_m)}$$

The equivalent inductance of two couple coils in parallel is given by

$$L_{eq} = \frac{L_1 L_2 - M^2}{L_1 + L_2 \mp 2M}$$

Example 10.1. *Two identical coupled coils in series has an equivalent inductance values of 0.084 H and 0.0354 H. Find the values of L_1, L_2, M and K.*

Solution. The equivalent inductance of two coupled coils in series is given by

$$L_{eq} = L_1 + L_2 \pm 2M$$

$\therefore \quad L_1 + L_2 + 2M = 0.084$

$\quad L_1 + L_2 - 2M = 0.035$

Subtracting, $\quad M = \dfrac{0.045}{4} = 0.01125$ H

Then $\quad L_1 + L_2 = 0.08 - 2 \times 0.01125 = 0.0515$

Since the two coils are identical, $L_1 = L_2$

$\therefore \quad L_1 = L_2 = 0.02875$ H

Then $\quad K = \dfrac{M}{\sqrt{L_1 L_2}} = \dfrac{M}{L} = \dfrac{0.01125}{0.02875} = 0.392.$

Example 10.2. *Find the vector values of the currents in the network of Fig. 10.9. Find also the power supplied by each source.*

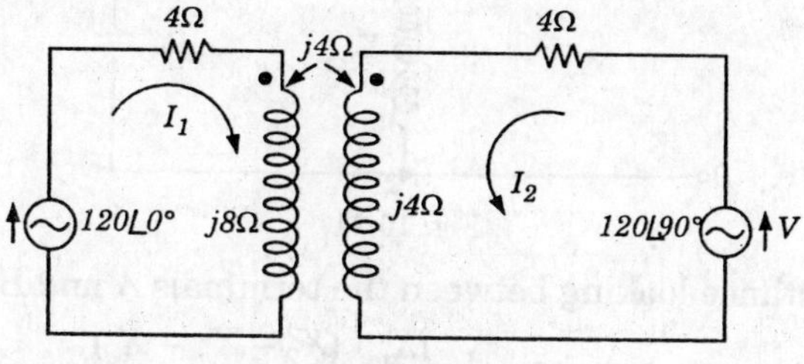

Fig. 10.9

Solution. The mesh equations are

$$120 + j0 = (4 + j8)\,I_1 + j4\,I_2$$

$$0 + j120 = +j4\,I_1 + (4 + j4)\,I_2$$

Solving for I_1 and I_2,

$$I_1 = \frac{\begin{vmatrix} 120 & j4 \\ j\,120 & 4 + j4 \end{vmatrix}}{\begin{vmatrix} (4 + j8) & j4 \\ j4 & (4 + j4) \end{vmatrix}} = \frac{480\,(2 + j1)}{j48}$$

$$= (10 - j20) \text{ Amps.}$$

$$I_2 = \frac{\begin{vmatrix} 4 + j4 & 120 \\ j4 & j120 \end{vmatrix}}{j48} = \frac{-960}{j48} = j20$$

Power delivered by the sources.

$$P_1 = \text{Re}\,[120 \times (10 + j20)] = 1200\ W$$

$$P_2 = \text{Re}\,[j120\,(-j20)] = 2400\ W$$

Example 10.3. *X_1 and X_2 are the self reactances of the two windings, X_m is the mutual reactance and X_c is the capacitive reactance of the circuit shown in Fig. 10.10. Show that this network behaves with respect to the terminals A and B, as an open circuit or as a short circuit according as $X_c = X_2$ or $X_c = (X_1 X_2 - X_m^{\,2})/X_1$.*

Solution. The equivalent circuit for the coupled circuit is drawn in Fig. 10.11.

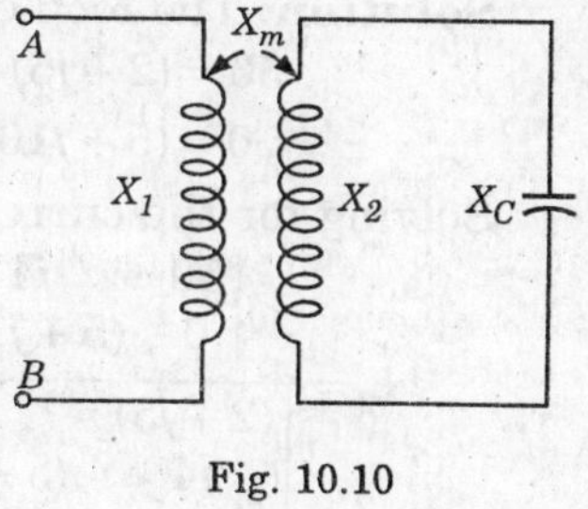

Fig. 10.10

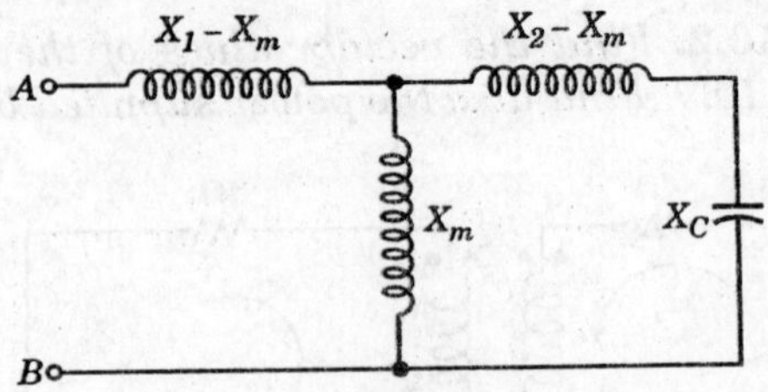

Fig. 10.11

The reactance looking between the terminals A and B is given by

$$X_{AB} = j\,(X_1 - X_m) + \frac{jX_m j\,(X_2 - X_m - X_c)}{jX_m + j\,(X_2 - X_m - X_c)}$$

$$= \frac{jX_1\,(X_2 - X_c) - X_m^{\,2}}{j\,(X_2 - X_c)}$$

The circuit behaves as an open circuit if X_{AB} is infinite and as a short circuit if X_{AB} is zero.

Therefore for open circuit, the condition is that

$$X_2 - X_C = 0 \quad \text{or} \quad X_2 = X_C$$

For short circuit, $X_{AB} = 0$ gives

$$X_1X_2 - X_1X_c - X_m^{\,2} = 0$$

or
$$X_c = (X_1X_2 - X_m^{\,2})/X_1$$

Example 10.4. *Calculate the current in the 5 ohms resistor for the coupled circuit shown in Fig. 10.12.*

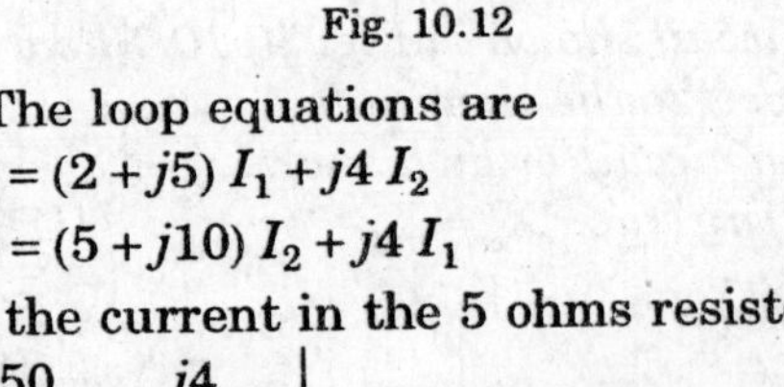

Fig. 10.12

Solution. The loop equations are

$$50 = (2 + j5)\,I_1 + j4\,I_2$$

$$0 = (5 + j10)\,I_2 + j4\,I_1$$

Solving for the current in the 5 ohms resistor,

$$I_2 = \frac{\begin{vmatrix} 50 & j4 \\ 0 & (5 + j10) \end{vmatrix}}{\begin{vmatrix} (2 + j5) & j4 \\ j4 & (5 + j10) \end{vmatrix}} = \frac{250 + j500}{-24 + j45} = 10.96\underline{/-178.5^\circ} \text{ A.}$$

EXERCISES

10.1. Two coupled coils of $L_1 = 0.9$ h and $L_2 = 0.4$ h have a coupling co-efficient $K = 0.8$. Find the mutual inductance M and the turns ratio N_1/N_2. **[Ans.** 0.48 h, 1.5]

10.2. Two coupled coils with $L_1 = 0.01$ h and $L_2 = 0.16$ h and $K = 0.5$ has $N_2 = 1000$ turns. The current in coil 1 is $i_1 = 10 \sin 400t$. Determine the voltage at coil 2 and the maximum flux set up by coil 1. **[Ans.** 80 cos 400t, 1×10^{-4} wb]

10.3. Find the voltage across the capacitance in the circuit of Fig. 10.13. **[Ans.** 7.9 ∠113.2° Volts]

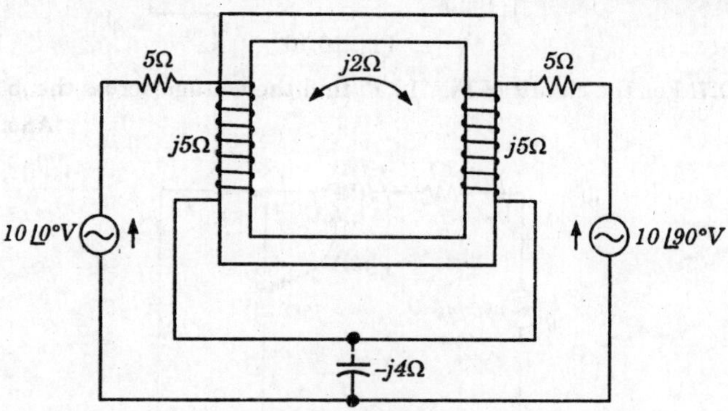

Fig. 10.13

10.4. In the coupled circuit of Fig. 10.14, find the voltage across the 5 ohm resistor. **[Ans.** 30.08 ∠ – 91.3° Volts]

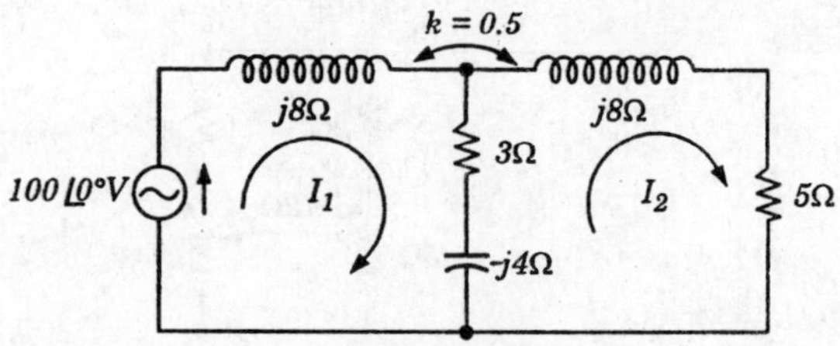

Fig. 10.14

10.5. In the coupled circuit of Fig. 10.15, find the value of the mutual reactance, if the power dissipated in the 4 ohm resistor is 52.3 watts. **[Ans.** $j3$ Ω]

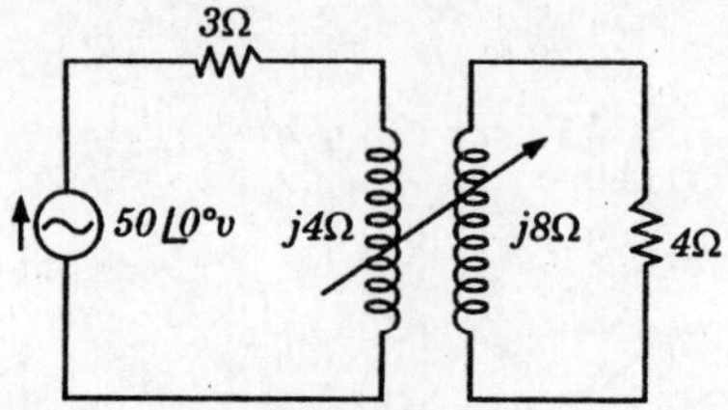

Fig. 10.15

10.6. Determine the value of "*K*" in the coupled circuit of Fig. 10.16, if the power dissipated in the 12 ohm resistor is 30 watts.

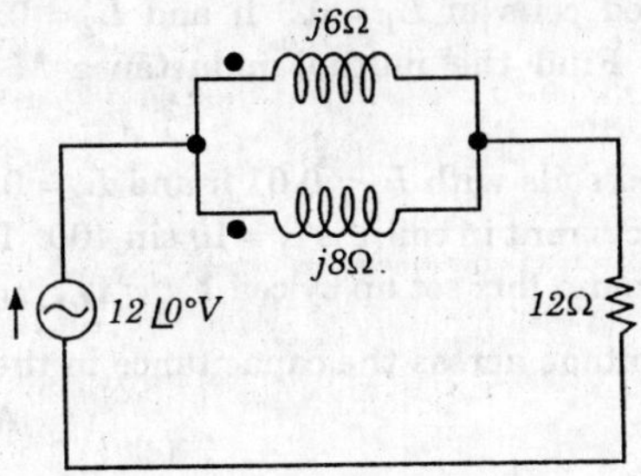

Fig. 10.16

10.7. For the circuit of Fig. 10.17 find the voltage across the *j*5 reactance.

[**Ans.** 25.2 ∠50°]

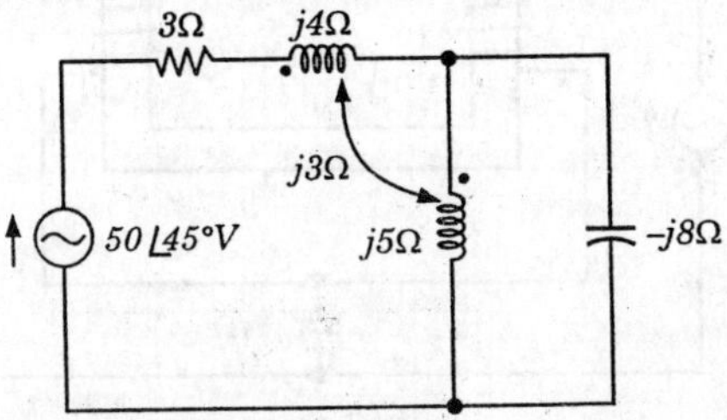

Fig. 10.17

10.8. Find the equivalent impedance of the coupled circuit of Fig. 10.18.

[**Ans.** 1 + *j*5]

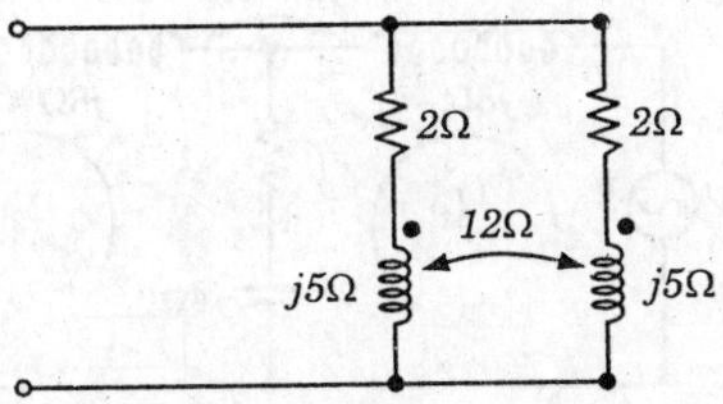

Fig. 10.18

ELEVEN

POLY PHASE CIRCUITS

A polyphase system consists of two or more single phase systems. The voltages or currents in the different single phase systems are not in phase. The commonest is the three phase system. Here the voltages of the three single phase systems differ in phase by 120 electrical degrees. The three voltages may be inter-connected ; they are of the same magnitude and frequency but differ in phase as shown in Fig. 11.1.

In a two phase system, the two voltages are displaced in phase by 90 degrees. In an n-phase system, n voltages equal in magnitude and frequency, are displaced from each other by $360/n$ electrical degrees.

Comparison Between Single Phase and Poly-phase Systems

A polyphase generator is larger, more economical per Mega-watt and operate at higher efficiencies than single phase generators. Transmission and distribution of power by three phase is cheaper and more efficient than by single phase lines. Polyphase motors produce uniform torque unlike single phase motors which produce pulsating torque. Polyphase motors are more efficient and more economical than single phase motors. Hence, the world over, generation, transmission and distribution of electric power is mainly poly-phase (and usually three phase).

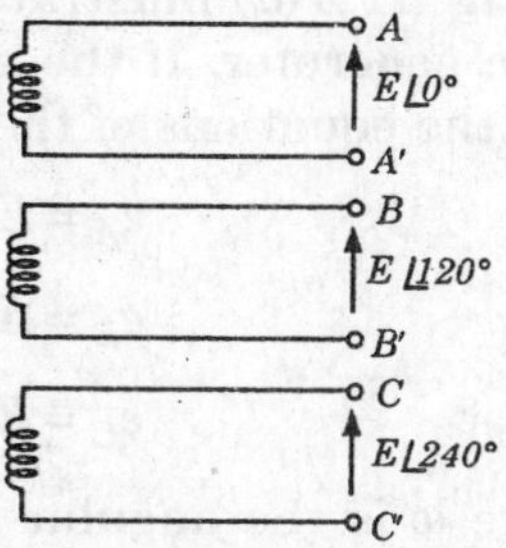

Fig. 11.1

Generation of Three-phase Voltages

All modern generators are three phase. They have three different windings which generate e.m.fs at phase difference of 120 degrees from each other.

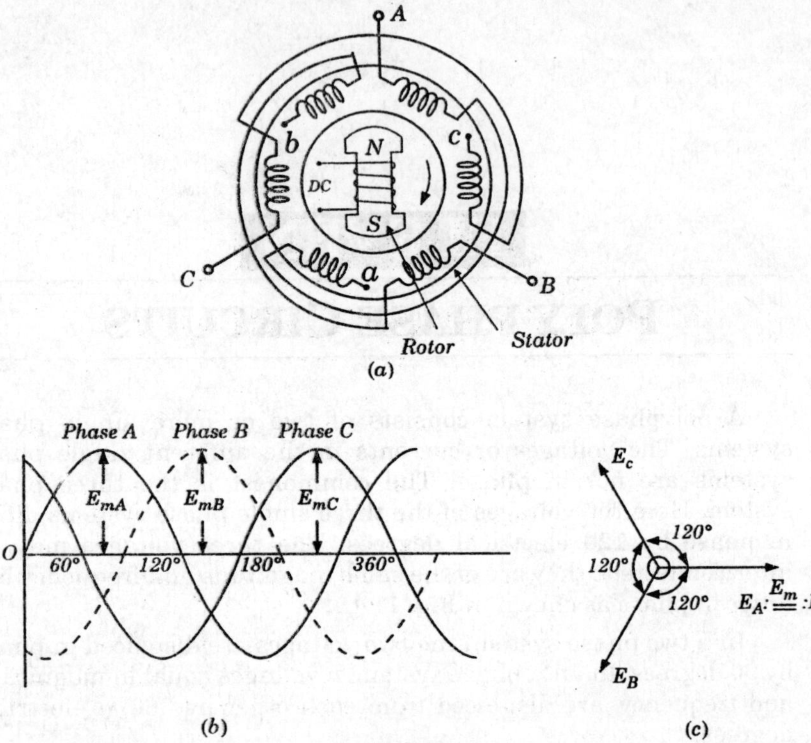

Fig. 11.2

Fig. 11.2 (*a*) illustrates the wave forms obtained from a three phase generator. If the emf of phase A is assumed as reference, then the equations of the three voltages may be written as

$$e_A = E_m \sin \omega t$$

$$e_B = E_m \sin (\omega t - 120°)$$

$$e_C = E_m \sin (\omega t - 240°)$$

where ω is the angular velocity of the rotor. The three voltages have equal magnitudes $\frac{E_m}{\sqrt{2}}$ but differ in phase by 120 degrees. They can be represented by the vector diagram shown in Fig. 11.2 (*b*) and may be written in polar form as

$$E_A = E \angle 0°$$

$$E_B = E \angle -120°$$

$$E_C = E \angle -240° = E \angle 120°$$

Phase Sequence

In the above three phase system, it is evident that the voltages of the three phases do not reach the maximum value at the same instant of time. The respective maxima are reached in some order. Here the B phase voltage follows the A phase voltage. The C phase voltage follows B. Hence the phase sequence is said to be ABC. Phase sequence of a polyphase system is the order in which the different phase quantities reach their maximum values. Anti-clockwise direction of rotation of vectors is of course assumed. We may use the double subscript notation for voltages as shown in Fig. 11.3.

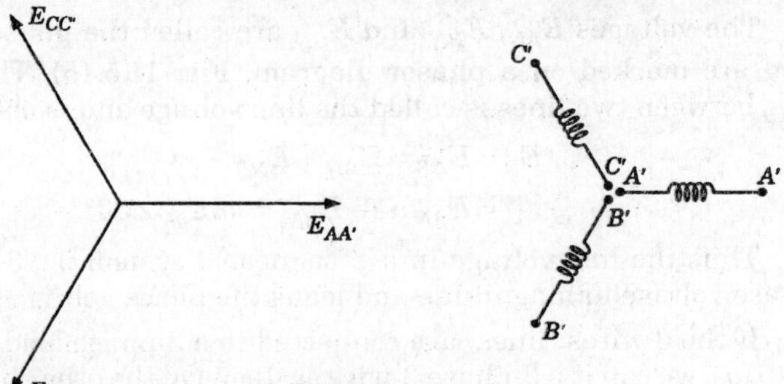

Fig. 11.3

Inter-connection of Three Phase Windings

A three phase system of voltages can be connected in the following three ways :

1. 3 independent connections
2. Star-connection
3. Delta connection.

1. **Independent connection.** In this, each phase supplies its load separately as in Fig. 11.4.

Six wires are required for such a system in which the three phases are completely independent of each other. The usual practice, however, is to inter-connect the windings to form a star or delta connection.

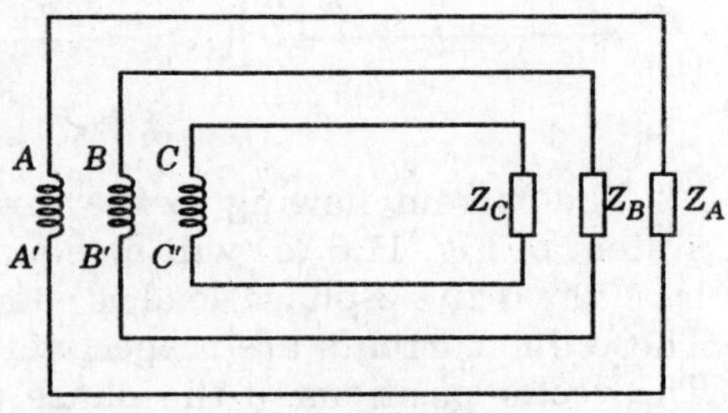

Fig. 11.4

2. **Star or Wye or Y-connection.** This is shown in Fig. 11.5 (a), the ends A', B' and C' being joined to form what is called the neutral point (N).

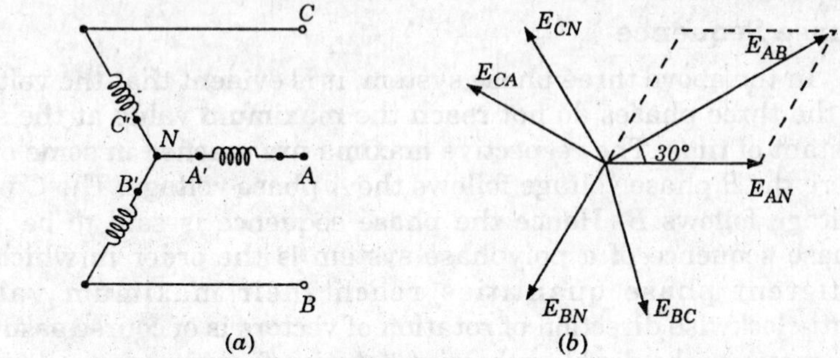

Fig. 11.5

The voltages E_{AN}, E_{BN} and E_{CN} are called the phase voltages and are marked on a phasor diagram, Fig. 11.5 (*b*). The voltage E_{AB} between two lines is called the line voltage and is obtained as

$$E_L = E_{AB} = E_{AN} + E_{NB}$$

$$= E_{AN} + (-E_{BN}) = \sqrt{3}E_{ph} \angle 30°.$$

Thus the line voltage in a *Y* connected system is √3 times the phase voltage in magnitude and leads the phase voltage by 30°.

If the 3 wires (lines) are connected to a 3-phase load as in Fig. 11.6 (*a*), we call it a 3-phase 3-wire system. On the other hand, if the neutral wire is brought out and used as a fourth wire, it becomes a 3-phase 4-wire system, Fig. 11.6 (*b*).

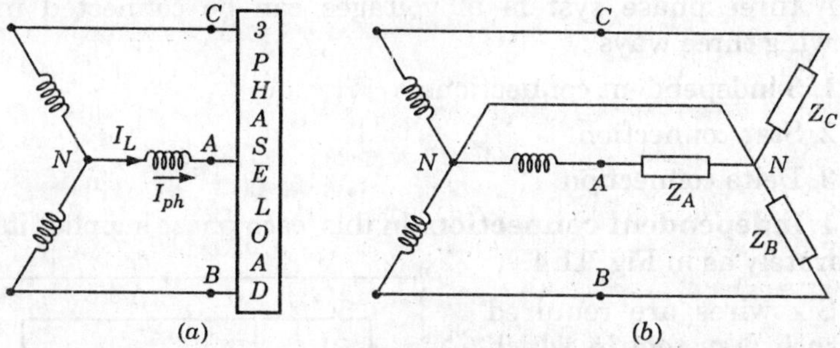

Fig. 11.6

The current flowing in the three lines of the 3-phase 3-wire system of Fig. 11.6 (*a*) will be equal in magnitude and displaced by 120°, if the 3-phase load is identical in all the three phases. These line currents are respectively equal to the phase currents. The vector positions of the phase currents relative to the phase voltages will depend on the power factor of the load. Fig. 11.7 shows three cases.

For a 3-phase 4-wire system, the current in the neutral wire is equal to the vector sum of the three line currents. When the load is

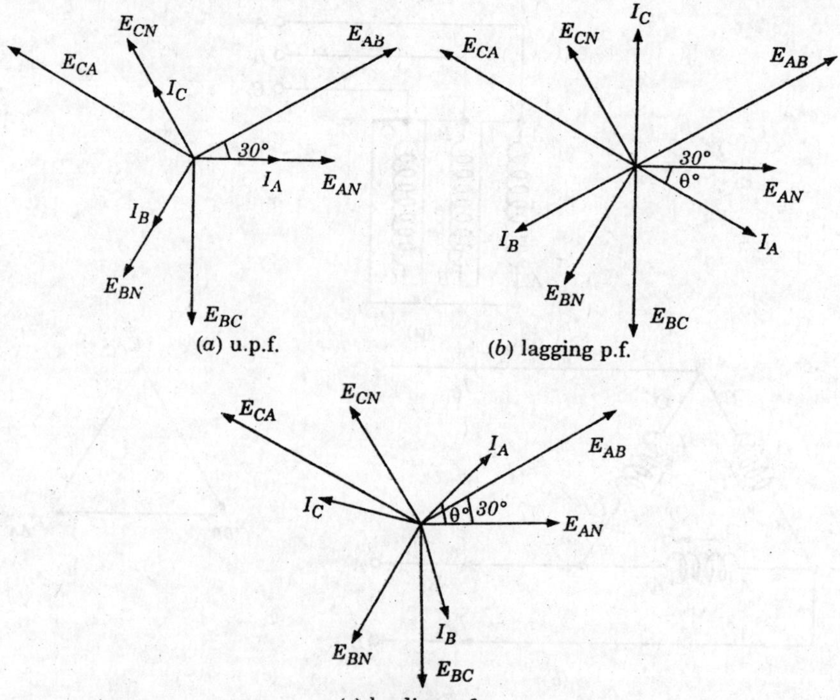

Fig. 11.7

balanced, this sum is zero. Therefore, the neutral wire in this case carries no current and may even be omitted.

The total power is equal to the sum of the powers in the individual phases. In the balanced case,

Total Power $= P_t = 3\, E_{ph}\, I_{ph} \cos\theta$

$= \sqrt{3}\, E_L\, I_L \cos\theta$

Thus, for a star connected system,

$$E_L = \sqrt{3}\, E_{ph}$$

$$I_L = I_{ph}$$

$$P_t = \sqrt{3}\, E_L\, I_L \cos\theta$$

$$= 3\, E_{ph}\, I_{ph} \cos\theta.$$

3. **Delta or Δ or mesh Connection.** If the 3 windings (or phases) are connected as in Fig. 11.8 (*a*) (*i.e.* the end of one phase to the start of another), then we get a closed winding. This is called the mesh connection (Δ connection) of Fig. 11.8 (*b*).

The vector voltages $E_{AA'}$, $E_{BB'}$ and $E_{CC'}$ add to zero as shown in Fig. 11.8 (*c*). Therefore, no current will flow in the closed loop of the

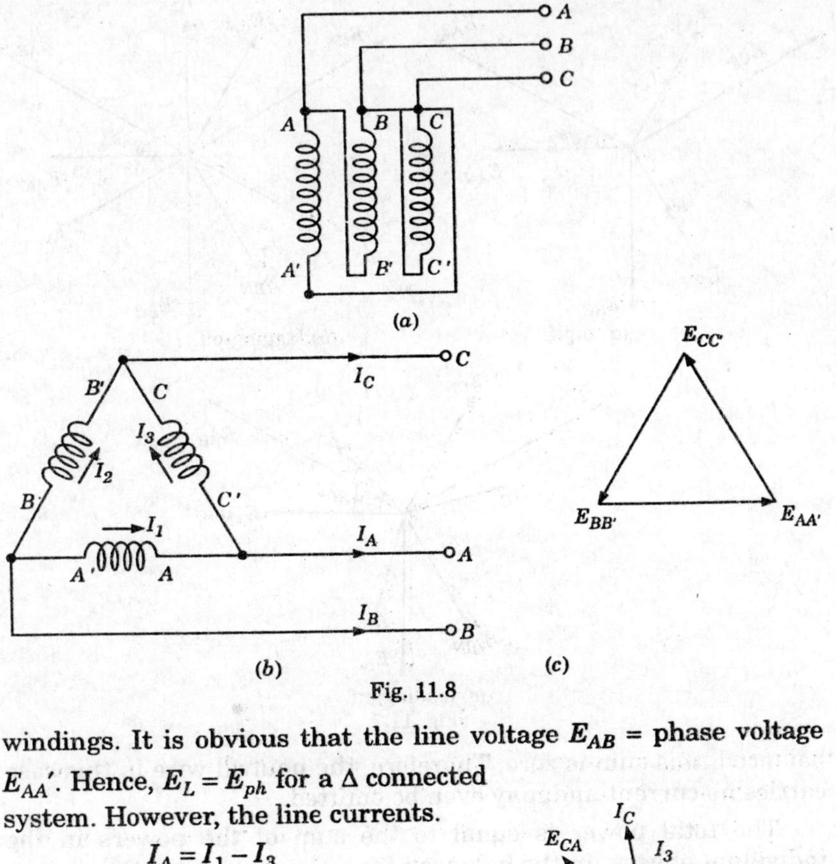

Fig. 11.8

windings. It is obvious that the line voltage E_{AB} = phase voltage $E_{AA'}$. Hence, $E_L = E_{ph}$ for a Δ connected system. However, the line currents.

$$I_A = I_1 - I_3$$

$$I_B = I_2 - I_1$$

and $$I_C = I_3 - I_2$$

As before, from the phasor diagram, it is evident that

$$I_{line} = \sqrt{3}\, I_{phase} \quad \text{(Fig. 11.9)}$$

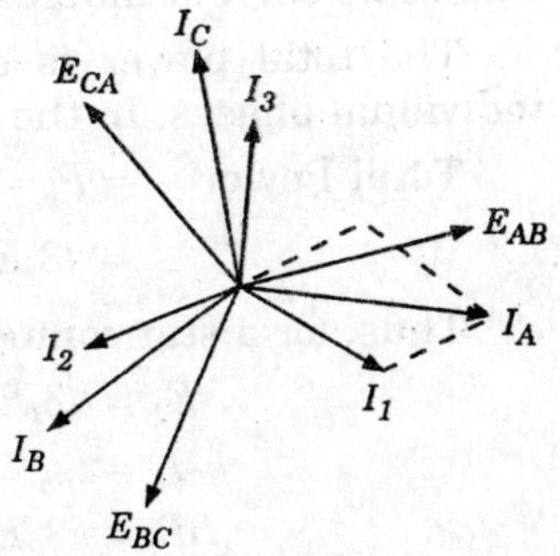

Fig. 11.9

Total power

$$= 3E_{ph}\, I_{ph} \cos\theta$$

$$= \sqrt{3}\, E_L I_L \cos\theta, \quad \text{as before.}$$

Example 11.1. *Each phase of a 3 phase alternator produces a voltage of 6,351 volts and can carry a maximum current of 315 amperes. Find the line voltage, maximum line current and total KVA capacity of the alternator if it is (a) Y (b) Δ connected.*

Solution. (*a*) *Y* Connection

$$E_L = \sqrt{3} \times E_{ph}$$
$$= \sqrt{3} \times 6{,}351 = 11{,}000 \text{ Volts}$$
$$I_1 = I_{ph} = 351 \text{ amps.}$$

$$\text{Total capacity} = \sqrt{3}\, E_L\, I_L \text{ Voltamperes}$$
$$= \sqrt{3} \times \frac{11{,}000 \times 315}{1000} \text{ kVA} = \mathbf{6000\ kVA.}$$

(*b*) Δ Connection

$$E_L = E_{ph} = 6{,}351 \text{ Volts}$$
$$I_L = \sqrt{3}\, I_{ph} = \sqrt{3} \times 315 = 545.6 \text{ Amps}$$

$$\text{Total capacity} = \sqrt{3} \times \frac{6351 \times 545.6}{1000} \text{ kVA} = \mathbf{6{,}000\ kVA}$$

Balanced 3 Phase Loads

In this chapter, we shall consider only a balanced set of voltages either connected in star or delta. The load, however, may be balanced or unbalanced, connected again in star or delta. We shall first consider the case of balanced loads. We may treat this case as single phase circuits and work only in phase quantities of voltage, current, power etc.

Example 11.2. *A 3 phase 400 volts supply is given to a balanced star connected load of impedance 8 + j6 ohms in each branch. Find the line current, power factor and total power, for the circuit of Fig. 11.10.*

Solution.

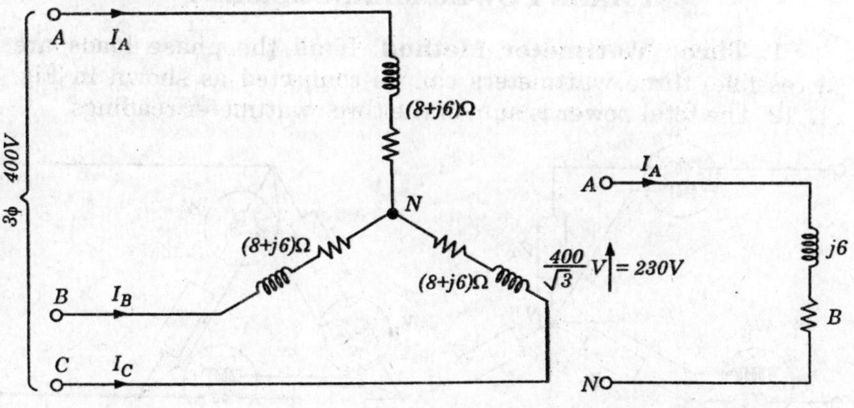

(*a*) (*b*) Single phase equivalent

Fig. 11.10

$$I_{phase} = \frac{230}{8 + j6} = \frac{230 \angle 0^\circ}{10 \angle 36.9^\circ} = 23 \angle -36.9^\circ \text{ Amps.}$$

$$I_{line} = I_{phase} = 23 \text{ Amps}$$

Power factor $= 0.8$ lag

Total Power $= 3E_{ph}\, I_{ph} \cos\theta$

$= \sqrt{3}\, E_L\, I_L \cos\theta = \sqrt{3} \times 400 \times 23 \times 0.8 =$ **12.7 kW.**

Example 11.3. *Repeat Problem 11.2 for the same load but Δ connected.*

Solution. $I_{ph} = \dfrac{400}{8 + j6} = 40 \angle -36.90°$

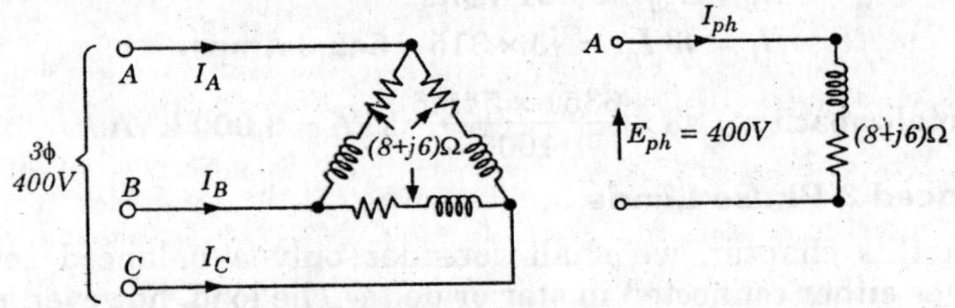

(*a*) (*b*) Single phase equivalent

Fig. 11.11

$$I_{line} = \sqrt{3}\, I_{ph} = \sqrt{3} \times 40 = 69.3 \text{ Amps}$$

Power factor $= 0.8$ lag.

Total power $= \sqrt{3} \times E_L I_L \cos\theta$

$= \sqrt{3} \times 400 \times 69.3 \times 0.8 =$ **38.4 kW.**

3-PHASE POWER MEASUREMENT

1. **Three Wattmeter Method.** If all the phase leads are accessible, three wattmeters can be connected as shown in Fig. 11.12. The total power is sum of the three wattmeter readings.

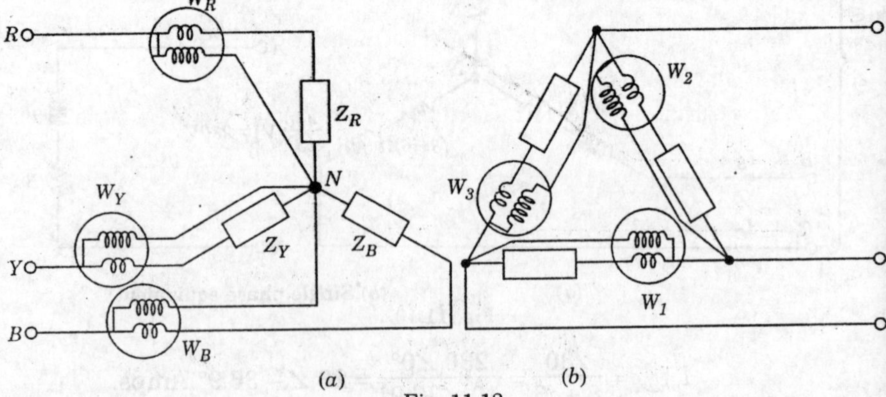

(*a*) (*b*)

Fig. 11.12

The above scheme is seldom used. The connections are difficult to make because usually the delta may not be broken and also the star point may not be available.

2. **Two Wattmeter Method.** A more convenient method is to use two wattmeters and this method is valid whether the load is balanced or not. Consider the two wattmeters as shown in Fig. 11.13 for the star connected load.

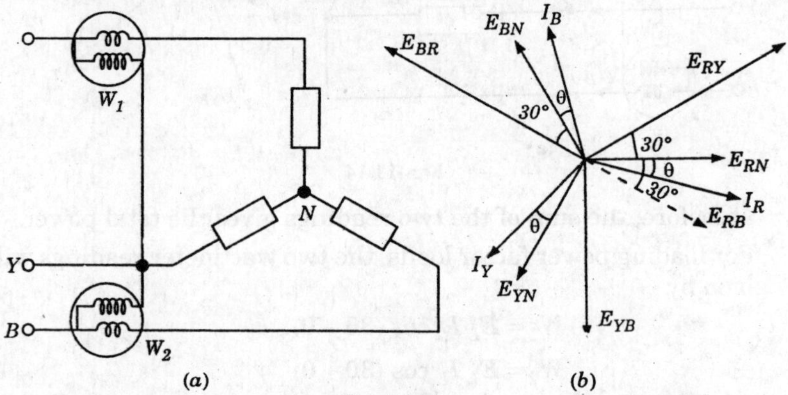

Fig. 11.13

The current coils of the two wattmeters are connected in R and B lines, and the pressure coils across RY and BY. The phasor diagram is drawn in Fig. 11.13 (b), for a lagging power factor. The wattmeters will indicate the following values :

$$W_1 = E_{RY} I_R \cos (30 + \theta) = E_L I_L \cos (30 + \theta)$$

$$W_2 = E_{BY} I_B \cos (30 - \theta) = E_L I_L \cos (30 - \theta)$$

$$\text{Hence } W_1 + W_2 = E_L I_L [\cos (30 + \theta) + \cos (30 - \theta)]$$

$$= \sqrt{3} E_L I_L \cos \theta$$

Thus the sum of the two wattmeter readings gives the total power.

Consider a balanced delta connected load with the wattmeter connections made as before. The connections and the phasor diagram are shown in Fig. 11.14.

The wattmeter readings are given by

$$W_1 = E_{RY} I_R \cos (30 + \theta) = E_L I_L \cos (30 + \theta)$$

$$W_2 = E_{BY} \cdot I_B \cdot \cos (30 - \theta) = E_L I_L \cos (30 - \theta)$$

$$\text{Hence } W_1 + W_2 = \sqrt{3} E_L I_L \cos \theta$$

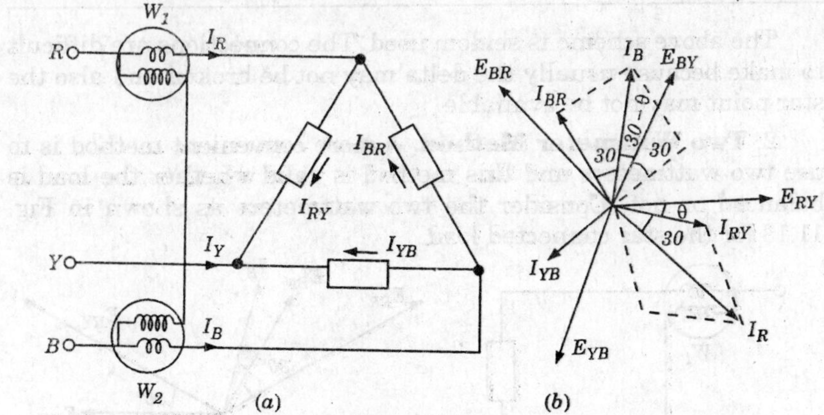

Fig. 11.14

As before, the sum of the two readings gives the total power.

For leading power factor loads, the two wattmeter readings will be given by

$$W_1 = E_L I_L \cos(30 - \theta)$$

$$W_2 = E_L I_L \cos(30 + \theta)$$

The effect of power factor variation on the meter readings is tabulated below. (Where P is the total power).

Power factor	θ	*Lagging*		*Leading*	
		W_1	W_2	W_1	W_2
1.0	0	0.5 P	0.5 P	0.5 P	0.5 P
0.866	30°	0.333 P	0.667 P	0.667 P	0.333 P
0.707	45°	0.211 P	0.789 P	0.789 P	0.211 P
0.5	60°	0	*P*	*P*	0
0.174	80°	– 1.135 P	2.135 P	2.135 P	– 1.135 P

The load power factor can be obtained from the two wattmeter readings. For lagging power factor

$$W_1 + W_2 = \sqrt{3}\, E_L I_L \cos\theta$$

and $$W_2 - W_1 = E_L I_L \cos(30 - \theta) - \cos(30 + \theta)$$

$$= E_L I_L \sin\theta$$

Therefore, $$\frac{W_2 - W_1}{W_1 + W_2} = \frac{\tan\theta}{\sqrt{3}}$$

or $$\theta = \tan^{-1}\left[\frac{\sqrt{3}\,(W_2 - W_1)}{W_1 + W_2}\right]$$

3. **Power Measurement with Single Wattmeter.** The total power in 3-phase balanced loads can be measured by the following methods.

(*a*) **Potential Lead Shift Method.** The wattmeter current coil is connected in the R line as shown in Fig. 11.15 (*a*) and the pressure coil is connected between R and Y first and then shifted from Y to B so that it is connected between R and B. For the first connection, the reading is

$$W_1 = E_L I_L \cos (30 + \theta)$$

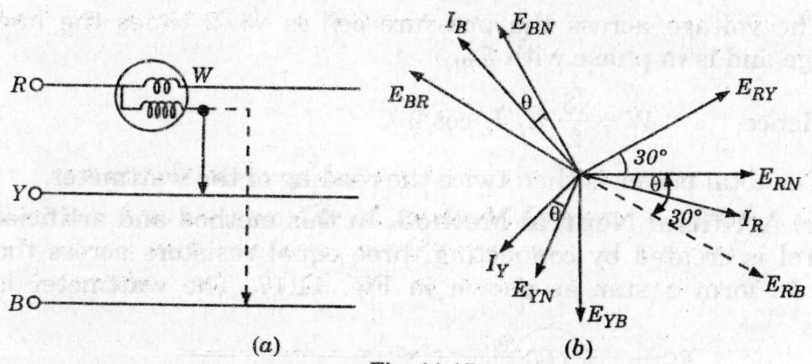

Fig. 11.15

For the second connection, the wattmeter reading is

$$W_2 = E_L I_L \cos (30 - \theta)$$

Hence the total power is sum of the two readings. By simply shifting one of the potential leads between two lines, the total power can be measured with a single wattmeter.

(*b*) **T-Method.** In this method the current coil is in R line. The pressure coil is connected between line R and the mid-point of two equal resistors connected between Y and B, as shown in Fig. 11.16.

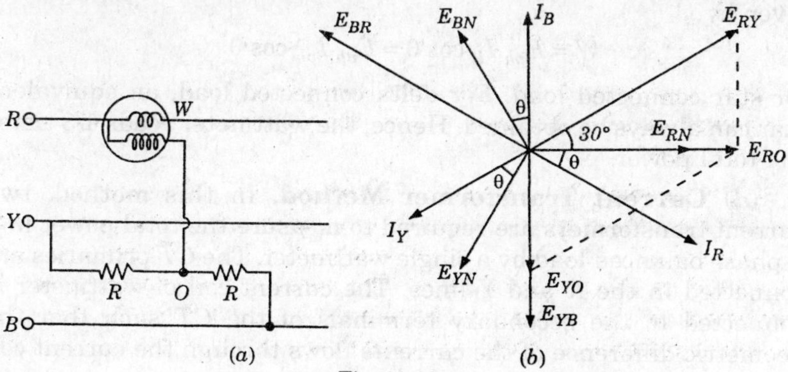

Fig. 11.16

The wattmeter reading is given by

$$W = E_{RO} I_R \cos \phi$$

when ϕ is the angle between E_{RO} and I_R

$$E_{RO} = E_{RY} + E_{YO}$$

But $E_{YO} = \frac{1}{2} E_{YB}$

Therefore, $E_{RO} = | E_{RY} | \angle 30° + | E_{RO} | \angle -90°$

$$= \frac{\sqrt{3}}{2} E_{RY} \Big| \angle 0°$$

The voltage across the pressure coil is $\sqrt{3}/2$ times the line voltage and is in phase with E_{RN}.

Hence $W = \frac{\sqrt{3}}{2} E_L I_L \cos \theta$

The total power is then twice the reading of the wattmeter.

(*c*) **Artificial Neutral Method.** In this method and artificial neutral is created by connecting three equal resistors across the lines to form a star as shown in Fig. 11.17. The wattmeter is

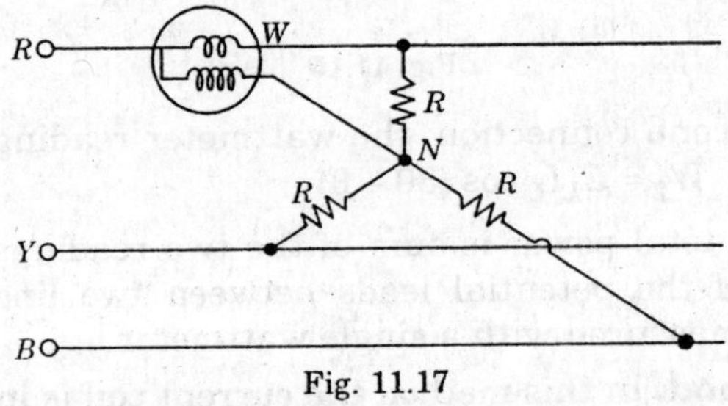

Fig. 11.17

connected as shown with the current coil in the line R and pressure coil across R and the artificial neutral N. The wattmeter reading is given by

$$W = E_{ph} I_L \cos \theta = E_{ph} I_{ph} \cos \theta$$

for star connected load. For delta connected load, an equivalent star can always be obtained. Hence, the wattmeter reads 1/3 times the total power.

(*d*) **Current Transformer Method.** In this method, two current transformers are required to measure the total power in a 3-phase balanced load by a single wattmeter. The CT primaries are connected in the R and Y lines. The current coil of wattmeter is connected to the secondary terminals of the CT such that the geometric difference of the currents flows through the current coil

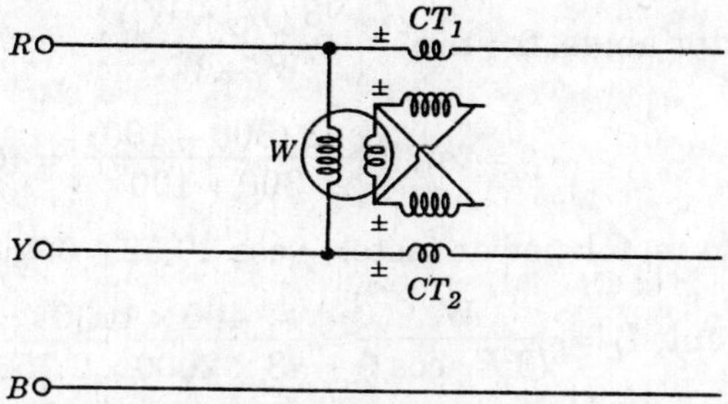

(a)

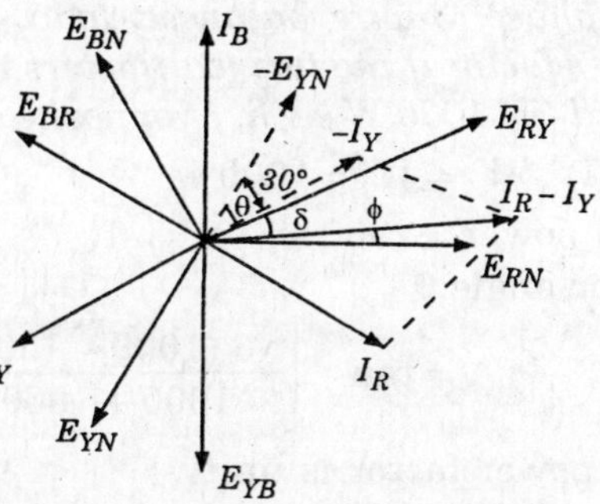

(b)

Fig. 11.18

of wattmeter as shown in Fig. 11.18 (*a*). Referring to the phasor diagram, drawn for lagging power factor star connected load and assuming unity *CT* ratio, the wattmeter reading is given by

$$W = E_L \mid I_R - I_Y \mid \cos \delta$$

Now $\quad \mid I_R - I_Y \mid = I_L$

The angle between E_{RN} and $I_R - I_Y$ is given by

$$\phi = 30 - \theta = 30 - \delta$$

Hence the angle between E_{RY} and $(I_R - I_Y)$ is θ

Therefore, the wattmeter reading is

$$W = \sqrt{3}\, E_L I_L \cos \theta$$

which is the total power. If the *CT* ratio is not unity the wattmeter reading must be multiplied by the *CT* ratio.

Example 11.4. *The power input to a 2000 V, 50 Hz, 3-phase motor is measured by two wattmeters which indicate 300 kW and 100 kW respectively ; calculate (a) the input power (b) power factor and (c) the line current.*

Solution. Power input = 300 + 100 = 400 kW

$$\text{Power factor angle, } \theta = \tan^{-1}\left[\frac{\sqrt{3}\,(W_2 - W_1)}{W_1 + W_2}\right]$$

$$= \tan^{-1}\left[\frac{\sqrt{3}\,(300 - 100)}{300 + 100}\right] = 40.59°$$

Hence, the motor power factor = cos 40.52 = 0.756

$$\text{Line current, } I_L = \frac{W}{\sqrt{3}\,E_L \cos\theta} = \frac{400 \times 1000}{\sqrt{3} \times 2000 \times 0.756} = \mathbf{152.7\ A.}$$

Example 11.5. *Two wattmeters are connected to measure the power in a 3-ophase, 3-wire balanced load. Determine the total power and power factor if the two wattmeters read (i) 1000 W each, both positive and (ii) 1000 W each, of opposite sign.*

Solution. (*i*) $W_1 = W_2 = 1000$ w

Hence total power = 2000 w

Power factor angle θ

$$= \tan^{-1}\left[\frac{\sqrt{3}\,(1000 - 1000)}{1000 + 1000}\right]$$

Hence, the power factor is unity.

(*ii*) $W_1 = 1000$, $W_2 = -1000$

Total power = 0

$$\text{Power factor angle, } \theta = \tan^{-1}\left[\frac{(1000 - 1000)\sqrt{3}}{1000 + 1000}\right] = 90°$$

Hence, the power factor is zero.

Unbalanced Loads

Consider the unbalanced delta connected load as shown in Fig. 11.19 (*a*). Assume, a phase sequence of *RYB*. The line voltages are

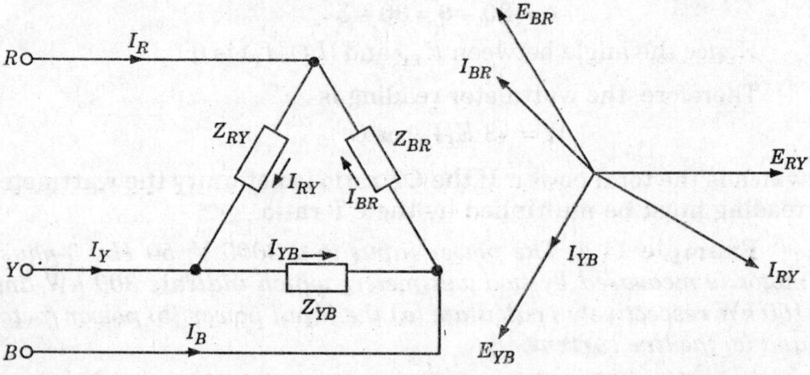

Fig. 11.19

balanced and for a delta connection, the phase voltages are the same as the line voltages.

Hence the phase currents

$$I_{RY} = \frac{V_{RY}}{Z_{RY}}, \quad I_{YB} = \frac{V_{YB}}{Z_{YB}} \quad \text{and} \quad I_{BR} = \frac{V_{BR}}{Z_{BR}}$$

Then $I_R = I_{RY} - I_{BR}$

$$I_Y = I_{YB} - I_{RY}$$

$$I_B = I_{BR} - I_{YB}$$

From the above expressions, the line currents and power consumed by each phase and hence the total power can be obtained. If the phase sequence is *RBY*, then the phasor diagram of voltages and currents is shown in Fig. 11.20. If the phase sequence is different, for the same load impedance, the line currents are entirely different. Hence, for the analysis of unbalanced delta connected loads, the phase sequence is important.

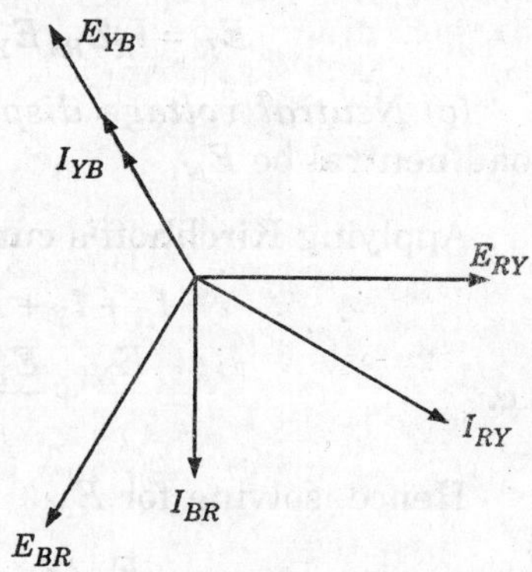

Fig. 11.20

Star Connected Load

Consider a 3-phase, 3-wire star connected unbalanced load. The following methods are used for analysis of such networks.

(*a*) *Equivalent delta method.* In this method, the unbalanced star load is replaced by an equivalent delta connected load and then it can be solved as before. The equivalent delta load impedances can be obtained by star-delta transformation.

(*b*) *Mesh method.* In this method, two mesh currents are chosen as shown in Fig. 11.21. Then the mesh equations are written as

$$E_{RY} = I_1 Z_R + (I_1 - I_2)\, Z_Y$$

$$E_{YB} = (I_2 - I_1)\, Z_Y + I_2 Z_B$$

The above equations are solved for I_1 and I_2. Then

$$I_R = I_1, \quad I_Y = I_2 - I_1 \quad \text{and} \quad I_B = -I_2$$

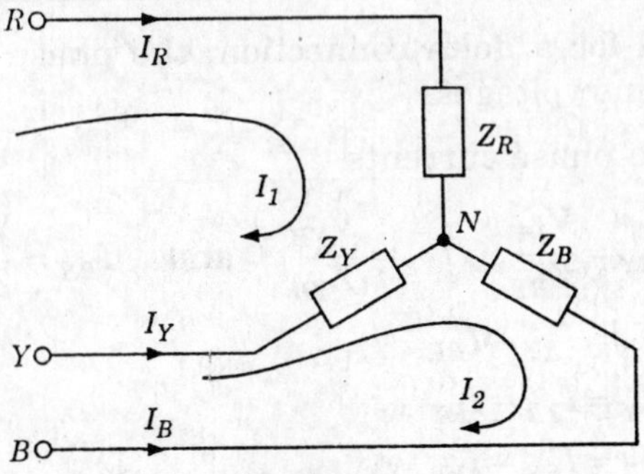

Fig. 11.21

The load phase voltages can be calculated from

$$E_R = I_R Z_R, E_Y = I_Y Z_Y \text{ and } E_B = I_B Z_B$$

(c) *Neutral voltage displacement method.* Let the voltage of load neutral be E_N.

Applying Kirchhoff's current law to the node N

$$I_R + I_Y + I_B = 0$$

i.e. $$\frac{E_R - E_N}{Z_R} + \frac{E_Y - E_N}{Z_Y} + \frac{E_B - E_N}{Z_B} = 0$$

Hence, solving for E_N

$$E_N = \frac{E_R/Z_R + E_Y/Z_Y + E_B/Z_B}{1/Z_R + 1/Z_Y + 1/Z_B}$$

From the above expression, the potential of the load neutral above that of the generator neutral can be obtained. Once E_N is calculated, the line currents and load phase voltages and power can be easily computed.

Unbalanced 3-Phase 4-Wire Star Connected Load

In this system, the potential of the load neutral is fixed to that of the generator neutral by the connection of the neutral wire. By this, the load phase voltages are same as the generator phase voltages. Hence, the line currents are given by

$$I_R = E_R/Z_R, \; I_Y = E_Y/Z_Y \text{ and } I_B = E_B/Z_B$$

where E_R, E_Y and E_B are balanced phase voltages. Hence, the analysis of unbalanced 3-phase, 4-wire star load is very simple provided, the impedances of the lines and neutral wire are negligible. If not, the mesh method can be used to solve the network.

Example 11.6. *Determine the line currents for the unbalanced delta connected load shown in Fig. 11.22 if the phase sequence is (i) RYB and (ii) RBY.*

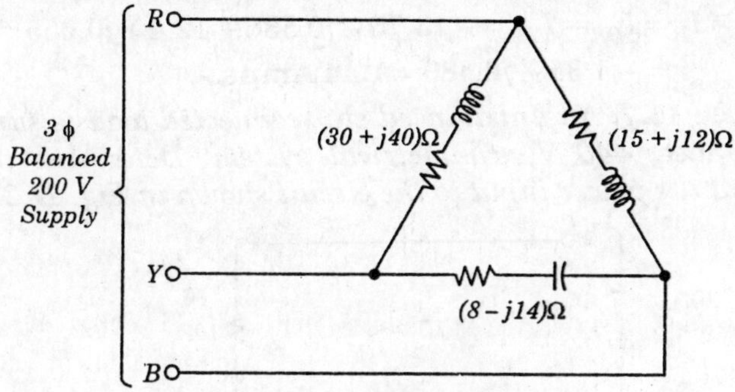

Fig. 11.22

Solution. (*i*) **Phase sequence RYB**

$$I_{RY} = \frac{200 \angle 0°}{30 + j40} = \frac{200\,(30 - j40)}{30^2 + 40^2}$$

$$= (2.4 - j3.2) \text{ Amps.}$$

$$I_{YB} = \frac{200° \angle -120°}{8 - j14} = \frac{-100 - j173.2}{8 - j14}$$

$$= \mathbf{(6.25 - j10.7)\ Amps.}$$

$$I_{BR} = \frac{200 \angle 120°}{15 + j12}$$

$$= \frac{-100 + j173.2}{15 + j12} = \mathbf{(1.57 + j10.3)\ Amp.}$$

Hence, $I_R = I_{RY} - I_{BR} = 2.4 - j3.2 - 1.57 - j10.3$

$$= 0.83 - j6.99 = \mathbf{7.05\ Amps.}$$

$$I_Y = 6.25 - j10.7 - 2.4 + j3.2$$

$$= 3.85 - j7.5 = \mathbf{8.43\ Amps.}$$

$$I_B = 1.57 + j10.3 - 6.25 + j10.7$$

$$= -4.68 + j21 = \mathbf{21.5\ Amps.}$$

(*ii*) **Phase Sequence RBY.**

$$I_{RY} = \frac{200 \angle 0°}{30 + j40} = 2.4 - j3.2$$

$$I_{YB} = \frac{200 \angle +120°}{8 - j14} = -12.4 - j0.055$$

$$I_{BR} = \frac{200 \angle -120°}{14 + j12} = -13.76 - j0.536$$

Hence $I_R = I_{RY} - I_{BR}$

$$= 2.4 - j3.2 + 13.76 + j0.536$$

$$= 16.16 - j1.664 = \mathbf{16.25\ Amp}$$

$$I_Y = I_{YB} - I_{RY} = -12.4 - j0.055 - 2.4 + j3.2$$

$$= -14.8 + j3.145 = \mathbf{15.13\ Amps}$$

$$I_B = I_{BR} - I_{YB} = -13.76 - j0.536 + 12.4 + j0.055$$

$$= -1.36 - j0.489 = \mathbf{1.44\ Amps.}$$

Example 11.7. *An unbalanced star connected load is supplied from a 3-phase, 440 V, symmetrical system. Determine the lie currents and the power input to the circuit shown in Fig. 11.23.*

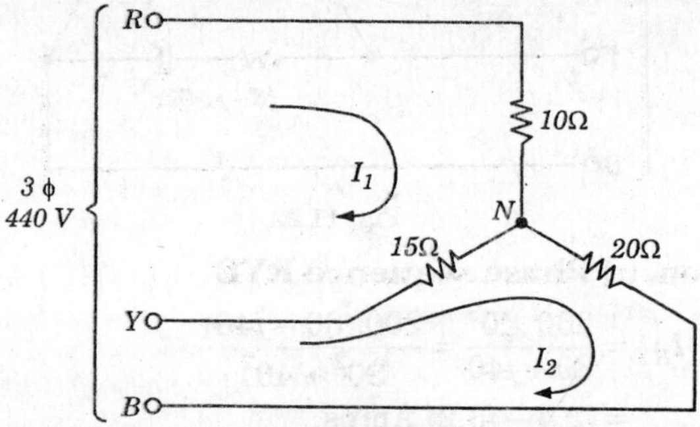

Fig. 11.23

Solution. We shall use the mesh method to solve this problem. The R phase voltage of the generator is taken as reference and the loop currents I_1 and I_2 are as shown.

The loop equations are given by

$$V_{RY} = 440\ \angle 30° = 10\ I_1 + 15\ (I_1 - I_2)$$

$$V_{YB} = 440\ \angle 30° - 120° = 15\ (I_2 - I_1) + 20\ I_2$$

i.e. $\quad 25I_1 - 15I_2 = 440\ (0.866 + j0.5)$

$$-15I_1 + 25I_2 = -j440$$

Solving the above equations

$$I_1 = 20.51 + j1.68$$

$$I_2 = 8.79 - j11.85$$

Hence $\quad I_R = I_1 = 20.51 + j1.68 = \mathbf{20.5\ Amps.}$

$$I_Y = I_2 - I_1 = -11.72 - j\ 13.53 = \mathbf{17.9\ Amps.}$$

$$I_B = -I_2 = -8.79 + j11.85 = \mathbf{14.7\ Amps.}$$

The power input to the network is equal to the sum of the phase powers and is given by

$$P = I_R{}^2 R_R + I_Y{}^2 R_Y + I_B{}^2 R_B$$

$$= (20.5)^2 \times 10 + (17.9)^2 \times 15 + (14.7)^2 \times 20$$

$$= \mathbf{13{,}350\ watts.}$$

Power Measurement in Unbalanced Load

The total power flowing into an unbalanced 3-phase load can be measured by a two wattmeter method as discussed below.

Consider a star connected load as shown in Fig. 11.24.

At any instant of time, the total power flowing into the load is given by

$$p = e_{RN} i_R + e_{YN} i_Y + e_{BN} i_B$$

But for a 3-phase, 3-wire star connected load,

$$i_R + i_Y + i_B = 0$$

from which $i_Y = -i_R - i_B$

Hence $p = e_{RN} i_R - e_{YN}(i_R + i_B) + e_{BN} i_B$

$$= (e_{RN} - e_{YN})\, i_R + (e_{BN} - e_{YN})\, i_B$$

$$= e_{RY} i_R + e_{BY} i_B = W_1 + W_2$$

The total power at any time is shown to be sum of the two wattmeter readings. Therefore, the two wattmeters connected properly as shown will measure the total average power as well.

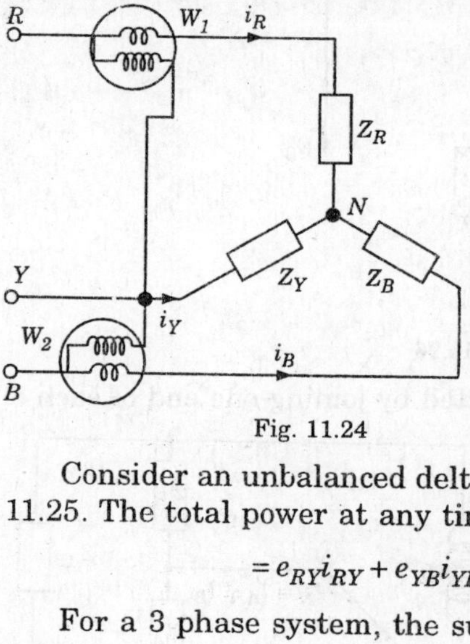

Fig. 11.24

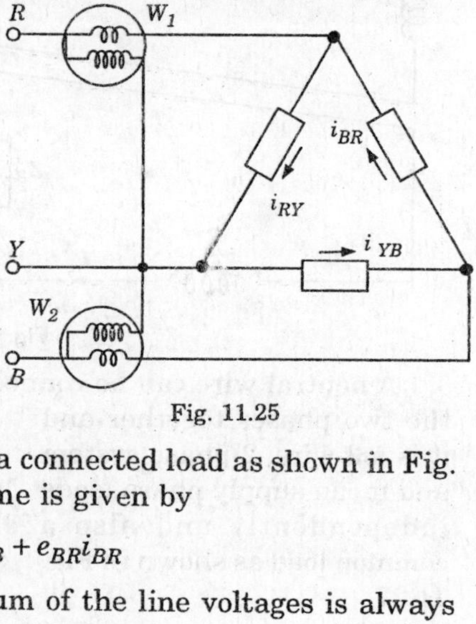

Fig. 11.25

Consider an unbalanced delta connected load as shown in Fig. 11.25. The total power at any time is given by

$$= e_{RY} i_{RY} + e_{YB} i_{YB} + e_{BR} i_{BR}$$

For a 3 phase system, the sum of the line voltages is always zero.

i.e. $e_{RY} + e_{YB} + e_{BR} = 0$

from which $e_{BR} = -e_{RY} - e_{YB}$

Hence $p = e_{RY} i_{RY} + e_{YB} i_{YB} - (e_{RY} + e_{YB})\, i_{BR}$

$$= e_{RY}(i_{RY} - i_{BR}) + e_{YB}(i_{YB} - i_{BR})$$

$$= e_{RY}i_R + e_{YB}(-i_B)$$
$$= e_{RY}i_R + e_{BY}i_B = W_1 + W_2$$

The total power at any time is sum of the two wattmeter readings. Obviously, therefore, the two wattmeters properly connected, always measure the total power flowing into a 3-phase system, whether it is balanced or unbalanced and whether it is star or delta connected.

Two Phase System

Two phase system is one in which there are two voltages and two currents which are equal in magnitude and frequency and displaced in phase by 90°. In two phase, the following systems are obtained. When two sources are insulated, it is four-wire, two-phase system and act independently supplying individual single phase load as shown in Fig. 11.26.

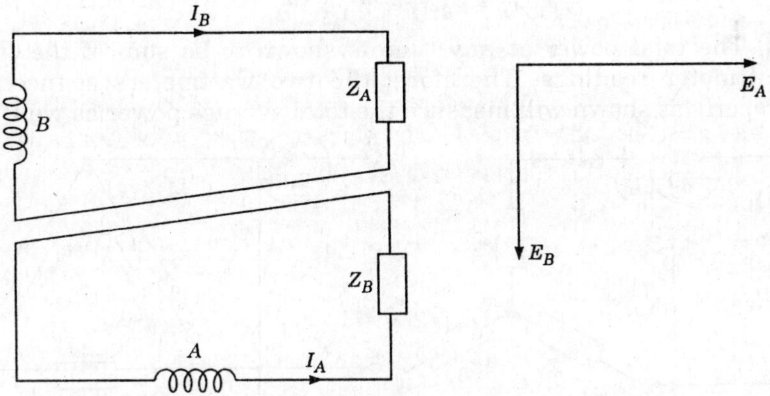

Fig. 11.26

A neutral wire can be connected by joining one end of each of the two phases together and it is a 3-wire, 2-phase system and it can supply phase loads independently and also a common load as shown in Fig. 11.27.

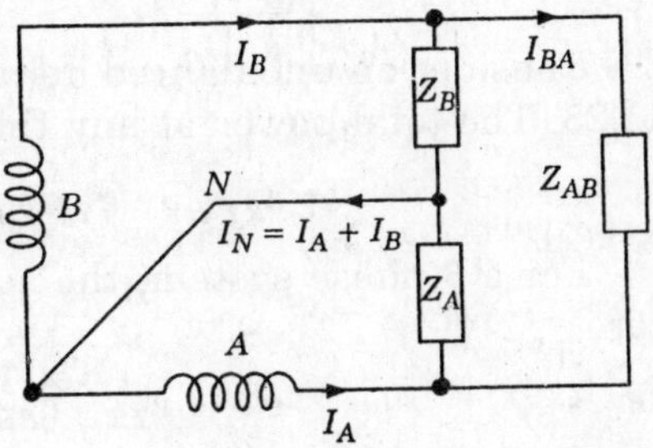

Fig. 11.27

The voltage across lines is √2 times the phase voltage and the current in the neutral wire is √2 times the line current.

EXERCISES

11.1. Each phase of a 3-phase star connected load consists of a pure resistance of 100 Ω in series with a capacitance of 31.8 μF. Calculate the power absorbed, total kVA and power factor when connected to a 400 V, 3 phase, 50 Hz supply. [**Ans.** 0.57 kW, 0.8 kVA, 0.707]

11.2. Each branch of a delta connected load has a resistance of 16 ohms and an inductive reactance of 12 ohms in series. Calculate the line current and total power when connected to a 400 V, 3 phase supply.

[**Ans.** 34.64 Amp. 19.2 kW]

11.3. A total 3-phase power of 100 kW is transmitted over a transmission line of impedance $(1 + j2)$ Ω/phase. The voltage between lines of the balanced 3-phase load is 11 kV. The load pf. is 0.8 lagging. Find the line voltage and p.f. at the sending end. [**Ans.** 11.025 kV, 0.8]

11.4. The power flowing into a balanced three-phase inductive load, measured by the two wattmeter method are 2000 W and 1000 W. The line voltages are 400 V, 50 Hz. Determine the total power, kVA and the power factor of the load. [**Ans.** 3.0 kW, 3.15 kVA, 0.95]

TWELVE

SYMMETRICAL COMPONENTS

In the previous chapter, the analysis of polyphase systems, in particular, 3-phase system was discussed. The solution of problems involving unbalanced loads becomes more difficult especially with complex impedances. One of the most powerful tools to deal with unbalanced circuits is the method of symmetrical components, first discussed by Dr. C.L. Fortescue in 1918. According to Fortescue's theorem, any set of unbalanced three-phase phasors can be resolved into three sets of balanced phasors called symmetrical components. They are :

1. Positive sequence components consisting of three phasors equal in magnitude displaced from each other by 120° and having the same phase sequence as the original unbalanced phasors.

2. Negative sequence components consisting of three phasors equal in magnitude, displaced from each other by 120° and having a phase sequence opposite of the original unbalanced phasors.

3. Zero sequence components consisting of three phasors equal in magnitude and with zero phase displacement from each other.

If *a*, *b* and *c* are used to denote the three unbalanced phasors with phase sequence *abc*, the positive sequence will have a phase sequence of *abc* and negative sequence components *acb*. Subscripts

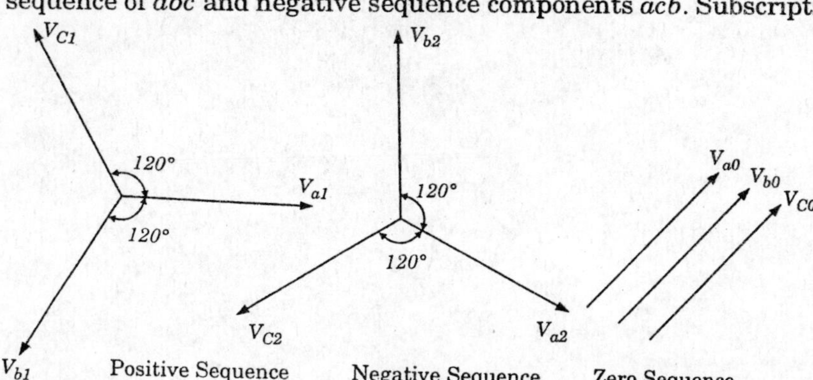

Fig. 12.1

1 is used for positive sequence, 2 for negative sequence and 0 for zero sequence. If the original unbalanced voltages are V_a, V_b and V_c then the positive sequence voltages will be denoted by V_{a1}, V_{b1} and V_{c1} the negative sequence voltages by V_{a2}, V_{b2} and V_{c2} and the zero sequence voltages by V_{a0}, V_{b0} and V_{c0} and the phasor diagrams will be as shown in Fig. 12.1.

The unbalanced phasors of voltages or currents are resolved into their symmetrical components and, therefore, the original phasors are the sums of the respective components and are given by

$$V_a = V_{a1} + V_{a2} + V_{a0}$$
$$V_b = V_{b1} + V_{b2} + V_{b0}$$
$$V_c = V_{c1} + V_{c2} + V_{c0}$$

Operators

The operator j has already been dealt with in A.C. circuits, which causes a rotation through 90° in the counter clockwise direction. From the above definition, the following functions are obtained :

$$j = 1\angle 90^\circ = 1\angle -270^\circ = 0 + j1 = +j$$
$$j^2 = j \cdot j = 1\angle 180^\circ = 1\angle -180^\circ = -1 + j0 = -1$$
$$j^3 = j \cdot j^2 = 1\angle 270^\circ = 1\angle -90^\circ = 0 - j1 = -j$$
$$j^4 = j \cdot j^3 = 1\angle 360^\circ = 1\angle 0^\circ = 1 + j0 = 1$$
$$j^5 = j \cdot j^4 = j$$

The letter a is used to define an operator which causes a rotation of 120° in the counter clockwise direction. Therefore, the following functions are obtained with the a operator :

$$a = 1\angle 120^\circ = 1\,(\cos 120 + j \sin 120)$$
$$= -0.5 + j0.866$$
$$a^2 = a \cdot a = 1\angle 240^\circ = -0.5 - j0.866$$
$$a^3 = a \cdot a^2 = 1\angle 360^\circ = 1 + j0$$
$$a^4 = a \cdot a^3 = a = -0.5 + j0.866$$
$$1 + a + a^2 = 1 - 0.5 + j0.866 - 0.5 - j0.866 = 0$$

Relationship Between Symmetrical Components and Unbalanced Phasors

From the definition of symmetrical components and with reference to the phasor diagram of Fig. 12.1, the following relations are obtained.

$$V_{a1} = V_{a1} \qquad V_{a2} = V_{a2} \qquad V_{a0} = V_{a0}$$
$$V_{b1} = a^2 V_{a1} \qquad V_{b2} = a V_{a2} \qquad V_{b0} = V_{a0}$$
$$V_{c1} = a V_{a1} \qquad V_{c2} = a^2 V_{a2} \qquad V_{c0} = V_{a0}$$

Therefore, the unbalanced voltages become

$$V_a = V_{a0} + V_{a1} + V_{a2}$$
$$V_b = V_{a0} + a^2 V_{a1} + a V_{a2}$$
$$V_c = V_{a0} + a V_{a1} + a^2 V_{a2}$$

or in matrix form

$$\begin{bmatrix} V_a \\ V_b \\ V_c \end{bmatrix} = \begin{bmatrix} 1 & 1 & 1 \\ 1 & a^2 & a \\ 1 & a & a^2 \end{bmatrix} \begin{bmatrix} V_{a0} \\ V_{a1} \\ V_{a2} \end{bmatrix}$$

Let
$$A = \begin{bmatrix} 1 & 1 & 1 \\ 1 & a^2 & a \\ 1 & a & a^2 \end{bmatrix}$$

then
$$A^{-1} = 1/3 \begin{bmatrix} 1 & 1 & 1 \\ 1 & a & a^2 \\ 1 & a^2 & a \end{bmatrix}$$

Hence the symmetrical components are obtained as

$$\begin{bmatrix} V_{a0} \\ V_{a1} \\ V_{a2} \end{bmatrix} = 1/3 \begin{bmatrix} 1 & 1 & 1 \\ 1 & a & a^2 \\ 1 & a^2 & a \end{bmatrix} \begin{bmatrix} V_a \\ V_b \\ V_c \end{bmatrix}$$

or
$$V_{a0} = 1/3\,(V_a + V_b + V_c)$$
$$V_{a1} = 1/3\,(V_a + a V_b + a^2 V_c)$$
$$V_{a2} = 1/3\,(V_a + a^2 V_b + a V_c)$$

Thus given three unbalanced phasors, the symmetrical components phasors can be resolved from the above relations. If required, the other components, V_{b0}, V_{c0}, V_{b1}, V_{c1}, V_{b2} and V_{c2} can be obtained. The above relations are true for any set of related phasors like voltages, currents, forces etc.. The symmetrical components and the original phasors can be obtained by analytical or graphical method.

In a three phase system, the sum of the three line to line voltages is always zero. Hence the zero sequence components can never be present in the line voltages whatever be the degree of unbalance. But the sum of the three phase voltages is not necessarily zero and, therefore, zero sequence voltages can be present in phase voltages.

In a three phase star connected system, the sum of the line current is equal to the current in the neutral, *i.e.* $I_n = I_a + I_b + I_c = 3I_{a0}$. If there is no neutral wire, I_n is zero and hence zero sequence currents cannot flow in the lines. In delta connected loads, there is no neutral and, therefore, line currents do not contain zero sequence components. However, there can be zero sequence components in the phase currents, which will be circulating in the closed delta.

Power in Terms of Symmetrical Components

The power flowing into an unbalanced three-phase load can be obtained in terms of the symmetrical components of voltages and currents. The complex power $S = P + jQ = V \cdot I^*$. For a three-phase system

$$S = V_a I_a^* + V_b I_b^* + V_c I_c^*$$

$$= [V_a \; V_b \; V_c] \begin{bmatrix} I_a \\ I_b \\ I_c \end{bmatrix}^*$$

where * indicates, the conjugate.

Let $\quad [V] = \begin{bmatrix} V_{a0} \\ V_{a1} \\ V_{a2} \end{bmatrix}$ and $[I] = \begin{bmatrix} I_{a0} \\ I_{a1} \\ I_{a2} \end{bmatrix}$

Then, in terms of symmetrical components,

$$S = (AV)_t \cdot (AI)^* = V_t A_t \cdot A^* I^*$$

$$= [V_{a0} \; V_{a1} \; V_{a2}] \begin{bmatrix} 1 & 1 & 1 \\ 1 & a^2 & a \\ 1 & a & a^2 \end{bmatrix} \begin{bmatrix} 1 & 1 & 1 \\ 1 & a & a^2 \\ 1 & a^2 & a \end{bmatrix} \begin{bmatrix} I_{a0} \\ I_{a1} \\ I_{a2} \end{bmatrix}$$

$$= 3\,(V_{a0} I_{a0}^* + V_{a1} I_{a1}^* + V_{a2} I_{a2}^*)$$

Thus the power in a three-phase system is equal to three times the sum of the powers due to positive, negative and zero sequence components.

Example 12.1. *A system of unbalanced three-phase voltages are given by 100 V, j200 V and (–100 – j160) V. Determine the three symmetrical components of the system.*

Solution. $V_R = (100 + j0)$ V

$V_Y = (0 + j200)$ V

$V_B = (-100 - j160)$ V

and phase sequence is *RYB*.

The zero sequence component of R-phase is given by

$$V_{RO} = 1/3\,(V_R + V_Y + V_B)$$
$$= 1/3\,(100 + j200 - 100 - j160) = j13.33 \text{ V}$$
$$V_{R1} = 1/3\,(V_R + aV_Y + a^2V_B)$$
$$= 1/3\,[100 + (-0.5 + j0.866)(j200) + (-0.5 - j0.866) \times (-100 - j160)]$$
$$= 1/3\,(100 - j100 - 173.2 + 50 + j80 + j86.6 - 138.56)$$
$$= 1/3\,(161.76 + j66.6) = (53.92 + j22.2) \text{ V}$$
$$V_{R2} = 1/3\,(V_R + a^2V_Y + aV_B)$$
$$= 1/3\,[100 + (-0.5 - j0.866)(j200) + (-0.5 + j0.866)(-100 - j160)]$$
$$= 1/3\,(461.76 - j106.6) = (153.92 - j35.53) \text{ V.}$$

Example 12.2. *Determine the unbalanced phase voltages V_a, V_b and V_c in a circuit where*

$$V_{a1} = 50\,\angle 0°,\; V_{a2} = 10\,\angle 90° \text{ and } V_{a0} = 10\,\angle 180° \text{ V.}$$

Solution. $V_a = V_{a1} + V_{a2} + V_{a0}$

$$= 50 + j10 - 10 = (40 + j10) \text{ V.}$$
$$V_b = V_{a0} + a^2V_{a1} + aV_{a2}$$
$$= -10 + (-0.5 - j0.866)\,50 + (-0.5 + j0.866)\,j10$$
$$= -10 - 25 - j43.3 - j5 - 8.66$$
$$= -(43.66 + j48.3) \text{ V}$$
$$V_c = V_{a0} + aV_{a1} + a^2V_{a2}$$
$$= -10 + (0.5 + j0.866)\,50 + (-0.5 - j0.866)\,j10$$
$$= -10 - 25 + j43.3 - j5 + 8.66$$
$$= (-26.34 + j38.3) \text{ V.}$$

Example 12.3. *The current flowing in the line 'a' supplying a delta connected load is 100 amp. With the current in line a as reference and assuming that line c is open, find the symetrical components of line currents.*

Solution. The line currents are as shown in the Fig. 12.2.

$$I_a = 10\,\angle 0°,\; I_b = -100\,\angle 0° \text{ and } I_C = 0$$
$$\therefore \quad I_{a0} = 1/3\,(I_a + I_b + I_c) = 0$$
$$I_{a1} = 1/3\,(I_a + aI_b + a^2I_c)$$

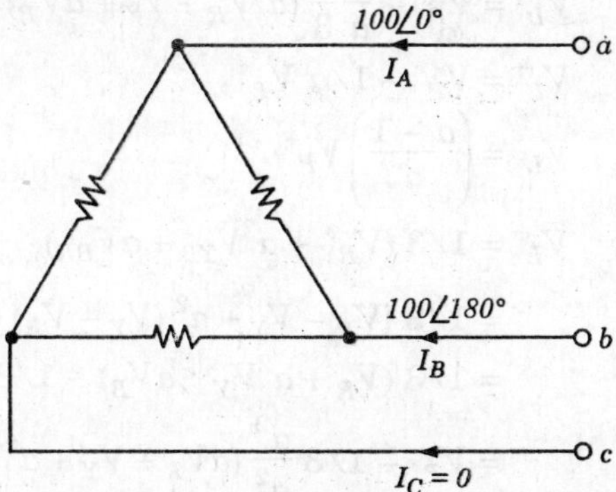

Fig. 12.2

$$= 1/3\ [100 + (-0.5 + j0.866)\ (-100)]$$
$$= 1/3\ (150 - j36.6) = (50 - j28.8)$$
$$= \mathbf{57.8 \angle -30° \text{ Amps.}}$$
$$I_{a2} = 1/3\ [100 + (-0.5 - j0.866) \times (-100)]$$
$$= 50 + j28.87 = \mathbf{57.8 \angle 30° \text{ A.}}$$

Example 12.4. *If in a 3-phase 4-wire unbalanced system of voltages V_P^+ and V_P^- denote the positive and negative sequence components of the drop from the R line to neutral and V_L^+ and V_L^- denote similar quantities of the drop from R line to Y line show that*

$$V_L^+ = \frac{a-1}{a} V_P^+$$

and $$V_L^- = \frac{a^2-1}{a} V_P^-$$

where $a = 1 \angle 120°$

Solution. If V_R, V_Y and V_B are the phase voltages, then the line voltages are given by

$$V_{RY} = V_R - V_Y, \quad V_{YB} = V_Y - V_B \quad \text{and} \quad V_{BR} = V_B - V_R$$

Then the positive sequence component of line voltage

$$V_{RY}^+ = V_L^+ = 1/3\ (V_{RY} + aV_{YB} + a^2 V_{BR})$$
$$= 1/3\ [V_R - V_Y + a\ (V_Y - V_B) + a^2\ (V_B - V_R)]$$
$$= 1/3\ [(V_R + aV_Y + a^2 V_B - (a^2 V_R + V_Y + aV_B)]$$

But the positive sequence voltage of R phase voltage V_P^+ is given by

$$V_P^+ = 1/3\ (V_R + aV_Y + a^2 V_B)$$

$$\therefore \qquad V_L^+ = V_P^+ - \frac{a}{a}\frac{1}{3}(a^2V_R + V_Y + aV_B)$$

$$V_L^+ = V_P^+ - 1/a\ V_P^+$$

i.e. $$V_L^+ = \left(\frac{a-1}{a}\right) V_P^+$$

Similarly $$V_L^- = 1/3\,(V_{RY} + a^2V_{YB} + aV_{BR})$$

$$= 1/3\,[V_R - V_Y + a^2\,(V_Y - V_B) + a(V_B - V_R)]$$

$$= 1/3\,(V_R + a^2V_Y + aV_B) - 1/3\,(aV_R + V_Y + a^2V_B)$$

$$= V_P^- - 1/3\,\frac{a^2}{a^2}\,(aV_R + V_Y + a^2V_B)$$

i.e. $$V_L^- = V_P^- - \frac{1}{a^2}V_P^- = \frac{a^2-1}{a^2}V_P^-$$

Example 12.5. *An unbalanced 3-phase network of pure resistance draws currents of 5, 5 and 7.07 amperes respectively from the R, Y and B lines of a 3φ, balanced supply. Find the symmetrical components of the line currents, if the load is delta connected.*

Solution. The sum of the line currents should add up to zero in a 3-phase system. Taking the line current in *R* phase as reference and for the *RYB* phase sequence, the phasor diagram of current is shown in Fig. 12.3.

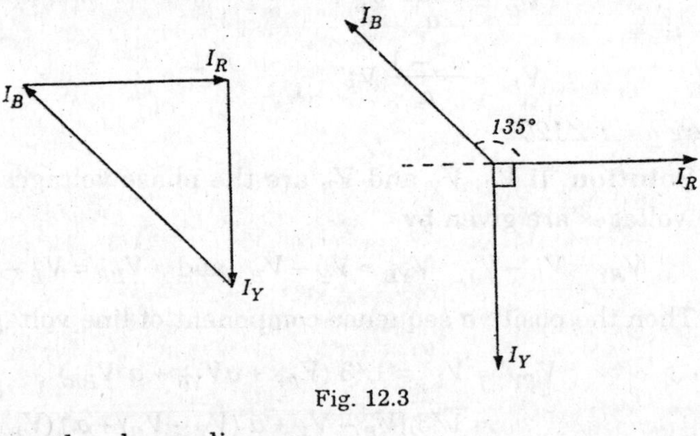

Fig. 12.3

From the phasor diagram

$$I_R = 5\angle 0°$$

$$I_Y = -j5$$

$$I_B = 7.07\angle 135° = -5 + j5$$

$$I_{R0} = \frac{I_R + I_Y + I_B}{3} = 0$$

$$I_{R1} = 1/3\ [5 + (-0.5 + j0.866)(-j5) + (0.5 - j0.866)(-5 + j5)]$$

$$= (5.22 + j1.443)\ \text{A}$$

$$I_{R2} = 1/3\ [5 + (-0.5 - j0.866)(-j5) + (-0.5 + j0.366)(-5 + j5)]$$

$$= (0.387 - j1.443)\ \text{A}$$

EXERCISES

12.1. The unbalanced currents in the R, Y and B leads of a 3-phase supply are given by 100, 141.4 and 200 Amps respectively. Find the sequence components of the currents.

[**Ans.** $I_{R0} = 0$, $I_{R1} = (126.2 + j57.8)$ A, $I_{R2} = -(26.5 + j57.8)$ A]

12.2. Show that the power associated with an unbalanced 3-phase system of voltages and currents is thrice the total power associated with the symmetrical components of these voltages and currents.

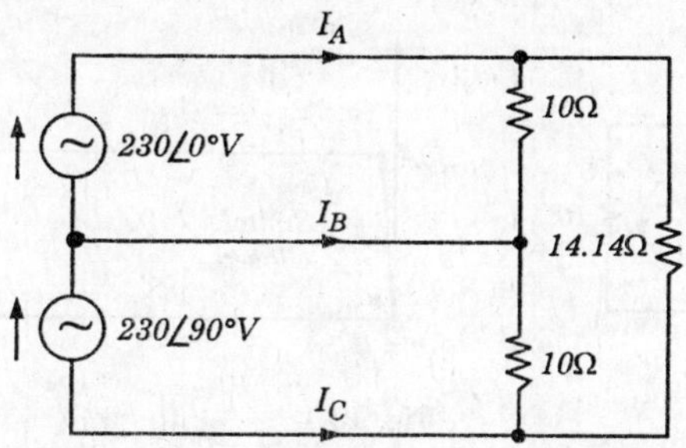

Fig. 12.4

12.3. Find the symmetrical components of the line currents for the system shown in Fig. 12.4. [**Ans.** $I_{A0} = 0$, $I_{A1} = (1.525 + j6.225)$, $I_{A2} = (36.67 + j0.08)$]

12.4. Resolve the unbalanced currents into their sequence components.

$I_R = 12 + j24$, $I_Y = 16 - j2$, and $I_B = -4 - j6$.

[**Ans.** $I_{R0} = (8 + j5.33)$, $I_{R1} = (0.845 + j15.11)$ and $I_{R2} = (3.155 + j3.56)$]

12.5. Determine the unbalanced phase voltages given

$V_{a1} = (50 + j0)\ V$; $V_{a2} = (0 + j10)\ V$ and $V_{a0} = (-10 + j0)\ V$.

[**Ans.** $V_a = (40 + j10)$ V, $V_b = -(43.66 + j48.3)$ V, $V_c = (-26.34 + j38.3)$ V]

THIRTEEN

CIRCUIT TRANSIENTS

When a circuit is switched from one state to another, the current in the circuit changes. The change will depend on the properties of the circuit.

If an e.m.f. of 200 volts is applied to a 10 ohm pure resistor as in Fig. 13.1 (*a*) the current rises abruptly, almost instantaneously to its steady value of 20 Amps as in Fig. 13.1 (*b*).

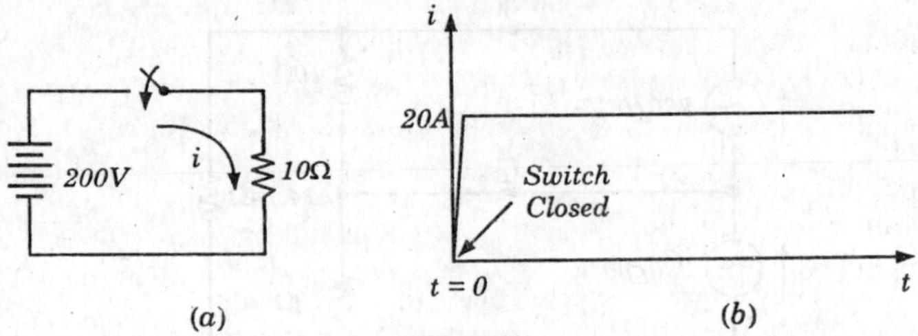

Fig. 13.1

If the same resistor is coiled around a magnetic core, the 20 Amps current value is reached only after a long time (Fig. 13.2). This is because time is required to store energy in the magnetic core.

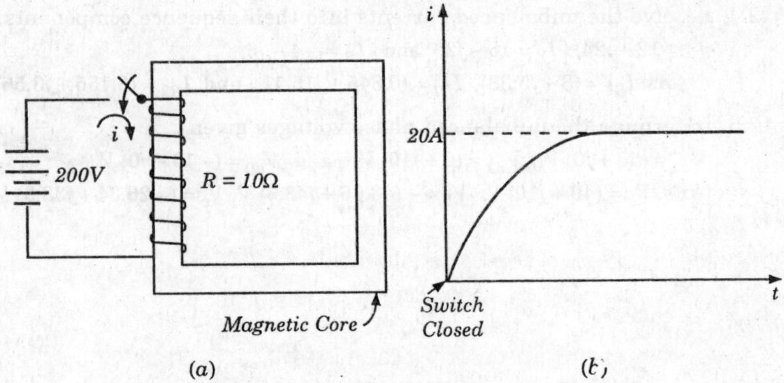

Fig. 13.2

If this circuit is switched off, because time is required to dissipate the stored magnetic energy, the current of 20 Amps dies down to zero only after a long time.

In the circuit of Fig. 13.2, while the current is rising to its final steady value of E/R, magnetic energy is continually being stored in the magnetic substance at a progressively diminishing rate. The magnetic energy tends to prevent any rise in current. This is similar to the case of a cycle tube being pumped up. As the air pressure in the tube increases it acts to prevent further pumping of air.

The property of an electric circuit to oppose any change in value of the current has already been explained as inductance. This property causes the current to lag behind the applied voltage so that the ultimate E/R value is reached to only after a lapse of time.

Laplace Transformation

In circuit transients, we often come across integro-differential equations as shown in this chapter. We shall adopt the Laplace Transform technique for solving such equations. The purpose of this book is not to deal with Laplace Transformation in detail. A brief resume is given here.

Advantages of Laplace Transformation Technique

The classical method of solving ordinary differential equations is rather involved. In the classical method, the complementary function and particular integral have to be determined and finally the arbitrary constants have to be obtained from known initial conditions. The Laplace Transform method is superior to the classical method due to the following reasons :

(*a*) It simplifies functions-Lapalce Transformation transforms exponential and trigonometric functions into simple algebraic functions.

(*b*) It simplifies operations. Laplace transformation transforms differentiation and integration, respectively, into multiplication and division. It transforms integro differential equations, into algebraic equations which are easier to handle. Laplace transformation is similar to logarithmic transformation, which converts multiplication and division into simple addition and subtraction. Laplace transformation deals with functions where as Logarithmic transformation deals with numbers.

(*c*) The arbitrary constants need not be determined separately. In solving a differential equation, by the Laplace Transformation method, the solution comes out complete.

(*d*) It makes use of step and impulse responses. If we know the response of a system to a step or impulse input, then the response of the system to any other input can be determined.

The Laplace Transform of a function $f(t)$ is defined by

$$F(s) = \int_0^\infty f(t)\, e^{-st}\, dt$$

$F(s)$ is the Laplace Transform of $f(t)$; s is a new variable which is complex,

and is written for sonvenience by the following cymbolic notation.

$$F(s) = \mathcal{L}[f(t)]$$

When the integral exists, $f(t)$ is said to be Laplace Transformable. The inverse Laplace Transformation is written for convenience as

$$f(t) = \mathcal{L}^{-1}[F(s)]$$

Laplace Transformation of Some Important Functions

1. A constant step function $f(t) = E$. The step function is normally represented as $f(t) = E\, u(t)$, $u(t)$ stands for a unit step function as in Fig. 13.3.

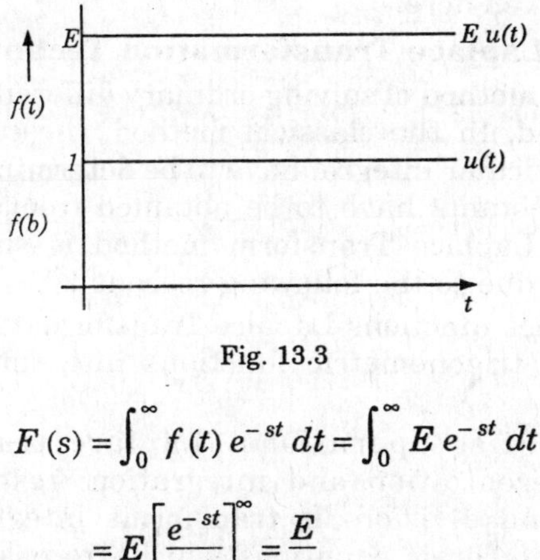

Fig. 13.3

$$F(s) = \int_0^\infty f(t)\, e^{-st}\, dt = \int_0^\infty E\, e^{-st}\, dt$$

$$= E\left[\frac{e^{-st}}{-s}\right]_0^\infty = \frac{E}{s}$$

2. The Exponential function e^{at}

$$\mathcal{L}[e^{at}] = \int_0^\infty e^{at}\, e^{-st}\, dt = \int_0^\infty e^{-(s-a)t}\, dt$$

$$= \frac{1}{s-a}$$

3. The sine function, $\sin \omega t$.

When know $\sin \omega t = \dfrac{e^{j\omega t} - e^{-j\omega t}}{2j}$

$$\therefore \qquad \mathcal{L}\,[\sin \omega t] = \frac{1}{2j}\,\mathcal{L}\left[e^{j\omega t} - e^{-j\omega t}\right]$$

$$= \frac{1}{2j}\left[\frac{1}{s - j\omega} - \frac{1}{s + j\omega}\right] = \frac{\omega}{s^2 + \omega^2}$$

4. The consine function cos ωt.

$$\cos \omega t = \frac{e^{j\omega t} + e^{-j\omega t}}{2}$$

$$\mathcal{L}\,[\cos \omega t] = \frac{1}{2}\,\mathcal{L}\left[e^{j\omega t} + e^{-j\omega t}\right]$$

$$= \frac{1}{2}\left[\frac{1}{s - j\omega} + \frac{1}{s + j\omega}\right] = \frac{s}{s^2 + \omega^2}$$

5. Power of t, t^n

$$\mathcal{L}\,[t^n] = \int_0^{\infty} t^n\, e^{-st}\, dt = \frac{n\,!}{s^{n+1}}$$

Theorem. The Laplace Transform of $e^{-\alpha t}$ times a function is equal to the Laplace Transform of that function with s replaced by $(s + \alpha)$.

$$\mathcal{L}\,[e^{-\alpha t} f(t)] = F(s + \alpha)$$

Two simple theorems will now be stated.

Theorem. The Laplace Transform of sum of two functions is equal to the sum of the Laplace Transform of the individual functions.

That is $\mathcal{L}\,[f_1(t) + f_2(t)] = \mathcal{L}\,[f_1(t)] + \mathcal{L}\,[f_2(t)]$

Theorem. The Laplace Transform of $k\,f(t)$ is equal to k. $\mathcal{L}\,[f(t)]$, where k is a constant.

$$\mathcal{L}\,[k\,f(t)] = k\,\mathcal{L}\,[f(t)]$$

Theorem. If a function $f(t)$ and its derivative $f'(t)$ are both Laplace Transformable and if $\mathcal{L}\,[f(t)] = F(s)$, then

$$\mathcal{L}\left[\frac{df(t)}{dt}\right] = \mathcal{L}\,[f'(t)] = s\,F(s) - f(0+)$$

As an extension,

$$\mathcal{L}\left[\frac{d^2 f}{dt^2}\right] = \mathcal{L}\,[f''(t)] = s^2 F(s) - s\,f(0+) - f'(0+)$$

$$\mathcal{L}\left[\frac{d^n f}{dt^n}\right] = s^n F(s) - s^{n-1} f(0+) - s^{n-2} f'(0+) \text{ -- } f^{(n-1)}(0+)$$

Theorem If $\mathcal{L}[f(t)] = F(s)]$, then

$$\mathcal{L}\left[\int_0^t f(t)\,dt\right] = \frac{F(s)}{s}$$

Table of Laplace Transforms

	$f(t)$	$F(s)$
1.	$u(t)$	$\frac{1}{s}$
2.	e^{-at}	$\frac{1}{s+a}$
3.	e^{at}	$\frac{1}{s-a}$
4.	$\sin \omega t$	$\frac{\omega}{s^2+\omega^2}$
5.	$\cos \omega t$	$\frac{s}{s^2+\omega^2}$
6.	$e^{-at} \sin \omega t$	$\frac{\omega}{(s+a)^2+\omega^2}$
7.	$e^{-at} \cos \omega t$	$\frac{s+a}{(s-a)^2+\omega^2}$
8.	t	$\frac{1}{s^2}$
9.	t^n	$\frac{n!}{s^{n+1}}$
10.	$\frac{df(t)}{dt}$	$sF(s) - f(0^+)$
11.	$\int f(t)\,dt$	$\frac{F(s)}{s} + \frac{f^{-1}(0^+)}{s}$
12.	$f(t-t_1)$	$e^{-t_1 s} \cdot F(s)$
13.	te^{-at}	$\frac{1}{(s+a)^2}$
14.	$\sinh \omega t$	$\frac{\omega}{s^2-\omega^2}$
15.	$\cosh \omega t$	$\frac{s}{s^2-\omega^2}$
16.	$f_1(t) + f_2(t)$	$F_1(s) + F_2(s)$

Solution of a Second Order Linear Differential Equation

Consider the equation $\frac{d^2 i}{dt^2} + b\frac{di}{dt} + ci = f(t)$

where b and c are known constants and $f(t)$ is a given Laplace Transformable function. To solve this equation, and find $i(t)$, let us take Laplace Transforms on both sides. Then,

$$sI(s) - si(0) - i'(0) + b[sI(s) - i(0)] + cI(s) = F(s)$$

The values of $i(0)$ and $i'(0)$ are necessary for solving the differential equation.

$$[s^2 + bs + c]\,I(s) = F(s) + si(0) + i'(0) + bi(0)$$
$$= F(s) + i(0)(b + s) + i'(0)$$
$$I(s) = \frac{1}{s^2 + bs + c}[F(s) + i(0)(b + s) + i'(0)]$$

To get $i(t)$, we have to find the Laplace inverse of $I(s)$. This will depend also on the initial conditions $i(0)$ and $(i'(0)$.

Inverse Laplace Transform

Consider $F(s)$ given by

$$F(s) = \frac{s^m + a_{m-1}s^{m-1} + \ldots\ldots a_1 s + a_0}{s^n + b_{n-1}s^{n-1} + \ldots\ldots b_1 s + b_0}$$

The co-efficients a_i's and b_i's are all real and m and n are positive integers. $F(s)$ is always a proper fraction, so that in our circuit theory problems $m < n$.

The general method is to write $F(s)$ in partial fractions as

$$F(s) = \frac{K_1}{s - s_1} + \frac{K_2}{s - s_2} + \ldots \frac{K_j}{s - s_j} + \ldots \frac{K_n}{s - s_n}$$

where $s_1, s_2, \ldots s_j \ldots s_n$ are the roots of the denominator function and are assumed distinct. We shall consider the case of repeated roots (multiple roots) later. The typical constant (residue) K_j is given by

$$K_j = [F(s)(s - s_j)] \text{ with } s = s_j$$

Knowing all the residues, $f(t)$ may be written using the table of Laplace transform as

$$f(t) = K_1 e^{s_1 t} + K_2 e^{s_2 t} + \ldots + K_j e^{s_j t} + \ldots K_n e^{s_n t}$$

Example 13.1. *Find*

$$\mathcal{L}^{-1}\left[\frac{s}{s^2 + 5s + 6}\right]$$

$$F(s) = \frac{s}{s^2 + 5s + 6} = \frac{s}{(s + 2)(s + 3)} = \frac{K_1}{s + 3} + \frac{K_2}{s + 2}$$
$$K_1 = [F(s)(s + 3)]_{s = -3}$$
$$= \left.\frac{s(s + 2)}{(s + 2)(s + 3)}\right|_{s = -3} = \left.\frac{s}{s + 2}\right|_{s = -3} = -3$$

Similarly $\quad K_2 = -2$

$$\therefore \quad f(t) = 3e^{-3t} - 2e^{-2t}$$

Example 13.2. *Find*

$$\mathcal{L}^{-1}\left[\frac{s}{s^2 + 2s + 5}\right]$$

Solution. Roots of the denominator

$$= \frac{-2 \pm \sqrt{4 - 20}}{2} = -1 \pm j2$$

$$\therefore \quad \frac{s}{s^2 + 2s + 5} = \frac{s}{(s + 1 - j2)\,(s + 1 + j2)}$$

$$= \frac{K_1}{(s + 1 - j2)} + \frac{K_2}{(s + 1 + j2)}$$

$$K_1 = \left.\frac{s}{s + 1 + j2}\right|_{s = -1 + j2} = \frac{-1 + j2}{j4} = \frac{1}{4}(2 + j1)$$

When the roots are complex conjugate, $K_2 = K_1^*$

$$K_2 = \frac{1}{4}(2 - j1)$$

$$\therefore \quad F(s) = \frac{1}{4}\left[\frac{2 + j1}{s + 1 - j2} + \frac{2 - j1}{s + 1 + j2}\right]$$

and $$f(t) = \frac{1}{4}\left[(2 + j1)\,e^{(-1 + j2)\,t} + (2 - j1)\,e^{(-1 - j2)\,t}\right]$$

$$= \frac{1}{4}e^{-t}\left[2e^{j2t} + je^{j2t} + 2e^{-j2t} - je^{-2jt}\right]$$

$$= e^{-t}\left[\cos 2t - \frac{1}{2}\sin 2t\right]$$

Case of multiple roots.

Let us take an example to consider this case.

Example 13.3. *Find*

$$\mathcal{L}^{-1}\left[\frac{s + 2}{s\,(s + 1)^2\,(s + 3)}\right]$$

Solution. The denominator has 4 roots ; 2 simple and one double

2 simple roots at $s = 0$ and $s = -3$ and one double root at $s = -1$

$$\therefore \quad F(s) = \frac{K_1}{s} + \frac{K_2}{(s + 1)^2} + \frac{K_3}{(s + 1)} + \frac{K_4}{(s + 3)}$$

K_1 and K_4 are found in the usual way.

$$K_1 = F(s)\, s\Big|_{s=0} = \frac{2}{3}$$

$$K_4 = F(s)\,(s+3)\Big|_{s=-3} = \frac{1}{12}$$

K_2 can also be found in the same way.

$$K_2 = F(s)\,(s+1)^2\Big|_{s=-1} = -\frac{1}{2}$$

K_3 is found in the following way.

$$K_3 = \left\{\frac{d}{ds}\left[F(s)\,(s+1)^2\right]\right\}_{s=-1}$$

$$= \left\{\frac{d}{ds}\left[\frac{s+2}{s\,(s+3)}\right]\right\}_{s=-1}$$

$$= \frac{s\,(s+3) - (s+2)\,(2s+3)}{s^2\,(s+3)^2}\Bigg|_{s=-1}$$

$$= \frac{-2-1}{4} = -\frac{3}{4}$$

Hence $$F(s) = \frac{2/3}{s} - \frac{3/4}{s+1} - \frac{1/2}{(s+1)^2} + \frac{1/12}{s+3}$$

$$\therefore \quad f(t) = \frac{2}{3} - \frac{3}{4}e^{-t} - \frac{1}{2}te^{-t} + \frac{1}{12}e^{-3t}$$

Example 13.4. *Find*

$$\mathcal{L}^{-1}\left[\frac{1}{2s^2\,(s^2+4)}\right]$$

Solution. The denominator has four roots :

1 double roots at $s = 0$

2 Complex conjugate roots at $s = \pm j2$

$$\therefore \quad F(s) = \frac{K_1}{s^2} + \frac{K_2}{s} + \frac{K_3}{s+j2} + \frac{K_4}{s-j2}$$

$$K_1 = F(s)\, s^2\Big\}_{s=0} = \frac{1}{8}$$

$$K_2 = \left\{\frac{d}{ds}\,[f(s)\, s^2]\right\}_{s=0}$$

$$= \frac{1}{2}\,\frac{(s^2+4)\times 0 - 1\times 2s}{(s^2+4)^2}\Bigg|_{s=0} = 0$$

$$K_3 = F(s)\,(s+j2)\Big|_{s=-j2} = \frac{1}{2s^2\,(s-j2)}\Bigg|_{s=-j2}$$

$$= \frac{1}{2\,(-j2)^2\,(-j4)} = -j\left(\frac{1}{32}\right)$$

$$K_4 = +j/32$$

Hence $$F(s) = \frac{1/8}{s^2} - \frac{j/32}{s+j2} + \frac{j/32}{s-j2}$$

$$= \frac{1/8}{s^2} - \frac{j}{32}\left[\frac{s - j2 - (s + j2)}{s^2 + 2^2}\right]$$

$$= \frac{1/8}{s^2} - \frac{1}{32}\left(\frac{4}{s^2 + 2^2}\right)$$

$\therefore$ $$f(t) = \frac{1}{8}\,t - \frac{1}{16}\sin 2t$$

If a root is repeated thrice, then the residues are calculated as follows :

$$F(s) = \frac{Nr\,(s)}{(s - s_1)^3} = \frac{K_1}{(s - s_1)^3} + \frac{K_2}{(s - s_1)^2} + \frac{K_3}{(s - s_1)}$$

$$K_1 = F(s)\,(s - s_1)^3\Big|_{s = s_1}$$

$$K_2 = \left\{\frac{d}{ds}\,[f(s)\,(s - s_1)^3]\right\}_{s = s_1}$$

$$K_3 = \frac{1}{2\,!}\left\{\frac{d^2}{ds^2}\,[F(s)\,(s - s_1)^3]\right\}_{s = s_1}$$

Example 13.5. *Find*

$$\mathcal{L}^{-1}\left[\frac{3s + 1}{5s^3\,(s - 2)^2}\right]$$

Solution. There are 5 roots *viz.*,
3 roots at $s = 0$ and 2 roots at $s = 2$

$\therefore$ $$F(s) = \frac{K_1}{s^3} + \frac{K_2}{s^2} + \frac{K_3}{s} + \frac{K_4}{(s - 2)^2} + \frac{K_5}{(s - 2)}$$

$$K_1 = F(s)\,s^3\Big|_{s = 0} = \frac{1}{20}$$

$$K_2 = \left\{\frac{d}{ds}\,[F(s)\,s^3]\right\}_{s = 0}$$

$$= \frac{1}{5}\,\frac{(s - 2)^2\,3 - (3s + 1)\,2\,(s - 2)}{(s - 2)^4}\Bigg\}_{s = 0}$$

$$= -\frac{1}{5}\,\frac{3s + 8}{(s - 2)^3}\Bigg|_{s = 0} = +\frac{1}{5}$$

$$K_3 = \frac{1}{2\,!}\left\{\frac{d^2}{ds^2}[F(s)s^3]\right\}_{s=0}$$

$$= -\frac{1}{10}\left[\frac{(s-2)^3 \times 3 - (3s+8)\,3\,(s-2)^2}{(s-2)^6}\right]_{s=0}$$

$$= -\frac{1}{10}\left[\frac{3\,(s-2) - 3\,(3s+8)}{(s-2)^4}\right]_{s=0}$$

$$= -\frac{1}{10}\left(\frac{-30}{16}\right) = \frac{3}{16}$$

$$K_4 = F(s)\,(s-2)^2\Big|_{s=2} = \frac{3s+1}{5s^3}\Big|_{s=2} = \frac{7}{40}$$

$$K_5 = \left\{\frac{d}{ds}\left[F(s)\,(s-2)^2\right]\right\}_{s=2} = \frac{1}{5}\left[\frac{s^3 \times 3 - (3s+1)\,3s^2}{s^6}\right]_{s=2}$$

$$= -\frac{3}{16}$$

$$\text{Hence } F(s) = \frac{1/20}{s^3} + \frac{1/5}{s^2} + \frac{3/16}{s} + \frac{7/40}{(s-2)^2} - \frac{8/16}{(s-2)}$$

$$\therefore \quad f(t) = \frac{1}{40}t^2 + \frac{1}{5}t + \frac{3}{16} + \frac{7}{40}te^{2t} - \frac{3}{16}e^{2t}$$

Initial and Final Value Theorems

It is sometimes necessary to determine the initial and final values of the output of a system even before the final solution is arrived at. In many cases, the initial and final values alone may be required. In all such cases if we are to determine the output response and then substitute $t = 0$ or $t = \infty$, it will be tedious and if we can determine the initial and final values before taking inverse Laplace Transforms, the work is simplified. Two theorems help us in this regard.

Initial Value Theorem. If $f(t)$ and $f'(t)$ are both Laplace Transformable, then the initial value of $f(t)$ is

$$f(0+) = \underset{t \to 0+}{\text{Lt}}\;[f(t)] = \underset{s \to \infty}{\text{Lt}}\;[sF(s)]$$

Final Value Theorem. If $f(t)$ and $f'(t)$ are Laplace Transformable, then the final value of $f(t)$ is

$$\underset{t \to \infty}{\text{Lt}}\;[f(t)] = \underset{s \to 0}{\text{Lt}}\;[sF(s)]$$

The final value theorem does not apply when $f(t)$ is a periodic function. For example, it cannot be used to determine the final value of say, $\sin(\omega t + \theta)$ as $\sin \infty$ has no definite value.

Example 13.6. *Given*

$$I(s) = \frac{s+3}{s^2+4s+8}$$

find the initial and final values of i(t)

Initial Value

$$\underset{t \to 0}{\text{Lt}} [i(t)] = \underset{s \to \infty}{\text{Lt}} [sI(s)]$$

$$= \underset{s \to \infty}{\text{Lt}} \left[\frac{s(s+3)}{s^2+4s+8}\right] = \underset{s \to \infty}{\text{Lt}} \left[\frac{s^2+3s}{s^2+4s+8}\right] = 1$$

Final Value

$$\underset{t \to \infty}{\text{Lt}} [i(t)] = \underset{s \to 0}{\text{Lt}} [sI(s)] = \underset{s \to 0}{\text{Lt}} \left[\frac{s(s+3)}{s^2+4s+8}\right] = 0$$

R.L. Transients (DC)

An *R-L* circuit is shown in Fig. 13.4 connected to a battery through a switch. The current during the time interval before the steady conditions are reached is called transient current.

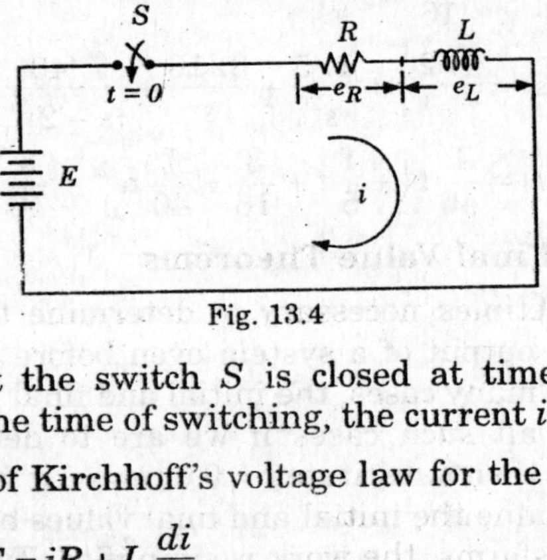

Fig. 13.4

Assume that the switch *S* is closed at time $t = 0$ and also assume that at the time of switching, the current *i* is zero.

Application of Kirchhoff's voltage law for the loop gives

$$E = iR + L\frac{di}{dt}$$

which may be solved for *i*

This is a differential equation and we shall solve it using Laplace Transformation technique. Taking Laplace Transforms on both sides of the equation

$$RI(s) + L[sI(s) - i(0)] = \frac{E}{s}$$

where $I(s) = \mathcal{L}(i)$

We know that just before closing the switch, the current $i(0) = 0$

The equation reduces to

$$RI(s) + LsI(s) = \frac{E}{s}$$

$$I(s) = \frac{E}{s(R+sL)} = \frac{E/L}{s(s+R/L)} = \frac{K_1}{s} + \frac{K_2}{s+\frac{R}{L}}$$

$$K_1 = sI(s)\Big|_{s=0} = \frac{E}{R}$$

$$K_2 = I(s)\left(s+\frac{R}{L}\right)\Bigg|_{s=-\frac{R}{L}} = -\frac{E}{R}$$

Hence $$I(s) = \frac{E/R}{s} - \frac{E/R}{s+R/L}$$

$\therefore$ $$i(t) = \frac{E}{R} - \frac{E}{R}e^{-\frac{Rt}{L}} = \frac{E}{R}\left[1 - e^{-\frac{Rt}{L}}\right]$$

The current is said to rise exponentially as shown in Fig. 13.5.

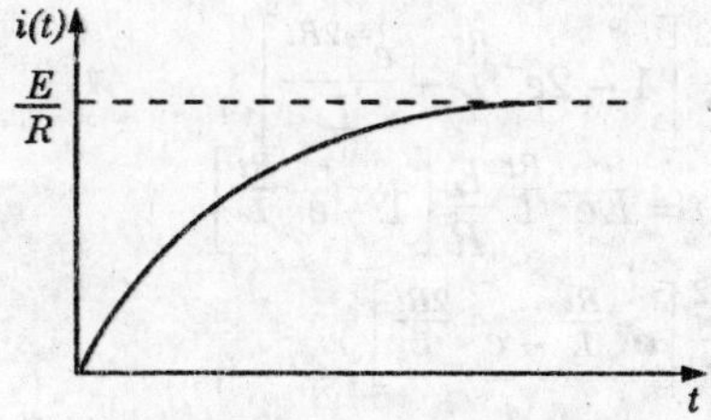

Fig. 13.5. R.L. Transient

The final value of the current may be obtained by substituting $t = \infty$ in equation for $i(t)$

$$i(t)\Big|_{t\to\infty} = \frac{E}{R} \text{ Amps.}$$

The plot in Fig. 13.5 shows the transition period during which the current varies from $i(0)$ to $i(\infty)$ or the steady state value. To determine the current at any time t_1 after the switch has been closed, we have to substitute $t = t_1$ in the equation.

Consider $t = T = L/R$ seconds.

$$i\Big|_{t=T} = \frac{E}{R}\left(1 - e^{-\frac{R}{L}\frac{L}{R}}\right)$$

$$= \frac{E}{R}(1 - e^{-1}) = 0.632\,\frac{E}{R}$$

$$= 63.2\% \text{ of the final value.}$$

In a circuit in which the current is increasing to a final steady value, the time (T) taken to reach 63.2% of the final value is called the time constant of the circuit.

The transient voltages across the elements of the circuit are obtained from the current. The expression for the voltage across the resistor is

$$e_R = Ri = R\,\frac{E}{R}\left(1-e^{-\frac{Rt}{L}}\right)$$

$$= E\left(1-e^{-\frac{Rt}{L}}\right)$$

$$e_L = L\,\frac{di}{dt} = L\,\frac{d}{dt}\left[\frac{E}{R}\left(1-e^{-\frac{Rt}{L}}\right)\right]$$

$$= Ee^{-\frac{Rt}{L}}$$

The instantaneous power in each element is given as

$$p_R = e_R i = \frac{E^2}{R}\left(1-e^{-\frac{Rt}{L}}\right)^2$$

$$= \frac{E^2}{R}\left[1-2e^{-\frac{Rt}{L}}+\frac{e^{-2Rt}}{L}\right]$$

$$p_L = e_L i = Ee^{-\frac{Rt}{L}}\,\frac{E}{R}\left[1-e^{-\frac{Rt}{L}}\right]$$

$$= \frac{E^2}{R}\left[e^{-\frac{Rt}{L}}-e^{-\frac{2Rt}{L}}\right]$$

The total power

$$p_T = P_R + P_L = \frac{E^2}{R}\left(1-e^{-\frac{Rt}{L}}\right)$$

The energy stored in the magnetic field of the coil is obtained as an integration.

$$W_L = \int_0^\infty p_L\,dt = \int_0^\infty \frac{E^2}{R}\left(e^{-\frac{Rt}{L}}-e^{-\frac{2Rt}{L}}\right)dt$$

$$= \frac{1}{2}\frac{E^2}{R}\left[\frac{L}{R}\right] = \frac{1}{2}L\left(\frac{E}{R}\right)^2 = \frac{1}{2}LI_{ss}^{\ 2}$$

where I_{ss} is the final steady state current.

RL-Decay Transient

Consider the circuit of Fig. 13.6. The switch S is previously in position 1 and has been there till steady state conditions are reached. The current then flowing is $i = E/R$ Amps. At $t = 0$, the switch is turned to position (2), which removes the source and puts a short circuit across the RL series branch. The application of Kirchhof's voltage law to the closed circuit gives us the equation.

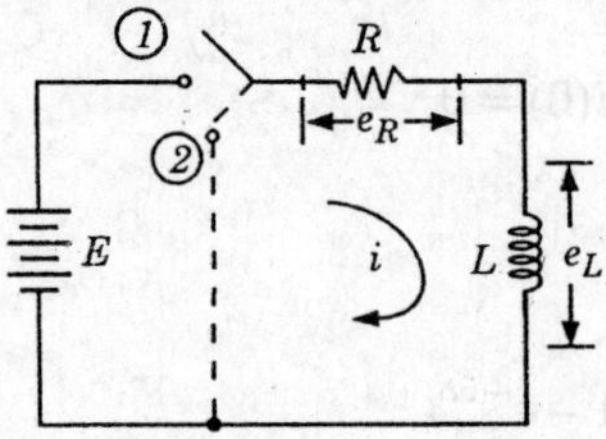

Fig. 13.6

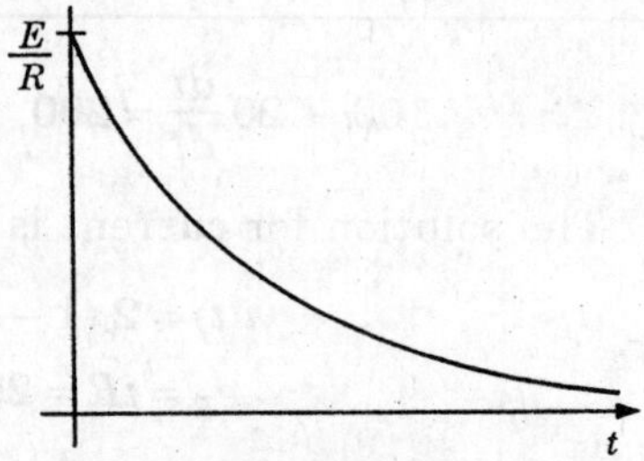

Fig. 13.7. Decay of current in an R-L circuit.

$$iR + L\frac{di}{dt} = 0$$

and this equation is to be solved subject to the initial condition that $i(0) = E/R$

Taking Laplace Transform on both sides

$$I(s)R + L\,[sI(s)] - i(0)] = 0$$

where $$I(s) = \mathcal{L}\,[i(t)]$$

$$I(s)\ [(R + sL)] = L\,\frac{E}{R}$$

$$I(s) = \frac{LE}{R}\left(\frac{1}{R + sL}\right) = \frac{E}{R}\left[\frac{1}{(s + R/L)}\right]$$

$$i(t) = \mathcal{L}^{-1}[I(s)] = \frac{E}{R}\,e^{-Rt/L}$$

The exponential decay is shown in Fig. 13.7.

Here again, at time $t = T = L/R$ seconds,

$$i(T) = \frac{E}{R}\,e^{-1} = 0.368\,\frac{E}{R}$$

$$= 36.8\% \text{ of the initial value.}$$

For a decaying case like this, the time constant is defined as the time required to reach 36.8% of the initial value.

Example 13.7. *A series RL circuit with R = 100 ohms and L = 20 h has a DC voltage of 200 volts applied through a switch at t = 0. Find (a) the equation for the current and voltages across the different elements (b) the current at t = 0.5 seconds (c) the current at 1 sec and (d) the time at which* $e_R = e_L$

Solution. The differential equation for the circuit is

$$100i + 20\frac{di}{dt} = 200, \qquad i(0) = 0$$

The solution for current is

$$i(t) = 2\,(1 - e^{-5t})$$

$$e_R = iR = 200\,(1 - e^{-5t})$$

$$e_L = L\frac{di}{dt} = 200\,e^{-5t}$$

$$i\,(t = 0.5) = 2\,(1 - e^{-5 \times 0.5})$$

$$= 2\,(-e^{-2.5}) = 1.836 \text{ A}$$

$$i\,(t = 1) = 2\,(1 - e^{-5}) = 1.987 \text{ A}$$

$$e_R = e_L$$

$$200\,(1 - e^{-5t}) = 200\,e^{-5t}$$

$$200 = 400\,e^{-5t}$$

$$e^{-5t} = 0.5$$

$$-5t = \log 0.5 = -0.693$$

$$t = 0.1386 \text{ sec.}$$

Example 13.8. *In the series circuit shown in Fig. 13.8, the switch is closed on position 1 at t = 0. At t = 1 milli-second, the switch is moved to position 2. Obtain the equations for the current in both intervals and draw the transient current curve.*

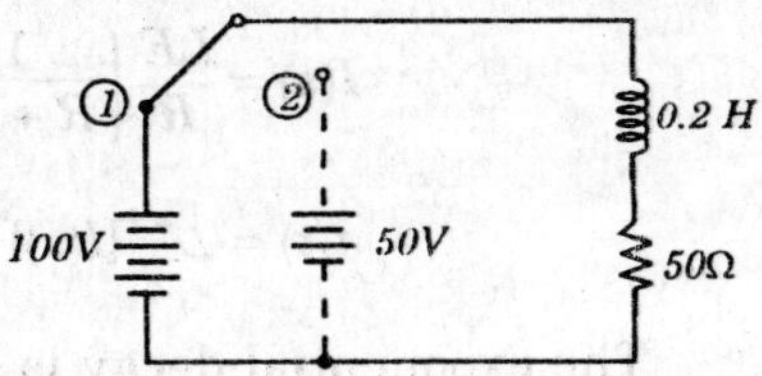

Fig. 13.8

Solution. When the switch is in position 1, the current equation is

$$i = E/R\left(1 - e^{-Rt/L}\right) = 2\,(1 - e^{-250t})$$

This is valid upto $t = 0.001$ sec.

At $\quad t = 0.001$ sec,

$$i = 2\,(-e^{-250 \times 0.001}) = 2\,(1 - e^{0.25}) = 0.4424 \text{ A.}$$

When $t = 0.001$ sec, the switch is moved to position 2. We shall assume that this is done at $t' = 0$ sec. The applied voltage is 50 V and the differential equation is

$$50\,i + 0.2\frac{di}{dt'} = 50$$

The initial condition for solving this equation is

$$i(0) = 0.4424 \text{ A}$$

Taking Laplace Transforms on both sides of this equation

$$50\,I(s) + 0.2\,[sI(s) - 0.4424] = \frac{50}{s}$$

$$50\,I\,(s) + 0.2s\,I(s) = \frac{50}{s} + 0.08848$$

$$\therefore \qquad I(s) = \frac{50 + 0.08848s}{s\,(50 + 0.2s)} = \frac{50 + 0.08848\,s}{0.2s\,(s + 250)}$$

$$= \frac{250 + 0.4424\,s}{s\,(s + 250)} = \frac{K_1}{s} + \frac{K_2}{(s + 250)}$$

Solving for K_1 and K_2

$$I(s) = \frac{1}{s} - \frac{0.5576}{s + 250}$$

$$\therefore \qquad i(t') = 1 - 0.5576\,e^{-250t}$$

$$t' = 0 \text{ implies } t = 0.001 \text{ sec.}$$

The equation for current may be rewritten using t itself as

$$i = 1 - 0.5576\,e^{-250\,(t - 0.001)}$$

Thus
$$i = 2\,(1 - e^{-250t})\;;\; 0 < t \le 0.001 \text{ sec}$$
$$i = 1 - 0.5576\,e^{-250\,(t - 0.001)}\;;\; t \ge 0.001$$

The transient current is shown in Fig. 13.9.

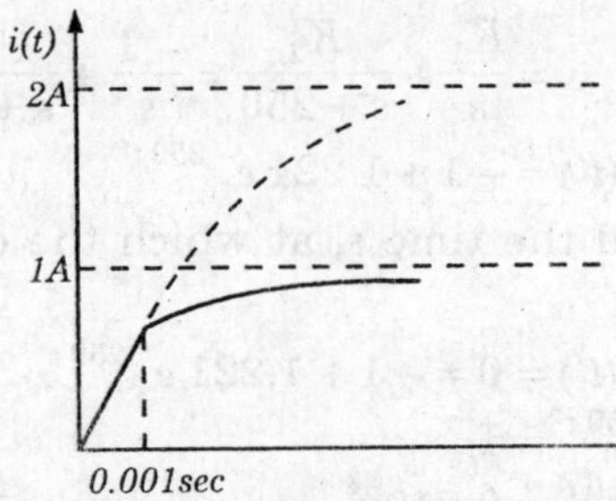

Fig. 13.9

Example 13.9. *In the circuit of Fig. 13.10, the switch S is closed at time t = 0 on position 1 and changed over to position 2 after 1 milli sec. Find the time at which the current is zero and reversing its direction. Assume that the change over of switch from 1 to 2 takes place in zero time.*

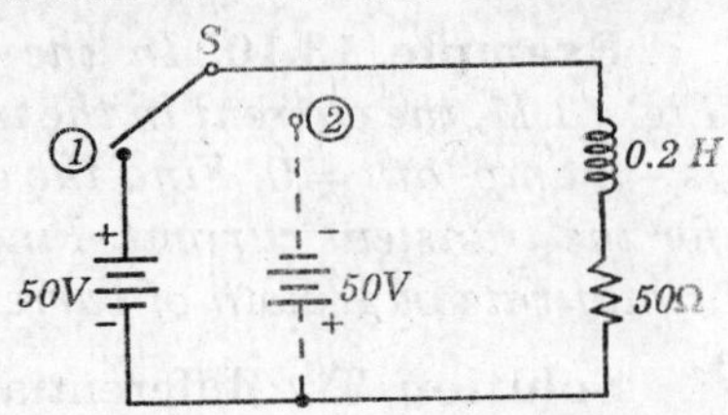

Fig. 13.10

Solution. When the switch is closed on to position 1, the differential equation of the circuit is

$$50i + 0.2\frac{di}{dt} = 50 \; ; i(0) = 0$$

∴ The equation for the current i

$$= \frac{50}{50}\left[1 - e^{-\frac{50t}{0.2}}\right]$$

$$i = 1 - e^{-250t} \; ; 0 < t \leq 0.001$$

At $t = 0.001$

$$i = 1 - e^{-250 \times 0.001} = 0.221 \text{ A.}$$

At $t = 0.001$ (or $t' = 0$), the switch is moved to position 2. The differential equation for the circuit is

$$50i + 0.2\frac{di}{dt'} = -50 \; ; i(0) = 0.221 \text{ A}$$

Taking Laplace Transform on both sides,

$$50\, I(s) + 0.2\, [sI(s) - 0.221] = -\frac{50}{s}$$

$$I(s)\,(50 + 0.2s) = -\frac{50}{s} + 0.0442$$

$$I(s) = \frac{-50 + 0.0442s}{0.2\, s\,(s + 250)} = \frac{-250 + 0.221\, s}{s\,(s + 250)}$$

$$= \frac{K_1}{s} + \frac{K_2}{s + 250} = \frac{-1}{s} + \frac{1.221}{s + 250}$$

Hence $i\,(t') = -1 + 1.221\, e^{-250t'}$

We need to find the time t, at which the current is zero and reversing.

$$i\,(t') = 0 = -1 + 1.221\, e^{-250t'}$$

i.e. $1.221\, e^{-250t'} = 1$

$$e^{-250t'} = 0.819$$

$$t' = 7.987 \times 10^{-4} \text{ sec}$$

or $t = 0.001 + 7.987 \times 10^{-4}$

$$= \mathbf{0.0017987\ sec.}$$

Example 13.10. *In the circuit of Fig. 13.11, the current in the inductance is – 6 amp. at t = 0. Find the expression for the transient current. Find also the initial rate of growth of current.*

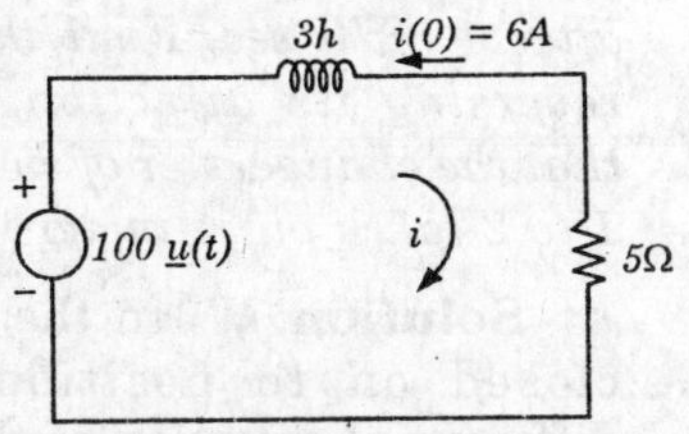

Fig. 13.11

Solution. The differential equation for the circuit for $t > 0$ is

$$Ri + L\frac{di}{dt} = 100\ ;\ i(0) = -6$$

$$5i + 3\frac{di}{dt} = 100$$

Taking Laplace Transforms on both sides of this equation

$$5I\ (s) + 3[sI(s) - i(0)] = \frac{100}{s}$$

$$5I(s) + 3\ [sI(s) + 6] = \frac{100}{s}$$

$$I(s)\ (5 + 3s) = \frac{100}{s} - 18$$

$$\therefore \qquad I(s) = \frac{100 - 18s}{s\ (5 + 3s)} = \frac{100 - 18s}{3s\ (s + 5/3)}$$

$$= \frac{\frac{100}{3} - 6s}{s\ (s + 5/3)} = \frac{K_1}{s} + \frac{K_2}{(s + 5/3)}$$

$$= \frac{20}{s} - \frac{26}{(s + 5/3)}$$

Hence $\quad i(t) = 20 - 26\, e^{-5/3t}$

Rate of growth $= \dfrac{di}{dt} = (-26)\left(-\dfrac{5}{3}\right)e^{-\frac{5}{3}t}$

Initial rate $= \left.\dfrac{di}{dt}\right|_{t=0} = \dfrac{130}{3}$

$= \mathbf{43.333\ Amps/sec.}$

Example 13.11. *A D.C. voltage is applied to a series RL circuit by closing a switch. The voltage across L is 100 volts at t = 0 and drops to 13.5 volts at t = 0.02 sec. If L = 0.1 h, find the value of R.*

Solution. $\quad e_L = Ee^{-\frac{Rt}{L}}$

At $t = 0$, $\quad e_L = 100 = Ee^{-0} = E$

At $t = 0.02$, $\quad e_L = 100\, e^{-R \times \frac{0.02}{0.1}} = 13.5$

$\therefore \quad R = \mathbf{10\ ohms.}$

Example 13.12. *In the circuit of Fig. 13.12, switch S_1 is closed at t = 0 and switch S_2 is opened at t = 0.2 sec. Find the expression for the transient current for the two intervals.*

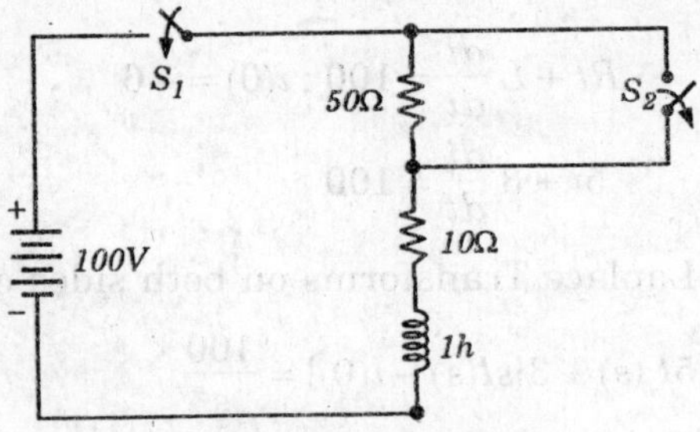

Fig. 13.12

Solution. When switch S_1 is closed at $t = 0$ (S_2 is still closed and the 50 ohms resistor is short circuited), the differential equation is

$$10i + 1\frac{di}{dt} = 100 \; ; i(0) = 0$$

$$\therefore \quad i = \frac{100}{10}\left[1 - e^{-10t}\right] = 10\left[1 - e^{-10t}\right]$$

At $t = 0.2$ sec, $\quad i = 10\,[1 - e^{-2}] = $ **8.65 Amps.**

The switch S_2 is opened at $t = 0.2$ sec ($t' = 0$). The differential equation for the circuit for $t > 0.2$ sec is

$$60\,i + \frac{di}{dt'} = 100 \; ; i(0) = 8.65 \text{ A}$$

Taking Laplace Transform on both sides,

$$60\,I(s) + sI(s) - 8.65 = \frac{100}{s}$$

$$(s + 60)\,I(s) = \frac{100}{s} + 8.65$$

$$I(s) = \frac{100 + 8.65\,s}{s\,(s + 60)} = \frac{K_1}{s} + \frac{K_2}{(s + 60)}$$

$$= \frac{1.67}{s} + \frac{6.98}{s + 60}$$

or

$$i(t') = 1.67 + 6.98\,e^{-60\,t'}$$

$$i(t) = \mathbf{1.67 + 6.98}\,e^{-60\,(t - 0.2)}$$

Example 13.13. *In the circuit of Fig. 13.13, the switch has been in position 1 for sufficient time to establish steady state conditions. The switch is then moved to position 2. Find the energy dissipated in the resistors during the transient.*

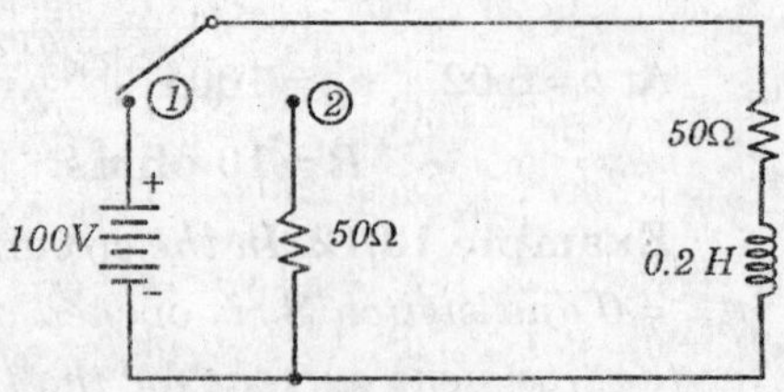

Fig. 13.13

Solution. When the switch is in position 1, the steady state current will be 100/50 = 2 Amps. After the switch is moved on to position (2), the differential equation is,

$$50\,i + 50\,i + 0.2\frac{di}{dt} = 0 \;;\; i(0) = 2\text{ A}$$

Taking Laplace Transform on both sides of the equation,

$$100\,I(s) + 0.2\,[s\,I(s) - 2] = 0$$

$$I(s)\,(100 + 0.2\,s) = 0.4$$

$$I(s) = \frac{0.4}{0.2s + 100} = \frac{2}{s + 500}$$

$$\therefore \quad i(t) = 2e^{-500\,t}$$

Energy dissipated in the resistors, is

$$\int_0^{\infty} i^2(t)\,Rdt$$

$$\mathcal{E} = \int_0^{\infty} 4e^{-1000t} \times 100\,dt$$

$$= \frac{400}{-1000}\left[e^{-1000t}\right]_0^{\infty} = 0.4 \text{ Joules.}$$

RC Transient

Consider the RC series circuit with a DC voltage applied through a switch as in Fig. 13.14. Let the capacitance have an initial charge of Q_0 coulombs.

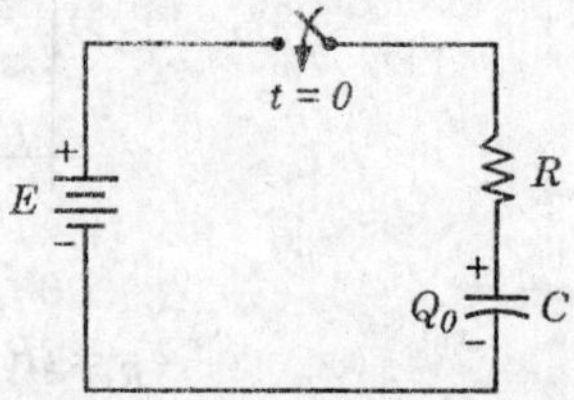

Fig. 13.14

The initial voltage on the capacitor

$$= V_0 = \frac{Q_0}{C}$$

Applying Kirchhoff's voltage law to the circuit, we get

$$iR + \frac{1}{C}\int idt + V_0 = E$$

(If the polarity of V_0 is reversed, the sign of V_0 will be negative).

Equation may be re-written as,

$$iR + \frac{1}{C}\int i\,dt = E - V_0$$

There is no loss in generality in assuming

$$V_0 = \frac{Q_0}{C} = 0$$

$$\therefore \quad iR + \frac{1}{C}\int i\,dt = E$$

This is an integral equation, to solve this, we shall take Laplace Transform on both sides.

$$RI(s) + \frac{1}{C} \cdot \frac{I(s)}{s} = \frac{E}{s}$$

$$\left(R + \frac{1}{sC}\right) I(s) = \frac{E}{s}$$

or
$$I(s) = \frac{E}{s\left(R + \frac{1}{sC}\right)} = \frac{E}{sR + \frac{1}{C}}$$

$$= \frac{E}{R\left(s + \frac{1}{RC}\right)}$$

$\therefore$
$$i(t) = \frac{E}{R} e^{-(t/RC)}$$

The initial value of the current is E/R amperes, and the final steady state value is zero Ampers. The current curve is shown in Fig. 13.15.

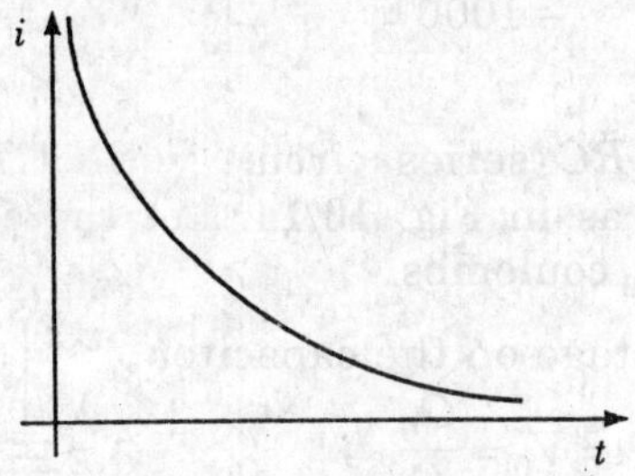

Fig. 13.15

$$e_R = iR = E\,\varepsilon^{-t/RC}$$

$$e_C = \frac{1}{C}\int_0^t i(t)\, dt = \frac{E}{CR}\int_0^t \varepsilon^{-t/RC}\, dt$$

$$= -E\left[\varepsilon^{-t/RC}\right]_0^t = E\left[1 - \varepsilon^{-t/RC}\right]$$

e_c increases and when $t = \infty$ (steady state condition)

e_c is equal to the applied voltage and opposing it.

The current i, then becomes zero.

$$P_R = e_R i = \frac{E^2}{R}\,\varepsilon^{-2t/RC}$$

$$P_C = e_C i = \frac{E^2}{R}\left[\varepsilon^{-t/RC} - \varepsilon^{-2t/RC}\right]$$

The energy stored in the capacitor is obtained by integrating P_C from zero to infinity

Energy stored in the capacitor

$$= \frac{E^2}{R}\int_0^\infty \left[\varepsilon^{-t/RC} - \varepsilon^{-2t/RC}\right] dt$$

$$= \frac{E^2}{R}\left[-RC\varepsilon^{-t/RC} + \frac{RC}{2}\varepsilon^{-2t/RC}\right]_0^\infty$$

$$= \frac{1}{2}CE^2$$

At $\quad t = RC$ sec, $i = \frac{E}{R}\varepsilon^{-1}$

= 36.8% of the initial current.

Hence time constant

$= T = RC$ seconds.

Decaying Transient

Consider the circuit of Fig. 13.16. The switch has been in position 1 for sufficient time to establish steady state conditions and at $t = 0$ is moved to position 2.

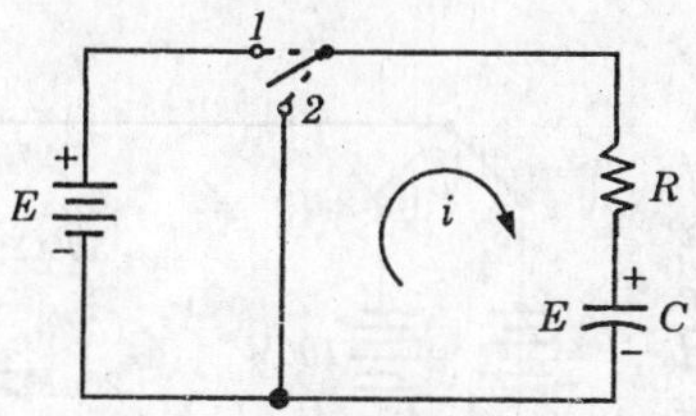

Fig. 13.16

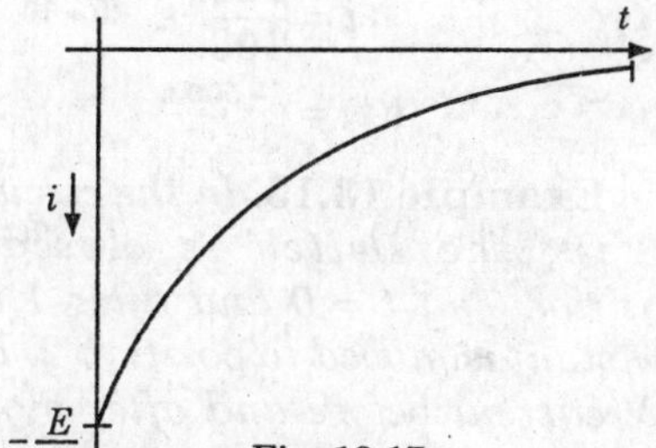

Fig. 13.17

Before the switch is moved to position 2, the capacitor gets charged to the voltage E with the polarity as shown.

The differential equation of the circuit is

$$iR + \frac{1}{C}\int i dt + E = 0$$

Taking Laplace Transform on both sides.

$$I(s)\left(R + \frac{1}{Cs}\right) = -\frac{E}{s}$$

and the solution is as before

$$i = -\frac{E}{R}\varepsilon^{-t/CR}$$

The current curve is drawn in Fig. 13.17.

Example 13.14. *The 20 μf capacitor in circuit of Fig. 13.18 has an initial charge $Q_0 = 0.001$ coulombs as shown. The switch is closed at t = 0. Find the transient current.*

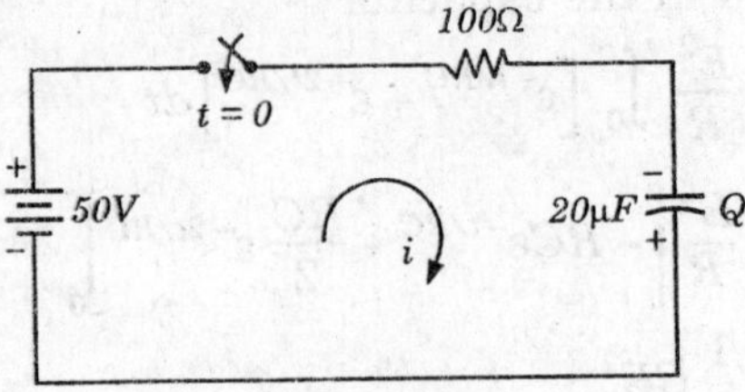

Fig. 13.18

Solution. The differential equation is

$$100i + \frac{1}{C}\int i\,dt - \frac{Q_0}{C} = 50$$

$$100\,i + \frac{1}{C}\int i\,dt = 50 + \frac{0.001}{20 \times 10^{-6}}$$

or
$$100i + \frac{1}{C}\int idt = 100$$

Solving which by Laplace Transform Technique ; we get

$$i = \frac{100}{100}\,\varepsilon^{-\frac{t}{20 + 10^{-6} \times 100}}$$

$$\mathbf{i(t) = \varepsilon^{-500\,t}}$$

Example 13.15. *In the circuit of 13.19, the switch is closed on position 1 at t = 0 and after 1 time constant is moved to position 2. Find the current before and after moving to position 2. Assume no initial charge on the capacitor.*

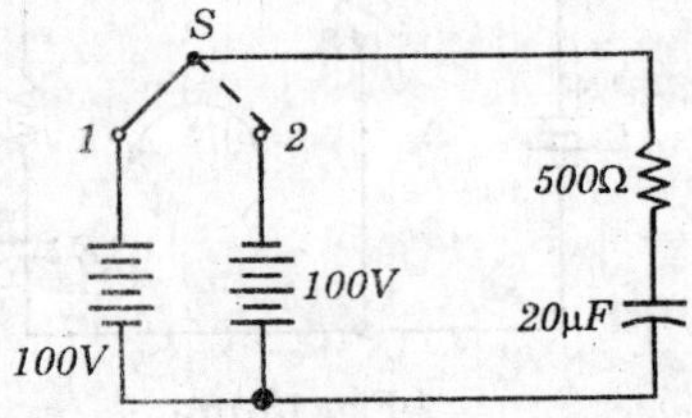

Fig. 13.19

Solution. When the switch is on position 1, the current expression as usual is

$$i = \frac{100}{500}\,e^{-\frac{t}{500 \times 20 + 10^{-6}}} = 0.2\,\varepsilon^{-100t}.$$

This continues until $t = RC = 500 \times 20 \times 10^{-6} = 0.01$ sec. The current at $t = 0.01$ sec.

$$i(t) = 0.2\,\varepsilon^{-100 \times 0.01} = \mathbf{0.0736\ Amps.}$$

The capacitor then has a voltage of $e_c = E\,(1 - \varepsilon^{-t/RC})$

$$e_C = 100\,[1 - \varepsilon^{-1}] = 63.2 \text{ Volts}$$

The switch is then closed on to position 2 at $t' = 0$ or $t = 0.01$ sec.

Then equation for the circuit is

$$500i + \frac{1}{C}\int i\,dt' + 63.2 = -100$$

or
$$500\,i + \frac{1}{C}\int i\,dt' = -163.2$$

$$i = \frac{-163.2}{500}\,\varepsilon^{-100t'}$$

$$= -0.3264\,\varepsilon^{-100t'} = -0.3264\,\varepsilon^{-100(t-0.01)}$$

At $t' = 0$, ($t = 0.01$ sec)

$$i = -\mathbf{0.3265 \text{ Amp.}}$$

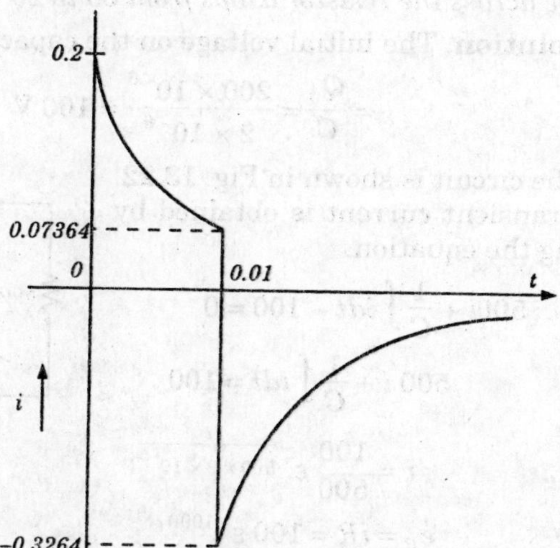

Fig. 13.20

The transient current is shown in Fig. 13.20.

Example 13.16. *The RC series circuit in Fig. 13.21 has an initial charge $Q_0 = 2 \times 10^{-2}$ coulomb as shown. Find the transient current if the switch is closed at t = 0.*

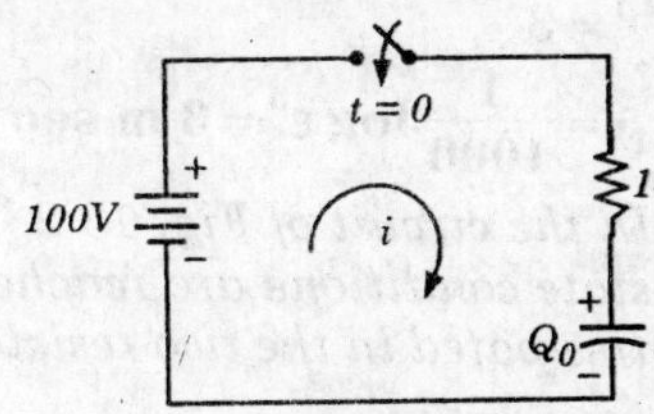

Fig. 13.21

Solution. After closing the switch, the equation for the circuit is

$$Ri + \frac{1}{C}\int i dt + \frac{Q_0}{C} = E$$

$$10i + \frac{1}{C}\int i dt + \frac{2 \times 10^{-2}}{100 \times 10^{-6}} = 100$$

i.e.
$$10i + \frac{1}{C}\int i dt = -\ 100 \text{ V}$$

or solving,
$$i(t) = \frac{-\ 100}{10}\ \varepsilon^{-\frac{t}{RC}} = \mathbf{-\ 10\ \varepsilon^{-100\,t}.}$$

Example 13.17. *A capacitor of 2 μF with an initial charge $Q_0 = 200 \times 10^{-6}$ coulomb, is connected across the terminals of a 500 ohm resistor at t = 0. Calculate the time in which the transient voltage across the resistor drops from 60 to 20 volts.*

Solution. The initial voltage on the capacitor

$$= \frac{Q_0}{C} = \frac{200 \times 10^{-6}}{2 \times 10^{-6}} = 100 \text{ V}$$

The circuit is shown in Fig. 13.22. The transient current is obtained by solving the equation.

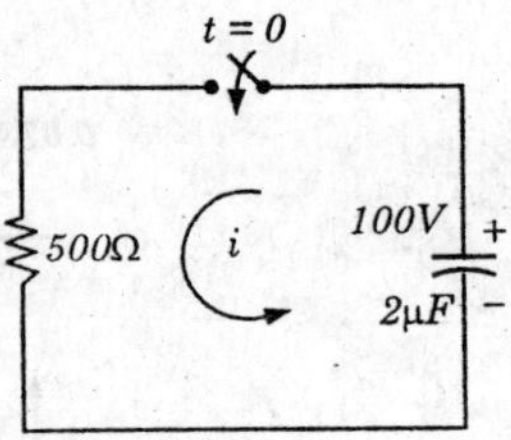

Fig. 13.22

$$500i + \frac{1}{C}\int i dt - 100 = 0$$

$$500\ i + \frac{1}{C}\int i dt = 100$$

$$\therefore \qquad i = \frac{100}{500}\ \varepsilon^{-\frac{t}{500 \times 2 \times 10^{-6}}}$$

$$e_R = iR = 100\ \varepsilon^{-1000\,t}$$

Let $e_R = 60$ V at $t = t_1$ and 20 V at $t = t_2$

$$100\ \varepsilon^{-1000\,t_1} = 60$$

$$100\ \varepsilon^{-1000\,t_2} = 20$$

Dividing,
$$\frac{e^{-1000\,t_1}}{e^{-1000\,t_2}} = 3$$

or
$$\varepsilon^{1000\,(t_2 - t_1)} = 3$$

or
$$(t_2 - t_1) = \frac{\mathbf{1}}{\mathbf{1000}} \mathbf{\log \varepsilon^3 = 3\ m\ sec}$$

Example 13.18. *In the circuit of Fig. 13.23, the switch S is in position 1 till steady state conditions are reached and then moved to 2. Find the energy dissipated in the two resistors. Show that this* *is equal to the energy stored in the capacitor before moving the switch.*

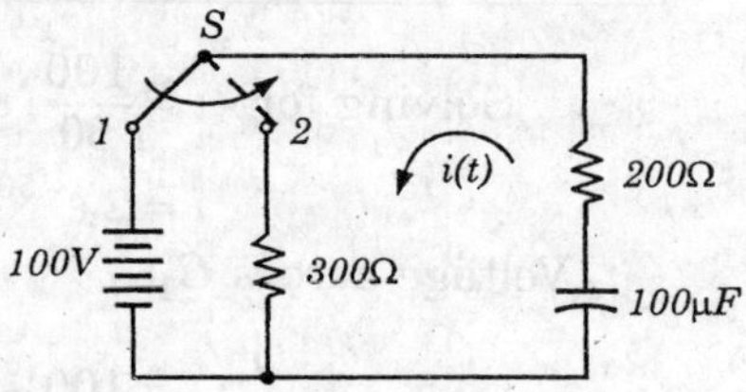

Fig. 13.23

Solution. When steady state conditions have been reached in position 1, the capacitor has a voltage of 100 V across it. On moving the switch to 2, the equation for the circuit is

$$200\, i + 300\, i + \frac{1}{C}\int i\, dt - 100 = 0$$

$$500\, i + \frac{1}{C}\int i\, dt = 100$$

$$i = \frac{100}{500}\, \varepsilon^{-t/(500 \times 100 \times 10^{-6})} = 0.2\, \varepsilon^{-20\,t}$$

Energy dissipated in the resistors

$$= \int_0^\infty i^2 R\, dt = \int_0^\infty 500 \times 0.2 \times 0.2\, \varepsilon^{-40\,t}\, dt$$

$$= -0.5\left[\varepsilon^{-40\,t}\right]_0^\infty = -0.5\,[0 - 1] = 0.5 \text{ Joule.}$$

Energy previously stored in the capacitor

$$= \tfrac{1}{2}\, CE^2 = \tfrac{1}{2} \times 100 \times 10^{-6} \times 100 \times 100 = \mathbf{0.5\ Joule.}$$

Example 13.19. *C_1 in Fig. 13.24, has an initial charge $Q_0 = 12 \times 10^{-4}$ coulombs. While C_2 has no initial charge. The switch is closed at $t = 0$, find the current transient, and the final voltage of capacitor C_1.*

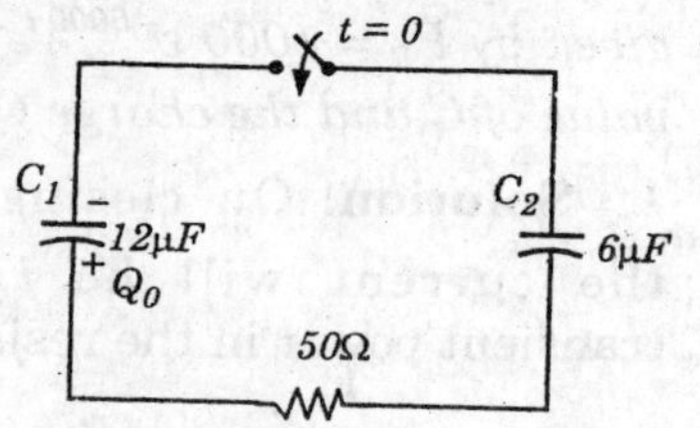

Fig. 13.24

Solution. The initial voltage on C_1

$$= \frac{Q_0}{C} = \frac{12 \times 10^{-4}}{12 \times 10^{-6}} = 100 \text{ volts}$$

When the switch is closed,

$$\frac{1}{C_1}\int i\, dt + 50\, i + \frac{1}{C_2}\int i\, dt = 100$$

$$50\, i + \frac{1}{C}\int i\, dt = 100$$

where $$\frac{1}{C} = \frac{1}{C_1} + \frac{1}{C_2} = \frac{1}{12} + \frac{1}{6} = \frac{1}{4}$$

$$C = 4\mu\text{F}$$

$\therefore$ Solving for $i = \dfrac{100}{50}\ \varepsilon^{-500\,t}$

$$i = 2\,\varepsilon^{-500\,t}$$

Voltage across C_1

$$= 100 - \frac{1}{C_1}\int_0^t i(t)\,dt$$

$$= 100 - \frac{10^6}{12}\int_0^t 2\varepsilon^{-500\,t}\,dt$$

$$= 100 - \frac{2\times 10^{+6}}{12\times 500}\left[\varepsilon^{-500t}\right]_0^t$$

$$= 100 - \frac{100}{3}\left[1-\varepsilon^{-500t}\right]$$

Final voltage across C_1,

$$= 100 - \frac{100}{3} = \mathbf{66.7\ volts.}$$

Example 13.20. *In the RC circuit of Fig. 13.25, the capacitor has an initial charge of Q_0 coulombs. When the switch is closed at t = 0, the transient power in the resistor is given by $P_R = 1000\ \varepsilon^{-5000\,t}$. Find the value of C and the charge Q_0.*

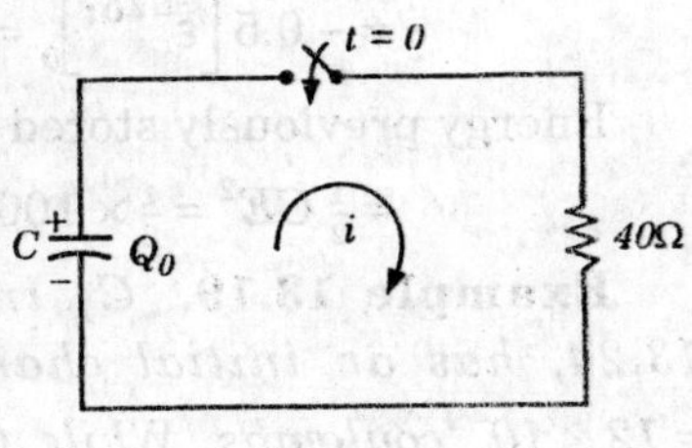

Fig. 13.25

Solution. On closing switch, the current will be $i = I\varepsilon^{-t/RC}$; transient power in the resistor $= e_R\, i$

$$= iRi = i^2R = 1000\,\varepsilon^{-5000\,t}$$

$$\therefore \qquad i^2 = \frac{1000^{-5000\,t}}{40}$$

$$i = 5\varepsilon^{-2500\,t}$$

This is of the form

$$i = \frac{E}{R}\,\varepsilon^{-t/RC}$$

$$\therefore \qquad \frac{E}{R} = 5$$

$$E = 40\times 50 = 200 \text{ volts} = \frac{Q_0}{C}$$

$$\frac{1}{RC} = 2500$$

$$\therefore \quad C = \frac{1}{2500 \times 40} = 10^{-5} = 10\ \mu F$$

$$Q_0 = EC = 200 \times 10 \times 10^{-6} = 2000 \times 10^{-6} \text{ Coulombs.}$$

Example 13.21. *In the series RL circuit of Fig. 13.26, the applied voltage is $e = 100\ \varepsilon^{-50t}$. Find*

(a) the resulting current and

(b) the initial rate of change of current.

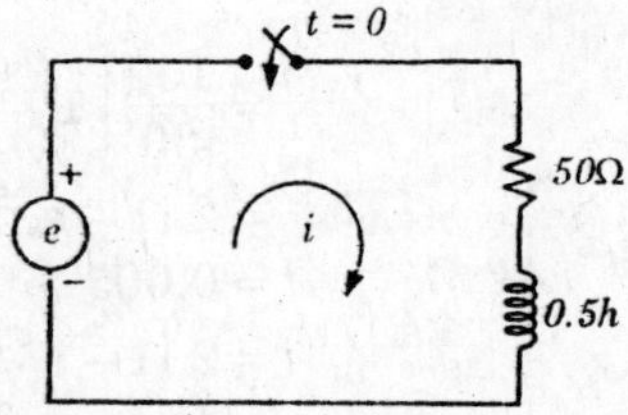

Fig. 13.26

Solution. On closing the switch, the application of Kirchhoff's voltage law gives.

$$(a) \qquad 50i + 0.5\frac{di}{dt} = e = 100\ \varepsilon^{-50t}$$

$$i(0) = 0$$

On taking Laplace Transform on both sides

$$50\ I(s) + 0.5\ sI(s) = \frac{100}{s+50}$$

$$I(s) = \frac{100}{(s+50)\ (0.5\ s+50)} = \frac{200}{(s+50)\ (s+100)}$$

$$= \frac{4}{(s+50)} - \frac{4}{(s+100)}$$

$$\therefore \qquad i = 4\ \varepsilon^{-50t} - 4\ \varepsilon^{-100t}$$

$$(b) \qquad \frac{di}{dt} = -200\ \varepsilon^{-50t} + 400\ \varepsilon^{-100t}$$

Initial rate of change of current

$$= \left(\frac{di}{dt}\right)_{t=0} = -200 + 400 = 200 \text{ Amps/sec.}$$

Example 13.22. *In the circuit of Fig. 13.27, switch 1 is closed at t = 0 and then after 5 milliseconds, switch 2 is opened. Find the transient currents.*

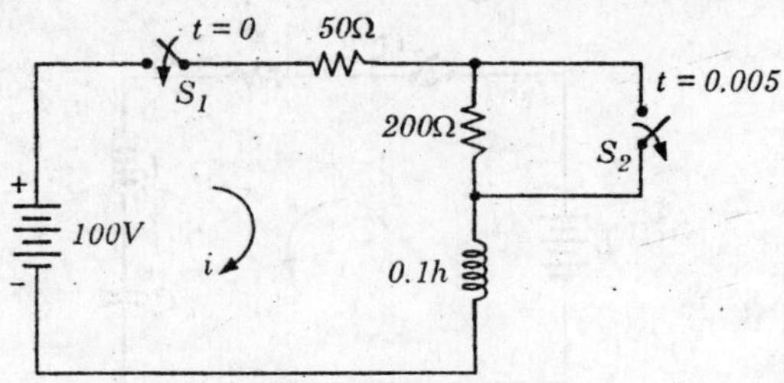

Fig. 13.27

Solution. With S_1 and S_2 closed, the voltage is applied to the circuit and the 200 ohms resistor is shorted.

The current i

$$= \frac{100}{50}\left[1 - \varepsilon^{-\frac{500}{0.1}t}\right]$$

$$= 2\,[1 - \varepsilon^{-500t}] \qquad 0 < t < 0.005$$

At $\quad t = 0.005$

$$i = 2\,[1 - \varepsilon^{-500 \times 0.005}]$$

$$= 2\,(1 - \varepsilon^{-2.5}) = 1.836 \text{ A}$$

At this time ($t = 0.005$ and $t' = 0$), S_2 is opened the differential equation, then is

$$250i + 0.1\frac{di}{dt'} = 100\,;\ i(0) = 1.836$$

Taking L.T. on both sides

$$250I(s) + 0.1[s\,I(s) - 1.836] = \frac{100}{s}$$

$$I(s)\,(250 + 0.1s) = \frac{100}{s} + 0.1836$$

$$I(s) = \frac{100 + 0.1836\,s}{s\,(0.1\,s + 250)} = \frac{1000 + 1.836\,s}{s\,(s + 2500)}$$

$$= \frac{K_1}{s} + \frac{K_2}{(s + 2500)} = \frac{0.4}{s} + \frac{1.436}{(s + 2500)}$$

$$i(t') = 0.4 + 1.436\,\varepsilon^{-2500t}$$

$$i(t) = 0.4 + 1.436\,\varepsilon^{-2500\,(t - 0.005)}, \text{ for } t > 0.005 \text{ sec.}$$

RLC Transients

The application of Kirchhoff's voltage law to the series RLC circuit of Fig. 13.28, yields the equation

$$Ri + L\frac{di}{dt} + \frac{1}{C}\int i\,dt = E$$

(assuming no initial charge on the capacitor)

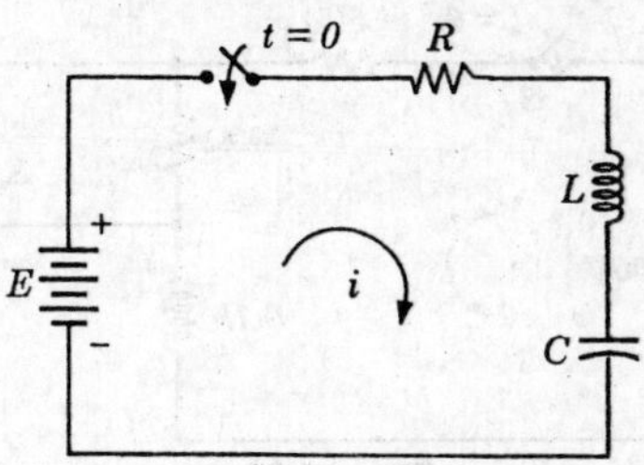

Fig. 13.28

This is an integro-defferential equation. Taking Laplace Transforms on both sides,

$$RI(s) + L[sI(s) - i(0)] + \frac{I(s)}{Cs} = \frac{E}{s}$$

Assuming $i\,(0) = 0$, we get

$$RI(s) + sLI(s) + \frac{1}{Cs}I(s) = \frac{E}{s}$$

$$I(s) = \frac{E}{s\left(R + sL + \frac{1}{Cs}\right)}$$

$$= \frac{E}{s^2L + sR + \frac{1}{C}} = \frac{\frac{E}{L}}{s^2 + \frac{R}{L}s + \frac{1}{LC}}$$

The roots of the denominator are

$$= -\frac{R}{2L} \pm \sqrt{\left(\frac{R}{2L}\right)^2 - \frac{1}{LC}} = \alpha \pm \beta$$

where $\qquad \alpha = -\dfrac{R}{2L}$

and $\qquad \beta = \sqrt{\left(\dfrac{R}{2L}\right)^2 - \dfrac{1}{LC}}$

Looking at the discriminant, it is obvious that there are three possibilities.

Case 1. Discriminant positive.

$$\left(\frac{R}{2L}\right)^2 > \frac{1}{LC}$$

The two roots are real and distinct. The denominator has the roots $(\alpha + \beta)$ and $(\alpha - \beta)$ and we may write

$$I(s) = \frac{K_1}{s - (\alpha + \beta)} + \frac{K_2}{s - (\alpha - \beta)}$$

K_1 and K_2 may be determined as before and i expressed as

$$i = K_1\,\varepsilon^{(\alpha + \beta)\,t} + K_2\,\varepsilon^{+(\alpha - \beta)\,t}$$

$$= \varepsilon^{\alpha t}\;[K_1\,\varepsilon^{\beta t} + K_2\,\varepsilon^{-\beta t}]$$

The current is said to be overdamped [see Fig. 12.29 (a)]

Case 2. Discriminant zero

$$\left(\frac{R}{2L}\right)^2 = \frac{1}{LC}$$

The two roots are equal. The solution is the critical damped case [Fig. 13.29 (*b*)].

$$I(s) = \frac{K_1}{(s-\alpha)^2} + \frac{K_2}{(s-\alpha)}$$

and $$i = K_1\, t \cdot \varepsilon^{\alpha t} + K_2\, \varepsilon^{\alpha t} = \varepsilon^{\alpha t}\, [K_1 t + K_2]$$

Case 3. Discriminant negative

$$\left(\frac{R}{2L}\right)^2 < \frac{1}{LC}$$

The roots then become complex conjugate and if we define

$$\beta = \sqrt{\frac{1}{LC} - \left(\frac{R}{2L}\right)^2}$$

then the roots are $(\alpha + j\beta)$ and $(\alpha - j\beta)$

$$I(s) = \frac{K_1}{s-(\alpha+j\beta)} + \frac{K_2}{s-(\alpha-j\beta)}$$

$$\therefore \quad i(t) = K_1\, \varepsilon^{(\alpha+j\beta)\,t} + K_2\, \varepsilon^{(\alpha-j\beta)\,t} = \varepsilon^{\alpha t}\, [K_1\, \varepsilon^{j\beta t} + K_2\, \varepsilon^{-j\beta t}]$$

K_1 and K_2 are complex and are also conjugate of one another.

$$K_2 = K_1^{*}$$

Hence i may be rewritten

$$i = \varepsilon^{\alpha} t\ [A \cos \beta t + B \sin \beta t]$$

This solution shows that the current is oscillatory and at the same time decays in a short time as $\alpha = -R/2L$ is always negative [Fig. 13.29 (*c*)].

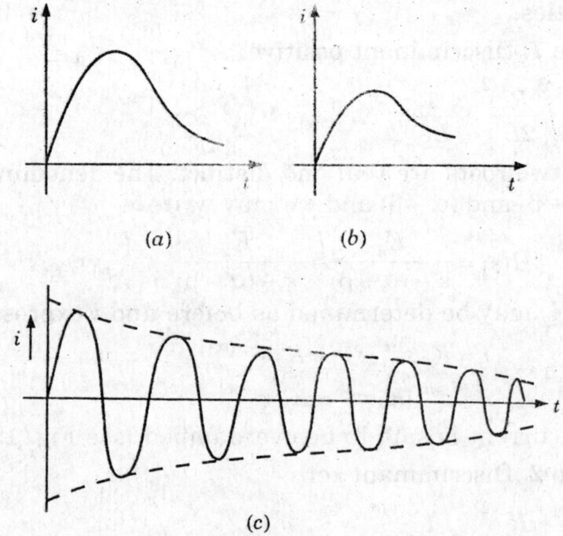

(*c*)

Fig. 13.29

Example 13.23. *A series RLC circuit with R = 1000 ohms, L = 0.1 h, and C = 100 μF has a DC voltage of 200 Volts applied to it at t = 0 through a switch. Find the expression for the transient current. Assume initially relaxed circuit conditions.*

Solution. When the switch is closed, the integro-differential equation for the circuit is

$$100i + 0.1\frac{di}{dt} + \frac{1}{100 \times 10^{-6}}\int i dt = 200$$

(all initial conditions zero)

Taking Laplace Transforms on either side, we get

$$100\, I(s) + 0.1[sI(s) - i(0)] + \frac{1}{100 \times 10^{-6}} = \frac{200}{.s}$$

$$I(s)\left[100 + 0.1\, s + \frac{10^4}{s}\right] = \frac{200}{s}$$

$$I(s) = \frac{200}{s\left(100 + 0.1\, s + \dfrac{10^4}{s}\right)} = \frac{2000}{s^2 + 1000\, s + 10^5}$$

The roots of the denominator are

$$\frac{-1000 \pm \sqrt{(1000)^2 - 4 \times 10^5}}{2} = -\,112.7 \text{ and } -\,887.3$$

$$\therefore \qquad I(s) = \frac{2000}{(s + 112.7)\,(s + 887.3)} = \frac{2.582}{(s + 112.7)} - \frac{2.582}{(s + 887.3)}$$

Hence $i(t) = 2.582\, \varepsilon^{-112.7t} - 2.582\, \varepsilon^{-887.3t}$

Example 13.24. *What value of capacitance in Example 13.23 will make the above circuit critically damped ? Find the transient current using this value of capacitor.*

Solution. The circuit is critically damped if the discriminant is zero *i.e.* when

$$\left(\frac{R}{2L}\right)^2 = \frac{1}{LC}$$

i.e.

$$\frac{R^2}{4L^2} = \frac{1}{LC}$$

$$C = \frac{4L}{R^2} = \frac{4 \times 0.1}{100^2} = 40\ \mu f$$

under this condition,

$$100i + 0.1\frac{di}{dt} + \frac{1}{40 \times 10^{-6}}\int i dt = 200$$

Taking L.T. on both sides and applying zero initial conditions,

$$I(s)\left[100 + 0.1\,s + \frac{25 \times 10^3}{s}\right] = \frac{200}{s}$$

or $$I(s) = \frac{2000}{s^2 + 1000\,s + 25 \times 10^4} = \frac{2000}{(s + 500)^2}$$

$\therefore$ $$i = 2000\,t\varepsilon^{-500\,t}$$

Example 13.25. *A series RLC circuit with R = 300 ohms L = 1 h and C = 100 μF has a constant voltage of 50 V applied to it at t = 0. Find the maximum current value. Assume zero initial conditions.*

Solution. After the switch is closed,

$$300i + 1 \times \frac{di}{dt} + \frac{1}{100 \times 10^{-6}} \int idt = 50$$

Laplace Transforming (with zero initial conditions)

$$I(s)\left[300 + s + \frac{10^4}{s}\right] = \frac{50}{s}$$

$$I(s) = \frac{50}{s^2 + 300s + 10^4}$$

The roots of the denominator are

$$\frac{-300 \pm \sqrt{(300)^2 - 4 \times 10^4}}{2} = -38.2 \text{ and } -261.8$$

$\therefore$ $$I(s) = \frac{50}{(s + 38.2)\,(s + 261.8)} = \frac{0.224}{(s + 38.2)} - \frac{0.224}{(s + 261.8)}$$

$$i = 0.224\,\varepsilon^{-38.2t} - \varepsilon^{-261.8t}$$

When the current is maximum, $\frac{di}{dt} = 0$

$\therefore$ $$\frac{di}{dt} = 0.224\left[(-38.2)\,\varepsilon^{-38.2t} + 261.8\,\varepsilon^{-261.8t}\right] = 0$$

i.e. $$261.8\,\varepsilon^{-261.8t} = 38.2\,\varepsilon^{-38.2t}$$

$$6.8534 = \varepsilon^{223.6\,t}$$

or $$t = 0.00861 \text{ sec.}$$

Substituting $t = 0.00861$ in the expression for current,

$$i_{max} = 0.224\,[\varepsilon^{-0.329} - \varepsilon^{-2.254}]$$

$$= \mathbf{0.1377\ Amp.}$$

Example 13.26. *A series RLC circuit with R = 5 Ω, L = 0.1 h and C = 500 μf has a D.C. voltage of 100 Volts applied at t = 0 through a switch. Find the resulting current transient.*

Solution. The integro-differential equation for the circuit after closing the switch is

$$5i + 0.1\frac{di}{dt} + \frac{10^6}{5000}\int idt = 100$$

Assuming zero initial conditions and taking Laplace Transforms on both sides,

$$5I(s) + 0.1\,sI(s) + 2000\frac{I(s)}{s} = \frac{100}{s}$$

$$I(s) = \frac{100}{0.1\,s^2 + 5s + 2.000} = \frac{1000}{s^2 + 50s + 20{,}000}$$

The roots of the denominator are

$$= \frac{-50 \pm \sqrt{2500 - 80{,}000}}{2} = -25 \pm j\,139.2$$

$$\text{Hence } I(s) = \frac{1000}{(s + 25 - j\,139.2)\,(s + 25 + j\,139.2)}$$

$$= \frac{K_1}{(s + 25 - j\,139.2)} + \frac{K_2}{(s + 25 + j\,139.2)}$$

$$\therefore \quad i(t) = 3.592\,\varepsilon^{-25t}\,[\varepsilon^{j\,139.2\,t} - \varepsilon^{-j\,139.2\,t}]$$

$$= \mathbf{7.184\,\varepsilon^{-25\,t}\,\sin 139.2\,t.}$$

A.C. Transients

R.L. circuit

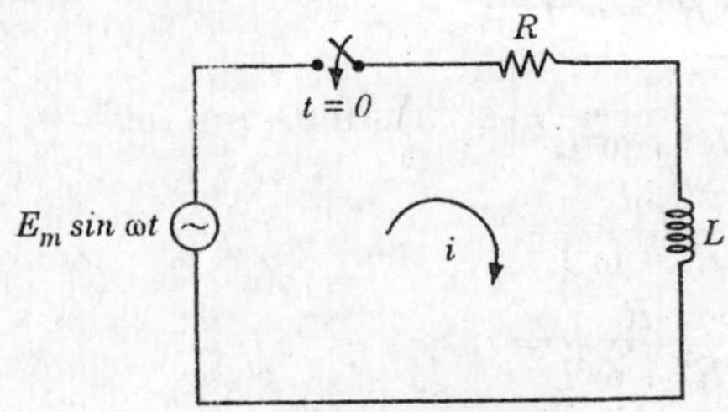

Fig. 13.30

Consider the circuit of Fig. 13.30 where a sinusoidal voltage $E_m \sin \omega t$ is applied to the series RL circuit at $t = 0$, through a switch. We shall assume that the initial current in the circuit is zero. The differential equation of the circuit is

$$iR + L\frac{di}{dt} = E_m \sin \omega t$$

Taking Laplace Transform on both sides

$$RI(s) + sLI(s) = \frac{E_m\,\omega}{s^2 + \omega^2}$$

$$I(s) = \frac{E_m\,\omega}{L\left(s + \frac{R}{L}\right)\left(s^2 + \omega^2\right)}$$

$$= \frac{K_1}{\left(s + \frac{R}{L}\right)} + \frac{K_2}{(s + j\omega)} + \frac{K_3}{(s - j\omega)}$$

$$K_1 = \frac{E_m\,\omega}{L\left(\frac{R^2}{L^2} + \omega^2\right)} = \frac{E_m\,\omega L}{R + \omega^2 L^2}$$

$$K_2 = \frac{\omega\,E_m}{L\,(R - j\omega)\,(-\,2\,j\omega)} = -\,\frac{E_m\,(\omega L - jR)}{2\,(R^2 + \omega^2\,L^2)}$$

$$K_3 = K_2^{\,*} = \frac{E_m\,(\omega L + jR)}{2\,(R^2 + \omega^2 L^2)}$$

$$\therefore \quad i = E_m \frac{\omega L}{R^2 + \omega^2 L^2}\,\varepsilon^{-\frac{R}{L}t} - \frac{E_m}{2\,(R^2 + \omega^2 L^2)}\left[(\omega L - jR)\,\varepsilon^{-j\omega t} + (\omega L + jR)\,\varepsilon^{+j\omega t}\right]$$

$$= \frac{\omega_L \cdot E_m}{R^2 + \omega^2 L^2}\left[\varepsilon^{-\frac{R}{L}t} - \omega L \cos \omega t + \frac{R}{\omega L} \sin \omega t\right]$$

$$= E_m \cdot \frac{1}{\sqrt{R^2 + \omega^2 L^2}}\left[\varepsilon^{-\frac{R}{L}t} \sin\theta - \sin\theta \cos \omega t + \cos\theta \sin \omega t\right]$$

$$= E_m \frac{i}{\sqrt{R^2 + \omega^2 L^2}}\left[\varepsilon^{-\frac{R}{L}t} \sin\theta + \sin(\omega t - \theta)\right]$$

where $\sin\theta = \dfrac{\omega L}{\sqrt{R^2 + \omega^2 L^2}}$

$$\cos\theta = \frac{R}{\sqrt{R^2 + \omega^2 L^2}}$$

or $\quad \theta = \tan^{-1}\left(\dfrac{\omega L}{R}\right)$

If the applied voltage is of the form $E_m \sin(\omega t + \phi)$, then in the solution, we substitute for ωt the value $(\omega t + \phi)$. The current is given by

$$i = \frac{E_m}{\sqrt{R^2 + \omega^2 L^2}} \cdot \left[\varepsilon^{-\frac{R}{L}t} \sin(\phi - \theta) + \sin(\omega t + \phi - \theta)\right]$$

where θ is defined as before.

RC Circuit

In Fig. 13.31, assuming initially relaxed conditions, we may write for $t > 0$

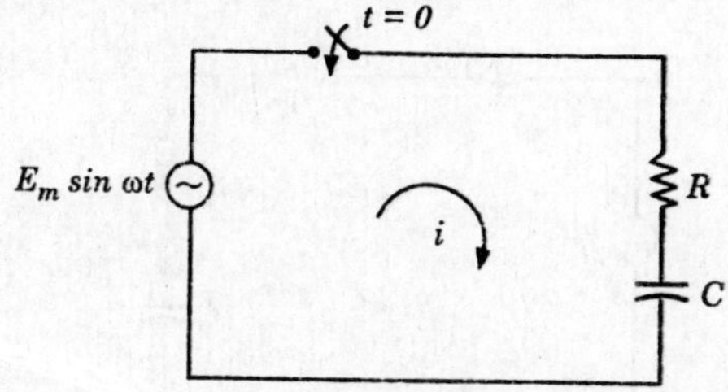

Fig. 13.31

$$iR + \frac{1}{C}\int i dt = E_m \sin \omega t$$

On taking Laplace Transforms on both sides,

$$R\,I(s) + \frac{I(s)}{s} = \frac{\omega E_m}{s^2 + \omega^2}$$

$$I(s)\left(R + \frac{1}{sC}\right) = \frac{\omega E_m}{s^2 + \omega^2}$$

$$I(s) = \frac{\omega E_m \cdot s}{R\left(s + \frac{1}{RC}\right)(s^2 + \omega^2)}$$

$$= \frac{K_1}{s + \frac{1}{RC}} + \frac{K_2}{(s + j\omega)} + \frac{K_3}{s - j\omega}$$

$$K_1 = \frac{-E_m \cdot \frac{\omega}{RC}}{R\left(\omega^2 + \frac{1}{R^2C^2}\right)} = -\frac{\omega C E_m}{1 + \omega^2 C^2 R^2}$$

$$K_2 = \frac{\omega C\, E_m\,(1 + j\omega CR)}{2\,(1 + \omega^2 C^2 R^2)}$$

$$K_3 = K_2^*$$

$$\therefore \quad i(t) = -\frac{\omega C\, E_m}{1 + \omega^2 C^2 R^2} \cdot \varepsilon^{-\frac{t}{CR}} + \frac{E_m}{\sqrt{R^2 + 1/(\omega^2 C^2)}} \sin(\omega t + \theta)$$

where $\theta = \tan^{-1}\left(\frac{1}{\omega CR}\right)$

RLC Circuit

The switch in the series *RLC* series circuit of Fig. 13.32 is closed at $t = 0$. We are interested in an expression for the current from then on (we shall assume all initial conditions to be zero).

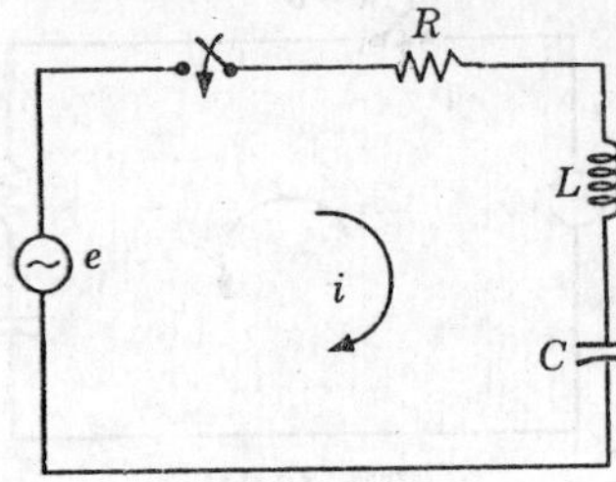

Fig. 13.32

After the switch is closed, we get the following equation by applying Kirchhoff's voltage law.

$$iR + L\frac{di}{dt} + \frac{1}{C}\int i\,dt = E_m \sin \omega t$$

on Laplace Transforming,

$$RI(s) + LsI(s) + \frac{I(s)}{Cs} = E_m\left(\frac{\omega}{s^2+\omega^2}\right)$$

$$I(s) = \frac{E_m\,\omega}{\left(R + sL + \frac{1}{sC}\right)(s^2+\omega^2)}$$

$$I(s) = \frac{E_m\,\omega\, s/L}{\left(s^2 + \frac{R}{L}s + \frac{1}{LC}\right)(s^2+\omega^2)}$$

The 4 roots of the denominator are

$$\pm j\omega \text{ and } -\frac{R}{2L} \pm \sqrt{\left(\frac{R}{2L}\right)^2 - \frac{1}{LC}}$$

i.e.

$$\pm j\omega \text{ and } \alpha \pm j\beta$$

where

$$\alpha = -\frac{R}{2L}$$

$$\beta = \sqrt{\frac{1}{LC} - \left(\frac{R}{2L}\right)^2}$$

The type of solution will depend on the value $\left[\left(\frac{R}{2L}\right)^2 - \frac{1}{LC}\right]$.

There are as before 3 possible cases.

Case 1. $\left(\frac{R}{2L}\right)^2 > \frac{1}{LC}$:

In this case, the roots are real and distinct and we may proceed as before to obtain the partial fraction expansion and the inverse Laplace Transform.

Case 2. $\left(\frac{R}{2L}\right)^2 = \frac{1}{LC}$

Here, the 2 roots ($\alpha \pm \beta$) become identical and equal to α only. This is a case of 2 repeated roots and the procedure for solution has already been indicated.

Case 3. $\left(\frac{R}{2L}\right)^2 < \frac{1}{LC}$

The roots are complex conjugates as already indicated in the case of D.C. R.L.C. transient.

The expression for the steady state current will be of the form

$$i_{ss} = \frac{E_m}{\sqrt{R^2 + (\omega L - 1/\omega C)^2}} \sin(\omega t \pm \theta)$$

where $\theta = \tan^{-1}\left[\frac{\omega L - 1/\omega L}{R}\right]$

This may be written in the familiar form

$$i_{ss} = \frac{E_m}{\sqrt{R^2 + (X_L - X_C)^2}} \sin(\omega t \pm \theta)$$

The expression for total current will then be the sum of i_{ss} and one of the expressions in the *DC–RLC* transient case. The three cases result as before in overdamped, critically damped and under damped (oscillatory) solutions.

Example 13.27. *A series RL circuit with R = 100 ohm L = 1h has a sinusoidal voltage source 200 sin (500 t + ϕ) applied at a time when ϕ = 0.*

(*a*) *Find the expression for the current.*

(*b*) *At what value of angle ϕ must the switch be closed so that the current directly enters the steady state.*

Solution. When the switch is closed, the differential equation for the circuit is

$$100i + 1\frac{di}{dt} = 200 \sin 500\, t$$

Taking Laplace Transforms on both sides under zero initial conditions,

$$100I(s) + sI(s) = \frac{200 \times 500}{s^2 + (500)^2}$$

$$I(s) = \frac{100000}{(s + 100)(s^2 + 250000)}$$

$$= \frac{K_1}{s + 100} + \frac{K_2}{s + j500} + \frac{K_3}{s - j500}$$

$$K_1 = 0.385$$

$$K_2 = -\frac{(5 - j1)}{26}$$

$$K_3 = -\frac{(5 + j1)}{26}$$

$\therefore$
$$i = 0.385\,\varepsilon^{-100t} - \frac{1}{26}\left[(5 - j1)\,\varepsilon^{-j500t} + (5 + j1)\,\varepsilon^{+j500t}\right]$$

$$= 0.385\,\varepsilon^{-100t} - \frac{\sqrt{26}}{13}\left[\frac{5}{\sqrt{26}}\cos 500t - \frac{1}{\sqrt{26}}\sin 500t\right]$$

$$= 0.385\,\varepsilon^{-100t} - 0.3922 \sin(500\,t - \theta)$$

where $\theta = \tan^{-1}(5) = 78.69°$

$\therefore$ $i(t) = 0.385\,\varepsilon^{-100t} - 0.3922 \sin(500t - 78.69°)$

(*b*) If $\phi \neq 0$, the solution for current would have been

$$i = 0.385 \sin(\phi - 78.69)\, e^{-100t} - 0.3922 \sin(500t + \phi - 78.69°)$$

If $(\phi - 78.69°)$ is a multiple of 180°, then the transient will be zero *i.e.*

$$\phi = 78.69 + n(180°),$$
$$n = 0, 1, 2, \ldots$$

Example 13.28. *In the circuit of Fig. 13.33 find the current. Assume initial charge on the capacitor is zero.*

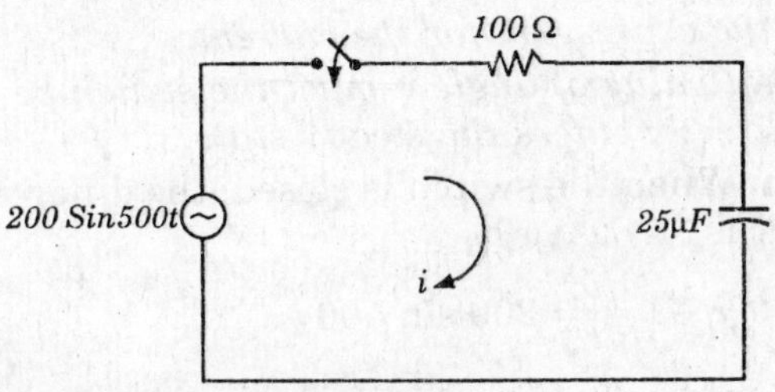

Fig. 13.33

Solution.

$$100\, i + \frac{1}{25 \times 10^{-6}} \int i dt = 200 \sin 500t$$

Taking Laplace Transforms on both sides,

$$100I(s) + \frac{40000\, I(s)}{s} = 200 \frac{500}{s^2 + 500^2}$$

$$I(s)\left[100 + \frac{40000}{s}\right] = \frac{100000}{s^2 + 500^2}$$

$$I(s) = \frac{100000}{\left(100 + \frac{40000}{s}\right)(s^2 + 500^2)}$$

$$= \frac{1000\, s}{(s + 400)\,(s^2 + 500^2)}$$

$$= \frac{K_1}{(s + 400)} + \frac{K_2}{(s + j500)} + \frac{K_3}{(s - j500)}$$

$$K_1 = \frac{-400}{41} = -0.976$$

$$K_2 = \frac{1000\,(-j500)}{(400 - j500)\,(-j1000)}$$

$$= \frac{5}{4 - j5} = \frac{5\,(4 + j5)}{41}$$

$$K_3 = \frac{5\,(4 - j5)}{41}$$

$$\therefore \quad i(t) = -0.976\, \varepsilon^{-400t} + \frac{5}{41}\left[(4 + j5)\, \varepsilon^{-j500t} + (4 - j5)\, \varepsilon^{-j500t}\right]$$

$$= -0.976\, \varepsilon^{-400t} + \frac{10}{\sqrt{41}}\left[\frac{4}{\sqrt{41}} \cos 500t - \frac{3}{\sqrt{41}} \sin 500t\right]$$

$$= -0.976\, \varepsilon^{-400t} + 1.564 \sin(500t + 38.7°)$$

Natural frequency and damping ratio. Consider the series *RLC* circuit excited by a source. We have seen that the response (current) depends on the relative values of R, L and C. We have also seen that there are three cases *viz.*, over-damped, critically damped and under damped. The frequency of the current is found to be β. given by

$$\beta = \sqrt{\frac{1}{LC} - \left(\frac{R}{2L}\right)^2}$$

The natural frequency of oscillation of the circuit is given by,

$$\omega_n = \frac{1}{\sqrt{LC}}$$

For critical damping

$$\left(\frac{R}{2L}\right)^2 = \frac{1}{LC}$$

or the value of resistance required for critical damping is

$$R_c = 2\sqrt{L/C}$$

The ratio $\sigma = \dfrac{\text{Value of resistance in the circuit}}{\text{Resistance for critical damping}}$

$$= \frac{R}{R_c} = \frac{R}{2\sqrt{L/C}}$$

is called the damping ratio.

Hence, $\beta = \sqrt{\omega_n^2 - \omega_n^2\sigma^2} = \omega_n\sqrt{1-\sigma^2}$

While ω_n is called the natural frequency, β is called the damped frequency of oscillation. When $\sigma = 1$, it corresponds to critical damping. When the value of $\sigma > 1$, we have over-damping and when $\sigma < 1$, under-damping.

Decrement or logarithmic decrement. It has been already shown that *RLC* circuit gives a response of the form,

$$i(t) = Ae^{\alpha t}\sin(\beta t + \phi)$$

where β is the damped frequency of oscillations. The period of such a wave is given by

$$T = \frac{2\pi}{\beta}\text{ seconds}$$

As the current decays, it is interesting to note the amount of decay in amplitude per cycle. The ratio of the amplitudes of the wave (see Fig. 13.34) during two successive cycles is given by the factor,

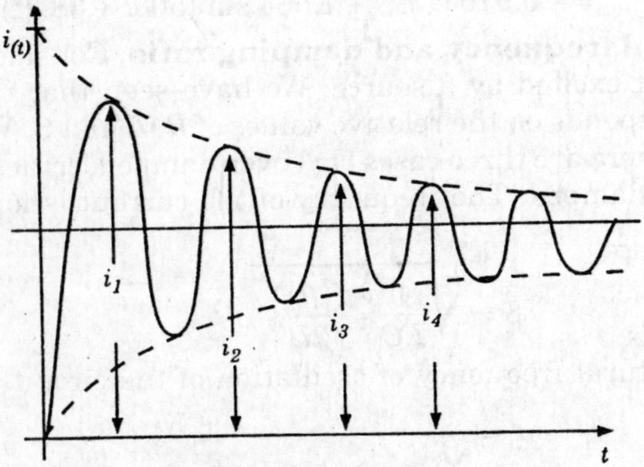

Fig. 13.34

$$\nu = \frac{i_1}{i_2} = \frac{i_2}{i_3} = \frac{i_3}{i_4} = \dots e^{xT} = e^{2\pi\alpha/\beta}$$

On taking natural logarithm of this factor, we have

$$\Delta = \log_e \nu = \frac{2\pi\alpha}{\beta} = \frac{2\pi\alpha}{\omega_n \sqrt{1-\sigma^2}}$$

The factor Δ is called "logarithmic decrement" or very often the "decrement" of the circuit. The reciprocal of Δ, equals the number of the cycles (or periods) for the amplitude to decay by the factor $\frac{1}{e} = 0.368$.

For highly oscillatory circuits (low damping), σ is small and σ^2 can be neglected and the decrement becomes

$$\Delta = \frac{2\pi\alpha}{\omega_n} = \frac{2\pi\ R/2L}{1/\sqrt{LC}} = \pi R\sqrt{\frac{C}{L}}$$

The quality factor of a circuit is given as

$$Q = \frac{\omega_n L}{R} = \frac{1}{R}\sqrt{\frac{L}{C}}$$

But $\quad \Delta = \pi R\ \sqrt{C/L}$.

Hence the logarithmic decrement and quality factor of a circuit can be related as $\Delta = \pi/Q$.

EXERCISES

13.1. Find the Laplace Transform of the following function :

(a) $e^{-at} \cosh \omega t$ (b) $e^{-2t} \cos 3t$ (c) te^{-at} (d) $\cos 100t$ (e) $\sinh t$

[**Ans.** (a) $\frac{s+a}{(s+a)^2+\omega^2}$ (b) $\frac{s+2}{(s+2)^2+9}$

(c) $\frac{1}{(s+a)^2}$ (d) $\frac{s}{s^2+100^2}$ (e) $\frac{1}{s^2-1}$]

13.2. Find the inverse Laplace Transform of the following functions :

(a) $\frac{s}{(s+2)(s+1)}$ (b) $\frac{3}{s(s^2+6s+9)}$

(c) $\frac{s}{(s^2+4)(s+5)}$ (d) $\frac{s+5}{s^2+2s+5}$ (e) $\frac{2s+4}{s^2+4s+13}$

[**Ans.** (a) $2e^{-2t} - e^{-t}$ (b) $1/3 - 1/3\ e^{-3t} - te^{-3t}$

(c) $\frac{5}{29} \cos 2t + \frac{2}{29} \sin 2t - \frac{5}{29} e^{-5t}$

(d) $\varepsilon^{-t} (\cos 2t + 2 \sin 2t)$ (e) $2e^{-2t} \cos 3t$]

13.3. A $2F$ capacitor initially charged to 100 V is suddenly connected to a circuit consisting of a 0.4 ohm resistance in series with a 4 H inductance at $t = 0$. Find the maximum value of the current and the instant at which it occurs.

13.4. Find the initial value of the current whose Laplace Transform is

$$I(s) = \frac{3s^2 + 1}{(s^2 + 4)(2s + 3)}$$

[Ans. 1.5 amp.]

13.5. Find the Laplace Transform of the current supplied by the source when the switch is closed at $t = 0$ for the initially relaxed circuit shown in Fig. 13.35. Hence find the initial and final values of this current.

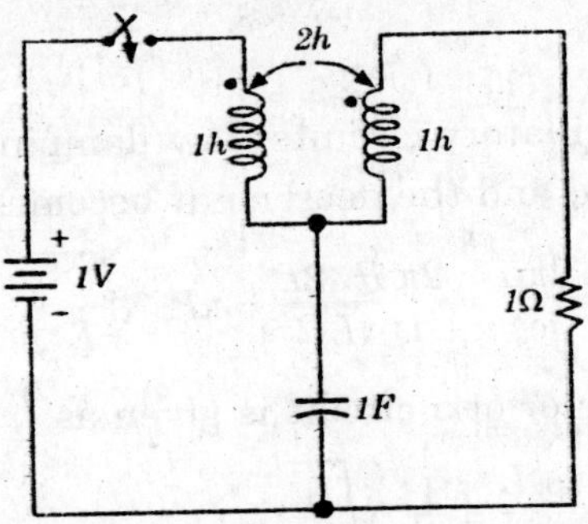

Fig. 13.35

$$\left[\textbf{Ans. } I(s) = \frac{1 + s + s^2}{s\,(1 - 2s + s^2 - 3s^3)}\ ;\ i(0) = 0,\ i(\infty) = 1 \text{ Amp.}\right]$$

13.6. Find the Laplace Transform of the current supplied by the source shown in Fig. 13.36. The network has no stored energy in it prior to closing the switch.

[Ans. $10\,(1 + 1.5s)/(s + 2)\,(1.5 + s + 1.5\,s^2)$]

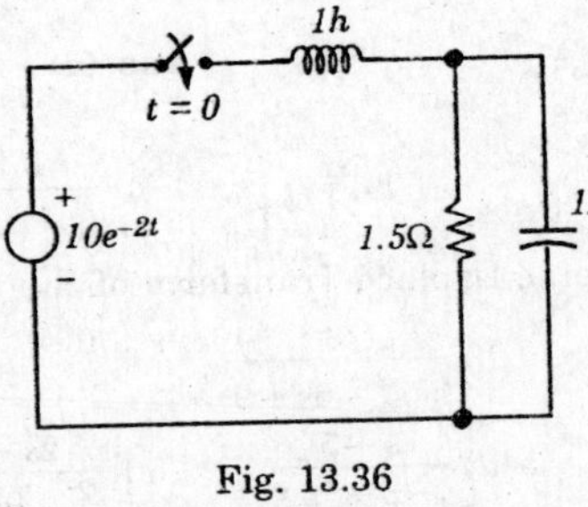

Fig. 13.36

13.7. The two throw switch in the network shown in Fig. 13.37 is kept in position 1 for a long time and then thrown into position 2 at $t = 0$. Find the current through the inductor from $t = 0+$ and onwards.

[Ans. $i(t) = 4\varepsilon^{-t/2} + 18\,t\varepsilon^{-t/2}$]

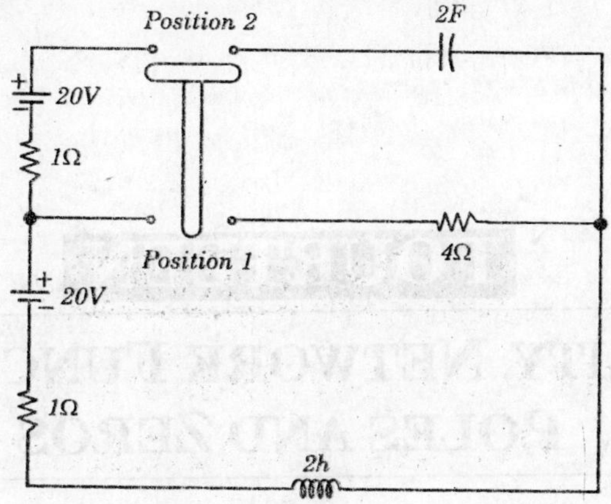

Fig. 13.37

13.8. Find the time varying voltage v(t) whose Laplace Transform is given by

$V(s) = \frac{1}{(s^2+1)^2}$. Find also $\int_0^{\infty} v(t)\, e^{-3t}\, dt$

$\left[\textbf{Ans.}\ \frac{1}{2}(\sin t - t\cos t),\ \frac{1}{25}\right]$

13.9. A step D.C. voltage is applied to an *RLC* series circuit. Obtain the conditions under which the transient current will be unidirectional or oscillatory. What would be the final value of the current ?

$\left[\textbf{Ans.}\ \text{Unidirectional}: \left(\frac{R}{2L}\right)^2 \geq \frac{1}{LC},\ \text{Oscillatory}: \left(\frac{R}{2L}\right)^2 < \frac{1}{LC},\ 0\right]$

13.10. If $R = 40$ ohms, $L = 0.2$ h and $C = 100\ \mu$F are connected in series and a step voltage is applied to the circuit, find the damping ratio and frequency of damped oscillations. **[Ans.** 0.447, 200 Hz**]**

13.11. An *R-L-C* series circuit has inductance of 20 mh and a capacitance of 0.5 μF. Find the values of *R* for the transient current in the circuit to have a damping ratio of 0, 0.5, 1.0 and 2.0. **[Ans.** 0, 100, 400, 800 Ω**]**

FOURTEEN

DUALITY, NETWORK FUNCTIONS, POLES AND ZEROS

Duality. Two electrical networks which are governed by the same types of equations are called dual networks or duality is said to exist between them. Consider the current voltage relations for the *RLC* series and parallel networks shown in Fig. 14.1.

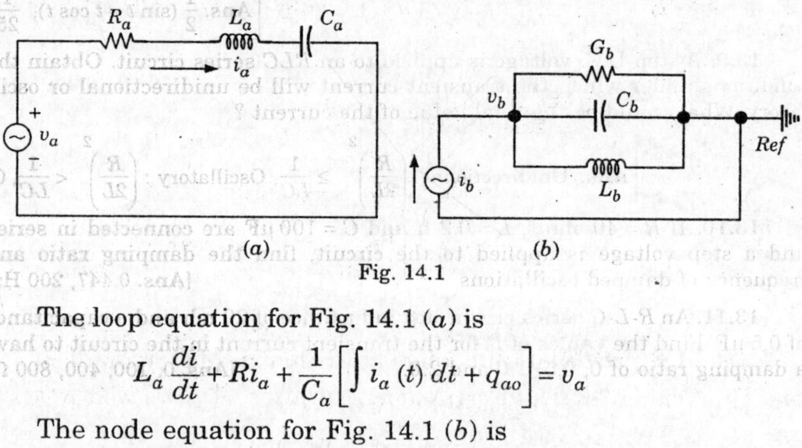

(*a*) (*b*)

Fig. 14.1

The loop equation for Fig. 14.1 (*a*) is

$$L_a \frac{di}{dt} + Ri_a + \frac{1}{C_a}\left[\int i_a(t)\,dt + q_{ao}\right] = v_a$$

The node equation for Fig. 14.1 (*b*) is

$$C_b \frac{dv_b}{dt} + G_b v_b + \frac{1}{L_a}\left[\int v_b(t)\,dt + \phi_{bo}\right] = i_b$$

Similarity is at once noticed, by comparing the above equations. In fact, the solution of the first equation will be identical to that of the second when the following changes are made :

$$L_a \longrightarrow C_b \qquad R_a \longrightarrow G_b \qquad C_a \longrightarrow L_b$$

$$v_a \longrightarrow i_b \qquad i_a \longrightarrow v_b \qquad q_{ao} \longrightarrow \phi_{bo}$$

Therefore, the series and parallel circuits shown are duals. Only planar networks have duals. A network is said to be planar if it can be laid on a plane without any branch crossing each other.

Table of Conversion of Dual Networks

Original Network	*Dual Network*
Loop current	Node voltage
Voltage source	Current source
Inductance	Capacitance
Capacitance	Inductance
Resistance	Conductance
Loop method	Node method
Closed switch	Open switch

Dot Method. The dual network is obtained by the dot method described below.

1. A dot is placed in each independent loop of the original network. These dots placed inside the loops correspond to independent nodes in the dual network.

2. A dot is placed outside the given network which will correspond to the reference node of the dual network.

3. All the dots are connected by dotted lines crossing all the branches. The dotted lines should cross only one branch at a time. The dual elements will form the branches connecting the corresponding nodes in the dual network.

4. The voltage rise in the direction of a clockwise loop current corresponds to a current flowing towards the independent node in the dual network and a clockwise current in a loop corresponds to a positive polarity at the dual independent node.

The dot method of obtaining the dual network is illustrated in the example below.

Example 14.1. *Construct the dual network for the network shown in Fig. 14.2.*

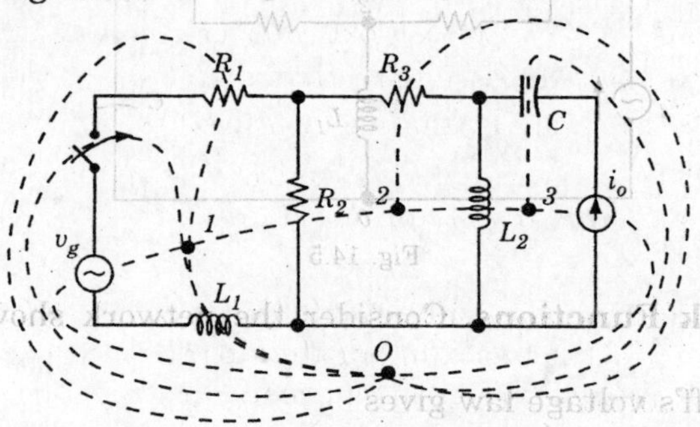

Fig. 14.2

Solution. In Fig. 14.2 are shown, three independent dots and the 0 dot outside the network. Dotted lines connecting the dots crossing each element are also shown. The dual network is then drawn in Fig. 14.3 with three independent nodes 1, 2 and 3 with 0 as the reference node.

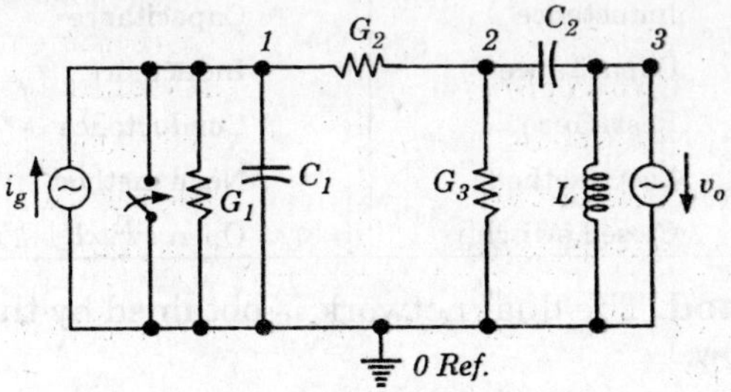

Fig. 14.3

Example 14.2. *Draw the dual of network shown in Fig. 14.4.*

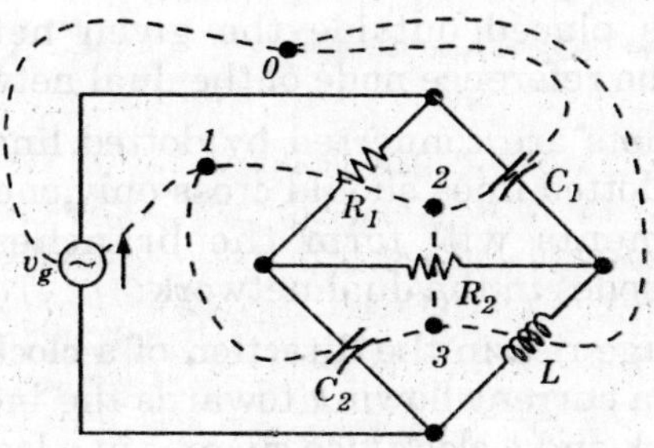

Fig. 14.4

Solution. The dual is shown in Fig. 14.5.

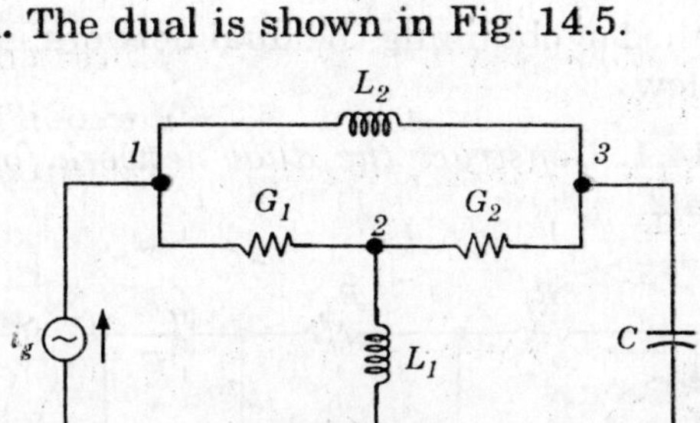

Fig. 14.5

Network Functions. Consider the network shown in Fig. 14.6.

Kirchhoff's voltage law gives

$$V = I\left(j\omega L + R + \frac{1}{j\omega C}\right) = I \cdot Z(j\omega)$$

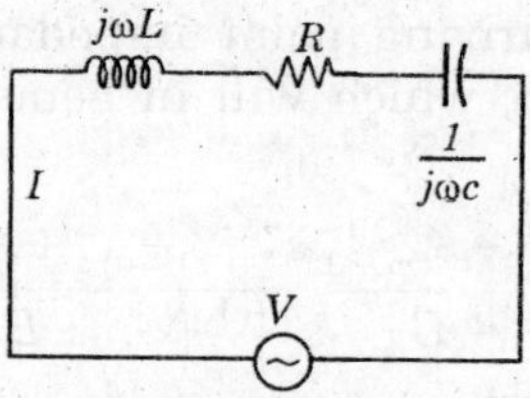

Fig. 14.6

where $Z(j\omega) = j\omega L + R + \dfrac{1}{j\omega L}$ is the impedance,

which is a function of the real frequency ω. Then time function of current is given by

$$i(t) = R_o\left[\frac{V \cdot e^{j\omega t}}{\left(j\omega L + R + \dfrac{1}{j\omega C}\right)}\right]$$

Complex Frequency. In the last chapter, network transients are discussed using Laplace Transform technique, where the Laplace variable $s = \sigma + j\omega$, is called the complex frequency. $\sigma = 0$ describes the steady state behaviour and $s = \sigma + j\omega$ describes the transient behaviour.

Impedance Function. It is the ratio of Laplace Transform of voltage to current. It is also called the operational impedance. For Fig. 14.6, the impedance function is obtained when s is substituted for $j\omega$ in Z.

$$Z(s) = sL + R + \frac{1}{sC}$$

It is a network function which may be considered as a generalised form of impedance in the following sense. It is a function of $s = \sigma + j\omega$.

The network function has no physical meaning in itself but it is instrumental in the study of network analysis and synthesis (Realization).

For a real frequency $s = j\omega$, $Z(j\omega)$ is an impedance in the true sense. $Z(s)$ is simply called an impedance function. In the same way, $Y(s)$ is called an impedance function. In the same way, $Y(s)$ is called an admittance function. Network functions can in general be ratios of Laplace Transforms of currents, voltages, voltage and current or current and voltage.

To obtain the impedance function, R, L and C in a network are replaced by R, sL and $1/sC$ respectively.

The transfer and driving point impedance functions of any network can be derived, which will in general be a ratio of two polynominals, say

$$W(s) = \frac{A_m s^m + A_{m-1} s^{m-1} + \ldots + A_1 s + A_0}{B_n s^n + B_{n-1} s^{n-1} + \ldots + B_1 s + B_0}$$

Poles and Zeros. The poles and zeros of a network function are defined as the values of s for which the function approaches infinity and zero respectively. The network function $W(s)$ can be factored into

$$W(s) = \frac{A_m (s - z_1)(s - z_2) \ldots (s - z_m)}{B_n (s - p_1)(s - p_2) \ldots (s - p_n)}$$

For $s \longrightarrow p_1$ (*i.e.* s approaches p_1), $W(s) \longrightarrow \infty$ p_1 is, therefore, a pole of $W(s)$. Similarly $p_2, \ldots p_3, \ldots$ are poles of $W(s)$. As $s \longrightarrow z_1$, $W(s) \longrightarrow 0$. Hence z_1 is a zero of $W(s)$. If $p_1 = p_2$, then $W(s)$ is said to have a pole of order 2 at $s = p_1$ and if $z_1 = z_2$, then $W(s)$ has a zero of order 2 at $s = z_1$.

Poles and zeros at infinity. The network function $W(s)$ can also be written in the form,

$$W(s) = \frac{s^m}{s_n}\left[\frac{A_m + A_{m-1}\frac{1}{s} + A_{m-2}\frac{1}{s^2} + \ldots + \frac{A_0}{s^m}}{B_n + B_{n-1}\cdot\frac{1}{s} + B_{n-2}\cdot\frac{1}{s^2} + \ldots + \frac{B_0}{s^n}}\right]$$

As $s \longrightarrow \infty$, the terms inside the brackets approach a constant value, say K

$$K = \frac{A_m}{B_n}$$

$$\text{Therefore, limit of } W(s) = \lim_{s \to \infty} \frac{s^m}{s_n} \cdot K = K \lim_{s \to \infty} \frac{s^m}{s^n}$$

The following observations can now be made.

1. For $m > n$, $W(s)$ has a pole of order $(m - n)$ at infinity in the s-plane. For $m > n$, and as $s \to \infty$, $W(s) \to \infty$.

2. For $m < n$, $W(s)$ has a zero of order $(n - m)$ at infinity. For $m < n$ and as $s \to \infty$, $W(s) \to 0$.

3 For $m = n$, $W(s)$ has neither poles nor zeros at ∞. Given the poles and zeros of a network function in the finite region of s-plane, the poles and zeros at infinity are always implied.

Pole-Zero Configuration. The pole-zero configuration of a network function is a graphical representation of the locations of its poles and zeros in the *s*-plane. Any network may be described by its behaviour say, transient or steady state response or by its network function. The network characteristics and behaviour are characterised by the pole-zero configuration.

The nature of response etc. are determined by the pole-zero plots. For synthesis of electrical networks, the pole-zero plot is instrumental in the solution of the problem.

Example 14.3. *Determine the driving point impedance function for the network shown in Fig. 14.7.*

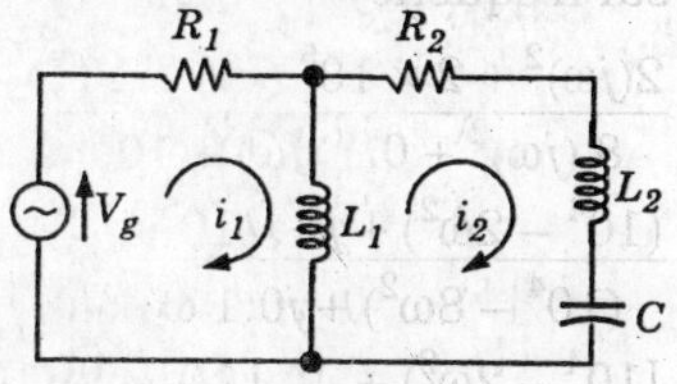

Fig. 14.7

Solution. The driving point impedance function is the ratio of Laplace transform of $v_g(t)$ to the Laplace Transform of $i(t)$.

The loop equation for the network are (after transforming)

$$V_g(s) = I_1(s)\, R_1 + sL_1\, [I_1(s) - I_2(s)]$$

$$0 = I_2(s)\left(R_2 + sL_2 + \frac{1}{Cs}\right) + sL_1\, [I_2(s) - I_1(s)]$$

Solving for $I_1(s)$

$$= \frac{\left[(L_1 + L_2)s + R_2 + \frac{1}{Cs}\right] V_s(s)}{(L_1 s + R_1)\left[(L_1 + L_2)s + R_2 + \frac{1}{Cs}\right] - {L_1}^2 s^2}$$

$$\therefore \quad \frac{V_g(s)}{I_1(s)} = Z(s) = \frac{(L_1 s + R_1)\left[(L_1 + L_2)\, s + R_2 + \frac{1}{Cs}\right] {L_1}^2 s^2}{(L_1 + L_2)s + R_2 + \frac{1}{Cs}}$$

Example 14.4. *Determine the number of poles and zeros of*

$$W(s) = \frac{20(s^3 + 6s^2 + 13s + 20)}{s^2 + 4s + 5}$$

Solution. Factorising,

$$W(s) = \frac{20\,(s + 4)\,(s + 1 - j2)\,(s + 1 + j2)}{(s + 2 - j)\,(s + 2 + j)}$$

Hence the zeros of $W(s)$ are

$$z_1 = -4, Z_2 = -1 + j2 \text{ and } z_3 = -1 - j2$$

and poles are $p_1 = -2 + j$ and $p_2 = -2 - j$

For this function, there is a pole of order 1 at ∞.

Example 14.5. *The operational impedance of a network is given by*

$$Z(s) = \frac{2s^2 + 2 \times 10^5 s + 10^4}{8s^2 + 0.1s + 10^4}$$

Find the frequency at which this network behaves as a pure reactance and find the value of the reactance.

Solution. For real frequency $s = (j\omega)$.

$$\therefore \quad Z(j\omega) = \frac{2(j\omega)^2 + 2 \times 10^5 (j\omega) + 10^4}{8(j\omega)^2 + 0.1(j\omega) + 10^4}$$

$$= \frac{(10^4 - 2\omega^2) + j2 \times 10^5 \omega}{(10^4 - 8\omega^2) + j0.1\omega}$$

$$= \frac{[10^4 - 2\omega^2) + j2 \times 10^5 \omega] [(10^4 - 8\omega^2) - j0.1\omega]}{(10^4 - 8\omega^2)^2 + (0.1\omega)^2}$$

For the network, to behave as a pure reactance, the real part of $Z(j\omega)$ must be zero.

i.e. $\quad (10^4 - 2\omega^2)(10^4 - 8\omega^2) + 2 \times 10^4 \omega^2 = 0$

or $\quad 16\omega^4 - 8 \times 10^4 \omega^2 + 10^8 = 0$

Solving, $\quad \omega = 50$ rad/sec.

The imaginary part of $Z(j\omega)$ gives the reactance value

$$\therefore \quad X = \frac{(10^4 - 8\omega^2)\, 2 \times 10^5 \omega - (10^4 - 2\omega)\, 0.1\omega}{(10^4 - 8\omega^2)^2 + 0.01\,\omega^2}$$

$= -$ **1000 Ω.**

Example 14.6. *Find the driving point impedance function for the network shown in Fig. 14.8.*

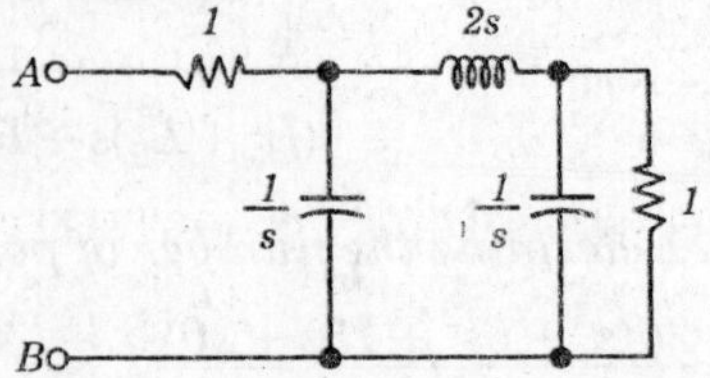

Fig. 14.8

Solution. The driving point impedance is determined as the impedance looking between points A and B. In the above figure, the impedance function is obtained by application of series parallel combination of impedances.

$$\therefore \quad Z(s) = 1 + \cfrac{\left(\cfrac{1}{s}\;\cfrac{2s + \cfrac{1}{s}\cdot 1}{1+\cfrac{1}{s}}\right)}{\left(\cfrac{1}{s} + 2s + \cfrac{\cfrac{1}{s}}{1+\cfrac{1}{s}}\right)}$$

$$= 1 + \frac{2s\,(1+s) + 1}{2s^2\,(1+s) + s + (1+s)}$$

$$Z(s) = \frac{2s^3 + 4s^2 + 4s + 2}{2s^3 + 2s^2 + 2s + 1}.$$

EXERCISES

14.1. Obtain the dual of the network shown in Fig. 14.9.

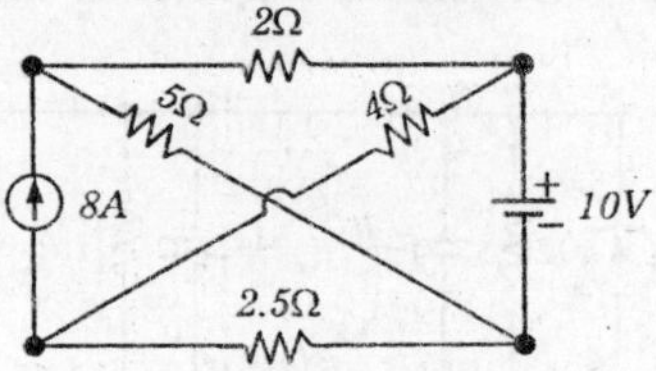

Fig. 14.9

14.2. Obtain the dual network of Fig. 14.10.

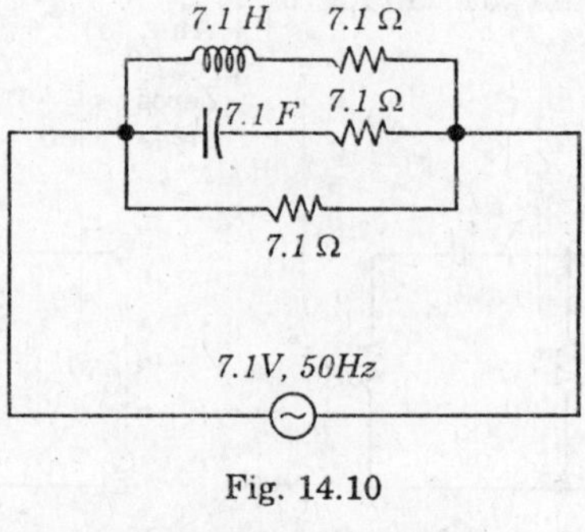

Fig. 14.10

14.3. Find the operational impedance for the networks shown in Fig. 14.11, between terminals *A* and *B*.

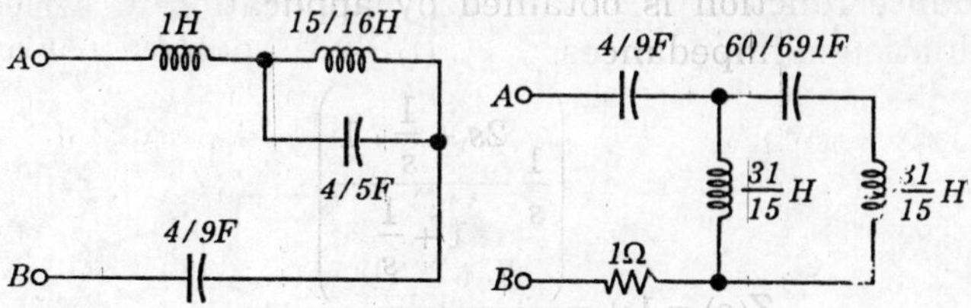

Fig. 14.11

$$\left[\textbf{Ans. } (a)\ \frac{(s^2+1)(s^2+2)}{s(s^2+4)} \quad (b)\ \frac{(s^2+1)(s^2+2)+s(s^2+4)}{s(s^2+4)}\right]$$

14.4. Determine the poles and zeros of the functions given below :

(*i*) $$W(s) = \frac{(s^2+1)(s^2+2)}{s(s^2+4)}$$

(*ii*) $$W(s) = \frac{(s^2+s+1)}{2s^3+2s^2+s+1}$$

(*iii*) $$W(s) = \frac{2s^2+s+1}{s(s^2+s+3)}$$

14.5. Obtain the network function $E(s)/I(s)$ for the network shown in Fig 14.12.

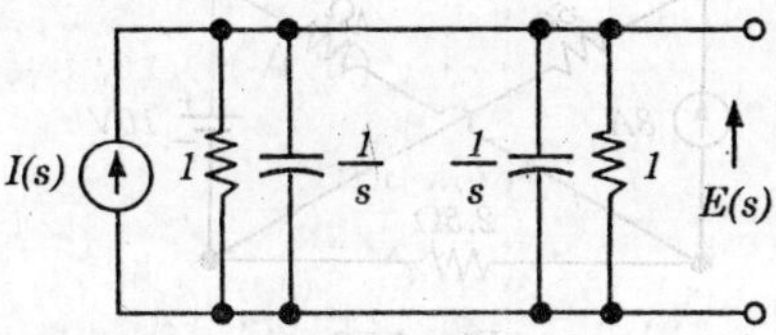

Fig. 14.12

14.6. Obtain the driving point impedance function for the networks shown in Fig. 14.13 and find the poles and zeros.

$$\left[\textbf{Ans. } (a)\ \frac{s^2+3s+1}{2s^2+s} \quad (b)\ \frac{s+1}{s^2+2s+2}\right]$$

Zeros : $s = -2.62, -0.38$ Zero : -1
Poles : $s = 0, -0.5$ Poles : $-1 \pm j1$

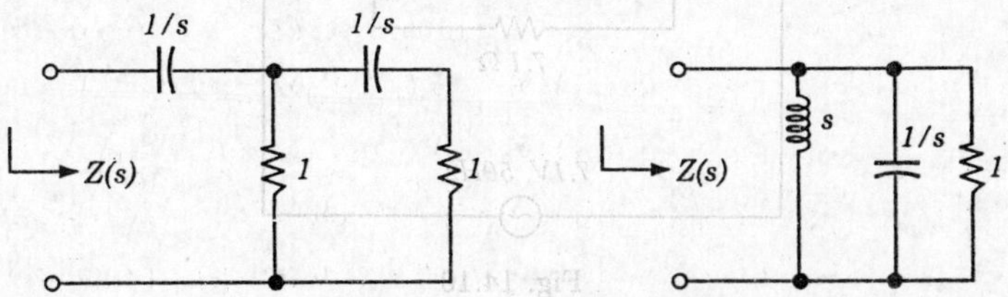

(a) (b)

Fig. 14.13

14.7. Determine the input impedance for the network shown in Fig. 14.14.

$$\left[\textbf{Ans. } \frac{(s^2+2s+s+1)}{s\,(s^2+s+1)}\right]$$

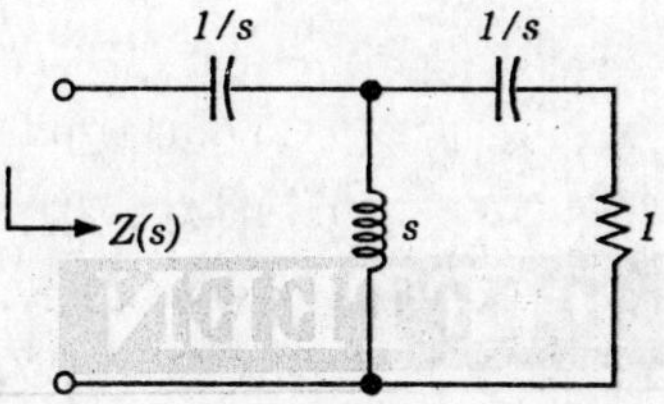

Fig. 14.14

FIFTEEN

TWO-PORT NETWORKS

Introduction. The circuits that we have seen so far are of the single-port type (Fig. 15.1).

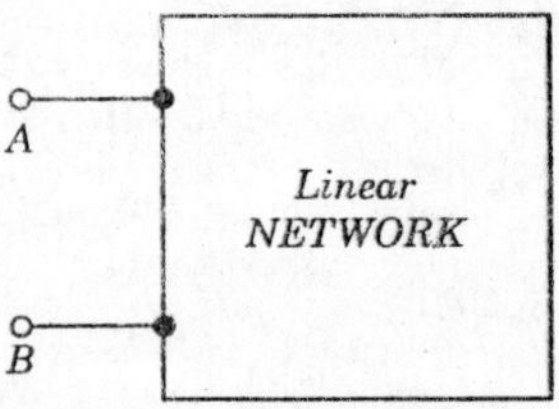

Fig. 15.1. One-port network.

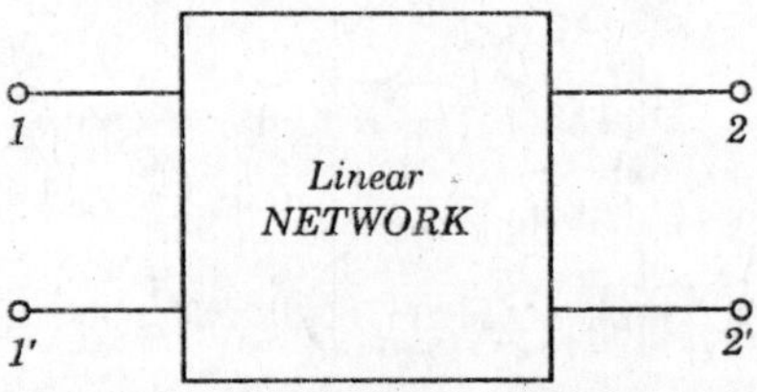

Fig. 15.2. Two-port network.,

AB is said to be the port where we may connect the voltage or current source. This port is generally known as the input port.

However, a large number of practical networks like transformers, electrical power transmission and distribution networks, communication networks, automatic control systems, electronic circuits, etc. are characterised by general networks having two ports (or two pairs, Fig. 15.2). The ports are called 1-1′ and 2-2′. One is called the input port and the other the output port. In such networks electrical energy signal enters the input port and is acted upon by the network and then leaves the output port. The terminal pair where the signal enters the network is called the input port and the terminal pair where it leaves the network is called the output port.

In this chapter, the methods of analysis of two port networks are discussed. The current and voltage relationships at the two ports of the network are described by various parameters in the following sections. It is assumed that the networks consist of linear elements and contain no dependent sources.

One port network. Consider the one port network shown in Fig. 15.1, consisting of linear passive elements. An ideal voltage source V_1 is applied at the terminals 1-1′ resulting in a current flow of I_1 Amps. Writing a set of loop equations and solving for the loop current I_1 by determinant method, we have

$$I_1 = \frac{I}{\Delta_z}\begin{vmatrix} V_1 & Z_{12} & Z_{1n} \\ 0 & Z_{22} & Z_{2n} \\ \cdots & \cdots & \cdots \\ 0 & Z_{n2} & Z_{nn} \end{vmatrix}$$

or more concisely, $I_1 = \dfrac{V_1\,\Delta_{11}}{\Delta_z}$ ...(15.1)

The ratio of V_1 to I_1 is defined as the driving point impedance for the one port network.

Hence $Z_{in} = V_1/I_1 = \Delta_z/\Delta_{11}$ ...(15.2)

If the one port network is excited by a current source at the terminals 1-1′ and the resulting voltage of the node 1 is V_1 with respect to 1′ then the ratio of I_1 to V_1 is defined as the driving point admittance.

In order to determine Y_{in}, it will be more convenient to write the nodal equations as $I = YV$.

Then solving for V_1, by determinant method, we get

$$V_1 = I_1 \frac{\Delta_{11}}{\Delta_y}$$

Hence $Y_{in} = \dfrac{I_1}{V_1} = \dfrac{\Delta_y}{\Delta_{11}}$ ...(15.3)

Example 15.1. *Find the driving point impedance Z(s) for the network shown in Fig. 15.3.*

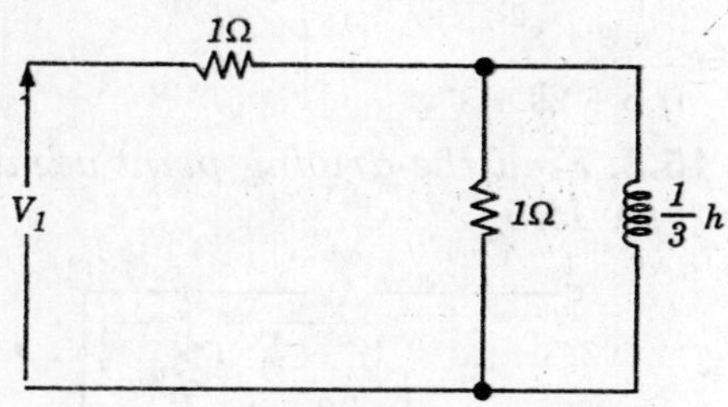

Fig. 15.3

Solution. The driving point impedance

$$Z(s) = \frac{V_1}{I_1}$$

This can be obtained by series parallel combination of the impedances.

i.e. $$Z(s) = 1 + \frac{1.1/3\,s}{1+\frac{1}{3}s} = 1 + \frac{s}{3+s} = \frac{3+2s}{3+s}$$

Example 15.2. *Find the driving point impedance Z(s) for the network shown in Fig. 15.4.*

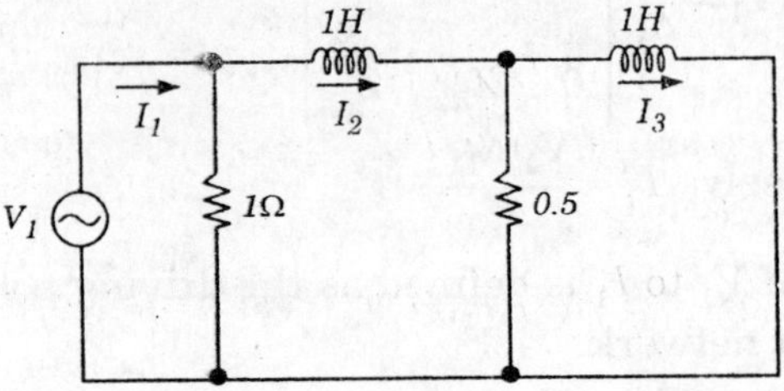

Fig. 15.4

Solution. Writing the equations in matrix form, we have

$$\begin{bmatrix} V_1 \\ 0 \\ 0 \end{bmatrix} = \begin{bmatrix} 1 & -1 & 0 \\ -1 & 1.5+s & -0.5 \\ 0 & -0.5 & 0.5+s \end{bmatrix} \begin{bmatrix} I_1 \\ I_2 \\ I_3 \end{bmatrix}$$

Solving for I_1

$$I_1 = \frac{\begin{vmatrix} V_1 & -1 & 0 \\ 0 & 1.5+s & -0.15 \\ 0 & -0.5 & 0.5+s \end{vmatrix}}{\begin{vmatrix} 1 & -1 & 0 \\ -1 & 1.5+s & -0.5 \\ 0 & -0.5 & 0.5+s \end{vmatrix}}$$

$$= \frac{V_1\,[(1.5+s)\,(0.5+s) - 0.25]}{(1.5+s)\,(0.5+s) - 0.25 - 0.5 - s} = \frac{V_1(0.5+2s+s^2)}{s+s^2}$$

$$\therefore \quad Z(s) = \frac{s+s^2}{0.5+2s+s^2}$$

Example 15.3. *Find the driving point admittance of the network shown in Fig. 15.5.*

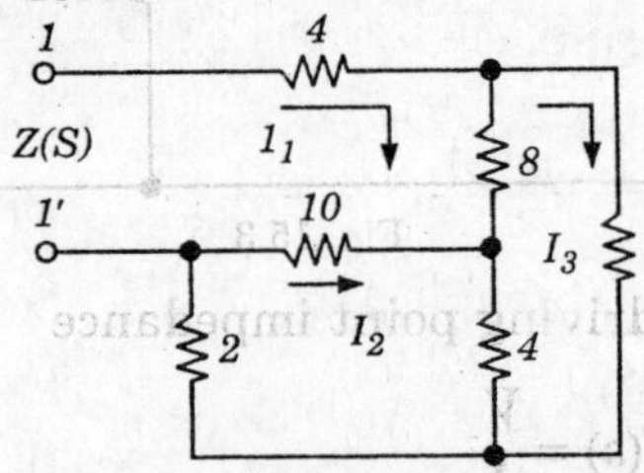

Fig. 15.5

Solution. Writing the loop equation by inspection with a source voltage V_1 applied between $1 - 1'$, we have

$$\begin{bmatrix} V_1 \\ 0 \\ 0 \end{bmatrix} = \begin{bmatrix} 22 & -10 & -8 \\ -10 & 16 & -4 \\ -8 & -4 & 18 \end{bmatrix} \begin{bmatrix} I_1 \\ I_2 \\ I_3 \end{bmatrix}$$

Therefore, $$I_1 = \frac{\begin{vmatrix} V_1 & -10 & -8 \\ 0 & 16 & -4 \\ 0 & -4 & 18 \end{vmatrix}}{\begin{vmatrix} 22 & -10 & -8 \\ -10 & 16 & -4 \\ -8 & -4 & 18 \end{vmatrix}}$$

$$I_1 = \frac{272\, V_1}{2520}$$

Therefore, $Z_i = \mathbf{9.265\ ohms}$

and $Y_i = \mathbf{0.108\ mho}$.

Two port networks. Consider the linear bilateral two-port network shown in Fig. 15.2, with current and voltage at the input terminals as V_1, I_1 and V_2, I_2 at the output terminals. The internal connection of the network elements are not generally shown ; but this is given in terms of a set of parameters called two-port network parameters. These parameters express the inter-relationship between V_1, I_1, V_2 and I_2. They are Z-parameter, Y-parameter, h-parameter and $ABCD$ parameter, image parameter etc. These parameters and their inter relationship are discussed in the following sections.

Admittance parameters : (Y-Parameters). Consider the two port network with source voltages V_1 and V_2 applied at the two ports and let there be n loops, with loop currents $I_1, I_2 \ldots I_n$. Writing the loop equations, we get

$$\begin{bmatrix} V_1 \\ V_2 \\ \vdots \\ 0 \end{bmatrix} = \begin{bmatrix} Z_{11} & Z_{12} \cdots & Z_{1n} \\ Z_{21} & Z_{22} \cdots & Z_{2n} \\ \vdots & \vdots & \vdots \\ Z_{n1} & Z_{n2} & Z_{nn} \end{bmatrix} \begin{bmatrix} I_1 \\ I_2 \\ \vdots \\ I_n \end{bmatrix} \quad \ldots(15.4)$$

or $$V = ZI$$

The loop currents I_1 and I_2 can be solved as the ratio of two determinants as,

$$I_1 = V_1 \frac{\Delta_{11}}{\Delta} + V_2 \frac{\Delta_{21}}{\Delta}$$

$$I_2 = V_1 \frac{\Delta_{12}}{\Delta} + V_2 \frac{\Delta_{22}}{\Delta} \quad ...(15.5)$$

where Δ is the determinant of the impedance matrix Z and Δ_{11}, Δ_{12} etc. are co-factors of Z.

The above equations can be rewritten as,

$$I_1 = Y_{11} V_1 + Y_{12} V_2$$
$$I_2 = Y_{21} V_1 + Y_{22} V_2 \quad ...(15.6)$$

where the Y's are the proportionality constants, called the Y parameters. The Y parameters can be obtained from direct inspection of the above equations.

Let V_2 be zero. (Output port shorted)

Then $I_1 = Y_{11} V_1$

$I_2 = Y_{21} V_1$

Hence $Y_{11} = I_1/V_1$, with $V_2 = 0$

$Y_{21} = I_2/V_1$, with $V_2 = 0$ ...(15.7)

Similarly if we make

$V_1 = 0$ (input port shorted), we have

$I_1 = Y_{12} V_2$

$I_2 = Y_{22} V_2$

Hence $Y_{12} = \dfrac{I_1}{V_2}$, with $V_1 = 0$

$Y_{22} = \dfrac{I_2}{V_2}$, with $V_1 = 0$ ...(15.8)

Since, these parameters are obtained by short circuiting, either the output or input port, the Y parameters are called as the short circuit admittance parameters. Y_{11} is short circuit input admittance, Y_{22} is the short circuit output admittance and Y_{12} and Y_{21} are the short circuit transfer admittances. Thus the Y parameters of two-port network can be obtained by short circuit method or from the loop impedance matrix.

Impedance parameters (Z parameters). Consider a two port network having n independent nodes. Let currents I_1 and I_2 be injected at the nodes 1 and 2, with respect to the reference node (1′ and 2′). Let the resulting voltages of all the nodes be $V_1, V_2 \ldots V_n$. Writing the node equations, we have

$$\begin{bmatrix} I_1 \\ I_2 \\ \vdots \\ 0 \end{bmatrix} = \begin{bmatrix} Y_{11} & Y_{12} \cdots & Y_{1n} \\ Y_{21} & Y_{22} \cdots & Y_{2n} \\ \vdots & \vdots & \vdots \\ Y_{n1} & Y_{n2} \cdots & Y_{nn} \end{bmatrix} \begin{bmatrix} V_1 \\ V_2 \\ \vdots \\ V_n \end{bmatrix} \quad \text{...(15.9)}$$

i.e. $I = YV$

The voltages V_1 and V_2 can be solved as the ratio of two determinants.

i.e.

$$V_1 = \frac{\Delta_{11}}{\Delta_y} I_1 + \frac{\Delta_{21}}{\Delta_y} I_2$$

$$V_2 = \frac{\Delta_{12}}{\Delta_y} I_1 + \frac{\Delta_{22}}{\Delta_y} I_2 \quad \text{...(15.10)}$$

where Δ_y is the determinant of the Y matrix and Δ_{11}, Δ_{12}, etc. are its cofactors.

The above equations can be rewritten as

$$V_1 = Z_{11} I_1 + Z_{12} I_2$$

$$V_2 = Z_{21} I_1 + Z_{22} I_2 \quad \text{...(15.11)}$$

where Z_{11}, Z_{12}, Z_{21} and Z_{22} are constants of the network, called the Z-parameters.

The Z-parameters can be obtained from the network Z matrix, as the ratio of two determinants. They can also be defined by letting I_1 or I_2 to zero.

Thus when $I_2 = 0$ (open circuit of output port)

$$V_1 = Z_{11} I_1 \text{ and } V_2 = Z_{21} I_1$$

Hence,

$$Z_{11} = \frac{V_1}{I_1}\bigg|_{I_2=0}$$

$$Z_{21} = \frac{V_2}{I_1}\bigg|_{I_2=0} \quad \text{...(15.12)}$$

Again when $I_1 = 0$ (open circuit of input port)

$$V_1 = Z_{12} I_2 \text{ and } V_2 = Z_{22} I_2$$

Hence,

$$Z_{12} = \frac{V_1}{I_2}\bigg|_{I_1=0}$$

$$Z_{22} = \frac{V_2}{I_2}\bigg|_{I_1=0} \quad \text{...(15.13)}$$

The conditions $I_1 = 0$ and $I_2 = 0$ correspond to open circuit of respective ports. Therefore, the Z-parameters are known as open circuit impedance parameters.

Hybrid parameters (h-Parameters). The use of hybrid parameters is well suited for the analysis of transistor circuits. The hybrid parameters are defined by writing a pair of equations relating V_1 and I_2 in terms of I_1 and V_2 as,

$$V_1 = h_{11} I_1 + h_{12} V_2$$
$$I_2 = h_{21} I_1 + h_{22} V_2 \qquad ...(15.14)$$

The constants h_{11}, h_{12}, h_{21} and h_{22} are called the h-parameters.
When $I_1 = 0$ (Open circuit of input port)

$$V_1 = h_{12} V_2 \text{ and } I_2 = h_{22} V_2$$

or $$h_{12} = \left.\frac{V_1}{V_2}\right|_{I_1 = 0} = \text{ open circuit voltage gain}$$

$$h_{22} = \left.\frac{I_2}{V_2}\right|_{I_1 = 0} = \text{ open circuit output admittance} \qquad ...(15.15)$$

When $V_2 = 0$ = (short circuit of output port)

$$V_1 = h_{11} I_1 \text{ and } I_2 = h_{21} I_1$$

or $$h_{11} = \left.\frac{V_1}{I_1}\right|_{V_2 = 0} = \text{ short circuit input impedance} \qquad ...(15.16)$$

$$h_{21} = \left.\frac{I_2}{I_1}\right|_{V_2 = 0} = \text{ short circuit forward current gain}$$

Since the parameters correspond to either impedance, admittance, voltage gain or current gain, they are called the hybrid parameters.

Inverse hybrid parameter : (g-parameters). The defining equations for the two-port network in terms of inverse hybrid parameter are

$$I_1 = g_{11} V_1 + g_{12} I_2$$
$$I_2 = g_{21} V_1 + g_{22} I_2 \qquad ...(15.17)$$

As before, the g-parameters can be obtained as

$$g_{11} = \left.\frac{I_1}{V_1}\right|_{I_2 = 0} \quad \text{and} \quad g_{12} = \left.\frac{I_1}{I_2}\right|_{V_1 = 0}$$

$$g_{21} = \left.\frac{V_2}{V_1}\right|_{I_2=0} \quad \text{and} \quad g_{22} = \left.\frac{V_2}{I_2}\right|_{V_1=0} \qquad \text{...(15.18)}$$

Transmission parameters (ABCD Parameters). In power and communication systems, it is always convenient to express the sending end (input) voltage and current in terms of the receiving end (output) voltage and current or *vice versa*. The corresponding constants used to represent the two-port network are called transmission parameters or *ABCD* parameters.

The defining equations are

$$V_1 = AV_2 - BI_2$$
$$I_1 = CV_2 - DI_2 \qquad \text{...(15.19)}$$

In the two-port network representation, the convention is that the current at port 2 enters into the network. But in transmission lines the current at the receiving end (port 2) will flow out from the network. Hence in the two-port network equations, the negative sign is used for the current terms.

The *ABCD* parmeters can be obtained by open circuit and short circuit tests at port 2.

With $I_2 = 0$ (Open circuit of port 2)

$V_1 = AV_2$ and $I_1 = CV_2$

With $V_2 = 0$ (short circuit of port 2)

$V_1 = -BI_2$ and $I_1 = -DI_2$

Hence, we have

$$\frac{1}{A} = \left.\frac{V_3}{V_1}\right|_{I_2=0} = \text{Open circuit voltage gain}$$

$$\frac{1}{C} = \left.\frac{V_2}{I_2}\right|_{I_2=0} = \text{Open circuit transfer impedance}$$

$$-\frac{1}{B} = \left.\frac{I_2}{V_1}\right|_{V_2=0} = \text{Short circuit transfer admittance}$$

$$-\frac{1}{D} = \left.\frac{I_2}{I_1}\right|_{I_2=0} = \text{Short circuit current gain}$$

...(15.20)

Inverse ABCD parameters. Inverse *ABCD* parameters are used to represent the voltage and current at port 2 in terms of voltage and current at the port 1.

The defining equations are

$$V_2 = A'V_1 - B'I_1$$
$$I_2 = C'V_1 - D'I_1 \qquad ...(15.21)$$

where A', B', C' and D' are called the inverse transmission parameters and can be evaluated as before.

RELATIONSHIP BETWEEN DIFFERENT PARAMETES

Given one set of parameters for a two port network, all the other parameter sets can be easily obtained.

Y-parameters in terms of Z-parameters. The Y-parameter equations are given by Equations (15.7 and 15.8). From the Z-parameters equations (15.12) and (15.13), we get

$$I_2 = V_2 - Z_{21}\, I_1/Z_{22}$$

Substituting the above equation in (15.11),

$$V_1 = Z_{11}\, I_1 + Z_{12}\,(V_2 - Z_{21}\, I_1)/Z_{22}$$

Therefore, $$I_1 = \frac{V_1}{Z_{11} - \dfrac{Z_{12}\,Z_{21}}{Z_{22}}} - \frac{Z_{12}/Z_{22}}{Z_{11} - \dfrac{Z_{12}Z_{21}}{Z_{22}}} V_2$$

$$= Y_{11}V_1 + Y_{12}V_2$$

Hence, $$Y_{11} = \frac{Z_{22}}{Z_{11}Z_{22} - Z_{12}Z_{21}}$$

and $$Y_{12} = \frac{-Z_{12}}{Z_{11}Z_{22} - Z_{12}Z_{21}}$$

$$I_2 = \frac{-Z_{21}}{Z_{11}Z_{22} - Z_{12}Z_{21}} V_1 + \frac{Z_{11}}{Z_{11}Z_{22} - Z_{12}Z_{21}} V_2$$

$$= Y_{21}V_1 + V_{22}V_2$$

Therefore, $$Y_{21} = \frac{-Z_{21}}{Z_{11}Z_{22} - Z_{12}Z_{21}}$$

$$Y_{22} = \frac{Z_{11}}{Z_{21}Z_{22} - Z_{12}Z_{21}}$$

Thus the above equations can be used to obtain the Y-parameters from Z-parameters.

Z-parameters in terms of Y-parameters. From the Y-parameter equations, the expression for voltages V_1 and V_2 are obtained and comparing with the Z-parameter equations, we can get the following relations.

$$Z_{11} = \frac{Y_{22}}{\Delta} \quad \text{and} \quad Z_{21} = \frac{-Y_{21}}{\Delta}$$

$$Z_{12} = \frac{-Y_{12}}{\Delta} \quad \text{and} \quad Z_{22} = \frac{Y_{11}}{\Delta}$$

where $\Delta = Y_{11}Y_{22} - Y_{12}Y_{21}$

h-parameters in terms of Y-parameters

h-parameter equations are

$$V_1 = h_{11}I_1 + h_{12}V_2$$
$$I_2 = h_{21}I_1 + h_{22}V_2$$

Y-parameter equations are

$$I_1 = Y_{11}V_1 + Y_{12}V_2$$
$$I_2 = Y_{21}V_1 + Y_{22}V_2$$

From the first Y-parameter equation we can solve for V_1 as

$$V_1 = \frac{I_1}{Y_{11}} - \frac{Y_{12}}{Y_{11}}V_2$$

Therefore $h_{11} = \frac{1}{Y_{11}}$; $h_{12} = \frac{-Y_{12}}{Y_{11}}$

Using V_1 in the second Y-parameter equation, we get

$$I_2 = \frac{Y_{21}}{Y_{11}}I_1 - \frac{Y_{21}Y_{12}}{Y_{11}}V_2 + Y_{22}V_2$$
$$= \frac{Y_{21}}{Y_{11}}I_1 + \left(Y_{22} - \frac{Y_{21}Y_{12}}{Y_{11}}\right)V_2$$

Therefore $h_{21} = \frac{Y_{21}}{Y_{11}}$

$$h_{22} = \frac{Y_{11}Y_{22} - Y_{12}Y_{21}}{Y_{11}}$$

ABCD parameters in terms of Z-parameters

$ABCD$ parameter equations are

$$V_1 = AV_2 - BI_2$$
$$I_1 = CV_2 - DI_2$$

Z-parameter equations are

$$V_1 = Z_{11}I_1 + Z_{12}I_2$$
$$V_2 = Z_{21}I_1 + Z_{22}I_2$$

From the second Z-parameter equation, we can solve for

$$I_1 = \frac{V_2}{Z_{21}} - \frac{Z_{22}}{Z_{21}}I_2$$

Substituting this in the first equation, we get

$$V_1 = \frac{Z_{11}}{Z_{22}} V_2 - \frac{Z_{11}Z_{22}}{Z_{21}} I_2 + Z_{12} I_2$$

Comparing the above equations with *ABCD* parameter equations, we get

$$A = \frac{Z_{11}}{Z_{22}}$$

$$B = \frac{Z_{11}Z_{22} - Z_{12}Z_{21}}{Z_{21}}$$

$$C = \frac{1}{Z_{21}}, \; D = \frac{Z_{22}}{Z_{21}}.$$

In the same way, other relationship can be obtained from the different sets of parameter equations for two-port networks.

Symmetry and Reciprocal two port networks. A two port network is said to be symmetrical if the network characteristics are not changed whenever the two ports are interchanged. The condition for symmetry in terms of Z-parameters is that $Z_{11} = Z_{22}$.

A two port network is said to be reciprocal if transfer impedances Z_{12} and Z_{21} are equal.

Equivalent T and π section models of two port network. The transmission lines are generally represented by π or T equivalent circuits. A general two-port network can also be represented by such T or π networks as shown in Fig. 15.6.

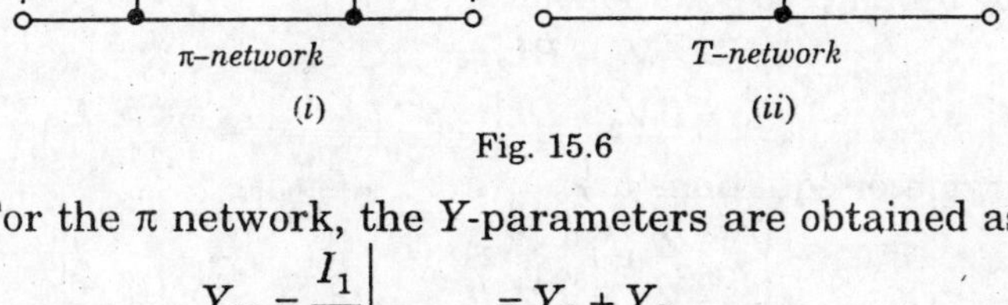

Fig. 15.6

For the π network, the Y-parameters are obtained as

$$Y_{11} = \left.\frac{I_1}{V_1}\right|_{V_2=0} = Y_1 + Y_2$$

$$Y_{21} = \left.\frac{I_2}{V_1}\right|_{V_2=0} = -Y_3$$

$$Y_{12} = \frac{I_1}{V_2}\bigg|_{V_1=0} = -Y_3, \quad Y_{22} = \frac{I_2}{V_2}\bigg|_{V_1=0} = Y_2 + Y_3$$

Hence $\quad Y_3 = -Y_{21} = -Y_{12}$

$$Y_1 = Y_{11} + Y_{12} \qquad \text{...(15.22)}$$

$$Y_2 = Y_{22} + Y_{12}$$

For the T network, the impedance parameters are

$$Z_{11} = \frac{V_1}{I_1}\bigg|_{I_2=0} = Z_1 + Z_2$$

$$Z_{21} = \frac{V_2}{I_1}\bigg|_{I_2=0} = Z_3$$

$$Z_{22} = \frac{V_2}{I_1}\bigg|_{I_1=0} = Z_2 + Z_3\ ; \quad Z_{12} = \frac{V_1}{I_2}\bigg|_{I_1=0} = Z_3$$

Hence $\quad Z_3 = -Z_{12}$

$$Z_1 = Z_{11} + Z_{12} \qquad \text{...(15.23)}$$

$$Z_2 = Z_{22} + Z_{12}$$

Special networks. Some special networks encountered in circuit analysis are the ladder, lattice, bridged T and parallel T

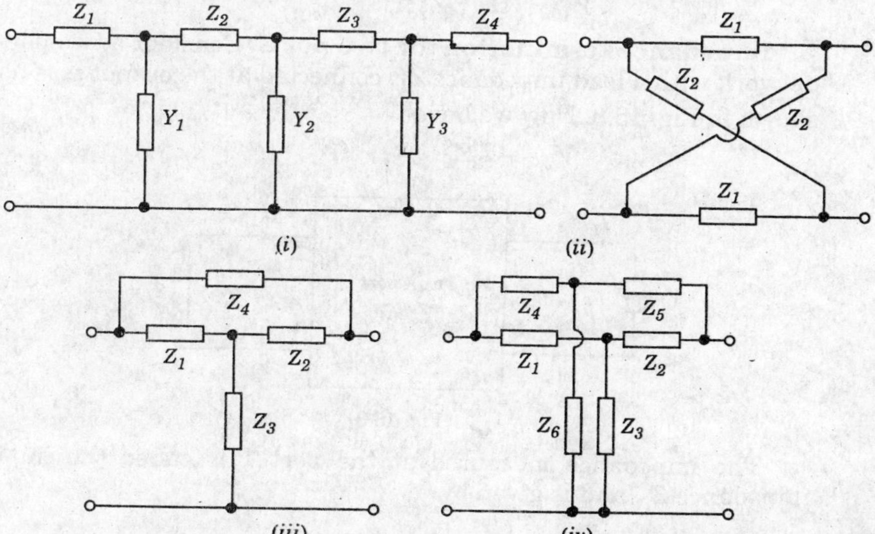

Fig. 15.7

networks, as shown in Fig. 15.7. The parameters for such two port networks can be obtained by the application of Kirchhoff's laws.

Open circuit and short circuit impedances. Consider a two port network represented by its *ABCD* parameters.

When the output port is opened the impedance measured at input port is called the open circuit impedance Z_{10}. When port 1 is opened, the impedance measured at port 2 is called the open circuit impedance Z_{20}. In the same way, the impedance measured at a port with the other port short circuited is called the short circuit impedance such as Z_{1s} and Z_{2s}.

The *ABCD* parameter equations are

$$V_1 = AV_2 - BI_2$$

$$I_1 = CV_2 - DI_2$$

Therefore, in terms of *ABCD* parameters the open circuit and short circuit impedances are obtained as

$$Z_{10} = \frac{A}{C}, \; Z_{1s} = \frac{B}{D}$$

$$Z_{20} = \frac{D}{C}, \; Z_{2s} = \frac{B}{A} \qquad \text{...(15.24)}$$

From the above equations, we get

$$\frac{Z_{1s}}{Z_{10}} = \frac{BC}{AD} = \frac{Z_{2s}}{Z_{20}} \qquad \text{...(15.25)}$$

Impedance termination for two ports. Consider a two-port network with a load impedance Z_L, connected at the output port as shown in Fig. 15.8. Now we have

$$V_2 = -I_2 Z_L$$

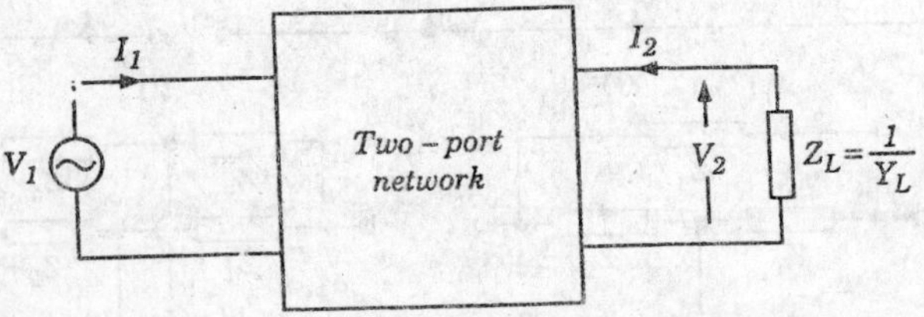

Fig. 15.8

The impedance measured at the port 1 is called the input impedance Z_{i1} and is given by

$$Z_{i1} = \frac{V_1}{I_1}$$

In terms of Z-parameters, the network equations are

$$V_1 = Z_{11} I_1 + Z_{12} I_2$$

$$V_2 = Z_{21} I_1 + Z_{22} I_2 = -I_2 Z_L$$

Therefore $\quad I_2 = -\dfrac{Z_{21} I_1}{Z_{22} + Z_L}$

Hence $\quad V_1 = Z_{11} I_1 - \dfrac{Z_{12} Z_{21} I_1}{Z_{22} + Z_L} = \left(Z_{11} - \dfrac{Z_{12} Z_{21}}{Z_{22} + Z_L}\right) I_1$

Therefore, $\quad Z_{i1} = \dfrac{V_1}{I_1} = \dfrac{Z_{11} Z_{22} - Z_{12} Z_{21} + Z_{11} Z_L}{Z_{22} + Z_L}$ ...(15.26)

In the same way, the input impedance in terms of other parameter sets can be easily obtained.

Output impedance. If the input port is terminated with an impedance Z_L the driving point impedance measured at the output port is called the output impedance Z_{i2}.

Image parameters. Consider a two-port network with impedance terminations. If the impedance seen at port one is Z_{i1} with an impedance Z_{i2} terminated at port 2 and simultaneously, the impedance seen at port 2 is Z_{i2} with an impedance Z_{i1} terminated at port 1, then the two impedance Z_{i1} and Z_{i2} are called the image impedances of the two port network, as shown in Fig. 15.9.

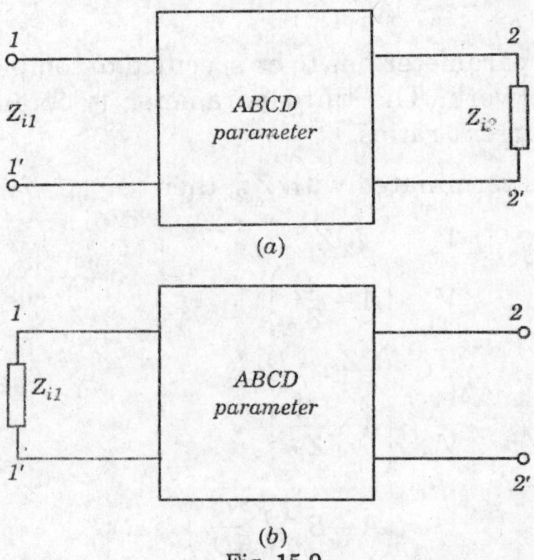

Fig. 15.9

Image impedance in terms of ABCD parameters. In terms of $ABCD$ parameters, we have

$$Z_{i1} = \frac{V_1}{I_1} = \frac{AV_2 - BI_2}{CV_2 - DI_2}$$

But $$V_2 = -Zi_2I_2$$

Therefore, $$Z_{i1} = \frac{-AZ_{i2} - B}{-CZ_i - D} = \frac{AZ_{i2} + B}{CZ_{i2} + D} \quad ...(15.27)$$

From (15.9), we have

$$V_2 = \frac{DV_1}{AD - BC} + \frac{BI_1}{AD - BC}$$

$$I_2 = \frac{CV_1}{AD - BC} - \frac{AI_1}{AD - BC}$$

Hence $$Z_{i2} = \frac{V_2}{I_2} = \frac{DV_1 - BI_1}{CV_1 - AI_1}$$

But $$V_1 = -Z_{i1}\, I_1$$

Therefore, $$Z_{i2} = \frac{DZ_{i1} + B}{CZ_{i1} + A} \quad ...(15.28)$$

Solving for Z_{i1} and Z_{i2}, we have

$$Z_{i1} = \sqrt{\frac{AB}{CD}}$$

and $$Z_{i2} = \sqrt{\frac{BD}{AC}} \quad ...(15.29)$$

One more parameter has to be specified to completely describe a two-port network. The third parameter is obtained from the voltage and current ratios.

If port 2 is terminated with Z_{i2}, then

$$V_2 = -I_2\, Z_{i2}$$

and $$V_1 = \left(A + \frac{B}{Z_{i2}}\right) V_2$$

$$I_1 = (CZ_{i2} + D)\, I_2$$

Hence $$\frac{V_1}{V_2} = \left(A + \frac{B}{Z_{i2}}\right)$$

$$= \left(A + B\sqrt{\frac{AC}{BD}}\right)$$

$$= \left(A + \frac{\sqrt{ABCD}}{D}\right)$$

Similarly $\quad \dfrac{I_1}{I_2} = -\left(C\sqrt{\dfrac{BD}{AC}} + D\right) = -\left(D + \dfrac{\sqrt{ABCD}}{A}\right)$

Then $\left(\dfrac{V_1}{V_2}\right)\cdot\left(\dfrac{-I_1}{I_2}\right) = \left(A + \dfrac{\sqrt{ABCD}}{D}\right)\left(D + \dfrac{\sqrt{ABCD}}{A}\right)$

$$= AD + 2\sqrt{ABCD} + BC = (\sqrt{AD} + \sqrt{BC})^2$$

$$\sqrt{\frac{-V_1 I_1}{V_2 I_2}} = \sqrt{AD} + \sqrt{BC} = \sqrt{AD} + \sqrt{AD - 1}$$

Since $\quad AD - BC = 1$

Define $\quad \sqrt{AD} = \cosh\theta$

then $\quad \sqrt{AD - 1} = \sinh\theta$

Hence $\quad \sqrt{\dfrac{-V_1 I_1}{V_2 I_2}} = \cosh\theta + \sinh\theta = e^{\theta}$ ...(15.30)

or $$\theta = \ln\sqrt{\frac{-V_1 I_1}{V_2 I_2}} = \frac{1}{2}\ln\left(\frac{-V_1 I_1}{V_2 I_2}\right)$$

Here θ is called the image transfer constant, and is used as the third parameter. We know that,

$$V_1 = Z_{i1} I_1 \qquad V_2 = -Z_{i2} I_2$$

$$\therefore \quad \theta = \frac{1}{2}\left(\ln\frac{Z_{i1}}{Z_{i2}} + \ln\frac{I_1}{I_2}\right)$$

Other forms in which θ can be expressed are

$$\theta = \cosh^{-1}\sqrt{AD} = \sinh^{-1}\sqrt{BC}$$

or $$\theta = \tanh^{-1}\sqrt{\frac{BC}{AD}}$$

Image Parameters in Terms of Open Circuit and Short Circuit Impedances. We know that,

$$Z_{i1} = \sqrt{\frac{AB}{CD}} \quad \text{and} \quad Z_{i2} = \sqrt{\frac{BD}{AC}}$$

$$\theta = \tanh^{-1}\sqrt{\frac{BC}{AD}}$$

Already it is shown that

$$Z_{1o} = \frac{A}{C}$$

$$Z_{1s} = \frac{B}{D}$$

Therefore, $\quad Z_{1o} Z_{1s} = \dfrac{AB}{CD} = Z_{i1}^{\,2}$

$$Z_{20} = \frac{D}{C} \quad \text{and} \quad Z_{2s} = \frac{B}{A}$$

Therefore, $Z_{20}\, Z_{2s} = \dfrac{BD}{AC} = Z_{i2}^{\;2}$

Thus $\quad Z_{i1} = \sqrt{Z_{10}\, Z_{1s}} \quad \text{and} \quad Z_{i2} = \sqrt{Z_{20}\, Z_{2s}}$ ...(15.31)

$$\theta = \tanh^{-1}\sqrt{\frac{Z_{1s}}{Z_{10}}} = \tanh^{-1}\sqrt{\frac{Z_{2s}}{Z_{20}}} \qquad ...(15.32)$$

The image transfer constant θ, in general will be complex. The real part of θ is called the image attenuation constant and the imaginary part is called the image phase constant. For symmetrical network, the image impedances will be equal and is called the characteristic impedance Z_0 and θ is called the propagation constant. Thus for symmetrical networks $A = D$ and

$$Z_{i1} = Z_{i2} = Z_0 = \sqrt{B/C} \qquad ...(15.33)$$

$$\theta = \gamma = \frac{1}{2} \ln \sqrt{\frac{-V_1 I_1}{V_2 I_2}}$$

$$= \frac{1}{2} \ln \sqrt{\frac{-Z_0 I_1^{\;2}}{Z_0 I_2^{\;2}}} \qquad ...(15.34)$$

$$\gamma = \alpha + j\beta \qquad ...(15.35)$$

α is attenuation constant measured in neper/sec.

β is phase shift constant measured in rad/sec.

Also, $\quad \gamma = \cosh^{-1}\sqrt{AD} = \cosh^{-1} A$ ...(15.36)

For symmetrical networks

$$A = \cosh\gamma$$
$$B = Z_0 \sinh\gamma$$
$$C = \frac{1}{Z_0}\sinh\gamma \qquad ...(15.37)$$

Impedance Matching. Consider the Thevenin's equivalent circuit of a general two-port network with respect to the output port as shown in Fig. 15.10. Let the output port be terminated with a load impedance Z_L.

The power transferred to the load will be maximum when $Z_L = Z_s^{*}$ (Maximum Power Transfer Theorem). The output impedance of the two port network with source connected at the input port is matched with the load impedance for maximum power transfer. This is generally referred to as impedance matching.

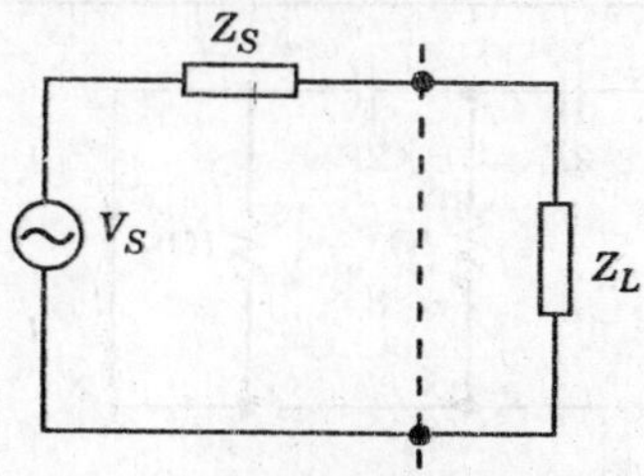

Fig. 15.10

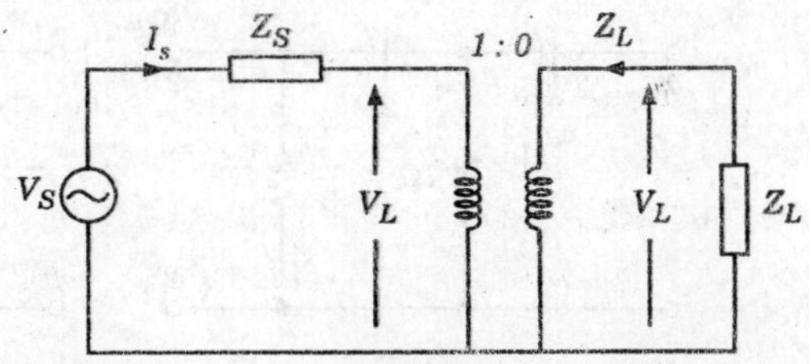

Fig. 15.11

The maximum power transfer to the load can also be obtained by inserting a transformer in between the load and the output port of the two port network as shown in Fig. 15.11.

From the circuit of Fig. 15.11, we have,

$V_L = aV_s$, where 'a' is the ratio of voltage transformation of the ideal transformer.

The load impedance Z_L referred to the primary side is

$$Z_L' = \frac{Z_L}{a^2} = |Z_L'| \angle\theta$$

The power is

$$P_L = P_L' = |I_s^2| Z_L' \cos\theta$$

$$= \frac{|V_s^2| Z_L' \cos\theta}{(R_s + |Z_L'| \cos\theta)^2 + (X_s + |Z_L'| \sin\theta)^2}$$

$$= \frac{V_s^2 \dfrac{|Z_L|}{a^2} \cos\theta}{\left(R_s + \dfrac{|Z_L|}{a^2}\cos\theta\right)^2 + \left(X_s + \dfrac{|Z_L|}{a^2}\sin\theta\right)^2}$$

For a given Z_L, the power P_L is a function of a. Hence by adjusting the transformation ratio a, the power P_L can be varied.

Hence, differentiating P_L with respect to a, and equating to zero and upon simplification, we get $a = \sqrt{\dfrac{Z_s}{Z_L}}$ for maximum power transfer.

Example 15.4. *Find the Y-parameters for the RC ladder network shown in Fig. 15.12 (a).* *(BDU 1983)*

Solution. The Y-parameter equations are

$$Y_{11} = \left.\frac{I_1}{V_1}\right|_{V_2 = 0} \quad \text{and} \quad Y_{12} = \left.\frac{I_1}{V_2}\right|_{V_1 = 0}$$

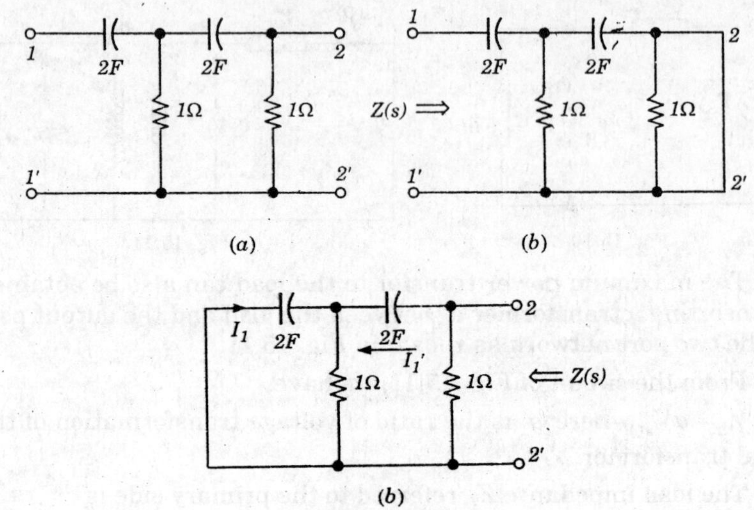

Fig. 15.12

$$Y_{22} = \left.\frac{I_2}{V_1}\right|_{V_2=0} \quad \text{and} \quad Y_{21} = \left.\frac{I_2}{V_2}\right|_{V_1=0}$$

(*i*) Short circuiting the terminals 22′ ($V_2 = 0$, Fig. 15.12 *b*)

$$Z(s) = \frac{1}{2s} + \frac{1.1/2s}{1 + 1/2s} = \frac{1 + 4s}{2s + 4s^2}$$

$$I_1 = V_1/Z(s) = V_1 \frac{2s + 4s^2}{1 + 4s}$$

Therefore, $Y_{11} = \dfrac{I_1}{V_1} = \dfrac{2s + 4s^2}{1 + 4s}$

$$I_2 = -I_1 \frac{1}{1 + \dfrac{1}{2s}} = V_1 \frac{4s^2}{1 + 4s}$$

$$Y_{21} = \frac{I_2}{V_1} = -\frac{4s^2}{1 + 4s}$$

(*ii*) Short circuiting the terminals 11′ [$V_1 = 0$, Fig. 15.12 (*c*)]

$$Z(s) = \frac{\left(\dfrac{1}{2s + 1} + \dfrac{1}{2s}\right) \cdot 1}{\dfrac{1}{2s + 1} + \dfrac{1}{2s} + 1} = \frac{1 + 4s}{4s^2 + 6s + 1}$$

Hence $\quad I_2 = \dfrac{V_2}{Z(s)} = V_2 \cdot \dfrac{4s^2 + 6s + 1}{1 + 4s}$

Therefore, $Y_{22} = \dfrac{4s^2 + 6s + 1}{1 + 4s}$

$$I_1' = \frac{I_2 \cdot 1}{1 + \dfrac{1}{1 + 2s} + \dfrac{1}{2s}} = \frac{I_2 \cdot 2s\,(2s + 1)}{4s^2 + 6s + 1}$$

$$I_1 = \frac{-I_1' \cdot 2s}{2s + 1} = \frac{-I_2\, 4s^2}{4s^2 + 6s + 1}$$

$$\frac{I_1}{V_2} = \frac{-4s^2}{1 + 4s}$$

Example 15.5. *Find Y_{21} for the network shown in Fig. 15.13.*

(MAD, 1982)

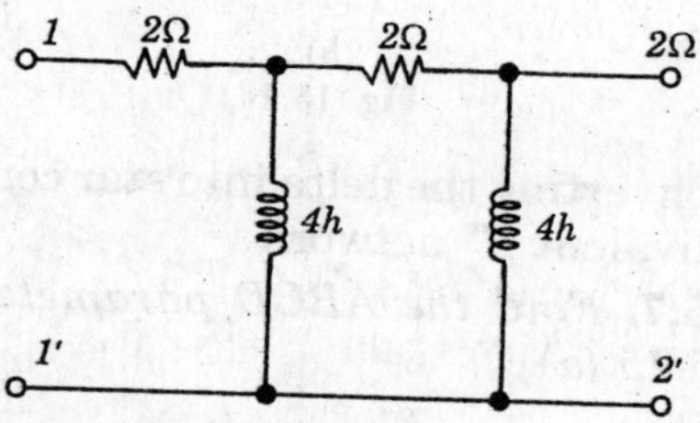

Fig. 15.13

Solution. $Y_{21} = \left.\dfrac{I_2}{V_1}\right|_{V_2 = 0}$

(*i*) Short circuiting the terminals 22′, we get

$$I_1 = \frac{V_1}{2 + \dfrac{4s \times 2}{4s + 2}} = \frac{V_1\,(4s + 2)}{16s + 4}$$

$$I_2 = -I_1 \cdot \frac{4s}{2 + 4s} = \frac{-4s}{2 + 4s} \cdot V_1 \frac{2 + 4s}{4 + 16s}$$

$$I_2 = \frac{-s\,V_1}{1 + 4s}$$

Therefore, $\dfrac{I_2}{V_1} = \dfrac{-s}{1 + 4s} = Y_{21}.$

Example 15.6. *Find the equivalent 'T' network for the bridged network shown in Fig. 15.14 (a).* *(BDU, 1984)*

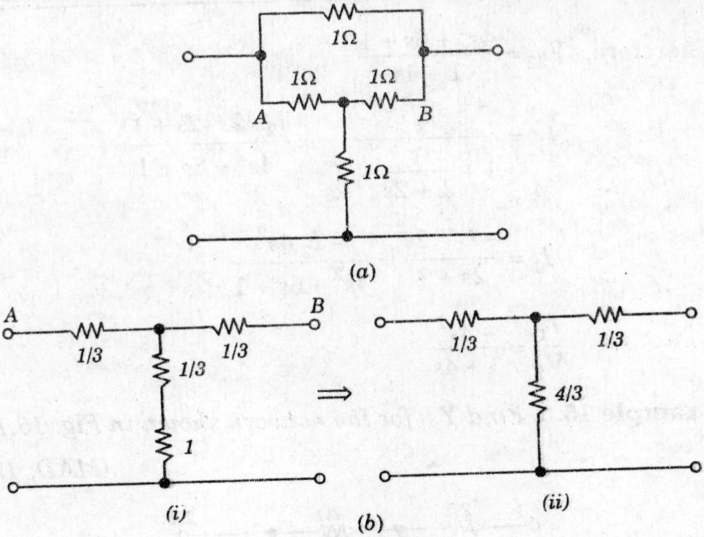

Fig. 15.14

Solution. Converting the delta into star connection, Fig. 15.14 (*b*) gives the equivalent '*T*' network.

Example 15.7. *Find the ABCD parameters for the network shown in Fig. 15.15 (a).* (BDU, 1985)

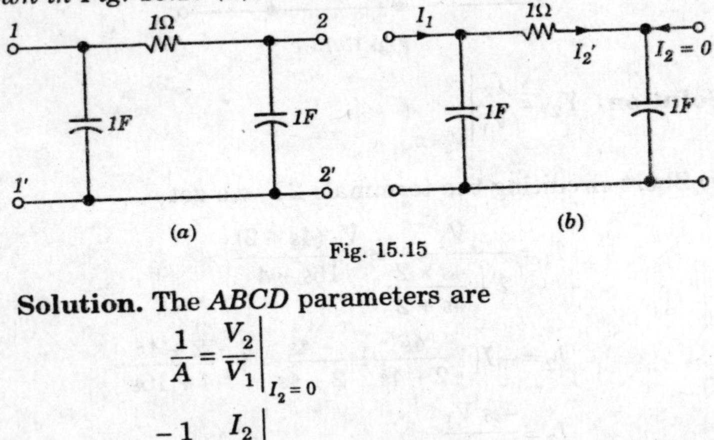

Fig. 15.15

Solution. The *ABCD* parameters are

$$\frac{1}{A} = \left.\frac{V_2}{V_1}\right|_{I_2 = 0}$$

$$\frac{-1}{B} = \left.\frac{I_2}{V_1}\right|_{V_2 = 0}$$

$$\frac{1}{C} = \left.\frac{V_2}{I_1}\right|_{I_2 = 0}$$

$$\frac{-1}{D} = \left.\frac{I_2}{I_1}\right|_{V_2 = 0}$$

(*i*) Open circuit of port 22′ [$I_2 = 0$, Fig. 15.15 (*b*)]

$$I_1 = \frac{V_1\left[\frac{1}{s} + 1 + \frac{1}{s}\right]}{\left(\frac{1}{s} + 1\right)\frac{1}{s}}$$

$$I_2' = \frac{I_1 \cdot \frac{1}{s}}{\frac{1}{s} + 1 + \frac{1}{s}} = V_1 \frac{s}{1+s}$$

$$V_2 = I_2' \cdot \frac{1}{s} = \frac{V_1}{1+s}$$

Therefore, $$A = \left.\frac{V_1}{V_2}\right|_{I_2=0} = 1 + s$$

and $$\frac{1}{C} = \left.\frac{V_2}{I_1}\right|_{I_2=0} = \frac{1}{s\,(1+2s)}$$

or $$C = s + 2s^2$$

(*ii*) Short circuit of port 22′ ($V_2 = 0$)

$$I_1 = \frac{V_1}{\frac{1 \cdot 1/s}{1 + 1/s}} = V_1 (1 + s)$$

$$I_2 = -I_1 \frac{1/s}{1 + 1/s} = V_1$$

Hence $$D = \frac{I_1}{I_2} = -(1+s)$$

and $$B = \frac{V_1}{I_2} = -1$$

Thus $$A = 1 + s\ ;\ B = -1$$

$$C = s + 2s^2\ ;\ D = -(1+s)$$

Example 15.8. *Determine the admittance parameters for the network shown in Fig. 15.16.*

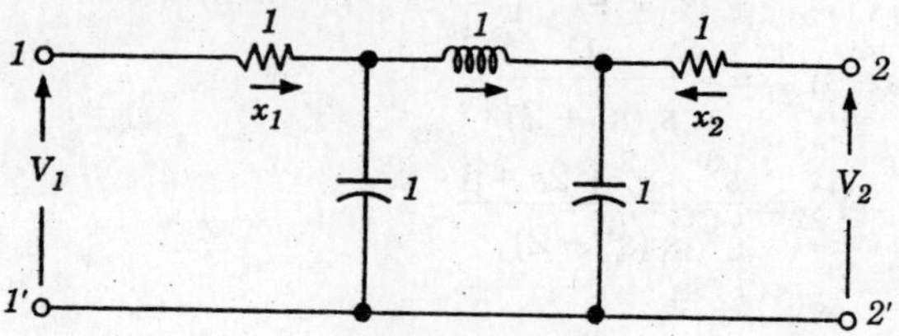

Fig. 15.16

Solution. $Y_{11} = \left.\dfrac{I_2}{V_1}\right|_{V_2=0}$

$$Y_{21} = \left.\frac{I_2}{V_1}\right|_{V_2=0}$$

Writing the loop equation with loop currents as shown, we get

$$\begin{bmatrix} V_1 \\ V_2 \\ 0 \end{bmatrix} = \begin{bmatrix} 1+1/s & 0 & -1/s \\ 0 & 1+1/s & -1/s \\ -1/s & -1/s & s+2/s \end{bmatrix} \begin{bmatrix} I_1 \\ I_2 \\ I_3 \end{bmatrix}$$

From the third equation,

$$I_3 = \frac{\dfrac{I_1}{s} + \dfrac{I_2}{s}}{s + 2/s}$$

Substituting in first equation,

$$V_1 = (1 + 1/s)\, I_1 - 1/s \left[\frac{I_1}{s} + \frac{I_2}{s}\right] \Big/ \left(s + \frac{2}{s}\right)$$

$$= \left[1 + 1/s - 1/s \frac{1}{(s^2+2)}\right] I_1 - \frac{I_2}{s\,(s^2+2)}$$

$$\text{Therefore } Y_{11} = \frac{s\,(s^2+2) + s^2 + 2 - 1}{s\,(s^2+2)}$$

$$= \frac{s^3 + s^2 + 2s + 1}{s\,(s^2+2)}$$

and $$Y_{12} = -\frac{1}{s\,(s^2+2)}$$

$$V_2 = (1 + 1/s)\, I_2 - 1/s \frac{(I_1 + I_2)}{s^2+2}$$

$$= \frac{-I_1}{s\,(s^2+2)} + \left[1 + \frac{1}{s} - \frac{1}{s\,(^2+2)}\right] I_2$$

$$\text{Therefore, } Y_{21} = -\frac{1}{s\,(s^2+2)}$$

and $$Y_{22} = \frac{s^3 + s^2 + 2s + 1}{s\,(s^2+2)}.$$

Example 15.9. *Obtain the hybrid parameters for the network shown in Fig. 15.17 (a).* *(MAD, 1983)*

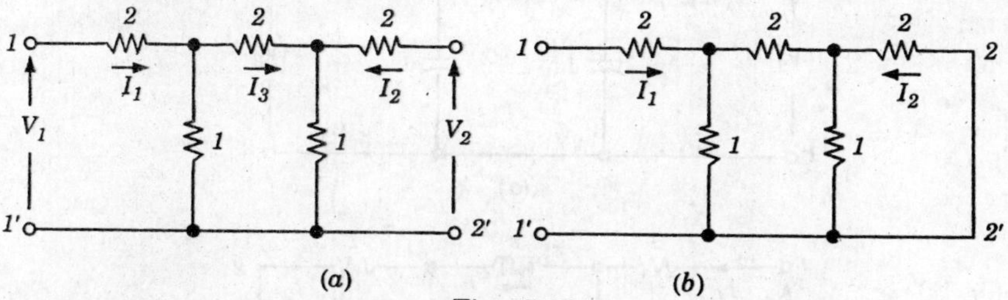

Fig. 15.17

Solution. (*i*) Short circuiting the terminal 22′ [$V_2 = 0$, Fig. 15.17 (*b*)]

$$I_1 = \frac{V_1 / \frac{(2\times 1)}{3} + 2}{(1+2+2/3)} + 2 = V_1 \times 11/30$$

$$h_{11} = \left.\frac{V_1}{I_1}\right|_{V_2=0} = \frac{30}{11}\ \Omega$$

$$I_2' = I \cdot \frac{1}{1+8/3} = \frac{3I_1}{11}$$

$$I_2 = -I_2' \cdot \frac{1}{3} = -\frac{I_1}{11}$$

Therefore,
$$h_{21} = \left.\frac{I_2}{I_1}\right|_{V_2=0} = -\frac{1}{11}$$

(*ii*) Open circuiting the terminals 11′ [$I_1 = 0$, Fig. 15.17 (*a*)]

$$I_2 = V_2 \cdot \frac{4}{11}$$

$$h_{22} = \frac{I_2}{V_2} = \frac{4}{11}\ \Omega$$

$$V_1 = I_2 \frac{1}{4} = V_2 \cdot \frac{4}{11} \cdot \frac{1}{4} = \frac{V_2}{11}$$

Therefore,
$$h_{12} = \frac{V_1}{V_2} = \frac{1}{11}.$$

Example 15.10. *Find the Y parameters for the network shown in Fig. 15.18 (a).*

Solution. (*i*) After short circuiting port 2 and redrawing the circuit using complex impedances, we have Fig. 15.18 (*b*).

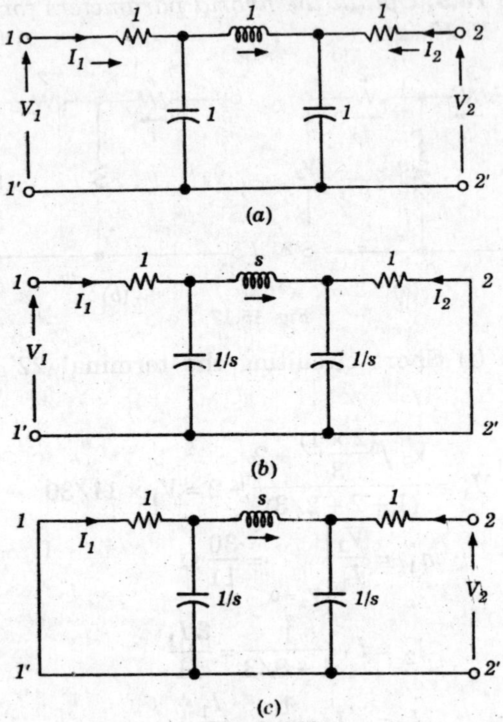

Fig. 15.18

$$Z(s) = \frac{\left[\dfrac{1 \times \dfrac{1}{s}}{1 + \dfrac{1}{s}} + s\right] \cdot \dfrac{1}{s}}{\left[\dfrac{1/s}{1 + \dfrac{1}{s}} + s + 1\right]} + 1$$

$$= \frac{s^3 + 2s^2 + 3s + 2}{s^3 + s^2 + 2s + 1}$$

$$Y_{11} = \left.\frac{I_1}{V_1}\right|_{V_2 = 0} = \frac{1}{Z(s)} = \frac{s^3 + s^2 + 2s + 1}{s^3 + 2s^2 + 3s + 2}$$

$$I_2' = \frac{I_1 \times \dfrac{1}{s}}{\left(\dfrac{s^3 + s^2 + 2s + 1}{s\,(s+1)}\right)} = \frac{I_1\,(s+1)}{s^3 + s^2 + 2s + 1}$$

$$I_2 = \frac{-I_1(s+1)}{s^3+s^2+2s+1}\,\frac{1/s}{(s+1)/s}$$

$$= \frac{-I_1}{s^3+s^2+2s+1} = \frac{-V_1}{s^3+2s^2+3s+2}$$

$$\text{Therefore, } Y_{21} = \left.\frac{I_2}{V_1}\right|_{V_2=0} = -\frac{1}{s^3+2s^2+3s+2}$$

(*ii*) By shorting port 1, we can similarly workout for Y_{12} and Y_{22}, Fig. 15.18 (*c*).

Since the circuit is symmetrical,

$$Y_{12} = Y_{21} = -\frac{1}{s^3+2s^2+3s+2}$$

$$Y_{22} = Y_{11} = \frac{s^3+s^2+2s+1}{s^3+2s^2+3s+2}.$$

Example 15.11. *A two-port network has the following open circuit and short circuit impedances*

$$Z_{10} = 900\ \Omega,\quad Z_{20} = 1000\ \Omega,\quad Z_1 s = 650\ \Omega$$

Find the parameters of the T equivalent circuit to represent the two port network.

Solution. Let the T network be as shown in Fig. 15.19.

$$Z_{10} = Z_1 + Z_3 = 900 \qquad \text{...(1)}$$

$$Z_{20} = Z_2 + Z_3 = 1000 \qquad \text{...(2)}$$

$$Z_1 s = Z_1 + \frac{Z_2 Z_3}{Z_2 + Z_3} = 650 \qquad \text{...(3)}$$

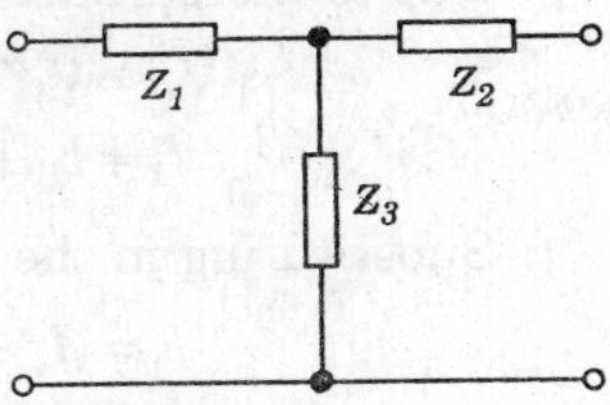

Fig. 15.19

From (1) $Z_3 = 900 - Z_1$,

$$Z_2 = 1000 - 900 + Z_1 = 100 + Z_1$$

Therefore,

$$650 = Z_1 + \frac{(100+Z_1)(900-Z_1)}{1000}$$

i.e. $$650 \times 1000 = 1000\,Z_1 + 90000 + 800\,Z_1 - Z_1^2$$

$$650000 = 1800\,Z_1 + 90000 - Z_1^2$$

$\therefore$ $$Z_1 = \mathbf{400\ \Omega}$$

From (1) $400 + Z_3 = 900$

Therefore, $Z_3 = \mathbf{500\ \Omega}$

From (2) $Z_2 + 500 = 1000$

Thefefore, $Z_2 = \mathbf{500\ \Omega}$

Example 15.12. *Two-port networks may be connected in series or in parallel. When two such networks are connected in parallel find the parameters of the overall network.*

Solution. It will be easy to obtain the parameters of an equivalent two-port network of two networks in parallel, if we use the Y parameter representation as shown in Fig. 15.20.

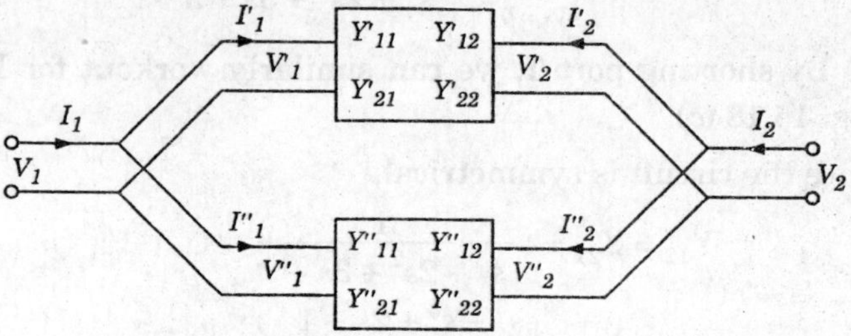

Fig. 15.20

From the above figure,

$$I_1' = Y_{11}'V_1' + Y_{12}'V_2'$$
$$I_2' = Y_{21}'V_1' + Y_{22}'\,V_2'$$

and
$$I_1'' = Y_{11}''\,V_1'' + Y_{12}''\,V_2''$$
$$I_2'' = Y_{21}''V_1'' + Y_{22}''\,V_2''$$

Due to the parallel connection, we have

$$V_1' = V_1'' = V_1 \quad \text{and} \quad V_2' = V_2'' = V_2$$
$$I_1 = I_1' + I_1'' \quad \text{and} \quad I_2 = I_2' + I_2''$$

Substituting in the above equation,

$$I_1 = (I_1' + I_2'')$$
$$= (Y_{11}' + Y_{11}'')\,V_1 + (Y_{12}' + Y_{12}'')\,V_2$$
$$= Y_{11}\,V_1 + Y_{12}\,V_2$$
$$I_2 = (I_2' + I_2'') = (Y_{21}' + Y_{21}'')\,V_1 + (Y_{22}' + Y_{22}'')\,V_2$$
$$= Y_{21}\,V_1 + Y_{22}\,V_2$$

The Y-parameters of two networks in parallel are obtained as the sum of the Y-parameters of the two networks.

i.e.
$$Y_{11} = Y_{11}' + Y_{11}'' \qquad Y_{21} = Y_{21}' + Y_{21}''$$
$$Y_{12} = Y_{12}' + Y_{12}'' \qquad Y_{22} = Y_{22}' + Y_{22}''.$$

If the two networks are connected in series as shown in Fig. 15.21, the equivalent circuit parameters can be obtained in terms of the *ABCD* parameters.

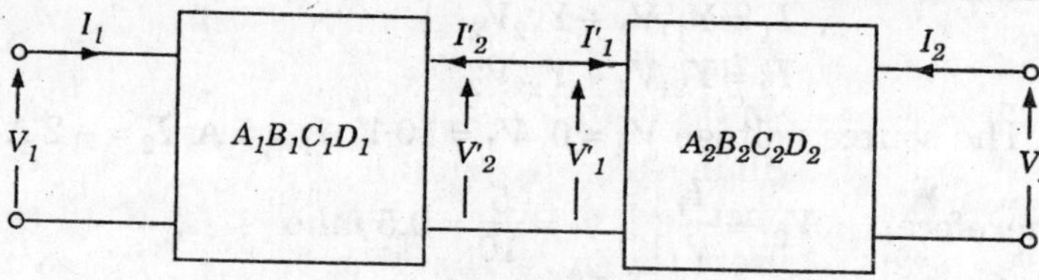

Fig. 15.21

The transmission parameter equations in matrix form are

$$\begin{bmatrix} V_1 \\ I_1 \end{bmatrix} = \begin{bmatrix} A_1 & -B_1 \\ C_1 & -D_1 \end{bmatrix} \begin{bmatrix} V_2' \\ I_2' \end{bmatrix}$$

$$\begin{bmatrix} V_1' \\ I_1' \end{bmatrix} = \begin{bmatrix} A_2 & -B_2 \\ C_2 & -D_2 \end{bmatrix} \begin{bmatrix} V_2 \\ I_2 \end{bmatrix}$$

For the series connection, we have

$$V_2' = V_1' \text{ and } I_1' = -I_2'$$

$$\therefore \quad \begin{bmatrix} V_1 \\ I_1 \end{bmatrix} = \begin{bmatrix} A_1 & -B_1 \\ C_1 & -D_1 \end{bmatrix} \begin{bmatrix} A_2 & -B_2 \\ C_2 & -D_2 \end{bmatrix} \begin{bmatrix} V_2 \\ I_2 \end{bmatrix}$$

$$= \begin{bmatrix} (A_1A_2 + B_1C_2) - (A_1B_2 + B_1D_2) \\ (C_1A_2 + D_1C_2) - (C_1B_2 + D_1D_2) \end{bmatrix} \begin{bmatrix} V_2 \\ I_2 \end{bmatrix}$$

The equivalent *ABCD* parameters are given by the above matrix.

Example 15.13. *The following measurements were made on a two port network.*

(i) With port 2 short circuited, a voltage of 10 V applied to port 1 results in $I_1 = 5$ A and $I_2 = -2$ A.

(ii) With port 1 shorted, a voltage of 5 V applied at port 2 results in $I_1 = -1$ A and $I_2 = 2$ A. The reference direction of currents, I_1 and I_2 are into the network. (Fig. 15.22).

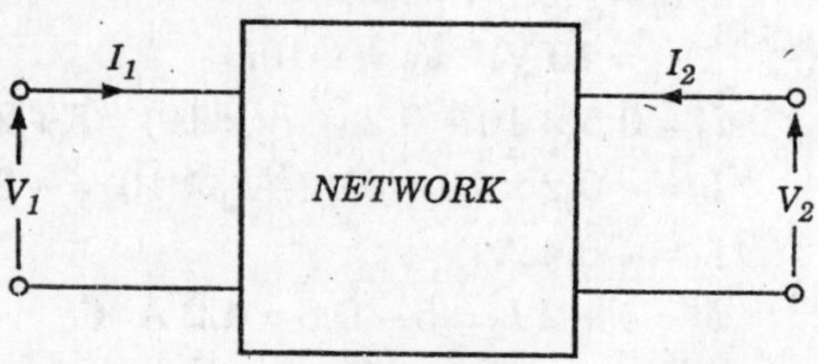

Fig. 15.22

Compute the Y-parameters for this network and write the Y-parameter equations. Compute the voltage across 10 Ω resistor connected at port 2.

Solution. The *Y*-parameter equations are

$$I_1 = Y_{11}V_1 + Y_{12}V_2$$
$$I_2 = Y_{21}V_1 + Y_{22}V_2$$

(*i*) The source voltage $V_2 = 0$, $V_1 = 10\ V$, $I_1 = 5$ A, $I_2 = -2$ A

Therefore, $\quad Y_{21} = \left.\dfrac{I_1}{V_1}\right|_{V_2=0} = \dfrac{5}{10} = 0.5$ mho

and $\quad Y_{21} = \left.\dfrac{I_2}{V_1}\right|_{V_2=0} = \dfrac{-2}{10} = -0.2$ mho

(*ii*) The source voltage

$$V_1 = 0, \quad V_2 = 5\text{ V}$$
$$I_1 = -1\text{ A}; \quad I_2 = 2\text{ A}$$

Therefore, $\quad Y_{12} = \left.\dfrac{I_1}{V_2}\right\}_{V_1=0} \dfrac{-1}{5} = 0.2$ mho

and $\quad Y_{22} = \left.\dfrac{I_2}{V_2}\right|_{V_1=0} = \dfrac{2}{5} = 0.4$ mho

(*iii*) With the 10 Ω resistor connected across the port 2, we have the Fig. 15.23.

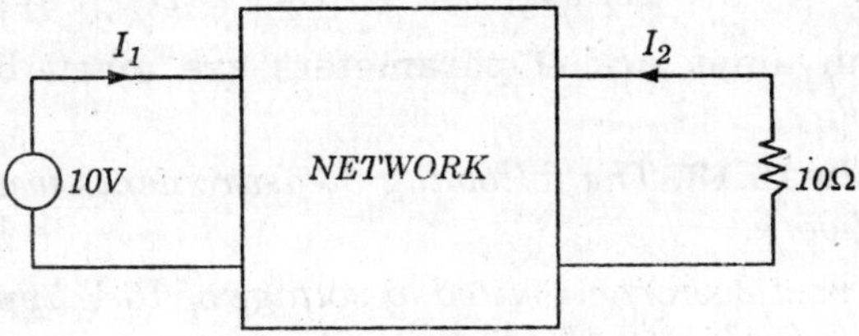

Fig. 15.23

Therefore the equations are rewritten as,

$$I_1 = 0.5\ V_1 - 0.2\ V_2$$
$$I_2 = -0.2\ V_1 + 0.4\ V_2$$
$$V_1 = 10\text{ V}, \quad V_2 = -10I_2$$

Therefore, $\quad I_1 = 0.5 \times 10 - 0.2\,(-I_2 \times 10) = 5 + 2\,I_2$

$$I_2 = -0.2 \times 10 + 0.4\,(-I_2 \times 10) = -2 - 4I_2$$

$\therefore \quad I_2 = -0.4$ A

and $\quad I_1 = 5 + 2\,I_2 = 5 - 0.8 = \mathbf{4.2\ A}$

Therefore, $\quad V_2 = 10 \times 0.4 = \mathbf{4\ V}$.

Example 15.14. *The Z parameters of a two-port network are*

$$Z_{11} = 30\ \Omega,\ Z_{22} = 10\ \Omega,\ Z_{12} = Z_{21} = 15\ \Omega,$$

Find the ABCD parameters.

Solution. The *ABCD* parameters in terms of *Z* parameters are

$$A = \frac{Z_{11}}{Z_{21}} = \frac{30}{15} = 2$$

$$B = \frac{\Delta_Z}{Z_{21}} = \frac{75}{15} = 5,$$

(Since $\Delta_z = Z_{11}Z_{12} - Z_{12}Z_{21} = 30 \times 10 - 15 \times 15 = 75$)

$$C = \frac{1}{Z_{21}} = \frac{1}{15} = 0.066$$

and $$D = \frac{Z_{22}}{Z_{21}} = \frac{10}{15} = 0.66$$

Therefore, $V_1 = 2\,V_2 - 5\,I_2$

$$I_1 = 0.066\,V_2 - 0.66\,I_2$$

Example 15.15. *The following equations give the currents I_1 and I_2 at the two ports of a two port network. Find the ABCD parameters.*

$$I_1 = 0.05\,V_1 - 0.4\,V_2$$

$$I_2 = -\,0.4\,V_1 + 0.1\,V_2$$

Solution. $Y_{11} = 0.05$

$$Y_{12} = -\,0.4 = Y_{21}$$

$$Y_{22} = 0.1$$

$$\Delta_y = Y_{11}Y_{22} - Y_{12}Y_{21}$$

$$= 0.05 \times 0.1 - 0.4 \times 0.4 = -\,\mathbf{0.155}$$

Therefore, $$A = \frac{-Y_{22}}{Y_{21}} = \frac{-0.1}{-0.4} = 0.25$$

$$B = \frac{-1}{Y_{21}} = -\frac{1}{-0.4} = 2.5$$

$$C = \frac{-\Delta_y}{Y_{21}} = \frac{-0.155}{-0.4} = 0.3875$$

$$D = \frac{-Y_{11}}{Y_{21}} = \frac{-0.05}{-0.4} = 0.125$$

Example 15.16. *Find the Y-parameters of the following resistive network (Fig. 15.24 a).*

Solution. (*i*) Short circuiting terminal 22′ [$V_2 = 0$, Fig. 15.24 (*b*)]

$$Y_{11} = \left.\frac{I_1}{V_1}\right|_{V_2=0} \quad \text{and} \quad Y_{21} = \left.\frac{I_2}{V_1}\right|_{V_2=0}$$

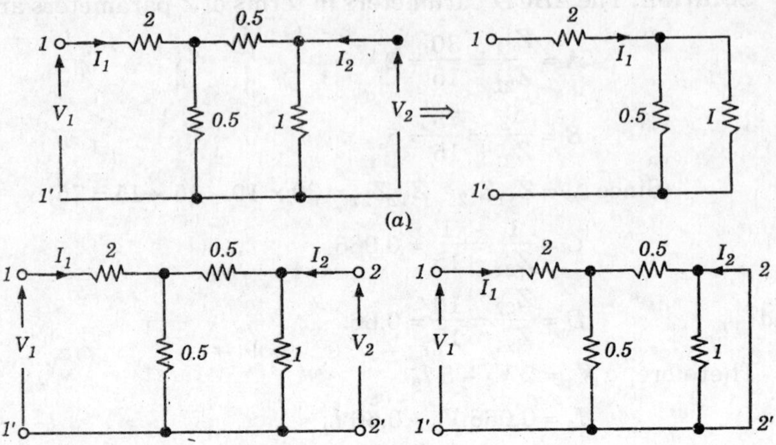

(a)

(b)

Fig. 15.24

From Fig. 15.24 (*b*),

$$I_1 = \frac{V_1}{2 + \dfrac{0.5 \times 0.5}{2}} = \frac{V_1}{2.25}$$

Therefore, $\quad Y_{11} = \dfrac{I_1}{V_1} = \dfrac{1}{2.25} = \mathbf{0.444\ mho}$ and $Y_{21} = \dfrac{I_2}{V_2}$

$$I_2 = \frac{-0.5\, I_1}{2.25}$$

Therefore, $\quad Y_{21} = \dfrac{-0.5}{2.25} = -0.22$ mho

(*ii*) Short circuiting the terminal 11′ ($V_1 = 0$)

$$R = \frac{0.9}{1.9} = 0.4737 \text{ mho}$$

$$Y_{22} = \frac{I_2}{V_2} = \frac{1}{0.4737} = 2.11 \text{ mho} \qquad \left[\because\ I_2 = \frac{V_2}{0.4737}\right]$$

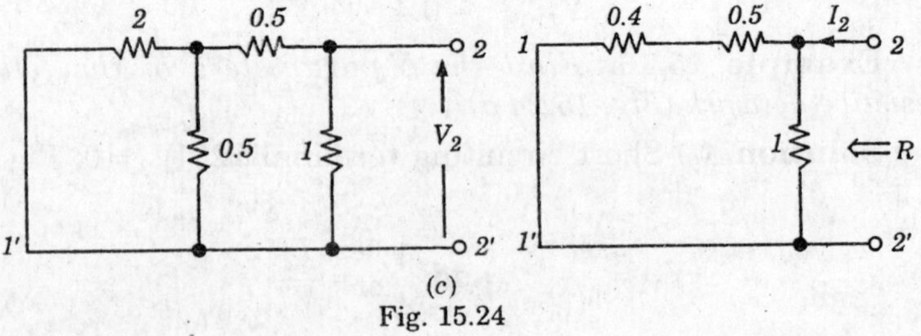

(c)

Fig. 15.24

$$I_1 = \frac{I_2\, 0.5}{1.9 \times 2.5} = \frac{\dfrac{V_2}{0.4737} \times 0.5}{4.75}$$

$$\therefore \qquad Y_{12} = \frac{I_1}{V_2} = -\,0.22 \text{ mho.}$$

Example 15.17. *Find the Z-parameters for the previous problem.*

Solution. The Z-parameter equations are,

$$Z_{11} = \left.\frac{V_1}{I_1}\right|_{I_1 = 0} \quad \text{and} \quad Z_{21} = \left.\frac{V_2}{I_1}\right|_{I_2 = 0}$$

$$Z_{12} = \left.\frac{V_1}{I_2}\right|_{I_1 = 0} \quad \text{and} \quad Z_{22} = \left.\frac{V_2}{I_2}\right|_{I_1 = 0}$$

(*i*) With the current $I_2 = 0$ (*i.e.* on open circuiting port 2), we have from Fig. (15.25 *a*).

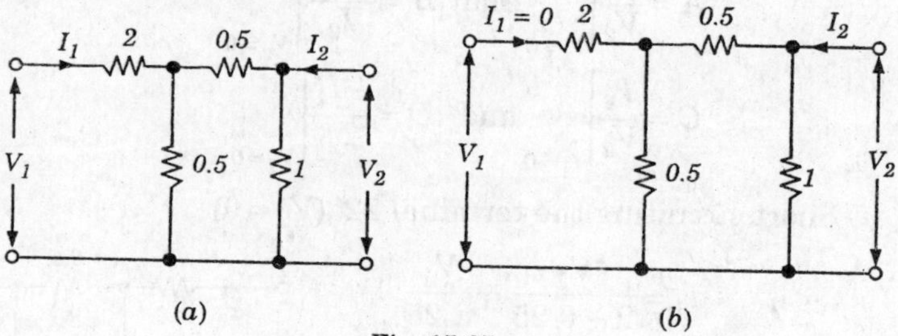

Fig. 15.25

$$I_1 = \frac{V_1}{2 + 0.375}$$

$$Z_{11} = \frac{V_1}{I_1} = 2.375\ \Omega$$

$$V_2 = \frac{I_1\, 0.5}{2}$$

Therefore, $\quad Z_{21} = \dfrac{V_2}{I_1} = 0.25\ \Omega$

(*ii*) With the current $I_1 = 0$, (*i.e.* on open circuiting port 1) from Fig. (25.25 *b*), we have

$$I_2 = 2V_2$$

Therefore, $\quad Z_{22} = \dfrac{V_2}{I_2} = \dfrac{1}{2} = 0.5\ \Omega$

$$V_1 = 0.5\ V_2$$

$$I_2 = 2V_2$$

Therefore, $$Z_{12} = \left.\frac{V_1}{I_2}\right|_{I_1=0} = \frac{0.5\ V_2}{2V_2} = 0.25\ \Omega.$$

Example 15.18. *Find the ABCD parameters for the network of Fig. 15.26 (a).*

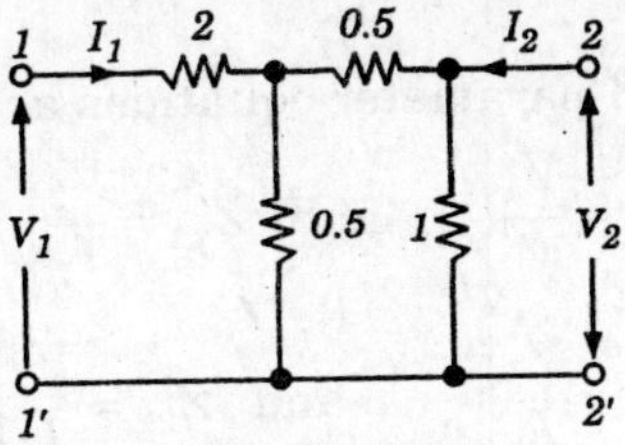

Fig. 15.26 (a)

Solution. The *ABCD* parameters are,

$$A = \left.\frac{V_1}{V_2}\right|_{I_2=0} \quad \text{and} \quad B = \left.\frac{-V_1}{I_2}\right|_{V_2=0}$$

$$C = \left.\frac{I_1}{V_2}\right|_{I_2=0} \quad \text{and} \quad D = \left.\frac{-I_1}{I_2}\right|_{V_2=0}$$

(*i*) Short circuiting the terminal 22′ ($V_2 = 0$)

$$I_1 = \frac{V_1}{2+0.25} = \frac{V_1}{2.25}$$

$$I_1' = -I_2 = I_1 \times \frac{1}{2} - \frac{V_1}{4.5}$$

$$I_2 = -\frac{V_1}{4.5}$$

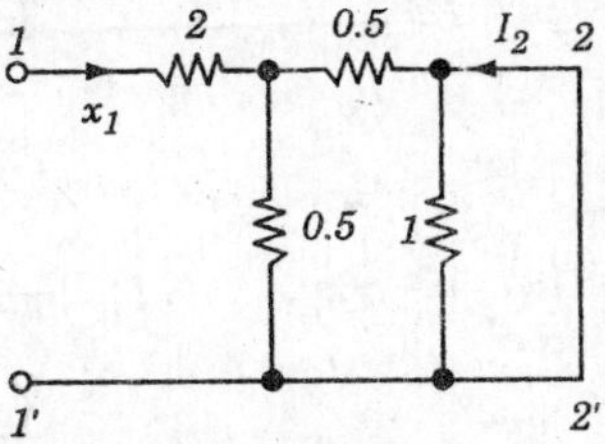

Fig. 15.26 (b)

Hence, $$B = -\left.\frac{V_1}{I_2}\right|_{V_2=0} = 4.5$$

and $$D = -\left.\frac{I_1}{I_2}\right|_{V_2=0} = \frac{V_1/2.25}{V_1/4.5} = 2$$

(*ii*) Open circuiting port 2 (*i.e.* $I_2 = 0$)

$$I_1 = \frac{V_1}{2 + \frac{0.5 \times 1.5}{2}} = \frac{V_1}{2.375}$$

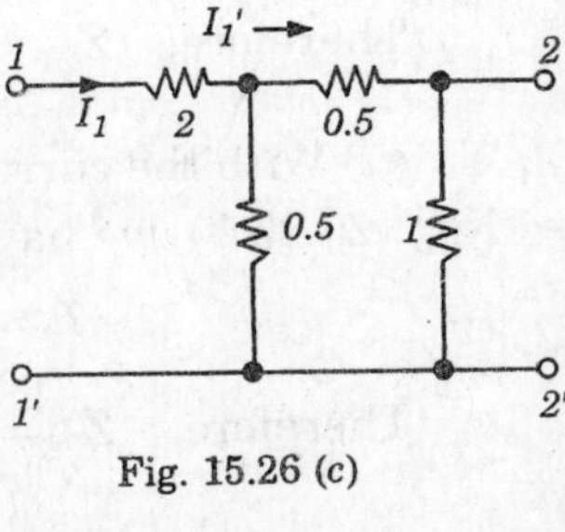

Fig. 15.26 (c)

$$I_1' = I_1 \times \frac{0.5}{0.5 + 1.5} = \frac{V_1 \times 0.5}{2.375 \times 2} = \frac{V_1}{9.5}$$

$$V_2 = I_1' \times 1 = \frac{V_1}{9.5}$$

Therefore, $$A = \left.\frac{V_1}{V_2}\right|_{I_2 = 0} = 9.5$$

and $$C = \left.\frac{I_1}{V_2}\right|_{I_2 = 0} = \frac{V_1/2.375}{V_1/9.5} = 4$$

Check : $AD - BC = 9.5 \times 2 - 4.5 \times 4 = 1.$

Example 15.19. *Find ABCD parameters for the network shown in Fig. 15.27.*

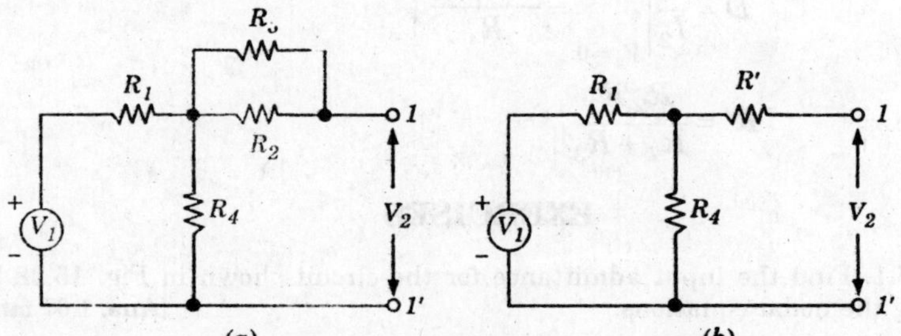

Fig. 15.27

Solution. Fig. 15.27 (*b*) shows the simplified network where R' replaces the parallel combination of R_2 and R_3.

(*i*) Open circuiting the terminal 11′ (*i.e.* $I_2 = 0$)

$$I_1 = \frac{V_1}{R_1 + R_4}$$

$$V_2 = I_1 R_4 = \frac{V_1 R_4}{R_1 + R_4}$$

Therefore, $$A = \left.\frac{V_1}{V_2}\right|_{I_2 = 0} = \frac{R_1 + R_4}{R_4}$$

and $$C = \left.\frac{I_1}{V_2}\right|_{I = 0} = \frac{1}{R_4}$$

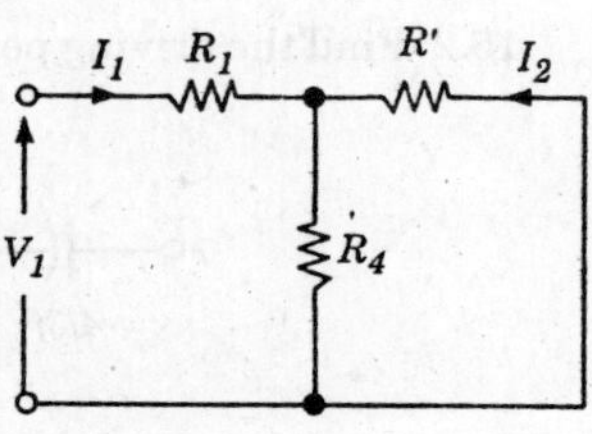

Fig. 15.27 (c)

(*ii*) Short circuiting the terminal 11′ (*i.e.* $V_2 = 0$)

$$I_1 = \frac{V_1}{R_1 + \dfrac{R' R_4}{R' + R_4}} = \frac{V_1 (R' + R_4)}{R_1 R' + R_1 R_4 + R' R_4}$$

$$I_2 = -I_1 \times \frac{R_4}{R' + R_4}$$

$$I_2 = -\frac{V_1 (R' + R_4) R_4}{(RR' + R_1 R_4 + R' R_4)(R' + R_4)}$$

$$= -\frac{V_1 R_4}{R_1 R' + R_1 R_4 + R' R_4}$$

Therefore, $B = -\left.\dfrac{V_1}{I_2}\right|_{V_2 = 0} = \dfrac{R_1 R' + R_1 R_4 + R' R_4}{R_4}$

and $D = \left.\dfrac{I_1}{I_2}\right|_{V_2 = 0} = \dfrac{R' + R_4}{R_4}$

where $R' = \dfrac{R_2 R_3}{R_2 + R_3}$

EXERCISES

15.1. Find the input admittance for the circuit shown in Fig. 15.28 by writing the nodal equations. **[Ans. 1.67 mho]**

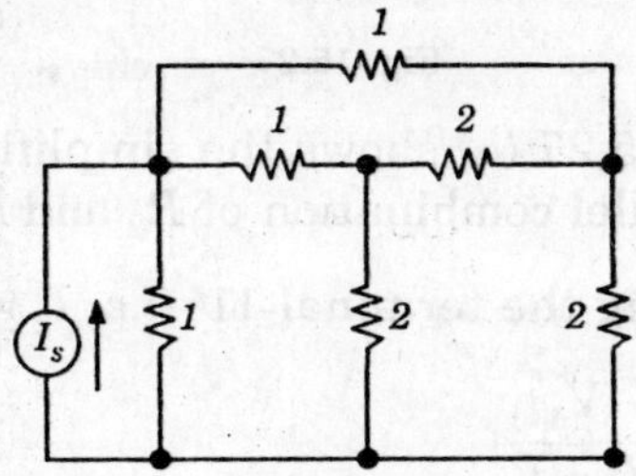

Fig. 15.28

15.2. Find the driving point impedance for the circuit shown in Fig. 15.29.

$$\left[\textbf{Ans.}\ \frac{2(s^2 + 4s + 3)}{s(s^2 + 6s + 8)}\right]$$

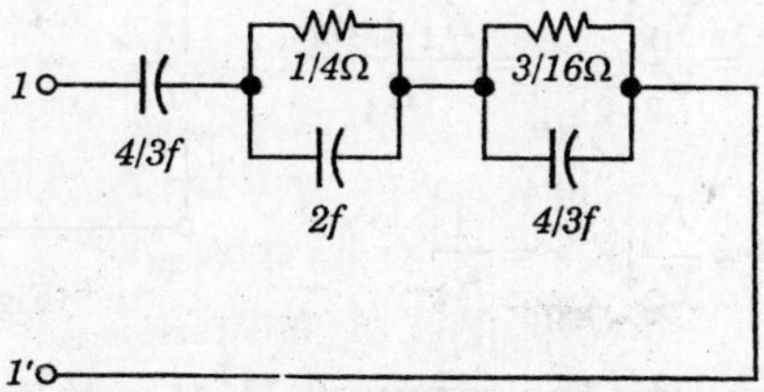

Fig. 15.29

15.3. Find the Y-parameters for the following circuits.

[**Ans.** $Y_{11} = 1/8$ mho, $Y_{21} = -62.5$ mho, $Y_{22} = 3/32$ mho]

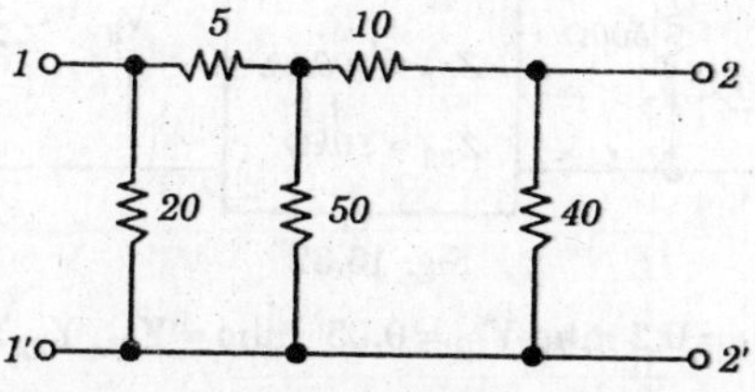

Fig. 15.30

15.4. Find the Y-parameters for the circuit shown in Fig. 15.31.

$$\left[\textbf{Ans. } Y_{11} = \frac{2s\,(1+2s)}{4s+1},\quad Y_{21} = \frac{-4s^2}{4s+1} = Y_{12}\right]$$

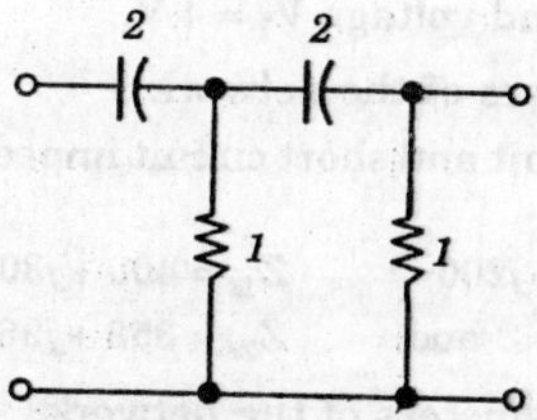

Fig. 15.31

15.5. The following measurements were obtained from a two-port network.

(*i*) With port 2 short circuited, a voltage of 15 volts applied to port 1 results in $I_1 = 2$ A and $I_2 = -0.5$ A.

(*ii*) With port 1 short circuited, a voltage of 10 volts applied to port 2 results in $I_1 = -3$ A and $I_2 = 1.2$ A.

Find the Y-parameters for the network.

With a 5 volts source connected across port 1, find the voltage across a 15 Ω load resistor connected across port 2.

15.6. Find the Y-parameters for the network having the following Z-parameters.

$$Z_{11} = 23\ \Omega,\ \ Z_{12} = Z_{31} = 20\ \Omega,\ \ Z_{22} = 15\ \Omega.$$

15.7. A two port network is terminated with a load impedance of $(3 + j4)\ \Omega$ at port 2. Find the input impedance if the Y-parameters are

$$Y_{11} = 5 \text{ mho},\ Y_{12} = -1 \text{ mho} = Y_{21} \text{ and } Y_{22} = 1 \text{ mho}$$

15.8. For the circuit shown in Fig. 15.32 determine the value of the R_L for maximum power delivered to it.

[**Ans.** 10.83 kΩ]

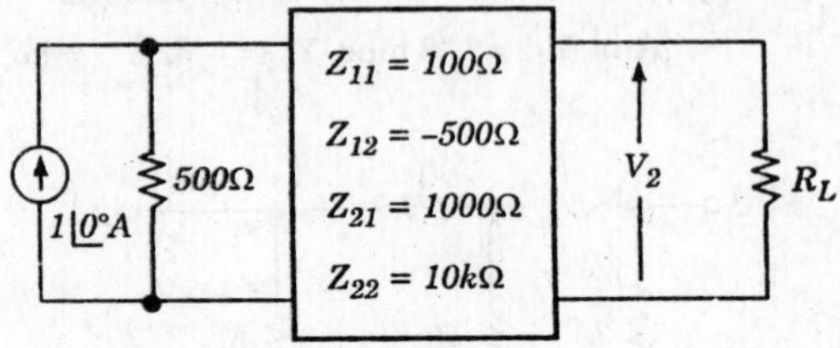

Fig. 15.32

15.9. Given, $Y_{11} = 0.2$ mho $Y_{12} = 0.05$ mho $= Y_{21}$, $Y_{22} = 0.3$ mho, calculate the Z-parameters.

15.10. The following readings were obtained, as a result of measurements on a two-port network.

(*i*) With port 2 open circuited, a voltage of 10 V applied at port 1 resulted in current $I_1 = 3$ Amps and voltage $V_2 = 7$ Volts.

(*ii*) With port 1 open circuited, a voltage of 10 V applied at port 2 resulted in current $I_1 = 2$ Amps and voltage $V_1 = 4$ V.

Find the Z-parameters of the network.

15.11. The open circuit and short circuit impedances of a two port network are ,

$$Z_{10} = 500 + j200 \qquad Z_{1s} = 400 + j300$$
$$Z_{20} = 400 \quad \text{and} \quad Z_{2s} = 358 + j96.$$

Find the image parameters of the network.

[Ans. $Z_{i1} = 452 + j254$, $Z_{i2} = 382 + j50$, $\theta = 1.0635 + j\,(0.715 \pm n/2\pi)$]

15.12. The Z-parameters of a two port network are $Z_{11} = 10\ \Omega$, $Z_{22} = 20\ \Omega$, $Z_{21} = Z_{12} = 5\ \Omega$. Find the $ABCD$ parameters of the two port network.

[Ans. $A = 2$, $B = 35$, $C = 0.2$, $D = 4$]

15.13. Derive the h-parameters in terms of $ABCD$ parameters.

15.14. Find the $ABCD$ parameters for the network shown in Fig. 15.33.

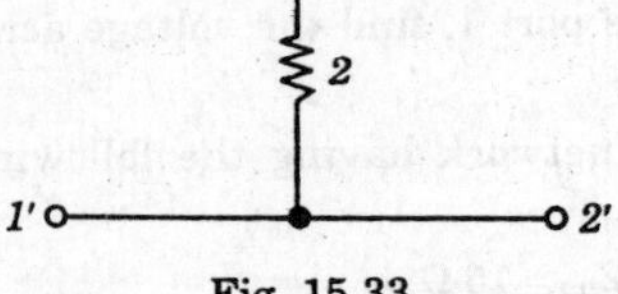

Fig. 15.33

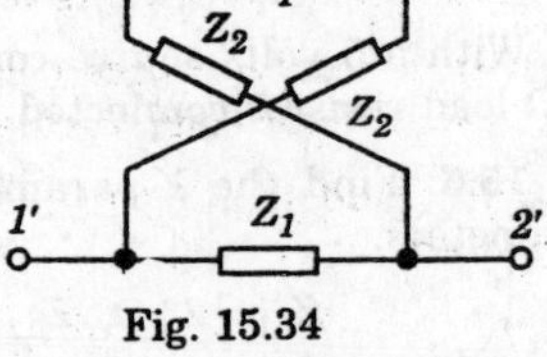

Fig. 15.34

$$\left[\textbf{Ans. } A = 2s + 1/2s = D,\ B = \frac{1+4s}{2s^2} \text{ and } C = 2\right]$$

15.15. Find the Z-parameters for the lattice network shown in Fig. 15.34.

$$\left[\textbf{Ans. } Z_{11} = \frac{Z_1 + Z_2}{2},\ Z_{12} = Z_{21} = \frac{Z_2 - Z_1}{2},\ Z_{22} = \frac{Z_1 + Z_2}{2}\right]$$

15.16. The Y-parameters of a two-port network are :

$$Y_{11} = 0.5 \text{ mho}, Y_{22} = 0.25 \text{ mho}, Y_{12} = Y_{21} = 0.4 \text{ mho}$$

Find the Z and $ABCD$ parameters of the network.

15.17. A two port network is terminated with a load resistance of 5 Ω at the output port. Calculate the input impedance if the $ABCD$ parameters are $A = 5$, $B = -3$, $C = 6$ and $D = -2$. **[Ans.** $Z_1 i = 0.786$ Ω**]**

15.18. Find the h-parameters for the network shown in Fig. 15.35.
[Ans. $h_{11} = 15$ Ω, $h_{12} = 0.5$, $h_{21} = -0.5$, $h_{22} = 0.15$**]**

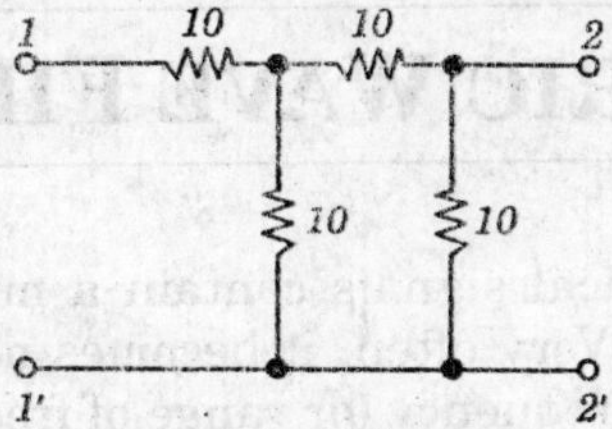

Fig. 15.35

15.19. Find the image parameters for the network shown in Fig. 15.36.
[Ans. $Z_{i1} = 2.24$, $Z_{i2} = 1.79$, $\theta = 1.45$**]**

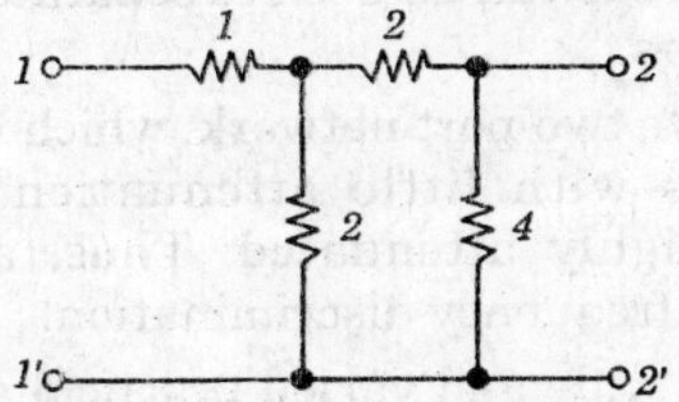

Fig. 15.36

15.20. The following measurements were made on a two-port network : with port 2 short circuited, a voltage of 10 ∠0° at port 1 results in a current of $I_1 = 2.5 \angle 0°$ and $I_2 = -0.5 \angle 0°$. With port 1 short circuited the same voltage applied at port 2 results in $I_2 = 1.5$ A, Find the π-equivalent circuit parameters for the two port network. **[Ans.** $Y_1 = 0.2$, $Y_3 = 6.05$, $Y_2 = 0.1$ mho**]**

15.21. A two-port network has the following $ABCD$ parameters :

$$A = 5, B = 50 \text{ Ω}, C = 0.2 \text{ Ω and } D = 2$$

Calculate the image parameters of the network.

SIXTEEN

ELECTRIC WAVE FILTERS

Sometimes, electrical signals contain a mixture of signals of different frequencies. Very often, it becomes necessary to apply a signal of a particular frequency (or range of frequencies) alone to a net work. It then becomes essential to filter out (or separate) signals based on their frequency. A device which does this job is called an electric wave filter. The frequency characteristics of certain types of networks can be used to separate electrical signals of different frequencies.

A filter is a passive two-port network, which will pass a desired band of frequencies with little attenuation, the rest of the frequencies being highly attenuated. Thus, a filter possesses definite properties of frequency discrimination.

Filters have very wide and varied practical applications. They are used in the areas of communication, automation, measurement and many other fields of engineering which make use of the principle of frequency discrimination. An ideal filter is one which permits undistorted transmission of a certain band of frequencies and suppresses all other frequency signals.

Inductance and capacitance are the simplest form of filters. Blocking capacitors are used in electronic circuits to discriminate between dc and high frequencies. Inductance coils can be used to pass dc and practically eliminate very high frequencies. (MHz)

Classification of Electric Wave Filters

1. Depending upon the spectrum of frequencies which they pass, filters can be classified into low pass, high pass, band pass and band elimination filters.

2. Depending upon the number of its L, T or π sections, a filter can be a simple or a composite filter.

3. According to the characteristics, they can be classified as constant K-filter, m-derived filter etc.

4. According to the type of element, they can be classified into a reactive (L and C), piezoelectric etc. filters.

The minimum number of elements in a filter is two (L section). Filter networks are generally set up as a symmetrical T to π section, which are regarded as the combination of L sections as shown in Fig. 16.1 with series impedance $Z_1/2$ and shunt admittance $2Z_2$

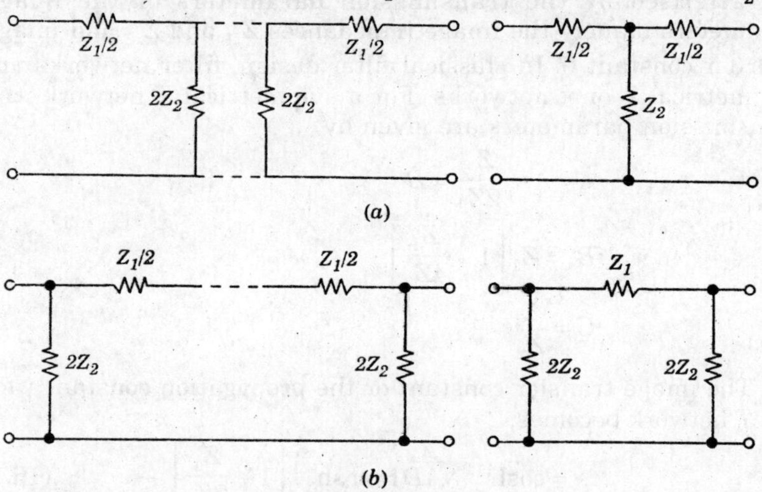

Fig. 16.1

A practical filter should follow the characteristics of an ideal filter. The difference in characteristics between an actual filter and an ideal filter is due to the improper matching between the terminal load conditions and losses in the filter networks. An ideal

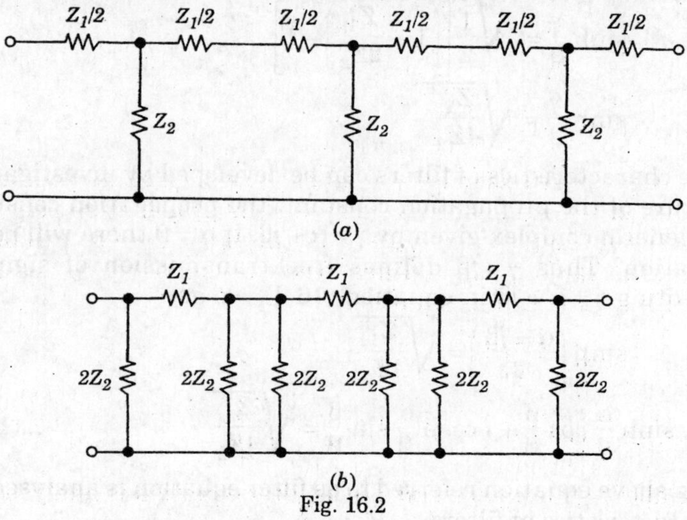

Fig. 16.2

filter will be a network of pure reactance elements. A tandem connection of several T or π sections will give rise to a ladder network as shown in Fig. 16.2.

Ideal Filter. A filter may be considered as a two port network, with passive reactance elements. Therefore the filter may be characterised by the transmission parameters or the image parameters namely the image impedances Z_{i1} and Z_{i2} and image transfer constant θ. In classical filter design, filter networks are symmetrical T or π networks. For a symmetrical T network, the transmission parameters are given by

$$A = 1 + \frac{Z_1}{2Z_2} = D$$

$$B = Z_1\left[1 + \frac{Z_1}{4Z_2}\right]$$

$$C = \frac{1}{Z_2}$$

The image transfer constant or the propagation constant γ for the T network becomes,

$$\gamma = \cosh^{-1}\sqrt{AD} = \cosh^{-1}\left[1 + \frac{Z_1}{2Z_2}\right] \qquad ...(16.1)$$

We know that

$$\sinh\frac{\gamma}{2} = \frac{1}{2}(\cosh\gamma - 1)$$

Hence for the T network,

$$\sinh\frac{\gamma}{2} = \sqrt{\frac{1}{2}\left[\left(1 + \frac{Z_1}{2Z_2}\right) - 1\right]}$$

or $$\sinh\frac{\gamma}{2} = \sqrt{\frac{Z_1}{4Z_2}} \qquad ...(1\text{6}$$

The characteristics of filters can be developed by investigating the nature of the propagation constant. the propagation constant γ is in general complex given by $\gamma = \alpha + j\beta$. If $\alpha = 0$ there will be no attenuation. Thus $\gamma = j\beta$ defines free transmission of signals. Substituting $\gamma = \alpha + j\beta$ in equation (16.3), we get

$$\sinh\left(\frac{\alpha + j\beta}{2}\right) = \sqrt{\frac{Z_1}{4Z_2}}$$

or $$\sinh\frac{\alpha}{2}\cos\frac{\beta}{2} + j\cosh\frac{\alpha}{2}\sin\frac{\beta}{2} = \sqrt{\frac{Z_1}{4Z_2}} \qquad ...(16.4)$$

The above equation referred to as filter equation is analysed for the characteristics of filters.

Consider that Z_1 and Z_2 represent reactive elements of the same type (with inductance or capacitance), then the radical on right hand side of Eq. (16.4) will be a real number.

Hence the imaginary part of Eq. (16.4) will be zero, *i.e.*

$$\cosh\frac{\alpha}{2}\sin\frac{\beta}{2} = 0$$

$\cosh\frac{\alpha}{2}$ cannot be zero for any α. So that,

$$\sin\frac{\beta}{2} = 0, \text{ i.e., } \beta = n\ \pi \text{ for } n = 0, 2, 4...$$

and $$\cos\frac{\beta}{2} = 1$$

Therefore, the Equation (16.4) becomes,

$$\sinh\frac{\alpha}{2} = \sqrt{\frac{Z_1}{4Z_2}}$$

the attenuation for this case is

$$\alpha = 2\sinh^{-1}\sqrt{\frac{Z_1}{4Z_2}} \qquad ...(16.5)$$

The condition $\frac{Z_1}{4Z_2} > 0$ implies that the signal will be attenuated. The frequency range over which $\frac{Z_1}{4Z_2} > 0$, is called the attenuation band.

If Z_1 and Z_2 are elements of opposite type (one inductance and the other capacitance) the right hand side of Equations (16.4) is purely imaginary.

Thus $$\sinh\frac{\alpha}{2}\cos\frac{\beta}{2} = 0$$

which means either

$$\sinh\frac{\alpha}{2} = 0$$

or

$$\cos\frac{\beta}{2} = 0$$

From the first condition, we get $\alpha = 0$ implies unattenuated transmission of signals. The frequency range over which this condition is satisfied is called pass band or transmission band.

$$\cosh\frac{\alpha}{2} = 1$$

and $\qquad \sinh \frac{\beta}{2} = \sqrt{\left|\frac{Z_1}{4Z_2}\right|}$

or $$\beta = 2 \sin^{-1} \sqrt{\left|\frac{Z_1}{4Z}\right|} \qquad ...(16.6)$$

From Equation (16.6), we have the condition that

$$\left|\frac{Z_1}{4Z_2}\right| < 1$$

For pass band, there are two conditions to be satisfied, namely that

$$\frac{Z_1}{4Z_2} < 0 \quad \text{and} \quad \left|\frac{Z_1}{4Z_2}\right| < 1$$

or $$-1 < \frac{Z_1}{4Z_2} < 0 \qquad ...(16.7)$$

If $\frac{Z_1}{4Z_2} < 0$ but the magnitude is greater than one, then the condition $\cos \frac{\beta}{2} = 0$ will be valid, from which $\sin \frac{\beta}{2} = \pm 1$

or $\qquad \beta = (2n - 1)\,\pi, n = 1, 2, ...$

This corresponds to attenuation band and the attenuation is given by

$$\alpha = 2 \cosh^{-1} \sqrt{\left(\frac{Z_1}{4Z_2}\right)}$$

Alternate method. For the symmetric T network, shown in Fig. 16.3, terminated in a load, Z_L, the input impedance is

$$Z_{in} = \frac{Z_1}{2} + \frac{Z_2\left(\frac{Z_1}{2} + Z_L\right)}{Z_2 + \frac{Z_1}{2} + Z_L}$$

$$= \frac{Z_1}{2} + \frac{Z_2\,(Z_1 + 2Z_L)}{Z_1 + 2\,(Z_2 + Z_L)} \qquad ...(16.8)$$

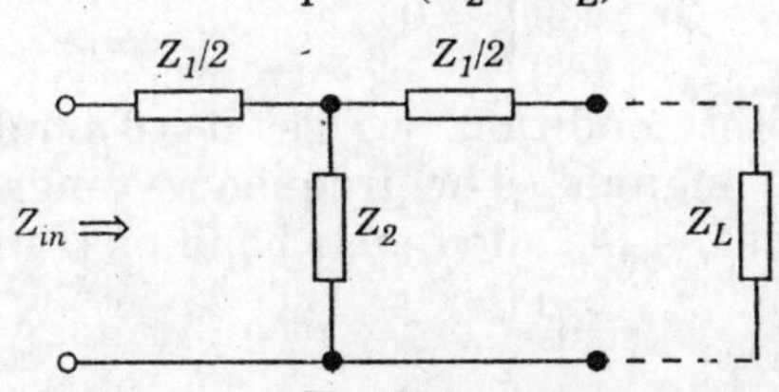

Fig. 16.3

The image impedance Z_I is defined as the load impedance such that

$$Z_{in} = Z_L \qquad \text{...(16.9)}$$

Substituting $Z_{in} = Z_L = Z_I$ in Equation (16.8). We have

$$Z_I = \sqrt{\frac{Z_1 Z_2 + Z_1^2}{4}}$$

$$= \sqrt{Z_1 Z_2 \left(1 + \frac{Z_1}{4Z_2}\right)} \qquad \text{... (16.10)}$$

Assume $Z_1 = jX_1$ and $Z_2 = jX_2$ (the sign of X_1 and X_2 will indicate whether the element is inductive or capacitive).

On substituting,

$$Z_I = \sqrt{-X_1 X_2 \left(1 + \frac{X_1}{4X_2}\right)} \qquad \text{...(16.11)}$$

In such a filter, for pass band frequencies, Z_I is purely resistive and for stop band frequencies Z_I is purely reactive. Only when Z_I is resistive can the network accept power from a source and transfer the power to the load. Remember that the coupling filter network is itself made up of only reactive elements and hence lossless.

There are two possibilities :

(*a*) Both X_1 and X_2 are of the same type, *i.e.* both series and shunt arms are either L or C. In this case X_1 are X_2 are both of the same sign and Z_I will always be purely imaginary. This implies that there is no possibility of a pass band.

(*b*) When X_1 and X_2 are of the opposite type ; one is inductive and the other capacitive. Here X_1 and X_2 are of opposite signs.

Hence the sign of Z_I^2 will depend on $1 + \dfrac{X_1}{4X_2}$.

For Z_I to be real (pass band), $1 + \dfrac{X_1}{4X_2}$ should be positive.

As X_1 and X_2 are of opposite signs, $\dfrac{X_1}{4X_2}$ is negative. Hence the condition for pass band is that $\dfrac{X_1}{4X_2}$ is greater than — 1.

Of course, since $\dfrac{X_1}{4X_2}$ in negative, we may write

$$-1 < \frac{X_1}{4X_2} < 0 \quad \text{for pass band} \qquad ...(16.12)$$

and
$$\frac{X_1}{4X_2} < -1 \quad \text{for stop band} \qquad ...(16.13)$$

Hence, we may conclude for pass band to exist, the shunt and series arms should be of the opposite type.

The same can be proved in an identical manner for the symmetrical π network also.

Cut off Frequencies. The filter network changes its behaviour from pass band to stop band over a frequency range. The frequency at which a filter network changes from a pass band to stop band or *vice-versa* is called the cut off frequency. These frequencies are obtained when

$$\frac{Z_1}{4Z_2} = 0$$

or
$$Z_1 = 0 \qquad ...(16.14)$$

and
$$\frac{Z_1}{4Z_2} = -1$$

or
$$Z_1 + 4Z_2 = 0 \qquad ...(16.15)$$

where Z_1 and Z_2 are reactances of opposite types.

Attenuation. The attenuation of a network is measured in terms of decibels or nepers. The decibel or bel (fundamental unit) is a measure of power ratio. If P_2 is output power and P_1 is the input power of a network, then attenuation in bel is $\log_{10} \frac{P_2}{P_1}$.

More convenient unit to measure attenuation is the decibel given by,

$$\text{attenuation in dB} = 10 \log_{10} \frac{P_2}{P_1} \qquad ...(16.16)$$

If the powers are associated with the same input and output impedances for the two port network, then

$$\text{attenuation in dB} = 10 \log_{10} \left(\frac{E_2}{E_1}\right)^2$$

$$= 20 \log_{10} \left(\frac{E_2}{E_1}\right) = 20 \log \left(\frac{I_2}{I_1}\right) \qquad ...(16.16)$$

The neper is the ratio of voltages or currents. Two voltages or currents differ by one neper, when one of them is 'e' times as large as the other. Hence the attenuation in neper

$$= \ln\left(\frac{I_2}{I_1}\right) = \ln\left(\frac{E_2}{E_1}\right)$$

$$\text{Attenuation in dB} = 20\log_{10}\left(\frac{I_2}{I_1}\right) = \frac{20\ln\left(\frac{I_2}{I_1}\right)}{\log_{10} e}$$

$$= 8.686 \ln\frac{I_2}{I_1} \qquad \text{...(16.17)}$$

Then attenuation in dB = 8.686 (attenuation in nepers).

Characteristic Impedance. The characteristic impedance for a T network is given by

$$Z_{0T} = Z_I = \sqrt{\frac{B}{C}} = \sqrt{Z_1 Z_2\left(1 + \frac{Z_1}{4Z_2}\right)} \qquad \text{...(16.10)}$$

We have already seen that for pass band, X_1 and X_2 are of opposite signs, and $-1 < \frac{X_1}{4X_2} < 0$. Therefore the characteristic impedance Z_{0T} will be real and equal to R_0 given by

$$R_0 = \sqrt{X_1 X_2\left(1 - \frac{X_1}{4X_2}\right)}$$

If such a filter is terminated with a load, $Z_I = Z_o$, the power will be transmitted without attenuation. Also if the filter is supplied by a source with a source impedance, R_o, matching Z_L, maximum power will be transmitted to the load without any attenuation.

If X_1 and X_2 are of opposite sign and $\frac{X_1}{4X_2} < -1$ the characteristic impedance Z_{0T} is a pure reactance. If the network is terminated with its reactance Z_0, power cannot be transmitted.

Consider now, the π section. $Z_o\pi = \frac{Z_1 Z_2}{Z_{0T}}$. The behaviour of $Z_{O\pi}$ will be same as that of Z_{OT} for pure reactance. Hence the conditions developed for pass and stop bands referring to the T section will hold good for π section as well.

Types of filters. Let us consider the different types of filters. According to frequency characteristics we have (1) low pass (2) high pass (3) band pass and (4) band elimination filters.

A low pass filter is one in which the pass band extends from $f = 0$ to the cut off frequency f_c and beyond which the network attenuates.

A high pass filter is one in which the pas band extends from $f = f_c$ to infinite frequency. Below f_c, the signals are cut-off.

Band pass filter is one in which the pass band extends from $f = f_1$ to $f = f_2$. The frequency signals from $f = 0$ to $f = f_1$ and from $f = f_2$ upto infinity are attenuated. A band pass filter can be obtained by cascading a low pass and high pass filter provided the cut off frequency of the low pass filter is greater than the cut off frequency of the high pass filter.

Band elimination filter is obtained by paralleling a low pass and a high pass filter provided the cut off frequency of the low pass filter is smaller than the cut off frequency of the high pass filter. The frequency characteristics are shown in Fig. 16.4.

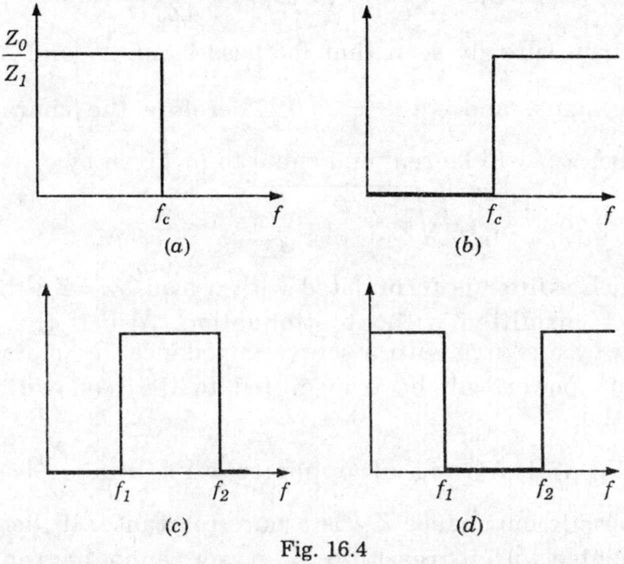

Fig. 16.4

Constant k filter. Prototype filters are called constant K-filters. They are simple T or π section filters satisfying the following relation between the series impedance Z_1 and shunt impedance Z_2 :

$$Z_1 Z_2 = k^2 \qquad ...(16.18)$$

where k is a constant.

Z_1 and Z_2 will be of opposite nature and hence $Z_1 Z_2$ will be a real constant.

Therefore, $$Z_1 Z_2 = R_o^{\,2} \qquad ...(16.19)$$

and R_o is called the design impedance.

Low pass constant k-filter. The low pass filter is shown in Fig. 16.5. The total series impedance is $Z_1 = j\omega L$ and shunt impedance $Z_2 = \dfrac{1}{j\omega C}$.

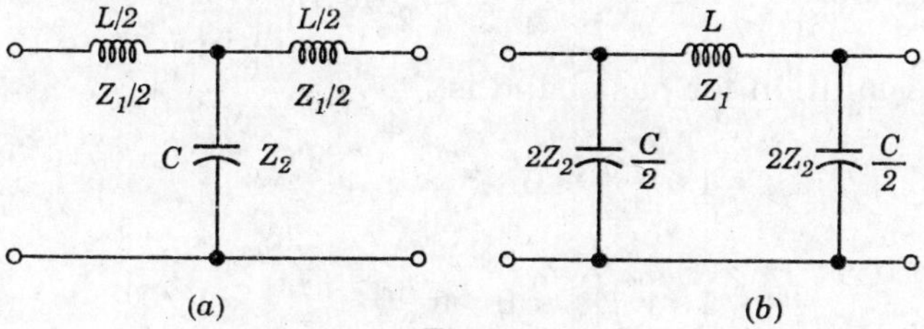

Fig. 16.5

$$Z_1 Z_2 = j\omega L \cdot \frac{1}{j\omega C} = \frac{L}{C}$$

Therefore, $R_o = \sqrt{L/C}$

$$\frac{Z_1}{4Z_2} = \frac{j\omega L}{4} \cdot j\omega C = -\frac{\omega^2 LC}{4}$$

The cut off frequencies are obtained from Equations (16.14) and (16.15)

$Z_1 = j\omega L = 0$ gives $f_1 = 0$ (lower cut off frequency)

$Z_1 + 4Z_2 = 0$ gives $j\omega_c L + \dfrac{4}{j\omega_c C} = 0$

$\omega_c^{\,2} LC = 4$ or $f_c = \dfrac{1}{\pi\sqrt{LC}}$ (second cut off frequency) ...(16.20)

This filter section will pass all the frequencies from 0 to f_c as shown in Fig. 16.6.

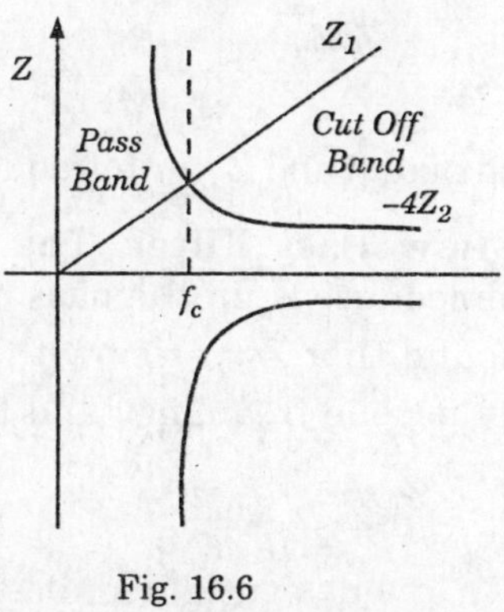

Fig. 16.6

The effect of frequency variation on γ can be obtained from

$$\sin\frac{\gamma}{2} = \sqrt{\frac{Z_1}{Z_2}}$$

$$= \sqrt{\frac{-\omega^2 LC}{4}} = \frac{1}{2} j\omega\sqrt{LC}$$

The condition for pass band is,

$$-1 < \frac{Z_1}{4Z_2} < 0$$

i.e.
$$-1 < \left(\frac{-f}{f_c}\right)^2 < 0 \quad \text{or} \quad 0 < \left(\frac{f}{f_c}\right)^2 < 1$$

$$\beta = 2\sin^{-1}\sqrt{\frac{Z_1}{4Z_2}} = 2\sin^{-1}\left(\frac{f}{f_c}\right)$$

In the pass band $f/f_c < 1$, $\alpha = 0$, $\beta = 2\sin^{-1}\left(\frac{f}{f_c}\right)$

In the stop band $f/f_c < 1$, and $\alpha = 2\cosh^{-1}\left(\frac{f}{f_c}\right)$ and $\beta = \pi$

The characteristic impedance of T-section low pass filter is

$$Z_{OT} = \sqrt{Z_1 Z_2\left[1 + \frac{Z_1}{4Z_2}\right]}$$

$$= \sqrt{\frac{L}{C}\left[1 - \omega^2\frac{LC}{4}\right]}$$

or
$$Z_{OT} = R_o\sqrt{1 - \left(\frac{f}{f_c}\right)^2} \qquad \text{...(16.21)}$$

For π section filter,

$$Z_{0\pi} = \frac{Z_1 Z_2}{Z_{OT}} = \frac{R_o}{\sqrt{1 - (f/f_c)^2}} \qquad \text{...(16.22)}$$

The variation of α, β and Z_o with frequency is shown in Fig. 16.7.

Design of Low Pass Filter. The load resistance and the characteristic impedance Z_o in the pass band should match. From Fig. 16.7, it is found that Z_o varies with frequency. Matching can be achieved only for one frequency and that is zero frequency.

Then $\quad Z_{OT} = Z_{O\pi} = R_a$

But for a LPF, $\quad R_o = \sqrt{L/C}$

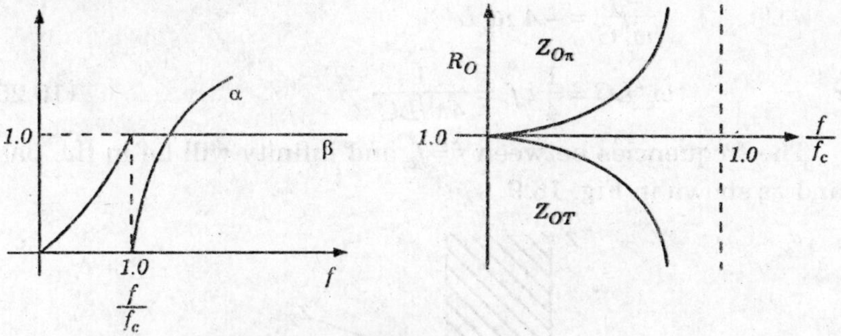

Fig. 16.7

At the upper cut off frequency, f_c

$$Z_1 = -4Z_2$$

i.e. $$\pi^2 f_c^{\,2} LC = 1$$

Substituting $R_o^{\,2} = L/C$, we get

$$\pi^2 f_c^{\,2} R_0^{\,2} C^2 = 1$$

Hence $$C = \frac{1}{\pi f_c R_o} \quad \text{...(16.23)}$$

and $$L = \frac{R_o}{\pi f_c} \quad \text{...(16.24)}$$

Using the above two equations, the *LPF* can be designed which will transfer maximum power only at zero frequency. The cut off from pass band to stop band is not sharp.

Proto Type High Pass Filter. A constant *k*-prototype *HPF* is shown in Fig. 16.8, with series impedance $Z_1 = -j/\omega C$ and shunt

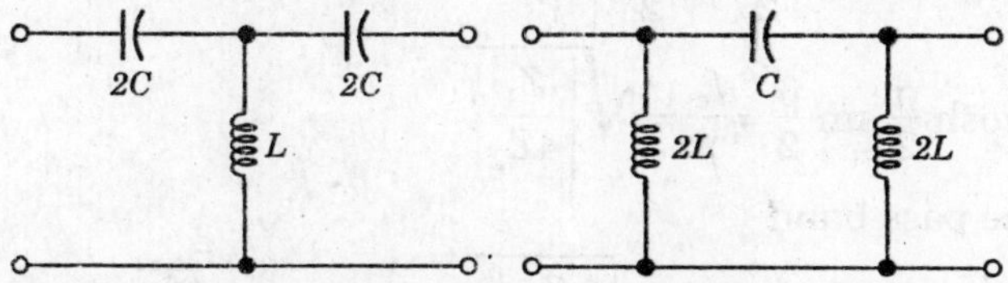

Fig. 16.8. *T* and π section *HPF*.

impedance $Z_2 = j\omega L$. Then $Z_1 Z_2 = L/C$ which indicates that it is constant *k* type filter.

Hence, we have $R_o = \sqrt{L/C}$

The cut off frequencies are obtained from $Z_1/Z_2 = 0$ and $\dfrac{Z_1}{4Z_2} = -1$. The second cut off frequency is infinity. The first cut off frequency is obtained from

$$\frac{-j}{\omega_c C} = -4\,j\omega_c L$$

or $$\omega_c^2 LC = \frac{1}{4}\,;\, f_c = \frac{1}{4\pi\sqrt{LC}} \qquad ...(16.25)$$

The frequencies between $f = f_c$ and infinity will lie in the pass band as shown in Fig. 16.9.

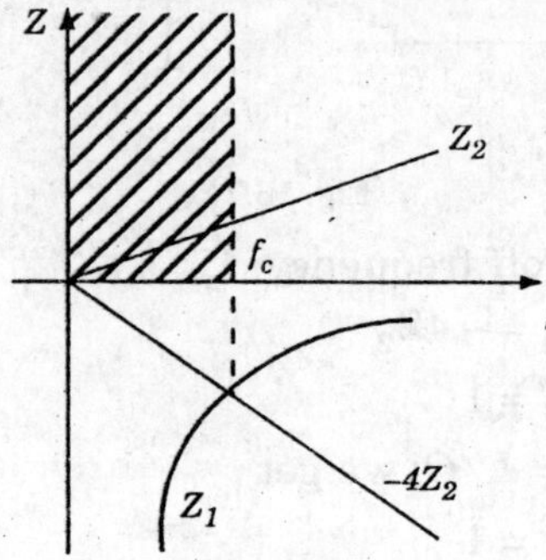

Fig. 16.9

Attenuation and phase shift. We know that

$$\sin\frac{\gamma}{2} = \sqrt{\frac{Z_1}{4Z_2}} = \sqrt{\frac{-1}{4\omega^2 LC}}$$

$$= j\,\frac{1}{2\omega\sqrt{LC}} = j\,\frac{f_c}{f}$$

i.e. $$\sinh\frac{\alpha}{2}\cos\frac{\beta}{2} + j\cosh\frac{\alpha}{2}\sin\frac{\beta}{2} = j\,\frac{f_c}{f}$$

Therefore, $\sinh\dfrac{\alpha}{2}\cos\dfrac{\beta}{2} = 0$

$$\cosh\frac{\alpha}{2}\sin\frac{\beta}{2} = \frac{f_c}{f} = \sqrt{\left|\frac{Z_1}{4Z_2}\right|}$$

In the pass band

$$\alpha = 0,\ \ \beta = 2\sin^{-1}\sqrt{\left|\frac{Z_1}{4Z_2}\right|} = \pm\, 2\sin^{-1}\sqrt{\frac{f_c}{f}}$$

At $f = f_c$, $\beta = \pm\, 2\sin^{-1}(1) = \pm\,\pi$ ...

In the attenuation band,

$$\beta = -\pi$$

$$\alpha = 2\cosh^{-1}\sqrt{\frac{Z_1}{4Z_2}} = 2\cosh^{-1}\sqrt{\frac{f_c}{f}}$$

Characteristic Impedance :

$$Z_{OT} = R_o \sqrt{1 - \frac{1}{4\omega^2 LC}} = R_o \sqrt{1 - \left(\frac{f_c}{f}\right)^2} \quad \text{...(16.26)}$$

$$Z_{O\pi} = \frac{R_o}{\sqrt{1 - (f_c/f)^2}} \quad \text{...(16.27)}$$

The variation of α, β in Z_o with frequency is shown in Fig. 16.10.

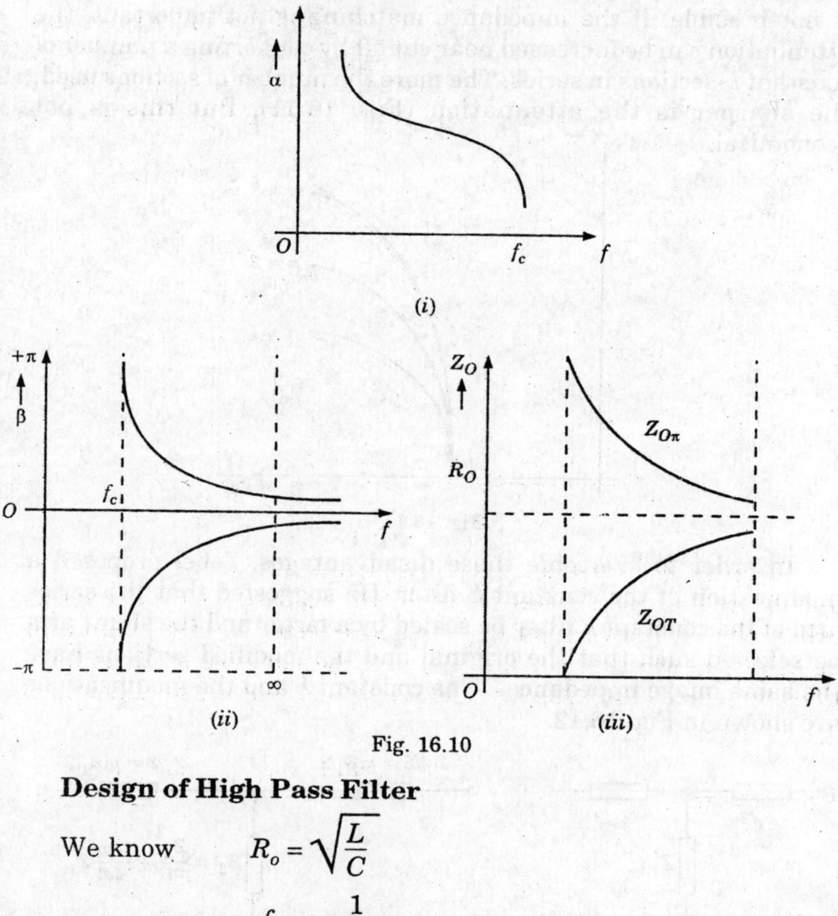

Fig. 16.10

Design of High Pass Filter

We know $R_o = \sqrt{\frac{L}{C}}$

$$f_c = \frac{1}{4\pi \sqrt{LC}}$$

Solving for L and C, we get

$$L = \frac{R_o}{4\pi f_c} \quad \text{...(16.28)}$$

$$C = \frac{1}{4\pi f_c R_o} \quad ...(16.29)$$

m-Derived Filter. The constant k proto type filters are very simple to design but suffer from two major drawbacks. The attenuation does not rise very sharply at cut off so that frequencies just beyond the pass band are not appreciably attenuated. This is shown in Fig. 16.11. Also the characteristic impedance varies very widely over the pass band, so that satisfactory impedance matching is not possible. If the impedance matching is not important, the attenuation can be increased near cut off by connecting a number of constant k-sections in series. The more the number of sections used, the sharper is the attenuation (Fig. 16.11). But this is not economical.

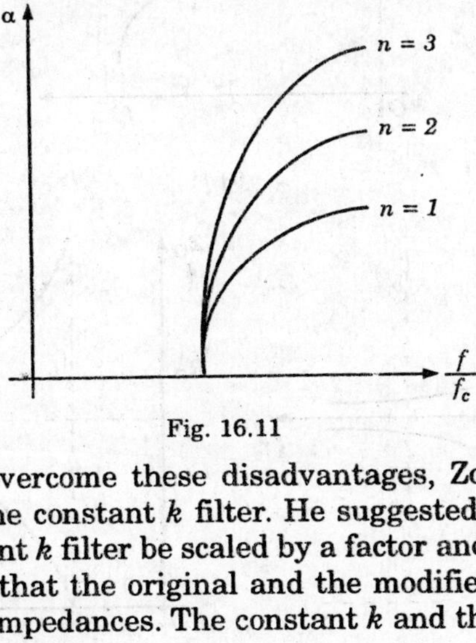

Fig. 16.11

In order to overcome these disadvantages, Zobel proposed a modification of the constant k filter. He suggested that the series arm of the constant k filter be scaled by a factor and the shunt arm be selected such that the original and the modified sections have the same image impedances. The constant k and the modifications are shown in Fig. 16.12.

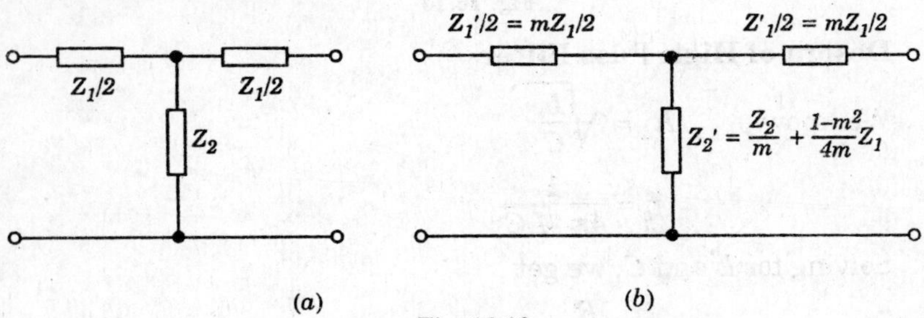

Fig. 16.12

Here, $\quad Z_1' = mZ_1 \quad ...(16.30)$

In order that the two sections have the same image or characteristic impedance,

$$Z_2' = \frac{Z_2}{m} + \frac{1-m^2}{4m} Z_1 \qquad \text{...(16.31)}$$

The shunt arm thus becomes a *L-C* combination (*i.e.*, a resonant circuit). At the resonant frequency of the shunt arm, it becomes a short circuit, thus allowing no signal to pass through ; *i.e.*, the attenuation is infinite. This frequency is thus termed f_∞ and will be higher than f_c for the L.P.F. The attenuation at other frequencies may be low and the performance of the filter can be improved by combining a constant *k* filter section and the *m*-derived filter. For the low pass filter, the constant *k* and the *m*-derived filters are shown in Fig. 16.13.

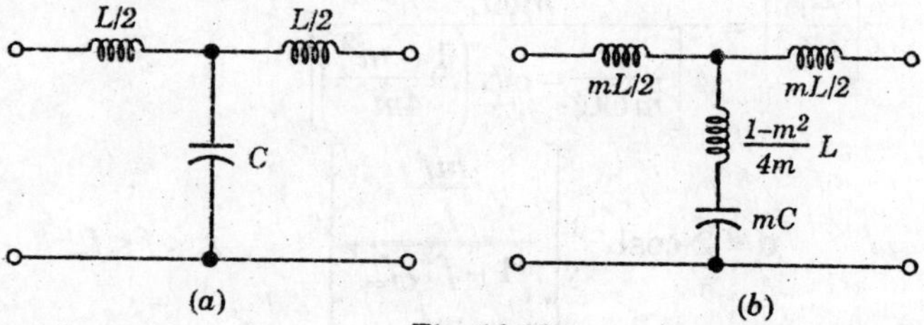

Fig. 16.13

Since *m* is an arbitrary constant, it is possible to design an infinite number of filters meeting the conditions on Z_o and f_c. But the two impedances in the shunt arm should be of opposite nature. This means $(1 - m^2)/4m$ must be positive. Thus *m* must be always chosen such that $0 < m < 1$.

Design of m-Derived Low Pass Filter. The design specification should give the cut off frequency f_c, the frequency of infinite attenuation, f_∞ and the design impedance, R_o. The cut off frequency for L.P.F. is

$$f_c = \frac{1}{\pi\sqrt{LC}}$$

At f_∞, the shunt arm will be constant.

i.e.,
$$\frac{Z_2}{m} = \frac{1-m^2}{4m} Z_1$$

or
$$\frac{1}{2\pi f_\infty mC} = \frac{1-m^2}{4m} 2\pi f_\infty L$$

Therefore,
$$f_\infty = \frac{1}{\pi\sqrt{1-m^2}} LC$$

or $$f_\infty = \frac{f_c}{\sqrt{1-m^2}} \qquad ...(16.32)$$

from which $$m = \sqrt{1-\left(\frac{f_c}{f_\infty}\right)^2} \qquad ...(16.33)$$

The value of 'm' is calculated from the above equation. The values of L and C are obtained as for the low pass constant k filter. The variation of attenuation in stop band is given by

$$\alpha = 2\cosh^{-1}\sqrt{\left|\frac{Z_1'}{4Z_2'}\right|} \qquad f_c < f < f_\infty$$

and $$\alpha = 2\sinh^{-1}\sqrt{\left|\frac{Z_1'}{4Z_2'}\right|} \qquad f_\infty < f$$

$$\left|\frac{Z_1'}{4Z_2'}\right| = \frac{m\omega L}{4\left[\frac{1}{m\omega C} - \omega L\left(\frac{1-m^2}{4m}\right)\right]}$$

$\therefore$ $$\alpha = 2\cosh^{-1}\left[\frac{\frac{mf}{f_c}}{\sqrt{1-f^2/f_\infty^2}}\right] \qquad f_c < f < f_\infty$$

and $$\alpha = 2\sinh^{-1}\left[\frac{\frac{mf}{f_c}}{\sqrt{f^2/f_\infty^2 - 1}}\right] \qquad f_\infty < f \qquad ...(16.34)$$

The phase shift in pass band is

$$\beta = 2\sin^{-1}\sqrt{\frac{Z_1'}{4Z_2'}}$$

$$= 2\sin^{-1}\frac{mf/f_c}{\sqrt{1-f^2/f_c^2\,(1-m^2)}} \qquad ...(16.35)$$

In the stop band, upto f_∞, β has the value of π. Above f_∞, β drops to zero as the shunt arm becomes inductive. These variations are shown in Fig. 16.14.

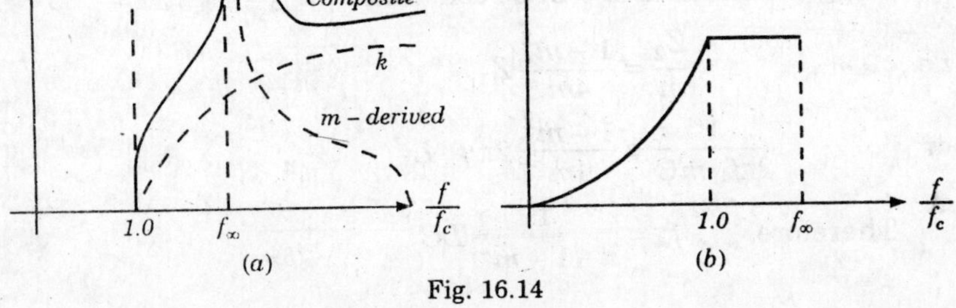

Fig. 16.14

m-Derived π Section Filter. The 'm' derived π section filter is shown in Fig. 16.15. The characteristic impedance is given by,

$$Z_{O\pi} = \frac{Z_1 Z_2}{Z_{OT}}$$

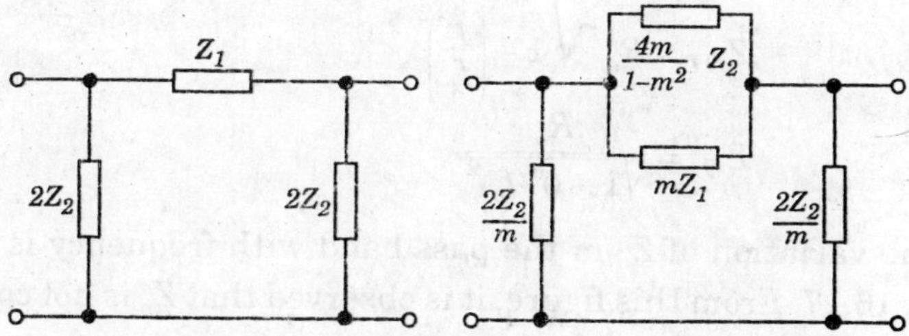

(a) Constant-k (b) m-derived

Fig. 16.15

For proper matching, the characteristic impedance of proto type and m derived filter sections should be equal. Assuming the shunt arm impedance $Z_2' = Z_2/m$, the series arm impedance Z_1' is obtained by equating the characteristic impedances.

i.e.
$$\frac{Z_1' \dfrac{Z_2}{m}}{\sqrt{Z_1' (Z_2/m)(1 + Z_1 m/4Z_2)}} = \frac{Z_1 Z_2}{\sqrt{Z_1 Z_2 (1 + Z_1/4Z_2)}}$$

Solving for Z_1' we get

$$Z_1' = \frac{1}{\dfrac{1}{mZ_1} + \dfrac{1}{\dfrac{4m}{1-m^2} Z_2}} \quad ...(16.36)$$

The series arm impedance Z_1' consists of two impedance in parallel ; one is mZ_1 and the other $\left(\dfrac{4m}{1-m^2}\right) Z_2$ as shown in Fig. 16.15 (b).

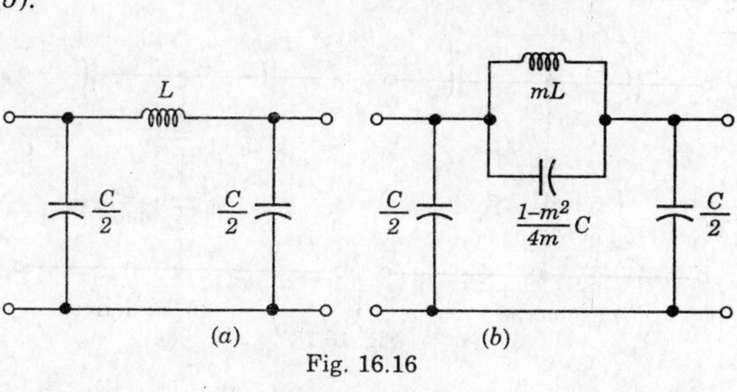

(a) (b)

Fig. 16.16

The m derived π section low pass filter and photo type filter are shown in Fig. 16.16.

The Variation of Characteristic Impedance. For a low pass filter, the characteristic impedance

$$Z_{OT} = R_o \sqrt{1 - \left(\frac{f}{f_c}\right)^2}$$

and $$Z_{O\pi} = \frac{R_o}{\sqrt{1 - (f/f_c)^2}}$$

The variation of Z_o in the pass band with frequency is shown in Fig. 16.17. From this figure, it is observed that Z_o is not constant over the pass band.

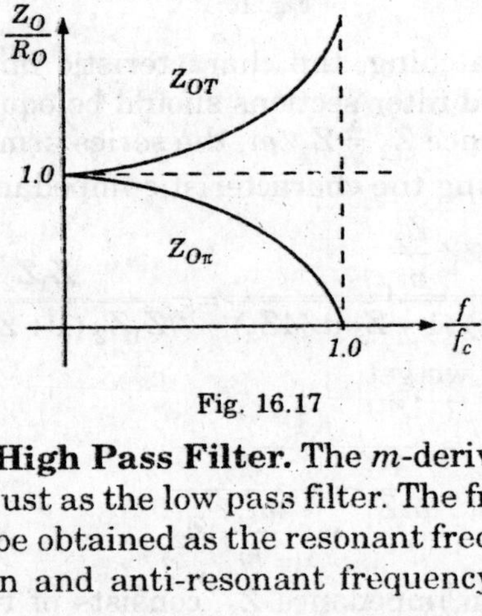

Fig. 16.17

m-Derived High Pass Filter. The m-derived high pass filter can be designed just as the low pass filter. The frequency of infinite attenuation can be obtained as the resonant frequency of the shunt arm for T-section and anti-resonant frequency of series arm for π-section.

The prototype and m derived high pass filter with T-section is shown in Fig. 16.18.

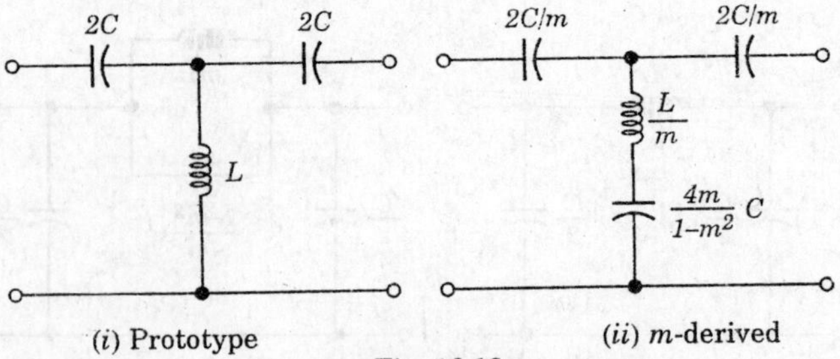

Fig. 16.18

The frequency of infinite attenuation is obtained from

$$\frac{\omega_\infty L}{m} = \frac{1}{\frac{4m}{1-m^2}\omega_\infty C}$$

or $$\omega_\infty^2 = \frac{1-m^2}{4LC}$$

But $$\omega_c = \frac{1}{2\sqrt{LC}}$$

Therefore, $$\omega_\infty^2 = (1-m^2)\,\omega_c^2$$

or $$f_\infty = f_c\sqrt{(1-m^2)}$$

Therefore, $$m = \sqrt{1-\left(\frac{f_\infty}{f_c}\right)^2} \quad ...(16.37)$$

The proto type and m-derived π-section high pass filters are shown in Fig. 16.19.

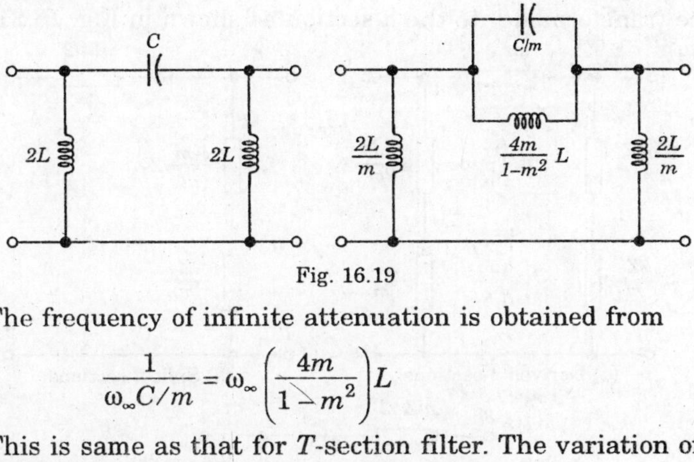

Fig. 16.19

The frequency of infinite attenuation is obtained from

$$\frac{1}{\omega_\infty C/m} = \omega_\infty\left(\frac{4m}{1-m^2}\right)L$$

This is same as that for T-section filter. The variation of α, β and Z_o with frequency is shown is Fig. 16.20.

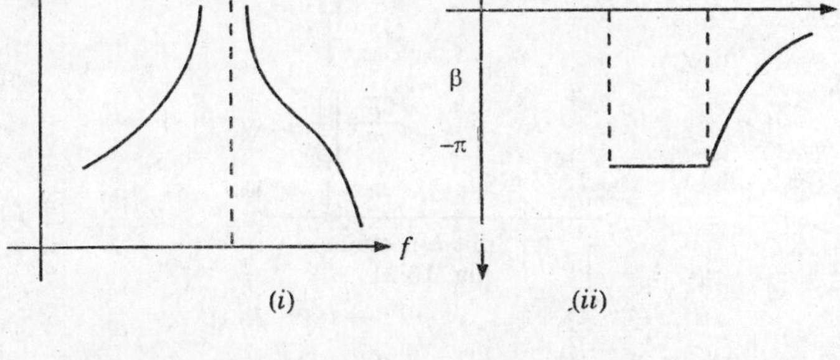

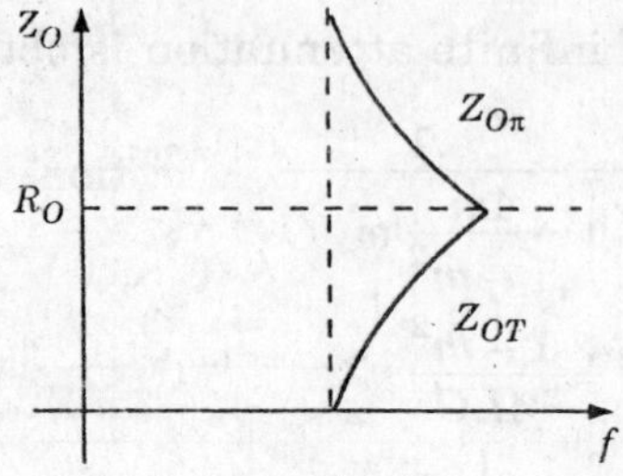

(iii)

Fig. 16.20

Termination with m-derived Half Filter. The first drawback namely the attenuation not being sharply increasing near the cut-off frequency, for the proto type filter is overcome by the m derived filter. But the second drawback is not eliminated ; *i.e.* the characteristic impedance Z_o is not constant over the entire pass band. Zobel has shown that by proper m derived L section terminations, a good impedance matching can be achieved, over the entire pass band. Consider the m derived T section filter which can be transformed into the π-section as shown in Fig. 16.21 (a).

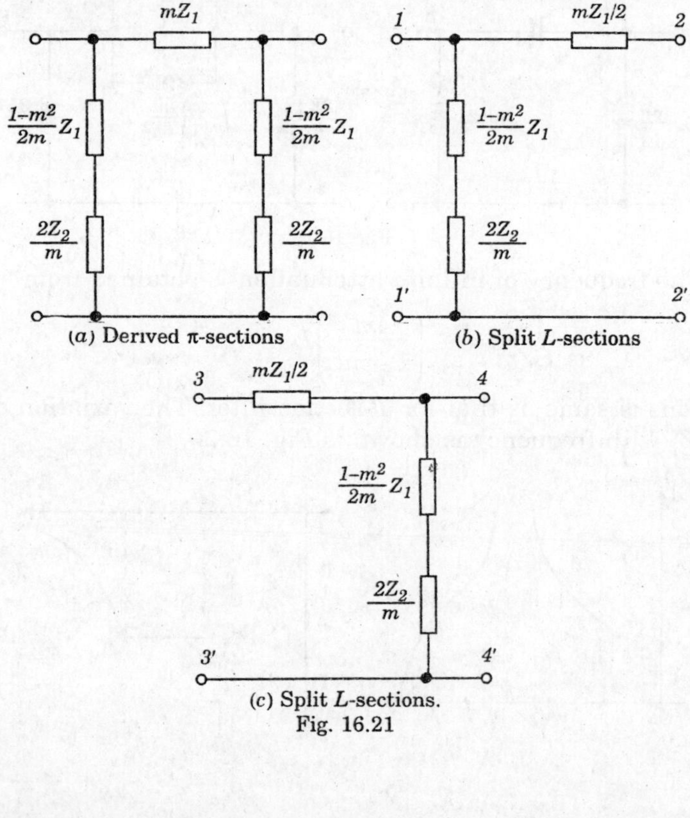

Fig. 16.21

This can further be split up into two L-sections as shown in Fig. 16.21 (b) and (c).

The image impedance of the left half section at 11′ is obtained from

$$Z_{1i} = \sqrt{Z_{10}\, Z_{1s}}$$

$$= \sqrt{\frac{(1 - m^2/2m\, Z_1 + 2Z_2/m)\,(1 - m^2/2m\, Z_1 + 2Z_2/m)\, mZ_1/2}{1 - m^2/2m\, Z_1 + 2Z_2/m + mZ_1/2}}$$

$$= \left(\frac{1 - m^2}{2m} Z_1 + \frac{2Z_2}{m}\right)\sqrt{\frac{(mZ_1/2)^2}{(1 - m^2)\, Z_1{}^2/4 + Z_1 Z_2 + m^2 Z_1{}^2/4}}$$

$$= \left(\frac{1 - m^2}{2m} Z_1 + \frac{2Z_2}{m}\right)\frac{mZ_1}{2}\sqrt{\frac{1}{Z_1 Z_2 (1 + Z_1/4Z_2)}}$$

$$= \left\{\frac{1 - m^2}{4} Z_1{}^2 + Z_1 Z_2\right\}\sqrt{\frac{Z_1 Z_2}{1 + (Z_1/4Z_2)}}$$

$$Z_{1i} = \left(1 + \frac{1 - m^2}{4}\frac{Z_1}{Z_2}\right) Z_{O\pi}$$

Similarly, the image impedance between terminals 22′ is obtained from

$$Z_{2i} = \sqrt{Z_{2o} Z_{2s}}$$

$$= \sqrt{\left(\frac{mZ_1}{2} + \frac{1 - m^2}{2m} Z_1 + \frac{2Z_2}{m}\right)\frac{mZ_1}{2}}$$

$$= \sqrt{Z_1 Z_2\left[1 + \frac{Z_1}{4Z_2}\right]} = Z_{OT}.$$

The image impedance between terminals 33′ will be same as Z_2 and $Z_{4i} = Z_{1i}$.

For a low pass filter,

$$Z_1 = j\omega L, \quad Z_2 = \frac{1}{j\omega C}$$

$$Z_{O\pi} = \frac{R_o}{\sqrt{1 - (f/f_c)^2}}$$

Therefore, $$Z_{1i} = \left[1 + (1 - m^2)\frac{j\omega L}{4}(j\omega C)\right]\frac{R_o}{\sqrt{1 - (f/f_c)^2}}$$

$$Z_{1i} = \left[1 - (1 - m^2)\frac{f^2}{f_c{}^2}\right]\frac{R_o}{\sqrt{1 - (f/f_c)^2}} = Z_{4i}$$

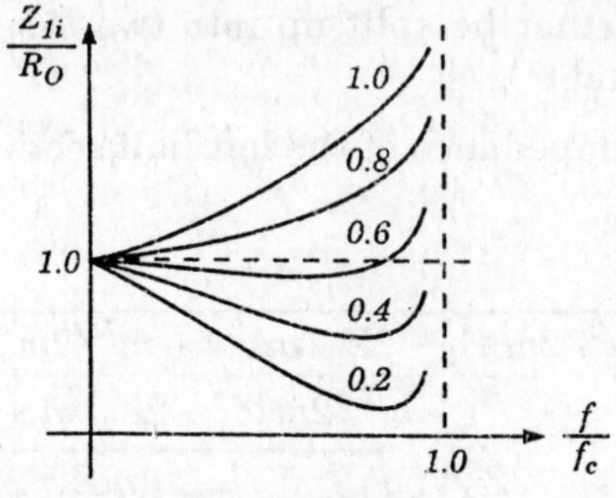

Fig. 16.22

$$Z_{2i} = Z_{3i} = \sqrt{\frac{j\omega L}{j\omega C}\left(1 + \frac{j\omega L}{4j\omega C}\right)} = R_o\sqrt{1 - \left(\frac{f}{f_c}\right)^2}$$

The image impedance, Z_{1i} is plotted against frequency in the pass band for different values of m as shown in Fig. 16.22. It is seen from the figure that for a value of $m = 0.6$, nearly a constant value of Z_{1i} equal to R_o is obtained over 85% of the pass band. Hence, a source with R_o can be matched satisfactorily at the terminals 11′ over most of the pass band.

Similar variation with m can be developed for the HPF.

Likewise a load of value R_o may be connected between terminals 44′ with a satisfactory matching. The prototype and m derived T section designed for a design impedance of R_o may be inserted, between terminals 22′ and 33′. The overall characteristic impedance will be very nearly constant at R_o except near cut off. All sections will be matched to maximum power transfer over atleast 85% of the pass band. The complete m derived filter section will be as shown in Fig. 16.23.

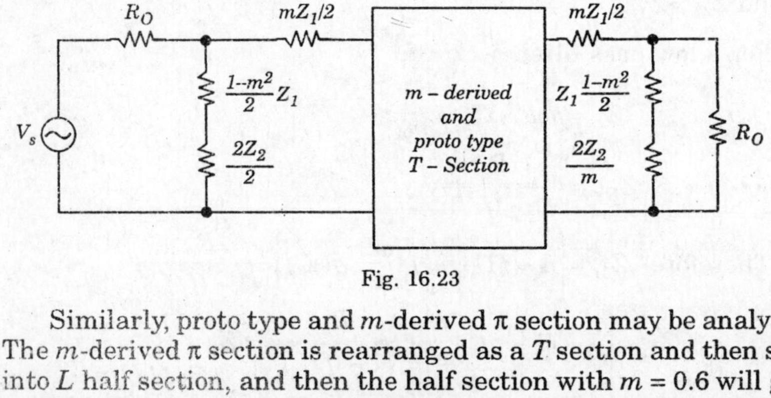

Fig. 16.23

Similarly, proto type and m-derived π section may be analysed. The m-derived π section is rearranged as a T section and then split into L half section, and then the half section with $m = 0.6$ will give satisfactory matching. The arrangement is shown in Fig. 16.24.

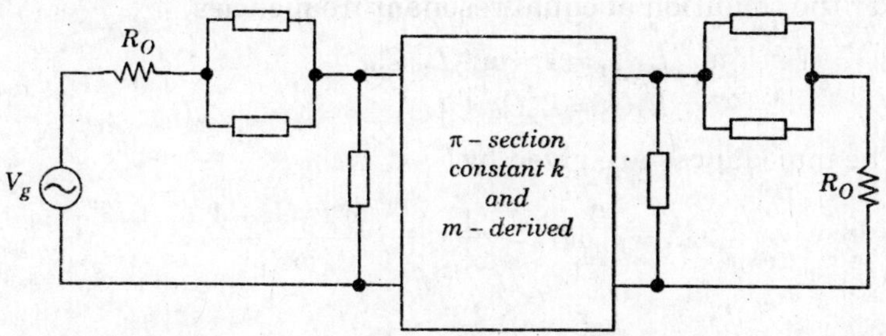

Fig. 16.24

Band Pass Filter. When it is desirable to pass a band of frequencies and block the frequencies on both sides of the pass band, we can combine a low pass and a high pass filter in series such that the cut off frequency of the low pass filter is higher than that of the high pass filter. But in practice, it is more economical to combine the low pass and high pass sections into a single filter section, called a band pass filter as shown in Fig. 16.25.

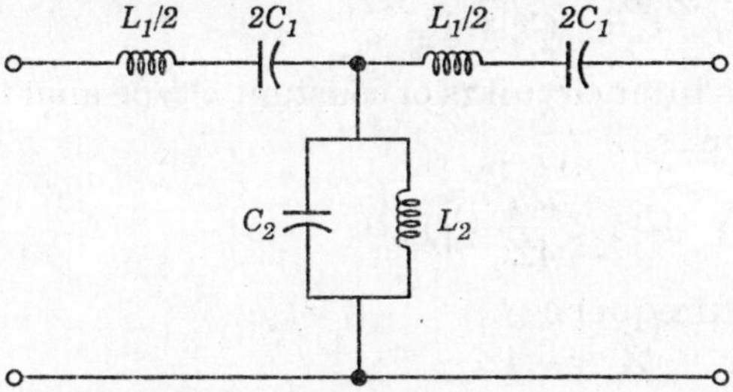

Fig. 16.25

In Fig. 16.25, the series arm is adjusted for series resonance and the shunt arm is adjusted for anti resonance at the same frequency. (The reactance curve of the circuit is shown in Fig. 16.26).

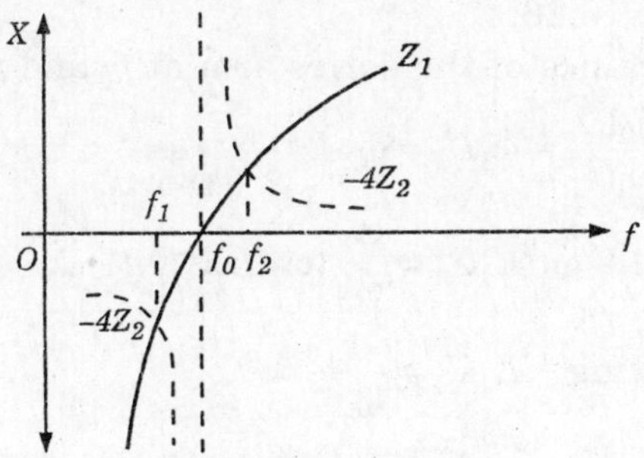

Fig. 16.26

For the condition of equal resonant frequencies,

$$\omega_o^2 L_1 C_1 = 1 = \omega_o^2 L_2 C_2$$

or
$$L_1 C_1 = L_2 C_2$$

The impedances are given by

$$Z_1 = j\left(\omega L_1 - \frac{1}{\omega C_1}\right) = j\,\frac{\omega^2 L_1 C_1 - 1}{\omega C_1}$$

and
$$Z_2 = \frac{j\omega L_2\left(-\frac{j}{\omega C_1}\right)}{j\omega L_2 - \frac{j}{\omega C_2}} = \frac{j\omega L_2}{1 - \omega^2 L_2 C_2}$$

Therefore, $Z_1 Z_2 = -\dfrac{\omega L_2 (\omega^2 L_1 C_1 - 1)}{\omega C_1 (1 - \omega^2 L_2 C_2)}$

But $L_1 C_1 = L_2 C_2$

Hence $$Z_1 Z_2 = \frac{L_2}{C_1} = \frac{L_1}{C_2} = R_o^2 \qquad \text{...(16.38)}$$

Thus, this filter circuit is of constant k type and, therefore, pass band condition is

$$-1 < \frac{Z_1}{4Z_2} < 0$$

At cut off frequency,

$$Z_1 = -4Z_2$$

or
$$Z_1^2 = -4Z_1 Z_2 = -4R_o^2$$

Therefore, $$Z_1 = \pm j\,2R_o \qquad \text{...(16.39)}$$

So at the lower cut off frequency $Z_1 = -j\,2R_o$ and at the upper cut off frequency $Z_1 = +j2R_o$, as shown by the reactance variation curve in Fig. 16.26.

The reactance of the series arm at f_1 and f_2 is given by

$$\frac{1}{\omega_1 C_1} - \omega_1 L_1 = \omega_2 L_1 - \frac{1}{\omega_2 C_1}$$

or
$$1 - \omega_1^2 L_1 C_1 = \frac{\omega_1}{\omega_2}(\omega_2^2 L_1 C_1 - 1)$$

Substituting $L_1 C_1 = \dfrac{1}{\omega_o^2}$

We have, $$1 - \frac{f_1^2}{f_o^2} = \frac{f_1}{f_2}\left(\frac{f_2^2}{f_o^2} - 1\right)$$

or $$f_o^2 (f_1 + f_2) = f_1 f_2 (f_1 + f_2)$$

or $$f_o = \sqrt{f_1 f_2} \qquad ...(16.40)$$

The frequency of resonance of the individual arms should be the geometric mean of the two frequencies cut off.

Design of Band Pass Filter. Let the filter be terminated in a load $R = R_o$. At the frequency $f = f_1$,

$$\frac{1}{\omega_1 C_1} - \omega_1 L_1 = 2R_o$$

or $$1 - \frac{f_1^2}{f_o^2} = 4\pi R_o f_1 C_1$$

Using $f_o^2 = f_1 f_1$, we can solve for C_1 as

$$C_1 = \frac{f_2 - f_1}{4\pi R_o f_1 f_2} \qquad ...(16.41)$$

and $$L_1 C_1 = \frac{1}{\omega_o^2}$$

Therefore, $$L_1 = \frac{R_o}{\pi (f_2 - f_1)} \qquad ...(16.42)$$

We know that, $R_o^2 = \dfrac{L_2}{C_1} = \dfrac{L_1}{C_2}$

Therefore, $$L_2 = C_1 R_o^2 \qquad ...(16.43)$$

$$L_2 = \frac{(f_2 - f_1) R_o}{4\pi f_1 f_2} \qquad ...(16.44)$$

$$C_2 = \frac{L_1}{R_o^2}$$

Therefore, $$C_2 = \frac{1}{\pi R_o (f_2 - f_1)} \qquad ...(16.45)$$

Thus the band pass filter can be completely designed using the above equations. It is also possible to obtain an m-derived band pass filter, by combining the m-derived low pass and high pass into one single circuit.

Band Elimination Filter. Band elimination filter is one in which a band of frequencies say from f_1 to f_2 is eliminated and the rest of the frequencies are passed. This can be achieved by combining a low pass filter and a high pass filter in cascade provided the cut off frequency of the low pass filter is below that of the high pass filter. But in practice, it is more economical to combine into one circuit as shown in Fig. 16.27.

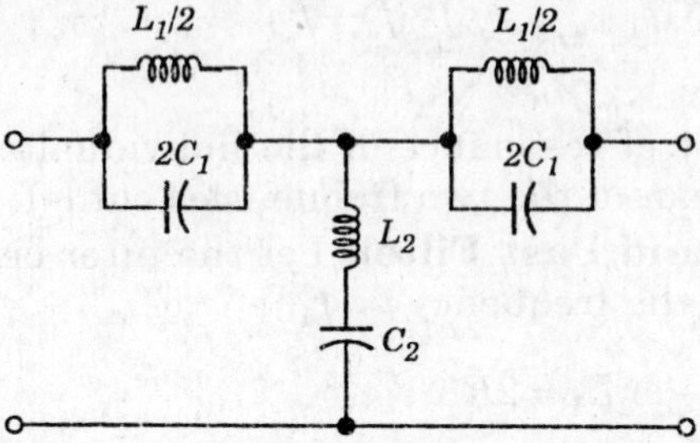

Fig. 16.27

As in the band pass filter, the series and shunt arms are made to antiresonate and resonate at the same frequency, f_o

The shunt impedance

$$Z_2 = j\omega L_2 - \frac{j}{\omega C_2}$$

and the series impedance

$$Z_1 = \frac{j\omega L_1\left(-\frac{j}{\omega C_1}\right)}{j\omega L_1 - \frac{j}{\omega C_1}} = \frac{\frac{L_1}{C_1}}{j\left(\omega L_1 - \frac{1}{\omega C_1}\right)}$$

Then $$Z_1Z_2 = \frac{j\left(\omega L_2 - \frac{1}{\omega C_2}\right)\frac{L_1}{C_1}}{j\left(\omega L_1 - \frac{1}{\omega C_1}\right)}$$

The resonant and antiresonant condition is

$$\omega_o^2 L_1C_1 = 1 = \omega_o^2 L_2C_2$$

i.e. $$L_1C_1 = L_2C_2$$

Hence $Z_1Z_2 = \frac{L_1}{C_2} = \frac{L_2}{C_1}$ is a constant equal to R_o^2 and also we can show that $f_o^2 = f_1 f_2$. The band elimination filter is thus of the constant k-type. For such a filter, the pass band condition is $-1 < \frac{Z_1}{4Z_2} < 0$. The cut off frequency is obtained from $Z_1 = -4Z_2$.

Multiplying both sides by Z_2 we get

$$Z_1Z_2 = -4Z_2^2 = R_o^2$$

Therefore, $Z_2 = \pm j R_o/2$ ...(16.46)

If the filter is terminated with a load $R_L = R_o$, at the lower cut off frequency

$$Z_2 = j\frac{1}{\omega_1 C_2} - \omega_1 L_2 = j\frac{R_o}{2}$$

i.e.
$$[1 - \omega_1{}^2 L_2C_2] = \frac{\omega_1 C_2 R_o}{2}$$

We know that $L_2C_2 = \dfrac{1}{\omega_o{}^2}$ and $f_o{}^2 = f_1 f_2$

$$\therefore \qquad 1 - \frac{f_1{}^2}{f_1 f_2} = \pi f_1 C_2 R_o$$

or
$$C_2 = \frac{f_2 - f_1}{\pi R_o f_1 f_2} \qquad \text{...(16.47)}$$

$$L_1 = C_2 R_o{}^2 = \frac{(f_2 - f_1)\, R_o}{\pi f_1 f_2} \qquad \text{...(16.48)}$$

Also,
$$f_0 = \sqrt{f_1 f_2} = \frac{1}{2\pi\sqrt{L_2 C_2}}$$

or
$$L_2 = \frac{1}{4\pi^2 C_1 f_1 f_2} = \frac{R_o}{4\pi\,(f_2 - f_1)} \qquad \text{...(16.49)}$$

$$C_1 = \frac{L_2}{R_o{}^2} = \frac{1}{4\pi R_o\,(f_2 - f_1)} \qquad \text{...(16.50)}$$

Using these equations, the band elimination filter can be designed given the two cut off frequencies and the design impedance.

Example 16.1. *Design a constant k low pass filter to cut off at 2 kHz with a characteristic impedance of 600 ohms.*

Solution. Using Equations (16.23) and (16.24),

$$C = \frac{1}{\pi f_c R_o} = 0.2653\ \mu\text{F}$$

and
$$L = \frac{R_o}{\pi f_c} = 95.5\ \text{mH}$$

The filter is shown in Fig. 16.28.

If we use a π filter, for the same specifications, we get the Fig. 16.29.

Example 16.2. *Design a constant k-high pass filter to cut off at 5 kHz. Assume a characteristic impedance of 600 ohms.*

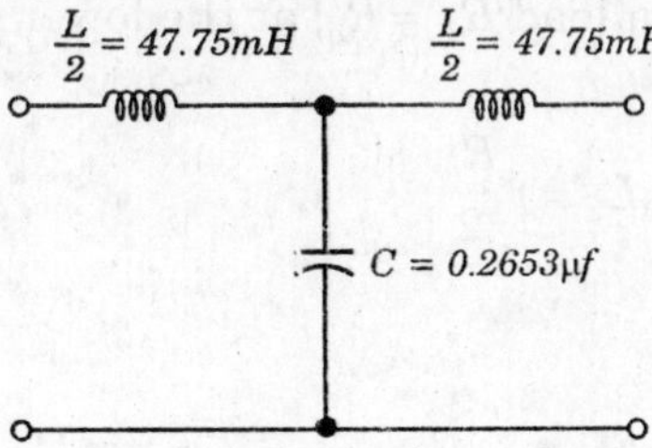

Fig. 16.28

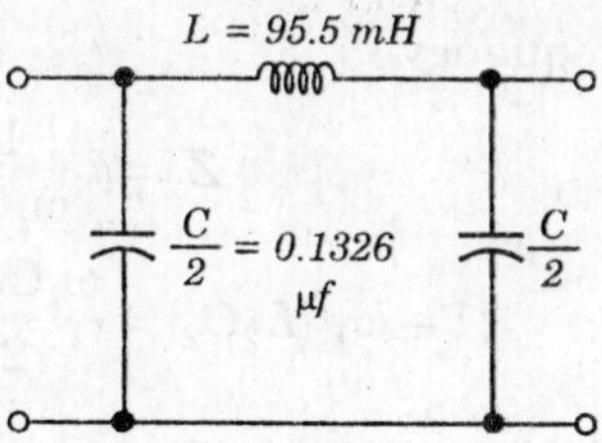

Fig. 26.29

Solution. From Eqs. (16.28) and (16.29)

$$L = \frac{R_o}{4\pi f_c} = 9.55 \text{ mH}$$

$$C = \frac{1}{4\pi f_c \, r_o} = 0.02653 \text{ μF}$$

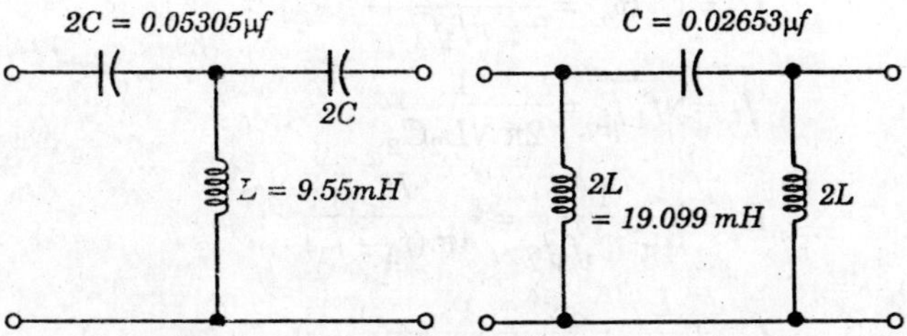

(a) (b)

Fig. 16.30

The T and π sections are shown in Figs. 16.30 (a) and (b).

Example 16.3. *In the example of 16.2, find the frequency at which the section will have an attenuation of 16 dB.*

Solution. From Equations (16.17), we know

Attenuation in dB = 8.686 × Attenuations in nepers.

Therefore, attenuation (nepers)

$$= \frac{\text{Attenuation in dB}}{8.686} = \frac{15}{8.686} = 1.727 \text{ nepers.}$$

$$\alpha = 2 \cosh^{-1} (f/f_c)$$

Therefore, $f/f_c = \cosh (\alpha/2) = \cosh 0.863$

$= 1.396$ (from tables)

Therefore, $f = 1.396 \times 2{,}000 = 2792$ Hz.

Example 16.4. *Design a constant k-LPF to cut off at 1000 Hz and a load of 500 ohms. Calculate the attenuation at 1500 Hz and phase shift at 50 Hz.*

Solution. $L = \frac{R_o}{\pi f_c} = 0.1592 \text{ H}$

and $C = \frac{1}{\pi f_c R_o} = 0.63662 \ \mu\text{F}$

The T section is shown in Fig. 16.31.

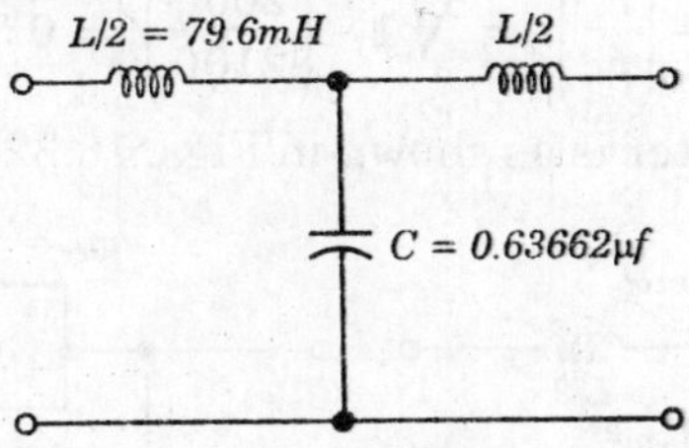

Fig. 16.31

Attenuation at 1500 Hz,

$$\alpha = 2 \cosh^{-1} (1500/1000)$$
$$= 2 \cosh^{-1} (1.5) = 1.925$$

Phase shift at 50 Hz,

$$\beta = 2 \sin^{-1} (50/1000) = 5.732°$$

Example 16.5. *Design a LPF of the constant k type to cut off at 1000 Hz with load impedance of 200 ohms. Find the attenuation constant at a frequency of 1,500 Hz and phase shift at 500 Hz.*

Solution. $L = \frac{R_o}{\pi f_c} = 63.66 \text{ mH}$

$$C = \frac{1}{\pi f_c R_o} = 1.59 \ \mu\text{F}$$

attenuation, α at 1500 Hz = 2 cosh (1500/1000) = 4.705

Phase shift, β at 1500 Hz

$$= 2 \sin^{-1} \frac{500}{1000} = 60°$$

Example 16.6. *Design a constant-k high pass filter to operate with a load of 200 ohms and have a cut off frequency of 5 kHz.*

Solution. $L = \frac{R_o}{4\pi f_c} = 3.18 \text{ mH}$

$$C = \frac{1}{4\pi f_c R_o} = 0.0796 \ \mu\text{F}.$$

Example 16.7. *Design an m-derived low pass filter of characteristic impedance, 600 ohms, and cut off frequency 2 kHz. The frequency of infinite attenuation, f_∞ is 2.1 kHz.*

Solution. The filter (of the constant k-type) has already been designed in Example 16.1. This has to be modified using the factor m

$$m = \sqrt{1 - \left(\frac{f_c}{f_\infty}\right)^2} = \sqrt{1 - \left(\frac{2000}{2100}\right)^2} = 0.305$$

The m-derived filter is as shown in Figs. 16.32 for T-section and 16.33 for π section.

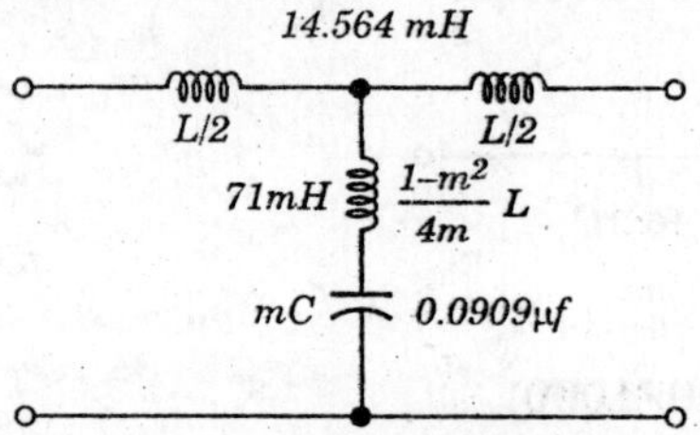

Fig. 16.32

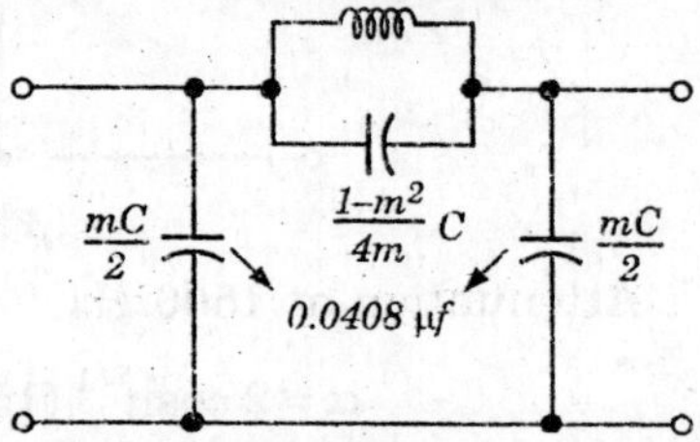

Fig. 16.33

Example 16.8. *Design an m derived filter to meet the specifications in Ex. 16.2. Use m= 0.35. Find also the frequency of infinite attenuation.*

Solution. In Ex. 16.2, the constant-k filter has already been designed. The m-derived filter sections are shown in Fig. 16.34 (a) and (b).

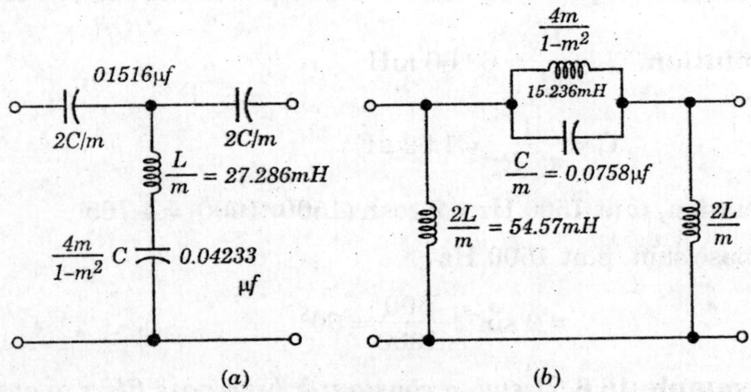

Fig. 16.34

Since, $m = \sqrt{1 - \left(\frac{f_\infty}{f_c}\right)^2}$

$$f_\infty = \sqrt{1 - m^2}\, f_c = 4.684 \text{ kHz}.$$

Example 16.9. *Design a low pass composite filter for $f_c = 2$ kHz and impedance 600 ohms. Frequency of infinite attenuation is 2.1 kHz. Provide half-section terminated for $m = 0.6$.*

Solution. The filter consists of a constant-k section, with a m-derived section to have infinite attenuation at 2.1 kHz. The end sections are half sections of m-derived structure with $m = 0.6$.

The values for constant k and m-derived have already been obtained in Problem 16.7. Fig. 16.35 shows the composite filter in its reduced form.

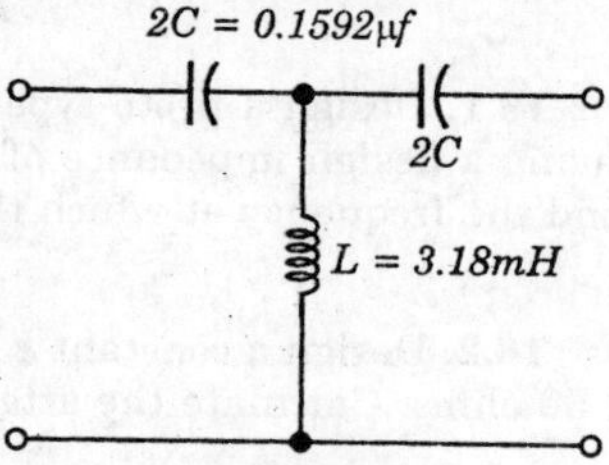

Fig. 16.35

Example 16.10. *Design a composite low pass filter to satisfy the following specifications.*

Cut-off frequency : *2 kHz*
Design impedance : *600 ohms*
Frequencies of infinite attenuation : *2.2 kHz and 4 kHz.*

Solution. The filter has three sections, *viz.*, a constant-k section with two m-derived sections to produce the transmission zeros at 2.2 kHz and 4 kHz. The end sections are half sections of m-derived structure with $m = 0.6$.

The constant k-section has already been designed (Ex. 16.1).

For $\quad f_\infty = 2.2 \text{ kHz}, \; m_1 = \sqrt{1 - \left(\dfrac{2}{2.2}\right)^2} = 0.4166$

for $\quad f_\infty = 4 \text{ kHz}, \; m_2 = \sqrt{1 - \left(\dfrac{2}{4}\right)^2} = 0.866$

Example 16.11. *Design a band pass filter with cut of frequencies of 2 kHz and 5 kHz and a characteristic impedance of 500 ohms.*

Solution. From Equations (16.41) to (16.45)

$$C_1 = \frac{f_2 - f_1}{4\pi R_o f_1 f_2} = 0.04775 \text{ μF}$$

$$L_1 = \frac{R_o}{\pi (f_2 - f_1)} = 53.05 \text{ mH}$$

$$L_2 = \frac{(f_2 - f_1) R_o}{4\pi f_1 f_2} = 11.94 \text{ mH}$$

$$C_2 = \frac{1}{\pi R_o (f_2 - f_1)} = 0.2122\ \mu\text{F}.$$

The values may be entered in Fig. 16.25.

EXERCISES

16.1. Design a proto type (constant k) low pass filter (T and π sections) having a design impedance of 600 ohms and a cut off frequency of 2000 Hz. Find the frequency at which the attenuation is 10 dB.

[**Ans.** $L = 95.5$ mH, $C = 0.2652\ \mu$F, $f = 2340$ Hz]

16.2. Design a constant k low pass filter to cut off at 1000 Hz with a load of 50 ohms. Calculate the attenuation at 1500 Hz.

[**Ans.** $L = 15.92$ mH, $C = 6.37\ \mu$F, $\alpha = 16.75$ dB]

16.3. Design a hpf to cut off at 1.5 kHz with R_o = 1000 ohms. What is the phase shift at 2500 Hz and the characteristic impedance ? What will be the attenuation at 1000 Hz ?

16.4. A π section lpf has a cut off frequency of 1 rad/sec and a load termination of 1 ohm. Design its elements.

16.5. Design a constant-k high pass filter with $f_c = 4$ kHz and $R_o = 600$ ohms. Design the corresponding m-derived filter to have infinite attenuation at 3.5 kHz.

16.6. A filter is required to pass all signals between 9.5 kHz and 10.5 kHz and attenuate the others with a load of 100 ohms. Design the elements.

16.7. Design a constant k lpf to cut off at 5 k rad/sec with a load of 100 ohms.

16.8. Design a composite lpf terminated by 600 ohms resistance. $f_c = 1000$ Hz. $f_\infty = 1250$ Hz.

16.9. Design a m-derived HPF with f_c = 2000 Hz and R_o = 600 Ω with very high attenuation at 1700 Hz.

16.10. A filter is to pass the band between 1250 Hz and 2000 Hz and is desired to load into a 400 ohm termination. Design a filter circuit.

16.11. Design a band elimination filter to cut the frequencies from 100 Hz to 5000 Hz and to have a design impedance of 600 ohms.

16.12. What is the cut off frequency of a LP Filter constant-k, π-section when the series arm is 20 h inductance and each shunt arm is 8 μF capacitor? Find also the characteristic impedance. [**Ans.** 1779 Hz, 1125 ohm]

16.13. Design a T-type attenuator to give 40 dB attenuation with R_o = 600 ohms.

16.14. Design a constant-k lpf for f_c = 7.5 kHz and R_o = 600 ohms.

16.15. Design a T section hpf with f_c = 10 kHz and R_o = 600 ohms. Find the characteristic impedance at 25 kHz and the attenuation at 5 kHz.

16.16. Design a π section constant-k hpf with f_c = 8 kHz and R_o = 600 ohms. Find also the characteristic impedance at 12 kHz and attenuation at 800 Hz.

SEVENTEEN

FOURIER SERIES

17.1. Introduction

In the earlier chapters, we have seen how to calculate the current (or response) in a circuit subjected to a sinusoidally varying voltage source. The steady state and transient responses of a circuit to sinusoidal excitations can be easily found using the techniques described in those chapters. But what if the applied voltage is not sinusoidal, but some arbitrary function ? How can we handle arbitrary excitation functions? Arbitrary waveforms (subject to certain conditions) can be split into a series of sinusoidal components. Arbitrary waveforms can therefore be discussed in terms of their frequency spectra. By superimposing the responses to the various sinusoidal components, we may obtain the overall response.

It will be seen that arbitrary periodic waveforms can be split into Fourier series of harmonic sinusoidal components. Non-periodic functions can be expanded into Fourier integrals.

17.2. Fourier Series

A function $f(t)$ is said to be periodic with period T, if

$$f(t + nT) = f(t), \qquad n = 1, 2, 3, \ldots$$

for all values of t. We have seen several periodic waveforms in Chapter 5. The French mathematician, J.B.T. Fourier stated, in 1822, that arbitrary periodic functions satisfying certain conditions can be expanded into an infinite trigonometric series consisting of sine and consine terms. The Fourier theorem states as follows : A periodic function $f(\theta)$ with period 2π that satisfies Dirichlet conditions, *viz.*

(*i*) that it has at most a finite number of discontinuities per period.

(*ii*) that it has at most a finite number of maxima and minima in a period and (*iii*) that the integral

$\int_{-\pi}^{\pi} |f(\theta)|\, d\theta$ exists and is finite, can be expanded into a Fourier series such that

$$f(\theta) = \frac{a_o}{2} + a_1 \cos\theta + a_2 \cos 2\theta + a_3 \cos 3\theta + \ldots$$
$$+ b_1 \sin\theta + b_2 \sin 2\theta + b_3 \sin 3\theta + \ldots$$
$$= \frac{a_o}{2} + \sum_{n=1}^{\infty} (a_n \cos n\theta + b_n \sin n\theta)$$

where the co-efficients a_o, a_n and b_n are given by

$$a_n = \frac{1}{\pi}\int_{-\pi}^{\pi} f(t) \cos n\theta\, d\theta, \quad n = 1, 2, 3, \ldots$$

$$b_n = \frac{1}{\pi}\int_{-\pi}^{\pi} f(\theta) \sin n\theta\, d\theta, \quad n = 1, 2, 3, \ldots$$

and $$\frac{a_o}{2} = \frac{1}{2\pi}\int_{-\pi}^{\pi} f(\theta)\, d\theta$$

which is the average value of the function $f(\theta)$, over a period.

If the given function is a function of time, as is usual in circuit problems, we have to modify the earlier equations accordingly. We substitute $\theta = \omega t$ here ω is the angular velocity equal to $2\pi f$ or $2\pi/T$ where T is the time period.

We then have

$$f(t) = \frac{a_o}{2} + \sum_{n=1}^{\infty} (a_n \cos n\omega t + b_n \sin n\omega t)$$

where $$a_n = \frac{2}{T}\int_{-T/2}^{T/2} f(t) \cos n\omega t\, dt, \quad n = 0, 1, 2, \ldots$$

and $$b_n = \frac{2}{T}\int_{-T/2}^{-T/2} f(t) \sin n\omega t\, dt, \quad n = 1, 2, 3, \ldots$$

The function $f(t)$ can also be expressed in alternate form, as follows :

$$f(t) = \frac{a_o}{2} + \sum_{n=1}^{\infty} C_n \cos(n\omega t - \alpha_n)$$

where $C_n = \sqrt{a_n^2 + b_n^2}$

and $\alpha_n = \tan^{-1}(b_n/a_n)$

Thus we have seen that an arbitrary periodic function satisfying the Dirichlet's conditions can be split into an average value plus harmonic components with a fundamental frequency and integral multiple of this frequency. If the magnitude of C_n is plotted with respect to the frequency, we have, what may be called the frequency spectrum. On the X-axis, we have, ω, 2ω, 3ω, 4ω etc., and the magnitude of each frequency component is marked

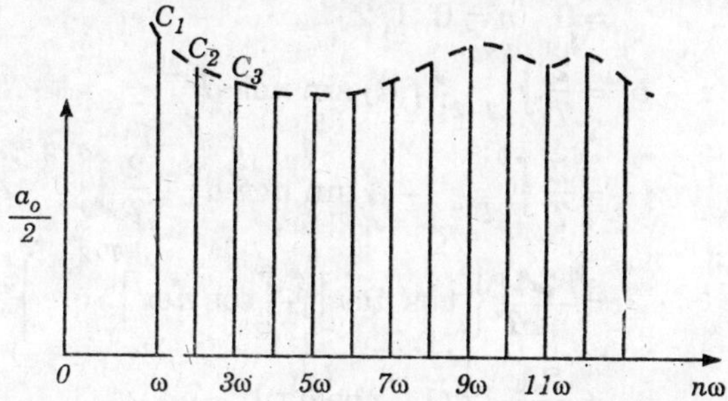

Fig. 17.1

as shown in Fig. 17.1. The values C_1, C_2, C_3 etc. exist only for integral values of ω. The component at $\omega = 0$ gives the average value. As T increases, ω decreases and the lines become closer. When $T \to \infty$ (the period becomes infinite, or in otherwords the function is non-periodic) the discrete spectrum of Fig. 17.1 becomes a continuous spectrum and the Fourier series becomes a Fourier integral. The method of handling non-periodic functions in discussed later in this chapter.

Example 17.1. *Find the Fourier series expansion and the frequency spectrum of the rectangular wave shown in Fig. 17.2.*

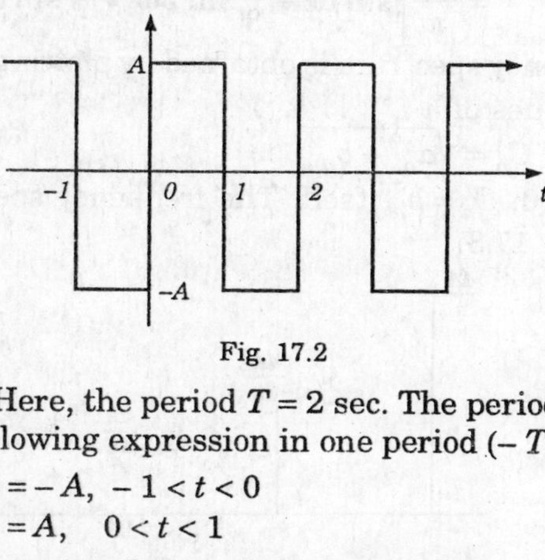

Fig. 17.2

Solution. Here, the period $T = 2$ sec. The periodic waveform is given by the following expression in one period $(-T/2$ to $T/2)$

$$f(t) = -A, \quad -1 < t < 0$$

$$f(t) = A, \quad 0 < t < 1$$

We now determine the co-efficients a_n and b_n.

$$a_n = \frac{2}{T}\int_{-T/2}^{T/2} f(t)\cos n\omega t\, dt$$

$$= \frac{2}{T}\int_{-T/2}^{0} -A\cos n\omega t\, dt + \frac{2}{T}\int_{0}^{T/2} A\cos n\omega t\, dt$$

$$= \frac{2A}{n\omega T}\left\{\left[-\sin n\omega t\right]_{-T/2}^{0} + \left[\sin n\omega t\right]_{0}^{T/2}\right\}$$

$$= 0, \quad n = 0, 1, 2, ..$$

$$b_n = \frac{2}{T}\int_{-T/2}^{T/2} f(t)\sin n\omega t\, dt$$

$$= \frac{2}{T}\int_{-T/2}^{0} -A\sin n\omega t\, dt + \frac{2}{T}\int_{0}^{T/2} A\sin n\omega t\, dt$$

$$= \frac{2A}{n\omega T}\left\{\left[\cos n\omega t\right]_{-T/2}^{0} - \left[\cos n\omega t\right]_{0}^{T/2}\right\}$$

$$= \frac{2A}{2n\pi}[2(1 - \cos n\pi)]$$

since $\omega T = 2\pi$

$$b_n = \frac{2A}{n\pi}(1 - \cos n\pi), \quad n = 1, 2, 3, \ldots$$

Hence, we may write the Fourier series as

$$f(t) = \sum_{n=1}^{\infty} \frac{2A}{n\pi}(1 - \cos n\pi)\sin n\omega t$$

$$= \frac{4A}{\pi}\sin \omega t + \frac{4A}{3\pi}\sin 3\omega t + \frac{4A}{5\pi}\sin 5\omega t + \ldots$$

$$= \frac{4A}{\pi}\left[\sin \omega t + \frac{1}{3}\sin 3\omega t + \frac{1}{5}\sin 5\omega t + \ldots\right]$$

The frequency spectrum is obtained by plotting C_n with respect to integral values of n

$$C_n = \sqrt{a_n^{\,2} + b_n^{\,2}}$$

Since $a_n = 0$, $C_n = b_n$ itself. The frequency spectrum is shown plotted in Fig. 17.3.

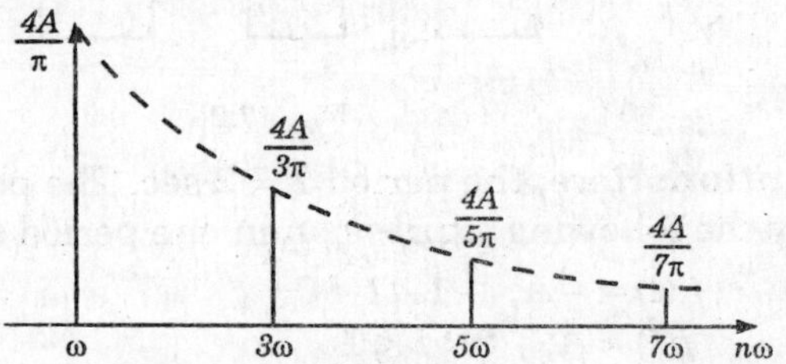

Fig. 17.3

17.3. Symmetry Conditions

In the previous problem, we have seen that the co-efficient $a_n = 0$ and in the Fourier expansion only the sine terms are present. Further, even amoung the sine terms, the even terms are absent. This is because the given functions satisfies some rules of symmetry. These will be discussed under two different categories : (*a*) Cosine or sine terms only and (*b*) even or odd terms only.

(*a*) **Cosine or sine terms only.** Consider a function satisfying the relationship

$$f(t) = f(-t).$$

Such a function is symmetric with respect to the *Y*-axis and is called an even function. When $f(t)$ is even,

$$b_n = \frac{2}{T}\int_{-T/2}^{T/2} f(t)\sin n\omega t\, dt$$

$$= \frac{2}{T}\left[\int_{-T/2}^{0} f(t)\sin n\omega t\, dt + \int_{0}^{T/2} f(t)\sin n\omega t\, dt\right]$$

$$= \frac{2}{T}\left[\int_{-T/2}^{0} f(-\alpha)\sin n\omega\alpha\, d\alpha + \int_{0}^{T/2} f(t)\sin n\omega t\, dt\right]$$

$$= \frac{2}{T}\left[\int_{0}^{-T/2} f(\alpha)\sin n\omega\alpha\, d\alpha + \int_{0}^{T/2} f(t)\sin n\omega t\, dt\right]$$

$$= 0$$

Here, we have replaced t by $-\alpha$ in the first integral. Thus, when $f(t)$ is even, $b_n = 0$ implying that no sine terms are present in its Fourier expansion.

Now consider a function satisfying

$$f(t) = -f(-t)$$

Such a function is called an odd function. For odd functions,

$$a_n = \frac{2}{T}\int_{-T/2}^{T/2} f(t)\cos n\omega t\, dt$$

$$= \frac{2}{T}\left[-\int_{-T/2}^{0} f(-\alpha)\cos n\omega\alpha\, d\alpha + \int_{0}^{T/2} f(t)\cos n\omega t\, dt\right]$$

$$= \frac{2}{T}\left[-\int_{0}^{T/2} f(\alpha)\cos n\omega\alpha\, d\alpha + \int_{0}^{T/2} f(t)\cos n\omega t\, dt\right] = 0.$$

Thus for odd functions, $a_n = 0$ and cosine terms are not present in the Fourier expansion.

(*b*) **Even or odd terms only.** A periodic wave $f(t)$ of period T contains only even harmonics if it has half-wave symmetry *i.e.* $f(t) = f(t \pm T/2)$

Such a function actually repeats itself every $T/2$ second. Its Fourier expansion consists of Cosine and sine terms but all odd terms are absent.

Similarly, a periodic wave $f(t)$ of period T contains only odd harmonics if it satisfies the relation

$$f(t) = -f(t \pm T/2)$$

The Fourier expansion consists of cosine and sine terms but all even terms are absent.

When a function is given to be split into its Fourier components, it is always worthwhile to analyse the symmetry conditions to determine which of the Fourier coefficients exist and which vanish. The table below summarises these conditions.

Table 17.1. Symmetry Conditions for $f(t)$.

Condition	*Property*
$f(t) = f(-t)$	cos terms only exist .... $b_n = 0$
$f(t) = -f(-t)$	sin terms only exist ... $a_n = 0$
$f(t) = f(t \pm T/2)$	even terms alone exist
$f(t) = -f(t \pm T/2)$	odd terms alone exist

Example 17.2. *Find the Fourier series expansion of the waveform shown in Fig. 17.4.*

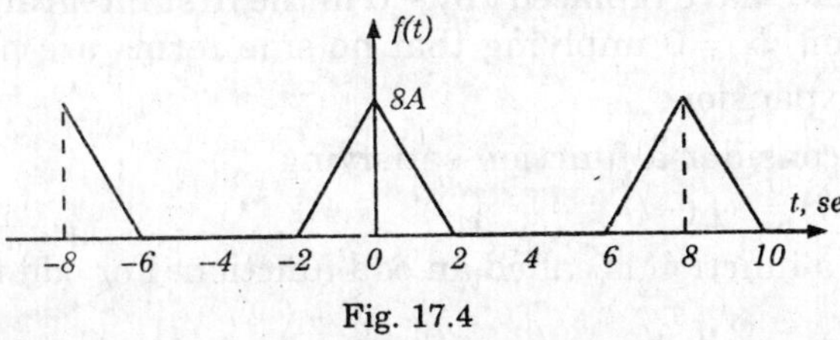

Fig. 17.4

Solution. $i(t)$ can be expanded into Fourier series as

$$i(t) = a_0 + \sum_{n=1}^{\infty} (a_n \cos n\omega t + b_n \sin n\omega t)$$

Since $i(t) = i(-t)$, the function is even, hence $b_n = 0$

$$f(t) = 8 + 4t, \quad -2 < t < 0$$
$$= 8 - 4t, \quad 0 < t < 2.$$

Hence $a_o = \dfrac{1}{8}\left[\int_{-2}^{0} (8 + 4t)\, dt + \int_{0}^{2} (8 - 4t)\, dt\right]$

$$= \frac{1}{8}\left[\left(8t + 2t^2\right)_{-2}^{0} + \left(8t - 2t^2\right)_{0}^{2}\right] = 2$$

$$a_n = \frac{2}{8}\left[\int_{-2}^{0} (8 + 4t) \cos n\omega t \, dt + \int_{0}^{2} (8 - 4t) \cos n\omega t \, dt\right]$$

$$= \frac{64}{n^2\pi^2} \sin^2 \frac{n\pi}{4} \quad \left(\text{since } 8\omega = 2\pi \text{ or } \omega = \frac{\pi}{4}\right)$$

Example 17.3. *Expand the sawtooth wave function shown in Fig. 17.5 into Fourier series.*

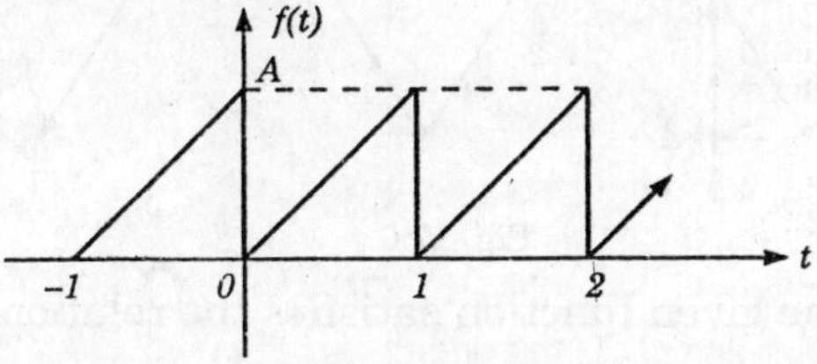

Fig. 17.5

Solution. The period is 1 sec

$$a_o = \frac{1}{T}\int_0^T f(t) \, dt = 1 \int_0^1 At \, dt = A$$

$$a_n = \frac{2}{T}\int_0^1 At \cos n\omega t \, dt$$

$$= \frac{2A}{Tn\omega}\left\{\left[t \sin n\omega t\right]_0^1 - \int_0^1 \sin n\omega t \, dt\right\}$$

$$= \frac{2A}{Tn\omega}\left[\frac{\cos n\omega t}{n\omega}\right]_0^1 = 0$$

$$b_n = \frac{2}{1}\int_0^1 At \sin n\omega t \, dt$$

$$= \frac{2A}{n\omega}\left\{\left[-t \cos n\omega t\right]_0^1 + \int_0^1 \cos n\omega t \, dt\right\}$$

$$= \frac{2A}{n\omega}\left\{-1 + \left[\frac{\sin n\omega t}{n\omega}\right]_0^1\right\}$$

$$= \frac{-2A}{n\omega} = \frac{-2A}{n \cdot 2\pi} = \frac{-A}{n\pi}$$

Therefore, $f(t) = \dfrac{A}{2} - \dfrac{A}{\pi} \sin \omega t - \dfrac{A}{2\pi} \sin 2\omega t - \dfrac{A}{3\pi} \sin 3\omega t \ldots$

$$= \frac{A}{2} - \frac{A}{\pi} \sum_{n=1}^{\infty} \frac{1}{n} \sin n\omega t$$

Example 17.4. *Expand the function given in Fig. 17.6 into Fourier series.*

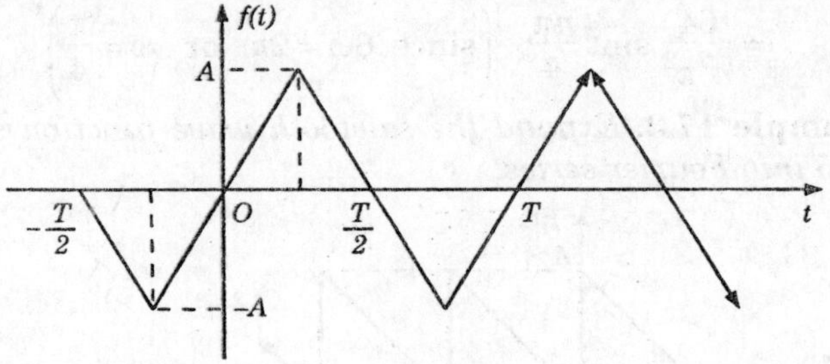

Fig. 17.6

Solution. The given function satisfies the relationship

$$f(t) = -f(-t)$$

Hence $a_n = 0$ for all n. Only sine terms are present

Also $f(t \pm T/2) = -f(t)$. Only odd harmonics are present.

$$b_n = \frac{2}{T} \int_{-T/2}^{T/2} f(t) \sin n\omega t \, dt$$

$$f(t) = -\frac{4A}{T}\left(1 + \frac{2t}{T}\right), \; -\frac{T}{2} < t < -\frac{T}{4}$$

$$= \frac{4At}{T}, \; -\frac{T}{4} < t < \frac{T}{4}$$

$$= 2A\left(1 - \frac{2t}{T}\right), \; \frac{T}{4} < t < \frac{T}{2}$$

$$\therefore \quad b_n = \frac{2}{T}\left[\int_{-T/2}^{T/4} -2A\left(1 + \frac{2t}{T}\right) \sin n\omega t \, dt + \int_{-T/4}^{T/4} 4\frac{At}{T} \sin n\omega t \, dt + \int_{T/4}^{T/2} 2A\left(1 - \frac{2t}{T}\right) \sin \pi\omega t \, dt\right]$$

It is left for the reader to work out this exercise. The value of b_n works out to

$$b_n = \frac{8A}{\pi^2 n^2} \qquad n = 1, 5, 9, \ldots$$

$$= \frac{-8A}{n^2 \pi^2} \qquad n = 3, 7, 11, \ldots$$

Hence $f(t) = \frac{8A}{\pi^2}\left(\sin \omega t - \frac{1}{3^2}\sin 3\omega t + \frac{1}{5^2}\sin 5\omega t \ldots\right)$

Example 17.5. *Find the trigonometric Fourier series for the periodic wave shown in Fig. 17.7.*

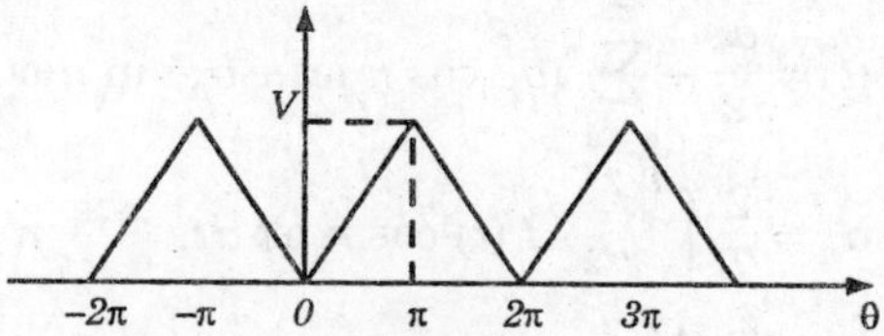

Fig. 17.7

Solution. $f(\theta) = \frac{a_o}{2} + \sum_{n=1}^{\infty}(a_n \cos n\theta + b_n \sin n\theta)$

Since $f(\theta) = f(-\theta)$, the function is even and $b_n = 0$

$$a_n = \frac{1}{\pi}\int_{-\pi}^{\pi} f(\theta)\cos n\theta\, d\theta = \frac{2}{\pi}\int_0^{\pi} f(\theta)\cos n\theta\, d\theta$$

$$= \frac{2}{\pi}\int_0^{\pi}\frac{V}{\pi}\theta\cos n\theta\, d\theta$$

as $f(\theta) = \frac{V}{\pi}\theta$ for $0 < \theta < \pi$

$$a_n = \frac{2V}{\pi^2}\left\{\left[\frac{\theta}{n}\sin n\theta\right]_0^{\pi} - \frac{1}{n}\int_0^{\pi}\sin n\theta\, d\theta\right\}$$

$$= \frac{2V}{\pi^2}\left(\frac{\cos n\theta}{\pi^2}\right)_0^{\pi} = \frac{2V}{n^2\pi^2}[\cos n\pi - 1]$$

For a_o, we cannot substitute $n = 0$ as it then leads to the 0/0 form. Hence,

$$\frac{a_o}{2} = \frac{2}{2\pi}\int_0^{\pi}\frac{V}{\pi}\theta\, d\theta = \frac{2V}{2\pi^2}(\pi^2/2) = \frac{V}{2}$$

and $a_n = 0$ for n even

$$= \frac{-4V}{n^2\pi^2} \text{ for } n \text{ odd.}$$

$$\therefore \quad f(\theta) = \frac{V}{2} - \frac{4V}{\pi^2}\sum_{n=1}^{\infty}\left[\frac{1}{(2n-1)^2}\cos(2\pi - 1)\theta\right]$$

$$= \frac{V}{2} - \frac{4V}{\pi^2}\left(\cos\theta + \frac{1}{3^2}\cos 3\theta + \frac{1}{5^2} + \cos 5\theta + \ldots\right)$$

Exponential Fourier Series. We may write the Fourier series in an alternate form with exponential terms. This from is more elegant and easier to handle. We shall start with the trigonometric form

$$f(t) = \frac{a_o}{2} + \sum_{n=1}^{\infty} (a_n \cos n\,\omega t + b_n \sin n\omega t)$$

where $$a_n = \frac{2}{T}\int_{-T/2}^{T/2} f(t) \cos n\,\omega t\, dt, \qquad n = 0, 1, 2, \ldots$$

$$b_n = \frac{2}{T}\int_{-T/2}^{T/2} f(t) \sin n\,\omega t\, dt, \qquad n = 1, 2, 3, \ldots$$

and $$\omega = \frac{2\pi}{T}$$

Since we know that

$$\cos \beta = \frac{e^{j\beta} + e^{-j\beta}}{2}$$

and $$\sin \beta = \frac{e^{j\beta} - e^{-j\beta}}{2j}$$

We may write $f(t)$ as

$$f(t) = \frac{a_o}{2} + \sum_{n=1}^{\infty} \left[a_n \frac{(e^{j\beta} + e^{-k\beta})}{2} + b_n \frac{(e^{j\beta} - e^{-j\beta})}{2j} \right]$$

With $\beta = n\omega t$

$$f(t) = \frac{a_o}{2} + \sum_{n=1}^{\infty} \left[\frac{(a_n - jb_n)}{2} e^{j\beta} + \frac{(a_n + jb_n)}{2} e^{-j\beta} \right]$$

$$f(t) = a_o + \sum_{n=1}^{\infty} \left(\alpha_n e^{jn\omega t} + \alpha_{-n} e^{-jn\omega t} \right)$$

where $$\alpha_o = \frac{a_o}{2}$$

$$\alpha_n = \frac{a_n - jb_n}{2}$$

and $$\alpha_{-n} = \frac{a_n + jb_n}{2}$$

while α_o is real, both α_n and α_{-n} are complex quantities

since $$\sum_{n=1}^{\infty} \alpha_{-n}\, e^{-jn\omega t} = \sum_{n=-1}^{-\infty} a_n\, e^{jn\omega t}$$

we may write $$(t) = \sum_{n=-\infty}^{\infty} \alpha_n \, e^{jn\omega t}$$

which includes α_o also.

Here $$\alpha_n = \frac{1}{T} \int_{-T/2}^{T/2} f(t) \, e^{-jn\omega t} \, dt$$

with n varying from $-\infty$ to ∞. The exponential form needs only one formula for all its coefficients and is more compact than the trigonometric form.

Example 17.6. *Find the exponential Fourier series for the function shown in Fig. 17.8.*

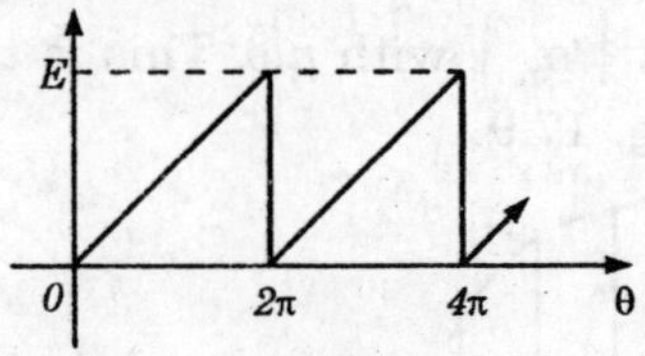

Fig. 17.8

Solution. $$f(\theta) = \frac{E\theta}{2\pi} \qquad 0 < \theta < 2\pi$$

$$f(\theta) = \sum_{n=-\infty}^{\infty} \alpha_n \, e^{jn\theta}$$

$$\alpha_n = \frac{1}{2\pi} \int_0^{2\pi} f(\theta) \, e^{-jn\theta} \, d\theta$$

$$= \frac{1}{2\pi} \int_0^{2\pi} \frac{E}{2\pi} \, \theta e^{-jn\theta} \, d\theta$$

$$= \frac{E}{4\pi^2} \left\{ \left[\theta \, \frac{e^{-jn\theta}}{-jn} \right]_0^{2\pi} - \int_0^{2\pi} \frac{e^{-jn\theta}}{-jn} \, d\theta \right\}$$

$$= \frac{E}{4\pi^2} \left[\frac{2\pi \, e^{-j^{2}\pi n}}{-jn} + \frac{e^{-j^{2} n\pi}}{n^2} - \frac{1}{n^2} \right]$$

Using the formula

$$e^{-j\alpha} = \cos \alpha - j \sin \alpha$$

and on simplification,

$$\alpha_n = \frac{jE}{2\pi n}$$

$$\alpha_o = \frac{1}{2\pi}\int_0^{2\pi} f(\theta)\,d\theta = \frac{1}{2\pi}\int_0^{2\pi} \frac{E}{2\pi}\,\theta\,d\theta$$

$$= \frac{E}{2\pi}$$

Hence $$f(\theta) = \frac{E}{2\pi} + \frac{E}{2\pi}\sum_{n=-\infty}^{\infty} \frac{j}{n}\, e^{jn\theta} \neq 0$$

To draw the frequency spectrum, we have to draw the amplitude versus integral values of $n\omega$. It will be remembered that amplitude

$$= \sqrt{a_n^{\,2} + b_n^{\,2}} = 2 \mid \alpha_n \mid$$

Hence we plot $2 \mid \alpha_n \mid$ with $n\omega$. This is tabulated below and shown plotted in Fig. 17.9.

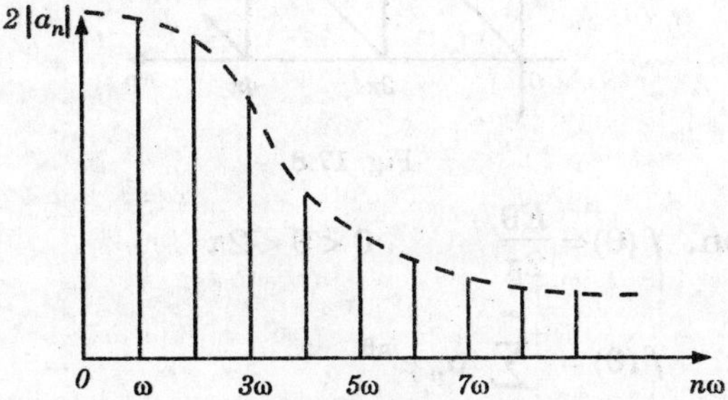

Fig. 17.9

n	0	1	2	3	4	5	6	7
αn	$\frac{E}{2\pi}$	$\frac{jE}{2\pi}$	$\frac{jE}{4\pi}$	$\frac{jE}{6\pi}$	$\frac{jE}{8\pi}$	$\frac{jE}{10\pi}$	$\frac{jE}{12\pi}$	$\frac{jE}{14\pi}$
$2\mid \alpha_n \mid$	$0.3183E$	$0.3183E$	$0.1592E$	$0.106E$	$0.0796E$	$0.0673E$	$0.053E$	$0.045E$

Example 17.7. *Find the exponential Fourier series of the half rectified sine wave shown in Fig. 17.10.*

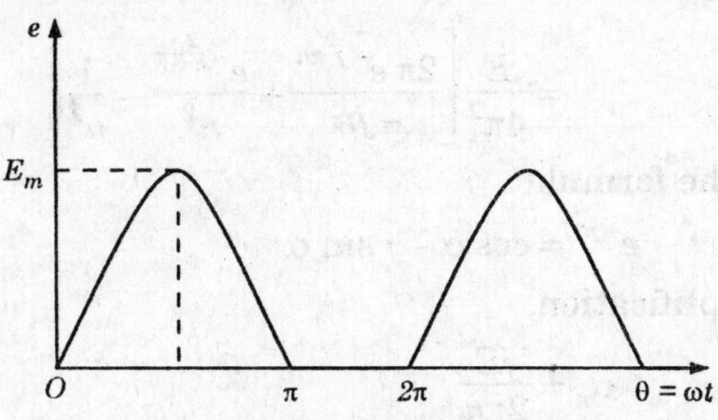

Fig. 17.10

$$f(\theta) = E_m \sin\theta \qquad 0 < \theta < \pi$$

$$= \sum_{n=-\infty}^{\infty} \alpha_n e^{-jn\theta}$$

where $$\alpha_n = \frac{1}{2\pi}\int_0^{2\pi} f(\theta)\, e^{-jn\theta}\, d\theta$$

$$= \frac{1}{2\pi}\int_0^{\pi} E_m \sin\theta\, e^{-jn\theta}\, d\theta$$

$$= \frac{E_m}{2\pi}\int_0^{\pi} \frac{e^{j\theta} - e^{-j\theta}}{2j}\, e^{-jn\theta}\, d\theta$$

$$= \frac{E_m}{j4\pi}\int_0^{\pi} [e^{j\theta(1-n)} - e^{-j\theta(1+n)}]\, d\theta$$

$$= \frac{E_m}{4\pi}\left[\frac{1}{1-n} + \frac{1}{1+n} - \frac{e^{j(1-n)\pi}}{(1-n)} - \frac{e^{-j(1+n)\pi}}{(1+n)}\right]$$

$$= 0 \text{ for } n \text{ odd}$$

$$= \frac{-V}{\pi(n^2-1)} \text{ for } n \text{ even}$$

Hence $$f(\theta) = \ldots - \frac{V}{15\pi} e^{-j4\theta} - \frac{V}{3\pi} e^{-j2\theta} - \frac{V}{3\pi} e^{j2\theta} - \frac{V}{15\pi} e^{j4\theta} - \frac{V}{35\pi} e^{j6\theta} + \ldots$$

Example 17.8. *Find the exponential Fourier series for the functions whose waveform is shown in Fig. 17.11.*

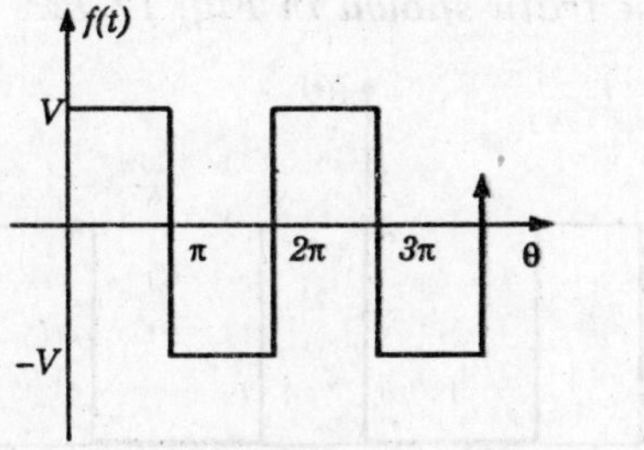

Fig. 17.11

Solution. $$f(\theta) = V \qquad 0 < \theta < \pi$$

$$= -V \qquad \pi < \theta < 2\pi$$

$$= \sum_{n=-\infty}^{\infty} \alpha_n e^{jn\theta}$$

where $$\alpha_n = \frac{1}{2\pi}\int_0^{2\pi} f(\theta)\, e^{-jn\theta}\, d\theta$$

$$= \frac{1}{2\pi}\left[\int_0^{\pi} V e^{-jn\theta}\, d\theta + \int_{\pi}^{2\pi} (-V)\, e^{-jn\theta}\, d\theta\right]$$

$$= \frac{V}{2\pi}\left\{\left[\frac{e^{-jn\theta}}{-jn}\right]_0^{\pi} - \left[\frac{e^{-jn\theta}}{-jn}\right]_{\pi}^{2\pi}\right\}$$

$$= \frac{jV}{2\pi n}\left[e^{-jn\pi} - 1 - e^{-j^2 n\pi} + e^{-jn\pi}\right]$$

$$= \frac{jV}{2\pi n}\left[2e^{-jn\pi} - e^{-j^2 n\pi^2} - 1\right]$$

$$= \frac{jV}{2n\pi}\left[(2\cos n\pi - j2\sin n\pi - \cos 2n\pi + j\sin 2n\pi - 1)\right]$$

$$= \frac{jV}{2n\pi}(\pm 2 - 2) \quad \begin{array}{l} + \text{ for } n \text{ even} \\ - \text{ for } n \text{ odd} \end{array}$$

$$= 0 \text{ for } n \text{ even}$$

$$= -\frac{j2V}{n\pi} \text{ for } n \text{ odd}$$

$$\alpha_o = \frac{1}{2\pi}\int_0^{\pi} V\, d\theta + \int_{\pi}^{2\pi} (-V)\, d\theta = \frac{V}{2}(\pi - 2\pi + \pi) = 0$$

Hence, $f(\theta) = \sum_{n=-\infty}^{\infty} \frac{-j2V}{n\pi} e^{jn\theta}$, n odd

$$= \frac{j2V}{n} \sum_{n=-\infty}^{\infty} \frac{-1}{n} e^{jn\theta}, \; n \text{ odd}$$

Example 17.9. *Find the exponential Fourier expansion for the rectangular pulse train shown in Fig. 17.12.*

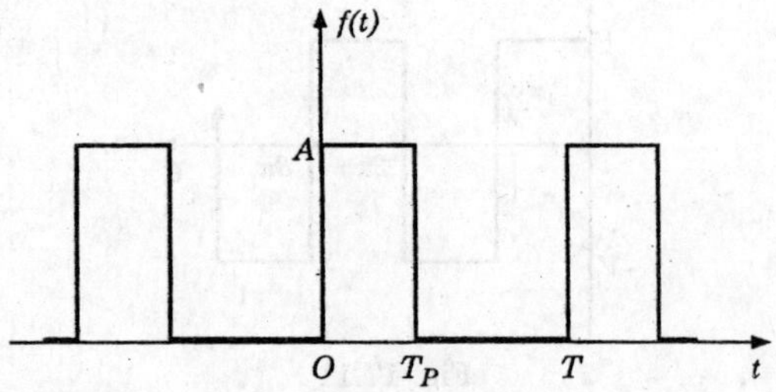

Fig. 17.12

Solution. $f(t) = A, \quad 0 < t < T_p$

$$= 0, \quad T_p < t < T$$

$$= \sum_{n=-\infty}^{\infty} \alpha_n\, e^{jn\omega t}$$

where, $\omega = \dfrac{2\pi}{T}$

$$\alpha_n = \frac{1}{T}\int_0^T f(t)\, e^{-jn\omega t}\, dt$$

$$= \frac{1}{T}\int_0^{T_p} A\, e^{-jn\,(2\pi/T)\,t}\, dt$$

$$= \frac{jA}{2n\pi}\left[e^{-jn\,2\pi\,T_p/T} - 1\right]$$

$$= \frac{A}{n\pi}\, e^{-jn\,\pi\,T_p/T}\, \sin\,(n\pi\, T_p/T)$$

Hence, $f(t) = \dfrac{A}{\pi}\displaystyle\sum_{n=-\infty}^{\infty} \frac{1}{n}\sin\,(n\pi\, T_p/T)\, e^{jn\,(2\pi/T)\,(t - T_p/2)}$

To obtain the frequency spectrum, we have to plot the amplitude $2 \mid \alpha_n \mid$ against $n\omega$

$$2 \mid \alpha_n \mid = \frac{2A}{n\pi}\left|\sin\left(n\pi\,\frac{T_p}{T}\right)\right|$$

Further for $n = 0$,

$$\alpha_o = \frac{1}{T}\int_0^{T_p} A\, dt = \frac{AT_p}{T}$$

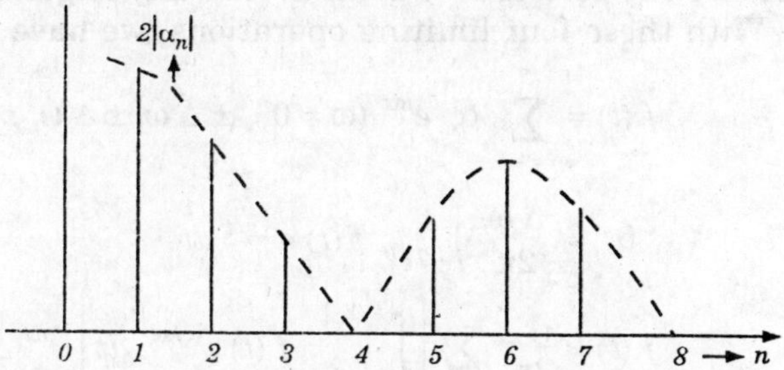

Fig. 17.13

Assuming $T/T_p = 4$, we may tabulate the following :

n	0	1	2	3	4	5
α_n	$A/4$	0.225 A	0.159 A	0.075 A	0	0.045A
$2\,\lvert\alpha_n\rvert$	$A/2$	0.45 A	0.318 A	0.15 A	0	0.09A

The spectrum is shown in Fig. 17.13.

Fourier Integrals and Transforms. Consider the frequency spectrum of the periodic rectangular pulse train. The spectrum is called discrete spectrum because it can be drawn only for integral values of n. The amplitude at any value of 'n' is the amplitude of the component whose frequency is n times that of the fundamental frequency, $1/T$. As the value of T increass, ω decreases as

$$\omega = 2\pi/T$$

The lines in the discrete spectrum become closer. In the limit as T increases indefinitely such that $T \to \infty$, ω tends to approach zero, the lines becoming so close that the discrete spectrum eventually becomes a smooth curve or a continuous spectrum. The implication of $T \to \infty$ is that the wave has a period approaching infinity or it is a non-periodic wave that never repeats itself. Thus, we arrive at the possibility of expressing non periodic (transient) functions in Fourier series form.

We shall begin with the exponential form of the Fourier series for a periodic function and let the period become infinite.

$$f(t) = \sum_{n=-\infty}^{\infty} \alpha_n \, e^{jn\omega t}$$

$$\alpha_n = \frac{1}{T}\int_{-T/2}^{T/2} f(t)\, e^{-jn\omega t}\, dt$$

As $\qquad T \to \infty, \quad \omega \to 0$

We shall represent the spacing between adjacent components by $\Delta\,\omega$. Hence the period, $T \to 2\pi/\Delta\,\omega$. Also any angular frequency $n\omega \to \omega$. With these four limiting operations, we have

$$f(t) = \sum_{\omega=-\infty}^{\infty} \alpha_\omega \, e^{j\omega t} \quad (\omega = 0, \; \pm\Delta\,\omega, \pm\Delta\,\omega, \ldots)$$

and
$$\alpha_\omega = \frac{\Delta\,\omega}{2\pi}\int_{-T/2}^{T/2} f(t)\, e^{-j\omega t}\, dt$$

i.e.
$$f(t) = \frac{1}{2\pi}\sum_{\omega=-\infty}^{\infty}\left[\int_{-T/2}^{T/2} f(t)\, e^{-j\omega t}\, dt\right] e^{j\omega t}\,\Delta\,\omega$$

$$= \frac{1}{2\pi}\int_{-\infty}^{\infty}\left[\int_{-\infty}^{\infty} f(t)\, e^{-j\omega t}\, dt\right] d\omega$$

as $\qquad T \to \infty, \; \Delta\omega \to d\omega$ and $\Sigma \to \int$.

This may be written as follows

$$f(t) = \frac{1}{2\pi}\int_{-\infty}^{\infty} g(\omega)\, e^{j\omega t}\, d\omega$$

where
$$g(\omega) = \int_{-\infty}^{\infty} f(t)\; e^{-j\omega t}\, dt$$

This pair of relationship is called the Fourier transform-pair ; $g(\omega)$ is called the Fourier transform of $f(t)$ and conversely $f(t)$ is called the inverse Fourier transform of $g(\omega)$.

We may also write this pair as

$$f(t) = \mathcal{F}^{-1}[g(\omega)] \text{ and } g(\omega) = \mathcal{F}[f(t)]$$

The Fourier transform, transforms a given function of time, $f(t)$ to a function $g(\omega)$ also called the spectrum function of $f(t)$. The inverse Fourier transform, transforms a function in the frequency domain to a function in the time domain.

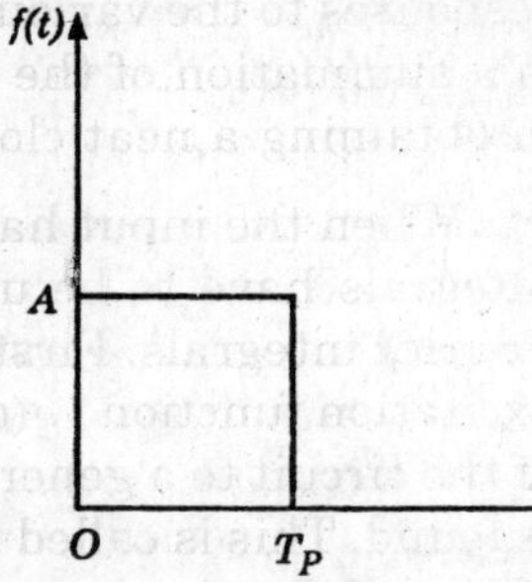

Fig. 17.14

Example 17.10. *Obtain the continuous spectrum (relative frequency distribution) of the single rectangular pulse shown in Fig. 17.14.*

Solution. We assume this function to have a period $T \to \infty$; *i.e.* the pulse never repeats itself. For this the continuous spectrum or frequency distribution is obtained by finding $g(\omega)$

$$f(t) = A,\ 0 < t < T_p = 0 \text{ elsewhere}$$

We know $g(\omega) = \mathcal{F}[f(t)] = \int_0^T Ae^{-j\omega t}\,dt$

$$= \frac{A}{-j\omega}\left[e^{-j\omega t}\right]_0^{T_p}$$

$$= \frac{A}{-j\omega}\left[e^{-j\omega T_p} - 1\right]$$

$$= \frac{2A}{\omega}\sin\frac{(\omega T_p)}{2}e^{-j\omega T_p/2}$$

The relative frequency distribution is a plot of $|g(\omega)|$ versus ω.

where $$|g(\omega)| = \frac{2A}{\omega}\left|\frac{\sin(\omega T_p)}{2}\right| = AT_p\left|\frac{\sin(\omega T_p/2)}{\omega T_p/2}\right|$$

The plot is shown in Fig. 17.15.

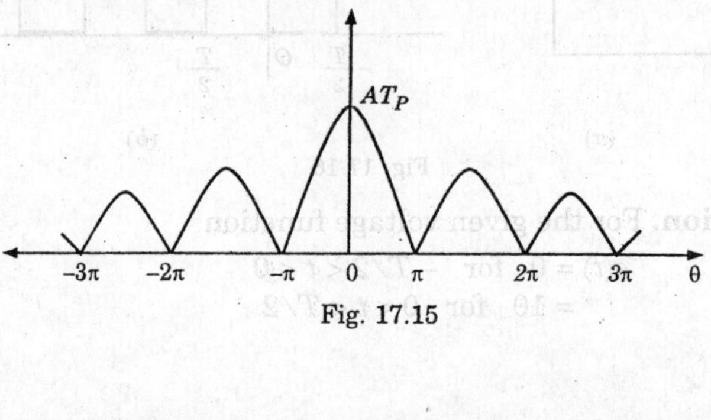

Fig. 17.15

Response by Fourier Methods. In this section, we shall discuss a procedure for obtaining the response of a circuit to an arbitrary forcing function (input) using Fourier methods.

If the forcing, function is periodic in nature, it can be expanded into Fourier series, the terms of which are harmonic components of the fundamental frequency of the given function. Having thus transformed, the given function of time into a function in the frequency domain, the response is obtained by superposing the responses to the various harmonic components. The total response is a summation of the component responses. The difficulty arises in obtaining a neat closed expression for the overall response.

When the input happens to be transient non-periodic, Fourier integrals have to be used. Four steps are involved in the use of Fourier integrals. First, we find the Fourier transform of the input excitation function ; $g(\omega) = \mathcal{F}[f(t)]$. Next, the steady state response of the circuit to a general component of frequency ω and amplitude is found. This is called the system function or the transfer function $H(j\omega)$ of the circuit to sinusoidal excitation. In the third step, the output for $g_i(\omega)$ as the input, is obtained as $g_o(\omega) = g_i(\omega)\ H(j\omega)$. Finally the output response is obtained as the inverse Fourier transform of $g_o(\omega)$ $f_o(t) = \mathcal{F}^{-1}[g_o(\omega)]$. This last step is in general quite difficult to evaluate.

The procedural steps will be illustrated by two examples.

Example 17.11. *The forcing function e(t) in the circuit shown in Fig. 17.16 (a) is the periodic rectangular wave shown in Fig. 17.16 (b). Determine the current in the circuit.*

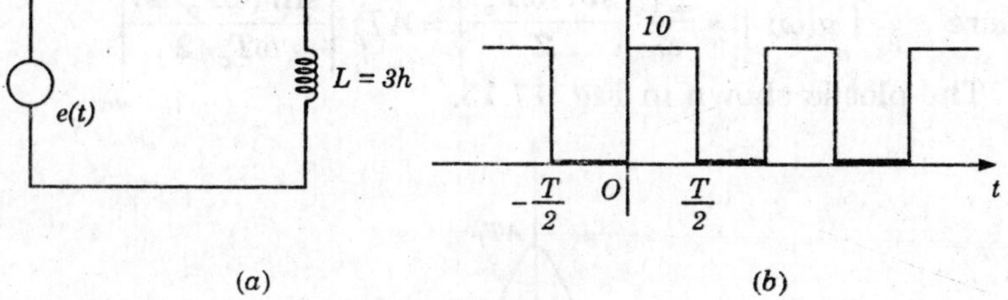

Fig. 17.16

Solution. For the given voltage function

$$e(t) = 0 \quad \text{for} \quad -T/2 < t < 0$$
$$= 10 \quad \text{for} \quad 0 < t < T/2$$

We may obtain the Trigonometric Fourier series as

$$e(t) = \frac{a_o}{2} + \sum_{n=1}^{\infty} (a_n \cos n\omega t + b_n \sin n\omega t)$$

where $$a_n = \frac{2}{T}\int_{-T/2}^{T/2} e(t) \cos n\omega t \, dt \quad n = 0, 1, 2, \ldots$$

and $$b_n = \frac{2}{T}\int_{-T/2}^{T/2} e(t) \sin n\omega t \, dt \quad n = 1, 2, 3, \ldots$$

Here $$a_n = \frac{2}{T}\int_{0}^{T/2} 10 \cos n\omega t \, dt$$

$$= \frac{20}{n\omega T}\Big[\sin n\omega t\Big]_0^{T/2}$$

Substituting $\omega T = 2\pi$, we have

$$a_n = \frac{10}{n\pi}[\sin n\pi] = 0$$

However, $a_o = 0/0$ form and must be found from

$$a_o = \frac{2}{T}\int_{0}^{T/2} 10 \, dt = 10$$

or $$\frac{a_o}{2} = \frac{10}{2} = 5 = \text{average value}$$

$$b_n = \frac{2}{T}\int_{0}^{T/2} 10 \sin n\omega t \, dt$$

$$= \frac{20}{n\omega T}\Big[-\cos n\omega t\Big]_0^{T/2} = \frac{10}{n\pi}[1 - \cos n\pi]$$

$$b_n = 0 \text{ for } n \text{ even and } b = \frac{20}{n\pi} \text{ for } n \text{ odd}$$

Therefore, $$e(t) = 5 + \frac{20}{\pi}\sum_{n=1}^{\infty} \frac{1}{n} \sin n\omega t$$

$$e(t) = 5 + \frac{20}{\pi}\sin \omega t + \frac{20}{3\pi}\sin 3\omega t + \frac{20}{5\pi}\sin 5\omega + \ldots$$

We shall find the steady state current in the circuit by finding the current due to the nth harmonic.

The nth harmonic voltage

$$= \frac{20}{n\pi}\sin n\omega t$$

$$\text{RMS Value} = \frac{20}{n\pi\sqrt{2}}$$

Impedance offered by $= R + jn\omega L$

the circuit to the nth harmonic $= 5 + j3n\omega$

$$= \sqrt{25 + 9n^2\omega^2} \;\underline{/\tan^{-1} 3n\omega/5} = |Z_n| \angle\phi$$

Current due to n^{th} harmonic

$$= \frac{20 \sin (n\omega t - \phi)}{n\pi \sqrt{25 + 9n^2\omega^2}}$$

Current due to d.c. component

$$= 5/5 = 1 \text{ amp}$$

Hence total current

$$= 1 + \sum_{\substack{n=1 \\ \text{odd}}}^{\infty} \frac{20 \sin (n\omega t - \phi)}{n\pi \sqrt{25 + 9n^2\omega^2}}$$

The current given above is the steady state current. Further it may be noted that as the value of '*n*' increases, the contribution of that particular harmonic to the total current decreases. In actual, numerical computations it may be necessary to include only a few terms.

Example 17.12. *In the circuit given in Fig. 17.17 (a), the applied voltage is the single half-sine voltage shown in Fig. 17.17 (b). Find the response $e_o(t)$.*

Solution. The given applied voltage is

$$e_a(t) = A \sin (2\pi/T)\, t = A \sin \alpha t$$

where $2\pi/T$ is a constant quantity.

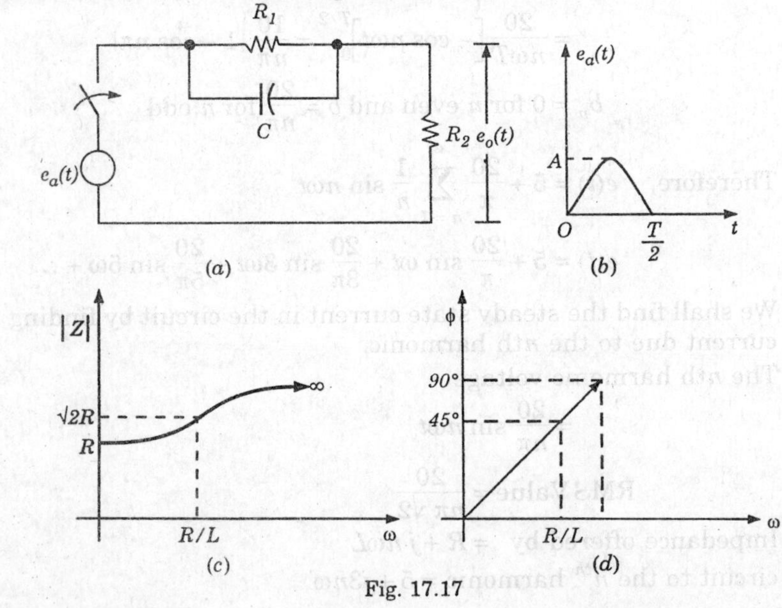

Fig. 17.17

The Fourier transform of $e_a(t)$ is

$$g_i(\omega) = \mathcal{F}[e_a(t)] = \int_0^{T/2} A \sin \alpha t \, e^{-j\omega t}\, dt$$

$$g_i(\omega) = \int_0^{T/2} A \sin \alpha t \, e^{-j\omega t}\, dt = \left(\frac{2A\alpha}{\alpha^2 - \omega^2} \cos \omega \frac{T}{4}\right) e^{-j\omega T/4}.$$

Next, we shall find e_o/e_a giving the transfer function $H(j\omega)$

$$H(j\omega) = \frac{R_2}{R_2 + \text{parallel combination of } R_1 \text{ and } C}$$

$$= \frac{R_2}{R_2 + \{R_1/(1 + j\omega CR_1)\}} = \frac{R_2(1 + j\omega CR_1)}{R_1 + R_2 + j\omega C R_3 R_2}$$

$$= \frac{R_2\sqrt{1 + \omega^2 C^2 R_1^{\,2}}}{\sqrt{(R_1 + R_2)^2 + \omega^2 C^2 R_1^{\,2} R_2^{\,2}}} < \phi$$

where $\theta_2 = \tan^{-1} \dfrac{\omega C R_1 R_2}{(R_1 + R_2)}$; $\theta_1 = \tan^{-1} \omega C R_1$

and $\phi = \theta_1 - \theta_2$

$$g_o(\omega) = g_i(\omega)\, H(j\omega)$$

$$= \left(\frac{2A\alpha}{\alpha^2 - \omega^2} \cos \omega \frac{T}{4}\right) e^{-j\omega T/4} \frac{R_2\, e^{j\phi}}{\sqrt{(R_1 + R_2)^2 + \omega^2 C^2 R_1^{\,2} R_2^{\,2}}}$$

$$= \frac{2A\,\alpha\, R_2\, e^{-j(\omega T/4 - \phi)}}{(\alpha^2 - \omega^2)\sqrt{(R_1 + R_2)^2 + \omega^2 C^2 R_1^{\,2} R_2^{\,2}}}.$$

The desired response $e_o(t)$ is the inverse Fourier transform of $g_o(\omega)$. This of course is a formidable task and we shall not attempt this.

EXERCISES

For each of the periodic waveform shown in Fig. 17.18 through 17.21.

(a) find the Fourier series expansion and

(b) sketch the frequency spectrum approximately to scale.

17.1

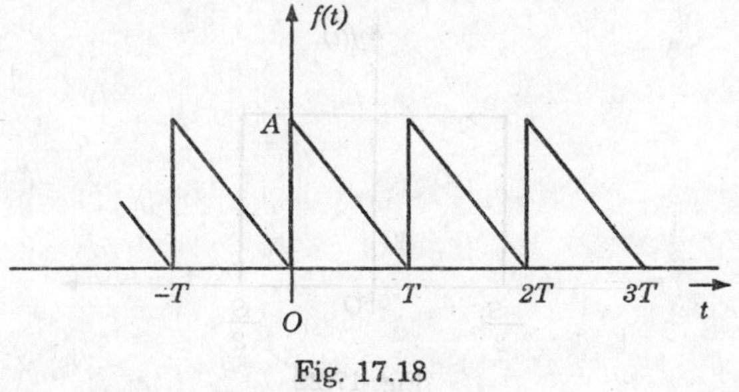

Fig. 17.18

17.2

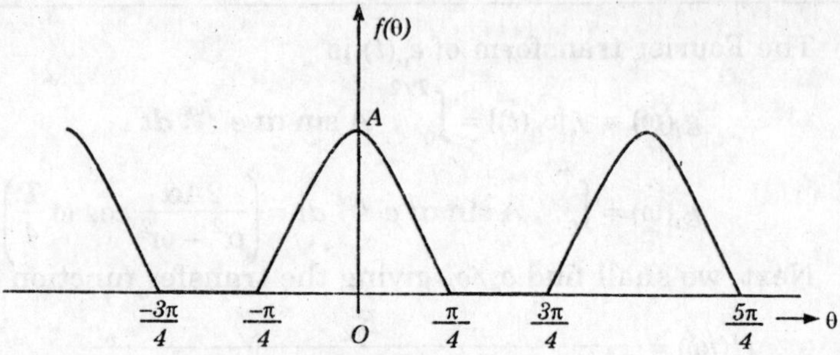

Fig. 17.19

17.3

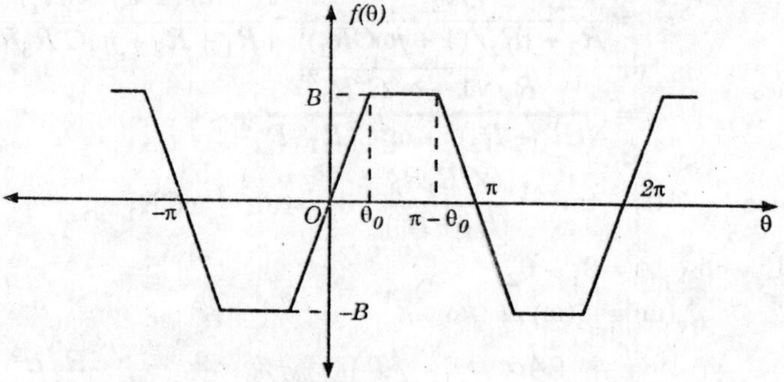

Fig. 17.20

17.4

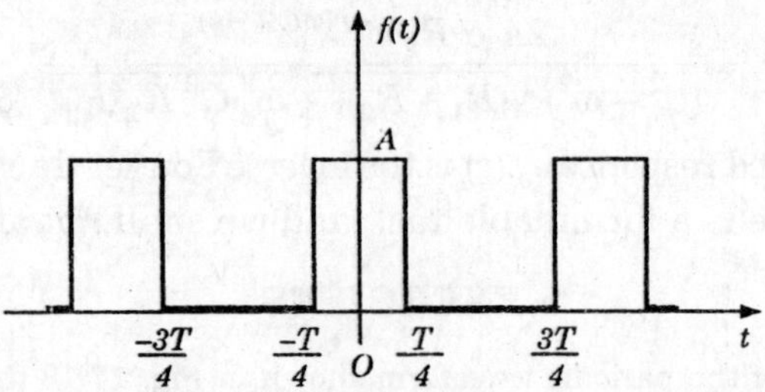

Fig. 17.21

17.5. Expand $f(x) = e^{-x}$ in a cosine series for the interval $0 < x < 2$.

17.6. Find the Fourier transform for the pulse shown below :

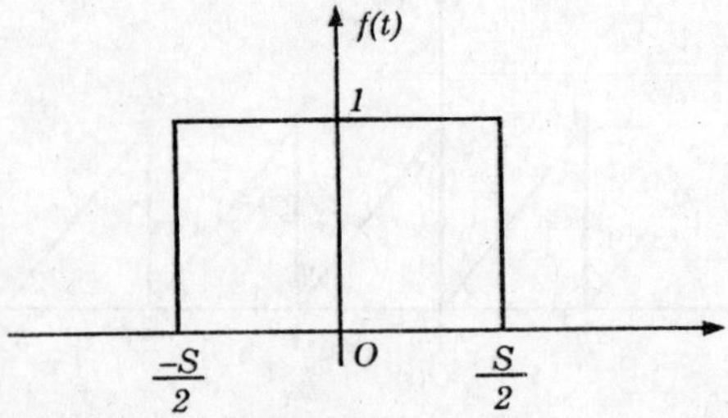

Fig. 17.22

17.7. Find the exponential Fourier series for the triangular wave form of Fig. 17.23 and sketch the line spectrum.

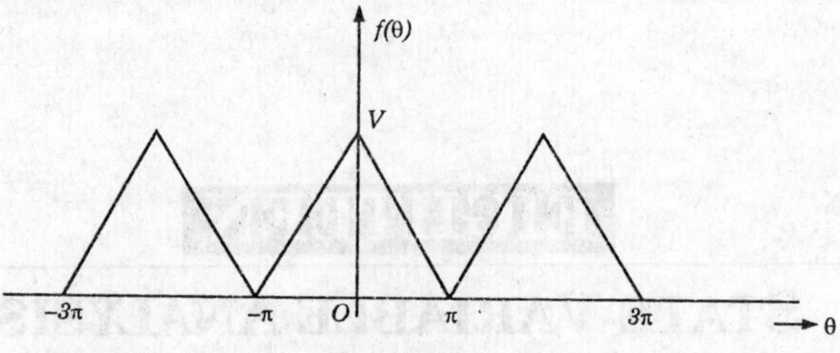

Fig. 17.23

17.8. Determine the Fourier transform of the waveform shown in Fig. 17.24.

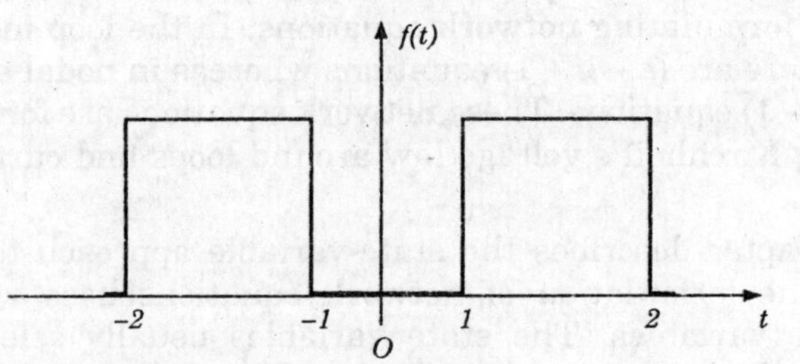

Fig. 17.24

17.9. Expand $f(x) = x^2$ in an exponential series for the interval $0 < x < 1$.

EIGHTEEN

STATE-VARIABLE ANALYSIS

Introduction. In the previous chapters, we have seen different methods of formulating network equations. In the loop method of analysis, there are $(e - n + 1)$ equations whereas in nodal analysis, we have $(n - 1)$ equations. These network equations are formulated by applying Kirchhoff's voltage law around loops and current law at nodes.

This chapter describes the state-variable approach to circuit analysis. The formulation of network equations uses what are called state variables. The state variables usually selected for network analysis are the capacitor voltages and the inductor currents as against loop currents and node voltages used hitherto.

For a large and complicated network with multiple inputs and outputs, the analysis and synthesis is a formidable task. The state variable approach is a streamlined technique simplifying the process considerably. Further, the state-variable formulation is particularly suited for computer applications. This formulation is also applicable to both linear and nonlinear circuits as well as to circuits with time-varying parameters.

State variables. Consider the network of Fig. 18.1. In this series *RLC* network, we would have considered the loop current for mesh analysis or node voltage (at some node) for nodal analysis.

For state-variable analysis, we shall choose the voltage V_C across the capacitor, and the current i_L in the inductor as the state variables.

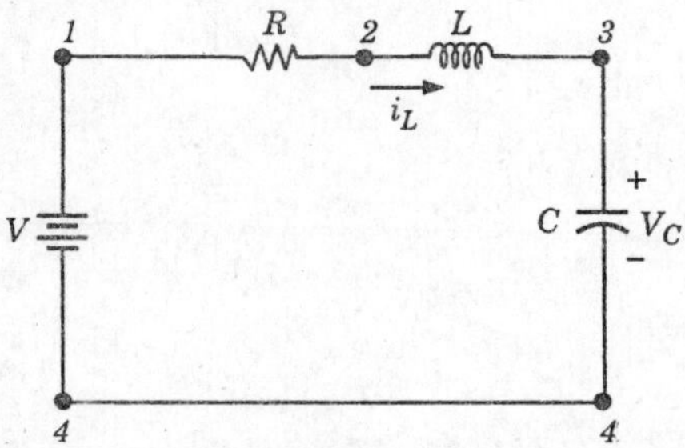

Fig. 18.1

By using the Kirchhoff's voltage law around the closed loop, we may write

$$L\frac{d_{iL}}{dt}+R_{iL}+V_C=V$$

or $$\frac{d_{iL}}{dt}=\frac{1}{L}(V-i_L R-V_C)$$

Also the voltage V_C may be obtained from

$$V_C=\frac{1}{C}\int i_L\,dt$$

or $$\frac{dV_C}{dt}=\frac{1}{C}i_L$$

These equations are said to be in state-variable form.

To generalise, the state variable equations are written in the form

$$\frac{dx_1}{dt}=a_{11}x_1+a_{12}x_2+\ldots+a_{m}x_n+b_1u_1$$

$$\frac{dx_2}{dt}=a_{21}x_1+a_{22}x_2+\ldots+a_{2n}x_n+b_2u_2$$

....

$$\frac{dx_n}{dt}=a_{n1}x_1+a_{n2}x_2+\ldots a_{nn}x_n+b_nu_n$$

where $x_1, x_2, \ldots x_n$ are the states and $u_1, u_2, \ldots u_n$ are the inputs.

Thus the state-variable form lends itself to generalisation of network equations for large networks with multi-inputs and also multi-outputs. More examples follow.

The concept of state perhaps originated from classical mechanics wherein the behaviour of a physical system containing particles is described by their positions and their corresponding velocities. The position and velocity variables, describe the complete state of the system and are called state variables.

"The state of a given physical system may be considered to be the minimal amount of information necessary to describe any future behaviour of the system".

We may write the generalised state variable equations in the form.

$$X=AX+Bu$$

where X is the vector of state variables, A is called the system matrix, u is the input vector and B is the input distribution matrix.

In the state variable formulation of equations describing the behaviour of a system, if the initial state of the system is known along with the inputs to the system in the time interval (t_o, t), then the state of the system at any time t can be computed. If for a network, the initial currents in the inductors and the initial voltages across the capacitors are known and the input is also given, then the state of the circuit is fully known at any other time. Hence, the capacitor voltages and the inductor currents are the state variables. These constitute the information necessary (along with the inputs) to determine the future behaviour of the circuit. The state of a circuit, in other words, consists of all relevant information regarding its past history required to predict the future behaviour. The number of state variables for a given network, therefore, is

$$n = n_c + n_l$$

where n_c is the number of capacitors and n_l is the number of inductors.

We may not be interested in all the state variables to form the output in a particular analysis. In such cases, the output vector Y may be expressed as

$$Y = CX \times Du$$

where C and D are constant matrices. The matrix C denotes how the state variables are related to the output and D indicates the direct connection, if any, between the output and input.

Example 18.1. *Consider the network shown in Fig. 18.2, write the state variable equations for the same.*

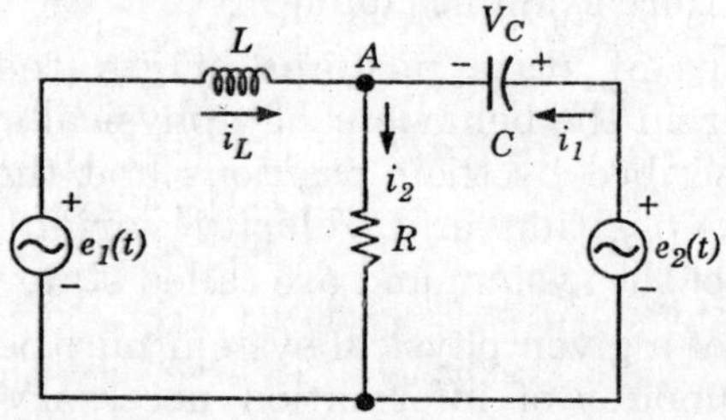

Fig. 18.2

Solution. Consider i_L and V_c as the state variables

For the outer loop, we have

$$L \frac{d_{iL}}{dt} = V_c - e_2 + e_1$$

or
$$\frac{d_{iL}}{dt} = \frac{V_c}{L} - \frac{e_2}{L} + \frac{e_1}{L}$$

For the node A, $i_L + i_1 = i_2$

i.e., $$i_L + C\frac{dV_c}{dt} = \frac{V_A}{R}$$

where V_A is the voltage of node A w.r.t. the datum

$$V_A = e_2 - V_c$$

Hence, $$i_L + C\frac{dV_c}{dt} = \frac{e_2 - V_c}{R}$$

or $$\frac{dV_c}{dt} = -\frac{i_L}{C} - \frac{V_c}{RC} + \frac{e_2}{RC}$$

These two equations can be written in the standard (normal) matrix form as follows :

$$\begin{bmatrix} \frac{di_L}{dt} \\ \frac{dV_c}{dt} \end{bmatrix} = \begin{bmatrix} 0 & \frac{1}{L} \\ \frac{-1}{C} & \frac{-1}{RC} \end{bmatrix}\begin{bmatrix} i_L \\ V_c \end{bmatrix} + \begin{bmatrix} \frac{1}{L} & \frac{-1}{L} \\ 0 & \frac{1}{RC} \end{bmatrix}\begin{bmatrix} e_1 \\ e_2 \end{bmatrix}$$

Thus, by applying Kirchhoff's voltage and current laws, and the voltage current relationships for the various elements, we may form the state-variable equations for simple circuits. However, for large networks with a number of loops, nodes and inputs, the selection of appropriate combination of loop and node equations by inspection becomes rather difficult. A step by step approach using network topological concepts is presented in this chapter.

Step-by-step Procedure

1. Draw the graph of the given network.

2. Select a tree containing the capacitors and voltage sources as its branches. The inductors and current sources must form the co-tree (links).

3. The state variables are the voltages across the capacitors and the currents through the inductors.

4. Write a node equation for each capacitor using Kirchhoff's current law.

5. Write a loop equation for each inductor using Kirchhoff's voltage law.

6. Each of these equations is manipulated until it involves only the variables selected in step 3 and the inputs. Voltage current relationships for each element may have to be used if necessary.

7. Convert the equations into the standard form.

Example 18.2. *Formulate the equations of the network shown in Fig. 18.3 (a).*

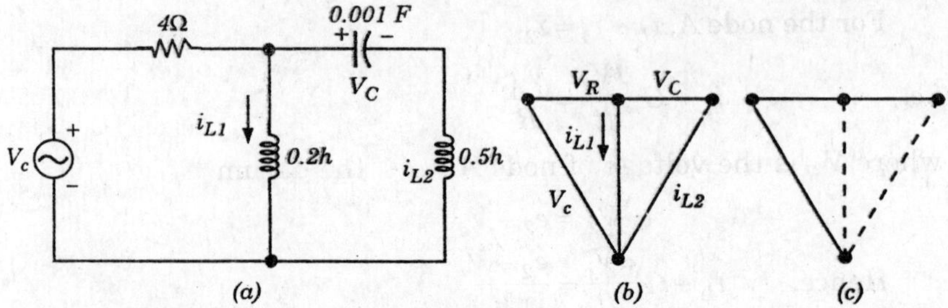

Fig. 18.3

Solution. The graph is shown in Fig. 18.3 (*b*) and a possible tree in Fig. 18.3 (*c*). The tree in Fig. 18.3 (*c*) includes the capacitor and the voltage source. The two inductor elements form the links. The state variables selected are V_c, i_{L1} and i_{L2}.

The node equation for the capacitance is

$$i_{L2} = 0.001 \frac{dV_c}{dt}$$

and the loop equations are

$$V_R + 0.2 \frac{di_{Li}}{dt} = V_s$$

$$V_R + V_c + 0.5 \frac{di_{L2}}{dt} = V_s$$

Since, $$V_R = (i_{L1} + i_{L2})\, 4,$$

we may re-write the above three equations as

$$\frac{dV_c}{dt} = \frac{i_{L2}}{0.001} = 1000\, i_{L2}$$

$$\frac{di_{L1}}{dt} = -\frac{4i_{L1}}{0.2} - \frac{4i_{L2}}{0.2} + \frac{V_s}{0.2}$$

$$= -20\, i_{L1} - 20 i_{L2} + 5V_S$$

$$\frac{di_{L2}}{dt} = -\frac{V_c}{0.5} - \frac{4i_{L1}}{0.5} - \frac{4i_{L2}}{0.5} + \frac{V_s}{0.5}$$

$$= -2\, V_c - 8i_{L1} - 8i_{L2} + 2V_s$$

These may be put in the standard form as

$$\begin{bmatrix} \dfrac{dV_c}{dt} \\ \dfrac{di_{L1}}{dt} \\ \dfrac{di_{L2}}{dt} \end{bmatrix} = \begin{bmatrix} 0 & 0 & 1000 \\ 0 & -20 & -20 \\ -2 & -8 & -8 \end{bmatrix} \begin{bmatrix} V_c \\ i_{L1} \\ i_{L2} \end{bmatrix} + \begin{bmatrix} 0 \\ 5 \\ 2 \end{bmatrix} V_s$$

Example 18.3. *Formulate the state equations in the normal form for the circuit of Fig. 18.4.*

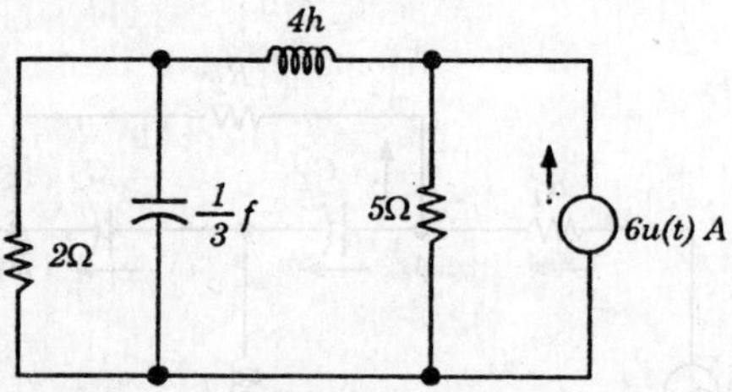

Fig. 18.4

Solution. The graph and a tree for the above circuit are shown in Fig. 18.5 (*a*) and (*b*) respectively.

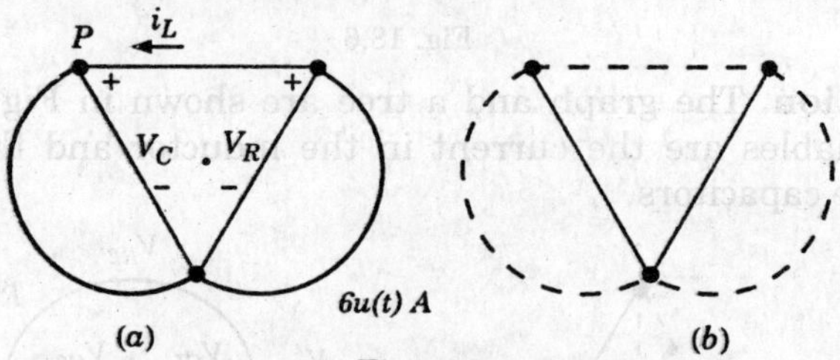

Fig. 18.5

Choosing V_c and i_L as the state variables and writing the loop equation including the inductor, we have

$$\frac{4\,di_L}{dt} + V_c = V_R$$

or
$$\frac{d_{iL}}{dt} = 0.25\ V_R - 0.25\ V_c$$

But, $$V_R = [6u\ (t) - i_L]\ 5 = 30\ u\ (t) - 5i_L$$

Substituting, $$\frac{di_L}{dt} = -\ 1.25\ i_L - 0.25V_c + 7.5u\ (i)$$

For the capacitor, we write the node equation at node P

$$i_L = C\frac{dV_c}{dt} + \frac{V_c}{2} = \frac{1}{3}\frac{dV_c}{dt} + \frac{V_c}{2}$$

Hence, $$\frac{dV_c}{dt} = 3i_L - 1.5\ V_c$$

Writing the two equations in matrix form, we have

$$\begin{bmatrix} \dfrac{di_L}{dt} \\ \dfrac{dV_c}{dt} \end{bmatrix} = \begin{bmatrix} -\ 1.25 & -\ 0.25 \\ 3 & -\ 1.5 \end{bmatrix}\begin{bmatrix} i_L \\ V_c \end{bmatrix} + \begin{bmatrix} 7.5 \\ 0 \end{bmatrix} u(t)$$

Example 18.4. *Obtain the state equations for the network shown in Fig. 18.6 in the normal form.*

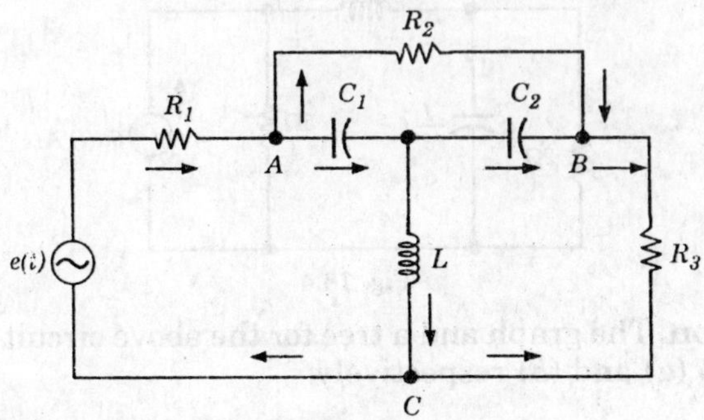

Fig. 18.6

Solution. The graph and a tree are shown in Fig. 18.7. The state variables are the current in the inductor and the voltages across the capacitors.

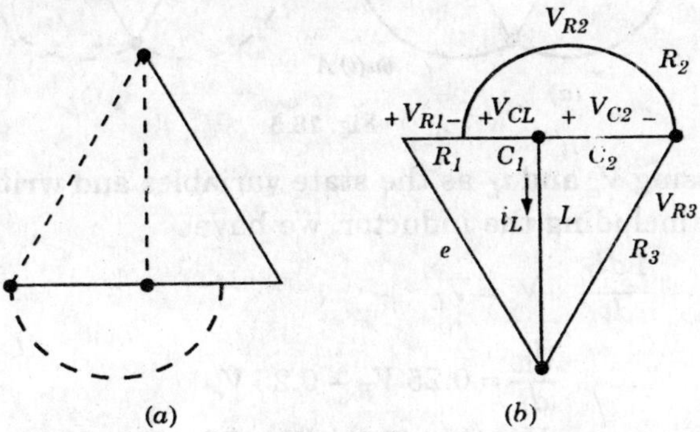

Fig. 18.7

As we add the link with the inductor, we may write the loop equation

$$L\frac{di_L}{dt} + V_{R1} + V_{c1} = e(t)$$

or
$$L\frac{di_L}{dt} = e(t) - V_{c1} - V_{R1}$$

Writing the node equation for C_1 (at node A),

$$\frac{V_{R1}}{R_1} = C_1\frac{dV_{c1}}{dt} + \frac{V_{c1}+V_{c2}}{R_2}$$

or
$$C_1\frac{dV_{c1}}{dt} = \frac{V_{R1}}{R_1} - \frac{V_{c1}+V_{c2}}{R_2}$$

Similarly for node B

$$\frac{V_{R3}}{R_3} = \frac{V_{c1} + V_{c2}}{R_2} + C_2 \frac{dV_{c2}}{dt}$$

or
$$C_2 \frac{dV_{c2}}{dt} = \frac{V_{R3}}{R_3} - \frac{V_{c1} + V_{c2}}{R_2}$$

From these equations, we have to eliminate V_{R1} and V_{R3} which are neither state variables nor the input function. We know, for node C

$$\frac{V_{R1}}{R_1} = i_L + \frac{V_{R3}}{R_2} \quad \text{or} \quad \frac{V_{R1}}{R_1} - \frac{V_{R3}}{R_3} = i_L$$

For the closed loop not involving R_2 and L

$$e(t) = V_{R1} + V_{c1} + V_{c2} + V_{R3}$$

or
$$V_{R1} + V_{R3} = e(t) - V_{c1} - V_{c2}$$

Solving for V_{R1} and V_{R3}, we have

$$V_{R1} = \frac{R_1}{R_1 + R_3} [e(t) - V_{c1} - V_{c2}] + \frac{R_1 R_3}{R_1 + R_3} i_L$$

$$= \frac{R_1}{R_1 + R_3} [e(t) - V_{c1} - V_{c2} + i_L R_3]$$

and
$$V_{R3} = \frac{R_3}{R_1 + R_3} [e(t) - V_{c1} - V_{c2} - i_L R_1]$$

Substituting, we have

$$\frac{di_L}{dt} = \frac{1}{L} [e(t) - V_{c1} - \frac{R_1}{R_1 + R_3} \{e(t) - V_{c1} - V_{c2} + i_L R_3\}]$$

$$= \frac{1}{(R_1 + R_3) L} [R_3 e(t) - R_3 V_{c1} + R_1 V_{c2} - R_1 R_3 i_L]$$

$$\frac{dV_{c1}}{dt} = \frac{1}{C_1} \left[\frac{1}{R_1 + R_3} \{e(t) - V_{c1} - V_{c2} + i_L R_3\} - \frac{V_{c1} + V_{c2}}{R_2} \right]$$

$$= \frac{1}{(R_1 + R_3) C_1} \left[e(t) + i_L R_3 - \frac{R_1 + R_2 + R_3}{R_2} (V_{c1} + V_{c2}) \right]$$

$$\frac{dV_{c2}}{dt} = \frac{1}{C_2} \left[\frac{1}{R_1 + R_3} \{e(t) - V_{c1} - V_{c2} - i_L R_1\} - \frac{V_{c1} + V_{c2}}{R_2} \right]$$

$$= \frac{1}{(R_1 + R_3) C_2} \left[e(t) - i_L R_1 - \frac{R_1 + R_2 + R_3}{R_2} (V_{c1} + V_{c2}) \right]$$

Putting these equations in the matrix form, we have the normal form given below :

$$\begin{bmatrix} \dot{i}_L \\ \dot{V}_{c1} \\ \dot{V}_{c2} \end{bmatrix} = \frac{1}{(R_1+R_3)} \begin{bmatrix} \dfrac{-R_1R_3}{L} & \dfrac{-R_3}{L} & \dfrac{R_1}{L} \\ \dfrac{R_3}{C_1} & -\dfrac{(R_1+R_2+R_3)}{R_2C_1} & -\dfrac{(R_1+R_2+R_3)}{R_2C_1} \\ -\dfrac{R_1}{C_2} & -\dfrac{(R_1+R_2+R_3)}{R_2C_2} & -\dfrac{(R_1+R_2+R_3)}{R_2C_2} \end{bmatrix} \begin{bmatrix} i_L \\ V_{c1} \\ V_{c2} \end{bmatrix} + \begin{bmatrix} \dfrac{R_3/L}{(R_1+R_3)} \\ \dfrac{1/C_1}{(R_2+R_3)} \\ \dfrac{1/C_2}{(R_1+R_3)} \end{bmatrix} e(t)$$

Example 18.5. *Obtain the state equations in normal form for the circuit of Fig. 18.8 (a).*

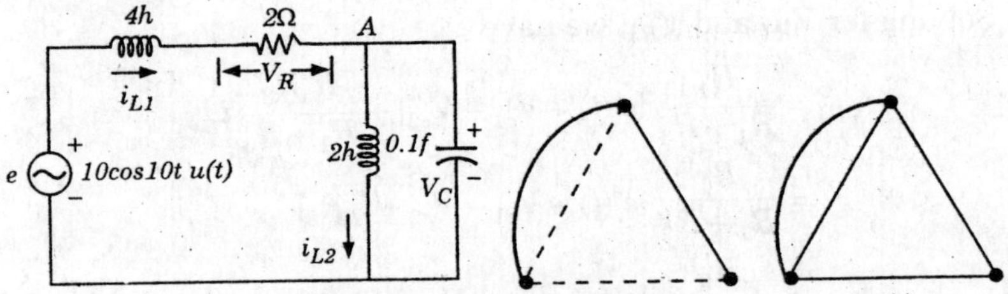

(a) (b) (c)

Fig. 18.8

Solution. Choose i_{L1}, i_{L2} and V_c as state variables.

For the capacitor, we write as node equation at A as

$$0.1\frac{dV_c}{dt} + i_{L2} = i_{L1}$$

For the $4h$ inductor, we write a loop equation (around the outer loop)

$$4\frac{di_{L1}}{dt} + U_R + V_c = 10 \cos 10t\, u(t)$$

We write a loop equation for the $3h$ inductor as follows L

$$\frac{2di_{L2}}{dt} = V_c$$

Also it may be noted $V_R = 2i_{L1}$. Substituting and re-arranging, we have,

$$\frac{di_{L1}}{dt} = \frac{10}{4}\cos 10t\, u(t) - \frac{V_c}{4} - \frac{2i_{L1}}{4}$$

$$\frac{di_{L2}}{dt} = \frac{V_c}{2}$$

$$\frac{dV_c}{dt} = \frac{i_{L1}}{0.1} - \frac{V_{L2}}{0.1}$$

The equations are put in standard form as

$$\begin{bmatrix} \frac{di_{L1}}{dt} \\ \frac{di_{L2}}{dt} \\ \frac{dV_c}{dt} \end{bmatrix} = \begin{bmatrix} -0.5 & 0 & -0.25 \\ 0 & 0 & 0.5 \\ 10 & -10 & 0 \end{bmatrix} \begin{bmatrix} i_{L1} \\ i_{L2} \\ V_c \end{bmatrix} + \begin{bmatrix} 2.5 \\ 0 \\ 0 \end{bmatrix} \cos 10t\, u(t)$$

Solution of the State Equation. The normal form of the state equation for a given circuit is

$$x = Ax + Bu$$

For the solution of this equation the initial condition of the state variables must be specified. This condition may be denoted as $x(0)$.

In the case of a scalar differential equation of form

$$\frac{dx}{dt} = ax + bu(t)$$

With a and b as constants, and $u(t)$ as a continuous function of time, the solution is obtained by taking Laplace transform on both sides.

$$sX - x(0) = aX + bu(s)$$

where X is the laplace transform of x and $u(s)$ is the laplace transform of $u(t)$.

Rearranging, $(s - a)\, X = x(o) + bu(s)$

Hence $$X = \frac{x(o)}{s-a} + b\,\frac{u(s)}{s-a}$$

When we take the laplace inverse, the first term gives $e^{at}x(o)$ whereas the second term can be obtained only through a convolution integral. Hence

$$x(t) = e^{at}x(o) + b\int e^{a\,(t-\tau)}\, u(\tau)\, d\tau$$

If we start at some initial time t_o, then this solution becomes

$$x(t) = e^{a(t-t_0)}\, X(t_0) + b\int_{t_0}^{t} e^{a(t-\tau)}\, u(\tau)\, d\tau$$

In the case of the matrix equation, we may similarly write

$$X(t) = e^{A\,(t-t_0)}\, X(t_0) + B\int_{t_0}^{t} e^{A\,(t-\tau)}\, u(\tau)\, d\tau$$

where $e^{A(t-t_0)}$ is the exponential matrix function and is called the state transition matrix.

The expression for e^A is given as

$$e^A = I + A + \frac{A^2}{2'} + \frac{A^3}{3'} + \ldots$$

where I is the identity matrix of suitable order.

EXERCISES

For the circuits shown below, obtain the state variable equations in the normal form.

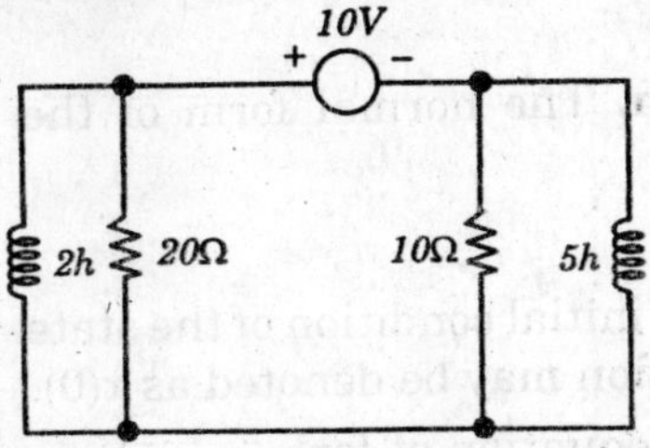

Fig. 18.9

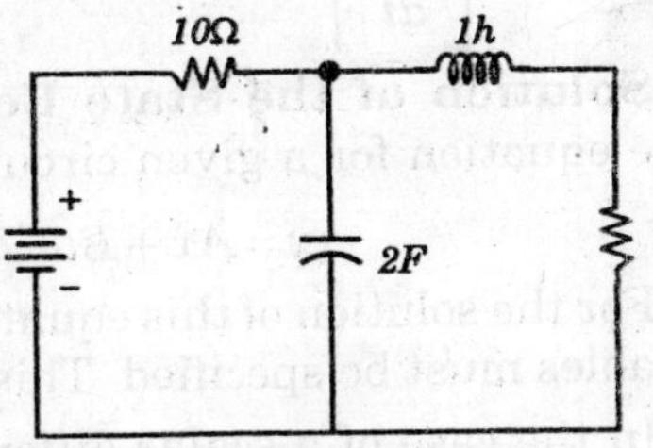

Fig. 18.10

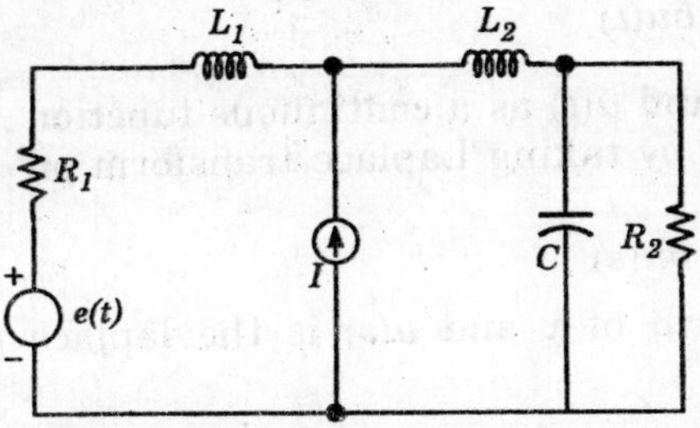

Fig. 18.11

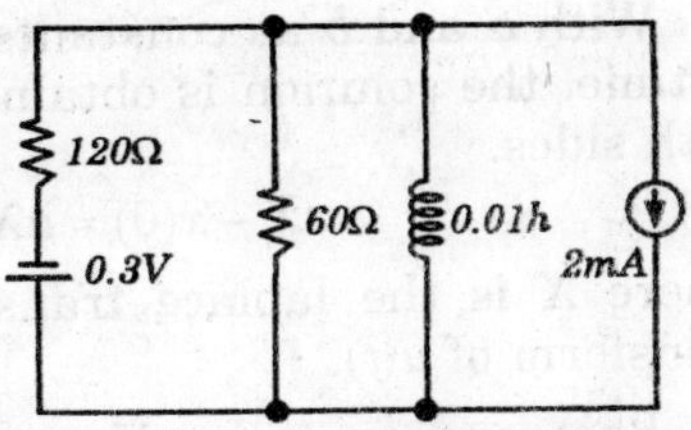

Fig. 18.12

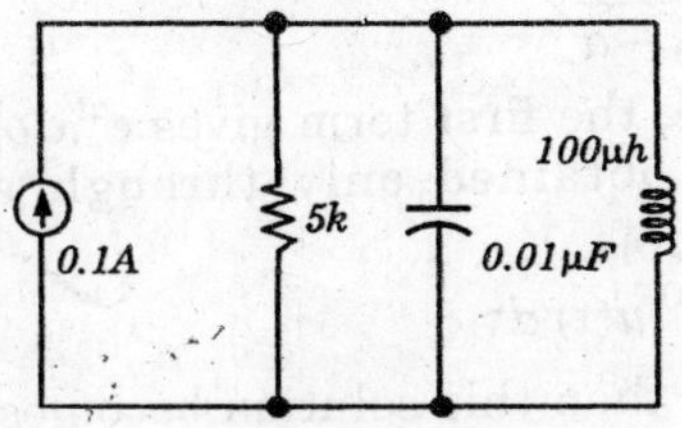

Fig. 18.13

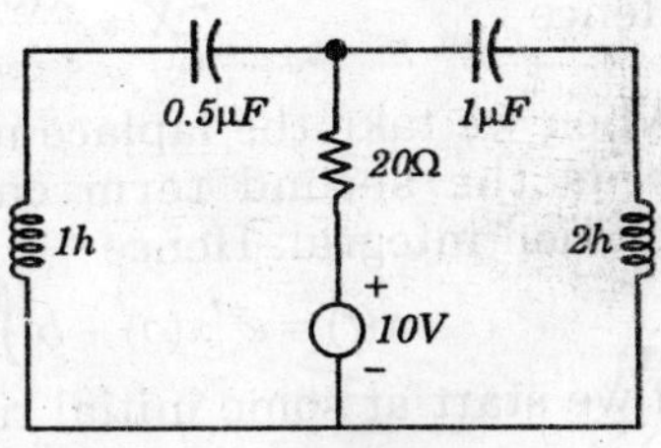

Fig. 18.14